1001 WEDDING IDEAS

SELLERS

PUBLISHING

Written by Tricia Spencer

Published by Sellers Publishing, Inc.

Copyright © 2012 Sellers Publishing, Inc.
Illustrations © jammydesign/iStockphoto
All rights reserved.

Sellers Publishing, Inc.
161 John Roberts Road, South Portland, Maine 04106
Visit our Web site: www.sellerspublishing.com
E-mail: rsp@rsvp.com

ISBN 13: 978-1-4162-0667-5
e-ISBN: 978-1-4162-0861-7
Library of Congress Control Number: 2012931313

10 9 8 7 6 5 4 3 2 1

Printed and bound in China

1001

WEDDING
IDEAS

THE ULTIMATE RESOURCE

FOR CREATING A WEDDING NO ONE WILL EVER FORGET

INSPIF **177.9** *d* HELP
S746
for the Mc *and Groom*

TRICIA SPENCER

CONTENTS

Part One: THE BIG-PICTURE DECISIONS

At first, planning your wedding may seem overwhelming, but here you'll find easy-to-follow advice and ideas on making your first big-picture choices.

If you are looking for a spectacular backdrop for your wedding, why not consider a natural wonder like Yosemite. Or is a special destination like Graceland your dream? Here's all the information you'll need to reserve an amazing setting.

Do you long for a country-western wedding? Or how about a speakeasy, Broadway, or eco-friendly theme? You'll find all the tips you need to create a memorable, one-of-a-kind, and personalized wedding.

It's showtime! These creative strategies will help you choose the right officiant, the ideal setting, and the perfect vows.

Part Two: THE WEDDING PARTY

Shopping for the wedding gown of your dreams? Fitting a dapper groom? Here are stress-free strategies.

From attendants' gifts to protocol for the flower girl and ring bearers, and even pets in the procession, help is here to guarantee a smooth ceremony and a happy wedding party.

Want to create a special (and fun!) rehearsal dinner? Rent a skybox, have a wine tasting, or throw a costume party!

Part Three: THE DETAILS

Part One

THE BIG-PICTURE DECISIONS

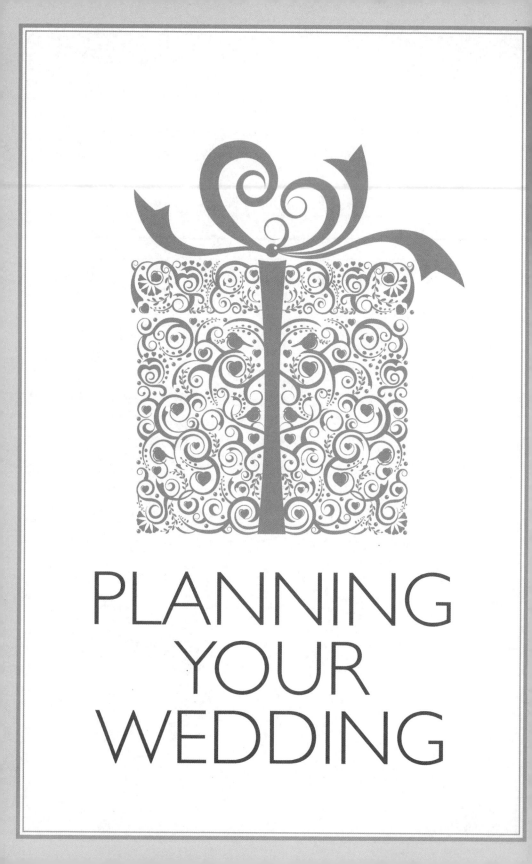

PLANNING YOUR WEDDING

Does it sometimes feel like entire governments have been created with less energy, deliberation, and organization than it takes to pull off a spectacular wedding? There's so much to do, so much to think about, so much to enjoy!

Wedding planning is supposed to be fun. Yet it's also a lot of work. But as Confucius said, "Choose a job you love, and you will never have to work a day in your life." That's what planning your wedding should be — a job you love.

If it's not in your nature to see all of the wedding-planning decisions through from start to finish, one of your earliest and most important decisions may be hiring the right wedding planner. Professional, well-respected wedding planners effectively assist brides and grooms who may or may not have a passion for the wedding-planning process. But whether you choose to work with a professional, or you set your own course, the ideas in this chapter will give you plenty of guidance and inspiration.

There are many options and issues to consider when planning your wedding. In subsequent chapters, you will find ideas, suggestions, and solutions for all of the major categories of wedding planning. But if you are looking for an overview of the wedding-planning process, or a wedding-related topic without a designated chapter, you will find it here.

As you begin to look at the "big picture" for planning your wedding, remember these two principles above all else:

1. It's never too early to plan.
2. Never make decisions without considering the alternatives.

With imagination and thoughtful preparation, you can create your dream wedding. So be inspired by the ideas that follow. Listen to your instincts, and remember that it's *your* wedding. When it's time for outside assistance, only employ people who you believe will help you achieve the perfect event. After all, the goal of wedding planning is to be able to look back on your wedding one day and say, "I wouldn't have changed a thing." If you can do that, you've had the wedding of a lifetime, just as you've always dreamed.

#1 *Engagement Celebration*

If the question has been popped and the affirmative answer has been given, it's official. You're engaged! An engagement party is now in order.

There's no need to rush. A few weeks after the successful proposal is the perfect time to celebrate.

The bride's parents traditionally host the engagement party, but anyone, even the bride and groom, can spearhead the occasion. It is nice, however, if someone else does the heavy lifting on their behalf.

Choose any party style — fancy, casual, full dinner, cocktails only, indoor, outdoor, huge and full of fanfare, or small and intimate. As long as it's fun, it's a success. The engagement party is likely the first time friends and family of both the bride and groom will interact, so make it warm and welcoming.

Don't invite guests to the engagement party if those guests will not be invited to the wedding, and address the issue of gifts on the engagement-party invitation. "No gifts please" tells guests that you're only interested in sharing the happy news, not in scoring both an engagement and a wedding gift. If engagement gifts are welcome, say nothing and let the guests decide. In either situation, don't open gifts at the party.

An engagement party is a time of bonding and celebration. Don't worry about fancy plans. Just have a blast.

#2 *It May Be Trendy, but Is It You?*

The funny thing about trends is their penchant for recycling. Today's big fad may have been all the rage in the flower-power 1960s, the Victorian 1800s, or even ancient Egypt. When it comes to wedding trends, the best one might be none at all.

It's hard to feel special if you follow the dictates of the latest captains of industry. Do you really care that some culinary impresario has decreed that black cake with white polka dots is the "trend" for wedding cakes, or that the latest fashion diva has nixed skinny-heeled shoes as "so last season"?

People who create trends are generally those who benefit financially from steering customers to something that's "new right now." You don't have to follow suit. It's your wedding, and every choice you make should be driven by what makes you happy. If you want open-toed shoes in the dead of winter, that's your call. If you'd love a big-skirted 1950s-style gown, so be it. If you've always dreamed of seeing your groom standing at the altar in a white tux, why should you sacrifice your dream because someone deemed white tuxes to be old news?

Think and decide for yourself. It's your wedding. Besides, whatever wedding choices you make, they're sure to be trendy sooner or later.

#3 *The Perfect Date*

Sometimes the wedding date is mandated by the availability of the venue or the officiant. But whether or not certain restrictions exist, date choices should be made with care.

Choosing a too-soon date adds stress to the wedding-planning process and may prohibit those who need ample notice from attending. Choosing a date during a volatile-weather season may impact the attendance of guests and the effectiveness of vendors.

To prevent sensory overload, you may wish to avoid sharing your wedding day with holidays, birthdays, anniversaries, and other dates of note. Giving your wedding a distinctive milestone date, with its own exclusive and special memories, means no emotional crowding on your anniversary.

A carefully considered date is the perfect launch to a spectacular wedding experience.

#4 *The Wednesday Wedding*

Most weddings are held on 1 of just 52 days a year — Saturdays. Choosing any other day of the week can trim wedding expenses and leave more money for the honeymoon.

Vendors who provide wedding products and services are eager to secure clients on nonprime wedding days, and that eagerness can translate into wedding-day bargains. Ceremony venues, reception halls, restaurants, hotels, caterers, musicians, limousine services, and almost all other wedding necessities cost less on a weekday. A non-Saturday wedding gives wedding couples a powerful supply-and-demand bargaining chip that, if used wisely, can ensure a spectacular wedding at a substantially reduced cost.

The downside of a non-Saturday wedding is guest attendance. Save-the-date notifications for a weekday wedding should go out as soon as possible after the date is chosen. But even with plenty of notice, some people may simply be unable to attend a nonweekend event. An evening wedding may help mitigate some guest attendance losses.

The choice comes down to what matters most. Is a more spectacular, less expensive wedding a viable option even though some guests will be unable to attend, or is the guest list the most important element of all? The answer to that question helps determine if a non-Saturday wedding will be the wedding of your dreams.

#5 Banish Pesky Worry

You already insure your car, your home, your health, and your life. Maybe it's time to insure your wedding day.

Insuring wedding events is now commonplace, and liability insurance may be required by ceremony and reception venues, especially if liquor is served.

Factor wedding insurance into the budget to protect against losses from accidents or damage at the ceremony or reception, and to provide peace-of-mind protection for everything from a catastrophic, new-puppy shredding of the gown to the failure of vendors to honor their commitments.

Check policy details to see what is and isn't covered, and explore different insurance providers. Thoroughly vet the one you choose by checking references, licenses, and company history.

Wedding insurance is not overly expensive, but it's an important consideration for the wedding budget. Unfortunately, as appealing as it may sound, coverage for "cold feet" is not offered.

#6 Here's a Tip — Say Thank You with Dollars

Tipping should always be about a job well done, and tips for wedding vendors and service providers should be increased or decreased according to actual service. Designate one person, perhaps the best man or father of the bride, to deliver tip envelopes to deserving recipients like these:

- hairstylists (15% to 20% of the fee, plus up to 5% for the shampoo assistant)
- valets (a dollar or two per car, to be divided among all valets)
- coat checkers (a dollar or two per guest, to be divided among all checkers)
- chauffeurs (15% to 25% of the transportation bill)
- makeup artists (15% to 20% of the fee)
- catering staff (up to 25% of the bill, to be divided among all catering staff)
- bartenders (15% to 20% of the bar bill if it's a cash bar, or up to 35% if guests are prohibited from tipping)
- restroom attendants (a dollar or two per guest, to be divided among all attendants)
- musicians ($20 to $30 per band member, and $35 to $75 for ceremony soloists or pianists/organists)
- officiates or officiants ($50 to $75 for civil service officiates if the ceremony is not conducted in a city-owned facility where tipping is prohibited, and $50 to $75 for religious

officiants, given as a donation to the house of worship or
to the officiant's designated charity)

Even florists, photographers, videographers, bakers, and seamstresses may sometimes deserve tips under exceptional circumstances, and a tipping list in the wedding budget means that no one will be inadvertently forgotten.

#7 *A Pleasant Rest for the Wedding Weary*

It's easy to concentrate on the big tasks of wedding planning and shortchange the not-so-crucial ones, but attention to the littlest details is where a wedding shines.

It's likely that most guests will make their way to the restroom at least once during the wedding festivities, and adding your own style to restroom décor is a welcome, unexpected touch.

Consider a wedding-themed floral arrangement for each ceremony and reception restroom. Display the bouquet alone or with a decorative array of flameless candles. A pleasant soap and a nice hand lotion in automatic dispensers, coupled with a basket of custom-printed paper hand towels, change the restroom experience. For a fun conversation piece, add a goofy wedding-couple photo in a quirky frame. A courtesy basket filled with essentials like safety pins, adhesive bandages, and travel-sized mouthwashes is a plus. And finally, upgrading the toilet tissue from razor-thin, corncob-scratchy commercial rolls to soft and supple, lap-of-luxury rolls is a kindness every guest will appreciate!

#8 *From Here to There with Functional Art*

Contrary to common perception, it's not only stubborn males who won't ask for directions. Women have also been known to wander aimlessly for far too long before seeking assistance. Fortunately, custom wedding maps keep all guests on the straight and narrow.

There are plenty of commercial Web sites offering "plug-in" customizing of wedding maps, but hiring a map artist to create a one-of-a-kind map will result in a useful, personal keepsake.

Artistically rendered maps can be as whimsical or as formal as you wish. They can include landmarks, points of interest for out-of-town guests, favorite restaurants, entertainment venues, and doggy day-care facilities. Incorporate wedding colors throughout or just as a decorative border. Fun tidbits like "Where the bride and groom first kissed" or "This is where we met!" can easily be woven into a custom-drawn map.

Artists who create unique wedding maps provide a master for color photocopying or make needed copies upon request. The original can be framed as a commemorative piece of art for the wedding couple's home.

Include the custom, keepsake wedding map in invitations and in welcome baskets for out-of-towners.

#9 *Engagement in the News*

After sharing your engagement news with friends and family, it's time for the newspaper announcement. Every newspaper has its own specific requirements, including word and photo limitations, deadlines, fees, and photo color guidelines. A local paper will likely cost significantly less than papers that enjoy a wider circulation.

Include the bride's, groom's, and all parents' names, plus hometown designations and a hint about the wedding date, such as, "A spring wedding is anticipated." Not specifying the exact wedding date helps prevent the public announcement from inadvertently being construed as an invitation, and from alerting criminals to exactly when you will be away from home.

Career and educational backgrounds for the bride and groom are frequently mentioned, but there's no need to divulge anything you don't wish to share. Simply say what matters to you.

Insert a formal or casual photo of the bride alone, one of the bride and groom together, or opt for no photo at all.

Hint! Want to get your announcement in the paper for free? If your wedding will be unique in a way that would be of interest to the newspaper's readers, contact the lifestyle editor of the paper and share your story. If your situation piques the editor's interest, your "announcement" could become a news article, complete with a professional writer and photographer and no bill to pay!

#10 *I Love You, Dad!*

You're excited about your impending marriage, and everyone is excited for you. But for Dad, if he's the one walking you down the aisle your wedding may feel like the sharpest of double-edged swords. When a father shares a close bond with a daughter, losing his little girl to the new man in her life is sometimes as painful as it is amazing. To add salt to the wound, dads are customarily ignored throughout the wedding-planning process, making their sense of loss even stronger. If you love him, show him!

Make a point of involving Dad in the process leading up to the wedding. Try a father-daughter picnic or a photo-booth session with just the two of you. Make him feel needed by giving him a special task, like tapping into his love of cars and encouraging him to help choose your wedding-day transportation. In any number of ways, let him know that, while you may be starting a whole new family, he will always be in your heart and in your life.

Remembering Dad during the hustle and bustle of wedding planning may be one of the greatest gifts you'll ever give him, and when the time comes for him to walk you down the aisle, he'll feel less like he's truly "giving you away."

#11 *Wedding-Day Loans — Yes? No? Maybe?*

Weddings are expensive, and it's understandable that skimping on the event you've dreamed about your whole life is not desirable. With wedding-day loans, you may not have to. But is taking out a loan for your wedding the right thing to do?

For couples with adequate financial wherewithal for the loan's payback, a wedding-day loan is more about convenience than about debt. But for couples with no financial windfall in sight, taking out a loan to cover wedding expenses may prove to be a painful way to begin the marriage.

Ask yourself if the wedding of your dreams is worth the sacrifices that will have to be made for months or years during the payback of the loan. Calculate how much interest will be paid over the life of the loan, then imagine what else could be purchased with that lost money.

Marriage discord caused by money issues is far too common, and the best wedding gift a couple can give themselves is to be honest about wedding expenses right from the start. A wedding-day loan may be helpful, but it should be entered into with four eyes wide open.

#12 *Dear Diary*

Tradition has taken a beating in modern times, but foregoing some traditions in favor of striking out in your own direction generates excitement. Traditional or unconventional, your wedding is yours to live and yours to share.

Keeping a diary from the moment of saying "Yes" to the last day of the honeymoon is a gift for yourself, and for the daughter you may someday have. For any young bride, the chance to know the littlest details of her mother's experience is a treasure.

The journey to the altar is filled with trials and frustrations, laughter and exhilaration, and lots of important decisions. Decades down the road, your diary will make your daughter's wedding experience even richer.

Write what you feel, not just what you do. Stuff a large envelope with snippets of the lace choices you pondered for days, or photos of the dozens of gowns you considered. Add a letter to your daughter, written right now while your own wedding glee is soaring, in which you promise to be with her on her own wedding day, even if the only way possible is in spirit.

A wedding diary has no downsides. It's a beautiful gift to yourself, and a beautiful gift to the daughter, or daughters, you may welcome someday.

#13 *Making the Most of the Bridal Show*

A vendor's purpose at a bridal show is to sell you a product or service. Your purpose at the bridal show is to seek inspiration and answers, and to do that effectively, preparation counts. The following tips can enhance both the fun and the usefulness of the bridal-show experience.

Take a friend who will help you organize promotional materials and business cards into large envelopes marked "yes," "no," and "maybe." (Don't throw out the "no" materials right away. You may change your mind!)

Wear only comfortable clothes and shoes.

Bring self-stick address labels for giveaway forms and vendor contact sheets. Use your own or your mother's address.

If no map and vendor list is provided at the door, use a notepad to record aisle and booth numbers of vendors you may wish to revisit. Retracing your steps to vendor booths at big shows can be an unpleasant challenge.

Wear appropriate undergarments for trying on gowns.

Be prepared to make deposits for those services or products you are definitely sold on. Show specials can provide exciting bargains.

Carry a phone or notebook computer with Internet access to compare something you see with something available elsewhere, and also use that online access to check reviews or vendor references.

Bridal shows are compact malls devoted to the things you want and need for your wedding. Preparation gives you greater clarity of mind and helps protect tired toes from unnecessary steps.

#14 *Who Pays?*

Weddings have come a long way from yesteryear, when young couples began marriage with virtually nothing to their names. Brides and grooms today are often older, living apart from parents, and more financially established. The old "rules" of who pays for what simply don't apply anymore. The groom's parents don't have to cover the costs of the officiant's fee, the license, the rehearsal dinner, and their share of the flowers while the bride's parents foot the bill for just about everything else. Modern wedding couples usually pay a portion or all of their own wedding expenses, with financial help from both families as agreed.

"Who pays for what" is a negotiation. Every parent wants to see a precious son or daughter enjoy a dream wedding. But no one, neither the wedding couple nor the parents, should be driven into financial hardship to do so.

When preparing the wedding budget, sit with each set of parents and detail areas where you will need financial assistance. Rather than assigning specific wedding costs, be open to accepting lump contributions. Perhaps the groom's parents can reasonably afford to share "X" amount, while the bride's parents can comfortably give "Y" amount. Accept the contributions with grace, use them to their best advantage, and don't worry that one may be greater than the other.

No one should expect 21st-century parents to follow archaic dictates about paying for wedding expenses. If you want a spectacular wedding, save for it. Parents usually respond to requests for help the best way they can.

#15 *The Charities of Your Choice*

The wedding-planning process is a perfect time to think about how your wedding can benefit your favorite charities. Donate flowers to hospitals or nursing homes, leftover food to soup kitchens, empty soft-drink cans and plastic bottles to scouts or schools in need of fund-raising tools, and decorations suitable for craft projects to after-school programs and day-care centers. There are plenty of ways to show compassion after the wedding.

Not every charity can accept tangible goods, but many can. Make a list of what you will likely have to donate, then contact a number of local charities and nonprofit facilities in your area to find homes for whatever items you wish to share. Enlisting the advice of local teachers, religious leaders, and volunteer organizations may be helpful in finding ideal matches and in coordinating delivery.

You will be busy enjoying your wedding night and your honeymoon, so be sure to assign someone to oversee the donation process on your behalf. The trappings associated with a wedding needn't go to waste, and it feels good to know they haven't.

#16 *Trimming the Guest-List Fat*

Like bellies at a beer fest, wedding budgets bloat from overindulging. Keeping the wedding budget in check is easier if you trim the wedding fat early.

It's a simple rule of thumb: the more guests you have, the more expensive the wedding. Every guest adds to the budget in multiple ways.

Compose your guest list without restrictions, then make a note next to each name, explaining why that guest should be invited. Honestly pinpointing the purpose of an invitation will help you pare the guest list down to size. You don't have to invite long-lost relatives you haven't seen in decades, or everyone in the office when you're only close to a couple of coworkers. Friends of friends and neighbors of neighbors can easily be eliminated. Make sure you're inviting someone for a reason that matters, not just to be nice or to keep the peace.

Learn to say, "I wish our budget allowed us to invite everyone, but it's not possible."

If a large guest list matters most, so be it. But if you need money to realize other wedding-day desires, not inviting every casual friend, coworker, or twice-removed relative can free up the money to make those desires a reality.

#17 *Taking It to the Bank*

One of the greatest assets a wedding budget can have is a designated wedding-planning bank account. It's far too easy to wander off budget when wedding expenses are paid with multiple credit or debit cards along with cash and checks. Trying to implement a budget only by tabulating receipts after the fact may doom the process.

A designated bank account provides an instant and clear picture of where the money is going. If you overspend in one area, you'll see it right away. But if you pay for that overexpenditure with a credit card, you will be far less likely to even realize you've overspent. Those excesses will multiply, and as time progresses you may find there's no money left to cover essentials you don't want to live without.

Opening a wedding-only bank account is an easy way to keep a firmer hand on the financial reins. Sticking to your budget ensures that important aspects of your wedding won't have to be sacrificed, and it adds tranquility to the spending process.

#18 *Prioritizing the Wedding Wishes*

Every bride and groom wants it all, but having it all is not always an option. Prioritization is crucial to effective wedding planning.

Begin by making a list of every wedding-day desire you've ever had, as if money were no object. Be thorough, and leave nothing off the list.

Once finished, choose the 25 most important items on the list, and record them on a new list. From that list, choose only your top 20. Repeat the process, eliminating five items each time, until only five remain. Now you've identified your true priorities.

Allocate the amount of money it will take to realize your top-five wedding-day desires. Once they are accommodated in the budget, do the same with the next five, and so on, until there's no more money to be allocated.

Prioritizing means you will have the money you need for the things that matter most. Don't worry about the items that get eliminated. It's your wedding. You should designate the bulk of your money for those elements your heart just can't live without.

#19 *Simple Acts of Kindness*

Thank-you notes are customarily sent in response to gift giving at the wedding. But long before the gift table becomes piled high with treasures, the bride and groom have received plenty of intangible gifts.

Keeping a daily journal will help you remember those who played a small but important role in the realization of your wedding dreams. Some will be hired contractors who go above and beyond on your behalf, like the seamstress who never lost her smile when you changed your mind a dozen times, or the gardener who labored tirelessly to prune the roses to perfection for your backyard wedding. Some will be family and friends, like the great-aunt who helped you locate that special antique candelabra or the neighbor's son who scooped the snow from your driveway so that you could make your final fitting.

Everyone likes to feel appreciated. A written note, a small basket of handmade cookies, or any heartfelt thank-you given to those whose simple acts of kindness contributed to your wedding day will make them, and you, feel fulfilled.

#20 *Marital Bliss Begins with Premarital Preparation*

A great, long-lasting marriage, like anything built to be worthy and eternal, requires a solid foundation.

Religious officiants frequently require at least one premarital counseling session. But for secular wedding couples interested in providing the best start to a lifetime together, a premarital marriage-education course may prove to be a great investment.

Preparing for future challenges by exploring them early identifies partners' strengths and potential weaknesses. Knowledge is power, and facing hard questions in advance of the wedding day highlights areas that may need work and instills a sense of shared responsibility and mutual understanding. Marriage prep is not therapy or counseling. It's education. Some states so value marriage-preparation courses that those who attend are entitled to reduced fees for marriage licenses.

Everything from conflict resolution to intimacy issues and shared goals is included in a marriage-education course, but the process will only be as effective as the instructor in charge. Always verify credentials and consider references.

A greater commitment means a greater chance of reaching that 50th wedding anniversary.

#21 *Do I Need a Professional Wedding Planner?*

That's a good question. Have you thrown the most awesome dinner parties ever, attending to every little detail with unbridled passion? Are you an on-the-job whiz at multitasking? Do your friends describe you as a control freak? If the answer to these questions is "yes," you may not need or want a professional wedding planner.

On the other hand, if forgetting to pick up the dry cleaning or losing your keys is a common occurrence, or if attending to the same task again and again drives you up a wall, a wedding planner could be a valuable investment.

Professional wedding planners add expense to the wedding budget, but on the other hand, they often have direct connections to vendors, resulting in discounts for services you couldn't have initiated on your own.

Two major reasons not to have a wedding planner are cost and the perceived loss of control over wedding-planning minutiae.

Two major reasons to absolutely have a wedding planner are reduced stress and the undeniable value of experience.

A wedding planner's greatest asset is the ability to listen. If the planner doesn't listen when being interviewed for the job, just say no. The one who listens best is the one who will best turn wishes into realities.

#22 *Passions before Pomp and Circumstance*

Wedding planning can make a groom's eyes glaze over. All that talk of lace and cakes and flowers is enough to chill even the warmest male toes, and it makes no sense to contribute to wedding-day cold feet.

While you huddle with designers and planners, encourage your groom to create and host his own wedding event. It can be anything he's passionate about, from a prewedding gathering at a football game to a bowling tournament for friends and out-of-town wedding guests. If he loves doing it, he'll love sharing it. It puts the wedding into perspective by weaving the monumental, life-changing occasion into the personal pleasures of everyday life, and it guarantees fun. Unlike the limited guest list of a bachelor party, the groom-hosted event can serve as a prewedding blast for any interested person on the wedding guest list.

Weddings don't have to be all about customs and traditions. Incorporating unexpected real-life activities into the schedule of expected wedding events is great for everyone. But a groom with wedding-detail-glazed eyes may appreciate it most.

#23 *Gifts You'll Want to Keep!*

Bridal registries aren't just for china, crystal, and silver anymore.

With the availability of the Internet and the versatility of mom-and-pop establishments, modern wedding couples can gently steer guests toward gifts the bride and groom truly covet. As a bonus, guests appreciate the guidance.

Registering at unique businesses inspires gifts that do more than set a nice table. Consider registering at retailers or service providers who offer the following:

- a health club or spa membership
- a remodel from a home-improvement store
- DVDs, CDs, or books
- a honeymoon or other destination trip
- flying, scuba, musical, or other lessons
- cooking or nutrition classes
- concert tickets
- a massage
- an online auction account
- charity donations
- eco-friendly upgrades
- health products
- a home down-payment account
- restaurant gift cards
- video games or computer applications
- coins for a coin collection
- stocks and bonds
- art

Whatever your passions, whatever your needs, where you register sets the tone. Guests may realize that toasters and blenders are not the greatest gifts for long-established couples marrying later in life, but you shouldn't expect them to read your minds about what a great gift might actually be. Help them. Register early, and register at a variety of places that feature gift options in all price ranges.

Gift registries work best when thoughtfully matched to the bride and groom's lifestyle.

#24 *All Limousine Companies Are Not Created Equal*

It's true. Not all limousines or limousine services are created equal.

To protect your day from unwelcome surprises, begin by asking the company the following ten questions when booking your transportation:

1. What is your state license number?
2. May I come to pick out the car I want?
3. How is the chauffeur attired?
4. Does the chauffeur have wedding experience?
5. Are there any fees above the quoted hourly rate?
6. Do you provide wedding decorations, and may I see them?
7. Do you permit custom decorations to be attached to the car?
8. What if we need the limo longer than anticipated?
9. Do you have references?
10. What is your policy on a disabled car and job farming?

All answers help ensure a joyful ride, but the answer to the last question is especially important. Working relationships between companies are a blessing in the event of a car breakdown, but some companies deliberately book jobs for more cars than they can handle then "farm" some jobs to another company for a percentage of the income. Hand picking a company and a specific limousine only to end up with something entirely different on your wedding day negates the research you put into hiring just the right service in the first place. Discuss farming policies up front and tell the limousine service that substitutions are unacceptable except in extraordinary and entirely unavoidable circumstances.

#25 *A Transportation Horse of a Different Color*

A traditional stretch limousine is awe inspiring, but maybe you're anything but traditional. Great news! There are plenty of creative options.

Everything from a horse-drawn Cinderella carriage to a motorcycle with a sidecar is available for today's adventurous wedding couples. If the reception is just a hop, skip, and a jump from the ceremony site, consider creating an unbelievable wedding-day video by using a bicycle built for two, a pair of wedding-decorated Segways, or a jazzed-up golf cart. Do you have an athletic wedding party? What a fun experience rollerblading to the reception would be!

If the reception is a fair distance from the ceremony site, there are vintage cars, street trolleys, funky buses, and even hayride wagons to get you there. In lieu of traditional limousines, try contacting car clubs. How incredible would it be to have a fleet of muscle cars or a matching parade of Model A's escorting the bride, groom, and wedding party to the reception?

Whether it has wheels, hooves, or sled runners, if it goes from here to there, it's wedding transportation.

#26 *Rice Is Nice but Natural Confetti Is Better*

Well-wishing rice has rained down upon brides and grooms for generations, but some venues will no longer permit rice on the premises. Fortunately, today's environmentally conscious wedding couples may choose beautiful, Earth-friendly "showers" that don't compromise local flora and fauna.

A decorated paper cone filled with dried flowers, leaves, or colorful herbs provides a safe and lovely alternative to rice. Just a gentle fan of the hand, and the "confetti" flies from the cone.

It's easy to make your own wedding confetti by pressing leaves into books or by drying flowers or herbs in a dehydrator. Once dry, simply turn the pieces into confetti with scissors or a paper punch. Use this fun project to turn children into CEOs of their very own "Wedding-Confetti Enterprise." Kids rarely get to contribute to wedding planning, but making natural confetti is right up their alley. Craft the cones from decorated paper stock or heavy wrapping paper and a few spots of paper glue. Adorn as desired.

Be sure to provide a recycle basket for empty cones!

#27 *Bubbles, Bells, and Sparkling Spells*

For the venue that doesn't permit showering the bride and groom with materials intended to land on the ground, blowing, ringing, or sparkling can preserve the "rice throwing" tradition without tossing a thing.

Bubbles blown by mouth or by the wave of a hand create a fairy-tale environment. There's no concern that the bubble solution will harm the Earth, but a bubble landing in an eye may cause it to sting. Not all solutions are derived from the same ingredients, so investigate the safety profile of different bubble products.

Tiny wedding bells or jingle bells attached to a seasonally inspired stick, like bamboo for summer or a pine twig for winter, fill the air with the sound of joyful celebration as the wedding couple passes by. To add visual excitement, top the stick with a long, thin ribbon that flutters with the wind.

Sparklers held high overhead create a magical spell. It is the fleeting essence of tiny fireworks bursting to life that gives sparklers their undeniably wedding-perfect allure. Bubbles, bells, and sparklers give rice an honest run for its money.

#28 *May I See Your License?*

A license to marry is mandated by states and counties nationwide, and each locale has its own unique set of requirements. The license comes with a compulsory "think about it" waiting period that is usually from one to seven days. The wait, however, is frequently waived under extenuating circumstances, like a soldier with only a two-day pass.

Many states have either reduced or eliminated the once-obligatory blood tests for marriage licenses, but other requirements remain standard. In most states, the bride and groom must be at least 18 years old and show valid IDs and certified copies of the dissolution of any previous marriages, and they must obtain the license together and in person. But states and counties routinely change requirements, so it's best to investigate licensing practices for the wedding location at least two months in advance of the planned wedding day. Most marriage bureaus supply handouts or post relevant information on the governing agency's Web site.

The marriage license can't be overlooked. As they say, "No job is complete until the paperwork is done."

#29 *Please Be Seated*

Creating a seating chart that keeps smiles on all faces is not the easiest task in the world. Of course, there is always the option of free seating, but free seating is a bit like high school, where the "cool kid" guests flock together while the "shy ones" try to fade into the scenery. Such a scenario is not conducive to a great event.

The object is to make each guest feel equally welcome, while also honoring special people in your lives.

Give the elderly and the disabled easily accessible seats closest to the restrooms and the buffet tables (if any). If the buffet tables and restrooms are on opposite ends of the room, seat them closest to the restrooms. Someone can always bring them a plate, but no one can visit the restroom for them.

Seat close family members nearest to the bride and groom.

Teens may sit with parents or at teen-only tables near the back of the room, where they can bond in the way that only teenagers do.

Children younger than 13 should always be seated with their parents. And as a courtesy, try to keep the littlest ones at tables that do not include elderly guests unused to rambunctious youngsters.

Unless otherwise instructed, separate by a mile those who were once, but are no longer, married or involved.

Incorporate solo guests into welcoming table groups. Never seat all single people together as if they were guest-list afterthoughts.

Consider personalities. Strive to make tablemates comfortable. Loud and boisterous isn't always a congenial counterbalance to shy and introverted, but commonalities, like those enjoyed by coworkers, easily breed free-flowing conversation.

Create your seating chart by designating individual chairs or by simply assigning tables, but do so after the benefit of thoughtful consideration.

#30 *Bless the Nanny*

Hiring a nanny or babysitting service for children at the wedding may prove to be one of your best wedding-planning decisions. Children have energy to spare, and without directing that energy, "oops" moments are inevitable. It's too much to ask that little ones simply sit quietly and do nothing. It's not in their nature, nor should it be. Addressing a child's need to be active by providing organized entertainment and interaction means happiness for everyone, especially the bride and groom.

Certain nanny or babysitting services have developed programs specifically for weddings. They provide activity bags that are gender specific, gender neutral, or customized to a particular wedding. Experienced workers watch over the children at both the ceremony and the reception, either in a designated separate room or in a specific corner set up just for the little ones. The number of nannies assigned is proportionate to the number of children to be cared for. Most services provide one worker for every three or four children.

Verify the reputation and licensing of any nanny or babysitting service, then sit back, relax, and know that everyone, even those who think playing hide-and-seek under the cake table would be a grand idea, will enjoy their day to the fullest.

#31 *Fill It with Hope and Other Stuff*

In centuries past, the hope chest held a bride's worldly household possessions, sending her to her groom with all the essentials necessary to create a home. A modern bride may not sit by the fire, hand stitching linens to add to her hope chest, but the concept of the chest remains exciting.

Shopping may have replaced embroidering and weaving, but there's still plenty to tuck away for a bride's new married life. Family heirlooms, cherished recipes, holiday ornaments, photos, diaries, treasured books, and mementos of family milestones nestle perfectly against the latest gadget snagged at a department store clearance event or that exquisite vase spotted at an estate sale.

Some hope chests are no more than cardboard boxes, while others are extraordinary pieces of furniture built to last a lifetime. Plain or fancy, a hope chest is a pleasure to tend.

#32 *Software to Save the Day*

While many companies sell wedding-planning software, and others offer certain online versions for free, it's important to remember that not all software is created equal. Comparison is key.

The most valuable software for DIY brides is mobile, private, reliable, and easy to use. Mobility matters because brides and grooms are always on the move. Utilizing software that does not require an Internet connection means never searching for Wi-Fi when shopping.

Your privacy is more vulnerable with online software, where gathered information is readily shared with wedding vendors far and wide. If you welcome unsolicited contacts, lax privacy is not a concern. But if receiving unwanted sales pitches isn't appealing, the privacy policy of the software provider is important. Software without Internet necessity is the most private. Online software and apps for mobile devices are the least private.

Reliability is important. Weddings often take years to plan, making software that has been purchased, installed, and tech supported by a major company a safer bet than software generated online by a small enterprise. Online companies come and go. You don't want to log on one day and discover an error message where your wedding details once were. If there is no procedure for independent backup, choose another software.

Ease of use goes without saying. Wedding software should require only rudimentary skills to operate. Complicated, lengthy procedures can add to wedding-planning stress, and that defeats the point of the "helpful" software.

Research, compare, and explore testimonials, then choose the software that supports your every need.

#33 *Wedding-Brunch Delight*

The morning-after wedding brunch is a let-your-hair-down final get-together that gives the newlyweds and their guests one last enjoyable interaction before the good-byes. There's no stress, just good food and good company, and the guest list can include anyone the bride and groom wish to invite. Parents may help, but the brunch is customarily hosted and funded by the wedding couple.

With a small guest list, an at-home brunch may be just the ticket. But for a brunch blessed with the pleasure of no preparation or cleanup, and one that is likely enlivened by entertainment and a unique ambiance, choose a well-established restaurant brunch.

Cruise brunches; jazz, piano, or gospel brunches; and hotel brunches with private dining rooms are all commonly available options. A bonus for booking your wedding brunch at a hotel is the probability of securing a package discount for events, meals, and rooms needed for guests.

The morning-after brunch isn't a must, but it is a pleasant way to add one last hurrah to the wedding experience.

#34 *Tick Tock!*

Who needs a wedding countdown clock? Everyone!

A wedding ticker is a countdown clock you add to your computer, cell phone, or other mobile device. Place the ticker on blogs or social network sites, in forums, on your Web site, or as a tag to your e-mails. Find a free ticker on the Web, fill in your details via an online form, and the site provides a code to copy and paste wherever you like. Use the same ticker in multiple places, or choose a different ticker for different applications. Some tickers are fairly plain, while others offer clever design choices and the ability to personalize them with a customized message.

Because time does fly when you're planning a wedding, a ticker keeps you focused. It won't be as easy to put off until tomorrow what should be accomplished today if the fleeting days are ticking away right before your eyes. It's also a clever reminder for guests who have their own details to address before your wedding.

Lost moments are never recovered. It's nice to have a little technological aid that reminds you of that.

#35 *Wedding Favors 101*

Wedding favors say "thank you" to guests. What should they express — elegance, distinction, whimsy, or something else? Do you want the favor to be useful and long lasting, or delectable but perishable? Do you want it personalized? Must all favors be the same? Are you partial to homemade gifts or to purchased ones? Should the favors enhance your wedding theme or convey a particular passion of the bride and groom?

Answering these questions before initiating your search will focus the selection process. Wedding favors should absolutely thank guests for coming, but it's a bonus if they also add ambiance to table décor. Men and women needn't receive the same favor, but it's okay if they do. Favors that come with presentation packaging save the time it would take to bag, box, tie, or otherwise secure individual favors. On the other hand, some favors, like mini topiaries or personalized wine glasses, require no packaging and still make a beautiful presentation. Ordering samples prevents disappointment. Sometimes a favor looks bigger, smaller, or different than advertised. It pays to hold it in your hand.

It's not the price of the favor that matters most. It's knowing that sincere thought underscored its selection.

#36 *Rocking the "Wedsite"*

The 21st century has gifted the planet with plenty of technological advances, but for wedding couples, one of the best is the chance to create a customized wedding Web site, affectionately known as a "wedsite."

Brides and grooms can now communicate with wedding guests from day one of their engagement without ever leaving their computers. Start by going online and selecting one of the many wedding Web site providers. Once you have chosen a domain name for your wedsite, the Web site provider assigns an Internet address and a template for uploading personal information. It's easy.

Web site prices range from free to a fixed monthly fee to a yearly flat rate, and comparison shopping ensures the best bang for the buck. There are online review sites that provide comparisons of many wedsites at once, making it easier to contrast the differences.

Options may include a text and content editor, a photo and video clips editor, blogs with RSS feeds, e-mail addresses, online RSVPs, electronic invites, thank-you card templates, event coordination tools, gift registries, and more. Not every wedsite has every feature, and some have plenty of positive testimonials while others aren't as well liked. Choose carefully, then enjoy the coordinating tools, the freedom of instant dissemination of information, and the excitement of watching your wedding planning unfold in living, online color.

#37 *Backyard Honeymoons*

Honeymoons don't have to involve umbrella drinks on a tropical island or a five-star hotel with bellhops who make more in daily tips than you paid for your entire honeymoon trousseau. America's backyard is full of honeymoon opportunities that move the spirit but don't rob you blind.

How about Crater of Diamonds State Park in Arkansas? Losing yourself in lush landscapes and prospecting for diamonds is great shared fun. Stay in a private lodge or in a cabin on the lake, and rent a boat to explore your surroundings. Crater of Diamonds is the only working diamond mine in the country that permits the public to dig to their heart's content and keep the diamonds and more than 35 other gems and minerals naturally occurring in the mine, no matter how valuable those finds turn out to be. And for pet-loving newlyweds, the park is completely pet friendly, even in the digging area of the mine. Or why not take a bed-and-breakfast tour? Some of America's bed-and-breakfast facilities are patterned after castles, while others are renovated, centuries-old homes full of vintage ambiance. Some are modern marvels set in the hearts of cities, and others are rustic and secluded. Within just a 200-mile radius around your home, it's entirely possible to hit some of America's sweetest bed-and-breakfast spots. The purchase of an up-to-date bed-and-breakfast guide or plotting a route online can lead to plenty of recreational opportunities perfect for newlyweds. The only truly necessary ingredients for a fabulous honeymoon are a husband and wife in love. With that kind of magic, even the humblest of surroundings are rich.

#38 *Getting to Know You*

You're getting married, so chances are you know each other pretty well, and you've probably already established a circle of mutual friends. But how well do you know each other's extended families?

The wedding-planning process is not only about the wedding day. It's about planning for a long married life. A crucial component of contentment throughout the decades is family harmony.

To be able to greet each of your intended's relatives with a personal remark, make an effort to learn about grandparents, aunts, uncles, and cousins before you meet them at the rehearsal dinner or reception. Saying to your new cousin Steve that you've always wondered what it would be like to hit the road at 100 miles an hour, before Steve has the chance to mention his occupation as a race-car driver, shows generous sincerity.

It's human nature to want to be thought of in kindness, and the simplest gesture goes a long way. Families at odds are a trial for any marriage, so whether you're the bride or the groom, get to know a little something about your new family before you meet them. The time spent asking each other about family members is time well spent.

#39 *Sweet-Dreams Book*

Brides often dream of their wedding day from the time they are little girls, so by the time the engagement really happens, each has a pretty good idea of what she wishes her big day to be. That's helpful. Score a wedding-planning edge when you approach every task with a dream book in hand.

Before meeting with vendors and suppliers, assemble your dream wedding on paper. Create a scrapbook of hair, makeup, gown, veil, and shoe photos clipped from magazines. Add fabric swatches culled from remnant pieces, hand sketches of perceived ceremony and reception layouts, and recipes of favorite dishes. The more defined your vision, the better your ability to negotiate with vendors.

A dream-wedding book won't translate every imagined concept into a reality, for your mind may change along the way, but when you start with tangible, hold-in-your-hand ideas, the path to turning lifelong dreams into wedding-day realities is easier to travel.

#40 *The "A" List*

Some wedding couples believe that keeping costs in check begins with the creation of an "A" and a "B" guest list. Wedding gurus even offer tips on how to be secretive enough to pull of an "A/B" guest-list scenario without getting caught in an embarrassing situation. In short, the process means that guests on the "A" list are invited, but for each who doesn't positively RSVP, a member of the "B" list gets an invite as if he or she was supposed to be invited all along. To pull it off, timing and secrecy matter.

Is an "A/B" guest list smart wedding planning, or is it the ultimate in bad taste? That's for you to decide. But the potential for hurt feelings is strong. It's no fun realizing you weren't the pick of the litter, and no one wants to be someone's "alternate."

Bad vibes spread like wildfire. If you hurt someone's feelings, don't expect him or her to keep quiet about it. Perhaps a viable alternative is to shave other expenses by choosing less pricey entrées, a smaller band, or a less expensive venue so that important people in your life can attend your wedding without being made to feel like an afterthought.

#41 *The Business of Home*

Weddings, showers, and rehearsal dinners at home are often intimate affairs attended by a select few guests. If so, it's likely no special permits will be necessary. But once you cross that fine line into a "large" gathering, your city or municipality may mandate permits for issues like excess parking or live entertainment. There may even be a fire inspection, an electrical or generator assessment (to confirm that power needs won't overwhelm the neighborhood), or an insurance or disabled-accessibility review.

The time to investigate permits is several months before the wedding date. Bureaucratic red tape takes time, and paperwork for wedding-related events cannot always be submitted online. Permits should be in hand before locking in rental equipment or vendor services for an at-home event.

Check with city or county offices to learn what permits are necessary. Take care of the business necessities early to determine if it's truly cost effective to celebrate at home. Sometimes the costs associated with permits and inspections exceed the price of renting a facility where all of that is someone else's concern.

#42 Wedding Mass Transit

Parking is sometimes the fly in the ointment of an otherwise spectacular wedding-venue choice. If the wedding is on a bluff with no off-road parking, or tucked inside a gated community that doesn't permit multiple guest cars, the solution is wedding-day mass transit.

Arrange for guests to park at a predesignated pickup site, like a carpool lot or a large commercial parking lot. Obtain permission from the store, office, or building management company in charge of the lot.

Hire a shuttle to ferry guests from here to there and back as needed. From a double-decker bus to a hay wagon, your "mass transit" can do more than move people. It can further your theme. For short distances, a smaller vehicle making multiple trips will work well. If the distance is several miles, a larger conveyance may prove more efficient and economical.

Parking problems don't have to torpedo your ceremony or reception venue choice. Just whittle them down to size with wedding mass transit.

#43 My Face, My Photos

Most professional photographers retain copyright to their work and sell prints and reprints, never negatives, for a wedding couple's personal use only. It's a conundrum. Photographers are artists entitled to residual income on their creative work. On the other hand, milking newlyweds to death over reprints feels unreasonable. Find a middle ground.

Search for a photographer who supplies a CD of all the day's high- and low-resolution photos, along with perpetual permission to print from and utilize the CD any way you wish, with the exception of selling the photos. Perpetual permission is for private use and may not include posting a wedding-movie montage derived from the photos on social-networking or public video sites, unless you see that such specific language is included in your contract. Sometimes the photographer will allow a release on public sites, as long as appropriate credit is given with each airing. For your part, agree not to sell your photos to photo banks, or anywhere else, with the intent of making income.

An all-encompassing CD of hundreds of images may carry a higher initial price tag than a photo album of pictures, but the ability to revisit the CD forever can outweigh the residual financial bite of having to buy prints again and again.

Another option is to agree to the photographer's copyright but not to agree to sign a model release. Without a model release, the photographer can't use your photos for any commercial purpose. Employ the model release as a bargaining chip. Agree to permit the photographer to sell your wedding photos for commercial uses in exchange for a reduced rate on the CD.

If the photographer doesn't agree to terms you deem important, move on and find another one. But be careful. Thoroughly study the work and reputation of any photographer willing to throw the copyright baby out with the bathwater. A photographer may voluntarily give up copyright for any number of reasons, but it isn't the norm, and you don't want to find out too late that the reason copyright wasn't an issue is that the photographer takes lousy pictures.

#44 *Brand-New Names*

Whether the (new) wife is taking her husband's name, the husband is taking his wife's, or both are planning to use a hyphenated last name, there's work to be done.

You will need to update these personal identifications:
    Social Security card (top priority)
    driver's license or state ID card
    voter registration card
    credit cards
    military ID
    passport
    frequent-flyer ID

You will need to notify these entities:
    banks, mortgage holders, landlords, and
      retirement account administrators
    health providers
    utilities
    insurance companies
    online affiliations like gaming, shopping,

and social networking sites
employers and licensing boards
clubs, memberships, and alumni associations
attorneys and power-of-attorney holders
the postal service

You will need to update these documents:
will
deeds
legal contracts
vehicle registrations

Obtain several certified copies of the marriage license. Some entities, like the Social Security Administration, require an original document and are unlikely to return it.

To prevent having to engage in the process all over again, don't apply for the name change until an after-wedding home address is established. Changing the name and the address at once saves everyone time and money.

#45 *Honeymoon Thank-You*

Of course you don't want to think about writing thank-you notes while on your honeymoon, but you could think about "saying" thank-you while celebrating your marital bliss. Let your camera and your ingenuity do the talking.

Write "Thank You!" in the sand, pose with your work, and snap a photo to later include with your thank-you cards. Or post the photo on your wedding Web site.

Take just one photo or create a photo journey that gives wedding guests a peek at your honeymoon adventures. Create funny, impromptu signs made from anything and everything, and include whatever message suits the moment.

Don't make it a chore that steals the magic. Be free spirited and impulsive, and say "Thanks," "We love you," or "Can you believe this?" whenever and wherever the mood strikes.

#46 *Advertisements at the Wedding?*

At first blush, that sounds just awful. But maybe it isn't.

Some wedding vendors would love the opportunity to put the name of their business in front of your guests, and they may offer a discount for the privilege of doing so.

This is not about erecting a neon sign or placing a garish display ad in the wedding program. It's about recognition. It could be as simple as adding a line to the end of the wedding program, such as: "Our floral pieces were arranged by My Favorite Florist of MyTown, MyState."

That simple line is unobtrusive but may translate to a discount on the overall cost of your floral bill. Or it may cover the cost of one bouquet or the ushers' boutonnières.

Don't relinquish the driver's seat. It's your wedding, and any form of advertising has to make sense to you. But asking vendors about bartering some of the costs in exchange for a direct mention to wedding guests may prove to be savvy wedding planning.

#47 *The Spice-Rack Shower*

If you're a bride with a home full of furnishings, chances are that traditional shower gifts may not make much sense. One can only use so many kitchen gadgets or bath sets. But there's something every food-loving bride-to-be cherishes: spices.

Drop a hint to the person throwing your shower that you've always dreamed of a well-stocked, international spice larder. Amassing a spice rack that goes beyond seasoned salt and garlic powder is expensive, but if unique and hard-to-find spices are purchased individually, there's no great financial burden on any one shower guest.

If cooking is a passion, spices make all the difference. Not all spices need to be fresh to be amazing, and a spice rack–themed shower is a surefire portal to a beautiful stash of delicious culinary inspiration.

#48 *And the Winner Is …*

You! Well, maybe not every time, but you won't ever be the winner if you don't enter the race. Contests sponsored by wedding vendors are slam-dunk, no-brainer paths to free supplies and services, but many brides simply ignore them. Of course, not everyone will win something, and obviously the vendor is holding the contest to amass a prospective client list, but who cares? If there are free rings, a cake, a gown, a bride's bouquet, a limo ride, or any other wedding necessity at stake, go for it.

It takes only moments to enter a contest, but the payoff could be a huge, budget-saving surprise. Like the lottery, someone will win something. It may as well be you.

#49 *Smoke Out*

More and more states have banned smoking inside commercial establishments, and for those states, prohibiting smoking at your wedding and reception comes with the territory. For other states, the decision is yours.

Fewer than 25% of Americans smoke. Unless your guest list is entirely drawn from that 25%, nonsmoking guests will attend. To a nonsmoker, even one cigarette, cigar, or pipe can cause discomfort. Smoke stench infiltrates formalwear fabrics, creates a mess of butts and ashes on tables, and opens up the potential for smoke burns on rented linens and supplies.

Even if the bride and groom smoke, smoking at the wedding comes with too many negatives to ignore. Handle the issue with elegant no-smoking signs, and set aside a comfortable designated area outdoors where smokers can take a break. Make it nice. Give it some décor and personality, and your smoking friends won't think less of you for not wanting a cloud of smoke hovering over the wedding cake.

#50 *A Task a Day*

It's easy to put off until tomorrow what could have been handled today. Unfortunately, the effects of procrastination have a way of piling up, until you find yourself overwhelmed and seriously stressed. Preparation brings comfort. Give yourself a daily goal, and to make accomplishing those goals easier, create a task-a-day wedding calendar.

Using your master timeline, break down all wedding-planning tasks into small increments. For example, your "shopping for the gown" segment could begin with:

- Monday, the 1st: Purchase wedding magazines.
- Tuesday, the 2nd: Complete review of at least one magazine, and denote dresses of interest.
- Wednesday, the 3rd: Visit a full-service fabric store to touch and examine gown fabric options.
- Thursday, the 4th: Complete review of additional magazines.
- Friday, the 5th: Visit gown designers' Web sites to study their style.
- Saturday, the 6th: Shop for undergarments to be used for trying on gowns.
- Sunday, the 7th: Rest!

A daily calendar keeps you going without scheduling too many tasks on any one day, virtually eliminating that rushed and panicked feeling so many brides experience.

#51 *New Best Friends*

When planning your wedding and honeymoon, you will deal with many new people. One of the paths to a successful wedding experience is the development of meaningful relationships. Always try to deal with the same person at any given establishment or service provider. Get to know each contact, and treat him or her with respect. Your effort will come back to you tenfold. It's a fact of life. If people care about more than the color of your money, they will work harder for you. But it's a two-way street. Taking a "you work for me!" approach, even if it's true, will likely earn you just enough effort to get the job done, and a "just scraping by" effort is not conducive to a great wedding. Look at situations from both your perspective and theirs. It's simple. Care about those you have hired, and they will care about your wedding and honeymoon happiness.

#52 *Belly-Filling Favors*

Glass jars purchased by the case don't look like much on their own. But fill them with something homemade and delectable, and you've created personal, memorable favors. Canning jars stuffed with cookies, fudge, or made-from-scratch pie fillings tease guests with the promise of an at-home treat once the wedding is over. Jelly jars of nuts, dried fruit, savory croutons, or fresh herbs look enticing on the table. Finish any filled jar with a ribbon and a bow, and if you wish, add a special message on a custom label you've printed from your own computer. Belly-filling favors are always a hit. They don't have to be fancy. They just have to be tasty.

#53 *Country Charm and Sweet Suburbia*

If you live and plan to marry in a big city, consider taking your nuptials on the road instead — not too far down the road, as just a hop, skip, and a jump away will suffice. Big-city venues are customarily far more in demand than those in smaller towns or rural communities, and moving your wedding and reception outside the city may shave precious dollars from wedding expenditures. Most guests don't mind driving up to an hour for your wedding, so why not choose facilities and services that offer beautiful amenities but for far less cost? In the bargain, you may find that getting married in a smaller community adds an element of warm surprise for you and your guests. Don't make the mistake of thinking that small-town vendors can't handle your needs. They can. And because they are located in a small community, without weddings piled on top of other weddings, chances are that you'll get the kind of dedicated, personal attention that is sometimes sacrificed to the lightning speed of big-city life.

#54 *Tantalizing Transfers*

For an unusually clever wedding favor, consider an iron-on transfer. With a good home printer, all it takes is a simple program and the right paper to make an iron-on transfer of virtually any photo or design. The paper is not expensive when purchased in bulk, and even in relatively small quantities, the cost is minimal. As with all things, the price goes down as the quantity goes up. Make just one design for everyone, or go the extra mile and mix up the designs to make them personal. When the transfer paper is printed and completely dry, gently roll the paper like a scroll, tie it with a ribbon, and tuck a sprig of lavender or a dried herb into the ribbon. The paper makes a nice presentation at each place setting, and guests will have a blast comparing the designs. By giving them transfers, you are giving them the option of ironing the design onto a T-shirt, pillowcase, tote bag, or whatever else their hearts desire. An iron-on transfer is full of possibilities, and the designs can be wedding centric or not, as you please.

#55 *Throwing Out the Net*

When it comes to wedding planning, the most common question is, "Where do I begin?" A great first step is to identify and then contact wedding vendors in your area. Use the Internet, phone book, and local Chamber of Commerce to compile your list of nearby florists, caterers, transportation services, reception halls, musicians, etc., and send each an inquiry letter. Stay organized, and use a filing and point system to catalog vendor responses. Rate the responses with one to five stars, and soon a vendor "winners" list will begin to emerge.

Your inquiry letter should be brief but sincere, such as:

Hello,

As a new bride-to-be I have just begun to plan my wedding. I am contacting wedding vendors in my area to learn all I can about available services. If you have information to share about your company, I would love to learn about you.

Thank you for your kind consideration.

Sincerely,

Jane Q. Bride

Be sure to include your mailing and e-mail addresses. Do not share your telephone number unless the vendor later lands on your "short list" of possible providers.

By reaching out, you are quickly separating those who are willing to go the extra mile from those who aren't. This blanket approach will also help to unearth smaller vendors who may do fabulous work for a lower price.

You will incur stationery and postage costs, but the potential benefits far outweigh your initial investment. Wedding events succeed or fail at the hands of vendors and suppliers. It pays to be proactive.

#56 *The Season of Engagement*

You got engaged during a blizzard, but you want your engagement photos to reflect the spring season of your wedding. How do you make that happen without going to a photo studio and standing before a backdrop? Engagement photos are often used as decorative accents at the wedding reception, as well as on engagement-party invites and in newspaper announcements. If you want to keep the seasonal theme consistent, have your photos taken in a location that keeps a season alive all year long. Indoor hotel gardens, beautiful fountains, and year-round arboretums can provide that spring or summer feel, even in the dead of winter. Remember to dress appropriately. Don't wear a sweater to a "summer" photo shoot. Conversely, even when it's sweltering outside, skating rinks and Christmas-tree farms can easily reflect that cool, winter ambiance. And don't discount retail facilities. Most home-improvement stores have year-round garden centers, and many department or specialty stores have a year-round "holiday" department. You'll need permission for photos in commercial facilities, but most will give their nod of approval. Just take a tip from the movie industry and tweak basic surroundings with props to create an illusion. When you use a natural setting instead of a photo-studio backdrop, your photos look real, and that's all you need.

#57 *Hidden Assets*

What talents and treasures do you have tucked away in your life arsenal? Do you have a small business? A degree? Practical experience and expertise? A garage full of wonderful doodads? You may be surprised to discover that you have something unique to offer others. If so, use that skill or that item to barter for wedding supplies and services any way and anywhere you can. Maybe it's possible to use your Web site–building savvy to help the limousine company upgrade its Web site in exchange for wedding-day livery service. Or perhaps those old tin signs tucked away in the attic are just the kind of décor items the rehearsal-dinner restaurant loves to feature. Bartering can reduce costs and make everyone happy in the process. Make a list of what you have to offer, both tangible and intangible, and take that list with you to every vendor meeting. Some vendors will have no interest in bartering, while others recognize the value right away. The smaller the enterprise, the more likely the proprietor will be open to bartering, as long as it's fair value for fair value. Don't try to barter a half a dozen old flowerpots to the florist in exchange for all the wedding florals. The best barter is one that makes both participants glad to do it. Bartering is as old as time. And even if you get only one vendor to play ball, you will likely save yourself a fair chunk of wedding-budget change.

#58 *The Photographer Test*

Is it enough to study a photographer's previous wedding work? The answer may be "yes," but there's one way to find out for sure. Ask the photographer to take a couple of photos of you during your initial consultation. Sadly, some professionals aren't professional at all and will use someone else's work as a promotional tool. Give the photographer the benefit of the doubt, but back it up with a wee test, and you'll feel better about putting that person in charge of your precious wedding-day photographic memories. Everything is digital these days, so he won't be wasting any film, just a moment or two of time. If those few unplanned snapshots don't make you happy, it may be time to wonder about all those gorgeous photos in the photographer's portfolio. The best way to find a photographer is through a referral by someone you know who has already experienced the photographer's services. But when that's not an option, and you are meeting a photographer without any knowledge of his work, it doesn't hurt to ask to see what the photographer can do on the spot.

#59 *Bridal-Shower Hotties*

Bridal-shower games don't have to be only about toilet-paper gowns and bridal-gift bingo. It's perfectly okay to push the envelope and have some outlandish fun — for instance, with a game of Bridal-Shower Hotties.

Cut out magazine pictures of hunky stars, athletes, dancers, singers, and politicians. To that pile, add one image of the groom. Place each picture in a large, opaque envelope and seal it, making sure there is one envelope per guest. Draw a little hint on each envelope — musical notes for a singer, an Oscar or Emmy statue for a screen or TV star, a flag for a politician, etc. For the envelope with the groom's picture, simply use a heart. The symbols are important. If guests don't show up and you have to pull envelopes from the game before beginning, you want to be sure not to pull the one with a heart. It must stay in the game.

At the shower, have guests choose an envelope and a pen from a basket. Tell everyone to leave the envelope sealed, then tell guests to imagine that their fairy Godmother has granted them 15 minutes completely alone with the hottie secreted inside their envelopes. Using the envelopes to write on, guests will list three things they would absolutely do in those fantasy 15 minutes. When everyone has completed their three intentions, go around the room and have each person read aloud what she wrote, still leaving all envelopes sealed. Once the group has finished, count to three, at which time everyone will open their envelopes and simultaneously reveal their fantasy hotties. All but one of the guests will be laughing, groaning, or screeching with glee over the hotties they discover, but one will get the groom's picture and surely not know how to react with the bride looking on. This game will be full of hilarious surprises and revelations, but none more so than when the groom's picture is revealed. That lucky and likely embarrassed guest is the winner of the game, and a prize will definitely be in order.

#60 *Bachelor Party 101*

In spite of what some think and what some movies depict, bachelor parties aren't required by law to be drunken blurs of debauchery. Mr. Groom-to-Be, if you're not a party animal at heart, consider a daytime bachelor event like a paintball game, water sports, tickets to a major-league sports event, or your own golf or poker tournament. After the daytime activities, hit up a nice restaurant or kick back in a pizza place, and make the alcohol optional. If you want to be roused from a drunken stupor by the stripper your buddies forced on you — the one your bride-to-be would definitely not like to know about — so be it. But if you're the kind of guy who can have fun without first draining a still, don't let the perception of a bachelor party get in the way of the one you would really enjoy.

#61 *Making a List, Checking It Twice*

One of the biggest wedding-day regrets is not having photos of particular people and events. Photographers may take hundreds of beautiful shots and still not get the ones you really wanted. A "must have" list is imperative. Begin with the guest list. Look at every name, and decide if a photo with that person is important to you. Those chosen people will lead your "must-have photos" list. If you want a candid shot of everyone on the guest list, make a note to have photos taken table by table during dinner. Go over the wedding-planning details and add the must-haves from that group, such as table centerpieces, the escort-card collection, ceiling décor, band members, etc. If you want unspoiled shots of the reception hall or ceremony venue, make sure those choices are on the list so that the photographer can capture them before the flood of guests arrives. Put every ceremonial function, like the sand ceremony, cake cutting, first dance, etc., on the list, and add special notes if necessary. For example, you may want a close-up of your unique toasting flutes in addition to the photo of you toasting.

Many experienced photographers will zero in on great shots you may not even think of, but those same talented photographers can't read your mind. If you want a photo of the groom tying his shoes before the wedding, you're probably going to have to spell it out. Keep a small notebook with you as your navigate your wedding plans, and every time a photo pops into your mind, jot it down. A comprehensive list helps to capture the magic and the memories, ensuring you get the wedding-day photo of you and Grandma that you so looked forward to.

#62 One Day Only

Instead of enlisting a wedding planner to shepherd the entire period of wedding planning toward its culmination, some couples opt for hiring a "day-of coordinator." The coordinator runs the show on the day of the wedding, and hopefully keeps that show running smoothly and on time. The goal is to lift the pressure from the bride and groom's shoulders so they can simply enjoy the experience. But a wedding-day coordinator will only be as effective as the wedding planning has been. Create a binder for the coordinator that spells out every detail of what should happen, from sunrise on the wedding day to the small hours of the reception's end. The coordinator can't be expected to wrangle the limos for the shuttle to the photo location if they don't know the destination or the time of departure, nor can they see to it that Grandma gets her photo op with you if you haven't listed such a photo on your "must-have photos" photographer's list. It makes no sense to spend good money on a coordinator then leave them in the dark.

As you plan your wedding, extract pertinent details from your wedding-planning notebook and transfer them into a detailed playbook for her. A "wedding-day playbook" in the hands of your coordinator is just as important to the success of the day as a playbook is to a football team heading into the Super Bowl. Without it, the day can quickly devolve into a series of missed opportunities.

#63 Sticking to Your Guns

Brides and grooms are pushed and pulled, stretched and squeezed, by well-intended advice. It's sad to hear newlyweds say that their one regret was not sticking to their guns. No one wants to hurt the feelings of mothers and others trying to help, but if there is one thing to remember, it's that the day belongs to the bride and groom. Every aspect of the wedding, including food, music, décor, entertainment, attire, and flowers — in short, every single thing — should feel absolutely right to the wedding couple. To help you tiptoe your way through the advice minefield, start your day with three morning affirmations. Say them in front of a mirror, and make it a not-to-be-missed ritual upon waking up:

1. Today I will enjoy my wedding adventures,
   for even the planning is precious.
2. I will be patient with advice-givers, for I know they mean well.
3. This wedding belongs to my intended and me, and in
   the end the decisions are ours, and ours alone, to make.

Speak with sincerity, and the affirmations will stick with you as you negotiate, shop, and plan, and in the end, you will have no postwedding regrets.

#64 *Into the Unknown*

What is the flip side of experience? It's inexperience, and that's just what you get when you hire unknown, unseasoned vendors who are just starting out. But you also get ambition, fresh visions, and a hunger for success. Vendors without much of a résumé to back up their business are eager to add notches to their belt, and they work hard, often at a significantly reduced rate. Since untried vendors want to build portfolios and customer testimonials, they need you as much as you need them. It is indeed possible to employ new vendors to your advantage. Since you won't have tons of referrals, long lists of testimonials, or mounds of photographic evidence upon which to base your decision, you will need to rely on what you see and what you ask. Has the vendor presented him- or herself as a professional, in spite of having markedly less experience than a seasoned counterpart? Has he worked for more established vendors before striking out on his own? Is he licensed, bonded, and insured? Has he formally studied his craft? Reliability is key. After the interview, are you comfortable that this person can execute the job effectively? Without a history, you will have to rely on pertinent questions, a contract, and your instincts. It may be too scary for some brides and grooms. But many who have taken a chance on an up-and-comer have saved money and uncovered great, raw talent in the process. Experience is valuable, but no one becomes experienced without first starting with a single step.

#65 *Scheduling around Nature's Call*

Restrooms exist for a reason. Everyone needs them. But what could be more frustrating than to have the videographer answering nature's call just as the cake-cutting ceremony commences? It is the job of the wedding planner, day-of coordinator, or reception host to make certain that no ceremonial event takes place without the presence of pertinent parties. But that responsibility is often mishandled, and miscues result, like the mother of the bride returning from the restroom to find her daughter and husband sharing the last two notes of their father-daughter dance. Missing that "once only" event will break her heart. Don't let this happen. Make a list of every person essential to each ceremony and reception event, whether those persons are family, guests, vendors, or service providers, then instruct your host, planner, or coordinator to delay events until all needed people are present. Some moments could later be restaged for the photographer, but events like the first dance or the sharing of the cake will never feel the same when restaged. Do it right the first time. A simple knock on the restroom door may make all the difference in the world.

#66 *Photography Tag Team*

Stuff happens, and disappointment turns into a sadness when the wedding-day photos or videos arrive with chunks of wedding-day life missing in action. To save money, some wedding couples opt only for photos or only for video and hire a single person to handle the task. So what happens when the batteries in the camera suddenly drop dead in the middle of the cake ceremony or the videographer doesn't discover they forgot to press the record button on the video camera until ten minutes after the officiant pronounces the couple husband and wife? Prevent the loss of even a moment of important wedding-day memories by having a backup person to assist the photographer and the videographer. This tag team can consist of two people from the same agency, each with his or her own camera, or your backup can come from designated friends and family members. It might not be perfect, but even a video captured with a cell phone will mean the world to you if the professional or his equipment temporarily fails. There is little about the wedding day more important than the photos and the video. Unlike the transient nature of just about everything else related to the wedding, photos and videos live forever. Protect the process. You'll thank yourself.

#67 *Words to Sleep On*

Even if they've lived together for years, brides and grooms usually spend the night before the wedding in separate locations. This absence adds to the beauty of the wedding day. There's simply nothing like that once-in-a-lifetime moment when the bride and groom first lay eyes on each other in their wedding-day finery. But the night before the wedding without your intended can be anxious, lonely, and fraught with sleeplessness. Help each other out. Make a pact to share a letter — him to you and you to him. Have your letters to each other delivered that night by a family member or friend. The words can be romantic and soul baring, or they can be funny and encouraging. Your personalities will dictate the tone. It feels good to be cared about, and when left to your own thoughts on the eve of something so monumental, a private sentiment that encourages, or a funny message that lightens the load, is the perfect dose of prewedding medicine.

#68 *Tax Boost*

Paying for a wedding is the hardest part. If you're blessed with the fine art of discipline, start socking away a piece of every paycheck from the moment you become engaged. Set up an interest-bearing savings account to be accessed only for wedding expenses. It sounds simple, but unfortunately, many aren't that disciplined. But there's another, seemingly less painful, way: taxes. Change the number of dependents on your paycheck to zero. You won't be garnering any interest on your money, but you are more likely to adhere to the plan if the money comes out before you see it. Keep your dependents at zero for as long as you can, and schedule your wedding for sometime after March in whatever year you choose, allowing you enough time to file your taxes and get your refund. You will file with your regular number of dependents, not zero, increasing any refund amount you would otherwise receive. Is this the ideal way to save money? No. But it's not a terrible way, either. Think of it as just one component of your plan to pay for your wedding without incurring a mountain of debt.

#69 *Let Her Shop till She Drops*

When is the right time to hire an "all things wedding" personal shopper? The answer is whenever it feels right and makes sense. Some brides want to personally search for every last wedding-related item, while others just want to make a decision based on a few hand-selected options. If shopping till you drop is not your ideal entertainment, entrust a personal shopper to handle the search. A "wedding-gown personal shopper" may or may not be the right choice for seeking out other wedding supplies. Gown shoppers are often focused only on attire, with the contacts to match. But it's perfectly fine to have more than one personal shopper, and saving yourself from endless hours of searching may be worth whatever investment you make.

Sometimes "free" is an option. Most major department and boutique stores have staff to assist you. When in doubt, call the store and ask if it offers a personal shopper service. Free or paid, your own personal shopper may be your ticket to dialing down the pressure.

#70 *A Gift from the Hand and the Heart*

Your wedding photo album can set you back a considerable penny or two, so replicating it as gift albums for parents and grandparents may be cost prohibitive. Don't forgo the idea. Construct the gift albums yourself instead. Begin with an inexpensive photo album or binder from a discount store, then cover it with leftover bridal fabric or decorative accent pieces from the wedding. Further the personal touch by embroidering the cover with whatever message you wish or by silk-screening a photo of you with your parents or grandparents onto the cover. Make it a memory book, and in addition to photos (or high-quality color photocopies, which cost less than prints and may look just as beautiful), include bits and pieces of this and that to represent the wedding experience, from before the ceremony to the honeymoon. Gift albums help to safeguard your memories. The loss of your wedding mementos in a natural disaster would not be as devastating if you knew other thorough and permanent compilations existed. No one will care that the album isn't fashioned of the finest leather with gold-leaf pages. Your thoughtful touch will likely make the gift albums worth more to those who receive them.

#71 *Club Power*

When working toward a fit and trim wedding budget, don't be afraid to wield your "club" power. What organizations do you belong to? Professional business groups, insurance companies, travel groups, and even book clubs have negotiated special price arrangements with vendors and service providers. Inquire about any discount affiliations for each store, service provider, or vendor. If you don't ask, you may not know that your roadside-assistance plan could get you a 20% discount at the rehearsal-dinner restaurant, or that your professional women's group affiliation might help you secure a reduced price on shoes. If you don't belong to a group with buying-power perks, think about joining one. It never hurts to expand your horizons, and the discounts may quickly offset any dues or fees associated with the club.

#72 *Piling Up*

Chaos is sure to follow the acquisition of wedding supplies if there's no plan in place for storing them. As boxes and bags of wedding supplies pile up, it's far too easy to misplace items you've searched long and hard to find. Fear not. Simply pack your treasures "to go" the moment you acquire them. Hit the local thrift shop and score a few inexpensive, clean, and sturdy suitcases. Suitcases stack and travel well, and that's ideal. Carefully and securely pack the bags with wedding supplies then store the suitcases together. Record the contents of each suitcase on a large hang tag attached to its handle. Everything will be catalogued, at hand, and ready to transport to the event. Because convenient suitcases make it so easy, any potential loss is nipped in the bud.

#73 *Lost? No Problem!*

Brides are regularly seen toting stuffed wedding-planning binders here, there, and everywhere. So what happens if you set the binder on the top of your car while you dig your keys out of your purse, only to get in and zoom off without remembering it's up there? That planner is scattered to the wind and crushed beneath rolling wheels before you even realize what happened. Binders can be left in dressing rooms, restaurant booths, or absolutely anywhere, proving why they should be just one component of wedding-planning organization. Even in the modern techno age, wedding-planning binders are still very valuable to a bride, but relying on one alone can bring heartbreak when something happens to your collection of notes, samples, contracts, appointment schedules, etc.

Back it all up. Save each e-mail correspondence to a dedicated wedding folder. Make a habit of photocopying or scanning hard copies of important documents, and duplicate written schedules and appointments in your cell phone, computer, or tablet. If your phone has a scanning app, use it, and use it often. When wedding planning, there's no worse feeling in the pit of your stomach than to realize that what you've already accomplished is all gone. With regular backups, that won't be a problem.

#74 *The Company Store*

Fortunately, the Depression-era practice of paying employees with scrip or tokens to be spent only at the employer's company store was eradicated in the 1950s. Yet a piece of that philosophy has become a common and disturbing trend with wedding venues. Somewhere along the way, many venues decided to form a pact with specific vendors then force wedding couples to use those vendors and those vendors only. Seriously? Don't do it. If a venue suggests using vendors with whom it has a wonderful working relationship, that's great. If a venue offers a package deal that gets you a discount if you use the vendors on its list, that's great, too. But if a vendor tells you that you MUST use its associated baker, caterer, florist, etc., you may wish to just walk away. How dare anyone tell you that you cannot choose your own cake stylist, or that you must choose only from the color palette of the in-house decorator? Some venues will permit outside vendors but charge you a fee for the privilege. Ugh. There are valid reasons for choosing venue-recommended vendors, but there's no valid reason for being forced to do so. Be wary of "company store" venues. Your wedding is no time to relinquish that kind of personal control unless, of course, that's your express desire.

7 5   *To Peek or Not to Peek*

What has become known as a "first look" is really just a preceremony photo session. The bride and groom see each other for the first time on the wedding day with only the photographer and/or videographer present to capture that priceless moment. It's done well before the ceremony so that, after the bride and groom spend a few moments together, the rest of the formal photos with the wedding party and parents can be accomplished before the wedding begins.

The first look may fly in face of tradition, but it has its upsides, like getting to go straight to your reception, where you can enjoy the cocktail hour with your guests. Its downside is the loss of that amazing look on your groom's face as the ceremony begins and you first crest the doorway at the other end of the aisle. There is also the very real possibility of accidental stains and snags during the photo shoots. So, it's a toss-up. Photographers are firmly camped on the side of a first-look session, because it gives them time to pose and stage and work without guests' getting in the way. Still, the ultimate choice is yours.

A third option is to enjoy the best of both worlds by taking prewedding photographs separately. The bride poses first with the bridesmaids, then with the groomsmen, then with the parents. Once finished, the bride returns to the bride's room to freshen up, and it's the groom's turn to follow the same scenarios. No photos are taken with the bride and groom together; these are reserved for the ceremony itself and the moments after. This approach effectively reduces the time needed for after-ceremony photos but keeps the tradition and the magic of seeing each other for the first time at the ceremony very much alive. In the end, there's no wrong decision, as long as you are happy with it. Carefully consider all options so that you won't begin your wedding with regret.

#76 *Honeymooning without a Brain*

Brides and grooms take a lot of things along on the honeymoon, and a good memory isn't always one of them. With all the excitement of being a newlywed, it's really easy to walk out the hotel door and leave precious belongings behind — belongings you may never see again.

Don't let it happen. While you still have your prewedding wits about you, make a list of every item you'll have in your suitcase, then tape the list to the inside cover. If you buy souvenirs along the way, add them to the list that night. With a list staring you in the face every time you open the suitcase lid, you are far less likely to ever forget something you've removed from the suitcase to stick in a drawer, a closet, or the hotel safe. If you don't want to list your grandma's gold pendant because it might alert thieves, give expensive items a code name: gold pendant = white toothbrush, or Jimmy Choo pumps = green handkerchief. Sticky-fingered maids or baggage handlers who see "white toothbrush" or "green handkerchief" won't be the least bit interested. The honeymoon is supposed to be a glorious adventure, but it's that very fact that makes important remembrances fly right out of your head. Let the list do the remembering, while you embrace the adventure.

#77 *Learning the Ropes*

Want to learn what to do and what not to do for your own wedding? Get firsthand experience by volunteering to help with other weddings. Wedding planners can always use an extra set of hands, and a volunteer who expects no payment is a tempting prospect for the planner (who is gaining a free "intern") and the bride (whom you will be helping to achieve the spectacular wedding of her dreams). In exchange, you will glean valuable ideas and learn how to avoid pitfalls in the wedding-planning process. A Brides Helping Brides co-op in your area benefits everyone. With brides lending a hand to other brides, knowledge is shared, details are addressed, and every bride wins. Don't be a bride who joins the "I wish I had known" list after the fact. Get out there and learn now.

#78 *Pay It Forward*

As a bride and groom, you are both discovering how quickly the expenses can shoot through the roof when planning a wedding. If only you'd had that knowledge when you were ten years old, just think how much you could have saved over the years. So when your wedding is over and you are settling into your new life, think of the children you will someday have, and create a wedding barrel for them. Each night, throw your change into the barrel, and forget it's there. There's no sugar-coating it. Dream weddings are expensive. Of course you must pay for living expenses and save for your children's college fund, but you can do those things and never miss the coins dropped into the barrel. One day, your children will be heart-warmed and grateful that you thought of their wedding at exactly the time of your own.

#79 *The Ballroom Ceremony*

With a ballroom ceremony and reception, there may be nowhere for guests to go between events, so how should the room be designed? Some wedding couples choose to align rows of chairs, thereby creating an aisle and an altar area for the ceremony. Unfortunately, at the conclusion of the ceremony, this configuration requires shuffling guests aside to set up the tables for the reception. If there is no large balcony or "cocktail" room available, scooting guests this way and that around workers won't be pleasant.

Consider a cabaret-style wedding instead. Go ahead and set up the room for the reception, but leave an open circle in the center of the tables for the ceremony. Guests will remain seated but will be close to the wedding couple as they say their "I dos." Keep centerpieces low so as not to restrict anyone's view. Guests may be surprised to find they are being seated at their tables before the ceremony, but no one will mind. Help them understand what to expect by attaching a program to each escort card, detailing how the day's events will unfold. Not only will your wedding be unique, your guests will enjoy the added comfort of table seating versus row seating.

#80 *Spoon It Up*

Add color and flair to your reception tables with a wedding favor that doubles as a place-card holder and a treat reservoir. Think spoon rests. Those valuable kitchen helpers come in a world of colors and designs, and some styles can be purchased inexpensively in bulk. Fill the bowl part with nuts, mints, or candies, and tie a combination place card/thank-you card to the handle. To help each guest find the correct seat, print the guest's name at the top of the card, then add a message of thanks below, making it clear that the spoon rest is a gift. From gingham to crystal, just about any theme can be matched. If eclectic is your choice, give each guest a different style of spoon rest, but with a common ribbon and delectable treat. Even guests who don't cook have a use for spoon rests. They also make great pocket-change collectors.

#81 Cake-Top Pipes

The twisting, turning, and embellishment of pipe cleaners provided many hours of childhood entertainment. Relive those moments with your bridal shower guests by staging a cake-topper contest. Your quest: Have each guest make a bride-and-groom cake topper completely from pipe cleaners. Pipe cleaners purchased in bulk are usually no more than a penny or two apiece, so choose a variety of shades. Guests can incorporate your wedding colors, your lifestyle or hobbies, or whatever their imaginations can conceive. If needed, feel free to share helpful hints. Play some fun vintage construction songs during the crafting, like "If I Had a Hammer" by Peter, Paul, and Mary or "Build Me Up Buttercup" by the Foundations. Set a time limit by playing a predetermined number of songs, and when all the toppers are finished, ask each guest to describe the inspiration for her piece. Then choose a winner, who will receive a prize. Immediately after the prize is awarded, gather the toppers and put them away. On your wedding day, use those pipe-cleaner cake toppers, in all their amusing and inventive glory, as part of a clever faux-cake display behind the guest-book table. Guests will surely enter your wedding reception with a chuckle on their lips.

#82 Alive and Well

For a favor everyone is likely to appreciate, consider a small potted plant. Nearly all homes have houseplants, and more are usually welcome. To keep the costs in check, buy the plants in their infancy. Green plants in two-inch pots are as inexpensive as plants come. Buy them several months early, and nurture them until the wedding day. By the time you present them to guests, they will no longer look like infant plants. Cover the pots in colored foil wrapping, and add a thank-you card on a card pick like those florists use. If a foil covering doesn't work with your décor, nestle the pot into anything from a cardboard gift box to a tiny burlap sack tied with bead-adorned raffia. Lots of wedding favors never make it home with guests. That's rarely true when speaking of a beautiful, living houseplant looking for a new home.

#83 Captured Emotions

When preparing your "must-have photos" list for your photographer, don't forget to request photos of your parents and grandparents, taken during your walk down the aisle and as you say your vows. The emotions playing upon the faces of those who raised you are something you will likely never get to see, if not for photos or video. You don't want to miss it. Avoid detracting from shots of you during the ceremony by assigning the family shots to a second photographer, or even to a friend with a good camera and good photographic instincts. Discuss it with your photographer and videographer. They will be able to help you formulate a plan for any situation that requires a camera to be literally facing two directions at once. But even if they work it out, which they will no doubt try their best to do, it never hurts to have someone seated close to your family who's willing to snap those candid shots that mean so much.

#84 *In a Land Far Away*

If a destination wedding has always been your heart's desire, begin with a long engagement. The more time you give your guests to arrange a major vacation that includes attending your wedding, the better the wedding day will be. Not surprisingly, it would be beyond the means of many guests to finance a significant trip inside of a year. But give those same guests two years to plan, save, request enough time off, and make necessary personal arrangements, and wedding attendance will definitely increase. Everyone loves a vacation, and your wedding is a great reason for guests to plan a trip they might not have allowed themselves to indulge in otherwise. Just remember the magic formula for a beautiful, well-attended destination wedding: the longer the distance, the longer the engagement. Follow that principle, and everyone wins.

#85 *We Care*

If you're planning a wild reception shindig with plenty of free-flowing alcohol, consider providing one or more designated-driver teams to assist guests who may have partied a bit too heartily. Each team would consist of two responsible, skilled drivers who consume only nonalcoholic beverages during the reception. One team member drives a guest home in the guest's own car while the other follows behind to provide the first driver a ride back to the reception. Hire professional drivers, or simply request that friends provide this service as their wedding gift to you. No wedding couple wants a drunk-driving incident to be associated with their wedding. While most wedding guests will not take you up on your offer, some may, and your "we care" attitude won't be lost on any of them.

#86 *My Wedding Storyboard*

Before a single movie camera rolls, every great film is first depicted on a storyboard — scene by scene, beginning to end. Why? It's because the storyboard keeps the director, the crew, and the actors on track. Brides and grooms create their own wedding storyboard for the exact same reason:

to stay on track. A picture really is worth a thousand words, and laying out all aspects of the wedding in pictures — in chronological order of wedding events — provides a priceless visualization of how everything should look and transpire. The pictures can be sketches, wedding scenes clipped from magazines or books, photos you've taken, or any combination of these materials. The storyboard doesn't have to be an actual freestanding board. It can be a scrapbook with the images in sequence, page by page. Spiral-bound wedding planners are great tools for nuts-and-bolts wedding-planning tasks, but they can't compare to actually seeing seeing your dream expressed in pictures. Take a cue from the movie industry and create your own wedding storyboard. Whether you use an expandable binder or the walls of your bedroom, a wedding storyboard keeps you focused on achieving the wedding you've always envisioned. Seeing is believing.

#87 *Prescription Protection*

Long before it's time to embark on the honeymoon, ask your doctor to give you a provisional prescription for the essential drugs you take every day. If your prescriptions come from certain chain pharmacies, refills can be obtained wherever you find a participating branch. But if you travel outside of your pharmacy's realm and you lose your prescription drugs, uncomfortable delays can ensue. A provisional travel prescription supplies a dosage no greater than the amount necessary for you to complete your trip. If you rely on crucial medications, it is far better to have that prescription in hand than to be caught unprepared. No newlywed needs to be bothered with tracking down prescriptions when there are so many wonderful honeymoon adventures to pursue!

#88 *Shower Me for Me!*

In the Art Deco era, themed bridal showers were all the rage. And why not? Themes provide instant direction for decorations, favors, food, and entertainment. But unlike ceremony and reception themes, which prove most successful when appealing to a broad spectrum of people, bridal-shower themes may be singular and focused solely on the bride.

Take any personal passion and turn it into your ideal bridal-shower theme. Help your shower hostess by discussing the things you love most. Whether it's an affinity for rainbows or one precious memory from high school, confiding in your bridal-shower hostess benefits everyone. Open communication means you'll get a shower way beyond paper wedding bells and nut cups, and your hostess gets instant relief from trying to figure out what would make you the happiest bride-to-be on Earth.

#89 *Mini Vacation for a Cause*

If you have a number of out-of-town guests needing accommodations, do them a favor by treating yourself. Test out the hotels. Call around and ask about group-rate discounts and amenities. Based on the information you receive, narrow the field of potential hotels to a smaller, preferred list, then pick a day and check in. There's no better way to know just how great or how miserable a hotel stay will be for your guests than to try it out yourself. Check in without telling anyone at the hotel why you are doing so. You don't want them to treat you differently just to get your wedding guests business. You want to experience the hotel just as your guests would. A few single-night hotel getaways, spread out over a few months during the wedding-planning process, help to ensure a pleasant experience for your guests and give you the opportunity to decompress from wedding-planning responsibilities. Win-win.

#90 *Legal Beagle*

Marriage creates a legal binding, and attention to business details must be an early part of wedding planning. The transition to married life means changes with banking, taxes, property, elder care, child care, wills, continuing education, business ownerships, debts, and more. While it is always wise to enlist the advice and guidance of attorneys, accountants, and other professionals when entering into legal agreements, couples can handle some issues fairly easily with the aid of legal-document software. Providing there are no disagreements as to what is to be listed on the forms, documents found online and at many office-supply retailers can be effective. The cost is minimal compared to creating the same agreements with the help of professionals. The downside is that you will get no customized advice from the software, nor will there be anyone to steer you toward topics you may not think of on your own.

For some couples, working with professionals right from the start is the wisest choice. For others, software and fill-in-the-blank legal forms work well, saving money in the process. Only you and your intended can choose which is best for you. The only wrong choice is not addressing legal concerns until after the wedding.

#91 *For Posterity*

Stuffing memories into a scrapbook used to be just a matter of affixing a memento to paper with tape, glue, or staples. But today, scrapbooking is an artistic enterprise, complete with specialty papers, adaptable borders, paint pens, cutouts, and embellishments of all kinds.

The bridal shower is a great place for everyone's inner artist to come out as they help create a wedding scrapbook for the bride. You provide the individual pages and the scrapbooking supplies of your choice, along with bits and pieces of the wedding-planning experience — fabric swatches, photos, notes, invitation and save-the-date samples, personalized napkins, etc. Anything and everything you've been accumulating, from the moment you said "yes" to the time of the shower, will be immortalized in a beautiful scrapbook made just for you by your closest friends and family. Let each shower guest choose three or four items to include on their page, and give everyone access to the supplies. Play some fun background music, make sure everyone has wet wipes, paper towels, and a TV tray or a table to work on, and let contagious imagination fill the room . . . and your book. Take a photo of each guest working on her special page, then add the photo to that page later. After the wedding, you will have even more material to contribute to your ever-expanding wedding scrapbook, but the creation of the early pages will be a special memory all its own.

#92 *Get Your Egg On*

For a clever wedding favor that is actually useful in your guests' homes, check out eggcups. Eggcups, in a variety of materials and styles, can be very inexpensive to purchase in bulk. Stuff them with goodies to transform each place setting. Insert a tulip baking cup in a silver-wire eggcup and fill it with candy, nuts, or even a little floral spray to add flair to the table and pizzazz to the favor. Or tuck chocolate-wafer sticks into a white ceramic cup for a clean, formal look. You can even place an egg in the cup — a decadent, gold-wrapped chocolate one, of course. The eggcup designs and the potential fillings are many, so find a combination that complements your reception décor. Add a clever thank-you card to each cup to identify them as gifts, not merely décor, and years from now, guests will remember your wedding every time they crack the shell of that three-minute breakfast egg.

#93 *Forever a Fan*

Fans are a dedicated bunch, and they love to express their enthusiasm. At your wedding, you can show your devotion to an artist, entertainer, or sport — and make wedding-favor hunting easier — by going straight to the source. An Elvis fan? Contact the gift shop at Graceland, learn what they may have that will suit your budget, and order directly. Can't live without cheering on your favorite football team? Visit the team's official Web site, and post what you're looking for on fan message boards. You never know who will volunteer information about a perfect, affordable, team-inspired gift. If a museum is dedicated to the object of your passion, you'll likely find a gift shop there as well. Just go online or call to ask. Fan-driven products come in all price ranges, and what is too expensive for a favor may make a great wedding-party gift. Don't rely on retail outlets alone. Go to the source to increase your odds of finding that one perfect favor that will please your guests and salute your favorite artist, entertainer, or sport in the process.

#94 *Scouring the Source*

When shopping for wedding supplies, it pays to think bigger than the wedding. If, for example, your reception venue or caterer does not supply card holders for table numbers or menus, check out restaurant or trade show suppliers. What may cost a few dollars from a bridal supplier may cost less than a dollar from a nonwedding supplier. Granted, you won't find wedding-themed holders at a restaurant or trade-show supply outlet, but you can always add a themed, decorative touch of your own. And dinnerware? You may find it possible to buy dinnerware for less than it costs to rent it. When the event is over, you can resell it or donate it to a soup kitchen or other worthy charity. When searching for supplies, think like a retailer. Who is their source? A little investigative work may squeeze extra dollars out of the budget for use on something you thought you would have to give up. It literally pays to consider the source.

#95 *Mad Hatter Hilarity*

Take a cue from Alice and her down-the-rabbit-hole friends, and have a bridal shower with a Mad Hatter theme. On shower invitations, instruct all attendees to wear a hat — the crazier the better. Serve lots of unusual teas, both hot and cold, and decorate with an array of teapots in all shapes, sizes, and conditions. Offer wedding-white cupcakes adorned with tiny clocks stopped at the time of the wedding.

Tweak traditional shower games to incorporate Mad Hatter elements. For example, instead of creating a toilet-paper gown for the bride, use that toilet paper to create wedding attire for white rabbits made from white foam or cardboard, and have the bride determine the winner. After all of the ladies have arrived and have had time to mingle in their wonderful hats, ask them to remove those hats and place them on a counter or table. Later, prop a number before each hat, and test the memories of your guests. Provide everyone with a pencil and a slip of paper that contains the names of all guests. Instruct everyone to write the number of the hat next to the name of the person who wore it through the door. No cheating! Award a prize to the guests, or guests, who most successfully tie the hats to their owners. And what Mad Hatter party would be complete without riddles? Go online and find some fun, wedding-inspired riddles to get shower guests thinking and laughing. A Mad Hatter theme for your shower just might make it more fun than any other shower your guests attend that year.

#96 *Shared Moments*

Because a wedding is such a life-changing milestone, it's a perfect time to reflect on all of those little moments that got you there. Create a journal for each of the people you love or simply wish to thank. Remember the special times you shared, or an important influence that person had on your life. There are commercial journals that lead you through a series of questions to help you form your thoughts. But it's just as easy, and less expensive, to simply purchase small books with blank pages, and write what you wish. Get books for everyone from your parents and your siblings to members of your wedding party, and encourage recipients to write about you, just as you will write about them. Exchange your books on the wedding day, or do so after the honeymoon so that wedding-day experiences can be included. If you wish, include a sheet with each blank book to suggest thoughts one might explore, such as "When we first met . . .," "What I love most about our time together . . .," "I laughed so hard when . . .," or "I always wish I had told you . . ." It doesn't matter how much or how little someone writes. It only matters that the words come from the heart.

#97 *Rock-Solid Favors*

With time but little money, you can create handy, customized wedding favors. Use rocks! Rocks make great paperweights and accents for potted plants. Find smooth rocks you can personalize by painting them with the guest's name and perhaps a touch of artistic expression, like a leaf, a flower, a heart, or a symbol related to your wedding theme. Once the art is dry, apply varnish all over the rock to give it a rich shine and to seal the paint in place. If you position one at each table setting, you won't need an additional place card. Just rest the rock on a thank-you card. So many wedding guests are accustomed to receiving a "trinket" favor they have no use for. It may prove refreshing to receive a lovingly designed, hand-painted rock that works inside or out to keep any number of life's necessities from flying away.

#98 *Elegant Upgrade*

Whether the favor is candy, nuts, or any morsel that can be sprinkled with edible gold or silver dust, it will look richer in a great jewelry box. Purchase wholesale-priced ring, earring, or bracelet boxes in bulk from a jewelry-packaging supplier. Clear plastic "crystal" boxes are especially elegant, but not expensive. Decide how many pieces of treats you plan for each guest, and purchase boxes in a size that suits your needs. Imagine how lovely your tables will look with real ring boxes at each place setting. (Of course, if you really want to go the extra mile with your wedding favors, make or purchase edible jewelry to enclose inside.) Shop around. Identical, beautiful boxes from different wholesalers can vary widely in price. But with a little shopping savvy and creative thinking, you can put together inexpensive favors that look fabulously rich.

#99 *Clang the Bell, Fire Up the Siren*

Everyone thinks of a limousine or a classic car as wedding-day transportation, but for wedding couples looking for an incomparable transportation experience, consider old service vehicles. Vintage fire engines, milk trucks, police cars, delivery wagons, ambulances, military transports, etc., will add their own special thrill to wedding-day excitement. Owners of such vehicles often love the opportunity to show them off. Check with parade organizers, who frequently maintain lists of vehicles that appear in local parades. Car-collector Web sites may also offer clues to where these gems are tucked away in your community. A limo is beautiful, but how exciting is it to experience a slice of history with its bell, whistle, or celebratory siren heralding the way just for you? Think old. Think service. Think "too much fun!"

#100 *Marriage under Glass*

Wedding-certificate holders are customarily made of metal and come with engraved wedding art and a place for an engraved personalization. The certificate is rolled up and stashed away inside, and all you ever see is the metal box. If you would rather see the certificate, but don't want to frame it and hang it on the wall, just roll it with the printed side out and slip it into a cylindrical glass vase. The certificate will automatically adjust to snuggle up to the inside of the glass. Top the vase with a round of lace and a ribbon, or if you prefer not to see the top, seal the top with a round acrylic disk and a dab of glue. Now you've turned your certificate into an artful conversation piece that fits anywhere and can be enjoyed anytime. If engraving is important to you, have the glass engraved, or have a charm engraved to add to the top. The certificate is special. You don't need to conceal it, unless you want to.

#101 *A Pig and a Hammer*

When saving for the wedding, even pennies count. One of the best ways to pack a pleasant surprise into the budget is to buy a huge piggy bank, but not a piggy with a cork. Piggy banks with easy access invite theft, and in this case, you would be the thief! When you dip into the bank for just a few coins to do this or that, you're literally robbing your own wedding of something special. Start early. Buy the biggest piggy you can find as long as there's no way to empty him except by taking a hammer to the fat fellow. If you have to smash your piggy, you will be far less likely to skim a little from his coffers here and there, and when it's time to spend on the wedding, he'll be heavy with coins, and even bills if you're so inclined. The key to realizing this wedding financial surprise is no early entry, and that means no prying coins from the hole with a coat hanger, either! A piggy, and a hammer, is a good beginning.

#102 *Newlywed Flash Cards*

Not all brides and grooms are enamored of public speaking, and giving a wedding-day speech may make your teeth grind. Help yourself out with a customized set of flash cards. When the spotlight is on you, it's easy to forget what you intended to say, and holding a paper speech in your hands doesn't necessarily make it flow any better. Simplify it. Take each element of your speech and assign it to a single 4" x 6" index card. In bold, black letters at the top of the first one, write THANKS. Then below it, list the people you need to thank at the beginning of the speech: guests, parents, in-laws, wedding party, etc. On the next card, write HONOR, and beneath it write the names of those you wish to acknowledge with a special tribute or a toast: maid of honor, best man, special helper, dear relative, lost relative, etc. A third card is LOVE, where you will note key points to share about your new spouse — the sincere and even funny reasons why you love him or her. Those three simple cards will help you give the perfect, not too long, not too short, wedding speech. When it's time to speak, you will set the cards upright behind the centerpiece on your table and refer to them as needed. But one more card is essential. On it you will write SMILE … LAUGH … SPEAK FROM THE HEART, because sometimes it's far too easy to forget to enjoy yourself, and it's your enjoyment that will make the speech a pleasure for listeners.

#103 *Wedding Builder*

You're not only creating a wedding, you're building one. So think like a builder, and mock it up. No successful builder works without plans, and if you want to ensure something will fit where you want it to go, or look the way you want it to look, you, too, should make a plan. One option is to use an online room-designing site to map out your ceremony and reception. A more old-school method is to make a cardboard model, complete with everything from tables to chandeliers. Whether you're designing online or sitting at your kitchen table with your cardboard and scissors, make your design to scale. You'll know quickly if the buffet table is going to block the view of the bride and groom for half of the guests, or whether you can squeeze in that floor fountain you really want. Mocking up your venues also helps with décor decisions. Work with colors. Cover your tables in fabric scraps, then add bits of contrasting fabric to represent different napkin color choices, and other splashes of color to represent flowers or centerpieces. What looks amazing in your head may not always look amazing throughout the venue. On the flip side, a mock-up may alert you to a dead zone that really could use some decorating assistance. Without a mock-up tool, you may not notice the problem until the wedding day, when it'll be too late to do anything about it. Give yourself the gift of a good plan.

#104 *December 26th*

What happens on December 26th? Sales! It is one of the most wonderful days of the year to shop for wedding décor. Christmas and wedding decorations share a lot of features. Bells, stars, and angels are just a few of the crossover items you can snag at a deep discount during Christmas closeouts. Later, use your finds at your summer, spring, winter, or fall wedding. Glittery white doves with feathered wings and fiber-optic lighting are just as wedding-day perfect as they are at Christmas, and the day after Christmas you can get them for a song. Don't forget small decorating essentials like glitter and ribbons, or seasonal wedding items like pinecones and icicles. And watch for display pieces. Does it matter if there's a Christmas tree on a beautiful candy dish? Not in the least. You simply line the dish with lace before filling it with candy. The day after Christmas is a shopping zoo, but if you're a smart shopper you can shave a bundle from your wedding budget by diving in and loading up.

#105 *Decoupage Doodling*

Decoupaging as a kid was a creative treat, but childhood activities fall by the wayside as grown-ups simply forget how exciting and fun it can be to create something from nothing. Your bridal shower is a great time to bring back the fun. Hit the thrift stores to collect old bridal magazines. Buy inexpensive flowerpots, crates, picture frames, birdhouses, and whatever else strikes your fancy, and get ready for a down-and-dirty decoupage contest. Forget grown-up tools — decoupage contestants must do it old-school with kid-friendly, round-tipped scissors and Popsicle sticks for smoothing. Say no to fancy decoupage glue — only white, slightly diluted school glue is allowed. Throw down some newspapers on tables or TV trays, and provide each shower guest with a small bottle of water and a rag. Tell guests their works of art will be judged on creativity and execution by the bride-to-be, and let the fun begin. To egg on the competitive spirit, be sure to call out the time as the clock winds down on the contest. Some of the art will be hot. Some will not. But a good or bad result is not the point — it's about diving in and letting the creative juices and the fun run wild. Of course, the bride-to-be should dive in, too. She just can't declare herself the winner.

#106 *New Life*

Help yourself. Help the environment. Help a new bride. You will do all of these things when you use the nonprofit, worldwide Freecycle Network. Sign up for free at Freecycle.org, then check local area listings for wedding supplies. When you finish with your own supplies, list leftover or reusable items on the site for other brides to find. There is no swapping or trading. There is no buying. Freecycle is all about recycling and reusing goods freely. The organization is highly respected, but that doesn't mean throwing caution to the wind. As with any interaction with those you don't know, take simple precautions like never going alone to pick up free items and not inviting others to your home to pick up items you have listed. There's always a public location where you can meet someone to receive or provide items. Most people are good and decent, just like you, but thinking "safety first" is always wise. The bottom line is that Freecycle can save you plenty of money on wedding supplies, perhaps by connecting you to a nearby newlywed with nowhere to store 75 bud vases from her own wedding. She just wants to move them along, and you need them to fill a void in your reception décor needs. It's a lovely win for you, for her, and for the Earth.

LOCATION

CHAPTER TWO • *Location*

"Location, location, location!" You may recognize this oft-spouted mantra as your realtor's favorite phrase, but it's a valuable doctrine for brides and grooms, as well.

The locations of your ceremony and reception play a significant role in the overall ambiance of the wedding day. The locations often dictate décor options or inspire ceremonial or entertainment ideas. They can also nip ideas in the bud when you realize that certain choices would be unworkable at a particular venue.

Choosing appropriate ceremony and reception locations is an early priority. You may have wonderful wedding plans dancing in your head, but without first securing your locations, your visions may not materialize as you imagined. Think of the architect who designs a glorious home made of carved stone. He impulsively purchases the heavy, expensive stone then discovers that the only available plot of land in town on which to build his spectacular house is at the edge of a beautiful river. When finished, the home is a masterpiece with a view that won't quit. Then the rains come, and that stunning stone creation, far too heavy for the saturated riverbank, just slip-slides away into the river. Location matters, and it matters first.

This chapter addresses location sites, both generic and specific. Some of the most wonderful wedding sites in the country are featured alongside general locations like gardens or campgrounds. You may not be planning a destination wedding, and you might think that reading about an amazing location six states away is a waste of time. It isn't. Even if you're marrying close to home, reading about other wedding locations can ignite ideas, spawn a theme, or inspire you to search for local facilities with something similar to offer.

Take a cue from successful realtors, and give location its due. You'll want to make sure you choose *the right place* to lay your foundation, before other wedding-day visions are set in stone.

#107 *Kimberly Crest House and Gardens*

Few mansions are as historically rich and as exquisitely preserved as the non-profit Kimberly Crest House and Gardens in Redlands, California. California weddings often come with Hollywood-style nuances, and a wedding at Kimberly Crest is no exception.

Carole Lombard, the beautiful silver-screen actress of the 1930s and wife of movie star Clark Gable, was a niece of the Kimberlys. Wedding couples walking the gardens may share a kiss in the exact same spot as this very famous couple.

Magic buffs may already know that the famed Magic Castle in Hollywood was built as a mirror image of Kimberly Crest, and music fans might recognize Kimberly Crest from Fleetwood Mac's "Big Love" music video.

From the picturesque petite French chateau mansion to the cascading fountains and panoramic terraces of the Italian gardens, Kimberly Crest is living history. Wedding guests who set aside the time to enjoy one of the docent-led afternoon tours in the days before or after the wedding will find much to appreciate.

A wedding can create a large carbon footprint, and knowing that dollars spent at Kimberly Crest are used exclusively for preservation is a bonus for brides and grooms who love the Earth and its human history.

Weddings are held from April through November. Volunteers staff Kimberly Crest, so a return communication by phone or e-mail is customary.

www.kimberlycrest.org — Web site

(909) 792-2111 — phone

info@kimberlycrest.org — e-mail

#108 *Yosemite*

More than a million years ago, a glacial mass of ice and snow sculpted the far-reaching vista now known as Yosemite. Located in central California, Yosemite National Park is a scenic wonder and an extraordinary backdrop for a wedding.

Weddings in the park are well-oiled machines spearheaded by Yosemite's Special Functions Department. Department wedding coordinators smooth the wedding-planning process while protecting the park's environment, wildlife, and visitors from any adverse impact.

With a nonrefundable deposit, weddings and park-catered receptions can be booked more than a year in advance. Site choices include the distinguished 1920s Ahwahnee Hotel, the 1879 National Historical Landmark Wawona Hotel, the rustic Curry Village Pavilion, and the Yosemite Lodge at the Falls, an environmentally conscious hotel situated just feet from the largest waterfall in North America.

Wedding couples can download a full-color brochure from the Yosemite Web site or request the brochure by mail. Every aspect of the wedding-planning process — from music policies and child care to vendor referrals and surcharges — is covered in detail.

Year-round, Yosemite literally offers its wedding couples the sun and the moon over breathtaking vistas.

www.yosemitepark.com — Web site

(801) 559-5050 — phone

YosEvent@dncin.com — e-mail

#109 *Cumberland Island National Seashore*

One of Georgia's crown jewels is its largest and southernmost island, Cumberland. Cumberland Island National Seashore Park offers mild, 60- to 80- degree temperatures year-round, making it a natural choice for outdoor weddings.

The island is rich with old settlement districts, undeveloped landscapes, wet marshes, and more than 50 miles of hiking trails. Cumberland is home to the oldest-known ceramics in America.

Park entrance fees and a wedding permit from the chief ranger are required. The choice of ceremony site is up to the wedding couple, but because a wedding is not allowed to restrict other park visitors' movements, visiting the island in advance to select a more private beach or inland area is advised. Since outdoor park events are restricted to one hour or less, an off-site reception may be desirable. But utilizing nearby hotel facilities, like the historically certified, turn-of-the-century Greyfield Inn, makes it easy to coordinate a park wedding, ferry transportation, and a reception.

Scheduling can take place anytime within the calendar year of the wedding but must occur at least ten working days before the ceremony. A required, nonrefundable deposit must accompany the permit application.

Nestled in the cradle of lapping waves, Cumberland Island is blessed with open, natural beauty. With its freedom of location choice, it is especially suited to smaller, more informal weddings, where the bride and groom consider nature to be a valued wedding guest.

www.nps.gov/cuis/index.htm — Web site

(912) 882-4336 (ext. 254) — Visitor Center phone

info@stmaryswelcome.com — Visitor Center e-mail

#110 *Old Tucson Studios*

One of the most delightful treasures of Tucson, Arizona, is Old Tucson Studios, where the tumbleweeds tumble and the Wild West comes alive. A wedding at Old Tucson is wrapped in layers of surprise.

Wedding vows can be exchanged in front of an 1880s mission façade in the town square, in the "Grand Palace Hotel" setting, or in Old Tucson's own rustic wedding chapel. Even transportation is a fun treat — wedding couples can arrive and depart by horseback, carriage, stagecoach, or train.

The studios are staffed with plenty of colorfully costumed characters bent on interrupting ceremony or reception proceedings, but ceremony surprises happen only at the will of the wedding couple. The reception, on the other hand, may hold surprises for everyone, especially the bride and groom.

On-site catering is available, and reception areas can hold from 75 to 400 guests. Wedding photos can feature everything from sweeping staircases to windswept streets, and guests are immersed in Wild West style from beginning to end.

"Dusty but deliciously spirited" describes the working film set and western theme attraction that is Old Tucson Studios, but "unforgettable" no doubt describes an Old Tucson Studios wedding.

> www.oldtucson.com — Web site
>
> (520) 883-0100 — phone
>
> guestrelations@oldtucson.com — e-mail

#111 *Crayola Factory and the National Canal Museum*

It isn't the world's largest (1,500-pound, 15-foot-long) crayon that stands out the most at the Crayola Factory located at Two Rivers Landing in Eason, Pennsylvania. It's the explosion of color. This is not Crayola's actual manufacturing plant, but rather an interactive visitor's center devoted to all things Crayola.

Weddings are prohibited during Two Rivers Landing business hours but can be held when businesses are closed for the day. Crayola Factory banquet areas seat up to 150 people, and uniquely Crayola options, like artfully presented crayon and marker demonstrations and a supply of crafts that allow guests to make on-the-spot wedding mementos, add creative spirit to a Crayola Factory wedding.

On the third floor of the building is the National Canal Museum, the only American museum dedicated to towpath canals. A towpath canal is a waterway in which boats are towed by mules or horses walking along the shore. The National Canal Museum banquet facility can host receptions of up to 400 guests, and for larger parties, the entire museum can be rented.

While the Crayola Factory is a naturally exciting venue for weddings with children on the guest list, it's also a source of fascination for the inner child in all adults. Weddings and receptions at the Crayola Factory and National Canal Museum are limited, so booking early is advised.

www.crayola.com/factory/ — Web site

(610) 559-6605 — phone

Use online contact form for e-mail inquiries

#112 *Glacier Gardens Rainforest Adventure*

May through September is the time to marry in one of America's most inventive botanical gardens. Glacier Gardens Rainforest Adventure in Juneau, Alaska, includes treasures of nature like untouched wilderness and waterfalls coexisting with artistically landscaped designs. The blooming plants and lush vistas create a gorgeous environment for framing a wedding.

Glacier Gardens was reclaimed from the devastation of a massive landslide, and at the hands of master gardeners Steve and Cindy Bowhay, it grew from a six-and-a-half-acre nursery into a more than 50-acre rainforest guided-tour adventure. Features include a cliff-face panoramic view of Juneau from Thunder Mountain, and an array of gorgeous, recycled, "upside down" trees with trunks buried in the ground and high-flying roots embellished with scores of flowering plants.

Weddings are held seven days a week at the Glacier Gardens Visitors Center. Events must be held after the close of daily tours and are generally limited to two hours.

Wedding guests who have not visited the gardens before may wish to arrive early and participate in a riding tour of the rainforest before the ceremony. Couples on certain Alaska cruises can prearrange a Glacier Gardens Rainforest Adventure wedding, then return to the ship to begin their honeymoon.

www.glaciergardens.com — Web site

(907) 790-3377 — phone

ggardens@ptialaska.net — e-mail

#113 *Wheeler Historic Farm*

Combine a functioning farm with a colorful historical heritage, and you get Wheeler Historic Farm in Salt Lake City, Utah, a 75-acre dairy farm brought back to its turn-of-the-century glory. To step onto the farm is to step back in time. Its preserved and restored buildings and wide-open spaces provide a wonderful backdrop for brides and grooms who embrace the culture of a simpler era.

Wedding-ceremony and reception locales are plenty. The Ice House can accommodate smaller weddings, and the Activity Barn, which can seat up to 200, comes with a full kitchen. The Stage area and four separate lawn areas can be customized to host small or large events. Farm rental sites can be rented individually in two-hour blocks of time, with no overall time limit. Renting a single farm facility will mean that other events maybe taking place simultaneously, and some noise overlap will naturally occur. On the other hand, wedding couples can rent out the entire farm if they so choose, and privately treat guests to a tour of the original farmhouse, a country hayride, and other unique farm features.

For pet-loving wedding couples considering a canine ring bearer, the farm is ideal. Dogs on leashes are always permitted, and with the farm's many resident animals, you never know when a family of ducks may check out the festivities or the whinny of a horse might sweeten the air.

The farm is open from dawn to dusk every day, and there's a campground on the property for out-of-town guests looking for a little rustic R&R.

www.wheelerfarm.com — Web site

(801) 264-2241 — phone

wheeler1@slco.org — e-mail

#114 *Trapp Family Lodge*

The hills were alive with songs from the heart when the von Trapp family fled Nazi-torn Austria in the early 1940s. Though the movie musical *The Sound of Music* chronicled the life that led to the departure from their homeland, it didn't show the final outcome of their journey. The family settled in Stowe, Vermont, and in 1950, they began welcoming guests to their Trapp Family Lodge.

Today's lodge is an alpine-influenced delight nestled on 2,400 acres of breathtaking beauty. Accommodations for guests include lodge rooms, private villas, and guesthouses, and pets are pampered with custom beds and treats.

Outdoor weddings at the Trapp Family Lodge may be held in the Wedding Meadow, surrounded by the lush rise of the Worcester Mountains, or on the concert stage against the shadows of the Nebraska Valley Mountain Range. Other outdoor venues include the Garden Court, located on the lodge's front lawn, and the Birches, an intimate birch grove well suited to smaller weddings. All outdoor weddings require the rental of a wedding tent as a precaution against inclement weather.

Indoor weddings are held in the beautifully detailed Mozart Room, the Salzburg Room, or the main dining room. The lodge takes pride in addressing individual wedding-party details so that every wedding is uniquely serviced.

A wedding at the Trapp Family Lodge is the epitome of raw beauty sweetened with refined grace.

> www.trappfamily.com — Web site
>
> (800) 826-7000 — phone
>
> Use online contact form for e-mail inquiries

#115 *Seattle Aquarium*

The ocean is the lifeblood of the Earth, and marrying at a location that celebrates this precious resource is wonderfully symbolic. A wedding at the Seattle Aquarium in Seattle, Washington, is an otherworldly adventure in which reception tables snuggle up to giant aquariums teeming with ever-moving ocean life. Aquarium feeding sessions and access to exhibits throughout the center add built-in entertainment, and a panoramic view of Elliott Bay and the Olympic Mountains just outside the aquarium's door provides a picturesque backdrop for wedding photos.

Wedding couples can choose an indoor ceremony, or they can marry on an outside deck where the relaxing, natural voices of Puget Sound soothe the senses.

The facility holds up to 800 guests, and all events and all cuisine served at the Seattle Aquarium are environmentally conscious and monitored by expert personnel. For brides and grooms who care about a world bigger than their own, a wedding attended by sea otters and fur seals is a revelation.

> www.seattleaquarium.org — Web site
>
> (206) 386-4321 — phone
>
> events@seattleaquarium.org — e-mail

#116 *Electra Cruises*

For wedding couples seeking all-inclusive wedding packages underscored by the thrill of the water, Electra Cruises in Newport Beach, California, has the goods.

For decades, Electra's inspired fleet of yachts has set sail with wedding couples and their guests, turning wedding events into extraordinary shipboard memories. The fleet features small and large vessels to accommodate weddings of up to 350 guests. From the modern, posh yacht with glass-domed decks to the vintage charm of a paddle-wheel riverboat, the Electra line covers any style preference, with each yacht boasting its own unique amenities and extras.

The cruise staff's years of experience and expertise alleviate wedding-planning stress for brides and grooms. All wedding packages include a four-hour cruise with necessary staff, permits, and emergency gear, plus a reception buffet with china, linens and silver, bar and bartender, officiant, wedding cake, photography, DJ entertainment, nautical wedding décor, a personal wedding coordinator, and flowers for the bride, groom, and the wedding cake. This one-stop, per-person-fee approach is perfect for on-board weddings, but Electra also works with preferred vendors to provide access to extras a wedding couple may desire.

Whether it's a sun-washed afternoon wedding, sunset nuptials, or a wedding under the stars, Electra Cruises provides the nautical magic.

www.electracruises.com — Web site

(800) 952-9955 — phone

info@electracruises.com — e-mail

#117 *Inn on the Riverwalk Bed-and-Breakfast*

Not all weddings are extravagant affairs with hundreds of guests, and when the wedding is destined to be intimate, a ceremony and reception at the Inn on the Riverwalk in San Antonio, Texas, may be just what the bride and groom ordered.

This 1916 Victorian bed-and-breakfast features 14 guest rooms, a dining room, and an outer deck just steps from the lushly bordered San Antonio River. The culinary and shopping delights of the San Antonio River Walk are but moments away. Weddings at the inn can accommodate up to 125 guests, and the prime river location, coupled with the relaxed pleasure of a B&B, make the facility suited to both your wedding and your honeymoon.

The inn has a wedding planner and an ordained minister on-site. Wedding packages can be all-inclusive, or select a la carte services instead.

Decorated championship bull rider Scott Kiltoff and his artist/realtor wife, Johanna Gardner, are hands-on owners at the Inn on the Riverwalk. Johanna's art, and art from other local artists, graces the interior of the inn, and Scott's passion for renovation keeps the inn ever evolving.

The Inn at the Riverwalk beautifully marries Victorian style with modern amenities, giving wedding couples a memorable exposure to both worlds.

www.innontheriverwalksa.com — Web site

(800) 730-0019 — phone

Use online contact form for e-mail inquiries

#118 *Chapel of Love at Mall of America*

A shopping mall may not be the first location that springs to mind when considering a wedding venue, but at the world-famous Mall of America in Bloomington, Minnesota, wedding couples have discovered the distinguished and quietly intimate Chapel of Love.

Wedding packages for the chapel range from very small ceremonies (with 12 or fewer guests) to larger ceremonies (of up to 70 guests). But a working partnership with the Park at Mall of America allows the Chapel of Love to accommodate weddings of between 50 and 350 guests and to provide private ballroom reception services. Ceremonies held at the Park take place on the stage, with an officiant and decorative floral pillars included. Reception amenities include tables with linens, exclusive ballroom use, mirror and candle centerpieces, and an on-site wedding coordinator.

Chapel of Love events are tightly scheduled, with most being allocated only an hour or less. Weekend weddings require an advance reservation, but weekday weddings are available with little notice. As long as the marriage license is ready, so is the Chapel of Love.

www.chapeloflove.com — Web site

(952) 854-4656 — phone

consultant@chapeloflove.com — e-mail

#119 *Manhattan Marriage Bureau at New York City Hall*

For most wedding couples, a wedding ceremony at city hall doesn't evoke visions of grandeur, but the Manhattan Marriage Bureau in New York City has found a way to give its brides and grooms an enhanced wedding environment for the price of a nice dinner for two.

What used to be an old DMV facility is now a pair of uniquely styled wedding chapels, complete with dressing rooms and a photo-op location that features a billboard-sized photo of the architecturally rich New York City Hall entrance. Award-winning designer Jamie Drake led the design renovations, incorporating wedding pastels like peach and lavender into the color schemes.

A streamlined process allows wedding couples to apply for their marriage license online, and the affiliated City Store sells wedding amenities such as ready-made bridal bouquets, faux rings, and disposable cameras, as well hairspray, tissues, and other wedding-day essentials. And if the wedding couple brings along an iPod, city officials will plug it in and fill the air with the couple's favorite music.

Brides and grooms can bring as many as 30 guests along for the nuptials, and though ceremonies at the Manhattan Marriage Bureau are just as brief as those held in city halls all around the country, New York's City Hall has transformed short and drab city-hall weddings into short and beautifully sweet ones.

www.cityclerk.nyc.gov — Web site

(212) 639-9675 — phone

Use online contact form for e-mail inquiries

#120 *Old World Village Church*

It may feel like a Bavarian wedding, but it's just southern California putting on European airs. Old World is an eight-acre shopping, dining, and entertainment village in Huntington Beach, California. Scores of buildings along cobblestone pedestrian streets house unique specialty shops, with upstairs living quarters for many European-born artisans and entrepreneurs. It is here that a small Christian church opens its doors to anyone from any denomination.

A beautiful stained-glass window above the altar and old-world, antique furnishings make the chapel exceptionally warm and welcoming. If the guest list is too large for the small chapel, or if the open air is desired, outdoor weddings for up to 350 people are held in Old World's gazebo garden.

Everyone will relish the richly delicious wedding cakes made at Old World by European culinary masters, and rental of the Festival Hall includes tables and chairs, a costumed event attendant, a security guard, and cleanup. Other reception services can be arranged with vendors of the wedding couple's choice, or Old World personnel can handle the necessary arrangements. The Old World German Restaurant provides catering, and menu choices include well-loved German selections, as well as Italian, Mexican, Hawaiian, and deli fare.

Dachshund races, oompah-pah bands flown in from Germany, art fairs, and street performances are just a few of the fun events routinely hosted at Old World Village. And for obvious reasons, an Old World wedding during Oktoberfest needs plenty of advance planning!

www.oldworld.ws — Web site

(714) 895-8020 — phone

info@oldworld.ws – e-mail

#121 *San Diego Zoo Safari Park*

Wedding photos never had it so good. A pride of lions enjoying the sun, cheetahs fleeting by, curious giraffes nibbling the treetops — these are just a few of the unconventional wedding guests brides and grooms may encounter when marrying at the San Diego Zoo Safari Park in San Diego, California.

If herds of rhinos on the horizon or exotic birds dappling the trees with rainbow colors sounds wedding-day exciting, the Safari Park is your venue choice. The park offers complete wedding services, including food and florals, unusual entertainment, and animal-print table linens. A standard wedding package is full of extras like admission for all guests, free parking, hors d'oeuvres served by butlers, an hour's worth of beer, wine, and soft drinks to kick off the reception, a buffet or sit-down dinner, Wild or Tame Jungle Juice for the toast, coffee, house florals, and for the wedding couple, a one-year membership to the San Diego Zoo Global society.

Indoor and outdoor ceremony and reception choices include the Heart of Africa and Hunte Nairobi Pavilion, the Lagoon Overlook and Mombasa Island Pavilion, the Treetops room, the Zoofari Party Area, and the Rondavel room.

With its natural vistas, lush tropical flora, and eclectic population of wild and wonderful animals, bridal couples and their wedding guests at the San Diego Zoo Safari Park may feel as if they've skipped the wedding and gone straight to the safari honeymoon.

www.sandiegozoo.org — Web site

(619) 685-3259 — phone

Use online contact form for e-mail inquiries

#122 *Graceland's Chapel in the Woods*

"Love Me Tender" is more than a classic Elvis love song. It's a sentiment that describes the ambiance at Graceland's Chapel in the Woods. Located adjacent to Elvis Presley's cherished Graceland home in Memphis, Tennessee, the quiet little chapel is capable of hosting up to 50 guests. Inside are antique church pews and a stained-glass window that replicates the beautiful panes found above the front door of the Graceland mansion.

The chapel includes a bride's dressing room and a small wedding-cake reception area, complete with a photo-friendly, hand-painted mural of Graceland. Dependent upon availability and approval, wedding couples can also request to have a photograph taken on the mansion grounds.

Graceland's event venues that can accommodate larger and longer receptions include the Pavilion, the Elvis Presley Automobile Museum, the Chrome Grill, Rockabilly's Diner, and covered or tented areas of the Plaza.

Uniquely Elvis decorations; customized swizzle sticks, glasses, and napkins; and Elvis- or musical-themed wedding favors are just a few of the unusual amenities available. Traveling guests can kick off their blue suede shoes across the street from the mansion at the one-of-a-kind Heartbreak Hotel.

Graceland's Chapel in the Woods is not about glitz and glamour. It's about serenity and warmth. All the Elvis-inspired fun is reserved for the reception.

www.elvis.com/graceland/ — Web site

(800) 238-2010 — phone

Use online contact form for e-mail inquiries or contact specialevents@elvis.com

#123 *The Cincinnati Observatory*

President John Quincy Adams dedicated the Cincinnati Observatory in 1843, and today this National Historic Landmark still houses the oldest professional telescope in the country.

For brides and grooms wishing for a wedding blessed by the stars, the Cincinnati Observatory offers both indoor and outdoor venues. Weddings must include fewer than 70 people if held inside or fewer than 100 for outside ceremonies. The facility is located in a residential neighborhood, and in deference to its neighbors, amplified music is not permitted outdoors. Because of the historical nature of the observatory, certain decorations are not permitted, but others, like freestanding florals and table decorations, are welcome.

Brides and grooms who choose to marry and celebrate at the observatory will appreciate the fact that event rental fees directly benefit the observatory's educational activities. Friends of the Observatory volunteers will help guide the wedding setup, and the bride and groom can give their guests a special gift — an astronomer/historian who will answer questions about the historic facility and the mysteries of the stars (the cost for this can be factored into the rental fees).

The only way to improve a nighttime wedding under the stars is to bring those stars closer. At the Cincinnati Observatory, wedding couples and their guests have that opportunity.

www.cincinnatiobservatory.org — Web site

(513) 321-5186 — phone

craig@cincinnatiobservatory.org — e-mail

#124 *Chateau Pomije*

Begin with a castle-like stone building, add mature vineyards, toss in the serenity of a peaceful pond, and top it all off with a functioning winery on more than 70 acres of picturesque landscape, and you've created a wedding-venue masterpiece.

Chateau Pomije in Guilford, Indiana, hosts weddings and receptions of up to 350 guests, with smaller rooms available for more intimate weddings. The on-site restaurant provides a full-service menu for catering, and wedding couples can opt for customized wine bottles to commemorate the occasion.

Wedding photos are blessed with the feel of an outing in the French countryside, and the outdoor gazebo provides a respite for brides and grooms who seek a quiet moment to take it all in.

The chateau is open year-round, and with its array of award-winning wines, turn-of-the-century fireplaces, and sweeping window views, it's the kind of wedding location brides conjure in their dreams.

www.cpwinery.com — Web site

(800) 791-9463 — phone

Use online contact form for e-mail inquiries

#125 *Royal Gorge Bridge and Park*

Colorado boasts some of the most beautiful landscapes the eye can behold, and wedding couples looking to add a breathtaking element to their ceremony would do well to consider Royal Gorge Bridge and Park in Cañon City, Colorado. Where else can you say "I do" from the world's highest suspension bridge? The bridge spans a gorge so deep that the Empire State Building could stand beneath it.

Holding a wedding at Royal Gorge means that guests can arrive days early or stay days late to experience all the gorge has to offer. Venue rates are reasonable, and brides and grooms won't have to spend an arm and a leg to add a dose of spectacular to an already amazing event.

If the height of the bridge gives you pause, don't fret. Weddings can also be held at other Royal Gorge facilities, like Juniper Junction, Big Horn Retreat, the Gazebo, Garden Terrace, Point Sublime, or Inspiration Point, all of which have views that stretch forever.

Parties of all sizes are accommodated, and the venue fee includes a reduced per-person rate for entrance to the park. Royal Gorge staff members know their park well, and the details of custom packages, catering, and other amenities are just a phone call away.

www.royalgorgebridge.com — Web site

(888) 333-5597 — phone

rgbsales@royalgorgebridge.com — e-mail

#126 *Classic Covered Bridges*

Of the more than 10,000 covered bridges built in the United States in the 19th and early 20th centuries, fewer than a thousand remain, and many of those are no longer on traffic routes. For wedding couples, forgotten bridges are a gift.

Covered-bridge weddings are full of quaint charm and living history. Some bridge caretakers permit both the wedding and the reception to take place on the bridge, and the extraordinary combination of white linen tablecloths against rustic wood is beautiful.

On other bridges, weddings are permitted outside the bridge only, with an open-air or tent reception nearby. And in some areas, a bridge wedding is permitted, as long as the reception is held at a separate local facility.

While a few are managed by private entities, most of America's covered bridges are maintained and overseen by the counties in which they are located. Contact the parks department of the state where you wish to marry to get a list of counties that host covered bridges. The Internet is also a quick tool for checking out photographs of the country's charming historical bridges.

For brides and grooms looking for a wedding as picturesque as a Rockwell painting, covered bridges deliver from every angle.

#127 *Thornewood Castle*

Less than 50 miles south of Seattle, Washington, lies one of America's greatest architectural treasures, Thornewood Castle. It was the late 1800s when local civic leader Chester Thorne indulged his passion for English Tudor design and began to build his own castle in America. Thorne purchased a 400-year-old Elizabethan manor in England, dismantled it, and with the help of three sailing ships, transported the historical structure piece by piece from the shores of England to the shores of the Pacific Northwest. Eventually he created a Tudor Gothic–style home worthy of a prince.

Thornewood Castle is 27,000 square feet of rich history, irreplaceable art, and gorgeous views, and it's a dream location for wedding couples. It's one of the few facilities in America where a bride and groom can enjoy the ceremony, the reception, and the honeymoon without leaving the premises and without losing the "castle" ambiance. Other facilities offer beautiful vintage exteriors, but the associated hotel rooms are often modern. At Thornewood Castle, the rooms are as steeped in old-world style as the grand exterior. From the centuries-old painted-glass windows, fountains, and statuary collections to the wood-dowel doors made of 500-year-old English oak, there's history and romance builtin to the bricks and mortar of Thornewood Castle.

Marry in the secret sunken garden, the Great Hall, or on the lawn overlooking American Lake. Wedding packages include extras like crystal-and-rose centerpieces and white linens, and a Thornewood wedding coordinator is on hand to oversee and provide assistance for wedding-day events.

For American brides and grooms looking for the royal wedding experience, a destination wedding in the countryside of England won't be necessary — just a trip to the beautiful Pacific Northwest.

thornewoodcastle.com — Web site

(253) 584-4393 — phone

info@thornewoodcastle.com — e-mail

#128 *Gardens*

The beauty of marrying in a garden is, well, the beauty. There's very little need to decorate for a ceremony that's held in the bosom of nature. Manicured lawns, sculpted shrubs, natural arches, and blooming flowers are blissfully part of the package, effectively whittling down the ceremony's decorating budget to a bare minimum. As long as Mother Nature cooperates and keeps the raindrops at bay, your garden wedding should be the magical event you dreamed of.

Spring and summer are perfect seasons for garden weddings, but if you're a fall or winter wedding couple, don't despair. Most sizeable cities have nurseries with year-round greenhouses, and some municipal arbo-

returns have at least part of their gardens under stationary roofing. Not all facilities will permit weddings on their premises in the off-season, but some will, creating the possibility of a gorgeous, cold-weather "garden" wedding.

To perfect a garden wedding, respect the environment and prepare for contingencies like insects, unexpected inclement weather, temperature variations, and uninvited guests of any species. And for photographs, always use a spotter. When those precious wedding-day photos arrive, you don't want to see tree branches shooting from your ears or your hairdo disappearing into a nest of climbing vines. A garden is an exquisite backdrop for photos, but a little human oversight guarantees a natural complement between you and nature's bounty.

#129 *Roy Rogers-Dale Evans Sunset Chapel*

Sunset Hills Memorial Park in Apple Valley, California, is not the only mortuary park in the country to hold weddings and other special events on-site, but it is surely one of the most unique. It is home to the Roy Rogers-Dale Evans Sunset Chapel, and the park is the final resting place of the King of the Cowboys and the Queen of the West. The park is nestled up against the desert hills in a peaceful setting away from city noise. A dining terrace graces the back of the chapel and overlooks a small lake with a central fountain, and to the right is an unusual green-grass-and-white-tent bridge.

Wedding receptions are held lakeside, on the terrace, on the covered bridge, or in the chapel, and full packages are available, including everything from food to sound to lighting. An experienced wedding coordinator is on the premises to help things go smoothly.

Richly designed and meticulously maintained cemeteries are as much a celebration of life as any place on Earth could be. Everyone who visits is filled with love and remembrance. Looking past the "memorial park" label opens up a world of wedding-site possibilities, and the Roy Rogers-Dale Evans Sunset Chapel is living proof. It's a beautiful location with a meaningful history, and couples will likely find much to love about their wedding experience there.

www.sunsethillsevents.com — Web site

(760) 247-0155 — phone

Use online contact form for e-mail inquiries

#130 Fairgrounds

Nearly all county and state fairgrounds have facilities that sit empty for most of the year. Unless your wedding coincides with the once-a-year fair or another big event held on the grounds, there's a good chance that you can secure a reasonably priced location for your wedding and/or reception.

Most fair buildings are basic structures without frills, but that simply means you can decorate and embellish any way you wish. At the fairgrounds, you won't have to worry about enough restroom facilities, parking, power, or about disturbing the neighbors with your lively band. And many buildings have an on-site kitchen for use by you or your caterer. There are also plenty of grassy areas if you'd like your wedding or reception to be an outdoor gathering.

When booking your fairground location, be sure to ask what permanent entertainments might be available. Sometimes it's just a matter of paying for the personnel necessary to open the giant slide or the merry-go-round, or to have a fair mascot or character entertain guests. Not all fairgrounds have permanent entertainments, but if they exist, why not try to incorporate them into your festivities? Fairground wedding events can be as elegant or as casual as you desire. They are a blank canvas just waiting for your artistic touch.

#131 Duke's Malibu

If you want that Hawaiian-beach ambiance and panoramic ocean vista without the expense of a trip to Hawaii or the grit of sand in your shoes, Duke's Malibu is ideal. Located in Malibu, California, Duke's is one of a chain of seaside restaurants dedicated to the memory of Duke Paoa Kahanamoku, who was born in 1890 and not only became an Olympic Gold Medal swimmer but was the "father of international surfing." All Duke's restaurants adhere to Duke's creed: "In Hawaii we greet friends, loved ones, or strangers with 'Aloha,' which means 'with love.' *Aloha* is the key word to the universal spirit of real hospitality, which makes Hawaii renowned as the world's center of understanding and fellowship. Try meeting or leaving people with 'Aloha.' You'll be surprised by their reaction."

It is that premise that makes Duke's Malibu stand out as a wedding and reception venue. The staff members incorporate the aloha spirit into every facet of their service. For weddings, the restaurant offers exotic sit-down or buffet meals, with all tables, chairs, linens, dinnerware, flatware, glassware, and votive candles included. The Moana Room at Duke's will accommodate up to 200 guests plus a dance floor. If no dance floor is desired, the room can seat up to 250 for a sit-down event or up to 400 for an appetizer event. A smaller room, the Board Room, is ideal for the bridal shower or rehearsal dinner. A beautiful setting blended with good food and the aloha spirit make Duke's feel like a faraway, tropical, destination-wedding site, even if you don't have to cross an ocean to get there.

www.dukesmalibu.com — Web site

(310) 317-6204 — phone

Use online contact form for e-mail inquiries

#132 *Campgrounds*

Some urban campgrounds really stretch the concept of "camping." They are no more than rows of concrete slabs with electrical, cable, and water hookups, often stuck out in the open without so much as a skimpy tree in sight, let alone a lick of privacy. Those campgrounds wouldn't make beautiful wedding and reception sites, but campgrounds in the woods, around lakes, or in the mountains make extraordinary wedding-event sites.

If you plan a campground wedding, it can easily be a multiday affair. Cabins, tents, motor homes, and camping trailers are all possible overnight accommodations for guests. Combine your wedding with a family reunion, or invite lots of family and friends and call it "The Bill and Sandy Wedding Vacation" (inserting your own names, of course). Most large campgrounds have facilities for gatherings. It may be a building or a covered picnic area, or you can erect tents as you wish.

If you have a campground wedding, be specific about what will and what won't be provided. Don't give your guests the impression that it's an all-expense-paid, three-day vacation if it isn't. Guests will incur the expense of camping and feeding themselves after the reception, but once you know how many will participate, you can negotiate a deal with the campground to get a reduced rate for everyone, especially if you choose to use the facility in the off-season. Those who don't wish to stay for a day or two don't have to. But for those who do stay, the festivities, games, cookouts, and good times carry on. Choose easy, rustic decorations and foods that taste good cooked over a campfire. Camping isn't for everyone, but a beautiful campground, with or without an overnight stay, can be a fun choice for the outdoor-loving bride and groom.

#133 *Country Estates*

If having separate ceremony and reception venues is not important to you, look to the countryside. Fabulous country estates exist just about everywhere, and many are occupied only part of the year, making them available for special-occasion rental. A big home that may come with a game room, pool, hot tub, garden, stable, etc., is an ultimate wedding venue.

Marry before a fireplace or in the garden, and give your guests country-living choices for the reception, like lawn games on the grass or board games on the veranda. Rent the estate for the day or for a wedding weekend. Tell all guests to bring casual clothes, and swimwear for the pool or hot tub. The home will be at your disposal, so changing areas will be convenient. Have a schedule for organized activities like honor dances or cutting the cake, but let the rest of the reception progress at everyone's leisure. Merely exploring the grounds will be an entertainment all its own. When renting an entire estate, be prepared for a sizeable security deposit, and be sure to assign overseers to help keep the day, or days, moving smoothly and safely for all guests. You'll find that the "country squire" lifestyle lends itself to a beautiful wedding experience.

#134 *Ghost Towns*

Ghost towns are more than dusty, Wild West relics. There are thousands of ghost towns scattered from coast to coast. Some ghost towns are owned by local governments or the state, while others are private property. Not all ghost towns are available for your wedding event, but many are. Imagine having your wedding celebration in a whole town named in your honor just for the day. How fun!

Ghost towns may or may not have any working facilities, so planning for a ghost-town wedding may mean bringing every essential with you, including portable restrooms — but this really isn't so different from the requirements of many outdoor weddings. Other ghost towns have been transformed into tourist attractions, and facilities are readily available. Still others may have just one or two buildings with power.

Find a list of the ghost towns in your state by checking online or with your state land-management office. Just think of the theme possibilities! The location of your ghost town, the industry or historical legacy it was known for, and whoever populated it are all wonderful starting points for choosing a theme.

#135 *Private Rail Cars*

Some wedding couples would prefer to invite 200 people to a traditional wedding celebration, while others would rather treat 25 people to an amazing wedding adventure. Either choice is perfectly wonderful.

But for those who choose adventure, a wedding on America's rails is something special. Private rail coaches can be chartered for any number of rail lines across the country. Think of it as a cruise on land, with sleeping and dining capability and spectacular, panoramic vistas unable to be seen via any other mode of transportation. Make it a one-day adventure, or take your guests on a multiday trip they'll never forget.

Private rail-car trips are subject to the availability of the train system, so plan well ahead to reserve your car and your attachment to the train. Some private charters charge a flat rate per car, while others opt for a per-person charge, based on variables such as the choice of foods and beverages to be stocked and requests for special accommodations. A great place to start is with a visit to AAPRCO (American Association of Private Railroad Car Owners) at aaprco.com. A wedding on the move is as thrilling and romantic as watching fireworks burst across the night sky.

#136 *Oak Lodge*

Who doesn't love maple syrup? With a wedding at Oak Lodge in Stahlstown, Pennsylvania, maple-syrup wedding favors are a natural.

Oak Lodge is nestled in a little village called Jimberg, and one of Jimberg's claims to fame is its production of pure maple syrup. But syrup is not Jimberg's only sweet pleasure. The little settlement of country buildings includes a log barn, a tavern, an 18th-century log cabin, a smokehouse, a maple-sugar shack, and best of all for wedding couples, a rustic log chapel. Jimberg is available in its entirety for weddings. There's no need to have a ceremony "here" with a reception "there" and lodging "elsewhere." This private mountain facility is ideal for couples wishing to have all their events in one place—for three days—including the rehearsal dinner, ceremony, wedding reception, and a bonus cocktail party.

The wedding couple gets to share the Eagles Nest, a 1,200-square-foot suite, while up to 15 of the bride's and groom's closest friends and family share the 6,000-square-foot Main Lodge. Marry in the chapel or outdoors, or even in the lodge, then use all of Jimberg as your reception venue. A waterfall, miles of woodsy trails, fishing, swimming, and glorious country quiet are mainstays. And extras? Oak Lodge is all about sharing. Wedding couples are provided with a keyboard and speakers, wall baskets to fill with flowers or greenery as they wish, a wireless microphone, tables, chairs, tents, and even a framed print of Oak Lodge for wedding guests to sign as a gift to the bride and groom. The facility can seat up to 120 wedding guests, if a large wedding is your choice. But for the wedding couple wanting to create an intimate, country-wedding weekend vacation for close friends and family, Oak Lodge may be an inspired choice.

www.oaklodgepa.com — Web site

(724) 593-2913 — phone

info@oaklodgepa.com — e-mail

#137 *Kentucky Derby Museum*

The Kentucky Derby Museum, located at Churchill Downs in Louisville, Kentucky, offers private elegance for wedding celebrations. Exclusive access to the museum is just one of the unique amenities available to wedding couples. Steeped in racing history, the Great Hall at the museum can accommodate hundreds of guests. It also features a towering, 360-degree screen where you may show the museum-provided, award-winning feature *The Greatest Race* or screen any filmed or slide-show creation of your own. You can even hire a bugler to play "Call to the Post" to announce the bride's arrival at the ceremony or the bride and groom's entrance into the reception. A reception rental also includes access to the museum exhibits for your guests.

The Kentucky Derby is an American institution, and its nonprofit museum is a beautiful facility. Wedding packages include many helpful necessities for use at the ceremony and the reception, and there are à la carte extras, like etched-glass wedding favors or a designated dance floor, to choose from.

You don't have to have a passion for horses to love the Derby experience, but if you do, a visit to the world-famous stables is also an option.

www.derbymuseum.org — Web site

(502) 637-1111 — phone

info@derbymuseum.org — e-mail

#138 *Renaissance Faires*

For the medieval-loving wedding couple, there's nothing quite as spectacular as marrying at a Renaissance faire. There are hundreds of them each year, all around the country. Some are modest and small, while others are enormous, elaborate undertakings complete with horses, jousts, magic, and historically appropriate rides.

The beauty of marrying at a Renaissance faire is that all of the décor is already in place, and there will be scores, if not hundreds, of costumed workers and participants to add to the illusion of traveling back in time. Heavy tankards of ale and hearty turkey legs are not a prerequisite for the wedding feast, but they sure are fun! And to fully capture that authentic medieval tone, a wedding couple should fashion their own garments and those of their wedding party to fit the era. Go ahead and encourage your guests to join in as well. So much of the enjoyment of a medieval wedding is the attire, and guests can wholeheartedly embrace the clothing of the period if they so choose. Renting medieval costumes may cost no more than traditional tuxedo rentals or dress purchases.

Weddings at Renaissance faires must be planned well in advance, with permission from faire administrators. Each faire is different, and its rules, requirements, and restrictions are unique. For example, some will offer weekend time slots for weddings, while others will allow weddings only on less crowded weekdays. But if you love the romance of medieval times, marrying on a Tuesday to make it happen is a very small price to pay. And think of the money you'll save on décor alone!

#139 *Weddings at Adventures On the Gorge*

If adventure is your cup of tea, consider On the Gorge in Lansing, West Virginia. Locals refer to the New River Gorge as the "Grand Canyon of the East," and sitting on the rim of that particular slice of heavenly nature is Adventures On the Gorge, an all-season adventure resort offering everything from zip-lining to white-water rafting, horseback riding, and paintball tournaments. Kayaking, fishing, hiking, mountain biking — whatever their adventure pleasure, wedding guests can easily entertain themselves before and after the wedding celebration. Imagine the fun and games available for the bachelor party or the bridal shower! Say "I do" with your feet planted firmly on the ground, or take those vows on a Treetops Canopy Tour platform high in the sky. With plenty of cabins for lodging, an in-house wedding planner, and an on-site caterer who doesn't mind serving pizza next to prime rib if that's your choice, brides and grooms looking for a wedding with exciting, personalized perks may find something wonderful — spring, summer, winter, or fall — in West Virginia.

www.weddingsonthegorge.com — Web site

(866) 920-1256 — phone

weddings@onthegorge.com — e-mail

#140 *L'Auberge de Sedona*

Sedona, Arizona, is known as "Red Rock Country," and its sprawling vistas and unusual clusters of rock formations make it a gorgeous natural setting for any wedding. L'Auberge de Sedona is a world-class resort nestled among the best views Sedona has to offer. Situated on the banks of Oak Creek and spread out over 11 acres, the hotel has been called one of the world's most beautiful facilities, and at the resort, brides and grooms have multiple location choices for their wedding or reception. For the eco-conscious wedding couple, it's good to know that L'Auberge de Sedona is environmentally forward thinking, practicing waste reduction, aggressive recycling, and composting of all organic waste created from landscaping and food services. The facility even maintains its own organic chef's garden to provide healthier produce for guests.

A wedding at L'Auberge de Sedona might take place beneath the trees on the Cottageside or Creekhouse lawns at Oak Creek, on the SpiritSong terrace with its stunning backdrop of Red Rock formations, or even in the Monet Ballroom. An on-site wedding specialist works closely with wedding couples on traditional wedding details as well as unique services such as spa packages, stargazing with their on-site telescope, or countryside tours. With its luxury hotel, private cottages, breathtaking natural setting, and full slate of entertainments, L'Auberge de Sedona is the very definition of a resort-wedding location.

> www.lauberge.com — Web site
>
> (928) 282-1661 — phone
>
> concierge@lauberge.com — e-mail

#141 *Oheka Castle*

On Long Island, just about an hour away from the heart of Manhattan, lies a castle that received the most expensive restoration in American history. After falling into disrepair from years of changing hands, New York's 1919 Oheka Castle, the second-largest residence ever built in America, was painstakingly resurrected over a span of 26 years, turning the structure into a beautiful hotel and gardens — and a stunning venue for weddings. The castle has even been featured in numerous movies and in TV programs like *Royal Pains*.

A wedding at Oheka Castle is a step back in time, replete with grandeur and romance. The castle's sweeping grounds include 23 acres of manicured lawns and natural flora. Ceremonies are held in the formal gardens, unless inclement weather sends them indoors. Since Oheka Castle hosts only one wedding per day, there is no rushed feeling for brides and grooms and their guests. Upper-floor guest rooms mean that the reception can spill over to breakfast, with guests already on the premises. A bridal suite is included for the newlyweds.

Oheka Castle is not for every budget, but even if a wedding and reception at the castle is not in the cards, it is possible to pay an hourly service fee to have wedding photographs taken on the grounds. Bridal shows are also held on the grounds, where you can gather inspirational wedding ideas in a gorgeous setting. Oheka Castle is located on Long Island's Gold Coast, in Huntington, New York.

> www.oheka.com — Web site
>
> (631) 659-1400 — phone
>
> events@oheka.com — e-mail

#142 *Beaver Meadows Resort Ranch*

If mountains that touch the sky are your passion, consider a wedding at Beaver Meadows Resort Ranch in Red Feather Lakes, Colorado. With no city-noise distractions, and with scores of beautiful, photogenic locations at hand, this 434-acre rural mountain ranch in the northern Rocky Mountains borders the vast Roosevelt National Forest and offers intimacy and wide-open spaces all at once.

Beaver Meadows Resort Ranch is a family-owned and operated facility that doesn't put on fancy airs. Instead, it concentrates on blending amenities with its natural surroundings. Because of its high, 8,400-foot altitude, temperatures will customarily be 10 to 15 degrees cooler than in nearby Fort Collins, and attire and events must adapt accordingly to the temperature and mountain breezes. To aid in planning a wedding with no unwelcome surprises, the Beaver Meadows Resort Ranch Web site posts average temperatures by month.

The resort's Reception Pavilion, with its large picture windows on all sides, sits on a special island in the North Fork of the Cache la Poudre River, overlooking a mountain pond. Amenities include everything from private use of facilities to outdoor picnic tables, decorating assistance, and an on-site event coordinator. For snow lovers, a winter wedding is absolutely possible. Lodging options, from condos to log cabins, abound, and an amphitheatre, catering, bar services, a homestead cabin, and even a group campfire are also available. Marrying in the mountains may require that unique considerations be addressed, but for those who love the clean, crisp beauty of hills and dales and the peaceful aura of flowing rivers and quiet ponds, a mountain wedding at Beaver Meadows Resort Ranch may be ideal.

www.beavermeadows.com — Web site

(800) 462-5870 — phone

info@beavermeadows.com — e-mail

#143 *Casinos*

Casinos are no longer the pride and joy of only Las Vegas and Atlantic City. Nearly every state now offers casino entertainment, and the vast majority of those casinos also offer wedding services. Casinos aren't just for destination weddings. Some, like Barona Casino near San Diego, California, offer a beautiful, freestanding chapel located on casino acreage. Others have designated chapel areas mere steps from the action or located inside the casino's accompanying hotel. Most offer private reception space as part of their wedding packages.

A wedding at a casino comes with obvious perks unavailable anywhere else. Those with attached hotels make it easy for wedding guests to extend the celebration after the reception by gambling or attending live shows before heading off to bed, without having to face a drive home. Even casinos without on-site hotels often have affiliations with local lodging and provide free shuttle transportation between the facilities. Arranging a reception feast is easy, because kitchens are already on the premises. Casinos routinely maintain a list of musicians and bands available for hire, many decorations are already in place, and the on-site professional staff is experienced in everything from floral displays to transportation. Casino personnel are masters at lightning-fast setups and teardowns of beautiful events, providing the comfort of knowing that your celebration will be ready when you are.

A casino wedding can be an easy, fun, and all-encompassing way to tie the knot. Just be sure to provide guests with a reception schedule, so that they aren't tempted to wander off and answer the call of the slot machines before the reception is over.

#144 *The Workplace*

You met at work. You share a passion for your work. You enjoy the people you work with. These are all reasons you might want to hold your wedding in the workplace. Not every company will permit workplace nuptials, but if they don't, you probably weren't considering having your ceremony there anyway. After all, places of business that truly support their employees are the most likely to say "yes" to on-site "I dos." If you decide to marry where you work, you can't keep it quiet. Holding your ceremony in the workplace means that any and all coworkers are welcome to share in the event.

Utilize quick-and-easy décor that can go up and come down in a matter of minutes. Designating one coworker to be responsible for each individual piece of décor makes this work beautifully. Twenty people affixing 20 large bows, then removing them after the ceremony, can be accomplished in the blink of an eye. Unless the business has a large conference room, on-site cafeteria, or meeting hall, you'll probably need to hold your reception elsewhere. But marrying among coworkers can be exceptionally fitting for those who love their jobs. It's by nature more casual than other ceremonies, but weddings should be about what makes the bride and groom smile. If that means marrying at work, so be it.

#145 *Sweet Apple Farm*

There's a gem of a wedding venue in Pell, Alabama, called Sweet Apple Farm, which is just 30 minutes from Birmingham and 90 minutes from Atlanta, Georgia. It's a place where deer can join the party, and it's ideal for wedding couples in love with life, nature, and each other.

Sweet Apple Farm is an 80-acre private estate of rolling hills, lush woods, and sweeping pastures, with facilities that have been lovingly restored and enhanced to create the perfect blend of natural beauty and wedding charm. From the super-private "1841 Log Cabin," with its antique brass bed, to the 4,500-square-foot Crystal Chandelier Barn, complete with a commercial prep kitchen, restroom, heaters, fans, dance floor, stage, and outside decks, Sweet Apple Farm offers amenities befitting both the bride and groom and its peaceful, rustic setting. There's also an on-site chapel, a country cottage, a screened-in pavilion, and the small, tranquil "Serenity Pond," where deer come to drink. Both indoor and outdoor weddings are available, and every wedding is approached with an eye toward creating a unique experience for the bride and groom, while protecting and preserving nature's gifts. Sweet Apple Farm is indeed a sweet spot for wedding couples.

www.sweetapplefarmal.com — Web site

(205) 338-4910 — phone

An e-mail address is not available for this facility

#146 *Festivals*

Whether it's a springtime hot-air balloon festival or a winter festival of lights, marrying at a well-loved festival adds a larger-than-life element to wedding events. Celebration is already in the air, and guests are treated to festival offerings in addition to a fabulous wedding.

You will need a festival location appropriate for the ceremony, as well as permission from festival sponsors. You will also need to plan the wedding and reception so that they will not interfere with the experiences of regular festival patrons. Providing your own insurance package may be necessary.

Let the theme of the festival be your decorative guide, and most of the décor will already be abundant. Place a block of tables near a festival entertainment stage, then make arrangements with festival food providers to feed your guests, negating the need for an outside caterer. With musical entertainment already slated, you won't need to hire a band for dancing, but because the band will not be there specifically for you, you won't have an emcee calling out special dances. No problem. Just use sign bearers hoisting "First Dance" or "Cake Cutting" or "Bouquet Toss" signs to silently but colorfully alert your guests to what's coming next.

Festivals thrive on a happy crowd, and since a wedding adds to the festival's revelry, festival organizers often embrace the idea and may even help you work out the details. A festival is a celebration for the masses. Your wedding is a celebration for you and your cherished guests. Combine the two, and both you and the festival may reap plenty of unusual and memorable benefits.

#147 *The Castle at Boston University*

Boston University, in Boston, Massachusetts, is home to a Tudor Revival mansion widely known as the Castle. Stunning architecture, a sweeping staircase, wood carvings, a stained-glass chandelier, and a view of the Charles River all add to the ambiance. With options such as the Great Hall, the Music Room, the Library, the Formal Dining Room, and a summertime patio, wedding couples can choose the venue combination that best suits their needs. Up to 92 people can be accommodated for a seated dinner and up to 125 people for a standing reception. Built long ago as a residence, the building's historic preservation means that this facility is not ADA wheelchair-accessible, and any impact that may have on your wedding celebration would need to be taken into account when considering the venue. Wedding packages include an on-site wedding coordinator, tables, chairs, a sound system, a private bridal suite, a baby grand piano, free guest parking, a coatroom, and custodial services. Special arrangements can also be made for use of the ground-floor BU Pub. "Catering on the Charles" provides food and beverage services, including chef-designed and custom menus. The Castle is a find for brides and grooms looking for a stately but romantic event.

www.bu.edu/castle/weddings/ — Web site

(617) 353-2934 — phone

castle@bu.edu — e-mail

#148 *Movie Theaters*

Movie theaters — old or new, popular chains or mom-and-pop places — routinely rent out theater space for private functions, including weddings. Imagine how much your guests would enjoy *en stadium* seating, where everyone sits in comfort and has a wonderfully unobstructed view of the bride and groom. A special movie can be played on the screen as the guests await the big moment. Some theaters will have unique film options from which to choose. Others may mandate that you acquire special films on your own and provide them to the theater to play during your event. Choose a real, full-length film, a short feature, a cartoon, or a personal wedding-themed film you've created. The screen can go dark during the ceremony or show a continuous-loop film of the sky, the ocean, a thousand flickering candles, or whatever else you wish.

Concessions can be included in rental fees if you'd like, and some theaters even offer sophisticated catering services. Movie theaters are suitable for ceremonies but less effective for receptions, as there is no room for guests to do anything but sit. Receptions could be held in the theater lobby or at another facility. Renting out an entire theater, including the lobby, is usually only possible during weekday, daytime hours, but it never hurts to ask about other times. Sometimes a local theater is just so empty during certain times that the proprietors would welcome a private party instead. Your best bet for this type of rental is an individually owned facility or a theater with multiple wings.

If you are real movie buffs and you don't care about reception events that customarily consume a lot of space, your reception could take place right inside the seating area, and could include a movie, a catered meal, and the wedding cake. You won't have a lot of dancing opportunities, but the romantic snuggling in the dark will be off the charts.

#149 *The B&O Station Banquet Hall*

What was once a train station for the B&O Railroad is now a beautiful event location, perfect for weddings. This Youngstown, Ohio, facility was built in 1905 and is documented in the National Register of Historic Places. It's located on the banks the Mahoning River near Mill Creek Park, providing beautiful scenery and its own park-like setting and pavilion for outdoor events. The building itself, with its solid brick structure, wrought-iron accents, and vintage lampposts, provides a gorgeous backdrop for wedding photos. Inside, there is a sweeping grand staircase and a rare tin ceiling. With the Youngstown Room, the Tunnel Room, and the Main Dining Area, the B&O Station can accommodate every bridal event, from the engagement party to the shower, and from the rehearsal dinner to the wedding and reception.

The step-back-in-time atmosphere of the B&O Station sets the stage for turn-of-the-century, elegant décor, but it is also the perfect venue for embracing a train or travel theme. There are no on-site wedding vendors, but the B&O Station has a working relationship with experienced local vendors ready to assist in all aspects of the planning.

There's something special about celebrating your wedding in a building with such a rich historical essence. Who waited at the station for that smoke-puffing locomotive to arrive? Where were they going? Wonder is a great conversation starter for wedding guests.

www.banquetatthebno.com — Web site

(330) 480-9859 — phone

manager@banquetatthebno.com — e-mail

#150 *Hagley Museum and Library*

Delaware is home to a lovely wedding venue, the Hagley Museum and Library in Wilmington. This nonprofit facility is devoted to the history of American enterprise, and is the home of the gunpowder works founded by E. I. DuPont in 1802. The grounds boast 235 acres of lush landscaping along the Brandywine River, along with a blend of vintage and modern structures, including an organic café.

The chateau-country ambiance is ideal for wedding celebrations. Photo opportunities include the original DuPont home, the riverbank, and a historic French heirloom garden. Wedding packages include an on-site event manager, use of the Soda House, and complimentary Hagley Museum tickets for all guests, which would serve as fitting wedding favors. Toscana Catering at Hagley delivers on-site dining packages that include an open bar service, a champagne toast, 54 choices of table-linen colors, butler-passed hors d'oeuvres, and fine dining or cocktail reception foods. Steeped in history and surrounded by beauty, a Hagley Museum and Library wedding and reception is one of Delaware's finest offerings.

www.hagley.org — Web site

(302) 658-2400 — phone

info@hagley.org — e-mail

#151 *Darby Field Inn*

If an intimate and romantic wedding is the desire, the Darby Field Inn of Albany, New Hampshire, delivers. Featuring services for elopements, small weddings of up to 20 people, and full wedding celebrations for parties up to 50 people indoors or 70 people outdoors, the Darby Field Inn specializes in making every wedding unique. For full weddings, the wedding package includes exclusive use of the entire inn for two days, with a country breakfast each morning. The innkeeper happens to be a Justice of the Peace, so even last-minute weddings are covered.

Marry in the gardens, before a roaring fireplace, or on the patio with a view of the White Mountains' Presidential Range. Get a relaxing couples' massage before the wedding, or take a stroll and embrace the serenity of nature before the excitement begins. The on-site restaurant offers an array of foods and beverages for your reception meal or cocktail service. And the elopement package even includes a bride's bouquet, groom's boutonnière, lamplight dinner, country breakfast, champagne, photos, and inclusion in the inn's Facebook and Web site photo galleries, so that your elopement can be shared with friends and family. The Darby Field Inn is a peaceful getaway venue that wedding couples with a small guest list may find to be a perfect fit.

www.darbyfield.com — Web site

(603) 447-2181 — phone

marc@darbyfield.com — e-mail

#152 *French Quarter Wedding Chapel*

The one and only wedding chapel in New Orleans's famous French Quarter is the French Quarter Wedding Chapel. It's small. It's quaint. It's fabulously unique. If your wedding is intimate, with fewer than 15 guests, you qualify to say "I do" in a chapel with more charisma than any small space has a right to claim. The high-beamed, 13-foot ceiling is covered with money. After being pronounced husband and wife, newly married couples sign a single denomination of currency to immortalize their first married signatures (not related to their legal wedding documents). The tradition began with a single excited bride and has carried forward ever since, filling the ceiling with currency from all over the world. Along with traditional and civil ceremonies, this special little chapel even offers handfasting. For larger weddings, arrangements can be made through the chapel for events held at other romantic New Orleans locations. An elopement package to the French Quarter Wedding Chapel includes usual amenities like a champagne toast and a little heart-shaped wedding cake, but also provides unusual pluses like a violinist, a romantic dinner for two, and a half-hour carriage ride through the French Quarter. Additional a la carte amenities may be added to the package as desired. Weddings in the French Quarter of New Orleans, Louisiana, may be kissed with a touch of magic because couples united there return years later to visit their money hanging from the ceiling . . . and they're still married.

www.frenchquarterweddingchapel.com — Web site

(866) 933-3864 — phone

info@frenchquarterweddingchapel.com — e-mail

#153 *Hocking Hills WeddingMoons at Getaway Cabins*

When the "I dos" are just about the two of you, and perhaps a small gathering of your closest loved ones, check out Hocking Hills WeddingMoons at Getaway Cabins in South Bloomingville, Ohio. Nestled in the forest of Hocking State Park, Getaway Cabins has short, sweet wedding ceremonies and elopements down to an art. Marry in the rustic gazebo or amidst the natural wonders of nearby Ash Cave. Available wedding indulgences include the Wedding Night Bed of Roses, a couples' massage, and a romantic dinner prepared and served in your own cabin by a traveling chef from the Grouse Nest. A personal wedding specialist is included in all price packages, and photography services, including Web site uploads, are available. Winter brides marrying at Hocking Hills can even borrow a white satin cape for the event. If the thought of being away from your furry critters, even to get married, is just not appealing, don't worry — they can come, too. And all cabins have fireplaces and hot tubs. Hocking Hills weddings provided by Getaway Cabins are designed to be the epitome of an affordable, carefree wedding experience. For some brides and grooms, that's the absolute best wedding feature of all.

www.hockinghillsweddingmoons.com — Web site

(740) 385-3734 — phone

getaway@getaway-cabins.com — e-mail

#154 *Rose Hill Inn*

A wedding with an "at-home" atmosphere doesn't have to be held at your own residence. Imagine marrying at the home of a favorite relative, if that relative happened to be the well-to-do owner of an 1860 Italianate villa. That's what it feels like to marry at Rose Hill Inn in Marshall, Michigan. Each of the six guest rooms is decorated with a specific floral theme, and breakfast is served fireside, beneath a crystal chandelier. Fine, delicate Haviland china over a lace tablecloth makes even ordinary yogurt feel elegant. All-inclusive elopement and wedding packages are available, or you can customize your wedding as you wish. The guest list is limited to 35 people indoors or 75 people in the outdoor Victorian gazebo. Very few wedding facilities are as beautiful in the winter as they are in the summer, but snow and ice only add to the timeless feeling of Rose Hill Inn. And for the groom who remembers his glory days as a Boy Scout, marrying at Rose Hill comes with some precious nostalgia. William Boyce, the founder of Boy Scouts of America, once owned this beautifully maintained and meticulously appointed bed-and-breakfast. A wedding at Rose Hill Inn is a wedding at home — away from home.

www.marshallweddings.com — Web site

(269) 789-1992 — phone

rosehillinnkeeper@cablespeed.com — e-mail

#155 *Nonprofit Facilities*

It's nice to know that your wedding dollars may do some extra good, and that's exactly the case when you choose to hold your ceremony or reception in the facilities of a nonprofit organization. Begin with your local area, and search for nonprofit and charity groups that may own or have exclusive use of buildings, gardens, or land. When you make your facility-rental donation, you will know that your money is going to preserve and foster the nonprofit group's contribution to the community. Don't be afraid to approach any organization, even if you think a particular facility doesn't host weddings. Perhaps they just never thought of doing so. From tree farms to natural-history museums, soup kitchens, and animal-welfare leagues, there are likely scores of nonprofit groups in your neighborhood who would benefit from having your wedding on the premises. Ask and you will learn.

#156 *Royale Orleans*

If it's a beautiful facility and minimal effort on your part that appeals to you, the Royale Orleans in St. Louis, Missouri, may be the celebration venue for you. This heartland facility has specialized in taking care of wedding couples for more than three decades and has perfected the art of providing what is needed before it's even asked for.

The Royale Orleans makes it easy to celebrate without sweating the small stuff. Wedding ceremonies include extras like aisle candles, a unity-candle stand, and a photogenic indoor rock garden and fountain. Receptions feature genteel southern décor, special lighting, a custom, mirrored cake table with candelabra, and a permanent dance floor. The Royale Orleans offers military discounts, and doesn't shy away from special wedding themes. And thanks to its large screen plus DVD-projection system, you can share your wedding and honeymoon videos with guests, making it especially ideal for celebrations following an elopement or a destination wedding. From cakes and stationery to ice carvings and an in-house nondenominational minister, the staff at the Royale Orleans knows weddings from start to finish, and sharing their expertise is what they do best.

www.royaleorleans.com — Web site

(324) 487-7006 — phone

info@royaleorleans.com — e-mail

#157 *Battleship* USS Alabama

Imagine how amazing it would be to hold your wedding celebration on the fantail of the *USS Alabama* battleship, docked in Mobile, Alabama. Launched in 1942 and retired in 1962, this World War II vessel is steeped in history and fascination. In addition to the open-air back deck, which accommodates 500 guests, smaller celebrations of up to 150 guests can be held in the Wardroom on the main deck. If you plan to invite everyone you've ever met in your life, the 36,000-square-foot Aircraft Pavilion onshore can hold up to 1,200 guests and still have room for its historic warplanes. A military wedding theme is a natural, but no more so than an ocean theme, a 1940s theme, a Dixieland jazz theme, or any other theme you envision. The sheer size of the ship will give your event a whopping dose of "wow" no matter what theme, colors, or activities you choose. It's a celebration venue literally without equal.

www.ussalabama.com — Web site

(251) 433-2703 — phone

See further contact information on Web site

#158 *Morikami Museum and Japanese Gardens*

For wedding couples looking to marry in a place of serenity, there's a fitting, romantic location within the Morikami Museum and Japanese Gardens in Delray Beach, Florida. Since the 1970s, this facility has preserved and promoted Japanese arts and culture. The six distinctive gardens were inspired by famous gardens of Japan, and each represents a different era. The Modern Romantic Garden, representing the late 19th and early 20th centuries, features an ingeniously designed hidden waterfall, while the Shinden Garden, representing the 9th through the 12th centuries, features bridges, lakes, and islands. Other gardens include the Paradise Garden, Early Rock Garden, Karesansui Late Rock Garden and the Hiraniwa Flat Garden.

Wedding events may include exclusive use of the Morikami terraces, lobby, and theater, together with portions of the gardens, dressing rooms, and a children's room with a Television and DVD player. Access to onsite rental staff, a wedding rehearsal site, and use of Roji-en: Garden of the Drops of Dew for formal portraits, are also available. Wedding couples also receive a one-year membership to the Morikami. In deference to the tranquil ambiance of the gardens, it is best to hold receptions elsewhere. But for that one precious moment in time when you become husband and wife, it is hard to beat the beautiful ambiance of the Morikami Museum and Japanese Gardens, which are known for their nurturing of nature and their profound respect for culture.

www.morikami.org — Web site

(561) 495-0233 — phone

morikami@pbcgov.org — e-mail

#159 *Schenley Park Skating Rink Banquet Hall*

Sometimes you must look no further than the city itself to find a wedding-reception pearl hidden there. That's the case in Pittsburgh, Pennsylvania, where the Schenley Park Skating Rink has an on-site banquet hall available for wedding receptions year-round. The skating rink is open from November through March, and gift certificates for a winter skate make great wedding favors. In the warmer months, miniature golf or other pleasures replace ice-skating, and the banquet hall provides an air-conditioned respite. Inside the banquet hall, wedding couples are free to use the facility's tables and chairs and its commercial kitchen. There are separate restrooms for men and women, a fireplace, and access to the balcony. With a standing capacity of 150 and a seated capacity of 128, most weddings would have ample space for their attendees to eat, drink, and be merry. The low facility-rental cost is a plus, and per-hour or all-day pricing is available. Schenley Park Skating Rink Banquet Hall is open seven days a week, and driving through beautiful, sprawling, historically rich Schenley Park en route to the reception is a treat all its own.

www.city.pittsburgh.pa.us/parks/schenley_skating_rink.htm#facilities — Web site

(412) 422-6523 — phone

#160 *Skunk Train*

Pair the rumble of a vintage train with stunning redwood scenery, and you've laid track for an amazing wedding experience. Wedding couples and their guests board the Skunk Train in either Fort Bragg or Willits, California, for an unforgettable trip to a remote location nestled in the majestic and romantic redwoods. Whether you choose the indoor Camp Mendicino Dining Hall or the outdoor Northspur Reception site for your celebration, you'll get white tablecloths and napkins, fresh bud vases on the tables, a cake-cutting service, and varied menus to choose from. Wedding ceremonies include white chairs and a bridal arch. The train itself provides an undeniably thrilling experience and unparalleled photo opportunities as it wends its way along the same "Redwood Route" it traveled in 1885. And no one minds a bit if the wedding party and guests show up in vintage attire befitting the train's historical legacy. Why is it called the Skunk Train? That's a great question for the conductor.

www.skunktrain.com — Web site

(866) 457-5865 — phone

See further contact information on the Web site

#161 *Clock Tower*

As the hands of time literally tick away, you say "I do" high inside the tower of the biggest clock in the city of Denver, Colorado. The Italian Renaissance–style Clock Tower, a nationally registered historic site, has been renovated into an event facility that boasts wraparound balconies with panoramic views of the mile-high city and five floors connected by straight and spiral staircases. The modern interior design is a stirring contrast to the century-old tower.

As if seeing the clock faces from behind is not exciting enough, the nuptials actually take place with those very faces as your incredible backdrop. Be selective with your guest list, because only 60 guests can be seated in the tower to share in your wedding ceremony. But what fun for those lucky 60!

Due to the tower's unique vertical layout, you can even dine floor-by-floor, rising or descending via the staircases to enjoy different functions or meal courses on separate floors. Since there are only stairs and no elevators, suitability for all guests must be taken into consideration, and the tower's architectural structure also means that the venue is not suitable for small children. But if your guest list permits you to embrace and enjoy this unusual venue high in the sky, wedding memories are no doubt destined to be … well, timeless.

www.clocktowerevents.com — Web site

(303) 877-0742 — phone

info@clocktowerevents.com — e-mail

#162 *The House of the Seven Gables*

The House of the Seven Gables is more than the inspired, 1851 Gothic novel by Nathaniel Hawthorne or the famed 1940 Vincent Price movie of the same name. The House of the Seven Gables is a real house built in 1668 that still exists today. Located on the harbor in Salem, Massachusetts, this home (now a museum) also boasts an 18th-century granite seawall and two ocean-side Colonial Revival gardens, making the facility a dream location for wedding couples looking for a gorgeous landscape or an ambiance with deep, deep roots in history.

The gardens are flush with fragrant blooms just as they were centuries ago. Wedding ceremonies and receptions at the Gables take place on the Seaside Lawn, with room for up to 200 seated dinner guests plus a dance floor. If the lawn is not your choice, indoor options include the large Plumsock Room or, for small, intimate affairs, the Hooper-Hathaway House, a 1682 colonial home near the Gables. Breathtaking views and a venue unlike anything else in the country afford brides and grooms the opportunity to take a step way back in time. To add an extra thrill for budding novelists or literature lovers on the guest list, Nathaniel Hawthorne's real home is just steps away from the imposing and awe-inspiring House of the Seven Gables.

www.7gables.org — Web site

(978) 744-0991 — phone

info@7gables.org — e-mail

#163 *Soldier Field*

When you think of stadiums, the playing field immediately comes to mind. And while holding your celebration right on the 50-yard line is an option, beautiful indoor options exist as well.

At Soldier Field in Chicago, Illinois, you'll find the enormous 1st Floor United Club, capable of accommodating 900 of your closest friends as they dine, dance, and celebrate with you. With 20-foot vaulted ceilings, large video walls and scattered fixed TVs, a sound system, a variety of furniture choices, security guards, cleaning service, setup, on-site and valet parking, and in-house catering with everything from sports foods to fine-dining cuisine and bar service, this site leaves you wanting for nothing. Of course, at its spacious size, it's not inexpensive, but if you're considering a wedding and a reception in one location with a considerable number of guests, the rental fee is less daunting.

Other venues include the 3rd Floor United Club for 150+ guests and the Colonnades, a covered outdoor area blessed with majestic columns and stunning views. And if you want to invite the entire Chicago Bears team to the wedding — in spirit only, of course! — consider renting the glass-enclosed, luxury Skyline Suite for your reception, timing it to occur during a game. There are also beautifully landscaped parkland sites at Soldier Field that can be rented for weddings and receptions.

With its extensive recycling program, Soldier Field takes important strides toward an Earth-friendly operation, and with an enterprise of its size, that's not easy. Any wedding couple would be proud to be a part of that effort.

www.soldierfield.net — Web site

(312) 235-7000 — phone

Use online contact form for e-mail inquiries

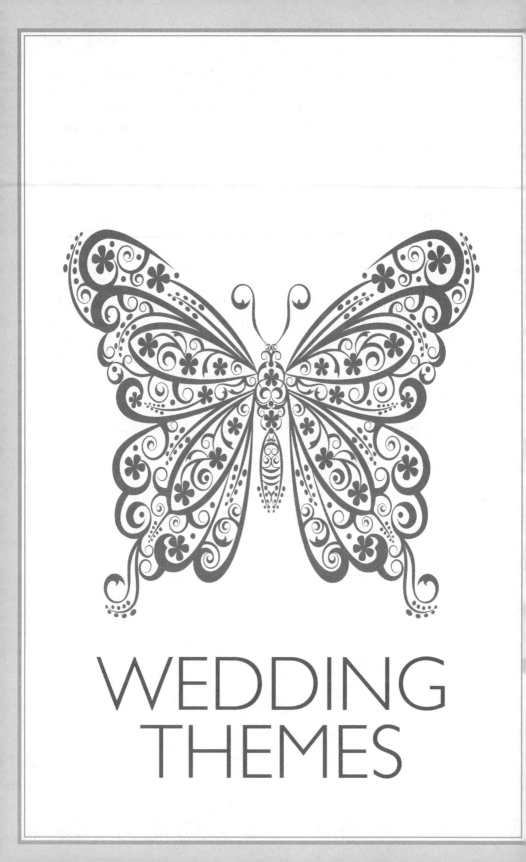

WEDDING THEMES

It used to be that a bride and groom joined together in matrimony, feasted with friends and family members, and went on their merry way. Later, wedding guests really couldn't remember a single detail of the wedding. That's because it was ordinary and predictable, like everyone else's wedding. But the use of distinctive themes in modern weddings has changed all that. Suddenly wedding events became impossible to forget. How perfect is that?

But remembrance isn't a wedding theme's only claim to fame. Themed weddings are easier to decorate, often substantially reduce costs, and highlight the personalities of the bride and groom. Some themes are just plain inexpensive to create, and for cash-strapped wedding couples, that's a blessed bonus.

This chapter is full of inventive themes and schemes. Not every last detail is defined. Instead, each theme is presented with just enough components to create a mental picture of what your wedding day might look like. Think of each idea as a campfire of smoldering kindling ready to be fully ignited into whatever theme strikes your fancy.

Once you choose a theme, study it from all angles. Research and learn everything you can about the core of the theme. Answer one important question: What is it that makes this a theme? When you arrive at the answer, the décor, food, drink, and favor possibilities begin to pop into your mind. Sometimes, when exploring a theme, there are so many options that it becomes more difficult to decide what not to use, rather than what you will use. Write down all of the possibilities, then prioritize. As your theme takes shape, add and subtract components until you have the perfect blend of "wedding" and "theme." Themes are like wedding-planning road maps. When you know where you're headed, life is so much easier.

#164 *The Hundred-Year Wedding*

As you look forward to your wedding day, the best first move may be to look back.

Going back exactly a hundred years to cultivate your wedding theme is like turning your wedding into one big treasure hunt of fun. It's also a fantastic way to involve the groom, his dad, his brothers, and his buddies in the wedding-planning process. If, for example, your wedding is in 2015, you'll surely want a 1915 touring car as your wedding-day limousine, and tracking one down is as much fun as riding in it! Searching for a certain vintage car, decorations, or other supplies is a great way to generate plenty of prewedding good times.

You'll need a 1915 love song for your first dance, and plenty of culinary delights of the day to feed your guests. Invite attendees to don period dress if they so choose, and assemble your own vintage wedding attire for an unforgettable experience. Produce some wedding-day photographs in black and white or sepia to further the theme, and use replica 1915 newspapers, complete with your wedding announcement and details of your wedding day, as wedding programs. 1915 trivia and world events complete the "newspaper."

A "hundred year" wedding is your own personal centennial celebration, and from concept to reality, hundreds of unusual memories will clamor for your attention.

#165 *Giddyup!*

Horse lovers need not leave their favorite steeds behind on their wedding day. Just host a pasture wedding! Blue skies, green grass, and wide-open spaces provide the perfect setting for horse lovers' nuptials.

Cover straw bales with saddle blankets to make great seating, and fashion aisles from additional bales, river rocks, split-rail fencing, or temporary hitching posts. The bride and groom can arrive on horseback if they choose, or if the wedding area is encircled with a protective outer fence, beloved horses can watch the festivities from a safe distance.

Offer a pony ride to keep children busy at the reception, and treat your guests to freshly grilled fare. For table décor, just visit the tack room. Halters trimmed with daisy leis and good-luck horseshoes make ideal centerpieces.

A horse-inspired wedding is comfortable and spectacular all at once. If you don't have your own horse or a pasture to put him in, try to find both through a willing horse aficionado, a local rancher, or a riding stable.

For any pasture wedding, be certain to create safe walkways to the ceremony, reception, and parking areas, and obtain appropriate insurance coverage.

Make a checklist. Put everything "horse" on it. Choose what you like best, and you're on your way to creating the ultimate horse lover's wedding.

#166 *Take Me Out to the Ball Game*

Wedding receptions don't have to be elegant. Some couples just want to have fun, and baseball-loving wedding couples can hit a home run with a baseball-themed reception.

Scour thrift stores for old baseball gloves, and turn them into table centerpieces by resting them on their backs and filling them with flowers or greenery. Tuck a baseball into the arrangement and add a small, framed photo of the wedding couple enjoying their favorite pastime. Mini scoreboards make great place cards for guest seating, and cups with a major league team's logo are ideal for the wedding bar.

Serve ballpark-style foods like hamburgers, hot dogs, nachos, peanuts, ice cream, popcorn, and other grab-and-go foods. A wedding cake fashioned from a tower of "baseball" cupcakes will give guests plenty to talk about!

Set up the band or DJ on a nice stretch of AstroTurf (some indoor/outdoor green carpeting will do the trick), and finish off the bandstand with a set of glitter-dusted throw-down bases.

As a treat for guests, encourage everyone to wear sneakers with their wedding-day attire. Even if the dress code of the day is tuxedo formal, the inclusion of sneakers will be a playful reminder of your theme.

And don't forget the seventh-inning stretch. Guests belting out a rousing rendition of "Take Me Out to the Ball Game" will be a highlight to remember!

#167 *Down on the Bayou*

Getting hitched at the edge of a swamp isn't the only way to give your wedding day that spicy Cajun flair!

Begin by relaxing your wardrobe requirements, because in Cajun fashion, comfort is king. Men needn't wear collars and can choose smartly styled, open-throat cotton shirts instead, while women enjoy the freedom of breathable, flowing dresses. Sandals replace toe-crunching formal shoes, and loosely woven hats complete ensembles for both men and women.

And oh the food! Brandy-and-milk punch, café brûlot, Louisiana crab cakes, smoked-mushroom pasta, sweet-potato-and-apple salad, and chicken-and-sausage gumbo are just a few of the amazing flavors designed to tickle guests' taste buds. Not all Cajun food lights a fire in your mouth, so make your menu as hot or as mellow as you wish, but remember that the true nature of Cajun food is its glorious use of spices.

Decorations don't have to consist of vinyl alligators hanging from the rafters. The simple but creative use of Spanish moss and aged wooden planks is enough to set the mood for your Cajun reception. Don't be afraid to combine rustic accents with elegant ones wherever you like. Instead of potted plants, use vine-wrapped fishing poles grouped upright in beautiful floor vases. Linen tablecloths sprinkled with a mixture of chili pepper and wedding-bells confetti, and topped with shrimp-boat or basket centerpieces, beautifully marry Cajun and wedding-day elements.

A Cajun-themed wedding will stick in your memory like jambalaya sticks to your ribs!

#168 *Beauty in Basic Black and White*

Black-and-white weddings are breathtaking. The absence of color doesn't merely evoke the essence of elegance. It provides a blank canvas for the imagination.

Images on early black-and-white TVs became colorized in the minds of the viewers, so that each person imagined the scene's details in a different hue. Black-and-white décor is beautifully minimalistic, but it also provides wedding guests the pleasure of their own perspective.

No wedding décor could be easier to create than one that is strictly black and white. Jet-black tablecloths topped with snowy white napkins or a white wedding cake surrounded by polished black stones is an awe-inspiring sight.

Black-and-white attire, all-white floral centerpieces accented with black candles, nests of black licorice topped with white-chocolate almonds at place settings, and floor-to-ceiling black or white drapes hung at intervals around the room create a striking sophistication.

#169 *All Aboard the Orient Express!*

A train-themed wedding fosters the romantic and adventurous spirit of a trip on the Orient Express. What could be more fun?

Invitations that resemble classic train tickets, programs styled like schedules, and aisle bouquets accented with ribbon-adorned train whistles are just a few of the inventive possibilities. Stacked vintage luggage decorated with old postcards of the world and topped with plants or floral arrangements sets the perfect reception tone. Luggage tags make ideal wedding favors, and an international smorgasbord is the ideal menu choice.

And how about a good old-fashioned Orient Express mystery? Sprinkle clues throughout the reception area that identify the bride, groom, and wedding-party members by tidbits not many would know. Guests can consider the clues then record their educated guesses on a slip of paper, sign it, and place it in a large brandy snifter. Near the end of the reception, the wedding couple draws one or more slips, and if the guesses are correct, winners receive a fun, train-themed prize.

All aboard!

#170 *Of Willows and Peacocks*

Lush green slopes dotted with weeping willows and strutting peacocks provide grand inspiration for a plantation-themed wedding.

Brides and bridesmaids in pastel hoop skirts, shielding delicate complexions with the aid of lace parasols, is the stuff of romance novels, but a modern bride can opt for a less vintage style and still have the plantation-themed wedding of her dreams. Flowing dresses that catch the whisper of the wind will fit the theme just as well as hoop skirts that come with a defiant will of their own.

Dogwoods, magnolias, mint juleps, candied pecans, Southern fried chicken, grits, hand fans, peacock feathers, and Dixieland jazz are all right at home at a plantation-themed wedding. Recreate the style of a sweeping plantation veranda at the reception through the use of white columns and wicker arches adorned with ferns and gardenias. Employ old wooden shutters as underliners for buffet dishes, or mount them upright as backdrops for photo collages of the wedding couple.

You don't have to be from the South to marry like a Southern belle. You simply have to enjoy the Southern spirit.

#171 *Wedding Kicks with Route 66!*

Couples who love nostalgia can bring a fun and fabulous flavor to their wedding with a Route 66 travel theme.

The old Route 66 captured the color and splendor of American life as it wound its way from windswept Chicago to the waves of the Pacific Ocean. En route, travelers could enjoy roadside attractions that dazzled the imagination, and dine on down home fare that warmed the belly and excited the taste buds. Take your guests on a virtual journey by re-creating the essence of Route 66 at your reception.

Look online for inspiring music ideas, table decorations, and favors. Old road signs add authentic flair, and butcher paper transformed into road maps from the eight states that host the old Route 66 turns tables into conversation pieces.

Fun foods can pay tribute to some of Route 66's craziest roadside attractions. Try "moon rock" cookies, "largest ball of twine" cheese balls, "three-headed monster" sandwiches, or "dollar diner" root-beer floats. Key chains or clever "Do Not Disturb" motel-style doorknob hangers are perfect wedding favors, and state-flower-filled convertible toy cars mounted atop old license plates make clever centerpieces.

#172 Mardi Gras!

Wrought iron, cool jazz, and shimmering purple, blue, green, and gold can get any party started. If your wish for your wedding guests is glamorous fun, a Mardi Gras theme is a surefire way to get there.

Bridesmaids dressed in rich purple and groomsmen wearing golden vests provide visually exciting counterpoints for the bride and groom at the altar. Tastefully infuse floral bouquets with colorful Mardi Gras beads and softly glittered feathers, and let handcrafted, decorated paper face masks mounted on dowels double as useful hand fans for guests.

Reception décor begins with a spectacular wedding cake adorned with Harlequin features. Linen-covered guest tables, accented with table runners made entirely from colorful metallic confetti, shine even brighter when topped with "gold doubloon" chocolate-coin wedding favors. Hurricane drinks from the bar and New Orleans-style cuisine on the buffet puts everyone in the Mardi Gras spirit, and with the air full of sweet Dixieland and Southern jazz, the biggest problem you may have is getting the party to end!

#173 Luck Be a Lady of Love!

You don't have to whisk your guests off to Nevada's crown jewel to enjoy a Las Vegas–themed wedding.

Las Vegas is oh so fun! From the good-luck wishes oozing from every decoration to the Las Vegas-unique, miniature-bay-shrimp cocktails everyone clamors for, Las Vegas is a world all its own.

If the idle-rich essence of old Vegas is the version you love, formal black-and-white with a touch of red and silver sets the perfect mood. Carry the theme forward with decorations that capture the glitz and glamour of a bygone Vegas era. Use chandeliers, stark white tablecloths contrasted with black linen napkins folded in spade and club shapes, catering personnel in black tie, and a single red rose commanding attention from the center of each table.

But if it's the whimsy and excitement of modern Vegas that speaks to you, lighten things up with bright colors and felt tablecloths topped with royal-flush centerpieces and roulette coasters that feature good-luck wishes from the bride and groom.

Whether your vision of Vegas is formal or fantastical, you'll find plenty of wedding favors, games, and supplies to choose from. There's one thing no one can deny. Las Vegas loves to share itself!

#174 *The Thanksgiving Wedding*

Dusty green, amber, chocolate, burnt orange, and ivory are just a few examples of the warm, inviting hues available to Thanksgiving brides.

Autumn is a time of transition, and it's a poignant time for two people to unite. Thanksgiving weekend is the most heavily traveled time of the year, and family members are likely already headed home. A wedding during Thanksgiving weekend could negate the need for a separate trip by friends and family to attend your nuptials.

Seasonal decorations and fall wedding favors are easy to imagine and easy to find. Infuse wedding foods with a fall twist, like pumpkin cake with cream-cheese filling or cranberry-orange spritzers from the bar.

A Thanksgiving wedding requires well-in-advance planning to ensure the availability of ceremony and reception venues, guest accommodations, and essential wedding vendors that may be called upon to service holiday-themed events.

When is getting married at Thanksgiving not the best idea? Perhaps it's when the groom is a die-hard football fan. You may not want to spend every anniversary watching the pigskin fly — unless, of course, you're an even bigger fan than he is.

#175 *Stir the Melting Pot!*

For a taste of worldly wonder, embrace unfamiliar but exciting wedding customs and traditions from other nations.

Wedding flowers are big budget busters, but if you borrow an old French tradition, wedding guests arrive at the wedding with flowers and floral decorations in tow. Imagine how inventive that could be. From a single bloom to a wildflower bouquet, your ceremony and reception flowers would be just as much a surprise to you as to your guests. You could always provide as many of your own flowers as you wish to ensure that your bridal bouquet is perfect, but for all other flower needs, you could let the floral tapestry be seeded by the creative contributions of your guests.

Venezuelan couples sometimes sing their wedding vows to each other. If the bride and groom are talented warblers, this is one tradition that could transform any wedding into something especially rare and wonderful.

From the brandy-soaked wedding fruitcakes of Ireland to the 13 coins a Spanish groom gives his bride to express his commitment, a melting-pot wedding can add unexpected flavors and magical moments to your wedding day.

#176 *FORE!*

Golf is a hugely popular pastime, and golf courses are gorgeous. What's not to love about a golf-themed wedding?

While it's natural to hold your wedding "on location," you don't really have to get married on the course or hold your reception in the clubhouse to have a golf-themed wedding. The theme can simply be tied to the bride and groom's love of the game.

A green-and-white color scheme begins the look, and filling the ceremony and reception with living plants, small trees, and "duck pond" fountains brings a subtle hint of golf to the décor. An aisle runner of indoor/outdoor faux-grass carpeting bordered with golf-ball buckets makes a strikingly beautiful aisle for the bride's walk to the altar. Tie white ribbons around the top of the buckets, and fill them with tightly packed white carnations to represent the golf balls.

Plenty of golf-themed wedding favors are commercially available, and centerpieces can include cleverly presented golf equipment like balls and tees. Real scorecards can serve as place cards.

Many golf courses offer wedding ceremony and reception services, but even if you're getting married in your own backyard or your reception is being held at the local VFW hall, it's the golf-loving spirit that turns your day into your very own "Masters" event.

#177 *I Pledge with All My Heart*

Becoming a U.S. citizen is a dream come true for many, and the day the pledge is taken and citizenship is realized is a great day for a wedding.

Just like a marriage, citizenship is a new beginning. Combining the two events creates a powerful celebration. It doesn't have to be the bride's or groom's citizenship at hand; it can be the naturalization of anyone who is close to the wedding couple's hearts.

The wedding theme can include special celebratory accents like sparklers for the wedding cake, a confetti toss during the cake cutting, and a specially designed corsage or boutonnière for the new citizen that matches the bride and groom's own flowers. Foods can include old-fashioned American fare like Boston baked beans, cornbread, blueberry muffins, roasted turkey, and pecan-pie tarts. Colorful centerpieces with flowers arced in the shape of rainbows over "hills and dales" of greenery represent the new land and a new day.

Friends and family already gather to celebrate with the new citizen. Attending a wedding at the same time can be a heartfelt gift from the bride and groom and for the bride and groom.

#178 *Bats at the Wedding!*

Halloween may not seem like the ideal time for a wedding, but many Halloween brides would challenge that notion.

Not all brides and grooms dream of a traditional wedding day, and a Halloween wedding promises plenty of unconventional fun. Make it as creepy as you wish, or forgo the creep factor altogether. From just borrowing the warm colors of the season for your Halloween wedding to loading it with spider-web-covered centerpieces and black-cat lanterns, how much or how little Halloween fright you include is up to you.

For delightful guest participation, invite them to dress in costume. Instruct them to come as wedding guests from other eras, or as sci-fi guests, or even dressed only in black. Plenty of wedding guests enjoy being told what to wear. It relieves the pressure to buy something new for the occasion, and costumes are easily fashioned from supplies found at thrift stores and garage sales.

Halloween weddings are usually semicasual or casual events and can cost less than other weddings to produce. A witch's-brew punch, pumpkin cupcakes, and candied apple wedges make great snacks, and inventive wedding cake possibilities are endless.

Bobbing for apples may not be on the Halloween wedding agenda, but dancing to the "Monster Mash" or "Thriller" is guaranteed to be a big hit!

#179 *The Art of Fine Art*

For a sophisticated and elegant reception, consider a fine-art theme. Springing for an original Chagall or a van Eyck may not be possible, but the works of most artistic legends are available in prints, at prices ranging from inexpensive to moderate.

Some of the world's most renowned artists have created wedding-inspired works. From smaller prints in tabletop frames to larger prints on easels, celebrate with wedding images from the 15th to the 21st century.

It's likely many of your guests have never seen a collection of fine wedding art, and a wedding-day gallery is a decidedly unique experience.

Splash your wedding colors onto palettes and turn them into underliners for glass-based centerpieces, and accent florals with artists' brushes. Use empty vintage picture frames to stylize the buffet or to highlight a custom drink at the bar, and give small, take-home picture frames as wedding favors.

After the wedding, give the art prints to friends and family members, but be sure to keep personal favorites for your new home.

Your fine-art theme doesn't have to revolve around weddings. Any subject matter can compose a theme. You might also consider contacting local artists who may be willing to loan or rent original works for the day.

#180 *Dragonfly Wings*

Dragonflies have four lovely iridescent wings, but the real beauty of the wings is their functionality. The forward wings and the back wings operate independently of each other to accomplish more effective movement. A bride and groom are like dragonfly wings — two independent people who, when married, combine their strengths to create a more effective shared life. The dragonfly's unique ability, together with its charm and allure, makes it one of the most symbolic of all wedding themes.

Water is important to the dragonfly's existence. Consider water fountains, water-filled bowls topped with floating candles or pond lilies, and floral sprays in water-filled vases to set the foundation for your dragonfly theme. Gathered and tied tall grasses tucked into floor urns or woven into garlands or arches provide large, effective backdrops for dragonfly accents, like bows or wings created from iridescent cellophane wrapping paper. Add just a hint of sparkle to tables by sprinkling iridescent glitter in table centers.

Use modern or vintage dragonfly jewelry to augment everything from centerpieces to the wedding cake, and choose dragonfly-themed wedding favors.

The beautiful aura of the dragonfly is easy to create and easy to admire.

#181 *Cupid's Gentle Touch*

Wedding venues and services are at a premium on Valentine's Day, so early planning is a must. Think of your Valentine's Day wedding as a living love letter.

A love letter isn't merely about the passion between a bride and a groom. It's about the love of family and friends, and that undeniable connection to what matters most in your life.

Instead of the expected pink-and-red color scheme, try something different. A day dedicated to the spectrum of love is the perfect time to dress the bridesmaids in white and the bride in rich magenta or deep purple. It's a day for looking beyond red roses tucked into a cloud of white baby's breath. Try variegated pink and white tulips nestled in purple heather instead. Worry less about chair décor and more about leaving a personal, artistic wedding-day message from the bride and groom on each guest's seat.

A Valentine's Day wedding doesn't have to be predictable or follow Cupid down a candy-heart rabbit hole. An original love-letter event makes your Valentine's Day wedding a from-the-heart gift to yourself and to your guests, and "from the heart" beats "heart décor" every time.

#182 *Fabulous Floor Show*

When well-dressed patrons arrived at the supper clubs of yesteryear, they knew they would stay until the wee hours. There would be rich food, velvety drinks, and a floor show of sultry, jazzy torch songs sung by divas with bright red lips, sophisticated hairdos, and lungs that wouldn't quit. Bring that supper-club glamour and excitement to your wedding reception.

Set the scene with white-linen-covered round tables, topped with short table lamps that cast just enough light to tickle the table's edge. Add chandeliers, vintage art, a polished dance floor, waiters in black tie, and a big-band ensemble fronted by an amazing vocalist, and your chic "supper club" will be the talk of the town.

"Cigarette girls" can work the room, but instead of cigarettes and cigars, have them offer red-wine lollipops and chocolate-covered mint sticks from their neck-strapped trays. Dinner is simple but elegant fare, served from silver platters or rolling serving carts.

Vintage supper clubs were an eclectic mix of the refined and the notorious, and it was that glamour-with-an-edge combination that made them so exciting. Strive to make your event authentic, and give your guests the pampered treatment.

#183 *Life Is a Star on Broadway!*

Go big or go home! That's the philosophy of every performance on the Great White Way known as Broadway, and it's that unstoppable reach for the stars that makes a Broadway-themed wedding so lively.

Broadway-style tickets make fun invitations, and wedding programs designed like playbills will reflect the show-going theme. Use a red carpet lined by small, white floor lights as a bold and beautiful alternative to the traditional white aisle runner.

At the reception, playbills from great Broadway shows are ideal table cards, and Broadway posters and theater masks, large and small, bring zest to the buffet or bar. Broadway-themed floral centerpieces accented with opera glasses transport seated guests to the "front row" of the action, and silver-star key chains or "neon sign" picture frames make great favors. And oh, the music choices! When you choose wedding songs from Broadway's musical legacy, you're choosing musical works by some of the greatest composers to ever live.

Be creative when considering reception venues. A Broadway-themed reception held in an old theater would be Tony Award worthy.

#184 *Ships Ahoy!*

You don't have to marry at the water's edge to celebrate a passion for ships. Whether it's the love of cruising, the thrill of a sailboat race, or the patriotic spirit of a fleet of navy vessels, a nautical atmosphere is easily created, even in the most landlocked venues.

Add maritime flavor by decoupaging photos of the wedding couple onto the rowing blades of vintage wooden oars then sticking them, handle first, into large, sea-colored floor pots. Line the walls with large, tricornered fabric "sails," with a small electric fan hidden behind each one to make it "catch the wind."

Miniature submarine periscopes rising from fishbowls filled with sea-inspired treasures and underwater florals are perfect centerpieces. Extend sparkle sand from the base of the fishbowls to underscore ship's wheel menu cards, and dot buffet and cake tables with beautiful coral pieces and lighthouse-shaped candles. Serve crab-puff hors d'oeuvres and at least one "catch of the day" entrée, and of course, instead of a traditional guest book, employ a captain's log.

And don't forget the fun! Never underestimate the delight of a remote-controlled boat race in a kiddie pool "ocean." Name one boat for the bride and one for the groom, and hold heats until everyone who wishes to captain a boat has had a turn. A player stays in the game as long as he or she is winning. In the end, only one will remain, and to the winner goes the spoils — the winning wedding boat!

#185 *Let the Sun Shine*

There's nothing like a kiss from the sun to foster hope and excitement on a beautiful spring morning. But even if the snow is blowing or the rain is falling, your ceremony and reception can still feel full of sunshine.

Choosing a sunshine theme for your wedding means weaving shades of yellow and gold with white and pale green. Think of the colors of a budding spring — nothing harsh, just soft, gentle hues.

Create bouquets and centerpieces from yellow and white flowers, accented with greens that are the color of new blades of grass. Visit a garden center to find interesting golden-sun wall art then use lighting that rises from the floor to the ceiling to illuminate each sun. Honeybees rely on the sun for navigation and are, symbolically, wedding day-ideal. Add realistic or artistic honeybees to the cake décor, napkin rings, and potted floor plants. Give window sun catchers or hanging prisms as wedding favors. And don't forget that there are hundreds of amazing songs about the sun and sunshine to make your wedding day even more memorable.

The sun gives life, and there's no reason that a warm, sunny spirit can't be the reigning theme of your wedding, no matter what the thermometer outside may reflect.

#186 *Shiver Me Timbers!*

As intensely disagreeable as their occupation was, pirates of old still maintain a mystical charm that refuses to disappear. Imagine a tall ship riding the waves, with the wind in her sails and treasure chests bursting at the seams on the quarterdeck.

A Treasure Island–themed wedding sets its sights on merriment. It's not for everyone, but for those brides and grooms wishing to treat guests to a day to remember, calling out the pirates can do the trick.

Just the word "pirate" spawns a cornucopia of ideas. Visualize a reception full of pirate booty, displayed with either an elegant touch or a funky flair. Generate festivity with message-in-a-bottle invitations, treasure-map programs, tropical-flower centerpieces accented with crossed cutlasses and white-and-gold Jolly Roger flags, and "peg-leg" easels with cartoon posters of the bride and groom in pirate scenes. Munch on eye-patch hors d'oeuvres and Caribbean entrées, and wash it all down with a signature "Yo Ho Ho" rum punch.

For a full-on party, invite guests to dress as pirates and wenches, and include reception games like treasure hunts and gold-coin tosses. To the winners goes the booty!

#187 *Splish! Splash!*

A pool-party wedding is the perfect antidote to sizzling summer heat. It's a semicasual event where the wedding party is dressed in tropical wedding finery, and the guests arrive in comfortable outdoor togs with swimsuits hidden beneath.

Imagine tables and chairs on the deck and lawn surrounding a sparkling pool. Add a steel band for some Caribbean flair and picnic tables laden with grab-and-go foods, and you won't have to think twice about whether or not the guests are enjoying themselves.

Hold the wedding at the pool's edge or on a deck, or build a small, platform stage in the yard that elevates the ceremony so that all guests can see every detail. A pool-party wedding works especially well for smaller gatherings, and where convenient access to a restroom and a changing area exists. If a home pool isn't feasible, consider renting the pool area of a hotel. Some facilities even rent pool enclosures for private events. Have a Plan B in case the weather doesn't cooperate, and make sure that safety precautions are in place, especially for any children in attendance.

Personalized beach towels or decorated bottles of sunscreen make great wedding favors, and when the afternoon wanes into the dark of night, candles floating on the pool turn everyone's thoughts romantic.

Sometimes wedding videos show guests without smiles, leaving the bride and groom to wonder too late what happened to the fun. The odds of seeing faces without smiles at a pool-party wedding are decidedly slim.

#188 *Celestial Exploration*

A nighttime wedding is perfectly suited for a celestial theme. Imagine twinkling constellations of lights overhead and long, flowing, midnight-blue drapes that circle the room. Before each drape hangs a dazzling waterfall of silver stars.

From shooting-star swizzle sticks at the bar to zodiac place cards on the tables, a celestial setting sparks the imagination.

A six-foot-tall half-moon creates a romantic photo backdrop for the wedding couple and their guests. White linen tablecloths covered with dark-blue overlays are both eye-catching and elegant, and centerpieces of white flowers settled onto mirror trays catch the light and give the illusion of tiny pools in a moonlit garden.

Celestial weddings lend themselves to graceful movement and subtle beauty. A bride wearing a crystal-accented gown that ebbs and flows as she walks or dances perfectly complements her darkly clad groom in a silver waistcoat.

When a celebration under the real stars is not an option, a celestial theme is truly the next best thing.

#189 *She's a Grand Old Flag*

Patriotism is a particularly popular wedding theme for military couples, but it's also an ideal fit for a wedding that falls near Memorial Day, the Fourth of July, Veteran's Day, or Labor Day.

When you think of a patriotic theme, the colors red, white, and blue jump to the forefront. But you don't have to abandon wedding-day elegance by adhering to such bright and bold colors. For a patriotic flair presented with wedding panache, simply substitute gold for blue and silver for red. Everything from flags, buntings, and bows to wall and table décor is just as patriotic without red or blue.

Fill upside-down, white military-style caps with white flowers and metallic ribbons, then add ornament-sized gold and silver bugles, tiny drums, and white doves of peace. Finish off the corners of all square tables with uniform epaulets.

Patriotic weddings love balloons. Tie bouquets of clear or white star-studded balloons into bundles secured with oversized bows, and float them in balloon columns around the room to add height and drama. Behind the head table, erect a balloon arch accented with gold and silver tassels.

Make your grand entrance at the reception to the military march of your choice, and treat guests to favors like flag lapel pins, dog-tag bookmarks, or eagle paperweights. And for the ultimate in patriotic weddings, make sure that every wedding supply, from the swizzle sticks to the wedding gown, is "Made in the U.S.A."

#190 *The Fantastic '50s!*

A wedding with a vintage 1950s theme is a roaring good time. If it's a summer wedding, consider an outdoor reception held at an old drive-in theater, and outfit the catering staff in crisp, white short-sleeved shirts with black pants and bow ties.

1950s brides wore full-skirted, fairy-tale gowns that turned every one of them into a queen, and it was the true dawn of bridesmaids' dresses resplendent with flowers, bows, and splashy sashes. Lace, rhinestones, and seed pearls ruled the day.

The '50s heralded the emergence of rock 'n' roll, and hundreds of songs full of love and innocence. Choose a live band in '50s attire to take older guests down memory lane, or opt for a jukebox filled with all the great '50s dance songs. A Frank Sinatra or Elvis Presley impersonator is a great surprise entertainer.

Instead of a traditional bar, set up a faux soda fountain that not only serves cocktails but also serves malts and fizzes. A candy table filled with vintage candies, like candy buttons on paper strips, rock candies, and flying-saucer bites, is guaranteed to tantalize the young and old alike.

Choose a '50s theme, then acquire decorations and attire via shopping excursions to thrift and antique stores. Now that's wedding-planning fun!

#191 *Romantic Greek Mythology*

Some of the most breathtaking gardens in the world feature spectacular cascades of flowers hanging from carved white columns, and statues of mythological gods reigning above manicured green hedges. It is that otherworldly magic that a Greek-mythology wedding theme inspires.

Is there anything more ethereal than a Grecian gown with its delicate flow and glittering trim? Every bride looks like a goddess in a one-shouldered, diaphanous wedding gown.

From tall, Grecian altar urns filled with waterfalls of purple flowers to wedding-program "scrolls" and sweeping garden vistas at the reception, a journey into the world of Greek mythology is worth taking.

Create a reception garden indoors or out by decorating with urns, columns, flowering trees, hedges, grapevines, statues, and fountains. Choose a general mythology theme that combines elements from many Greek gods, or focus only on Eros and Aphrodite, the Greek god and goddess of love.

Celebrate the labyrinths of Greek mythology by commissioning a maze decal on the dance floor, or by printing individual paper labyrinths for each guest to enjoy. Use hedging to create interesting walkways around the perimeter of the room, and arches to frame important areas like the head table, cake table, or your buffet of Greek delicacies. Candle-cluster centerpieces complete the romantic picture.

You don't have to suggest that guests wear togas, but it's always an option!

#192 *Boot-Scootin' Country Fun*

A country-western theme mentioned on a wedding invitation needs no explanation. Every guest knows what to expect and looks forward to the fun.

For wedding couples, a country theme reduces wedding expenses. Mason jars tied with a ribbon and filled with a few daisies easily replace costly centerpieces. Bolts of gingham, checkered, or bandana fabric can be cut into table runners, to be used alone or layered upon inexpensive white-denim tablecloths. Décor costs are minimal. Utilize online auctions or fun trips to flea markets, garage sales, and thrift shops to gather old cowboy boots, spurs, ropes, hats, buckles, wooden wagon wheels, tin cups, saddlebags, and cowboy art. It doesn't matter what condition the items are in — the older and more worn, the better!

Use miniature straw bales instead of ice to create sculptures, and instead of an open bar, fill washtubs and barrels with ice, beer, soda, and lemonade. Delicious and hearty country-style food sets you back a lot less than filet mignon or chicken cordon bleu, and a tiered display of cowboy-decorated cupcakes perfectly replaces the traditional, budget-killing wedding cake.

Personalize your event by having your own branding iron and rubber-stamp custom made, then use your "brand" to decorate everything from wooden planks to paper. And don't forget the "wanted" posters! Any creative-arts software will help you produce fun "wanted" posters of the bride and groom and members of the wedding party.

The only thing left to do is to spend some of your saved dollars on a hot country band, because rollicking, good music at a country-western wedding is the core of everyone's good time.

#193 *Winter-Holiday Bookends*

There's one time of year when families work just a little harder to get together: the holiday month between Thanksgiving and Christmas. By choosing a winter-holiday theme for your wedding and scheduling the wedding between the bookends of Thanksgiving and Christmas, you may get a leg up in several wedding-planning departments.

Out-of-town guests will incur only the expense of a single trip to enjoy both a holiday celebration with family and your wedding. Event venues are already richly decorated, which minimizes decorating costs. Holiday songs lend themselves to reception sing-alongs, and there's nothing like an entire room of people joining in song.

Infuse vibrant holiday colors into wedding attire and photo backdrops. Holiday feasts are easy to imagine and create, including seasonal treats like eggnog or warm mulled cider, and winter flowers like poinsettia blooms, pine sprigs, or autumn-hued maple leaves, unavailable at any other time of the year, inspire unusual bouquets and centerpieces.

The month between Thanksgiving and Christmas touches the heart, but it's traditionally a very busy time for everyone. A wedding during this season requires plenty of notice to family and friends, but when properly executed, it's a rewarding time to say "I do."

#194 *Cookies-and-Cutters Celebration*

Cookies are the number-one dessert in America, and rightly so. Who doesn't love a cookie? Choosing a cookie theme for your wedding means two things: your décor will be eaten, and your guests will be delighted.

From centerpieces to nut cups and even invitations, if it can be fashioned, it can be fashioned from cookie dough. Giant cookies with images or messages easily decorate walls and dangle from ceilings or tree branches. Cookie bouquets or gingerbread-cookie swans are clever, eye-catching centerpieces. Add a cookie diorama to the buffet table, and make cookie "plates" to hold everything from swizzle sticks to after-dinner mints. A cleverly decorated gingerbread bride and groom atop the wedding cake are inexpensive but adorable.

Cookie cutters are routinely used in kitchens around the country, and many cookie lovers collect them as a hobby. Incorporate cutters as wedding favors, or tie wedding-color-themed ribbons to them and put several different styles inside glass receptacles to create eclectic works of art. From starfish and dolphins for beach weddings to autumn leaves and pumpkins for fall weddings, cutters come in many shapes and sizes. If just the right design escapes your determined hunt, commission custom cookie cutters from a professional baker, or make them at home with cookie-cutter kits.

Cookies and cutters are as elegant or as whimsical as you wish, and when the guests leave, your cookie décor walks right out the door with them.

#195 *The Kiss of the Blarney Stone*

March hosts St. Patrick's Day, and it's a grand time for March wedding couples to embrace all the delights the holiday has to offer. Bagpipers and green-tinted bar drinks are a treat. Irish canapé hors d'oeuvres, Irish soda bread with a bacon and cabbage entrée, and Irish coffee with the wedding cake add just the right celebratory flavors. Music from an Irish harp at the ceremony and an Irish-jig dance contest at the reception ensure that the air is filled with lilting spirit.

Décor is a breeze, with top-hat flower vases, rainbow arches, shamrock accents, and even a leprechaun or two. Don't forget to add a pot of gold, filled with golden-wrapped candies and chocolate coins, to welcome guests at the guest-book table, and select Celtic toasting glasses as the perfect complement to the cake-cutting ceremony.

A March wedding color scheme doesn't have to be exclusively green. The Emerald Isle is enriched with a landscape of wildflowers and shrubs in purples, pinks, yellows, blues, and whites. Softly infusing beautiful greens with splashes of accenting colors doesn't distract from a March or St. Patrick's Day theme. It elevates it.

Legend has it that those who kiss the Blarney stone are soon blessed with the gift of gab. Spur lively conversation by adding your very own kiss-worthy Blarney stone replica.

#196 *The Passion of Romeo and Juliet*

In spite of the poison-and-dagger ending of Shakespeare's *Romeo and Juliet*, it is one of the greatest love stories ever told. To create a Romeo-and-Juliet-themed wedding, bypass the tragedy and create a celebration based on the undefeatable love of two people meant for each other. Hold your wedding — figuratively, of course — in the ancient and richly beautiful city of Verona, Italy.

Set the mood with appropriate costuming, or opt for wedding attire with a vintage, but not necessarily authentic, flair. Choose simple flowers gathered in natural bundles, and serve Italian foods inspired by 14th-century cookbooks. Tables groaning under the weight of vegetables, meats, fishes, cheeses, and olives, offered in wooden serving platters and metal bowls, add period ambiance to the wedding feast.

For decorating ideas, rent Franco Zeffirelli's stunning 1968 movie, *Romeo and Juliet*, and for musical inspiration, plunder the movie's soundtrack. It boasts some of the most hauntingly beautiful music ever recorded for a film.

And for the ultimate Romeo-and-Juliet experience, plan a destination wedding to Verona, Italy, where, since 2009, wedding couples have been permitted to marry in a civil ceremony at the real House of Juliet — balcony included.

#197 *Charity from the Heart*

Many brides and grooms arrange for charitable donations of leftover food, flowers, and other wedding supplies, but some want to do more. A charity wedding theme makes it happen.

Every aspect of the wedding will be charity driven. Instead of registering for china and linens, wedding couples register at their favorite charities, and traditional wedding gifts are replaced by donations from guests made in the bride's and groom's names. In reverse, gifts to charity made in the names of wedding guests, either individually or as a whole, substitute for typical take-home wedding favors.

Wedding supplies and services can be purchased from retailers who donate a portion of each sale to charity, and special sales events, like the Brides Against Breast Cancer wedding-gown tour, help wedding couples stick to their charitable goals and still have the wedding of their dreams.

Charity always begins at home, and renting from venues that really need the money, like a local garden, community center, or any facility that relies on donations for survival, furthers the charity cause where it matters most.

A charity wedding is about more than the bride and groom. It's a celebration of the bride and groom's world.

#198 *Crystal Wonders*

For a wedding that literally sparkles, choose a crystal theme, where everything from centerpieces to wall décor is made of glass. Even if it's only inexpensive cut glass or cut acrylic that resembles glass, the ambiance will feel like the embodiment of a fairy tale.

Use large brandy snifters filled with clear or colored crystals for centerpieces, and create crystal waterfalls from long strands of cascading glass beads. A crystal tree rising up from the center of a buffet is as beautiful as a running fountain, and artistic crystal chandeliers hung low as a backdrop for the cake table turns the cake into the star it's meant to be. Use a blown-glass cake topper and engraved crystal toasting glasses.

Crystal wedding favors are easy to find, and Swarovski crystal jewelry not only accents the bride and her bridesmaids, it can do double duty as napkin rings and embellishments for candles.

Crystal adds instant elegance, and the more you use, the richer the experience. A wedding ceremony or reception decked out in glass won't ever be forgotten. And the funny thing is that, while all that glass may look frighteningly fragile, most crystal pieces are strong and durable. Still, a crystal theme may not be appropriate for a wedding reception with children in attendance.

#199 *Treading Lightly upon the Earth*

Eco-friendly, green weddings begin with the small things, like recycled and tree-free paper goods, compostable straws and swizzle sticks, and Earth-inspired wedding favors such as seeds or tree saplings. Any diligence on behalf of Mother Nature is appreciated, but there's no reason not to think bigger. Here are some topics to consider:

Energy. Search for a venue that receives its electricity from wind, water, or solar power, or consider using the sun as your primary source of lighting. Changing to an outdoor, afternoon wedding can significantly reduce energy consumption.

Flowers. Choose in-season, chemical-free local flowers that don't require shipping. Opt for potted flowering plants for centerpieces, and use bamboo for décor.

Food. Celebrate community farmers and gardeners by utilizing recipes based on local food resources. Foods that don't travel far are fresher, more accessible, and require less packaging and refrigeration. Use organic foods, bamboo serving dishes, and plant-based utensils.

Attire. Renting minimizes the resources needed to make fabric and create clothing. Another eco-friendly option is an heirloom gown that is worn more than once. If a custom gown is your dream, use natural fabrics from sustainable sources.

Photography. Go digital, and work only with online proofs.

Transportation. Fuel and exhaust are great Earth offenders. Holding the ceremony and reception in a centrally located area reduces travel for everyone. For your wedding "limo," try a human-powered rickshaw or a pedicab, either of which will not only avoid pollution but add novelty to the wedding experience.

Carbon offsets. Purchasing carbon offsets that support wind farms and other renewable-energy technologies can effectively reduce your wedding's carbon footprint to zero.

"Reduce, reuse, recycle" is the mantra of the green movement. For an eco-friendly wedding, simply ask yourself, "How can I do it better?"

#200 *Victorian Grace*

A Victorian-themed wedding glows with regal opulence, and it's a girly-girl's dream come true. The Victorian era spawned an abundance of ruffles, lace, flowers, and lovebirds, and it embraced the genteel pleasure of tea and scones served on delicate, floral-patterned china.

Turn your wedding day into a Victorian fantasy with a richly adorned high-neck gown, delicate gloves, and lacy half-boots, and outfit the groom and his groomsmen in ascots and pocket watches. Give the reception a luxurious atmosphere by using fringed tablecloths, decorative iron benches, glistening candelabra, gorgeous flowers, and lush ferns. For place cards, scour antique shops for vintage spoons. Attach a parchment-paper name tag to each spoon's handle with a white ribbon, and nestle a colored sugar cube in the bowl of the spoon.

Choose wedding colors of white, ivory, gold, rose, and the palest of blues, and serve rich Victorian fare like fresh fruits, beef, game birds, fish, and vegetables in sumptuous sauces. Carry tussy-mussy bouquets, and add porcelain figurines to centerpieces. Give the wedding cake plenty of floral, lovebird, and lacy adornments, and create wedding programs in the style of cherub-themed Victorian valentines. Decorate walls and easels with Victorian-era landscapes, and don't forget to print select wedding photos in diffused black and white or sepia to capture the romance of the period.

To complete the Victorian immersion, hold the reception at a vintage inn or a manor home, furthering the illusion of a visit to Queen Victoria's parlor.

#201 *The Family Picnic*

When the wedding budget is extremely modest, it's a good time to remember the joy of a family picnic. Weddings don't have to follow rules. If a couple says "I do," it's a wedding. So pick a date then pick a park!

Make arrangements with park administration for your wedding event, and hold the ceremony and the reception in one place to cut down on venue expenses. Any huge backyard can substitute for a park.

Use inventive, outdoorsy invitations you create yourself, with nontraditional wording like:

> *Please join us at our fun-for-everyone*
> *"All Family" Picnic Wedding*
> *Dress casual, and bring the children!*
> *Fried chicken, potato chips, punch, and cake will be served.*
> *Please feel free to bring additional picnic foods*
> *for your family to enjoy, as well as blankets, lawn chairs,*
> *games, and other fun picnic stuff. Yes, we're getting married,*
> *but on our wedding day, every guest is family. We look forward*
> *to welcoming you to our "All Family" Picnic Wedding!*

Serving fried chicken, potato chips, punch, and cake is an inexpensive way to provide reception food for a lot of people. Adjust the food as your budget permits, to include tubs of sodas or dips for the chips, etc. By suggesting to families that they can bring their own favorite picnic foods as well, you are supplementing the reception's food offerings with no additional burden on the wedding budget.

Ensure that each invited family gets a table. Use picnic tables, card tables, or any table that's easily transported to the park or yard. Round up tables from family and friends if necessary, and cover them with shower curtains from a dollar store. Just cut off the hems and the grommets to turn the curtains into durable outdoor tablecloths.

Providing chairs is nice. Although some guests will be happy to spread out a blanket on a patch of grass to eat or watch the ceremony, some frown upon laying food dishes on the ground.

A "family picnic" wedding is fun without being overly expensive. But even with pockets full of money to spend, it's hard to deny the good times of a picnic wedding.

#202 *Tropical Treasure*

"The tropics" instantly conjures thoughts of gently swaying palm trees, sun-drenched white sands, exotic foods, and colorful, fruity drinks topped with tiny umbrellas. Whether your wedding is on the beach or in the heart of downtown, a tropical theme is a happy one.

To make the decorative budget happy as well, forget fancy and expensive tropical flowers as centerpieces and instead use real pineapples, which are historical symbols of welcome. Stud the body of the fruit with pearl-tipped corsage pins and glaze the green crown with sparkling sugar crystals. Nestle the adorned pineapple atop a bed of raffia, or in a lagoon of dry white rice, to give your tables a decidedly tropical and festive feel. Border the reception area in long, white, sheer curtain panels hanging from bamboo rods, and add discreetly placed small fans to make them softly flutter in the breeze. Use clusters of seashells to accent the buffet, bar, and guest-book table, and let real or battery-powered tea lights tucked into hollowed-out pineapples provide flickering ambiance for the cake table.

Serve skewered fruit chunks as appetizers and luau foods as entrées. Hibiscus-themed drink umbrellas and food picks and hibiscus designs on wrapped butter mints can be purchased in bulk at little expense.

Make every decision with the goal of creating an open and airy ceremony and reception, and your tropical theme will feel like a "getaway vacation" for your guests.

#203 *Otherworldly Encounters*

If you've always wanted an "out of this world" wedding, what could be more thrilling than a UFO theme?

Glowing UFO lamps with fiber-optic sprays are perfect centerpiece starters. Surround the lamps with odd and interesting greenery and a few "moon rocks" that you've emblazoned with "alien" graffiti. Hang twinkling star balls from the ceiling with clear fishing line to create your own galaxy, and employ lots of inexpensive neon necklaces and bracelets to bring otherworldly life to foil-wrapped potted plants and table settings with space-age-style dinnerware. The bar will be a big hit when drinks with clever space names are served in glowing neon glasses. Outfit your waitstaff in "alien server" uniforms, and weave metallic accents into linens.

You don't have to don costumes in lieu of traditional wedding attire unless that's your wish, because wedding finery against a backdrop of "alien invasion" makes the experience all the more surreal and fun. Just let your imagination guide you. After all, no one really knows what aliens or faraway galaxies look like. Be inventive, and create your own universe. And don't forget the robots!

#204 *Sky-High Nuptials*

For the bride and groom who love to soar, a helicopter-themed wedding may be just perfect. Exotic locales like Hawaii, Niagara Falls, Alaska, and the Grand Canyon join more urban locations like Las Vegas and New York City in offering helicopter ceremonies. In fact, you are likely to find a helicopter service conducting wedding flights in most metropolitan and tourist locations. You can actually marry during the flight, or be whisked away to marry in a location inaccessible by traditional transportation, like on a glacier, atop a waterfall, or at a volcano's edge.

A marriage in the sky is necessarily intimate, with room for the bride, groom, officiant, and one or two witnesses only. As soon as you return, you'll want to throw a nice, big reception for all those well-wishers who weren't airborne for the nuptials. Serve cupcakes with spinning pinwheel tops, and consider miniature crystal or molded-chocolate helicopters as favors. Keep the theme alive with centerpieces made from crystal helicopters and exotic flowers. Add plenty of decorative whirligigs, including a helicopter weathervane (destined to become a lifetime keepsake for your home), at the guest-book table. Display instant photos of your flight and wedding on easels, or incorporate them into an endless-loop slide show or video show. And clever "Come Fly with Us" reception-only invitations are a must!

#205 *We Hit the Lottery!*

Winning the lottery is a once-in-a-lifetime dream come true, but isn't that just what happened when, out of all the billions of people in the world, you and your intended found each other? It was the luckiest day of your life when you discovered love, so a lottery-themed wedding reception is just the ticket. Wedding favors are easy. Give one-dollar scratch-off tickets tucked in "Lucky in Love" envelopes, and pair them with unique and delicious treats. Be prepared to hear frequent cries of "Yippee!" as the cards are scratched. Those who don't have a winning card will still have a winning morsel with which to satisfy the sweet tooth. Use more lottery tickets to decorate centerpieces then give the centerpieces as prizes for reception activities like old-fashioned carnival games customized to the wedding couple. Serve festive foods like "Spin the Wheel" pizzas or "Powerball" meatballs.

A lottery theme is fun because winning is fun. Make every guest a winner by keeping unexpected excitement in motion, and your wedding reception will be a big win of its own.

#206 *Football Fantasy*

There's a reason the Super Bowl continues to be one of the most watched televised events in America. Football fans are crazy for the game! For brides and grooms whose autumn weekends never pass without attending or viewing a football game, there's no reason to forgo their football passion at the wedding. Some sports arenas are now permitting weddings on the premises. Check with the franchise to see if you can say "I do" on the 50-yard line or in the end zone of your favorite team's home turf.

For the reception, make each cake tier football shaped, and top it with a bride and groom sharing a kiss at the goalpost. Rally the football spirit with peanuts, hot pretzels, and nachos served from a "concession stand" near the bar. Many college team mascots are available for hire for special events, and your favorite mascot leading the way as you enter the reception is just plain fun. Think "football ticket" invitations and artificial-turf carpeting. And don't forget to incorporate team colors and game-day gear into everything from bouquets and centerpieces to wall art and linens. Invite real football players as a surprise for guests, and when it's time for the garter ceremony, let the groom slip a "Super Bowl ring" garter from beneath that gorgeous gown!

#207 *Speakeasy Whispers*

Prohibition. From 1920 to 1933, that word struck dread into the hearts of most Americans. Under the watchful eye of the Feds, no alcoholic beverages could be sold, so underground bars with innocuous exteriors began to sprout up like green grass pushing through cracked pavement. Like nature itself, social drinking simply couldn't be squashed. These incognito night spots became known as speakeasies, and admittance was restricted to patrons who could softly utter an ever-changing password to get in.

If the age of Prohibition, with its flapper-style gowns for women and zoot suits for men, sends your romanticism into overdrive, a speakeasy reception is for you. Set the tone with muted lighting sources and an oversized bar complete with bar stools. Dress bartenders in white shirts with armbands and suspenders, and give your drinks era-inspired names like Rotgut, Monkey Rum, and Tarantula Juice.

Fill your reception hall with the sounds of cool jazz, and use white flowers and red accents to offset the soft gray of your linens. A rented fog machine can mist the room occasionally, supplying "smoky" ambiance without choking your guests. Decorate with vintage posters, and pay homage to bootlegging by decking the hall with clusters of old boots stuffed with bottles and flasks. Put trivia cards on each table, inviting guests to match famous Prohibition gangsters with crimes and dates. And don't forget the password! Include a business-card-sized slip of paper bearing your "wedding speakeasy" password in your invitations. Make your unique speakeasy a step back in time, but with all the comforts of a modern wedding reception, and you'll tap the best of both worlds.

#208 *Flower-Power Peace and Love*

Oh, those flower power days of the 1960s. *Peace* and *love* were the catchwords of the day, and the infamous Woodstock music festival changed lives. The era spawned the Beatles and music's British invasion, and it was a time for simplicity of style. Hippies ruled. Fashion was loose and flowing, and headbands and flowers snuggled up to iron-flattened tresses and over-ratted bouffant hairdos.

If you dream of getting married barefoot in a flowing, white summer dress with a circlet of wildflowers in lieu of a veil, then a hippie-inspired, peace-and-love wedding is perfect for you. It's one of the most inexpensive themes to produce, for the more homemade the decorations and the more down-home the food, the better. Beaded macramé, peace symbols, and lots of unstructured wildflowers set the scene, while classic '60s songs set the tone. To immerse your guests in the attitude of the period, incorporate fringe, leather, paisley, smiley faces, sunflowers, tie-dye, lava lamps, mood rings, and printed horoscopes anywhere and everywhere. Instruct guests to don bell-bottoms and sandals, or any other casual clothes, like those they might wear to an evening summer concert. Casual dress means you can break out the Twister game and dance the "Twist" until the cows come home. And don't forget the "Make Love, Not War" place cards. The flower-power era is full of great, inclusive sentiments.

#209 *Joyful Christmas Wedding*

With whole cities decorating for the holidays, your guests will already be in a festive mood for your Christmastime wedding, and all those existing decorations make your job easier. Simply make your wedding and reception an extension of what already surrounds you. then add your own personal twist to the occasion.

Try a whitewashed ceremony with only white, gold, and silver décor, then enjoy an explosion of seasonal colors at the reception — the contrast will be striking. Enlist a "Kriss Kringle" to personally hand out a beautiful (or whimsical), customized ornament favor to each guest. Fill elegant or funny Christmas stockings with treats, and give the stockings as prizes for reception games or challenges. Hire a costumed caroling group for the cocktail hour, and position natural-twig reindeer boasting "Just Married" signs at the reception entrance.

From twinkling white lights and easily made polymer "snow" to faux icicles and halls filled with holly, the decorating basics are easy. Stretch beyond the basics with inventive treats like snowflake peppermint cocktails with candy-cane stir sticks, and miniature, popcorn-ball "snowballs," fashioned into snowmen for centerpieces and accents and piled high in small, decorative sleighs for snacking. The best Christmastime wedding is the one that embraces both the holiday spirit and the spirit of love that is inherent to every wedding. Make the wedding about you, with the glory of Christmas as your backdrop.

#210 *To Dream of Disney*

Whether you choose to marry at Disneyland or Disney World or thousands of miles away from either location, the wonderful world of Disney brings an unbeatable fairy-tale aura to your wedding day. Disney makes or licenses many wedding-related products, like cake toppers, cake-knife sets, invitations, favors, and decorations. But you can enhance your Disney theme with your own Disney-inspired creations as well. Generously glitter the top third of white pumpkins to use as centerpieces, and surround them with cute mice figurines in various "work" poses. Drape sheer, pale-blue fabric on vintage dress mannequins, then use wrapped wire to stretch out sections of the fabric. Place silk birds at the ends of the wires as if Cinderella's feathered little helpers were designing her gorgeous gown right there at your reception. Designate tables using the names of Disney attractions instead of numbers, and go to the online Disney store to order a Minnie Mouse–ears bride's hat and a Mickey Mouse–ears groom's hat to include in the head-table centerpiece. Choose a fairy-tale wand for the flower girl to carry, and don't forget how beautiful the song "When You Wish Upon a Star" would sound at the ceremony. A Disney theme fits extravagant or frugal weddings equally well, for the whole Disney concept is built on imagination, which doesn't cost a thing.

#211 *Behold the Wild Blue Yonder*

The love of flying endures among those who crave soaring above the clouds. From airline ground crews to flight attendants and pilots, and from crop dusters to military jet pilots, aviation is a way of life. If flying is high on your list, consider an aviation-themed wedding.

Imagine an "airplane" wedding cake with majestic wings that spread wide across the cake table, and visualize leaving the ceremony under a shower of paper airplanes launched from the hands of your special guests. "Airline ticket" invitations and "boarding pass" programs are ideal, as are "pilot's wings" place cards. Line the ceremony aisle with ropes of "runway lights." If possible, and if the weather permits, hunt for an empty airport hangar to host your reception. Small, private airports often have available facilities.

For reception décor, pair vintage airplane art with photos of the bride and groom to create interesting collages. Designate reception tables by using miniature flags and the names of international airports from around the world. Silver, white, and a cornucopia of blues is the perfect color scheme for an airplane wedding, and packaged peanuts are a must at the "runway" bar — where the "flight attendant" will, of course, be mixing "aviation" cocktails. And remember to have your emcee begin reception announcements with "This is your captain speaking!"

#212 *Fiesta!*

When you think of a fiesta, you think of bright colors, larger-than-life dances, scrumptious comfort foods, and spirited music. Fiestas are vibrant occasions, and you don't have to come from south of the border to love the joyful, celebratory environment of a fiesta wedding reception.

Wedding-party attire can embrace everything from elegant formalwear to colorful peasant dresses for the women and guayabera shirts and casual khakis for the men. Consider bouquets and boutonnières accented with vibrant chili peppers and cactus-themed centerpieces atop richly colored, serape-inspired tablecloths.

Big, bold, and brightly colored paper flowers can be draped over arches and gathered in floor or wall arrangements. String *papel picado* (intricately cutout paper) into garlands or mobiles to hang from tree limbs or over potted plants.

And what fiesta would be complete without a piñata? Piñatas stuffed with wedding favors are just as much fun for the young at heart as they are for the young of age. It's your wedding. Go a little "fiesta" or go all the way, right down to the dance of love and courtship — the Mexican Hat Dance. Treat guests to the unforgettable sounds of a mariachi band, and round out the festivities with mouth-watering Mexican recipes suitable for everything from appetizers to cocktails.

Everyone knows that a fiesta is a party. Once you embrace the fiesta spirit, good times are inevitable.

#213 *Hi-Tech Cool*

As new technologies grow, so does the number of hi-tech aficionados. If flash drives and 3-D TVs get your heart pumping, a hi-tech wedding theme may be an ideal fit.

Buy blank CDs in bulk, then use long ribbons to hang them from the ceiling in staggered lengths above the dance floor. The CDs will sparkle in the lights, and you will have an inexpensive but dazzling canopy for your dance floor. Use a home printer to print wedding-couple photos onto another batch of CDs, then use those CDs as place-card holders. The CDs can be data free, or you can actually record a mix tape or a funny story on them to turn them into favors as well. "Plug" a computer mouse into the base of your wedding cake, then rest the mouse on a custom wedding-day mouse pad. Pair flash drives with baby's breath and green leaves to make boutonnières, and weave accents of fiber-optic wire throughout bouquets and centerpieces. Scour secondhand stores or the Internet for old circuit boards and make them into collages, incorporating wedding-color accents. Set up a live Web feed of the festivities, and be sure to have monitors airing the podcast at the reception. And don't forget the artificial intelligence! Book the services of an interactive robot to delight and entertain your guests, and instead of a ring bearer, have your rings delivered by a remote-control figure or vehicle decked out in formal duds.

Geeks are newly cool, and there's no reason to hide your techno-gadget-loving tendencies from the world. If hi-tech is what makes you tick, let your wedding be as cutting edge as modern technology itself.

#214 *Woodsy Wonderland*

For those who prefer the company of living trees to the hustle and bustle of the city, a woodsy, deep-forest wedding theme is perfect. If you are actually marrying in the woods, nature will take care of itself. But if your wedding must take place indoors, it's still possible to transform the ceremony and reception venues into woodsy wonderlands.

Use real logs and branches to border the ceremony aisle and to create a ring around the head table, and incorporate moss, stones, and a water element into centerpieces. Imagine the tiers of your wedding cake decorated to resemble the trunks of trees, complete with love messages carved into the "bark." Choose a blown-glass tree for a cake topper, but mount the cake on a real, bark-intact, slice of tree trunk. Invite plenty of owls and other woodland-creature figurines to the party, mingling them with centerpieces or using them to hold signs or anchor table linens. Just after Christmas, hit the closeout sales and buy freestanding, lighted, white-wicker reindeer in various poses to create elegant, contrasting focal points amidst the earthy colors of your woodland décor. Heed your woodland theme by wearing free-flowing clothing that moves like a breeze in the treetops — no uncomfortable garments for anyone. Give your flower girl real leaves instead of rose petals to toss from her naturally woven basket, and choose squirrel-art nut cups for place settings. Further the delectable quotient by making your own sweet treats with the help of squirrel, owl, and bunny chocolate molds. Keep an unspoiled natural paradise in mind as you plan, and your woodsy wedding will be serene and beautiful, whether or not you're actually in the woods.

#215 *Spying High*

If it's excitement you crave, adopt a theme whose motto sends prickles of anticipation dancing across your skin with the sound of just three little words: "Bond, James Bond." These iconic words instantly bring to mind intrigue, stunning scenery, and fast cars, all wrapped in black-tie elegance and the savior faire of a martini, "shaken not stirred."

Make your spy-themed wedding thoroughly fun. Well before the wedding, dress the part and have photos taken of the two of you in "action" poses, then turn the photos into "movie posters" for the reception. For the utmost authenticity, contact a car dealership with an Aston Martin on the premises, and you might be allowed to pose with a "Bond" car, especially if you agree to add a line at the bottom of the reception poster, such as: "Aston Martin car provided by XYZ Motors."

Watch all of the 007 movies to extract ideas for décor, like female figurines made of shimmering gold (*Goldfinger*) for bar-area decoration or chess-piece place-card holders (*From Russia with Love*) at place settings. Use flowers and faux diamonds in oversized martini glasses as centerpieces, and identify each guest table with the names of Bond's nemeses. And don't forget the music. James Bond movie scores feature everything from background music appropriate for the cocktail hour to love songs perfect for special dances.

A spy movie and a wedding have a lot in common, with one significant difference. One provides a couple of hours of adventurous entertainment, while the other sets the stage for the adventure of a lifetime.

#216 *Jungle Paradise*

The lushness of the jungle translates to a visually exciting wedding reception. Tables covered in black-and-white zebra-print linens and surrounded by glossy, jet-black chairs are a sophisticated homage to African jungle life, while an Amazon rainforest theme would be vivid and colorful, with a more whimsical tone. Make your chosen jungle theme ring true by learning about the region. If it's the jungles of Africa you wish to re-create, take your cue from the wildlife — elephants, lions, tigers, etc. For the Amazon jungles, it's the brilliantly colored birds, butterflies, and tree frogs that reign supreme.

Jungle flora everywhere is lush, green, and wet, which you can emulate by adding faux dewdrops to vines and plants used as table runners or as wall or potted-plant décor. If real waterfalls aren't an option, simulate waterfalls by stringing strands of white lights between faux rock formations. Cover the light strands with a wide piece of sheer aqua-blue fabric that is fluffed between the rocks. The full fabric will add to the flowing-water illusion. For refreshments, serve "Jungle Juice" cocktails and foods made with spices that come from real jungle plants. Tropical flowers and tribal-mask focal points make beautiful centerpieces, and green crystal stemware ties your theme together no matter what linens or dinnerware you use. The jungle is alive with beauty and spirit. Infuse your reception with those elements to create a lush, vibrant paradise.

#217 *Abundant Apples*

Besides being delicious and nutritious, apples are gorgeous. They are hearty and durable, and their size gives them stature, making the creation of decorative pieces easy. You can incorporate a variety of colored apples or concentrate on a specific apple, like a red or green one, to drive the wedding theme. A green-apple wedding will look strikingly different than a red-apple wedding. The red apple is robust and well suited to fall and winter, while green apples evoke a softer ambiance and feel very spring- or summer-like. Pair green apples with a deep, rich color, like navy blue or wine, and red apples with light accents like pastels, silver, or gold.

Apples are perfect for both décor and dining. Affix a place card to a bamboo skewer, and insert the skewer into an apple to liven up place settings. Tumble apples into glass cylinders or crystal vases to create centerpiece art for dining, buffet, cake, and guest-book tables, and cluster larger glass floor vases filled with apples and apple blossoms into staggered-height floor art. Mini crab apples entwined with apple-blossom florals are inventive cake toppers, and a self-serve apple bar with skewers, chunked apple pieces, caramel, marshmallow crème, chocolate, melted red-hot cinnamon candy, crushed nuts, and other flavorful dipping sauces and toppings is a fun treat for wedding guests.

To really embrace the joy of the apple, hold the ceremony or reception in an apple orchard. For apple décor, you can't do better than a living apple tree!

#218 *Lucky Strikes!*

Bowlers love their game, and bowling alleys have come a long way over the years, making the bowling experience an especially enjoyable slice of life. If you and your intended are avid bowlers, share your passion. First check with local bowling alleys to determine what facilities are available for your reception. If leagues aren't playing, chances are that you can rent out all or a portion of the bowling alley for a reasonable price, especially with smaller establishments.

Use long guest tables, creating an "alley and pins" table runner for each. In the center of the table, arrange miniature bowling pins — two full sets, placed back-to-back on a base of greenery, with each "1" pin facing one end of the table. Drizzle two rows of black aquarium sand, extending away from the pins, to represent the gutters, then sprinkle dried flower petals between the two black-sand "gutters," creating a beautiful floral "alley." Be sure to include turkey on the dinner menu or buffet because, after all, a "turkey" in bowling is a really big deal! Invite guests to dress "bowling" casual, which they will love, and negotiate the use of shoes, balls, and alleys for guests for a designated portion of the reception. When someone rolls a strike, it's a signal for a newlywed kiss! A band or DJ can steer guests toward and away from the alleys as needed so that they may witness or participate in traditional reception events like a first dance or the cake cutting. A small, decorated cake is ideal for the cake ceremony, with "bowling ball" cupcakes served to the guests. Even if you can't hold your reception at a real bowling alley, a bowling wedding theme shares your passion, and may entice bowling novices to give your favorite fun game a try!

#219 *Fire and Ice*

If the bride or the groom is a firefighter, choose a fire-and-ice theme. Fire represents purity, passion, and creativity, and the cool temperance of ice is fire's perfect counterbalance. Ice and fire together create water, and water means "life" in every corner of the Earth.

If you can't hold the reception in an actual firehouse, bring the firehouse to you, with everything from the pole to the hats. Build centerpieces around firefighter's hats found at party-supply shops, weaving in glistening faux ice cubes as accents. A fire-engine ice sculpture on the buffet or dessert table captures the theme, and utilizing a small, decorated fire ax instead of a knife to cut the cake is a hoot. Use white-silk faux-flame torches for mood lighting, and invite plenty of stuffed-animal dalmatians to the reception to cozy up to potted plants and keep a watchful eye on the gift and guest-book tables.

Consider wearing a white bridal gown with a bold red accent and incorporating firefighter lapel pins into the boutonnières. You don't have to limit yourself to red and orange to pay tribute to the firefighter in your life. Whites and silvers with red and black accents are perfect. If it's the groom who is the firefighter, consider having him carry the bride into the reception "hero style." Guests will get a kick out of it! And don't forget the firehouse cuisine. What fire-and-ice wedding would be complete without firehouse chili and an ice-cold drink to wash it down? Fire and ice are as perfect a pairing as a bride and a groom.

#220 *To Dream of Angels*

It is said that, when an angel appears in your dreams, you've received a divine idea, and guardian angels are often credited with the big and little miracles of everyday life. For many, just thinking of angels brings a smile and lifts the spirits, and an angel-themed wedding does that, too. Imagine saying your vows beneath two stylized angels adorning your bridal arch, or cutting your cake where it rests between two extraordinary wings. From paper to fine crystal, angel décor is easy to find and easy to incorporate into centerpieces, table settings, favors, food, and stationery, as well as wall, ceiling, and floor art. An angel theme thrives in a sea of white, with only minimal color accents. A gently splashing angel fountain at the reception entrance sets the tone for the celebration to come, and lots of warm up-lighting completes the ambiance. And what could be more delightful for the angel lover's palate than a beautiful array of mouthwatering, lemon-kissed angel-food cupcakes?

#221 *Cartoon and Main Feature*

If you and your intended share a love of the cinema, go old-school, and choose a double theme for your reception. In a bygone era, movies were always preceded by a delightful cartoon. Tickle your guests by beginning the reception with a cartoon-themed cocktail party, complete with fun drinks and hors d'oeuvres. Include decorative touches, like embellished cocktail napkins and swizzle sticks, reflecting the cartoon of your choice.

Are you a fan of Sylvester and Tweety Bird? Or maybe Mickey Mouse is your favorite. You can choose any existing cartoon, or even create your own by turning the bride and groom into cartoon characters with their own animated adventure running on an endless video loop at the cocktail party. Make the cartoon the old-fashioned way, with art drawn on rapidly flipping pages, or go to a Web site like JibJab to create your own super-fun video cartoon.

Choose your favorite movie as the theme for the main reception activities, and use that movie as your blueprint for everything from décor to games. It doesn't matter if you pair Bugs Bunny with *Gone with the Wind*, or your personalized cartoon characters with *Love Story*. The double theme will work with any cartoon/movie combination. Erect a "movie marquee" easel in your reception hall with a "Tonight's Movie Cartoon Is:" sign, complete with art representing your cartoon choice. And when it's time for the cocktail party to end, remove that sign to reveal one that reads "Enjoy Tonight's Main Feature:" followed by the title and art depicting the movie you've chosen. Substitute photos of the bride and groom in the movie poster so it's clear that the wedding couple is tonight's main attraction. Fun and fantasy always pack an entertainment punch.

#222 *Abe and Mary and Friends*

Abe and Mary-Todd Lincoln's log cabin beginnings. Antony and Cleopatra's opulent, exotic palace. Guinevere and Sir Lancelot's star-crossed destiny. Bonnie and Clyde's hot guns and hot wheels.

One of the easiest ways to create a wedding theme is to first choose a famous couple from history, myth, or legend. Let passion be your guide, and select a couple that generates excitement for you. Learn all you can about the iconic twosome, then re-create their world as your wedding theme. From the wooden serving planks of Mary-Todd Lincoln's earliest kitchen to the swords and saddles employed by Sir Lancelot in the kingdom of King Arthur, ideas for wedding décor, food, attire, and accents will flow easily from all that surrounds the renowned pair. Costume shops, theater and party-supply stores, and even reenactment organizations are great resources for "period" re-creation. And don't forget fictional duos like Scarlett O'Hara and Rhett Butler, or Han Solo and Princess Leia. Every famous couple possesses its own special aura. Embrace it, and make it yours.

#223 *Steampunk Dreams*

Steampunk is, in a word, fun. The decidedly 20th-century term characterizes a lifestyle that springs from subgenres of science-fiction stories, especially those driven by steam-powered inventions. Let yourself be inspired by visionary tales like Jules Verne's 1870 literary giant, *20,000 Leagues Under the Sea*. Imagine the gadgets, the clothing, and the décor — the blend of the then-present time with futuristic machines that didn't yet exist. Gears and pipes are a decorative mainstay, and you can incorporate them into everything from centerpieces to hair adornments. Victorian-style clothing with outlandish accessories are a perfect fit, and mechanical arms holding buffet dishes are a treat. The beauty of a steampunk wedding is the opportunity to marry elegance to dreams. As long as it fits the era and pays homage to steam, anything goes, making the wedding-planning treasure hunt for decorative accents as entertaining as the wedding. And if you can't find what you're looking for, make it. No one will have a clue whether it's right or wrong, because the most important element of steampunk is unbridled imagination.

#224 *We're Engaged! We're Married!*

Surprise weddings trim the budget, thrill guests, and reduce wedding-planning stress to no more than a fleeting moment.

Your engagement party is the ideal time to unleash a surprise wedding. Guests are already gathered and in a celebratory mood. Some wedding couples prefer a long engagement, but for others, it's "What's the point in waiting? We're ready to be Mr. and Mrs.!"

Keeping the nuptials a secret is easy. No one needs to know except the wedding couple and the officiant, who will naturally be an invited guest. Greet your guests, then simply slip away long enough to change into whatever wedding finery you choose, and return to the party to make the "It's our wedding!" announcement.

Distribute a secret stash of bouquets and boutonnières to newly appointed wedding-party members. If uniformity matters, take along black choir robes for the best man and groomsmen, and blue ones for the maid of honor and the bridesmaids. Robes are easily donned over any regular clothing. A wedding cake delivered by a bakery at a predesignated time completes the wedding surprise.

Wedding planning for a big wedding is an unforgettable experience, but for some, seasoning the "I dos" with the element of surprise is even better.

#225 *Boogie-Woogie Bugle Bash!*

The 1940s saw the country go to war, but the nation was alive with hopeful spirit, as it reveled in a watershed of great big-band sounds. Swing was all the rage. The Andrew Sisters' megahit "Boogie Woogie Bugle Boy" was just one of the timeless songs of the era, which also produced crooners and jazz greats like Frank Sinatra, Ella Fitzgerald, and Benny Goodman. Legendary films like *Casablanca*, *It's a Wonderful Life*, and *Yankee Doodle*

Dandy ruled the cinema, along with those indelible Westerns starring singing cowboys Gene Autry and Roy Rogers.

Such classic music and films now provide great fodder for brides and grooms looking to recreate an incomparable ambiance for their wedding. A 1940s wedding is blessed with satin gowns, red lips, and men dressed in pinstriped suits. Apparel with a military influence also works well for a 1940s theme. The decade spawned delectable new foods like M&Ms and Chicago-style pizza — two great treats for wedding guests! Floral wallpaper art, ruffled-curtain room dividers, tin-canister bouquets, and centerpieces designed around old rotary telephones will help to make the step back in time complete. The 1940s is a grand era to "visit," even if you're far too young to remember its treasures firsthand.

#226 *Easter Parade*

When Irving Berlin wrote his classic, early-20th-century song, "Easter Parade," the actual "parade" had already been going on for decades. It was less of a parade and more of an after-church stroll along the boulevards, taken by well-to-do people dressed in their Sunday finery of extravagant hats and the latest fashions.

Today, the "Easter Parade" still exists, and it makes a wonderful inspiration for a wedding. Delicate prints and fabrics rule both attire and decorations. Light and breezy is the goal. Large, decorated hats are fun to create and can accent everything from walls to arches, and Easter baskets trimmed with spring flowers and filled with edible candy eggs are beautiful, lighthearted centerpieces. Consider an old-fashioned "Easter egg hunt" at the reception, but instead of hiding eggs, hide the wedding favors. Choose a menu that reflects your own traditional Easter Sunday dinner with all the trimmings. If you're having a church wedding, it will already be filled with Easter florals, helping to save on floral expenses. Porcelain bunny figurines are perfect adornments for the buffet table, and sparkling pastel balloons at the reception entrance welcome guests to your celebration with an instant promise of springtime fun. An "Easter Parade" –themed wedding is just full of storybook possibilities.

#227 *Country Living*

An old-fashioned "country living" wedding is a dream to produce. There are so many readily available options for locations, food, music, and décor that the biggest problem is not in figuring out what to use — it's in deciding what doesn't get used. Costs are often slashed significantly by replacing expensive "wedding" items with everyday "country" items. Try old weathervanes nestled in a bed of inexpensive greens and flowers instead of pricier floral centerpieces. Use old quilts hung from the ceiling to create a clever "cloud cover," or stretch them between potted shepherd's hooks to create faux walls. Forget fancy table linens, and opt for wood-plank tables adorned with a single lace runner instead. Forgo programs at the ceremony by printing the schedule on two weathered signs and placing one on each side of the seating area. Augment the signs with old duck-decoy pairs sporting top hats and bridal veils, and give personalized rain gauges as wedding favors.

A "country living" wedding is not a country-western wedding. It's not about cowboys. It's about a slice of the slower, simpler, and often sweeter side of life that comes from rural living. If you've never lived in the country, don't despair. Just grab your intended and take a drive. Country living is always just right around the bend.

#228 *Purple Reign*

Throughout history, Cleopatra and other royal dignitaries indulged their passion for purple by turning priceless dyes into purple garments so valuable they rivaled the worth of precious gems. Purple became synonymous with great wealth, but fortunately, today's wedding couples don't need coffers of gold to embrace the glory of purple.

A purple wedding theme incorporates color nuances from lilac to violetand from soft lavender to deep, vibrant, lose-yourself-in-it royal purple. Pair purple with white and metallic colors for a rich, opulent ambiance, or accent purples with pale pastels to create an undeniable air of romance. The rare lavender rose represents love at first sight and makes a perfect floral focal point for arrangements or bud vases. A splash of purple on a white wedding gown can be breathtaking, and a judicious use of purple foods and drinks turns ordinary dining into a fun adventure. Bridesmaids look fabulous in purple-hued gowns, and groomsmen sporting purple-toned ties or waistcoats set a stylish standard. Thankfully, you no longer have to rule a country to experience the wonder of purple. You simply have to love it.

#229 *Love Buzz*

Bumblebees boast a symbolic significance that crosses cultural divides. Because they represent immortality, wisdom, purity, rebirth, and community, the hard-working bumblebee is a fine theme for a wedding celebration.

Bumblebee décor is easy to envision and easy to acquire. From edible sugar bumblebees to rhinestone-studded specimens for centerpieces and floor trees, those industrious little yellow-and-black fellows bring the essence of sunshine to the celebration. If you prefer "refined" to "lighthearted and whimsical," simply change all yellow components to gold. Make all of your bumblebees gold-and-black, and add glitter to the golden parts if you wish. The spirited bumblebee looks downright dapper and distinguished when he's given the golden Midas touch! To further the elegance quotient, don't use eyes — it's the eyes that give the bees their cuteness. Without eyes, bumblebee décor is more artsy than merry.

The humble little bumblebee is extremely versatile. You don't even have to use bees at all to enjoy their symbolism. Decking out your reception in formal black with either yellow or gold accents gets the point across, with or without the addition of a single bee. But with bumblebees offering so many decorative opportunities, you'll surely want at least one hive-full sprinkled about.

#230 *Discovery Garden*

Plants enhance a beautiful décor. But while all plants are a decorative plus, unusual plants transform an ordinary garden theme into a wondrous and "wow" experience. Rare and exotic plants are more than part of the atmosphere — they become entertainment and conversation starters as guests discover them. You can even fashion a game around them by having everyone guess their identity, or by having guests give them funny but fitting names. The bride and groom decide the winners.

Purchase unusual plants for the wedding and reception, then use them as prizes or share them with family and friends. You can save money by planning ahead and growing many of the plants yourself; use full-grown plants as décor and baby plants as favors. If you don't expect to distribute the plants to guests, consider renting a variety of plants, to be returned after the celebration. Craft at least one menu item from an unusual plant and offer bar drinks with exotic plant names. There's nothing like a fabulous, creative garden to promote love and romance, and a discovery-garden theme is an inspired notch above ordinary.

#231 *The Wonder of Rainbows*

Sometimes a theme can be based simply upon a feeling, such as the one inspired by gazing upon a rainbow. Rainbows have the "sweet sigh" factor, evoking smiles of wonder and admiration. Legends from cultures around the world value rainbows as roadmaps leading to pots of gold, bridges to mystical lands in the sky, and even pathways to Heaven. But no matter what legend a rainbow spawns, the one thing it will always have is undeniable beauty — exactly what you get when you choose a rainbow theme.

The colors of a rainbow are red, orange, yellow, green, blue, indigo, and violet, but rainbows needn't hang everywhere for you to capture their essence. Just softly fold rainbow colors into centerpieces, napkins, and wall art. Hang strands of prisms where they will catch the light, and use water elements, like faux raindrops, on potted-plant leaves and flower petals. Ask a special-effects lighting wizard to create a rainbow effect across the ceremony or reception ceiling. Turn inexpensive little terra-cotta flowerpots into wedding favors by transforming them into "pots of gold" with golden paint. Stuff a scrap of white lace into the pot, allowing the edges to spill out over the rim then fill the pots with gold-wrapped candies. The white lace offers just the right visual contrast between the golden candy and the golden pot. Attach a wire handle if you wish, and include a thank-you card with a message such as: "We've found our pot of gold in each other. Thank you for making our find even richer." Serve colorful foods and rainbow-shaped cookies and breads. Rainbows may be fleeting, but their beauty and magic are wondrous.

#232 *Happy New Year!*

Roy Rogers and Dale Evans did it in 1947. Fifty years later, Will Smith and Jada Pinkett did it, too. What did they do? They married on New Year's Eve.

A New Year's Eve wedding is a joyful celebration wrapped in contagious excitement. It requires plenty of advance planning, and early save-the-dates are a must for guests. But if you plan well and secure necessary locations and vendors months or even years ahead, you can pull off a spectacular wedding and reception that gains momentum as the night marches on.

Creating your New Year's Eve theme is easy. The primary components of décor are sparkle and flair. Add sparklers to the wedding-cake ceremony, and remember that New Year's Eve is definitely a champagne occasion, so let the bubbly flow! Noisemakers are also great additions. Just be sure to pass them out late in the reception — you don't want your guests drowning out the band and reception events with whizzes, whoops, and siren squeals. A confetti or balloon drop at midnight is spectacular, and who needs Times Square? Just make your own "wedding ball" to drop during the midnight countdown. Since it's traditional to kiss the one you love just as the new year begins, be sure to have your photographer and videographer capture not only your midnight kiss but the kisses happening all over your reception — it's a rare and wonderful photo opportunity.

Whether you choose a black-tie night of glamour, or a more casual, focused-on-fun event, marry all the joys of a traditional New Year's celebration with your own wedding-day traditions. That perfect blend will be invigorating.

#233 *Cherry-Blossom Festival*

What could be more beautiful than a Japanese cherry tree in bloom? The life cycle of the delicate cherry blossom is far too brief, making its beauty all the more poignant. It's a living expression of the fleeting nature of life, reminding all who gaze upon it of the importance of celebrating precious moments, like your wedding.

A cherry-blossom theme is springtime perfect, and because cherry blossoms are so popular, you will have no difficulty finding appropriate printed materials, favors, and décor. But you can also add to the commercially available products by reaching deeper into the cherry blossom's historical Japanese roots. For example, hire a lute player for the ceremony, and add sake as a drink option at the reception. Serve a menu that is as light and delicate as the cherry blossom itself. Frame sheets of cherry-blossom wallpaper or wrapping paper then use the framed art to create inventive groupings on walls, easels, or tables. Use soft, flowing kimonos instead of drapes wherever drapery is needed. Long, arching cherry-blossom twigs make beautiful centerpieces, and potted, faux cherry trees are an ideal backdrop for the cake table. A cherry-blossom theme is light, airy, and welcoming. It's hard to get it wrong.

#234 *Daddy-O Cool*

Beatniks, those nonconformists of the '50s and '60s who loved poetry, jazz, and stylized art and who exemplified a bohemian lifestyle, could do your wedding proud. A beatnik wedding theme is custom made for wedding couples who embrace the philosophy of being different.

Capture the essence of a hole-in-the wall coffeehouse from half a century ago by using wooden tables without linens and adorning them with small sets of bongos instead of centerpieces. Feature a coffee bar, and when your jazz band isn't playing, invite anyone to take the stool on a small, dimly lit stage to read their poetry or sing their song. Provide a "language" primer on each table, instructing guests to freely sprinkle phrases like "Cool, man" or "Dig it" or "Way to go, Daddy-O" into conversations. And for total immersion, invite all guests to dress like beatniks. Most will love it, because it requires no dressing up and no pricey purchases, since simple, old black clothes are ideal. To help with wardrobe selections, include a photo collage of beatnik fashions (beatniks loved a good beret) on a separate sheet inside your poetry-book-style wedding invitations. A beatnik wedding is dressed down, not up, but that doesn't mean that the bride and groom can't be as spectacularly outfitted as they wish.

#235 Birds of a Feather

Imagine an aviary filled with the bold, vivid colors of beautiful, exotic birds. This bright yet softly cohesive scene captures the spirit of an exotic-bird wedding theme.

From the gorgeous spectacle of the proud peacock and the wonderfully intense, blended colors of a wild macaw to the formal countenance of a "tuxedo-clad" penguin and the sweet face of a hummingbird, bird-inspired wedding décor comes to life in a vibrant fashion. There are countless birds with special characteristics, which means that it's possible to choose extraordinary color palettes that just wouldn't work with any other theme.

You don't have to stuff every corner with a fake bird. Just use faux birds here and there, taking clues from their coloring, their lifestyle, and their habitat to create the illusion that you and your guests are experiencing their world. Cover foam shapes with birdseed to form tabletop sculptures, and turn birdbaths into living plant stands. Drape long swathes of sheer, sky-blue fabric across the ceiling, and rent a variety of living trees in pots to bring the birds' natural habitat indoors. Name your bar drinks after favorite birds, and make "lovebirds" your cake topper. And don't forget to have the band cut loose with a rousing version of "Rockin' Robin" to get those dancers on their feet. Later, a sweet, slow-dance rendition of "Blackbird" will give everyone an opportunity to cuddle.

#236 A Midsummer Night's Dream

Shakespeare was a creative fellow, and his vision for *A Midsummer Night's Dream* included some of the most inventive, and wedding-perfect, forest scenes ever imagined. Shakespeare penned his enchanted-forest play in the 16th century, and it's just as joyful nearly 500 years later.

You'll want lots of vines and leafy garlands, as well as trees of all sizes and shapes — silk or real. Stick to forest greens and other earthy colors, or whitewash everything for a completely different forest aesthetic. Flutes, harps, tinkling bells, and sparkling, winged insects are staples for centerpiece and tree adornments. Hang photos of the bride and groom, gently framed by silk fairy wings, from tree limbs or display them on tabletop easels. Nestle a feast of fruits, nuts, berries, and breads atop a "mossy" buffet during the cocktail hour. Hang five wind chimes in a tent-top formation above the cake table: one high in the center and one at each corner, connected by lush, gently sloping vines dotted with colorful silk butterflies. Add water elements, like tabletop fountains or fishbowls filled with blue water and topped with floating "lily pad" candles, to represent the sparkling pools of the forest. Use plenty of "pixie dust" glitter to dress tables and floors, and embrace a magician as the perfect entertainment.

The beauties of Shakespeare's forest are endless. Use many or just a few. If you need help, rent the 1999 film version of the masterpiece, starring Michelle Pfeiffer and Kevin Kline. You can even show it, without sound, in the background of your cocktail reception. *A Midsummer Night's Dream* is a delightful escape.

#237 *Hol-i-DAY*

If you're stuck for a wedding theme, check out your wedding date on one of the "wild and wacky holidays" Web sites. There are hundreds of holidays that don't get much publicity (or may not have a verifiable origin), but an "unusual holidays" Web site could be a great place to conjure up a wedding theme.

Are you marrying on December 8th? That's National Brownie Day! How about on July 13th? It's Barbershop Music Appreciation Day. Just think of the possibilities! Before choosing your wedding date, you may want to peruse a few "holiday" listing sites, and pick a day that will give your event a giant infusion of fun. If you've already picked a date, check out the holidays anyway. There just might be something unusual or interesting about your day that you'll want to include. On the other hand, you might want to avoid some days. November 27th is Pins and Needles Day, and brides and grooms already have enough of those!

#238 *A Spot of Tea?*

After a morning wedding, a high-tea theme may hit the spot for a reception that extends into the afternoon. High tea, afternoon tea, or any other kind of tea is not a typical American pastime, so you'll need to borrow ideas from friends across the Atlantic. Americans inevitably associate teatime with scones and crumpets, but in truth, high tea is a meal with both sweet and savory selections. It's actually "afternoon tea" (also known as "low tea"), which happens later in the day, during which the dainty stuff is served. High tea got its name from the food being served on high (dining-height) tables, rather than on the lower (coffee-table-height) tables of afternoon tea, and it was born in the working class, not the aristocratic one.

For your high-tea buffet, serve staples like salmon and pork pies, along with fun high-tea foods like bacon-and-onion pudding or Scotch eggs. Most of your guests will have never had the opportunity to enjoy such culinary fare. Serve your meal about mid to late afternoon, and provide plenty of wonderful tea selections, along with accompaniments like milk, lemon slices, sugar, cinnamon, mint, etc. Consider offering tea kits as wedding favors, and decorate with sturdy lace and floral centerpieces fashioned around vintage teapots. In keeping with the theme's working-class heritage, a single musician strikes the perfect musical note. And remember that at a tea of any sort, cups with saucers are an absolute must.

#239 *Nothing but the Best*

Every bride and groom wants only the best for their wedding. Choose "Nothing but the Best" as your wedding theme, and you shall have it. Simply examine every decorative, culinary, musical, or floral idea then zero in on the best part of it. What's the best part of a muffin? Hands down, it's the top, so instead of whole muffins, serve only muffin tops. The best part of a flower is no doubt the bloom, so use only blooms — no stems. The best part of icing the cake is licking the frosting bowl, so you treat guests to frosting-filled shot glasses. The best part of going to a party is the surprises discovered in the gift bag, so tuck your favors and other unexpected treats into clever bags. The best part of a musical set is the songs that bring back memories, so load the playlist with only those best-of-the-best songs that move and inspire. Whatever the act or the accent, root out the best aspect and feature it. Guests will get an absolute kick out of your "best of" theme. After all, your wedding day is already the best day ever.

#240 *Northern Lights*

Aurora borealis. Unless you live in, or travel to, the polar region at the top of the Earth, you may never get to experience the aurora borealis phenomenon up close, but those who have are somehow transformed by it. The lights may have scientific explanations, but their brilliant and ever-changing display of colors transcends science. When the lights flare, the mind doesn't care that the phenomenon is caused by naturally colliding electrons — the show is simply otherworldly.

It is that miracle-of-nature essence that a northern-lights theme brings to your wedding, one that springs from all things colorful and soft. A wedding gown of watered silk is perfect, as are midnight-blue table linens topped with iridescent organza table runners, especially those with colors that bleed softly into each other. Mood lighting is a must, since the right artificial lighting can work its magic on walls and ceilings, re-creating the ebb and flow and playful, teasing spirit of the northern lights. Serve a menu based on foods from the northern polar region, which would include dishes from Alaska, Canada, Greenland, Finland, Russia, Sweden, or Norway. And, of course, set up a self-serve ice-cream bar late in the evening. Feature purple heather in floral arrangements, and erect a beautiful ice sculpture to represent the frozen tundra. In lieu of wedding favors, make a charitable donation in each guest's name to help save the polar bears. You'll find that a northern-lights wedding theme is magical, romantic, and inviting, just as you'd hoped.

#241 *Timeless Moments*

Before you marry, there will be many timeless moments shared between the two of you. To honor those moments, choose "Timeless" as your theme. From beautiful vintage styles to sleek modern designs, clocks and calendars have served as methods of remembrance for hundreds of years. Fill your reception with clocks and calendars in all sizes, shapes, and ages. Remove the batteries, or let the vintage clocks wind down, then set the hands on each clock to reflect one perfect moment in time experienced by the bride or the groom individually or by the two of them together. Set calendars to a specific month or day that reflects a special memory. Beneath each clock or calendar, add a small, framed note, with or without a photo, describing what happened at that moment in time. Use classic, timeless quotes as table identifiers and only non-hybrid florals for centerpieces. Look to timeless toys for gifts and entertainment, like yo-yos personalized with wedding-couple stickers as favors, and hula hoops waiting in the wings to take a whirl on the dance floor. Serve foods that have stood the test of time, looking and tasting just as they did hundreds of years ago, like roast pork, cornbread, or mashed potatoes. Spell out the word "Timeless" in floral art behind the cake table. Love is timeless — why not let your wedding day say so?

#242 *Wonders of the Deep*

You don't have to be saying "I do" on a sandy beach to appreciate the teeming life far beneath the ocean's white-capped waves. A "Life of the Sea" theme is beautiful and invigorating, and whether your wedding is seaside or not, your reception can feel as if it is an extension of the ocean itself.

Make judicious use of blues, teals, and seafoam greens, and add water elements like fountains and water-filled bowls with floating candles and sprigs of seaweed. Use dolphin, whale, sea-horse, and other ocean-inspired statuary to decorate the buffet and guest-book tables. Add starfish and seashells to centerpieces, and provide an array of some especially delicious seaweed snacks. Ask a local seafood restaurant if you can acquire their discarded clamshells. Clean and dry them thoroughly, then use them to hold place cards. Of course, seafood is perfect for the menu, and your wedding cake, with its own aquatic decorations, can be placed atop a large, watercolor base painted to look like the sea.

#243 *Historically Romantic*

If you love curling up with a sweeping, romantic story set in a bygone era, you may love re-creating it as your wedding theme even more. Historical romances are brimming with wedding inspiration. They're called historicals because they incorporate facts into fictional stories, and those facts include the real scoop on everything from food and clothing to décor and entertainments. As an added bonus, many romance novels even contain one or more lengthy wedding scenes.

Imagine a wedding on the bow of a tall ship or on the shore of some distant land. You don't have to go there to experience it firsthand — you can replicate it by using a well-written romance novel as your wedding-planning guide. If you look closely enough, you'll find ideas and authentic details right there on the pages that you can apply to every aspect of your wedding. As you read, use a highlighter to document the colors, menus, unique clothing, décor, utensils, shoes, accessories, music, dances, and even the thoughts of the hero and heroine. Before you know it, your historical-romance wedding theme will simply begin to fall into place. All you must do is transform "fantasy" into "reality."

#244 *The Land of Oz*

Follow the yellow brick road to an amazing wedding and reception. What's more beautiful than the Emerald City? When you choose a *Wizard of Oz* theme, you open the door to gorgeous possibilities. Walk a Yellow Brick Road aisle runner that begins at the ceremony and later ends before a shimmering Oz backdrop at the reception. Make ruby-slipper centerpieces by covering old high heels with red glitter. Fill them with poppies and a miniature flying monkey made by adding pipe-cleaner wings to rubber vending-machine monkeys or to tiny stuffed-animal monkeys. A picnic basket with a stuffed "Toto" peeking out from one side is excellent as your card box on the gift table. Erect a balloon rainbow over the cake table, and use emerald gems on your cake. A scattering of plant stands filled with greenery and giant lollipops will add the fairy-tale effect, and bridesmaids can carry bouquets with a golden lollipop motif. Hire Dorothy, the Cowardly Lion, the Scarecrow, and the Tin Man from a party or singing telegram service to mingle with guests and encourage shy ones to get up and dance. Try tiny hot-air balloons as place cards and a replica of Dorothy's house, complete with the Wicked Witch's striped-stockinged feet beneath it, as the focal point for the buffet table. And don't forget the lighting. Lights with green lenses work wonders to elevate the overall "Oz" sensation. *The Wizard of Oz* is timeless, and the right blend of elegance and whimsy makes an "Oz" wedding just as timeless.

THE
CEREMONY

CHAPTER FOUR • *The Ceremony*

Since the dawn of modern western marriage, there has been a walk down the aisle, a pair of "I dos," and the pronouncement of "husband and wife." But modern wedding ceremonies offer much more than the familiar, basics.

This chapter addresses traditional and not-so-traditional aspects of the ceremony. From creative seating and aisle configurations to personalized vows and rehearsing the first kiss, you'll find ideas for turning your ceremony into a personal expression of who you are.

If you are marrying in a house of worship, ceremonial changes may require approval from the venue. If you are marrying anywhere else, permissions are usually required only if you plan to somehow alter the facility or impact the environment. When planning a wedding ceremony, follow your ABCs:

A. Select and confirm your location.

B. Ask for a written list of venue policies before signing on the dotted line.

C. Plan your ceremony according to the venue's requirements.

Trying to bend a venue to your will is far more difficult than learning up front what is or is not permissible, and then crafting your ceremony accordingly. But in all circumstances, if you want to deviate from the rules, it never hurts to ask. Even if you've been given written guidelines that prohibit a particular event you wish to include, inquire if an exception can be made. The worst that can happen is that the answer is "no." But compromises can sometimes be made that please both you and the facility.

The ceremony is the most important and meaningful component of your wedding day. With a little careful planning, there's no reason it shouldn't be all you wish it to be.

#245 *This I Vow*

Many wedding couples exchange personally written vows. But what if the wedding couple is blessed with only one eloquent writer? What about the poor counterpart who can mutter little more than, "I love you more than anything"? Writing unique vows is joyful for some and stressful for others.

Everyone hopes to make his or her partner feel like the only soul on the planet, but personal expression is often a challenge. The answer is to walk in the shoes of those who have gone before you.

The arts are a never-ending resource for beautiful words, and seeking inspiration from songs, poetry, books, movies, and plays is no less personal than writing the words from scratch. Who can lay a greater claim to love? Is it the person for whom the writing comes easily, or is it the one who spends hours or days searching for just the right combination of already written words?

Words alone are never truly original. They've all been said and said again. It's how those words are presented that counts. Whether the vows are written by one's own hand or culled from history, what they say doesn't matter nearly as much as the act of saying them. In the end, originality ranks only a distant second to "coming from the heart."

#246 *A Place of Honor*

Reserving priority seats for honored family members is a given. Both sets of parents should be ensured a front-row view of the ceremony. Divorced parents and their current spouses may share the front row if enough seats are available, or stepparents or birth parents may be seated directly behind the parents most responsible for raising the bride and the groom.

Grandparents are seated directly behind parents, and siblings and other family members are seated next to or behind them.

In addition to honored family members, there are other wedding guests who deserve VIP treatment. Seat elderly guests close to the front and on an aisle if possible. Aisle seats should also go to the disabled and to mothers with small children, who may need to carry a fussy little one from the room.

When blended families and complex feelings are involved, it's best to discuss the ceremony's seating arrangements in advance. For example, a stepmother who is closer to the groom than his birth mother should not be relegated to a lesser seat simply because her name is not on the birth certificate. Traditional etiquette is not as important in modern weddings as honoring true relationships, and finding a way to give all loved ones the priority seating they deserve will make the day more pleasant for everyone.

The mother of the bride is the most honored guest, followed by the mother of the groom. Ensure that they have the two best seats in the house, and the rest of the priority seating will be easier to envision.

#247 *A Kiss for Mom*

Whether you're the bride or the groom, chances are you wouldn't be who you are without your mom. Including her in the wedding ceremony, even if for only a brief moment of recognition, enriches the occasion.

At a prearranged point in the ceremony, both the bride and groom turn and approach the mother of the bride. The groom presents her with a single rose as a symbolic expression of family unity, and her acceptance of the rose is followed by a simultaneous kiss on the cheek from both the bride and the groom. The attention then turns to the mother of the groom. The bride presents her with the flower, and the same double kiss follows. Underscoring this simple act of inclusion with gentle background music or the lyrical voice of a soloist will add a poignancy that everyone, especially the proud mothers, will always remember.

#248 *Roundtable Readings*

A beautiful reading captures hearts and imaginations. A single person designated by the wedding couple typically performs a selected reading as part of the ceremony, but a reading is a wonderful opportunity to include many people who would cherish participating in the event.

Choose your material from the many available literary, poetic, or religious offerings, or write a piece yourself, then print the chosen text in a large, easy-to-read font on white parchment paper. Make as many copies as there will be readers, and divide the reading into sections. If you plan on six readers, divide the reading into six equal parts, and number the passages accordingly. Using a yellow highlighter, highlight a different section on each of the six sheets, and once you've chosen your readers, write their names next to the numbered, highlighted section they will read.

Prearrange a ceremonial cue that will instruct your guest readers to stand and begin the reading. An easy cue would be the turning of the bride and groom to face the guests. Once the bride and groom have turned, the readers rise, and the first reader begins, followed by numbers two through six. At the conclusion of the reading, the bride and groom simply turn back to resume other ceremonial procedures, and the readers sit back down.

Underscore the reading with only the sound of silence, or choose a background of chimes or a soft melody from a harp or flute.

Giving the sheets to your readers well in advance of the big day, to allow for practice and familiarity, facilitates a flawless shared reading on the wedding day.

#249 *Forever Unity*

Uniting the flames of two individual candles into the flame of a single unity candle is a lovely, symbolic gesture in a wedding ceremony. But to keep the "forever" alive, consider combining your unity candle with an anniversary countdown candle.

Countdown candles typically include a column of sequential numbers, that represent the accrued years of marriage. Unity candles are often embellished with sprigs of flowers and personalized with the names of the bride and groom and the wedding date. But with a little tweaking, a single candle may serve as both a ceremonial wedding-day candle and an anniversary candle for the years ahead.

Custom candles can include wedding designs on the front and countdown numbers on the back. Or you could make your own countdown candle by adding small jewelry findings to your unity candle. A column of tiny rhinestone hearts or little metal studs is easily affixed to the candle to represent the years without distracting from the wedding-day sentiment.

It's uplifting to have an anniversary candle to light for just a few shared moments each year, but knowing that the candle you light actually stood with you at the altar revives precious feelings that may have grown distant with time.

#250 *Bringing the Park to the Ceremony*

Instantly transform any wedding-ceremony venue into a park-like setting by replacing individual chairs with park benches.

Wedding or party-goods suppliers rent benches in a variety of styles. From Victorian elegance to country whimsy, park benches change the look and mood of a wedding ceremony.

Bench rentals are considerably more expensive than chair rentals, but you don't have to replace all the chairs. Just seat the front row of honored guests in benches, or utilize a single bench at each of the four corners of the guest area. Even a few benches can significantly enhance the ambiance.

If you're not destined to wed in the park, let stylish outdoor benches bring the magic of the park to you.

#251 *A Kiss Is Just a Kiss . . . or Is It?*

The action that follows the words "you may kiss the bride" seems pretty obvious, but you only get one shot at that first married kiss. Practice does make perfect.

Rehearsing the first kiss means that teeth will not clink, lips will not miss their mark, and the photographer will have a clear view for picture-perfect immortalization.

Decide on the style and the timing. Will the kiss be long and passionate? Short and sweet? Humorous? Surreptitiously hidden behind the bride's bouquet? Will both of your heads tilt to left or right? It's easy for a smaller head to disappear behind the tilt of a larger head, so practicing before a mirror will reveal the best view for guests and the photographer.

Finally, at the wedding rehearsal, tactfully ask your officiant if he or she would step aside after uttering the permission to kiss. If the officiant takes a large step to the left or to the right (whichever works best), there will be no third head in the photo, and only the ceremony's lovely background will frame that never-to-be-repeated first kiss.

Kissing practice is one of wedding planning's secret little treats.

#252 *Trees of Life*

Trees are a great natural treasure, and incorporating baby trees into the wedding ceremony creates a poignant, symbolic ritual for you and your guests.

Begin with an odd number of one- to two-foot-tall tree saplings in embellished 12-inch pots. Position them at the altar before the ceremony. If that number is 15, arrange seven trees in an arc on the bride's side of the altar and seven on the groom's side. A groomsman will position the 15th tree behind you, once you've taken your place before the officiant. The wedding party will fan out on the outside of the tree arcs.

At a predetermined point in the ceremony, you and your groom will each retrieve a decorative watering can placed next to the first tree and begin to water each pot on your respective sides. Start with the container closest to the back of the altar and work forward toward the sole tree in the center. A soft musical background provided by a vocalist or a musician adds harmony to the watering ceremony.

After watering each individual tree, arrive together to simultaneously water "your" tree. When finished, set the watering cans on the floor on either side of the tree, clasp hands, let the music fade away, and recite a pledge as one, such as, "As this tree grows fuller and stronger, so shall we."

Resume original places and proceed with the rest of the ceremony. After the wedding, give the baby trees to friends and family members to plant in your honor, keeping "your" tree to nurture for the next 50-plus years.

#253 *"Fatherly" Escorts*

In today's blended world, it's not uncommon for a bride to face a dilemma over who walks her down the aisle. Should she ask the birth father she saw on weekends or the stepfather she grew up with? Or maybe in spite of a father and a stepfather, it was her grandfather, oldest brother, or even a great aunt who taught her how to grow into the woman she is on her wedding day.

Avoid the stress that comes from exclusion by inviting them all to share in the task. It's a perfect solution for the bride with many important relationships.

Escorts enter just before the bride and station themselves at varying intervals along the aisle. The first escort delivers the bride to the second, the second to the third, and so on. At each handoff, the escort yielding his or her position falls in behind the bride and follows the procession to the altar, where all escorts simultaneously present the bride to the groom before taking their seats.

If there are only two "fathers," it's easy to honor them both by inviting one to walk to the bride's left and one to the right.

When it is impossible to choose just one escort from many deserving candidates, the best course of action may be simply to choose them all.

#254 *Mastering the Kneeling Bench*

Many religious wedding ceremonies incorporate kneeling during prayer, regardless of whether or not doing so is a religious guideline of that particular faith.

A single, softly padded bench meant for two may be used, or two individual benches positioned side by side or back-to-back, with the bride and groom facing each other, may be chosen instead.

Kneeling seems like an easy, worry-free action, but for brides, it's anything but simple. Tight gowns with sleek lines can make the kneeling bride look like a mermaid squirming to sun herself on a rock. Full-skirted gowns can cause the knees to rest too high in the skirt, pulling the bride forward until it's all she can do to keep upright. Slips and skirts can catch in high heels so that rising is accompanied by the sound of ripping fabric or, even worse, an off-balance barrel into her intended, the officiant, or the unforgiving floor.

Take precautions. Use both hands to slightly lift the gown just before kneeling, to prevent taut fabric from pulling or to avert a too-high-in-the-skirt impact from the knees. Make an effort to keep your heels pointed downward to avoid snagging, and never attempt to rise if anything feels wrong. To illuminate potential problems, practice kneeling while wearing your dress and shoes.

The issue isn't just about kneeling. It's about kneeling and rising with grace.

#255 *Soul of the Season*

Wedding ceremonies have a singular purpose: to unite two individuals into a couple. If that goal is met, the trappings surrounding the union can be anything you wish for them to be.

Brides often ask if it's appropriate to include seasonal activities in the wedding ceremony. During the winter holidays, can Christmas carols be sung in lieu of traditional love songs? Can the wedding party wear sandals or sneakers during hot summer months, even if the wedding is indoors? Is it okay to share a taste of something from the harvest instead of lighting a unity candle during the ceremony?

The answer to all seasonal questions is "yes." The season in which you marry is a relevant and sentimental aspect of the wedding day, and incorporating the best of the season into the ceremony makes perfect sense.

#256 *Long-Winded Wedding*

Several necessary components help determine how long the wedding ceremony will last, but adding too much to those components can transform what would have been a delightful wedding experience into one that feels more like teeth pulling. If guests are yawning, checking watches, squirming, or nodding off, the ceremony is either too long or too boring.

To prevent guests from silently wishing that the wedding would "get over already," adhere to a few basic principles. If the ceremony is going to be overly long, strive to make it as interesting and compelling as possible. Listening to an officiant giving a drawn-out speech is not going to be as enjoyable as watching the bride and groom interact in one ceremonial event or another.

If you fear that lengthy religious or cultural rituals will add tedium to the ceremony, offset the potentially dull parts with custom nuances. For example, incorporate musical interludes of familiar melodies before and after extensive stretches of talking or praying to refocus the mind, lighten the mood, and make the sitting-in-silence time feel shorter.

It's your ceremony, and whether it is long or short is your call. But it doesn't hurt to make it so special that guests will think the whole thing ended far too soon.

#257 *Who Shall Be Our Officiant/Officiate?*

If you and your intended share the same faith, deciding who will conduct the marriage ceremony is simpler. But today's brides and grooms often come from diverse backgrounds, and both the bride and groom may have a favorite religious officiant they prefer. How do you choose?

There's no rule against having more than one officiant, and sharing ceremony duties is a peaceful solution. If a joint ceremony is not possible, find an equitable compromise. For example, the bride's choice could conduct the marriage ceremony, and the groom's choice could baptize the couple's first child.

Deciding who gets the honor of marrying you is easier when all available avenues have been investigated. Every state authorizes different people to conduct marriages, and checking your state's options could offer alternatives, like the "Deputy for a Day" program in California, where even a friend of the wedding couple can receive a temporary license to legally marry them.

For the nonreligious, a civil ceremony with a city officiate is customary. An officiate differs from an officiant in that there is no religious component in the civil ceremony he or she conducts, whether that ceremony is conducted on city property or at an off-site location. Unlike religious officiants, civil officiates are usually unknown to the bride and groom. Choosing an officiate begins with a query to the local county clerk, whose office can provide a list of available officiates for hire.

#258 *Formally Yours*

The tone of the wedding experience is set by the tone of the ceremony.

Elegance and style are the core elements of a formal wedding. Daytime or nighttime, the bride wears a spectacular full-length gown, often with a long, dramatic train, and the groom embraces the distinction of black-tie attire. White-tie finery is reserved for the most formal of nighttime weddings.

Formal weddings usually include large wedding parties, and the attendants' attire follows the dictates of the bride's gown and the groom's tuxedo.

Although a formal wedding may be held anywhere, the dignified and structured nature of a church or a garden makes either one an ideal ceremony venue.

Receptions traditionally include sit-down dinners with full stemware and flatware table settings, imposing centerpieces, and top-of-the-line champagne.

A sea of glowing candelabra, gloves for the wedding party, a full orchestra, and limousines all around are just some of the embellishments reserved for formal weddings.

Formality may cost more, but if it will make your dreams come true, there's never a better time than your wedding day to splurge.

#259 *Semiformal — the Better Half*

The still sophisticated but more relaxed alternative to the formal wedding is the semiformal wedding. Think of a semiformal wedding as the "better half" of a formal wedding. Elegance still reigns, but the style is more comfortable.

The bride's gown may be full, tea, or ballerina length, and the groom may don either a tuxedo or a formal suit. Bridesmaids' dress lengths do not have to match the bride's gown. Groomsmen customarily dress the same as the groom, and the number of attendants overall is generally smaller than with a formal wedding.

Semiformal ceremonies often include elements and actions custom-designed by the bride and groom, and ceremony locations can include anything from churches to hotel chapels to riverboats. A sit-down dinner, a buffet, or a blend of both is acceptable for the reception meal, and a live band or a DJ may provide the music. Letting your hair down during the reception happens far more frequently at a semiformal wedding than at a formal one.

Semiformal weddings strive to take the loveliness of formality and wrap it in an ambiance of comfort. Understandably, this winning combination has become the most popular wedding-style choice.

#260 *The Informal "I Do"*

If fully formal or semiformal is just not your thing, an informal wedding may provide wedding-day bliss.

With an informal wedding, everything is a blank slate. The ceremony, whether officiated by a religious leader, a justice of the peace, or a legally qualified friend of the family, is often completely designed by the wedding couple to reflect their passions or points of view.

While any number is acceptable, the wedding party is usually small, with only two or three attendants on either side. The bride and her bridesmaids can choose to wear gowns or everyday dresses of any style.

The groom and groomsmen may opt for anything from suits to sport coats and slacks, or even slacks and a nice shirt.

Plenty of informal weddings take place on the beach or in a park, but they can be held virtually anywhere. Reception fare runs the gamut from a backyard barbeque to a prearranged dinner in a restaurant's banquet room to snacks and wedding cake at home.

Informality has its place. Not every wedding couple shares a desire for pomp and circumstance, and an informal wedding will still be a wedding to remember.

#261 *A Warm, Celebratory Glow*

Many have felt the impact of a stadium full of concertgoers waving lighter flames during a passionate song. It's a moving, emotional experience, and with today's battery technology, brides and grooms can experience the same all-encompassing tribute as part of the wedding ceremony.

Candle tapers and tea lights are now available in battery-operated models. The flick of a tiny switch brings all the ambiance of a real candle to the ceremony, without the risks of actual flame. Attach a beribboned note to each candle to tell the guest when to light it during the ceremony, and ushers can distribute the candles as guests are seated.

Have the candles raised during the lighting of the unity candle, during the first kiss, or at any number of designated moments throughout the ceremony.

Candlelight is magical, but for modern wedding couples, it does not have to be dangerous.

#262 *About-Face!*

The backside is not necessarily one's best feature, but that's the feature presented to guests by most wedding couples. If you want the love in your eyes to be the feature that shines, and not a flicker of light off your derrière, consider facing your guests during the ceremony.

Religious officiants may be less inclined to cooperate, because facing the altar may carry religious significance. But for other types of ceremonies, facing your guests is a viable option. As long as the officiant has no holes in his britches, he won't likely object to his backside being the one on display.

Facing your audience is a treat for each and every guest who witnesses your union, but it's an even greater reward for the bride and groom who get to see the expressions of loved ones as they bind their families together.

#263 *Ceremony Chair Care*

Whether in an outdoor garden or a hotel ballroom, chair decoration helps to set the right tone.

Chair covers come in a variety of fabrics, colors, and patterns, and are fashioned to fit folding, wooden, plastic, banquet, and other chair styles. The least expensive covering is usually the loose, tent-like cover that drapes the chair before being cinched with a sash and a bow. This method works, but unfortunately, varied hem heights often create an overall messy appearance. There is slippage from loose bows and inconsistent bulkiness from not gathering each chair's fabric identically. Furthermore, too-loose fabrics can catch shoe heels.

A better choice is a cover designed specifically for the exact style of chair used. A fitted cover may cost more, but the differences in appearance and usability are likely worth the added expense. Bows and sashes are sometimes included in chair rental fees.

Choose chair covers with safety, beauty, and comfort in mind. Choose rental companies that guarantee their products' condition and an all-inclusive final price that covers every associated cost. Verify policies regarding decorative additions like floral sprays, greenery, ribbons, etc.

Beauty is always in the eye of the beholder, but any eye appreciates rows of smartly dressed chairs.

#264 *Butterflies against the Sky*

A butterfly release during or just after the wedding ceremony is an inspiring sight. Like poetry in motion, butterflies carry a wedding couple's hopes and dreams skyward on gossamer wings. But the perfect butterfly release must always put the well-being of the butterflies first.

Choose a butterfly breeder with verifiable health and licensing certifications and a sterling reputation. To protect indigenous species, captive-bred butterflies cannot be released into all geographic areas. The Web site of the U.S. Department of Agriculture (USDA) maintains a specific state-by-state chart of permissible butterfly releases, including locations and butterfly species permitted.

Guidelines for temperature control, the time of day of the release, and other handling protocols must be strictly followed. If the safety of the butterflies cannot be assured, the release should not take place.

Less scrupulous breeders may transport butterflies in containers that expose them to potential harm. Be certain that shipping containers protect the butterflies from the elements, crushing, and each other.

Ceremonial-release containers must protect the butterflies from potential human error and be equipped with generous, wide openings that accommodate wing expansion.

The ascent of butterflies is touching, symbolic, and wedding perfect, but only if the butterflies live well before flying free.

#265 *On the Wings of a Dove*

The dove has long symbolized love and peace, and brides and grooms of yesteryear gifted each other with a white dove as a pledge of unity. The wedding-day release of this monogamous, gentle creature used to be reserved for royalty, but now every wedding couple can cap their ceremony with the uplifting vision of white doves sailing a blue sky.

Of course, they won't really be doves, since actual doves are unfit candidates for ceremonial release. With inadequate flying skills, a skittish demeanor, and a poor homing instinct, a release into unknown territory would subject doves to suffering, starvation, and an extreme vulnerability to predators. Real doves must never be used for a dove release. Fortunately, their snow-white pigeon cousins are perfect substitutes.

White homing pigeons, commonly referred to as doves, are the birds of choice for a dove release. They interact well with people and have extraordinary homing skills. As long as they are seasoned, healthy birds with many hours of flight time, they'll do your wedding proud and stay safe in the process. Use only a certified, licensed breeder who maintains meticulous health records for the flock, and who provides a dove handler on the day of the event.

Pigeons rely on sunlight for navigation and can only be released during daytime hours, no later than at least two hours before dusk. Accordingly, a dove release should never be considered for evening or sunset weddings.

The best release is the one that attends to the well-being of the birds, establishes a clear line of sight for wedding guests, and creates the heartfelt, meaningful moment for the bride and groom that the doves are there to represent.

#266 *The Elopement Ceremony*

Even if there are no guests to help you celebrate, the real secret to eloping is planning. Utilize the financial resources you would have spent on a big wedding, and plan an intimate but spectacular wedding at an exotic get-away locale. A huge perk of eloping is getting to say "I do" in a fairy-tale setting that would have been too expensive for a traditional destination wedding. Imagine marrying in the romantic shadows of the Eiffel Tower, feeling the exhilarating rush of the Australian Outback, or drinking in the breathtaking vista from the white sands of a Costa Rican beach. The world is your oyster. But even if your fairy-tale wedding is held close to home, planning ahead can make it the wedding of your dreams.

Know the legalities of the area where you plan to marry, including residency requirements, necessary documentation, health tests, licenses, and marriage validity. Prearranging permits, transportation, hotels, flowers, attire, and even excursions means a stress-free wedding free of the snarl of frustrations generated by unattended details.

The U.S. State Department provides an online travel-registration tool that triggers assistance in the event of an emergency on foreign soil. Registering and updating your itinerary on the agency's Web site takes only a few minutes, but it's a potentially lifesaving effort.

You decide to elope for your own reasons, but an elopement doesn't have to mean standing before a justice of the peace in dirty jeans and sneakers. With planning, it's whatever you wish it to be.

#267 Rehearsal Fine-Tuning

A wedding rehearsal covers the basics like who stands where, when to walk down the aisle, and at what points in the ceremony activities such as candle lighting or kneeling will occur. Make the ceremony a cut above by addressing the smallest details with vigor. Subtle nuances change the look and feel of the wedding, and enable the photographer and the videographer to do their jobs more effectively.

One of those nuances is presentation. Take a cue from actresses and professional models who never stand fully front when facing the paparazzi. There is always an angle, even if slight, factored into the pose. Ceremony photos look less attractive when wedding attendants face fully forward instead of assuming a stance turned a bit more toward the bride and groom.

Invite the photographer and videographer to the rehearsal, for their benefit and yours. Discuss positions, walking gaits, and potential pitfalls. For example, a groomsman may be prone to wearing an oversized watch face that could cause disruptive flashes when it catches the light. The time to learn such things is at the rehearsal, when there's still time to fix them. The wedding day is too late to realize that the tallest bridesmaid completely obscures a shorter one at the altar.

To ensure a smooth ceremony, take time at the rehearsal to hash out issues big and small.

#268 *Beautiful Cheat Sheets*

Pity the bride or groom who wrote personal vows then promptly forgot them. It's heartbreaking to intend to say so much, only to say so little when it's finally time to speak. Forgetfulness nips at the heels of nervousness, and standing at the altar with the world watching can rack the steeliest of nerves. So cheat. But do it beautifully.

Instead of relying on memory, write your vows on beautiful scrolls, then turn the scrolls into a ceremonial act by having them presented to you just before the vows.

Before wedding guests arrive, have an usher place the scrolls on a small silver or crystal tray and deposit the tray near the altar. When it's time, the flower girl or ring bearer retrieves the tray and presents the scrolls to the bride and groom. The unfurling of the scroll with both hands is visually dramatic, and having the scroll to cling to is comforting. Of course, holding hands will be impossible, so you must decide if not clasping hands during your personal vows is an acceptable sacrifice for the prevention of forgotten words. If holding hands is more important than remembering the words, then forgetfulness shouldn't be a worry or become a regret.

After the wedding, frame the scrolls for your bedroom wall and be reminded of your vows with the dawn of each sun and the glimmer of every moon.

#269 *Petals with Heart*

If a petal-strewn aisle is permitted at your ceremony venue, make it a participation event for all wedding guests.

In lieu of an aisle runner, provide a large bowl or basket of colorful petals at the ceremony entrance. As the ushers greet the guests, they instruct them to take a few petals to drop along the way as they are shown to their seats. Because guests are seated in different rows, the petals should naturally cover the length of the aisle.

The flower girl may add white petals just before the bride's entrance, or simply make her way to the altar with whatever beautiful accessory she carries.

With a shared petal-scattering experience, every guest becomes an honorary member of the wedding party.

#270 *Tears of Joy*

Even old curmudgeons have been known to sniffle at weddings, but for parents, grandparents, and siblings, those sniffles can easily turn into waterworks. Providing tissues for guests is a kindness, but for those closest to you, consider personalized keepsake hankies.

Personalize hankies for both men and women any way you wish, from the bride's and groom's names and wedding date to a personal message written just for the handkerchief's recipient.

Plenty of embroidery businesses customize handkerchiefs, or perhaps you have someone in the family blessed with needle skills. No matter how they are produced, they will matter to those who receive them.

#271 *One Final Proposal*

Sometimes there's no one to walk the bride down the aisle, or at least no one she wishes to ask. But there is one person perfect for the job: the groom.

A groom's feet aren't glued to the floor at the altar. He can move. To create a beautiful moment that guests won't be expecting, begin the ceremony with a repeat of the proposal. As the bride arrives at the back of the aisle, the groom leaves his position at the altar, walks to her, drops to one knee, and asks, "Will you marry me … now?" At her "yes," the groom rises, takes her arm, and escorts her to the altar.

It's not a catastrophe if there is no father, brother, or "other" to walk the bride down the aisle. It's an opportunity to seize the moment and turn the focus from something "missing" into something "memorable."

#272 *To Have and to Hold the Dearly Departed*

Even though a person is lost to this Earth, the love felt for him or her lives on. It feels right to remember that certain someone during one of the most important milestones in your life.

For each departed loved one, light a candle, add a heart ornament or a balloon to the bridal arch, or place a flower in a special vase. Presenters carry the candles, ornaments, balloons, or flowers to you at the altar, so that you may complete the remembrance ritual. Make the additions a silent part of the ceremony, without explanation to guests, or include the names of designated presenters in your program, identifying each departed person that the candle, ornament, balloon, or flower represents.

Love and loss is the circle of life. A remembrance ceremony honors all who are a part of your precious circle.

#273 *"Soleful" Speech*

Want to give your guests a chuckle or make them smile unexpectedly? If your ceremony involves kneeling, let your soles speak for your souls. The soles of the bride's and groom's shoes are the perfect place for a little visual surprise. Make a simple design, like intertwined hearts, or relay a message that only makes sense when the soles of all four shoes are exposed. For example, place the word "Our" on the bride's left shoe and the word "Love" on her right shoe, together with the word "Is" on the groom's left shoe and "Forever" on his right one, and to the guests it will read "Our Love Is Forever." Keep it warm, or opt for a message that will add fun and laughter, like "Caught" "Him!" on her shoes and "Caught" "Her!" on his. "Soleful" speech isn't for every wedding ceremony, but for some, it's a perfect dash of memorable.

#274 *The Language of Love*

Your vows are special and sacred, but some words that you wish you could say just aren't wedding-day appropriate. To mention something intimate without risking the embarrassment of onlookers, create your own language of love.

Long before the wedding day, coin your own words. For example, replace the word "body" with "bika" or "touch" with "feesha." If you stand before the altar and say, "The touch of your body is more than I ever could have imagined," you're likely to shock the officiant and drown your parents in an irreversible red blush. But if you say, "Nu feesha o san bika la carie tee meeko wey junnay," it will sound lovely and exotic to listening ears, even though they can't understand a word. Enjoy the best of both worlds by reciting most of your vows as usual then finishing with a sentiment from the language of love you have secretly created, a language heard by all but understood by only the two of you.

#275 *Walking the Path Forever*

When making arrangements for your ceremony, you'll discover that even disposable aisle runners can be costly. Instead of spending money on a one-time-use aisle runner, consider purchasing a real rug runner instead. Real rugs can be beautifully yet discreetly monogrammed to commemorate your wedding day, then enjoyed in the home for years to come. If the wedding-day runner is ultimately too long for your home, simply cut it, have the ends rebound, and you'll have multiple runners for use at home.

It's not necessary to walk upon a white runner, unless you specifically dreamed of doing so. In truth, a richly colored runner creates a stunning contrast to a white or ivory wedding gown. You may pay more for a real runner, but that stretch of carpet is more than just a wedding-day decorative accent. It's an investment in your home and your new marriage. Runners cut to any length are available at home-improvement stores and online. To score a great deal, watch for sales and check out the remnant bins!

#276 *A Generous Welcome*

Greet arriving wedding guests with a personalized welcome outside your ceremony venue. No one will wonder whether they've found the right spot if they see an oversized boxwood monogram gracing the lawn. Or choose something that celebrates your wedding theme. Try a carousel horse wearing a personalized, floral horse blanket to underscore your fairy-tale theme, or place a giant, personalized golden goblet on either side of the entranceway to reflect your Romeo and Juliet theme. Oversized lawn ornaments can be crafted from wood, wire, hard foam, or any material that lends itself to safe anchoring in or on the ground. Most churches and other ceremony venues will allow custom "welcome" art, as long as it's tasteful and safe for guests and the facility.

#277 *A Grand Entrance*

Unless the bride's approach is hidden from guests' view, it's hard to make a grand entrance at an outdoor wedding. Everyone can simply watch the bride make her way to her starting position, rendering the subsequent march down the aisle fairly anticlimatic.

So give yourself some doors. Check with a local stage theater or the theater department of a local college to inquire about renting a prop wall and doors. Erect the wall, leaving the doors open to form a welcome arch for wedding guests. Once all guests are seated, have ushers close the doors to await your arrival behind them. At the appropriate time, the ushers will open the doors, and your entrance will be as grand as if you'd made it from the doorway of a cathedral. If a stage wall is not available, use poles and heavy drapes topped with floral vines to make a curtained entranceway instead.

The reveal of the bride and her father or other escort is a thrilling part of the ceremony. There's no reason to sacrifice that moment simply because the wedding venue is "out of doors."

#278 The Perfect Blend

A wedding is all about uniting two people and two families. Then why adhere to the customary separation of guests? The old "bride's side" or "groom's side" seating can result in a lopsided venue that feels uncomfortable for the smaller side and forces guests on the larger side to sit farther back than necessary.

Just as you blend two families during the ceremony, blend the friends and relatives of those families through seating by rows and not by affiliation. If you wish to acknowledge those who are there for the bride and those who are there for the groom, do so with your wedding program. Print your programs with identical information on the inside, but finish some with a white-on-black cover and some with a black-on-white cover. The usher may ask guests "Bride?" or "Groom?" then give them the appropriate program. When those with predominantly white programs are seated next to those with predominantly black programs, you've done more than just equalize the audience seating — you've sparked curiosity and conversation.

#279 Ceremony in the Round

Nonchurch weddings lend themselves to inventive structure, for the "altar" can be anywhere you want it to be. One beautiful setting, easily created outdoors or in a hotel ballroom, is a "ceremony in the round." An elevated round stage is situated in the center of circular rows of seating. The "aisle" stretches from an entryway to one edge of the stage, culminating in a couple of steps for stage access and departure.

With the ceremony elevated and in the round, guests are much closer and have a greater ability to see and hear ceremonial events. For the wedding couple, the ceremony will feel inclusive, as if every friend and family member sitting in the seats is a part of the ceremony itself.

A stage large enough to accommodate the full wedding party would likely negate the intimacy of a ceremony in the round, and attendants would block the guests' view of the bride and groom. Instead of taking up positions on the stage, attendants can form two forward-facing lines on the aisle at the base of the steps, thereby creating a vanguard for the bride's entrance as well as for the newlyweds' exit. The stage need only be big enough to accommodate the bride, the groom, the officiant, and whatever ceremonial props are needed. Attendants will be only a few steps away, and soloists and musicians can position themselves on the outer fringes of the seating area. A ceremony in the round can feel like a warm, wedding-day embrace.

#280 *Ceremony Part Deux*

It's an age-old question: How do you invite only close family and friends to the ceremony but invite others only to the reception without hurting their feelings? Some people who are excluded from the ceremony will understand, while others will feel slighted and wonder, "If I'm not good enough for the ceremony, why should I care about the reception?" Whether you restrict the ceremony guest list to save money or just because you want the nuptials to be more intimate, you are left with some guests believing that they were only invited to the reception to bring a gift, not to share in the true joy of the day.

The solution is easy: repeat your vows at the reception. You will already be married, so there is no need for an officiant. But for those who could not attend the ceremony, your thoughtfulness will matter.

Just before the first dance, gather on the dance floor. Re-create your altar positions, but with the wedding attendants facing the guests, and you and your spouse facing each other. Have your emcee, bandleader, or reception host ask for everyone's attention. The room will grow silent, and without further explanation, you will repeat your vows, then turn to your guests and thank them for sharing in your moment. At the conclusion, the music of the first dance will begin, and as your attendants leave your side, you will take to the dance floor for the first time as husband and wife. This very early wedding-vow renewal will be an unexpected gesture of inclusion for all guests, going a long way toward smoothing ruffled feathers and soothing hurt feelings.

#281 *Gorgeous Courthouse "I Dos"*

Getting married at the courthouse or in a civil office with a justice of the peace sounds pretty utilitarian. It is. The surroundings are usually far from romantic. But they don't have to be. If you're planning a private, quick wedding with just a couple of close friends or family members as witnesses, you can still add beauty to the occasion. Of course, you likely won't be granted permission to spend hours adorning the courthouse or office, but you can still have decorations.

Pack everything you need in a tote bag, like a long length of sheer fabric that can be held by the witnesses and stretched out to create a draped, swag-style backdrop. Other perfectly portable decorations include battery-operated flameless candles, to be placed in a circle around the wedding couple, or large, colorful peacock feathers, fanned out to hide just about anything you don't want to show up in photographs. Such items are situated and removed in a matter of seconds. If you want it in your civil wedding, make it mobile and take it with you. As long as you don't waste time or attempt to attach something with an adhesive, no one from the facility will likely veto your beautiful adornments. As you look back on your civil wedding, you'll be glad you had a few decorative accents in tow.

#282 *The Sands of Time*

If you are planning a unity sand ceremony instead of the lighting of a unity candle, consider doing so with a custom hourglass kit. You still add sands of different colors, but when all is done, you will have created a very special ceremony keepsake. Carry the hourglass theme forward to your reception by incorporating hourglasses in a variety of shapes, sizes, colors, and materials into your centerpieces, and make them accessible so that guests can turn them at will. Like a tiny dry waterfall, the flutter of sand through an hourglass adds a gentle, subtle movement to table décor. With the flick of a wrist, an hourglass is forever flowing, just as a marriage is meant to be.

#283 *Beyond the Vows*

Writing your own vows is common, but what about the officiant's words? Can you write them too? The answer depends upon who marries you. Each religion has its own marriage-ceremony script, and a justice of the peace is usually pretty set in his or her way as well. Other officiants may be more open to your suggestions for crafting or modifying the ceremonial wording.

Most wedding couples don't realize that they can ask to change the officiant's words, but it's perfectly acceptable. It is your wedding, after all, and no one wants wedding words that just don't fit the life and the love of the bride and the groom. Write down what you would like the ceremony to say, or not say, then compare what you've written to what the officiant plans on saying. If they are worlds apart, share your concerns with the officiant. Remember, you can't expect the officiant to know that something bothers you if you don't speak up.

Even with religious leaders, you can ask to see the ceremony script and request certain alterations if they really matter to you. For example, the phrase "till death do us part" may make you uncomfortable, and changing that line to "for as long as it shall be" may alleviate discomfort. If something in the ceremony wording doesn't sit well, be your own advocate, and ask if it can be changed. If the answer is "no," the decision then becomes whether or not changing the wording means more to you than being married by that officiant in that particular venue.

#284 *Upside-Down World*

If you want your wedding to be completely different, do it in reverse. Instead of a ceremony followed by the reception, throw a huge reception with the ceremony as its final, crowning moment. Guests will be left with a lasting impression of your unity, and you will go to your wedding night with your vows still lingering on your lips.

You won't necessarily need to have both a ceremony venue and a reception hall. A single location works beautifully, and a ceremony-last wedding also opens the door to an after-breakfast or after-brunch wedding. If it's freshness — hair, makeup, attire, etc. — that concerns you, set aside a half hour just before the ceremony to rest and refresh. Your guests won't miss you, since they will be enjoying the reception entertainments.

Partying with your guests before you become husband and wife is a great way to kill off those pesky nerves. By the time you say "I do," the jitters will have dissipated. Going in reverse won't appeal to everyone, but for those who like to make the world their own private oyster, a backwards wedding day may be a beautiful thing.

#285 *Bull's Eye*

Up the "awe" quotient at your ceremony with a poignant, visual finish to your vows. After the last word is spoken, the groom opens his jacket to reveal a bull's-eye with a discreet Velcro™ center, positioned on his left chest. The bride slips a small, Velcro-backed heart from her bouquet, waistband, or sleeve, and presses it gently against the bull's-eye sitting squarely over her groom's heart. It only takes seconds, but the impact won't be lost on a single soul, as the groom rebuttons his coat and the officiant continues toward the pronouncement of husband and wife. Do it with a smile, or do it with a tear of emotion. It won't matter if the action is lighthearted or serious. Everyone in the room will feel the loving connection.

#286 *To Meet in the Middle*

Sometimes the bride simply doesn't want to be "given away" or escorted down the aisle at all. The idea of the groom already waiting at the altar, with all eyes on her, just isn't every bride's wish.

If that's you, make a different plan. Houses of worship often have a center aisle as well as two outer aisles bordering the pews. Have the attendants gather at the back of the main aisle. As they wait, the groom arrives and takes his place at the back of his outer aisle. Once he's in position, the bride makes her way to the back of her outer aisle. Done properly, the attendants will block both the bride's and groom's view of each other during this setup.

Once the processional begins, the attendants approach the altar via the center aisle, and as the last pair passes forward, the bride and groom will see each other for the first time. After the attendants are in place at the altar, the music changes, and the bride and groom simultaneously make their way to the front, to literally meet in the middle — a perfect symbolic gesture of the essence of marriage. It's a shared spotlight between the bride and the groom, and works just as beautifully in any indoor or outdoor ceremony setting where outer aisles exist or can be created. When using this approach, it's even more important for the photographer to attend the rehearsal. The photographer will have to be on the top of his or her game to capture both the bride and groom when they are walking so far apart. But the meeting in the middle will be a photographer's dream shot—a priceless moment.

#287 *Can You See Me Now?*

One of the hardest tasks your wedding photographer faces is capturing those precious moments at the altar. Brides and grooms usually face away from the camera, and the lighting at the altar is often the worst of any of the day's locations. Talk with your photographer and videographer, then consult the powers-that-be at your ceremony venue. Some churches and other facilities have supplemental lighting available. If your venue does not, inquire about what additional altar lighting is permissible. It's important to keep your photographer in the loop, because all lighting is not created equal, and some shades and intensities of light can make matters worse.

The best lights at the altar are those that simply create a soft, brighter glow surrounding the wedding couple. An altar can be dark. Make a plan to brighten it.

#288 *The Long and Winding Road*

When getting married in a house of worship, there's not much you can do about that straight-line walk to the altar. But if your wedding is outdoors or in a ballroom, the aisle can be anything you wish it to be. It doesn't have to be airport-runway straight from the back to the front — it can meander, like a gentle brook wending its way through a meadow.

Give your aisle vibrancy by using a colored carpet or cut tiles, and line its curves with stones, leaves, flowers, bows, or greenery. Use a single soft curve to make it interesting, or give it several curves, and a unique audience-participation flair, by designing your seating arrangement to accommodate a walkway between certain rows. Making your way to the altar with a side-to-side, but forward-moving, trek allows guests an "up close and personal" view of the bride as she passes by them. Later, guests will enjoy an inclusive thrill as the newlyweds pass back through the seating at the ceremony's end. Getting off the "highway" almost always offers the best scenic views. An unusual aisle is a ceremony scenic delight.

#289 *Fanfare!*

By now, every potential bride and groom has likely seen the YouTube®-famous video of a dancing wedding-party processional, complete with clever choreography and the shocked but smiling faces of the wedding guests. That razzle-dazzle entrance has since been personally tweaked and performed by many wedding parties. It's certainly not for everyone, but if giving your guests the "surprise!" treatment right from the start appeals to you, then a choreographed ballroom waltz or a robot dance down the aisle may tickle the fancy of you and your guests. If you wish, go beyond choreography, and let your creative juices flow. Perhaps the wedding party can roller-skate to the altar, or the groomsmen can deliver the bridesmaids, one by one, via a wheelbarrow.

When it's fun and fabulous fanfare you desire, the sky is the limit. But if, on the other hand, you love the idea of fanfare but deep down still crave the sanctity of a traditional ceremony, go ahead and have both. Walk the aisle as sweetly and as serenely as brides have for hundreds of years, then give the wildly entertaining fanfare free reign as the wedding party enters the reception instead.

#290 *Across the Aisle*

Whether in a church with pews or in a garden with rows of chairs, you can pass beneath a gorgeous archway on your way to the altar. Bamboo lends itself to bending into an arch, after a long soak in water. Once its shape is set, it will stay that way and be sturdy enough to support floral decorations. Helium-filled balloons make festive arches, and bits of greenery are easily woven throughout the balloons if desired. Inexpensive, snap-together tubular arches are also available to buy. Whatever materials are chosen for the arch they must be anchored at the end of one row, then arch over the aisle to the end of the matching row on the other side. Make your design open and airy, with just a few intermittent arches down the aisle, or make it into a denser pergola to create the illusion of a fantasy ceiling. Decorate sparsely on the upward lengths so that guests can easily see the processional and recessional. But the arched part is yours to adorn as richly as you wish. Arches are especially beautiful when interspersed with tiny white lights, and with battery-operated models, a lack of electricity is not a problem.

#291 *Video Vows*

If your ceremony venue permits a large video screen, why not share extraordinary video vows?

Before the wedding day, both the bride and the groom make a short video dedicated to their intended. Walk along a beach or sit beneath a willow tree as a friend records your special message, or set up the camera to record yourself. Be anywhere you wish, wearing what you wish, saying what you wish. Then, during the part in the ceremony where you would exchange personal vows, you would turn instead to the video screen to watch each other's video vows.

Why record your vows on video? Because it's relaxed, allowing words to be spoken that nerves might otherwise steal. It's more inventive, permitting you to share soul-deep reflections while visiting a location that means something to the two of you. It gives you the freedom to be you — not the wedding-day you, but the real, everyday you. Making individual video vows requires a great deal of trust in each other, but those heartfelt videos, fading from one to the other in a beautifully artistic, cinematic blend, can create a wondrous ceremonial moment.

#292 *We're Off!*

Exactly how happy are you to be married? After the pronouncement of husband and wife, you kiss, turn to be presented to your guests, then proceed with the recessional. You can simply walk out in a most dignified manner, or you can unleash all that pent-up excitement and go out with a bang.

A wild-and-crazy departure is fun for you and fun for your guests. One such exit involves a very well-known wizard. Link arms and skip left, then right, to "We're Off to See the Wizard" from *The Wizard of Oz*. Your wedding party will follow suit behind you. It's a rousing, fun song, and at that spectacular moment, you'll probably feel as if Oz is just around the corner anyway. Just don't be surprised if your guests share a skip or two on their way out as well. That's one contagious melody!

Part Two

THE WEDDING PARTY

GOWNS, ATTIRE & BEAUTY

CHAPTER FIVE • *Gowns, Attire & Beauty*

O h, the wedding gown. It is every bride's fantasy to be a queen for a day, and nothing turns that fantasy into reality more effectively than wearing the gown of your dreams. At no other time in life is there more emphasis on a woman's attire — or a man's, for that matter. The wedding day is inherently special, and spectacular attire is the right of every bride and groom.

But there's more than that gorgeous gown, dapper tuxedo, and perfect bridesmaid dresses to be addressed. There are shoes, jewelry, headpieces, and other accessories, as well as the beauty tools to bring them all together. That's what you'll find in this chapter — ideas that will work for you. From the top of your head to the tips of your toes, from the inside to the outside, if you're thinking about "appearance," this is the chapter to scour for inspiration.

There's much to consider when deciding on wedding-day attire for the bride, the groom, and the wedding party. Beyond fabrics and fashion there are personalities, body shapes, wearability, comfort, and costs to consider. But there will never be a wedding day do-over, so thoughtful decisions are vital.

Some of the ideas that follow explore different clothing, accessory, and beauty options, while others arm you with insights to help ward off unfortunate regrets. There are even those that simply make you wonder about a unique look or a technique worthy of further exploration.

To be the quintessential fairy-tale queen and king, and be surrounded by beautifully turned-out attendants, requires diligence. May you find some of that inspiration right here.

#293 *A Fine Foundation*

Too many brides have learned the hard way that ill-fitting undergarments can ruin the look and feel of a stunning wedding gown. Wedding photos don't lie, but they tell the truth far too late to change anything, and no bride wants a wayward bustline, a wrinkled waist, or bumpy, dimpled hips to be her wedding-day legacy.

Wedding gowns look their best when slipped over a smooth foundation. From the bra to the panty hose and all lingerie in between, it pays to be diligent in the selection of wedding-day undergarments. Avoid straps that dent the skin, seams that create ridges, and push-up supports that push too far and create jiggly mountains of cleavage or bulges of underarm skin with nowhere to hide. Steer clear of anything that causes discomfort. There's no equitable trade-off in substituting a seamless look for a pained facial expression.

The key to success is to find the right undergarment combination well in advance. Don't let your wedding day be the first time you put your entire under-and-over ensemble together. Finding out at the last moment that your underwear makes your backside resemble the surface of the moon won't create a wedding-day memory you'll be eager to remember.

#294 *It's a Secret*

Therapists know the value of documenting what you feel. Putting pen to paper and transforming your emotions from ethereal to tangible makes good things happen, and your wedding day is the perfect time to do just that.

Before your wedding, write what's in your heart. Record your goals for your new married life. Remember someone you've lost, or write an early message to the children you hope to someday have. Write about dreams or fantasies or promises you're determined to keep. When you're finished, carry your message with you to the very place your new married life begins — the altar.

No one needs to know but you. Tuck this private message away from all eyes. It's easy to sew a little pocket into the hem or waistband of a gown or a slip, or to designate a tuxedo pocket as the perfect message hideaway.

Carrying a secret blueprint of dreams throughout your wedding day will lift your soul, and a secret pocket filled with your innermost thoughts is gentle therapy at its best.

#295 *Changing My Mind Is My Prerogative!*

You've bought your gown, but now you've changed your mind about the color, and you're ready to whip out the box of dye. Be forewarned. Dying a wedding gown is not for the faint of heart.

Wedding gowns are customarily crafted from fabrics like satin, chiffon, organza, tulle, and laces, none of which can be dyed with much success. The best fabrics for dying are those that contain greater than 80% cellulose fiber, like cotton, hemp, linen, or rayon, and the likelihood that your gown is fashioned from such fabrics is slim. Additionally, even when dyed together, different types of fabrics absorb color differently, and a dyed wedding gown boasting multiple fabrics can result in clashing shades of whatever color you were hoping for.

If your heart is set on turning that white gown into pale peach or champagne, you should seek the advice of a fabric professional. You may be able to remove only one of the fabrics from the gown, dye it, and have the gown reassembled. The entire gown would not be the new color, but a touch of the color you covet would be included.

In the alternative, add a colored sash, bow, cuffs, or hemline to your gown. Adding colored accents is easier than trying to transform a gown entirely.

Before you tackle the dying option, check out one of the bridal-gown exchange sites on the Internet, and see about trading your gown for one that is already the color you want. Sometimes, the easiest solution is the best.

#296 *Mix-and-Match Bridesmaids*

Thankfully, it's become rare to see bridesmaids' dresses drowning in fields of oversized roses and rows of bows. Today's bridesmaid dresses are more after-the-wedding wearable, and some brides further encourage that wearability by allowing their bridesmaids to choose their own dresses. It's a generous gesture, but one that should be tempered with guidelines and the bride's final approval.

Be specific when setting options for bridesmaids' dresses. For example, there is a cornucopia of blue hues, but not all blend well. Different hues of any primary color can create an undesirable color clash at the altar. To resolve the issue, buy a bit of fabric of the color you like best and cut it into swatches for your bridesmaids to use when shopping for dresses.

Dress length and necklines should also be discussed. If it is acceptable for one bridesmaid to be in floor-length, one in tea-length, and one in a miniskirt, so be it. But that's not usually the image a bride is hoping for. Don't leave any details up to the bridesmaids' imagination, if you're looking for the perfect combination of wearability and wedding-day gorgeous.

Finally, instruct your bridesmaids to show you their dress, or a photo of it, before it's purchased. The goal is to have all bridesmaids in dresses that are personally flattering without having one that draws attention for being too different — or worse, one that adversely affects the bride's gown.

Mismatched bridesmaids' dresses can work beautifully, if their acquisition is thoughtfully managed.

#297 *Heirloom Gowns*

When it means the world to be able to wear great-grandma's fragile gown, you may need the expertise of a clothing restoration expert. Heirloom gowns can sometimes be reinforced to render the dress as wearable today as it was a hundred years ago, but someone with casual sewing skills should not attempt the process, and not every gown qualifies for restoration or reinforcement.

There are very few artisans who have the experience and talent to salvage vintage clothing. Begin your search by contacting your local museum curator and asking if he or she can provide a recommendation. When searching for an expert online, it's especially important to verify qualifications. Do not ship your heirloom gown to someone you cannot fully vet through every available resource.

If you do find a viable person and shipping is necessary, be sure to photo-document the dress from every angle, capturing every detail, before you send it. When you prepare the dress for shipment, pack a generous amount of plain white tissue between every fold and around the gown, making certain it cannot slide in the box when the box is moved. Insure the shipment for the gown's collectible value.

Some lucky brides' heirloom gowns are so well preserved that nothing special must be done before wearing them. For everyone else, the right expert and due diligence is the path to ensure a wedding-day gown blessed with priceless sentiment.

#298 *Designer Accessories at a Fraction of the Cost!*

Walking down the aisle wearing the crown jewels may be easier than you think — if you don't mind renting.

In today's fashion world, designer everything can be rented. Want to settle a diamond tiara over your tresses? Rent it. Want the latest Jimmy Choo shoes peeking out from beneath your gown? Rent them. Enjoy the use of virtually any luxury accessory for the price of a rental. Rent just for the wedding day, or extend the rental through the honeymoon.

Renting is not inexpensive, but it is far cheaper than purchasing an identical accessory. Establishments that rent luxury accessories require substantial deposits as protection against loss or damage. Deposits are generally refundable upon the item's return in good condition, but the deposit may make up-front costs a challenge. Be sure to thoroughly investigate any rental company, and carefully read every term in the rental contract before you sign it.

So go ahead and indulge in that emerald-and-diamond necklace, and while you're shopping, why not pick up a Rolex watch for the groom? Luxury accessories at your wedding are a thrill, even if only for a day.

#299 *Mad for Hats?*

When combined with just the right gown, a hat in lieu of a wedding veil can be a stunning choice. Consider a Roaring '20s, flapper-style cloche hat paired with an Art Deco gown; a studded, white cowgirl hat teamed with a flowing prairie dress; or a wide-brimmed, at-the-races hat matched to a Victorian gown. But while hats may be gorgeous, wearing them is tricky.

It's unlikely you will wear your hat throughout the reception, and unfortunately, fluffy hairdos and hats are mortal enemies. If you plan to wear a hat, choose a sleek hairstyle to avoid the horrid ring-around-the-head indentation hats frequently leave behind. Remember, the longer you wear the hat, the deeper the dent.

Another concern is the heat of a warm day. Some hats are specifically made to breathe, but many aren't. A perspiring scalp beneath your hat could lead to itching, and no bride wants to be caught digging at her head on her wedding day.

Hats do have a place in wedding attire, but advance experimentation with them is advised. Whip up your wedding-day hairstyle, then wear your hat for a couple of hours. Once it's removed, you will quickly know what to expect. A hat is a fabulous topper, as long as it doesn't leave you with the dreaded "hat hair" for your first wedded dance.

#300 *The Happy-Feet Dance!*

It's a fact. New shoes can kill your toes, rub your heels, and otherwise make your life miserable. But how do you break in new shoes without making them look like old shoes?

Purchase your wedding shoes as early as possible after deciding on your gown. The longer they are on the premises, the more chances you will have to break them in.

Don very thin socks (slightly thicker than panty hose), and slip your feet into your shoes. Now slide each foot and its shoe into a large slipper sock with a nonskid bottom, and go about your business around the house. You can walk for minutes or hours at a time and not worry about staining or marring the shoes, or even scuffing the soles. Ensconcing the shoes in durable, nonslip slipper socks will maintain their new appearance as they "learn" the contours of your feet.

Happy feet on your wedding day is a wedding gift to yourself!

#301 *Bespectacled Brides and Grooms*

The wedding day can present a dilemma for brides and grooms who wear glasses. Photographers often ask that glasses be removed for pictures. Eyeglasses can snag veils or reflect flickering lights at the altar, creating flashes that distract guests. But are those issues important enough for a bride or groom to sacrifice his or her clear sight and usual appearance on wedding day?

If the bride or groom sometimes wears contacts and at other times wears glasses, the answer is simple. Wear the contacts. But if either regularly wears glasses, the wedding day is no time to take the contact plunge and risk discomfort, unfamiliar vision, or a totally new look.

Eyeglasses are as important as any other wedding-day accessory, and are just as wedding-day appropriate. By planning ahead, it's feasible to purchase new glasses with your wedding in mind. Brides can choose a gently rounded frame to mitigate issues with the veil and earpieces that won't interfere with a special hairstyle. Antiglare lenses take care of errant flashes and reflections for either the bride or groom, and frame color and adornment can be chosen with the entire wedding ensemble in mind.

Sometimes when people who wear glasses take them off, they simply don't look like themselves anymore. That's not the image you want on your wedding day. Don't be afraid of your glasses. Embrace them!

#302 *Offer the Gentle Hand*

An extraordinary pair of gloves has the power to transform even the most budget-conscious gown into something much more. Brides have worn gloves throughout the ages, but today's brides have the luxury of choosing wedding-specific styles, such as Mousquetaire gloves, fingerless gloves, or pre-slit gloves (the latter two allow easy access for the ring exchange).

The formality and the time of day of the affair have long been reflected in the length of the glove. Wrist-length gloves are traditionally worn for morning or afternoon functions, while elbow-length gloves denote a twilight occasion. Over-the-elbow styles have always been reserved for the most formal of nighttime events. But modern brides have, with much success, pushed the envelope when it comes to accessorizing with gloves. Now it is widely accepted that, as long as the glove doesn't encroach on the sleeve of the gown, any length is appropriate at any time of day.

Bridal gloves are fashioned in a myriad of fabrics and styles. Simple, plain gloves are very effective when the gown is intricate, and gloves embellished with crystals, pearls, embroidery, beads, or gems easily add excitement to an understated gown.

You will wear your gloves during the ceremony, in the reception receiving line, and to dance the first dance with your groom. They should be removed to eat, drink, and cut the cake.

#303 *Bridal Veils by Hand*

Saving money on the bridal veil is possible when you create it yourself. Bridal magazines, bridal stores, and online veil photos can provide inspiration. Veils are usually plain or lace-bordered U-shaped pieces of tulle, with seed pearls or crystals attached after the veil is cut and fashioned.

Veil patterns are available at fabric stores, or you can opt to make your veil without a pattern. Working with tulle and lace may require practice. Use scrap pieces to experiment with cutting strokes, and cut only with finely honed scissors to avoid snagging.

Make a U-shaped template from poster board to support the tulle for cutting. After the template is drawn and cut, carefully lay the tulle across it and weigh the edges down with smooth and heavy objects, like books. Tulle is easily snagged. Avoid exposing it to roughly textured items.

Cut the tulle to match your template, and you've created a basic veil ready to be gathered onto a comb or a headband. Tulle is available in a variety of widths, and the more fabric you use, the fuller the veil.

Making your own veil pays homage to the ancient tradition of going to your groom in finery created by your own hand, and doing so may add a fair dose of pride and personal satisfaction to the wedding experience.

#304 *Ban the Greasepaint!*

One sad mistake that brides frequently make on their wedding day is presenting a face that isn't usually theirs. Too much makeup and incorrectly applied makeup are the antithesis of loveliness, and it's pretty important to present a face your groom will recognize.

A subtle hand will give you the epitome of wedding-day beauty. If you never wear false eyelashes, why do so on the one day when wedding photos will document you for all eternity? You don't want those photos to reflect someone you don't even know. Too-pink cheeks, too-stark lips, or too "anything" is taboo.

Experiment with makeup shades and applications many times before the wedding. Do it on your own or with the aid of a makeup artist. Take photos after each test. Study them, and soon the "right" you will emerge. When the wedding day comes, you will know exactly what to do, and you won't be tempted to go overboard. The best regret is the one you never have.

#305 *Gowns of a Different Color*

White was not always the chosen color for wedding gowns. Early brides wore rich, dark colors for their nuptials, and today's brides are rediscovering the impact that a gown with color can have.

Opt to add color to a white gown by adding a sash or a bodice overlay, or choose to wear a gown of any color that complements you. Colorful options are a blessing, especially for those brides whose complexions are not enhanced by white garments.

From deep purple to soft peach, colorful wedding gowns can transform a wedding. Queen Victoria may have led the white-wedding-gown tradition, but she did not make it law. A wedding gown should be what you want it to be, even if that means getting married in seafoam green or buttercup yellow.

With hued gowns, you open unique color-palette opportunities. Imagine the beauty of a winter bride at the altar in a deep-wine wedding gown, her attendants in pale rose, and the groomsmen in formal gray. It's not a typical wedding scene, but it is a spectacular one.

If breaking with tradition is your style, then a gown with color is the first possibility to explore.

#306 *Finessing Wedding-Day Jewelry*

All eyes are on the bride on the wedding day, and the goal should be to present a unified package of loveliness, with no glaring distractions to draw unwanted attention. The jewelry chosen for the wedding day should be simple and delicate, and it may be wise to forgo some jewelry altogether, like toe rings and ankle bracelets.

If you go to all the bother of a million-dollar smile, why divert your guests' gaze to a twinkle on your toes?

Don't be upstaged by your own jewelry. Jewelry should play a supporting role, not star in your wedding day. Think subtle and sincere when selecting earrings, a necklace, or jewels for your hair.

An heirloom piece is ideal. It's your "something old," and it adds emotional significance to the day.

Wedding-day jewelry is the perfect finishing touch, but only if approached with gentle reserve.

#307 *The Great-Legs Factor*

Full-length gowns are gorgeous, but brides with killer legs might want to opt for a shorter, more versatile wedding-day gown.

A short gown not only shows off shapely legs, it allows show-stopping shoes to shine.

There are logistical reasons for selecting a short gown, like eliminating the possibility of tripping on a hemline and not soiling a hemline that drags on the floor or ground. A short gown also keeps you cooler at a hot venue, may be less expensive than a full-length gown, and has more after-the-wedding possibilities. From tea length to mini, short gowns are perfect for some brides.

Even if your legs don't resemble a runway model's, a shorter gown and amazing shoes might be just what the stylist ordered. It's your wedding day. Choose what makes you happy.

#308 *Body by You!*

You're getting married. Perhaps you're wishing for the kind of fabulous figure that makes even a gunnysack look good. If that's what you want, there's only one way to get it: hard work.

An unhealthy obsession with weight loss or body sculpting is not required. But it is time to add at least a toning regimen to your schedule. An inch here or there can make a difference when it's time to don that beautiful gown.

A body in optimum health augments the radiant beauty that comes from the soul. Yoga, diet, meditation, aerobics, and light weight lifting all play a role in making the kind of subtle body changes you will notice and appreciate. Exercise is more fun when shared, so invite your maid of honor, your groom, or even your faithful dog to join your new regimen. Creativity is your friend. If you can't stand jogging, play softball. If bicycling makes you cringe, try swimming. Don't do boring exercises you hate, since statistics show that you will simply stop doing them before they deliver any benefit. Make your workouts fun and make them consistent. When you walk down that aisle, you'll be glad you made the effort.

#309 *Scent of a Woman . . . or a Man*

A mélange of perfumes, colognes, body lotions, antiperspirants, hair-care products, oils, and creams can quickly turn into chemical warfare, and no wedding day should be remembered for how strongly it smelled.

Choose a wedding-day fragrance and stick to it. For everything else that might potentially add to the olfactory mix, select unscented varieties. Emitting a strong odor in the receiving line, even if you consider the odor to be fabulous, is not endearing. Guests who sneeze, wheeze, and suffer from tearing, allergy-reddened eyes because of scent sensitivity can suffer needlessly when they attempt to wish you well or share a dance with you. Avoid the possibility of causing discomfort by applying your scent sparingly and asking wedding-party members to do the same.

A hint of a fresh and subtle scent is what every wedding entourage should aspire to.

#310 *Expressive Pearls*

Pearls are wedding-perfect bridal accessories, and they hold the distinction of appearing at more weddings than any other gem. The "something old" or "something borrowed" is often a cherished pearl heirloom necklace or a distinguished pair of pearl earrings.

The pearl's color adds its own traditional expression of character. From the "purity, peace, faith, and sincerity" meaning associated with white pearls to the "love, passion, generosity, and loyalty" of pink ones and the "independence, mystery, and prosperity" of black pearls, every color supports the essence of the wedding day.

A pearl's complemental effect is soft, never glaring, and pearls come in all price ranges, so every bride can enjoy them.

#311 *To Clutch or Not to Clutch*

Wedding gowns aren't fashioned with pockets to hold a woman's essentials, so even brides need handbags. But what style works best?

Most bridal purses are elegant but petite white clutches with a satin-sheen finish, although some pastel, metallic, and black clutches are preferred. A comb, a powder compact, a lipstick, a mirror, and some tissues are about all they can hold, and when more is needed, such limited space is challenging. Choosing a traditional purse with a larger capacity is not a crime. Not every bride must carry a delicate, white-satin bag, and a bag with a strap may prove to be more manageable throughout the day's events.

Reuse is also a consideration. For a suitable after-wedding purse, the typical white-satin bag may fall short. But a bag with color and a stylish finish that doesn't say "wedding" can serve you well on any number of occasions down the road, long after it's done its duty on the big day.

#312 *How Sweet the Crowning Jewels*

Every bride feels like a princess, and every self-respecting princess accessorizes with the finest jewels, including her favorite tiara.

Bridal tiaras vary in style and intensity: real gems or faux gems, richly colored stones or brilliantly white stones, small and subtle or tall and regal. Tiaras can be worn alone, or they can support an attached veil.

Plenty of bridal manufacturers create stunning tiaras, but don't forget thrift stores, antique shops, and online auctions, where gorgeous vintage tiaras with prong-set rhinestones can often be snapped up at reasonable prices.

A princess knows the value of versatility, and one of the best reasons to wear a tiara is the ability to add a veil for the pageantry of the ceremony, then wear only the tiara for the revelry of the reception.

#313 *Designer Patchwork*

Not every bride can afford a couture gown created especially for her. The incredible creations of famous designers are available to those who can pay for them, but for those who can't, the gown choices are either "off the rack" or "homemade." Expand those choices. Consider a patchwork gown.

Generations of wedding gowns find their way into consignment shops and thrift stores, and gown designers dispose of torn or soiled gowns they have no interest in repairing. Many of these dresses are available for a song. It matters little that the gown has a foot-long tear in the skirt when only its sleeves are of interest. Or why not strip that beautifully beaded bodice from the voluminous skirt of the gown you found online, and attach it to the svelte skirt of the gown you found at the consignment shop?

Seamstresses accustomed to working with bridal fabrics can part out a dress and reattach portions to create a stunning, one-of-a-kind "designer" gown just for you. Buying existing but imperfect gowns provides access to quality fabrics and adornments that may otherwise seem unaffordable.

Enlist the expertise of a seamstress before shopping. Not all fabrics mesh well, and knowing what to look for makes the search more productive. The beauty of this process is that most wedding gowns are fashioned from the same stable of fabrics, so finding pieces that blend seamlessly is easier than one might think.

Patchwork doesn't apply only to a quilt. A patchwork gown turns beautiful, individual components into couture art.

#314 *Black-Tie Elegance*

Choosing "black tie" for your wedding means that you expect your guests to dress within specific formal, elegant confines.

Black tie for men includes a black dinner or tuxedo jacket (white is an acceptable alternative for summer, if specified), matching black trousers without cuffs, a black cummerbund or a black waistcoat, a white shirt accented with a black bow tie, black patent-leather shoes over thin black socks, and shirt studs and cuff links of gold or pearl.

Black tie for women encompasses a finely styled dress in cocktail or calf length for a daytime wedding or a full-length gown for an evening wedding, delicate shoes with a matching or complementing handbag, fine jewelry, and fashionable hair and makeup.

Black-tie events are beautiful, but to guarantee that your guests dress according to your wishes, leave no doubt. Clearly indicate "Black Tie" on the invitation.

#315 *White-Tie Formality*

While black tie is elegant and refined, white tie is the ultimate in formality. For example, black tie is worn to accept a prestigious award, while white tie is worn to a heads-of-state dinner. If your wish is for the quintessential formal wedding, but you do not customarily move in wealthy circles, understand that guests will likely have to rent or buy attire to grant your white-tie wish.

White tie for men includes a black tailcoat with matching full-dress, satin-piped, and cuffless trousers, a white waistcoat, a white shirt with a stiff wing collar accented with a white bow tie, black patent-leather shoes over thin black socks, white silk button-on suspenders, and pearl studs.

White tie for women includes a full-length gown typically accented with rich, glitzy embellishments, fine jewelry, delicate shoes with or without adornments, a richly appointed evening handbag, and elegantly styled hair and makeup.

When choosing white tie, give guests as much notice as possible. White tie is the crème de la crème of celebration attire, and while the feeling it evokes may be priceless, actually acquiring it definitely comes with a price.

#316 *Fine but Not Fancy*

If black-tie elegance or white-tie formality is not your preference, you may choose to specify other designations on the invitation, such as "Semiformal," "Cocktail," "Informal," "Dressy Casual," or "Casual." Most weddings fall into one of these categories.

Semiformal dress means men may choose dark suits and ties with dress shoes, and women may opt for a nice cocktail or full-length dress, accompanied by tasteful jewelry, dressy shoes, and a coordinated handbag.

A cocktail preference means dress or business suits with ties for men, and that perfect "little black dress" or other cocktail-length dress for women.

An informal designation means men are permitted to wear a suit or simply a sport coat, with or without a tie, and women can be comfortable in any nice, shorter-length dress.

Dressy casual attire includes a sport coat with contrasting slacks for men, and a nice dress or pantsuit for women.

If the wedding is casual, the wardrobe of the day is a shirt and slacks for men, and a skirt or pants with a blouse, a pantsuit, or a casual dress for women. Casual shoes are acceptable for both genders.

#317 *Outfitting the Masses*

While white tie is no doubt spectacular, and there may never be another opportunity to experience such an event, choosing white tie for guests may require a rental cost for men and a purchase expense for women. To avoid financial discomfort, consider blended wedding attire. In this scenario, the wedding party wears white tie, but guests are permitted to wear black tie. This solves a host of problems, yet allows that fairy-tale white-tie experience for the bride and groom.

The blending of white tie with black tie works well, but be cautious about other blended styles. If the wedding party is formal, you surely don't want guests in casual attire. The best way to ensure adherence to specific attire is to spell out the rules on the invitation. Wedding guests take comfort in knowing what is expected of them.

Adding the word "optional" gives guests alternative choices. For example, "Black Tie Optional" tells guests that the wedding is formal, but that either black-tie or semiformal attire for wedding guests is welcome. "Optional" traditionally means no more than one step down from the designation, meaning that "Black Tie Optional" cannot descend all the way down to casual attire.

To make it easier for guests to comply, include the designated attire on the invitation and on your wedding Web site.

#318 *Wrapped in Comfort*

The wedding shawl was born of necessity. Old churches were unheated, causing shivering at the altar that wasn't spawned by love, excitement, or nerves. Indoor heat eventually solved the dilemma, but the versatile shawl persevered as a stylish wedding-day accessory.

Fashioned of any fabric and embroidered with matching or contrasting threads, a shawl enhances even the most rudimentary gown or adds a splash of needed color. Affix seed pearls, rhinestones, sequins, or crystal beads as desired, and use them to reinforce the wedding theme via a subtle monogram, custom design, or symbol of importance to the wedding couple. Shawls for bridesmaids unify the overall look, especially when attendants have chosen their own dresses.

Drape the shawl low on the back with the tails softly curling over the arms, or settle it gently over the shoulders. Don it or remove it throughout the day as desired, then take it home to wear again whenever you wish. Unlike the wedding gown, a bridal shawl easily joins your wardrobe. Wear it when it makes you happy, then one day give it to your daughter for her "something old" at her own wedding.

#319 *Spin the Wheel*

Not everyone has an artist's eye, but you shouldn't worry that you're not blessed with the ability to imagine the nuances of a color palette. Rely on a color wheel instead.

When choosing colors for the wedding and for wedding attire, the use of a color wheel inspires you and simplifies the job of identifying "what goes well with what." You may think you want blue and peach as your colors, then a look at a monochromatic wheel reveals new "wow" possibilities. A monochromatic wheel shows only the shades of one specific color, and the blue wheel may make you realize how stunning it would be to forget the peach and have each bridesmaid wear a different intensity of the same blue.

Other wheel options include an analogous wheel (showing two to six colors that fall next to each other on the wheel), a complementary wheel (exhibiting vibrant two-color matches), and a triad wheel (showing three colors that create a triangle shape on the wheel). Some combinations produce bold color statements, while others generate gentle blends.

When Sir Isaac Newton created the first prism-inspired color wheel in the 17th century, he likely had no idea that discerning brides would one day be able to use those wheels to create color combinations once reserved for the world's great artists.

#320 *Nails of Glory*

On your wedding day, it's important for your nails to be carefully groomed. After all, the ring will be slipped past those nails, in plain view of all watching eyes. Later, when you shake hands, cut the cake, raise a glass, or dazzle someone with your beautiful ring, your fingers will be on display.

The most appealing nails are those that complement the bride, not overpower her. Bright nails draw the eye, but nails with no color at all are equally distracting. Both extremes draw attention away from what should be a complete and balanced presentation. When choosing your color and nail style, remember that it's impossible to go wrong with exquisitely manicured nails, boasting just a hint of color.

Select your gown, then experiment with colors, shapes, adornments, sparkles, and nail jewelry, and after each unique application, hold your hand next to your gown and photograph it. After objectively viewing multiple combinations, the perfect one will rise to the top.

And don't forget your toes. A smart pedicure should follow the same tasteful color rule. Finally, share your nail revelations with your bridesmaids. Their nails should not outshine yours or detract from their attire.

Give your nails a meaningful supporting role. Just don't let them steal the show.

#321 *Hallelujah Hips*

If dieting and exercise hasn't vanquished every annoying little bump and bulge, consider wearing the perfect body shaping undergarment under your wedding-day finery.

Women value a form-fitting profile, and throughout history they've found creative, if sometimes painful, ways to trim and tuck errant flesh. From early 16th century "stays" and rib-crushing Regency-era "corsets", to hip-and-thigh-hugging 20th century girdles, generations of women have wiggled and squirmed their way into garments designed to beautifully reshape the body. Fortunately, 21st century brides can slim and smooth unwelcome body dimples with considerably less pain than early brides were forced to endure for beauty's sake.

Shapewear, in styles designed to contour everything from the whole body to isolated trouble spots, is available from manufacturers like Spanx, Maidenform, Bali, and many others. Before shopping for that special undergarment, ask friends for recommendations and read online customer reviews. Watch for repeated complaints of "rolling" (the garment should stay put in both standing and sitting positions without creating "muffin top" bulges), "sticking" (it shouldn't take a small army to remove it), and "comfort" (the wedding day is long; you don't want to be miserable in your clothes).

Experiment with body shaping choices early. Don't let your very first shapewear "tightening and tucking" experience happen on your wedding day. And don't forget the groom! If he's so inclined, shapewear for men is available, too.

#322 *Exceptional Wedding-Night Lingerie*

It's easy to choose wedding-night lingerie by first impression. But looking sexy on the hanger doesn't mean that frothy negligee is the one for you. Lingerie must look great, fit well, and represent the real you. Don't feel pressured to choose traditional white when you're a deep-purple kind of woman at heart. There are no rules on the wedding night. Choose hot and sexy or sweet and innocent, but choose with beauty and functionality in mind.

It's no secret that wedding-night lingerie is merely the prelude to nudity, so steer clear of fabrics that bunch up and stick to the skin like two socks in a static-cling war. Peeling off an unwieldy garment mid-kiss isn't all that enticing. And don't buy something two sizes too small in some misguided effort to make your new husband think you're teeny weeny. An ill fit makes you uncomfortable — you'll be preoccupied with tugging and adjusting your lingerie. Really, he's not going to wake up in the morning and study the size tag on your negligee.

Whether you're a size 2 or a size 42, you're already loved and in love, and your wedding night is no time to try to be someone else. Plus-size brides don't have to choose shapeless muumuus, and runway-model types aren't compelled to wear only three strategically placed bows. Body size doesn't define a woman, and it should not define the wedding night.

Choose lingerie that is special to you, and you alone.

#323 *Worldly Wedding Gowns*

Personalizing the wedding gown to honor one's heritage doesn't have to mean marrying in full cultural garb. The addition of one or more accent pieces can easily combine traditional cultural influences with modern wedding style.

Ethnic accents turn any off-the-rack gown into a custom work of bridal-gown art. Try draping a simple A-line gown with a colorful Indian sari, or adding a Spanish bolero jacket to a strapless dress. Hair adornments of Brazilian beads or a Swedish bridal crown address heritage without overpowering the overall look. Or choose a dress pattern that is culturally identifiable, like the unmistakable ribbon-wrapped bodice of a Grecian gown.

Cultural accents are a sincere nod of reverence to blended families. Altering or adorning existing gowns or men's attire with one or more cultural influences is an unspoken, welcome sign of respect and love.

#324 *The Forever Garter*

It's not a new idea. It's well documented that in the 1950s members of the Long Beach Bachelorettes shared a single garter. The blue garter was worn on the bride's wedding day, then returned to the organization for safe-keeping until the next bride needed it. Bachelorette clubs may have gone the way of the dinosaur, but this unusual tradition still has merit within families or close circles of friends.

There's something emotionally fulfilling about knowing your garter will foster repeated joy throughout lifetimes. Sharing it with relatives or closely bonded friends and handing it down through generations make this a meaningful tradition. Mark the garter's usage on a family tree, or keep a journal of its travels from sorority sister to sorority sister.

A forever garter isn't a wedding-day requirement, but it's a full-of-life experience that many may enjoy.

#325 *Beautiful Budget Bride*

Just because something is more expensive doesn't necessarily mean it's worth more, and skyrocketing prices can strain even the most flexible of budgets. To be a beautiful but frugal bride, practice tricks of the trade.

A gown purchased on sale is a good start, but extending your advantage by also scoring shoes, a veil, and accessories on sale is even better. Don't be afraid to negotiate. There's no harm in asking the bridal shop to discount the veil and gloves with the purchase of a gown. Cast your net far and wide to look for the best deals, and don't be swayed by hard-sell tactics.

For hair, nails, and makeup, investigate the offerings of local cosmetology schools. The rates are usually a fraction of commercial salon prices, yet you won't have to sacrifice expertise. Cosmetology schools are loaded with talented students supervised by cosmetology experts. The key is to visit the school several times in the months leading up to the wedding to connect with those who serve you best.

The biggest obstacle in a bride's quest to be both beautiful and frugal is impatience. Holding wedding-shopping excitement in check is no easy task, but you must fight the good fight. Imagine you are a lioness on the hunt, and adopt the philosophy of "wait, stalk, and seize." Soon you'll be spending all those saved dollars on a few extra honeymoon delights.

#326 *Bridal Fabrics That Softly Flutter*

Soft and airy wedding fabrics float as you move. For an ethereal, goddess-like feeling, choose chiffon. Chiffon is fashioned from real or synthetic silk, and its best feature is its "gentle waterfall" draping ability. Imagine chiffon as the fabric of angels.

Georgette is a silk that is often interwoven with cotton threads to produce a more durable fabric. It's textured and not as sheer as chiffon, but its tight weave creates a springy effect. It pairs well with satin trim.

Tulle is fine netting. It flows well and resists crushing, but it's rougher to the touch, making it more suitable for use as accents rather than construction.

Charmeuse is heavier than chiffon or georgette, but it pools beautifully at your feet. Art Deco gown designers used charmeuse to fabulous effect, and although it's made of silk, its satiny finish catches the light like a prism.

Organza shares commonalities with tulle, but its heavier weight makes it more suitable for dress construction. Some organza has a lovely translucent finish that looks opaque from certain angles, even though the fabric is sheer.

Silk is far and away the most popular wedding-dress fabric. It's a natural fabric that ebbs and flows with movement and blends well with a variety of other fabrics to create interesting designs. Silk also lends itself well to transformation. Crepe, for example, is merely a crinkled, twisted version of silk.

For a gown with that unmistakable fairy-tale flow, begin with gentle fabrics.

#327 *Bridal Fabrics of Regal Bearing*

If sophistication is your objective, and a regal gown with a sturdy character is your choice, certain fabrics possess that recognizable, stiff carriage that makes them worthy of a queen.

Satin is a smooth, heavy fabric derived from silk or polyester. It has a mild draping ability and a lustrous finish that supports adornment well. Its unflappable ability to hold its form makes it popular for very formal weddings.

Taffeta's charm is its rustle. When you want to be heard as well as seen, a crisp, shiny, and feminine taffeta is the choice. When taffeta was first introduced in the 14th century, it quickly became a sought-after fabric for ball gowns and judges' robes. Bridal gowns were a natural progression.

Peau de soie, which in French means "skin of silk," is a satin derivative with a medium to heavy weight. Its finish is duller than satin, but it's less likely to water spot in the event of a spill. It constructs and drapes beautifully.

Brocade is a heavy, raised-pattern material so sturdy that a gown fashioned from it can sometimes stand upright by itself. It's a very formal fabric that is often confused with its cousin, damask. Damask is also intrinsically patterned, but the design does not rise above the fabric.

Regal fabrics beget regal gowns, and in the hands of a talented designer and seamstress, these fabrics deliver the "queen for a day" experience in spades.

#328 *Timeless Beauty*

How do you know that someone was married in the '80s? You check out the hair!

Hair and makeup styles are far greater indicators of an era than attire or shoes. For wedding photos that won't make you cringe every time you walk past them, avoid the latest grooming fads.

You may feel all punk rock today, and think it's totally awesome to shave your head on one side and stick a flower where hair used to be, or to bling out your nose with a heart-shaped nose ring, but how about the many tomorrows to come? Will the punk feeling last? If the answer is "yes," then go for it. But if punk rock may not always rule your world, maybe the head shaving and the nose ring aren't wedding-day ideal after all.

Give it some thought, and ask yourself if trendy makeup and hairstyles are more important than "your style." Slicked-back, plastered-to-the-head hair may be all the rage, but if such a hair statement goes out of style, which sooner or later it's bound to do, your wedding photos will suddenly reflect a bride from an "era" instead of a bride for the ages.

Not being able to tell from the photos when the wedding took place is priceless.

#329 *To Bustle or Not to Bustle*

Sometimes wedding gowns are a lot to handle. A full skirt and a long train look fabulous progressing toward the altar, but later it may feel as if your dress is trying to wrestle you to the ground. There's a big difference between walking a straight line down the aisle and navigating your crowded reception.

To avoid tripping yourself and others with your voluminous attire, employ a bustle system of loops and discreet waistline buttons or hooks. Your gown may come with a bustle system already in place, or acquiring one may be an optional alteration.

Some brides believe a bustle will make sitting uncomfortable. It's a fair concern, depending upon how much fabric you gather at your backside. Usually, however, the fabric is spread in such a way that it's less of a "bunch" and more of a "waterfall," making the bustle a far better option than doing nothing.

To bustle or not to bustle is a personal choice for every bride with a full-skirted gown or a long, nondetachable train. But unless your goal is to be the star of an embarrassing funniest-video moment, it's risky to ignore yards of encroaching fabric that are threatend by everything from human feet to table legs.

#330 *Loop-the-Loop*

If a hands-free bustle isn't your style, consider a wrist or finger loop.
An elegant loop is attached to the underside of your gown or train, and unlike a sophisticated bustle system, the wrist or finger loop is easily attached at home.

Slip the loop over your wrist, and the fabric sweeps up to one side, allowing you to pursue reception activities without the encumbrance of excess material trailing behind you. A finger loop performs the same function by slipping over the middle finger like a ring.

The drawback to a loop is that you never have two completely free hands. While it is possible to eat, cut the cake, dance, etc., with a looped hand, doing so is often awkward. Furthermore, if the amount of fabric being swept up is plentiful, the weight of it constantly drags on the hand. To keep the fabric up, your hand must be up. For light, airy fabrics, this is easy, but for denser, thicker fabrics, it can quickly become tiresome. Loops work best with single-layered gowns that have no underskirt or excessively long train to lift.

#331 *Handle with Care*

Wedding-gown fabrics are most often made of delicate materials that are easily snagged. Handling of the gown happens repeatedly for one issue or another, not to mention the number of the times you haul it out to show it off to friends and family.

Fingernails or even rough skin can snare fabric and leave a disfiguring mark. The solution is simple. Buy a pair of thin, white cotton gloves, and never handle your gown without wearing them.

Further protective steps include banning jewelry when handling the gown and never letting the dress hem or train rest on the floor. Murphy's Law dictates that the lovely necklace you're wearing will find a way to entangle your gown's lace, or that just dropping the dress to the floor for a moment will turn it into an inadvertent duster. Dirt that's hard to see on the floor is all too apparent on a hem of pale fabric.

Your bridal gown is precious. Handle it with kid gloves, literally.

#332 *Quick Change*

It's become popular practice to have not one, but two, wedding-day outfits — the elaborate gown for the ceremony and a simpler dress for the reception. The theory is comfort. It's assumed that the bride cannot fully enjoy herself at the reception if miles of fabric encumber her, or if she's cinched into a bodice so tight that she can hardly breathe. There's merit in that viewpoint, and if changing into something more comfortable makes sense, do so.

If, however, that's not your perspective, don't buckle under some someone else's idea of what's "trendy" or "popular." You likely paid a lot of money for your wedding gown. You've waited for what felt like an eternity for your wedding day to arrive, and chances are you'll never wear the gown again. If wearing that beautiful creation until the cows come home is your wish, don't let "popular practice" get in the way. Enjoy every minute of it.

#333 *Wear-Again Gowns*

For bridal gowns and bridesmaids' dresses born to do double duty, consider styles with detachable skirts. A removable skirt is attached to the underside of a shorter dress to create a full-length gown. Once the formal occasion is over, the bottom length of the skirt is detached, leaving a beautiful cocktail dress. This system works especially well with ruffled layers, but it is also appropriate for any dress with a decorative hem that hides the thigh-to-floor (or knee-to-floor) skirt attachment.

Detachable skirts are a genuine kindness for bridesmaids who are customarily left with a never-to-be-worn-again dress taking up space in their closet, or the prospect of paying for alterations to turn the dress into something else.

Brides may choose a detachable skirt or opt for an overskirt. An overskirt augments a cocktail-length dress by attaching a matching full skirt and train at the waist. When properly fashioned, no one will know that the voluminous skirt can disappear in moments, leaving a classy cocktail dress beneath.

Some bridal-dress manufacturers carry limited lines of convertible, wear-again gowns. For a custom-made dress, investigate the convertible option with your designer or seamstress.

Rewearing a formal dress, or at least part of it, after the big day is definitely possible.

#334 *Try It! You Might Love It!*

A common mistake brides make when shopping for their bridal gown is letting the hanger do the talking. Gowns may look one way on hangers, but entirely different on the body. Disregarding a dress because of how it looks on the rack shortchanges your options.

You're a bride. Seize the moment and try on as many gowns as you wish. It's absolutely your prerogative to do so. Don many gowns over the course of several days, weeks, or months. Leave no stone, or hanger, unturned. A gown that appears one-dimensional and unremarkable on the rack may be so well suited to your body that it transforms itself, and you, into wedding magic.

#335 *The Buddy System*

When searching for your perfect gown, don't shop alone. It's fun to have company, and other opinions matter. Even with mirrors all around, "issues" will arise that only another interested eye can detect. You don't have to agree with the appraisal of friends and family, and the ultimate choice is yours to make, but relying solely on the feedback of salespeople is not wise.

Bridal-shop workers have a vested interest in selling product and may not be completely honest about how a particular gown suits you. It doesn't make their viewpoint worthless. It just makes it a bit more suspect than one coming from someone who cares about you.

To hear from many voices, change your shopping buddies as often as you like. In the end, yours is the deciding voice, but a peppering of different opinions is valuable.

#336 *The Bridal-Gown Photo Journal*

A digital camera is a bridal-gown shopper's friend. To make the right choice, you need to be able to compare looks side by side. Standing before a mirror in one gown at a time isn't as effective as seeing yourself in several different gowns at once. Photographs provide that option, without the use of mirrors that may secretly shave off a few pounds (as some clothing-store mirrors are notoriously reputed to do).

Have a friend take photos of you in your favorite gown choices at each bridal salon, then later review the photos together. You'll find that your ideal look draws your attention again and again.

Certain bridal shops won't allow photographs, even though the pictures would be no different than photos of the gowns that appear in catalogs or magazines. But you have a choice. Unless you simply must have a certain dress at a shop that doesn't permit photos, go to a store that allows you the freedom to make wise choices. In the alternative, ask the bridal shop if they would agree to photos taken with an instant camera that prints pictures on the spot. This eliminates the bridal shop's fear that you are a design-stealing spy bent on destroying its business. Study the photo array at the shop, then leave it behind in an envelope for your perusal at a later date. If the shop won't even accommodate that simple scenario, give your business to someone who will.

It's your wedding. You have every right to use modern tools, like photography, to help you make perfect decisions.

#337 *The Wicked World of Don't*

If you don't want to put on your gown on your wedding day only to discover that it just doesn't fit or feel right, try it on when you are in your best physical and emotional condition.

Don't shop during "Mother Nature's monthly visit" or after a night of beer and salty pretzels. Don't shop when you've reached the point of stress overload. Don't shop in granny panties and a sports bra that you would never be caught dead in on your wedding day. Don't shop in inappropriate shoes. Don't shop while wearing perfumes, deodorants, or makeup that would force store personnel to prohibit you from trying on the best gowns.

To achieve comfort and style perfection, don't live in the world of "don't." Shop smart.

#338 *A Groom's Perfect Fit*

Grooms who don't wear formalwear on a regular basis may balk at wearing the perfect tuxedo. Tuxedo trousers generally feel looser than the pants a man wears daily, making him think his tuxedo britches are too big. They're not, and trying to select formalwear the same way business slacks or blue jeans are chosen may result in an undesirable look on the wedding day.

The looser fit in tuxedo pants helps keep pleats sharp and pockets from bulging open. Yet it may feel strange, causing the groom to request a smaller size. Sales assistants should steer the groom and his groomsmen to the right formal fit, but many give in to a groom's assertion that the clothes "don't fit right" and do as the groom asks, even though they know better.

- Important considerations:
- Seams should not strain, and there should be no pulling across the jacket's shoulders.
- The cummerbund and waistband shouldn't slip or slide.
- Pant legs and shirtsleeves should be neither too long nor too short.
- Pants should rest gently across the top of the shoes, and shirtsleeves should edge just past the wrist.
- No more than an inch of shirt cuff should show beneath the jacket sleeve.
- The shirt's neck opening shouldn't gape or restrict, and a waistcoat should close smartly around the shirt without puckering or sagging.
- A cummerbund must settle over the trousers' waistline without curling up when the groom is seated.

A tuxedo's expected fit is a preshopping insight every groom and groomsman should possess.

#339 *Going to the Source*

Brides may not be allowed inside the inner sanctum of bridal-gown designers, but a personal shopper is.

Like a home designer who goes directly to building and decorating-supply sources to secure the latest and greatest in home décor, a personal bridal-gown shopper puts you on the cutting edge of emerging fashion by visiting gown designers on your behalf and locking in next year's gown before next year even arrives.

The shopper's fee is usually 15% to 25% over and above the cost of the gown, but there's often an equalizing effect from buying direct versus buying the same gown after it's released to retailers.

The caveat is that, unless you are interested in a very high-end gown, even your personal shopper won't be able to breach the hallowed halls of some designers. But personal shoppers do come with other benefits.

Professional shoppers already know what each local bridal shop has to offer. They know the best time to shop. They have an established relationship with retailers and the ability to negotiate discounts or bonuses on the customers' behalf. And unlike your mom, your sister, or your best friend, your shopper won't tell you a gown looks fabulous just to make you feel better.

The added expense of a shopper must be factored into the budget, but only hire someone who has dressed many brides. Without experience in the field, your shopper will have no shopping clout.

#340 *The Perfect Measure*

For perfectly flattering wedding attire, it's vital that the bride, groom, and attendants know their exact sizes. If possible, have measurements taken by a professional stylist or seamstress before commencing the search for wedding attire. It's far too tempting when wielding your own measuring tape to give it a little tug inward, and fudging on measurements is simply a no-no.

Print your measurements — including hat, shoe, and all relevant body-part sizes — on a card to carry with you. Sharing your measurements with the store consultant allows her to execute her job more efficiently and effectively, and you won't waste time being remeasured or being shown garments that are destined to fit you like an army tent.

Leave no significant body part out. From upper arms to inseams to neck sizes, every measurement matters.

#341 *Fake, Fake, Fake*

Can you buy a new Vera Wang gown on the Internet at half the price of one in the store? Maybe. But would it really be a Vera Wang design? Unlikely. Unless you're buying a secondhand Vera Wang dress from a private party, chances are that what you see and what you actually get will be decidedly different.

Fake designer gowns sell like hotcakes all over the Internet. When it's impossible to touch the material, check the stitching, or examine the label in person, the potential for fraud is high.

It's not always easy to identify a knockoff. But it's virtually impossible to do so when shopping only from online pictures. Sometimes disreputable sellers actually steal photos of real designer gowns to lure customers toward their fakes. Theft of designers' work is rampant. Is trying to score a gown for a fraction of what it should cost worth the risk, when you know that the gown has a good chance of arriving in sub-par condition?

Trimming the wedding budget is admirable, but perhaps the purchase of the wedding gown is not the place to gamble. Inadvertently breaking the law by purchasing a bootleg design may result in a dress that hangs like a burlap sack or splits at the seams during the first dance.

To buy a designer gown online, ensure its legitimacy by going directly to the designer's Web site. Otherwise, let extreme caution be your guide.

#342 *Wedding-Gown Design Maps*

Even if making your wedding gown completely from scratch is not your desire, gown patterns are beneficial. Patterns not only generate ideas, they offer paths to alterations that can make an off-the-rack gown feel couture.

Bridal-gown patterns are an asset in the gown-shopping process. Perusing the pattern books in a fabric store will help you visualize the construction of a gown, and when you see it piece by piece rather than as a whole, you begin to realize that you could "add a little something there" to create just the right elegant, whimsical, or fairy-tale feel you are looking for. The simple addition of a sash, bow, panel, pleat, appliqué, etc., can alter any gown's personality.

It's fine to wear a beautiful gown right off the rack, but if you want to give it your own personal touch, think of bridal-gown patterns as road maps to the customized gown of your dreams.

#343 *Look to the Label*

Brides need more information about their wedding gown than just its price. Labels are important, and they're the law. Original gown labels may disappear for a number of reasons, but where the dress originated, who made it, and what fabrics were involved in its construction are all pieces of information that help prevent negative repercussions. No bride wants to wind up with a shiny cotton blend when the dress was represented as silk. This issue is so important that the Federal Trade Commission (FTC) issued a brochure for brides entitled "Wedding Gown Labels: Unveiling the Requirements." Go to business.ftc.gov and enter "wedding gown labels" in the search box to read, print, or e-mail a copy of the brochure. Knowledge is power. Use it to your advantage.

#344 *Stressed Out!*

Most wedding gowns, whether vintage or modern, are conscientiously crafted to prevent unwanted splits and rips, but many, especially discount gowns, are mass produced with scant attention paid to avoiding flaws like dangling threads, unfinished seam endings, or mismatched alignments.

The best way to determine if a gown is fit enough to go the distance on your wedding day is to give it a stress test. Conduct a thorough visual and physical inspection by examining every inch with your eyes, a flashlight, and your smoothly gloved hands. If all is well, put on the dress and bend, twist, sit, reach, and squirm. Have your maid of honor or other assistant watch the seams, darts, and fastenings as you move. Stress is evident when the straining of seams or fabric occurs. If that happens, address the issue by choosing another gown or by working with a seamstress to reinforce problem areas. A wedding-gown stress test doesn't take long, and putting your gown through the paces can keep your first dance from becoming a wardrobe disaster.

#345 *Muslin — The First Line of Defense*

Wedding-gown fabrics are expensive and require specialized construction talents. When working with a custom-gown designer/dressmaker, a muslin sample is the first order of business. The creation of a muslin gown allows an initial fitting before the actual wedding-gown fabrics are cut. The sample gives both the bride and the gown creator the opportunity to make desired design changes or necessary fit adjustments before expensive bridal fabrics are compromised. So make this question the first thing you ask when considering a custom wedding gown: "Do you provide a muslin sample?" The ultimate decision of who makes your gown is up to you. A muslin sample for something so important in your life is a small but vital expense that can ultimately save money and prevent heartache.

#346 *The Beauty of a Cost-Cutting Gown*

The wedding gown is an enormous investment, and it is almost always worn just once. But it is possible to trim the wedding-gown budget without sacrificing elegance or style, and to end up with stunning wedding attire and a gorgeous gown for anniversaries and other special occasions down the road.

Begin with the purchase of an evening gown. A strapless, backless, or barely strapped gown without sleeves is ideal. It doesn't have to be white or ivory, but it can be. Once purchased, take the gown to a bridal dressmaker, and commission a beautiful jacket made with traditional bridal fabrics and accents. Depending upon the evening gown you've chosen, the jacket can be any length, from bolero to tuxedo, and even have its own train. It can be formal and sophisticated or ethereal and floating like a sheer shawl caught in a breeze. An experienced dressmaker will help you decide which jacket style best suits your evening-gown choice.

On your wedding day, you will look every inch the beautiful bride, but later, only the jacket will need packing away. The gown will be ready for the next big event in your life. And with the money you saved from choosing a bridal jacket over a bridal gown, you can add caviar and champagne to each and every honeymoon dinner or buy a beautiful piece of furniture for your home.

#347 *A Manly Upgrade*

Not every groom needs or wants a tuxedo for the wedding, especially when a nice, dark suit that can be worn again and again simply makes more sense. A vest and a tie elevate many nice suits to "wedding" status.

Any suit can be formally upgraded with the addition of a contrasting tie and waistcoat. White or ivory is the most obvious choice, and either will add just the right degree of wedding formality, but the color choice is truly unlimited. Sky blue, pastel green, rose, burgundy, or even royalty-inspired purple can change the look of an ordinary dark suit so much that most guests will think it was made for the wedding.

Whether the ties and coordinated vests are purchased or rented, the cost will be considerably less than purchasing or renting a tuxedo, and the burden of added expense and inconvenient fittings for the groom and his groomsmen won't be an issue.

Just like brides, grooms should wear what makes them happy on their wedding day.

#348 *The Veil Tale*

When it comes to wedding veils, brides face the old "which came first — the chicken or the egg?" dilemma. Do you choose a hairstyle and then choose a veil or choose a veil, and then fashion a hairstyle that works well with it?

Hairstyles change the appearance of a veil by altering its length, its fall from the crown of the head, and its flow. A last-minute decision to wear an upswept hairdo can actually shorten the veil's length by eight inches or more. That's a significant change to the overall appearance of the wedding ensemble. A too-flat hairdo can make the veil literally cling to the skin as it sweeps down from the crown of the head, creating strange, unflattering shadows on the face. And a modern, spiky hairdo can catch a veil and bunch it into uneven points that stick to your head and refuse to fall.

To avoid these issues, choose your gown, then your hairstyle, then your veil, and wear the actual hairstyle when you go veil shopping. Don't forget the "all sides" experiment. Never choose a veil from just looking forward into a mirror. To understand how a veil complements you, it must be viewed from the front, back, and both sides. Because all bodies and faces are different, something that appears quite beautiful from one direction may not necessarily look stunning from another.

#349 *A Hint of Black*

An all-white wedding gown is the most popular color choice for brides, but some brides have learned the secret of black. The world hasn't turned topsy-turvy — all-black wedding gowns are still rare. But black accents on white gowns are popular for a reason. The relief provided by a single black flower, a black bow with a jeweled center, or a black sash, with or without tails, gives white wedding gowns a whole new captivation. It's hard to look away from the striking contrast. Adding a black accent to that gorgeous white gown won't tickle every bride's fancy, but consider the option when gown shopping. See for yourself what a hint of black can do. It might just provide that perfect flair you didn't even know you were looking for.

#350 *Hairy Weather*

Keeping your hair natural and true to your personality is important, but in some cases, your most comfortable hairstyle just won't work with the wedding venue you've chosen. Blame it on the weather. High humidity can turn the hairspray on your upswept style into a sticky helmet of varnish, and marrying on a windy cliff will whip your long tresses about your face, so that in every photo you look like you're in the midst of a tornado.

Be prepared. Go online and view the area's weather history for your wedding day, then choose two hairstyles, an "A" choice and a "B" choice, ensuring that each will work with your headpiece. Make sure you have all essential tools at hand to change, or at least to tame, your hair in the event the weather becomes a challenge. If you arm yourself with a backup plan, unruly weather won't even have the opportunity to be your "un-*do*-ing."

#351 *Happy, Funny, Informal Feet*

Humor is a blessing. Comfort is a pleasure. Formal dress shoes can make one miserable. These are facts of life. But if your feet are happy and there's a smile on your face, the world just seems to rotate more smoothly. Enter wedding-day sneakers.

Plenty of wedding couples have discovered that happy feet are the perfect catalysts to a full-on, go-for-it, have-a-blast day. Bedazzle your wedding sneakers if you wish, or turn them into autograph canvases and let guests sign them for posterity. There's something uniquely compelling about a formal gown grazing the tops of sneaker-clad toes, or suits sporting the ultimate comfort shoes beneath their trouser hems. Most guests will get a kick out of the contrasting attire. A few will be appalled. Either way, who cares? If you want to give your feet and your wedding a gloriously comfortable and happy foundation, sneakers are at your service.

#352 *Wedding-Gown Afterlife*

What do you do with the wedding gown after the big day? On one hand, keeping it preserved, while knowing full well it is never to be worn again, is somehow comforting, in spite of the storage space it will consume. On the other hand, finding another use for the gown may make better sense. Very few wedding gowns are actually handed down through the generations. Brides simply want to choose their own attire. So what can you do with the gown besides selling it or giving it to charity? You can deconstruct it and turn it into items you will see and enjoy every day.

Lace makes wonderful sachets, and brocades are perfect for throw pillows. Trims can be salvaged and added to the special-occasion attire already in your closet, or they can be transformed into hair or handbag adornments. Use portions of the dress to make infant christening gowns, or use pieces of it to mat art or photographs. The more you spread the wealth of your gown throughout your daily life, the more wedding memories will be sparked. Keep the gown intact if you wish, or deconstruct and repurpose it. You will know which is the right choice for you.

#353 *Groom Couture*

Brides often spring for a custom gown while grooms dutifully head off to the tuxedo shop for their rented wedding-day finery. If clothes matter to the groom, why not look into custom work for him as well? It can be something as simple as a one-of-a-kind tie made especially for him, a custom-tailored shirt, or the creation of an entire ensemble, from tie to trousers. Some grooms couldn't care less about their attire, but there are those who appreciate being perfectly decked out. If your groom takes pride in his appearance, custom garments may make him feel like a king. He may just need to be pointed in the right direction, away from the rental facility.

#354 *Virtual Vision*

Technology has given brides some amazing tools. From the option to peruse wedding Web sites to shopping online for supplies from all over the world, planning a wedding today comes with a lot of conveniences previous generations of brides didn't enjoy.

One of the absolute best is the virtual-hairstyle tool. A bride can upload a photo of herself into a hairstyle program and change the style, color, and adornments to get a preview of possible wedding-day hairdos. Seeing your own image with hairstyles you might not have imagined is a gift. Once you've narrowed the styles down to a few, take those printed photos to your stylist for real-world experimentation. Technology opens doors. There's no reason brides shouldn't walk through them.

#355 *The Incredible Disposable Dress*

Wedding gowns cost a lot of money and look gorgeous for a day. Unfortunately, like a new car driven off the dealership lot, their value declines drastically the very next day. Still, the expense is worth it if you walk down the aisle in the gown of your dreams. But what if you could do that without the extreme expense? That may be possible with a disposable dress.

Gowns made of paper or water-soluble plastics, or even those made of organics, can change the wedding-gown experience in a big way. If you've ever watched fashion-design television shows, you know that clothing can be made from literally anything. Designers with skill and vision can create something out of modest or unconventional materials to give you a spectacular walk down the aisle without thousands of dollars in investment. Sure, the thought of saying "I do" in a gown of popcorn or origami roses isn't going to send every bride into fits of ecstacy, but for some brides, as well as their bridesmaids, being different is right up their live-for-the-moment alley.

#356 *Gallery of Complementary Fashion*

Sometimes brides are tempted to control the colors of their wedding guests' attire. They may have good intentions. For example, how beautiful would it be to see all the guests in only ivory and forest green at your winter wedding? But any attempt to control the attire of guests must be undertaken with care. Unless your guests are affluent, asking them to wear something other than what is considered customary wedding attire is an imposition. Forcing guests to buy clothes to match a color scheme is wrong, and if you do intend to dictate the shade of your guests' attire, the only reasonable choice is black. Almost everyone has something black in his or her wardrobe. But is an audience clad all in black really what you want for your wedding day? Probably not. So instead of requiring attire in a certain hue, distribute hand fans in a color that complements your theme. You will still look out to the gallery of guests and find a panorama of the desired color, but you will not offend or inconvenience your guests in the process.

#357 Wedding-Gown Fine Art

You will have your wedding photos and your videos, but if you want something wonderful to go with them, consider an artist's rendering of your wedding gown. Provide a photo of your gown to an artist who will recreate the dress in oils, charcoals, watercolors, or whatever medium you prefer. The gown portrait becomes a piece of irreplaceable art. And if you decide to give away, sell, or repurpose the real gown, you will always have the framed, fairy-tale version, and it will always be at its most beautiful.

#358 Shimmering Strands

Is hair tinsel perfect for a modern bride? If you're the kind of woman who loves bling, the answer may be "yes." On the other hand, if the idea of shimmering strands peeking through natural tresses feels tacky, the answer is probably no. Hair tinsel is no different from any other hair adornment. When used sparingly, it can be quite beautiful as it catches the light beneath your veil, and later as you spin about the dance floor with your new husband.

To decide if hair tinsel is right for your wedding day, experiment. In one of your practice hairstyle sessions, weave it into the hairdo and experience how it feels and looks. Take photos to see what happens when the flash hits it. Weave it into your best friend's hair so that you can step back and examine its effect objectively. Hair tinsel is not something to choose at the last minute. Think ahead. Practice with it. It may be just the finishing touch you've been looking for . . . or not.

#359 The PG-Rated-Gown Dilemma

Did you know that your wedding-gown choice is not entirely your own? At least that's the case when you marry in a house of worship. Some religious venues have attire restrictions. Wouldn't it be horrible to pay top dollar for your stunning backless gown only to discover that, if you wear it, you'll be forbidden to even walk down the aisle?

If you're planning a religious ceremony, check on your faith's policies. If you learn there are rules against strapless, backless, plunging, short, sheer, or other styles of gowns, look at it as an opportunity. For the ceremony only, add a piece that beautifully accents your gown. An opaque, lace shawl to cover your shoulders or a delicate cape to conceal your back works well and is easily removed for the reception.

Be sure to check with the venue before you make the mistake of purchasing an expensive gown that does not lend itself to supplemental pieces. A little investigative work in advance prevents a mad scramble to "fix it" later on.

#360 *Sock It to Him with a Kiss*

To ensure that your groom doesn't show up in his fine threads and shiny shoes sporting his favorite pair of NFL socks, send him wedding-day socks as a gift. Search for an elegant pair of socks that would complement his attire, then personalize them with a bit of embroidery or a permanent fabric pen. Draw a pair of lips in your favorite lipstick shade, or simply write an "I Love You" message. Put your private sentiment or art on the toe portion of the socks, and you will be the only ones who will know it's there. It's a loving gesture with a practical benefit. Your gift adds memories, and no team logos or weird patterns will wink from beneath his pant legs every time your groom takes a step.

#361 *Life Outside the Box*

The price to clean and preserve a wedding gown after the wedding often rivals the cost of the gown itself. When the preserved gown comes back to you, it's usually arranged on a bust form that makes it appear as if the bodice still conceals a living bosom. There are yards of acid-free tissue between the folds, and the gown is sealed in an acid-free box that may include a see-through lid. It's now a very expensive "white elephant" that women are even afraid to handle, for fear the box will somehow crack open and "kill" the preservation. So what do you really have? A box. A dress that can't see the light of day. And a crippling fear.

If that's not your desire for your gown, make a different choice. Don't clean it. Don't preserve it. Live with it. Do you ever wonder how all those gloriously fancy gowns from centuries past survived without a chemical bath and acid-free boxing? Besides, aren't those grass stains and champagne dribbles as much a part of the memories of your wedding day as the gown itself?

If your goal is a dress your daughter will someday wear, then go ahead and spend the money to clean and preserve it, even though the likelihood of her wanting to wear it is decidedly slim. Check with the Association of Wedding Gown Specialists for a referral in your area. Not all cleaners can competently handle your gown. But if you are keeping the dress for your own memories, keep it as is and let it age as you do. Frame it if you like, or just keep it in your closet to visit regularly. Preserved in a box for posterity, or part of your daily life and remembrances? You decide.

#362 *An Ascot, My Good Man?*

Who wears ascots? The answer is any 19th-century gentleman who followed the fashion-forward dictates of the legendary Beau Brummell. Two hundred years later, the ascot is still a handsome choice for grooms and groomsmen. Today's ascots may look slightly different than the puffy styles sported by Mr. Brummell, but the theory is identical. An ascot scarf is worn inside the shirt and covers the area of the chest where the shirt lays open. An ascot tie covers the same area, but rests atop a closed shirt.

The ascot tie is wedding perfect, especially for morning or early afternoon weddings. It is a formal accessory, but a bit less so than a traditional bow tie, and it looks especially appealing when fastened with an elegant ascot pin. What sets an ascot tie apart is its width. There is enough fabric to be tucked into the vest, creating a neat, stylish focal point. An ascot instead of a tie or a bow tie works well for the groom who embraces the look of gentry.

#363 *Hopeless Hanger Marks*

Hangers are unfriendly devices. Even the padded varieties seem to find a way to leave unsightly bumps and dents. Your gown would be far better off hanging on a mannequin, but not many household closets are stocked with department-store props.

But there is a solution, and maybe your football-loving nephew can help. Child-sized football shoulder pads make great supports for heavy gowns. Affix the pads to a wooden hanger, cover them with a thick T-shirt that has sleeves long enough to encase the pads, and slip the gown over the finished structure. The shoulder area of the gown will be as fully supported as if you were wearing it yourself. Hang your impromptu mannequin from a ceiling hook so that the dress skirt does not bunch against the floor, and your gown will be spared from those dreaded hanger marks. And remember, if you're going to cover your gown, avoid plastic bags. Use a muslin garment cover instead.

#364 *Color Splash*

What could look more beautiful than elegant white heels peeking from beneath your gown? How about elegant red heels, or forest-green ones? Colored shoes with a white wedding gown may not sound appealing to some, but before you make that judgment, try them on for size. The look can be extraordinarily breathtaking. A burst of color that only flashes as you take a step doesn't detract from the gown — it supports and highlights it. Colored shoes also allow you to more effectively weave seasonal influence into your attire. Choose just a hint of color, like a blush rose, or go for the bold statement that only deep-purple shoes could supply. Colored shoes are an exciting style option for modern brides.

#365 *In the Heat of the Night . . . and Day*

If you're an August wedding couple, chances are there's going to be heat. The same is true of a number of other months on the calendar, and wedding attire is often heavy, even when created with summer fabrics. Take clothing that doesn't breathe, and add a hot day, posing for photos, and managing stress, and you've got the perfect formula for a sweaty body.

You may wish to choose undergarments that can help. Moisture-wicking garments are very popular for athletes and anyone engaged in summer activities. They used to be bulky and ill suited for wearing beneath fine outerwear, but that's no longer the case. You can now find moisture-wicking underwear in attractive, thin styles that fit smoothly under a gown or tuxedo. It's mighty difficult to put on a smile and maintain your composure when a pool of sweat is gathering at the small of your back. Check out the different brands of moisture-wicking undergarments, and get relief from the heat. There's no need to worry that those mortifying pools of sweat will soak through your wedding attire for all to see.

#366 *Split the Difference*

If your plan is to wear six-inch heels down the aisle then switch to more comfortable shoes at the reception, beware of the "big trip." Gowns hemmed to accommodate high heels will suddenly be too long for lower-heeled shoes, creating the possibility of ending up on your nose instead of your toes while dancing or even while walking. Protect yourself by splitting the difference on the hem length. Pick a length that is a bit shorter than what you'd normally choose for pairing with your high heels and a bit longer than what you'd choose for the lower-heeled shoes. It won't be perfect, but it will be far better than tripping over your hem all night. No bride needs a wedding photo of herself tumbling across the dance floor.

#367 *His and Hers Crown Jewels*

Custom jewelry is fashioned from metals, crystals, precious gems, beads, and other materials. Some custom pieces are made by professional jewelry artisans, while others spring to life at the hands of a talented friend or family member with a passion for jewelry making.

However you choose to have it created, consider commissioning your custom wedding jewelry with an intertwined theme suitable for both him and her. Choose a pearl necklace with a monogrammed heart for her that complements pearl-studded, monogrammed cuff links for him. Or maybe you wish to use your jewelry as the splash of color and the matching motif for your respective wedding ensembles, such as an emerald "moon" bracelet for her and an emerald "moon" tie tack for him. Any shared design element will form a special connection between the two of you. In the eyes of your guests, it is merely beautiful jewelry, but to you, it's an unspoken but meaningful wedding-day bond.

#368 *Wedding-Ring Surprises*

There's no denying the beauty of traditional wedding bands and diamond rings. Yet so many wonderful ring options are available to today's brides and grooms that sticking with a tried-and-true wedding set is now an option, not a given.

Ceramic wedding rings by top jewelry designers have changed the face of rings both visually and functionally. Though very shatter- and scratch-resistant, ceramic rings are lightweight compared to their metal counterparts, adding comfort to everyday wear. They also lend themselves to distinctive customization unavailable with traditional rings.

Creating one-of-a-kind wedding-band designs from scratch is a growing business, as more and more wedding couples look to express their unique identity.

Other emerging ring concepts include marrying birthstones to diamond settings and crafting new rings from select pieces of vintage rings.

Merely choosing a diamond setting is no longer the end all of wedding-ring shopping. Brides and grooms who literally think outside the ring box will find amazing ring options unavailable at any other time in history.

#369 *Up and Coming*

There's nothing wrong with buying a wedding gown straight off the rack. Beautiful is beautiful — it doesn't really matter where that beauty came from. But if having a gown designed especially for you has been your dream since you were a little girl, maybe you should watch a little reality TV.

Old episodes of *Project Runway*, *The Fashion Show*, and *Fashion Star* are filled with talented, not-yet-made-it designers. Sure, you'll have to look beyond some of the out-there styles that only a runway model would wear, but if you look closely at the workmanship and vision of each designer, you may just find a diamond in the rough who would create your one-of-a-kind gown at a fraction of what an established designer might charge. Most reality-TV clothing designers can be located by entering their name into an Internet search engine. Some have online shops and already offer custom works. Others can be contacted via social networking sites. If you don't know the designers' names, enter the name of the TV show and the word "contestants" into a search engine. You'll find plenty of follow-up information on the designers. Look for designers whose clothes are, first and foremost, constructed well. Pay special attention to those who love to design gowns. And if the design contestant listened when fashioning a garment for a specific individual, that's golden. No bride needs a designer blinded by his own "it's all about me, fabulous me!" mantra. TV shows about fashion construction are perfect hunting grounds for brides looking for unique talent. And talented designers are always eager for new clients.

#370 *Shrug It On*

If you find a beautiful gown and try it on only to discover that you don't have the arms of a goddess, rest assured that you are not alone. In spite of the fact that most women's arms are not sculpted works of art, bridal fashions are often strapless or sleeveless. Finding a ready-made gown with sleeves is not always easy, but the problem is simple enough to rectify with the use of a beautiful shrug.

A shrug is basically a set of sleeves with just enough "top" to hold it on. It can be made in a bolero or turtleneck style, or simply cut away so that only the sleeves show from the front, leaving the neck and upper chest bare. The sleeves can even be attached to a stunning piece of jewelry that arcs over the shoulders. Any experienced seamstress can construct a shrug with short, three-quarter, or full-length sleeves that looks as if it originally came with your gown. You get to cover your arms, add another element that expresses your personality, and still buy that beautiful strapless gown that caught your eye. Those are a lot of benefits from one little garment.

#371 *Fabulous, Free Frontlet*

A tiara is worn on top of the head. A frontlet rests on the forehead. A frontlet works with most hairstyles and is customarily jeweled or crystal beaded. But the beauty of a frontlet is that you don't have to go out and buy one if you don't want to. Virtually any necklace can be transformed into a frontlet with the use of hidden hair clips.

Choose a necklace you already own, or rummage the thrift stores for extraordinary vintage pieces. Frontlets can also be crafted from a strip of exquisite lace adorned with a single, jeweled, brooch-style piece attached to the center front. Allow the frontlet to originate on the top of the head and fall gently over the forehead, or stretch it across the forehead from side to side. Forehead jewels aren't merely for those brides seeking a medieval look. Unusual frontlets add an elegant finishing touch to any number of bridal ensembles.

#372 *Gowns with Heart*

When choosing a wedding dress, think about the moments that brought you to the point of bridal-gown hunting. What were you wearing when you first met, first kissed, got engaged, or shared that one indelible experience you'll never forget?

To add heart to your gown, pay homage to a special memory by wearing an accessory worn during that earlier event, or by designing a gown that follows the style of the well-loved garments you wore that day. Even if you wore blue jeans and a tank top, it's possible to incorporate hints of that casual outfit into your gown. Perhaps you will choose a gown with the same neckline as the tank top, or trim the tails of the gown's sash with tiny blue hearts to represent the jeans. Everything, even beautiful clothes, means more when you are personally connected. Adding a bit of your romantic history to your gown may make you love it even more.

#373 *The Pants Dance*

Brides naturally dream of a beautiful gown for their wedding. But sometimes a pantsuit or a flowing, wide-legged pant is a bride's preferred choice. If you don't want to wear a dress, don't — some pants are so voluminous that they glide and flow like the skirt of a gorgeous gown, but they have the same benefits as a pair of tailored slacks. They offer a welcome freedom of movement and an inherent modesty that no gown can provide. A beautifully designed pantsuit may be especially fitting for a windy beach or mountain ceremony. And for those brides choosing one gown for the ceremony and another for the reception (or for just the second half of the reception), a beautiful, white pant-and-top ensemble may be just the ticket.

#374 *Beyond the Diamond*

Diamonds may be a girl's best friend . . . or not. There's no denying the glory of a diamond, but scores of other precious and semiprecious stones have a glory all their own. It pays to think beyond diamonds when considering wedding-day jewels. A bride who loves color will no doubt find stones that will make her heart flutter just as much as any diamond could. Sapphire, jade, ruby, emerald, aquamarine, amethyst, opal, garnet, topaz, turquoise, and tiger's eye are just a few wedding-perfect options that will continue to add beauty to your wardrobe for a lifetime. Choose birthstones if you wish, or simply choose those stones that catch your eye as you walk through the jewelry-store door. Diamonds are forever, but they aren't the only eternally appealing option. Other stunning stones also master the march of time.

#375 *Mine Alone*

Do you plan to keep your wedding gown forever? If so, consider giving it the ultimate personalization. Monogram it. Have your new married monogram, your wedding date, or whatever sentiment you wish embroidered on your gown. You can use color by adding the work to an unseen, underneath location, like on the inside of the hem, or you can make it visible, if only barely, by choosing color-matched embroidery, like white on white. Utilizing a thread that exactly matches the gown's hue will result in a raised impression that no one will see unless they are intimately close. But it will be there, and you will know it is there. Personalizing the gown is especially poignant if you plan to someday hand the gown down to future generations. It's sweet and sentimental.

#376 *Unveiled Veils!*

One of the most joyous and liberating aspects of being a modern bride is the decided lack of dictates. You are absolutely free to be you! And one way to express the real you is to don whatever white wedding dress makes you feel luscious, then pair it with a colorful veil.

Trim the edge of the veil in an accent color, or go for an entirely tinted veil. A rose-, blush-, or lilac-colored veil over a white gown is unexpected and gorgeous. A veil that is white at the top of the head, then gradually darkens as it moves downward, culminating in a vibrant color that lays against the back of your white gown can be breathtaking. You don't have to do the white-on-white thing unless that's your express wish. You're a modern bride. If you are "colorful" at heart, you can infuse color into your veil and add the element of beautiful surprise to your wedding attire.

#377 *Indelible Impressions*

If you're searching for wedding rings that fall somewhere between glittering diamonds and plain bands and you've always wanted rings as unique to you as your own DNA, check out fingerprint wedding bands. Impressions of the bride's and groom's fingerprints are forever immortalized on the inside or outside of beautiful gold or silver bands. Choose to have the groom's fingerprint on the bride's ring and the bride's fingerprint on the groom's ring, or keep each ring personal to its wearer. The fingerprint can consume just a portion of the ring's surface or encompass the whole ring. It can maintain its natural fingerprint shape or be stretched and manipulated into an artsy fingerprint design. Fingerprint rings are a distinctly modern, and extraordinarily personal, choice for 21st-century wedding couples.

#378 *Man Hands*

It isn't just the bride's hands taking center stage on the wedding day. The groom's hands will be touched, viewed, and photographed up close and personal, too. So what if he's a nail biter? Gnawed-on fingertips, male or female, simply aren't attractive. Brides can hide the problem with artificial nails if necessary, but grooms are generally reluctant to don fake nails, even though they do exist for men.

Presentable "man hands" begin with fingers sporting nice nails. For him to have well-manicured nails, he must begin working on them early, beginning with no more biting. If he can't or won't quit chewing his nails into gnarly stubs, get him a brush-on nail-biting deterrent. The taste is so horrible that the success rate is actually quite good. There are many on the market, so read the reviews carefully to determine which will work best for him. And if he still resists change, buy a set of fake nails for men and tape them to the refrigerator door. Just the sight of them might do the trick when all else has failed.

#379 *Saving Grace*

One of the most valuable wedding-day garments isn't actually a garment at all. It's the hankie.

Weddings are emotional. Tears and sniffles are common. Don't forget to tuck his-and-hers hankies into your wedding attire. With a soft, lacy hankie for her and a nice, crisp hankie for him, neither the bride nor the groom will be caught unprepared. Personalize or monogram the hankies if you wish.

Tissues catch the sniffles but waste away quickly, often leaving particles behind. Who wants bits of wet tissue clinging to an eyelash or stuck to an upper lip on their wedding day? A hankie is a saving grace that does its job well. All you have to do is remember to bring it.

#380 *Gone to Her Head*

From bridesmaids to moms and grandmas, deciding on the best hair adornments can be a challenge. Fascinators and combs are two beautiful options.

A fascinator is a decorative hair attachment secured to the hair with clips, pins, barrettes, or combs. It's comprised of a cluster of jewels, feathers, or ribbons that customarily sits to one side of the head. Think of it as the focal point of a hat, but without the hat. When nosegays or corsages aren't desired, a fascinator, or perhaps a hair comb adorned with a beaded crystal flower, may be a viable choice. Fascinators and combs also combine well with a nosegay or corsage, if the combination is not overwhelming.

When the sophistication of a hat is desired, but the tiring aspect of wearing one isn't, a fascinator is the perfect solution. If a floral touch would be a perfect accent but someone doesn't wish to be bothered with wearing or holding flowers, a crystal flower comb solves the problem. Fascinators and combs are decidedly cooperative.

#381 *Heel-to-Toe Splash*

It may cost a lot less to dress up a plain shoe than to buy an already embellished shoe. Shoe clips come in a variety of styles, including bows, feathers, glittering crystals, and gemstones. Some styles clip to the front of the shoe, while others clip to the heel. Any solid-color shoe is a candidate for embellishment, and if you purchase a plain shoe, you are more likely to find occasions to wear it after the wedding. With the quick addition of clips, shoes are easily customized for virtually any ensemble from the wedding day forward. Shoe clips help your feet take a turn toward loveliness.

#382 *On the Cuff*

Wedding cuffs are wide, no-latch bracelets made of everything from plain metal to crystals and diamonds. Jewelers and other retailers carry cuffs, but for your wedding you may want to seek out a jewelry artisan instead.

Having a cuff created just for you means that it will fit perfectly and be designed to directly complement your gown. A ready-made cuff may be too wide for a petite bride with a small wrist, completely overwhelming her arm and her look. A standard cuff may be too narrow for a bride of stature, not extending far enough up the arm and ruining the effect of the cuff. As with Goldilocks, the goal is to find the one that's "just right," and that's best achieved through custom work. If you don't know any jewelry makers, Etsy.com is a good place to begin your search. A beautiful wedding cuff may be the perfect final touch, but only if it looks as if it belongs.

#383 *Toasty but Tasteful*

It's often hard to predict the temperature at your wedding-reception venue, and sleeveless or strapless gowns expose a lot of flesh. If goose bumps aren't the accessory you wish to sport, a bridal cardigan may be the needed fix. Sweaters with an unmistakable bridal flair are available in all styles, from bolero to poncho to traditional, and in all sleeve lengths. If chosen wisely, a bridal cardigan can actually transform a wedding gown into something even more amazing.

There's no reason to be miserable if the wind blows, the temperature dips, or your nerves freeze the blood in your veins. Choose a classically styled, ready-made cardigan, or commission a custom one. A lovely cardigan is definitely preferable to wearing your new husband's tuxedo jacket, which happens all too frequently at weddings. He's suddenly underdressed, and you've turned your beautiful gown into the underlining of an oversized sack. If cold could be an issue, stave off the chills, beautifully.

#384 *Give Shoes the Boot*

Weddings are primarily about being delicate, elegant, and refined. That means polished shoes for men and dainty shoes for women, which are always a perfect complement to sophisticated attire. But if you're not necessarily the delicate type, try using your feet to unify the wedding party. Make a bold, unexpected fashion statement. Wear boots!

Beautiful ankle boots for the bride, ankle or taller boots for the bridesmaids, dress boots for the men, and adorable boots for the flower girl and ring bearer give the entire wedding party a uniquely cohesive flair. Unlike traditional wedding shoes, boots will get plenty of after-wedding use. This is not about utilitarian boots that you drag out of the closet when the first snow hits. This is about stylish, wedding-perfect boots that transform a look. Boots aren't for everyone, but they may be right for you.

#385 *Wonderful Wrists*

Gorgeous cuff links peeking from the sleeves make the man in the tuxedo more dapper, and engraved, precious-metal cuff links for the groom and his attendants are nice gifts. But if you want your groom and his attendants to be different from every other man of the day, make the cuff links yourself.

Cuff links are one of the easiest pieces of jewelry to make. Purchase commercially produced cuff-link backs, then top them with whatever adornment you wish. Alternatively, using instructions easily found online or at craft stores, make simple loop-and-bar cuff-link backs yourself. Gemstones, coins, glass, and even personal mementos are suitable cuff-link embellishments. You don't have to be a jeweler to do the job. You just have to follow a simple tutorial, and indulge your creative spirit.

#386 *Private Message*

Thinking ahead to the wedding night? Well, you know your intended surely is, so why not surprise him with a private little message?

Embroider a special sweet sentiment — or a funny one, or a seductive one, or any one you wish — onto your wedding-night lingerie. He'll be expecting to see a flower, a bow, or other girly-girl stuff, but will he be anticipating an artistically applied message right there on your body? Not very likely.

That brief message can be an icebreaker for those who need one, a stress reliever for those too nervous to relax, or an invitation to paradise for those who long ago broke the ice and learned to relax in each other's company. It's not a big surprise. It's just a thoughtful little wedding-night extra.

#387 *Au Naturel*

Sometimes finding just the right bra for that strapless, backless, or lace-topped gown is difficult, and after an exhaustive search, you may still end up with a bra that proves to be downright uncomfortable. It's time to consider going to the altar without one. It's not as decadent as it sounds. In fact, most wedding gowns are boned or so tightly fitted that they actually support you better than a typical bra. And the less you put between you and your gown, the less opportunity there will be for bulges, creases, and other undergarment-induced puckers.

Try it. Have a fitting with and without your bra, and experience the difference in look and feel. Bra size doesn't matter. It's how the gown fits that does, and even those with ample busts can forgo the bra if the gown hugs the body just right. Unless your gown is completely sheer, no one will know, and if going braless makes wearing your gown more comfortable, that's a good thing. Au naturel does have its advantages.

#388 *Well Undercover*

Concealer is used beneath finishing makeup to hide typical blemishes, but sometimes traditional cover-up products won't do the trick. When the spot, scar, or other discoloration just won't disappear, bring out the big guns. Use tattoo concealer. In seconds, a good-quality, waterproof, smudge-resistant tattoo concealer can hide birthmarks the size of battle-ships or obliterate an endless parade of dark spots caused by too much sun. To achieve a natural look, experiment long before the wedding day to find the right shade for your skin tone and to master the art of blending the concealer into your flesh. A mass of too-dark concealer against lighter skin, or too-light concealer on darker skin is not much of an improvement over a rash of blemishes. It's like wearing a neon sign that says, "Hey, look! I hid my blemishes right here!" You don't want that. You want the skin and the concealer to marry well, and if you happen to have a beloved tattoo that may not be as well loved by your mom or your minister, you'll be all set if you have that masterful tattoo concealer on hand. The ink can disappear for just a day, then reappear for the rest of your life.

#389 *Quick and Slick*

Getting your hair done just right for the wedding often requires significant time and effort. But if you're a bride who looks awesome in a smooth hairstyle or a hair bun, you can have the quickest hairdo in town on your wedding day. Just pull your hair back into either a flat or bun-style snood.

Snoods have adorned women's hair for centuries. They are fashioned of everything from heavily crocheted yarns to whisper-delicate crystal- or pearl-beaded strings. The "flat" snood gathers your hair but allows it to maintain a soft, "down" look. The "bun" snood fits over a smooth or curly bun at the nape of your neck, and that bun doesn't even have to be your own hair. A clip-on bun with a snood is so realistic that no one will even question it as an extension. The down-style snood has a decidedly vintage look, while the bun snood is indifferent to time. Both offer brides the opportunity to forgo hours of hair preparation and still look divine.

#390 *The Big Push*

Brides often wonder about adding that little extra something to their bustline on their wedding day. Should you or shouldn't you use bra inserts?

Of course, that's up to you, but you have to ask yourself if that extra bit of cleavage is worth any discomfort that might tag along with it. Not all inserts are comfortable for the long haul, and a wedding day is just that: long.

If you feel inserts are important, insist on those that are soft and natural, easily fit into your bra without peeking out, don't cause sweating, and don't transform you into a whole new person. A little enhancement is nice, but showing up on your wedding day two cup sizes larger than normal will just set tongues to wagging. And no matter how much the packaging claims that the inserts will stay put, don't believe it. Invest in some double-sided body tape. The last thing you need at a lively reception is to dislodge one of those rascals and watch it take flight across the dance floor. If you've never before worn inserts, buy several pairs long before buying the gown. Try them out, then select only the most comfortable and reliable performers.

#391 *Color Perfect*

Most bridal tiaras are crafted with glittering, clear rhinestones to give them a distinctly royal appeal. But not every bride is meant to simply glisten in the light. Some are meant to express their individuality in inventive ways. Colorful tiaras suit such a bride well. Blue, emerald, and purple stones elevate a tiara's expression, and the bride's, too. But it's black rhinstones that are, by far, the most dramatic. A black-stoned tiara, paired with black-and-clear rhinestone earrings and a matching necklace, creates a gorgeous contrast to a white, ivory, or pale-rose gown. It's been said that black goes with everything, and when it comes to tiaras, black not only "goes with," it transforms. When shopping for a tiara, give those with color a look. Maybe you're a bride who hasn't yet discovered her love of bold wedding-day accessories. Try them on and see for yourself.

#392 *Vegan Wear*

For a green wedding that follows through in all aspects, consider vegan attire. Don't let the earthy look of some vegan shoes and accessories fool you. Keep looking. Truly stunning vegan wear is out there. Mink is just one designer of fabulous, animal-free shoes. Conscious Clothing is just one purveyor of natural fiber clothing, and Ecco Bella is just one manufacturer of vegan cosmetics. There are more designers and manufacturers entering the field every day. It's no longer difficult to have a lovely wedding that is completely animal-free. If doing so matters to you, plenty of beautiful choices exist.

ATTENDANTS
& FAMILY

CHAPTER SIX • *Attendants & Family*

Wedding attendants are important people, and the most successful wedding-party relationships are those that begin with friendship. Asking someone to stand with you as you enter marriage means that he or she has a special role in your life. You bestow an honor upon the person you ask to join your wedding party, and his or her acceptance bestows a reciprocal honor upon you. That acceptance is soon followed by mutual obligations, duties, and responsibilities, all leading toward the ultimate goal of a carefree and jubilant event. Because attendants can so affect the outcome of the day, wedding-party selection is one of the most important decisions you will make.

This chapter's goal is to make the wedding-attendant experience sweet and successful for everyone. You will find ideas for everything from tasks and accessories to parties and ways to express your gratitude, all of which will help to ensure a beautiful, happy wedding party that functions well and makes the bride and groom's experience more joyful.

The wedding party doesn't have to be huge to be amazing. Sometimes just the inclusion of a maid or matron of honor and a best man is the ideal choice. When expenses are a concern, a moderately sized wedding party may be the answer. For other brides and grooms, a virtual army of attendants is what they've always envisioned for their perfect day. In spite of the old-fashioned belief that the number of attendants should be based on the size of the guest list or the time of day of the wedding, there are no right or wrong numbers. The most important thing is that your wedding party is composed of people you truly want to be there for you. When it comes to your wedding party, let your heart — and your budget — be your guide.

#393 *Must I Have Bridesmaids by the Score?*

Formulas that dictated how many bridesmaids a bride should have — one bridesmaid for every 45 guests or so — used to float around in wedding etiquette circles. Along the way, fortunately, wise brides decided to dump the formulas in favor of reality.

Bridesmaids' numbers are flexible, and are better decided by the heart and the purse strings than by archaic rules. There are two rules of thumb:

Have as many bridesmaids as you have women in your life who you wish to honor.

Have as many bridesmaids as you can afford.

Whether you have a maid of honor and a single bridesmaid or enough attendants to man a football team depends solely upon your wishes and your wherewithal. No one will think less or more of your wedding based on how many bridesmaids stand with you at the altar. The reasons for bridesmaid selection should be personal. There's no need to worry about numbers.

#394 *Schoolyard Pick*

Sometimes, due to cost or space constraints, it's simply not possible to have all of the attendants you wish you could have, and that means making difficult choices.

When choosing attendants, the bride and groom should first decide on a final quantity, then each prepare a preliminary but prioritized list of candidates. Both the bride's and the groom's list should include potential groomsmen and bridesmaids.

If the decision is four attendants each, then the top two names on each list are automatically included. But for the other 50 percent of the available slots, take a cue from grammar-school recess and alternate picks. Both the bride and groom will likely lose someone they wish they could have, but alternating picks makes the process equitable. Unless you opt for names in a hat, it's the friendliest and fairest way to choose.

Choosing all bridesmaids from the bride's family and friends while leaving out the groom's sisters, or omitting the bride's brother because the groom has three brothers of his own, can cause heartache and hurt feelings. To avoid ruffled feathers among those not chosen as attendants, consider inviting them to fulfill other wedding-planning or wedding-day roles. Where there's a will, there's always a way.

#395 *Side Heavy*

What happens to the wedding party if the bride has ten friends she can't live without, but the groom has only four best buds?

If symmetry and balance matter, and you don't want a long line of bridesmaids trailing off the dais while the row of groomsmen barely makes a dent on the carpet, employ a couple of tricks to even out the look.

An unequal number of bridesmaids and groomsmen is perfectly fine, but it can look awkward at the altar. Instead of the bridesmaids' standing shoulder to shoulder in one long line, consider having them stand front-to-back in two smaller, parallel lines. This is an easy way to make ten look closer to five.

On the groom's side, ask the groomsmen to stand a bit farther apart and turn slightly more toward the altar. This will elongate the line by replacing a thinner profile with a broader body view.

For entering and exiting, assign one groomsman to two or more bridesmaids, and have them walk as a group rather than having the groomsman offer an arm as an escort.

Another alternative is to throw convention out the window and split the attendants into two equal groups. Both bridesmaids and groomsmen would support the bride and the groom on his or her side. While it may seem a bit too inventive for those who cherish tradition, this wedding-attendant configuration is actually a very lovely look.

#396 *Wacky and Wonderful Wedding-Party Invites*

If having certain people in your wedding party is important, ask them. If you want them to grin from ear to ear, ask them with a big dose of creativity.

Inviting people to be bridesmaids and groomsmen should be as special as the relationship you share. Instead of a phone call, send a telegram, or create a funny DVD of friendship photos that invites them via a tour down memory lane. Create fake lottery scratch-off tickets that declare them winners of a coveted wedding-party spot, or present them with pizza-sized cookies that ask for the honor of their service in chocolate-chip lettering.

Explore the possibilities for unforgettable wedding-party invites by thinking big and thinking fun!

#397 *Partying When the Best Man Is a Woman*

Gender neutrality is a consideration when naming any wedding-party member, and having both men and women attendants on the bride's or groom's side is an increasingly popular practice. Most nontraditional attendants suffer no adversity with regard to wedding duties. But the one "best man" duty with which a "best woman" might feel uncomfortable is planning the bachelor party.

If the groom is okay with his "best woman's" attendance at the bachelor party, that's fine, but guys may just want to have fun, and a female friend in the mix changes the party dynamic. To resolve the issue, the best woman could plan the bachelor party but decline to attend. She would be invited to the bachelorette party instead. Or she could temporarily abdicate her position and delegate bachelor-party-planning duties to a groomsman.

The same scenario is workable in reverse if a "man of honor" is chosen instead of a "maid" or "matron of honor."

When choosing a best woman or a man of honor, brides and grooms should take care to make them feel comfortable with their role, even if it means that certain duties need to be handed off to another attendant. No one wants to feel awkward. Parties are meant to be carefree!

#398 *Honorary Solidarity*

It's very likely that you will have to make concessions when finalizing your wedding party. If you asked every beloved friend and family member to stand with you at the altar, you could easily end up with enough attendants to field opposing football teams. So how do you say, "I wish I could have you with me, too," when there are just so many important people in your life? Make them honorary attendants. Though they will have no duties, as wedding-party or house-party members do, you can still acknowledge their special place in your heart by connecting their wedding-day attire with yours. For example, if the groom will be wearing a forest-green tie, invite his circle of guys to add a touch of forest green to their wedding-day attire to show solidarity with him. If you are carrying a single red rose, invite those special women in your life to add something red or rose-themed to their wedding-day ensemble. There's no pressure to comply. It's just a personal, intimate way to bestow an honorary connection on those who cannot, for whatever reason, join the wedding party.

#399 *Merry Maid and Matron*

Many brides wish to honor both a cherished friend and a big sister by having both an unmarried maid of honor and a married matron of honor. When there is both a maid and a matron, sharing the responsibilities can keep the peace and make some duties easier to perform.

As the married honor attendant, the matron stands next to the bride during the ceremony, and the maid of honor stands next to her. Divide ceremony duties between them. The matron arranges the bride's gown, veil, and train at the altar (if there are no train bearers) and holds her bouquet, while the maid holds the groom's ring and any special prayers, readings, or customized ceremonial necessities.

Ask the maid and matron to share equally in prewedding tasks like the bridal shower, bachelorette party, shopping with the bride, helping the bridesmaids, etc. Both the maid and matron would give reception speeches, and both would receive special attendant gifts. Choose identical attire, or distinguish each ever so slightly with minor nuances.

It is certainly acceptable to engage dual honor attendants, and choosing both a maid and a matron of honor can be a blessing. A bride shouldn't have to worry that she must slight one cherished woman in her life for another who is equally special.

#400 *Shower Me with Joy and Laughter*

The maid of honor customarily hosts the bridal shower, but any friend or relative can step in if she is unable to do so. If the shower is a surprise event, the hostess will be planning it on the sly, but if it isn't, the bride's input on everything from the guest list to refreshments to party games should be welcomed.

Bridal showers aren't just for "showering" a bride with gifts for her new married life. At their heart, showers are occasions for bonding. Fielding humorous advice from long-married women and hearing fun, creative ideas for marital bliss from single friends are the shower events a bride will remember. It's the joy that matters most, and anyone hosting a bridal shower will do well to worry less about the peripheral details and more about ways to encourage a spirit of friendship and a foundation for laughter.

#401 *Taking the Bride's Luncheon on the Road*

A bride's luncheon honors her maid of honor and her bridesmaids, but it's perfectly acceptable to invite the mothers of the bride and groom. A typical luncheon takes place in a restaurant, with food, conversation, and bridesmaids' thank-you gifts taking center stage. But for a day to remember, consider taking the luncheon on the road.

Treat the girls to a variety of culinary experiences by planning a traveling tasting day. You would journey from one restaurant to another, perhaps enjoying appetizers at a Spanish restaurant, soups and salads at an Italian restaurant, entrées at a French restaurant, and desserts at a German restaurant. To create your "international" tasting tour, choose any ethnic foods you like, and take only the most scenic routes between establishments. Instead of a two-hour lunch, your bride's luncheon will last several hours and be filled with exciting new experiences.

Make specific arrangements with each restaurant, including special table décor and small, "themed" favors at each location. For transportation, hire a limo or enlist a friend with a van. Incorporate some scenic surprises into the ride, like funny signs you've created about each bridesmaid and posted along your route.

A bride's luncheon is always special, but there's no reason it can't be extraordinary.

#402 *The Helpful House Party*

In the South, where grand weddings are a staple, female friends and family members who weren't attendants but who helped with specific wedding tasks came to be known as the "house party."

Today's house parties aren't bound by geography, and they can include any number of men and women. As with the selection of wedding attendants, being asked to participate in house-party duties is an honor the bride and groom only bestow upon those they like and trust.

House-party members are detail specialists who provide assistance with prewedding and wedding-day tasks. For instance, one person may supervise the guest book and later oversee the serving of the cake, while another may direct limousine drivers, act as a liaison to the band, and keep the gift table neat and safe.

With hundreds of small wedding-planning details needing attention, house-party members are a blessing in the days leading up to the wedding, but on the day of the wedding, be sure to delegate only a few ceremony and reception responsibilities to each so that everyone can enjoy the wedding festivities.

House-party members can dress in a distinctive way that coordinates with wedding-party attire, or not, as you see fit.

Remember to thank house-party members with gifts of appreciation.

#403 *Ushering in the Smiles*

All too often, the seating process at a wedding ceremony resembles a funeral procession. Voices are hushed and heads are bowed as guests make their way to their seats. But there's a difference between sophisticated deference and a somber demeanor, and the persons responsible for setting the right tone are the ushers.

If the usher is stiff and serious, the guest will follow his lead. If he makes friendly eye contact and greets the guest with a smile, he will likely get a smile in return.

No bride or groom hopes for rigid guests who are secretly wishing for "it" to be over. You want everyone to enjoy your wedding as much as you do. It's not necessary to encourage dancing in the aisles or the batting of beach balls across the pews, but showing your guests that you don't expect them to sit silently and examine their fingernails while they await your arrival is a welcome kindness.

Improve the prewedding wait by giving your ushers your biggest smile and asking them to pass it on.

#404 *Dips, Flips, and Quips*

A journey to the dance studio guarantees bachelorette-party fun. Who wouldn't love to be twirled around the dance floor by a handsome dance partner?

Treating the women in your life to a dance lesson with pros is a recipe for unforgettable memories, and as a bonus, everyone picks up some new moves to share with significant others back home.

Bachelorette parties don't have to be just about barhopping and hangovers. Those elements are welcome if you want them, but why not make the bachelorette party a once-in-a-lifetime event?

A bonding, instructive, laugh-out-loud ballroom experience will give all of the ladies, not just the bachelorette, something to rave about.

#405 *Short Duty for Flower Girls and Ring Bearers*

Depending upon the age of the flower girl and ring bearer, the trip down the aisle may be all you should ask of them. Older children usually do fine standing at the altar with the rest of the wedding party, but younger ones may find that long stand difficult.

It's perfectly acceptable for the youngest wedding-party attendants to be retrieved by their parents after the petals are flung and the rings are delivered. Allowing little ones to sit with their parents may prevent unwelcome distractions during the ceremony. Once seated, reward the tiny attendants with a quiet surprise to keep them entertained, like a fabric picture book, a small stuffed animal, or a kaleidoscope.

When it's time for photos, small children who haven't grown weary from standing in silence will be fresh, rested, and more apt to deliver a picture-perfect smile instead of a picture-disrupting case of the fidgets.

#406 *Keeping the Train on Track*

The long train of an ultra-formal wedding gown requires the assistance of a train bearer or two. Train bearers carry the train as the bride walks down the aisle, then arrange it in a beautiful spray behind her at the altar.

The length of the train determines the number of train bearers. Some trains are so long that multiple hands are necessary to keep the fabric from tugging as the bride moves. Train bearers can be younger or older, but they are customarily between the ages of 9 and 14. They are dressed to complement the flower girl's and ring bearer's attire, and can wear formal gloves to help protect the delicate fabric of the train.

Rehearsal matters. Train bearers need practice to learn how to handle the fabric without crushing it and how to effectively display the train at the altar. The best way to ensure a grand entrance is to have the train bearers practice with a length of lightweight fabric. Even a king-sized microfiber sheet will substitute nicely for the real train. Envision a clock face superimposed over the train, and instruct your sole train bearer to walk behind the fabric tail, elevating it with one gloved hand holding the train at "five o'clock," and the other at "seven o'clock." If there are two train bearers, one will walk at the "five o'clock" position, and the other at "seven o'clock." No matter how many train bearers there are, they can easily match their positions on opposing sides of the "clock face."

To add balance and symmetry to the lift, choose an imaginary mark on each train bearer's body. For example, designate the bottom of the trouser pocket or the top of the cummerbund to be the height where the hands should be held. It's not easy to judge what would be "three feet off the floor" while walking, but it's easy to remember to hold the train at a level matching something specific on the body. When it's time to fan out the train behind the bride at the altar, begin with a "three o'clock" to "nine o'clock" stretch, and the rest of the train will easily smooth into place as the train bearers complete their task and back away to take their seats.

Short and medium-length trains rarely require a train bearer. If the bearers would be closer than ten feet behind the bride, they probably aren't needed.

#407 *Forever Photos*

You won't be the only one looking fabulous on your wedding day. Your attendants will also be sporting their finest and looking their best. So why not take the opportunity to give them a personal treat? Give them the gift of a photograph from the wedding photographer.

Your photographer doesn't care what he or she is directed to photograph, and if you wish for some of your photos to be exclusive to each wedding-party member, that shouldn't be a problem. It wouldn't consume a lot of time to take a head shot of each bridesmaid and groomsman, but the small time investment will be more than worth it when you present your wedding-party members with their professional photos. People frequently have no formal head shots for passports, ID cards, or social-networking pages, so a nice head shot is a great gift. Sharing your photographer with your wedding party for just a few, well-directed poses is an inventive and gracious way to say, "We really appreciate you."

#408 *You Light Up My Life*

Wedding attendants may do double duty as candle lighters, but normally two other individuals are selected specifically for the task.

Candelabras are an essential component of some wedding ceremonies, especially very formal ones, and the lighting of the candles is a lovely ritual. The candle lighters enter after the guests have been seated, and before the processional begins, to light candelabras at the altar, in the windowsills, or wherever they may be positioned. Each candle lighter works one side of the room, synchronizing their efforts to create a flowing, visual movement. Their work is usually underscored by soft music.

When all candles are lit, designated candle lighters take their seats and enjoy the ceremony. If the candle lighters are also members of the wedding party, they move to the back of the hall to assume their places in the processional.

Immediately following the recessional of the newlyweds and wedding party, the candle lighters snuff the candles as the guests file out.

Candle lighters can be of any reasonable age, as long as fire-safety protocol is observed. Some venues have restrictions on the number of candles permitted, and it's always wise to discuss the desired use of candles in the early stages of venue negotiations.

#409 *Groomsmen on Wheels*

Why the responsibility of decorating the wedding "getaway car" was ever delegated to men is an infinite mystery. But doing so falls squarely under the jurisdiction of the best man and the groomsmen.

If you don't want your vintage car or limousine to end up with "Just Married" painted in shoe polish on the rearview window and some leftover Christmas bows stuck to the door handles, it's a good idea to give the fellas a bit of guidance.

It's not that men are incapable of designing great decorations, or of affixing them properly; it's that most of them just don't think it's worth the bother. If you beg to differ, the best course of action is to gather up any decorations provided by the limousine service, purchase any additional decorations that you desire, and give all of the items to the male attendants, along with written instructions on how and where to attach them. Leave nothing to chance, and you'll be less likely to approach a vehicle that even the sorriest of parades would reject.

#410 *To the Bride and Groom!*

The best man and the maid of honor are both expected to toast the newlyweds at the reception, but often the toasts are so similar that one sounds like a copycat. And since the best man always goes first, it's the maid of honor who generally delivers a speech riddled with the same "great friend," "good person," "amazing people" rhetoric.

The cure for inadvertent repetition is communication. There's nothing wrong with the best man and the maid of honor sharing ideas for their toasts. In fact, bouncing ideas off one another will freshen both speeches.

There's no law that says a toast has to be "X" amount of minutes. A short toast full of energy and spirit is far better than a longer toast that rambles. If the best man and the maid of honor collaborate, redundancy is avoided, and each toast is a truly unique tribute.

Two heads are always better than one, and encouraging the two honor attendants to coordinate their messages can make the toasting experience the delightful memory it's intended to be.

#411 *A Rose Is Still a Rose*

Would you know who's who in the wedding party if your wedding planner asked who your "pageboy" will be?

As cultures have blended throughout history, certain words have floated to the top of the international word stew. Some words are readily understood. But others, because of their diverse origins, might leave you scratching your head, even in the context of a common event like a wedding. The following wedding-party identifications should help avoid confusion. Different names describe the same wedding-party member.

- maid of honor, matron of honor (when married),
  chief attendant, chief assistant, man of honor (if a man)
- best man, chief groomsman, chief assistant, best person
  or best woman (if a woman)
- bridesmaids, bridal attendants, honor attendants (if male)
- groomsmen, ushers, honor attendants (if female)
- train bearers, pages
- flower girls, flower attendants
- ring bearer, pageboy
- wedding party, bridal party, wedding attendants

A rose by any other name is still a rose, and such is true for the wedding party.

#412 *Rings on a Pillow*

A ring bearer's trek down the aisle, with his precious cargo tied to a pillow with a bow, is a symbolic march that adds delight to the processional. But for sanity's sake, it's wise to make the little fellow's cargo a lot more symbolic and a lot less precious.

Entrusting the real wedding rings to the ring bearer can instill fright in the bravest of brides and grooms. Ribbons may come untied, sending rings spinning into grates or under immoveable fixtures. Ring bearers have also been known to do unspeakable things to their pillows at the most inopportune times. No actual wedding rings should suffer the indignity of being wiped against a dripping nose or sat upon for a slip-and-slide down the aisle.

To prevent misfortunes, entrust the maid of honor and the best man to handle the transport and care of the real rings. Use the ring bearer's pillow to showcase a lovely fake ring set that is more than willing to take a sneeze for the team.

#413 *In the Hands of the Flower Girl*

She's an adorable, bona fide star of the wedding aisle as she makes her way to the altar with basket in hand. She's the flower girl. But today's flower girl doesn't have to settle for a white wicker basket filled with rose petals.

A little-girl purse adorned with removable bows is easily filled with petals or stemmed flowers, and keeping the purse postwedding is more fun than keeping a basket. A small treasure chest brimming with flowers also looks lovely as it's carried down the aisle, and it later becomes a jewelry box for your little miss to treasure at home.

An oversized bow with flowers on the streamers is lightweight and effortless for the littlest flower girls to manage, and Christmas-tree angels affixed with a ribbon handle on the back are a beautiful and spiritual alternative to the customary flower-girl basket.

Careful consideration of the flower girl's age helps determine what she should carry. Many venues prohibit the actual sprinkling of petals, so thinking beyond the traditional flower-girl basket is another way to individualize your wedding and make your flower girl happy, too.

#414 *A Bounty for Bridesmaids and Groomsmen*

While a delicate necklace, a bracelet, or earrings is certainly a fine gift for a bridesmaid, and every groomsman could use a silver money clip, there's no reason you must stick to the tried and true.

Identical gifts may prevent imagined hard feelings, but in truth, selecting gifts that are perfect for each individual attendant doesn't show preferential treatment — it's the ultimate example of equal treatment. Considering each man or woman's life when choosing a gift demonstrates respect for their friendship, as well as appreciation for their wedding-party service.

An engraved measuring cup for the cooking aficionado, a first-edition book by a favorite author for the passionate reader, or even a Star Wars collectible for the sci-fi fan in your midst are all ideal gifts based on the life and loves of the persons receiving them.

Wedding-party gifts don't have to be "wedding" oriented, and there's no such thing as a universal gift. Caring enough to go the extra mile enhances the pleasure of giving.

#415 *Gift Baskets All Around*

Bridesmaids and groomsmen aren't the only wedding-party participants to be thanked with a gift of appreciation, and individualized gift baskets thoughtfully express gratitude.

For the officiant, consider a basket that includes faith-inspired books of poetry, along with bookmarks and stationery. Add a few wrapped candies or other accents to give the basket flair. For the pianist or soloist, try a basket of teas with a musically themed cup or mug, and for the crochet-loving guest-book attendant, choose a basket of colorful yarns.

Gift baskets generously fill the role of thank-you gifts for attendants and helpers, but also excel as welcome gifts for out-of-town guests and as "We Love You" gifts for grandmothers and other dear hearts, especially when they include photos and meaningful items from the wedding couple's lives.

It's not necessary to think big. Small gift baskets fashioned by your own hand, and finished in colorful plastic wrap and a friendly bow, are every bit as enjoyable as professionally created baskets.

#416 *Groom Grooming by the Best Man*

Spearheading the bachelor party isn't the best man's most monumental task. Getting a spit-polished groom to the altar is. The months leading up to the wedding day are as physically important to the groom as to the bride, and it's a time for the best man to shine as the groom's "right arm."

Wedding preparation includes playing sports and working out together for fitness and relaxation. Exercise not only instills a sense of health, it clears the head and settles anxiety, making it a great ally in the war against wedding-day nerves.

An effective best man monitors the groom's schedule to ensure that dental, barber, and manicure appointments are kept. Great smiles take time to achieve, and any fixing, cleaning, or whitening should be done well in advance of the big day. The last haircut should be about a week ahead, so it doesn't have that "overly fresh-cut" look. And a prewedding manicure is ignored at great peril, since a groom's hands receive almost as much wedding-day scrutiny as the bride's.

Grooming the groom is not the best man's only responsibility, but it is the one with the greatest wedding-day payoff.

#417 *Bridesmaids Need Essentials, Too*

Just as the bride needs "stuff" with her on her wedding day, so do her bridesmaids. A lipstick, comb, tissues, powder, etc., need to be within reach for every attendant, but bridesmaids' needs are often overlooked. As a thoughtful gesture, provide them with coordinated bags.

Fabric drawstring bags are ideal, and they're easily made at home. A round of fabric, a drawstring-cord handle, and some stitching, and it's done. A small bag that slips over the wrist holds important essentials and accents the bridesmaid's ensemble.

Give an identical bag to all women of the wedding party, or add visual interest by making each one unique in fabric, color, or pattern.

#418 *The "Wedding Party" Party*

There's the bachelor party, the bachelorette party, the bridal or couples shower, and the rehearsal dinner, but none of those is just a cut-loose time for wedding-party members only. Wedding attendants have plenty of before-the-wedding and during-the-wedding responsibilities, and it's nice to acknowledge their commitment with a day of fun meant just for you and them.

Make it as informal as you wish, like a cocktail hour after work or a Saturday-morning breakfast. Or make a more dramatic splash. Introduce an element of spirited team rivalry, like a photo scavenger hunt — the bride and her attendants on one side versus the groom and his attendants on the other. The head of the losing team buys the drinks or springs for the pizza.

No matter how large or how small, your exclusive party opens the door to new bonds. That's a welcome benefit for all wedding-party members, who will be a happier and cohesive group on your wedding-day.

#419 *Sore-Thumb Attire*

There's a general rule of thumb when it comes to attire for the wedding party: don't stand out. No one on either side of the wedding couple should steal attention from the bride and groom. But religious dictates, cultural beliefs, and affiliations with uniformed entities, like the military, police, or firefighters, may preclude a harmonious look at the altar.

It's understandable that a naval officer might wish to wear his dress uniform instead of a tuxedo in his role as best man, or that a particularly devout bridesmaid might frown at putting flowers in her hair or wearing that strapless attendant dress you fell in love with.

To prevent one person from standing out like a dashingly attired sore thumb, you have two choices. One, allow all wedding-party members to express individuality, thereby reducing the impact of a lone person's differences. Two, be direct. Before inviting him or her to be in the wedding party, ask if following your wedding-attire wishes will create an uncomfortable personal issue.

You have the right to create the wedding look of your dreams, but you also have a responsibility to consider the feelings of those you care about. Addressing the issue up front wards off problems. Unless you're asking your attendants to wear something offensive, they will likely acquiesce to your wishes. If they don't, ask yourself what is more important: having that person with you as you marry or ensuring the look you really want? There's no wrong answer. There's only your honest preference.

#420 *Someone to Look Up To*

Think about it. The very grown-up bride gets an escort down the aisle, as do her equally mature attendants. The mighty groom stands at the altar, supported by his vanguard of able groomsmen. Only the tiniest, youngest attendants — the ring bearer and the flower girl — are asked to brave the long walk down the aisle alone. Does that seem fair?

Some flower girls and ring bearers will have no issue with that lonesome trek, but others may find it terrifying. If you have young ones who may experience fear instead of excitement as they face that solo journey, give them someone to look up to. Give them a grown-up escort of their own. A big brother or sister, a favorite cousin, a grandpa or grandma, or anyone the child feels comfortable with will do the trick. The older person grandly escorts the child down the aisle then simply takes a seat when finished. With someone to look up to, no tiny attendant will have to be the only one to walk alone, and no precious little face will have to grow wet with tears of anxiety.

#421 *An Act to Be Honored*

While the bride's escort is not considered an attendant, this individual is a very important part of the wedding party, and an even more important part of the bride's life. Whether this person is a father, brother, or uncle or even a special aunt, sister, cousin, or friend, the responsibility of walking the bride down the aisle is special.

Consider commemorating that role with the creation of a special lapel pin or brooch. It doesn't have to be elaborate — just a customized pin that can be worn on the wedding day, and any day thereafter as wished. It could bear a symbol of the wedding with the date engraved below it or a private message of love from the bride.

The father of the bride is the traditional escort, and a father both swells with pride and winces with loss on his daughter's wedding day. The thoughtful gesture of creating and giving a lasting token of the experience is a simple but meaningful way to say, "Thank you, and I love you."

#422 *Hello? I'm Hungry!*

Brides and grooms get so consumed by the wedding day that they often don't eat. That's understandable. You're nervous. But your attendants aren't racked with nerves, and they need sustenance. Wedding couples often plan the day down to the finest detail but never address feeding their attendants throughout the day. Food at the reception is a given, but bridesmaids and groomsmen invest many hours in the wedding day before it's time to dine at the reception.

Feed them. Make sure there is a generous spread of healthy snacks and bottled waters in both the bride's and the groom's dressing rooms. Whether it's muffins and fruit or a six-foot deli sandwich, be sure there is enough for everyone to enjoy. Don't let the "music" underscoring your vows to be the loud gurgling of hungry bellies.

#423 *Honor Parade*

Do you come from a big family with more nephews and nieces than you can shake a stick at? Instead of choosing to honor just two of them with the positions of flower girl and ring bearer, include them all by making them banner bearers.

Think about the award banners that precede the floats in the Rose Parade. Now imagine two little guys carrying a "Very Special Bridesmaids" banner before your attendants make their way down the aisle, or a "Sweet and Honorable Maid of Honor" banner before the maid of honor's entrance. For announcing the bride's arrival, choose a traditional message, like "Here Comes the Bride" or something clever that will amuse guests (and soothe your nerves in the bargain), like "Best in Show — Her Honor, the Bride."

The banners can say whatever you wish them to say, and they can be carried by any number of children. You can expand the banners to include the arrival of the flower girl and ring bearer, the seating of the parents, or the entrance of the groom and his groomsmen. It's your parade. Make the banners traditionally formal or delightfully fun to reflect the mood of the day.

#424 *Fido and Fifi down the Aisle*

Pets are members of the family, and it's not uncommon for brides and grooms to want to include precious critters in the wedding. Jennifer Hudson, Montel Williams, Gwen Stefani, Adam Sandler, and Ellen DeGeneres are just of a few of the many who have incorporated beloved pets into the wedding ceremony.

Whether it's a horseback ride for the bride and groom, a canine ring bearer, lovebirds on a swing, or a potbellied pig giving the bride away, there's always a way to include a pet who will enjoy the experience and not be frightened.

To make it work, you will need to choose a pet-friendly venue, socialize the animal to crowds, noise, and sudden movements, designate someone the animal knows to be your pet handler (to see to care, food, water, and restroom needs), and make arrangements for the pet to be returned safely to its home long before the day's events are over.

While a single wedding rehearsal is usually sufficient for human wedding party members to learn their ceremonial roles, a pet may need a bit more practice to learn what is expected of him. Patience and love are key.

Pets are the ultimate wedding personalization, and it's important to remember that the wedding day belongs to the bride and groom. If having Fido or Fifi at the wedding is important, don't worry about how others may view your decision. Nothing is worse than a wedding with regrets.

#425 *Big-Boy Rings*

Sometimes little guys want to feel like big guys, and carrying a fluffy pillow just doesn't cut it. Fortunately, there's no law that says ring bearers must deliver rings on something that's soft, satiny, and adorned with bows. Flower girls routinely carry something they get to keep, while the ring bearer's go home empty-handed. But if little Johnny conveyed those rings to the altar in the back of a toy truck, in a sand pail, or tied to the handle of an intergalactic light saber, he would feel like the king of the universe. Whatever boy-friendly item you choose can also be decorated to reflect your wedding theme, and in the end, you still get the ceremonial delivery of the rings, while the little guy feels ten feet tall bringing them to you.

#426 *Superheroes and Fairy Princesses*

Small children traditionally rate wearing fancy clothes right up there with eating their spinach. It's just not fun. And a ring bearer or flower girl spending the day tugging and frowning at their clothes is definitely not fun for the bride and groom. So why not let the young ones look great and be kids, too?

Add a black satin cape to the little guy's tuxedo, and he's no longer just a ring bearer. He's the RING BEARER SUPERHERO OF THE WORLD! A delicate set of wings turns your flower girl into a fairy princess right out of her storybooks. Suddenly, those fancy clothes are not only tolerated, they're wholeheartedly embraced. And with grumpiness averted, you'll enjoy more delightful photo opportunities and even sweeter memories.

#427 *Flower Girl or Bridesmaid?*

It's an age-old dilemma: What do you do with girls in the wedding party who seem too old to be flower girls but are just too young to be bridesmaids? There are no age restrictions in any wedding-party job description, but having a bridesmaid too young to wear the more adult attire and attend bridesmaid events can cause unnecessary complications. And while a ten-year-old girl could still be a flower girl, she may not be eager to accept the role at what she considers to be her advanced age. You could call her a junior bridesmaid, but that implies an involvement in bridesmaid functions. The perfect solution may be to give her a distinction all her own and call her your Bridal Belle or Bridal Miss.

This would be an honorary position, and as with most honorary positions, it's all about the title. But that doesn't mean you can't create some special perks and fun responsibilities to go along with the title. For example, your Bridal Belle could be delegated the honor of being your personal executive assistant during the dressing process on the wedding day. If someone knocks on the door asking to see you, they would have to ask your Bridal Belle first. Or if you wished to send a note to the groom's room, only your Bridal Belle would be entrusted to deliver it. She would wear an age-appropriate outfit that complements the bridesmaids' dresses, make the walk down the aisle just before the flower girl and ring bearer, and stand with the bridesmaids at the altar or take her seat with her parents, according to your preference. A special title means something to a young girl, and it relieves you of trying to figure out how to have a ten-year-old at the bachelorette party.

#428 *Young Fun*

Sometimes the youngest wedding-party members suffer from prewedding neglect. There's the engagement party, shower, bridesmaids' luncheon, bachelorette and bachelor parties, and so on. But these events are all for adults. What about the little ones? Where's their party? If you are having young people act as flower girl, ring bearer, train bearers, candle lighters, etc., why not show them some prewedding love, too?

One of the best things a wedding couple can do to help ensure the success of their wedding day is to get to know the children who will be participating. Take them to the beach, an arcade, or an amusement park, or just throw a party at your home for them and their parents, making the children the guests of honor. You can give the occasion wedding overtones, but the real theme is enjoyment and bonding. A get-together is especially helpful if there are young ones with whom you don't interact on a regular basis. The better they know and like you, the better they will perform on your wedding day. And more important, you will be properly thanking them for their participation, in a way that makes them feel as valued as their adult wedding-party counterparts.

#429 *Smiling in the Rain*

Are you marrying in a rainy spot? Rain can happen just about anywhere, but for some areas, it's pretty much a given. In many cultures, rain on the wedding day is considered good luck. But good luck aside, no bride wants to dampen that gorgeous gown.

Umbrellas are practical necessities, but if you think ahead, there's no reason those umbrellas can't be just as fabulous as the rest of your wedding-day attire. Leave the formal black versions to the men's side, and treat yourself and your bridesmaids to umbrellas that will actually add to the photo ops, not detract from them. Be bold and creative when choosing the bridesmaids' designs — the ladies' umbrellas don't have to be plain white. And for you, a colorful, heart-shaped or flower-shaped umbrella that frames you and your white gown in the rain can be downright gorgeous. Staying beautiful and dry is the goal. But even if the rain decides to hold off, you'll still have an extraordinary, photo-friendly prop you can later take to the reception, where guests can have photos made with it, too!

#430 *Sweet Spa Treatment*

Need a fun, functional, "extra something" gift for bridesmaids? Consider a comfy, luxurious salon robe.

During wedding preparations, it's nice to have something soft to slip on in the dressing room, when hair and makeup are the focal points. Salon robes are available in a range of prices. To make them even more special, create a personalized iron-on transfer on your computer, then iron one onto each robe. The designs could be all the same, or you could make each one unique to its recipient.

The robes protect clothing and provide modesty, and your dressing-room photos will show the camaraderie of the bride's team! There's always a good reason to don a salon robe, even at home, and bridesmaids will get to keep their robes to do just that.

#431 *Shuffle Up!*

If you're looking for an original gift for wedding-party members, give them a custom deck of playing cards. Any photo can be used to make cards, and the cards don't have to feel cheap and flimsy. Even Bicycle, one of the largest, oldest, and most respected card makers, creates quality decks of cards with whatever image you send them.

Make the cards wedding themed, poignant, or silly, but feature the wedding party as the focus of the photo, not necessarily the bride and groom. Perhaps you could choose a shot of you and the bridesmaids from the shower or from a dress-shopping excursion, and for the guys, perhaps the perfect choice is a photo of the groom and his attendants enjoying a Sunday afternoon football game. Imagine how surprised your wedding party will be to open their gifts and see their own smiling mugs staring back at them. It's not a frilly or elegant gift, but it's a great way to commemorate an important moment in time with an item that's fun for everyone.

#432 *Little Elegance*

Most girls, even little ones, love jewelry. If all of the bridesmaids will be wearing necklaces, chances are your flower girl will be longing for one, too. Make her necklace special. Choose a pretty locket and an appropriately sized chain. Well in advance of the wedding day, ask your florist for discarded petals representing the flowers that will be included in your bouquets. (Florists always have torn petals littering the workroom, and a few petals may as well go to you, rather than end up in the compost heap.) Press and dry the petals, then secure bits of them in a filigree locket to create a unique "flower girl only" necklace any young miss will love to wear. Locket contents can be changed as desired, and there's no reason your special little flower girl shouldn't have jewelry she can grow with.

#433 *Bold and Beautiful!*

Small, delicate earrings are generally the rule of thumb for bridesmaids, but should those earrings ever be big and bold instead? Of course! If the bridesmaids' dresses are already tailored to accent the neckline, and flattering, upswept hairdos are the plan, then bigger, more attention-grabbing earrings can replace a necklace and artistically complete the ensemble. Larger earrings, paired with hair that's drawn back from the face, take on a whole new decorative purpose, graduating from a subtle, supporting role to a starring one. When chosen with care, big, beautiful earrings can make the presentation of your bridal party especially unique and dazzling.

REHEARSAL
DINNER

CHAPTER SEVEN • *Rehearsal Dinner*

The wedding is imminent, you've practiced your "stand here" and "walk there" movements, and everyone in the wedding party knows exactly how to execute their wedding-day roles. You've done all you can to prepare. Now it's time to give stress the boot and embrace the pleasure of good company at your rehearsal dinner.

The rehearsal dinner is the perfect informal foil to the formal wedding day. You're gathered together with the wedding party, family members, and hand-selected guests. Forget the pomp and circumstance. Enjoy yourself!

In this chapter, you'll find ideas for entertainment, locations, décor, and other rehearsal-dinner considerations. A rehearsal dinner isn't the biggest star in the wedding show, but it is a valuable supporting player. There's every reason to fill the event with fun and intimate camaraderie.

The rulebook has been rewritten. As with every other aspect of a wedding, long-standing traditions aren't necessarily as cherished as they once were. Traditions are important if you wish them to be, but if you long to design a rehearsal dinner that doesn't follow customary dictates, do so. There is no one to prevent you, even if the bride and groom aren't hosting the event. The groom's parents have traditionally paid for and hosted the rehearsal dinner, but many modern wedding couples do it on their own, and with that responsibility comes a tremendous freedom to create a rehearsal dinner like no other. Even if the groom's parents pay for and host the dinner, feel free to express your desires to them. They can't know what you'd like if you don't speak up.

If the rehearsal dinner comes with delectable food, great conversation, a toast, and some fun surprises, it's a winner — no matter what venue, décor, and activities you choose.

#434 *Come on Down!*

The rehearsal-dinner guest list can grow like a weed if not closely watched. But you don't have to invite the whole world. The "must haves" include the members of the wedding party and their spouses, all parents, and the officiant plus his or her spouse. The "maybe" invites include house-party members, out-of-town guests, and anyone else you ask to join in.

Factor the "must haves" into the budget, then see if funds exist to accommodate the "maybe" invites. Don't feel bad for not inviting those not specifically involved in the rehearsal if you can't afford to do so.

On the other hand, instead of serving a pricey, formal dinner to a few guests, throw an old-fashioned backyard barbeque or a picnic in the park, and you can feed twice the number of people at a cost comparable to a smaller, sit-down function.

The rehearsal dinner is about friendly mingling and thanking those who help make the wedding day spectacular. Restrict the guest list as necessary, then concentrate on making the occasion the most enjoyable and relaxing wedding-day prelude ever.

#435 *Flexible Restaurants*

Rehearsal dinners commonly take place in restaurants, but if possible, choose a restaurant with an eye toward flexibility.

Unlike the more formal reception dinner, rehearsal dinners are pretty easygoing. Selecting a restaurant that will embrace an extension of your dinner-party hours, or your sudden desire to order an extra round of snacks not included in the original meal arrangements, can reap appreciated dividends.

If you choose a quiet night for your rehearsal dinner, the restaurant is more likely to be adaptable. Don't expect any restaurant to let you go with the flow if it's the establishment's prime dinner night. Some will be more amenable than others. You simply have to ask about flexibility before making a reservation. When all is said and done, you'll be glad you thought to book a restaurant that's willing to bend a little.

#436 *Sit Here*

Are assigned seats necessary for rehearsal dinners? No. On the other hand, they have their advantages. With assigned seating, the burden is not on the guest to decide whom to sit next to, and guests who arrive late never have to interrupt the festivities by scouring for an empty seat.

Assigned seats also smooth the proceedings by coinciding with a predetermined order of toasts, making it less likely that someone is forgotten. Clever table place cards add to the party atmosphere and provide a memento for the scrapbook.

Rehearsal-dinner assigned seating is not imperative, but it does come with some very nice perks.

#437 Who's the Boss?

Generally speaking, persons bearing the cost of the rehearsal dinner are permitted to design it any way they see fit. The bride and groom may not have the final word on what transpires, but in most cases their wishes are considered.

If the wedding couple is paying for the rehearsal dinner, it will naturally include whatever features they desire. But what if the costs are shared? If, for example, the bride and groom are kicking in some dollars, but the groom's parents are shouldering the bulk of the expense, who's the boss?

When more than one head full of ideas is involved, conflicts can ensue. If the groom's mother wants to restrict toasts to only select guests, but the bride wants to open the floor to all, it can be especially difficult to reach a compromise if one party is paying a larger portion of rehearsal-dinner costs. That party may feel entitled to the final say. But while there is no rule of etiquette that clearly defines duties by monetary split, and common sense may indicate that whoever pays more gets to say more, the happiness of the wedding couple should always be the primary concern.

Even if the wedding couple isn't contributing any money at all to the rehearsal dinner, no host or hostess should insist on any feature that would cause the bride and groom dismay. That doesn't mean that the wedding couple has the right to add expense through special requests, but it means that, on issues of utmost importance, the bride and groom get to have the final word.

#438 Rehearsal-Dinner Budget Savers

Sometimes there's little left in the budget for the rehearsal dinner, and even when the dinner tab is being picked up by a traditional host, like the groom's family, looking for ways to save can be important. Here are a few alternatives that easily cut costs down to size:

- Hold the dinner at home instead of at a commercial facility.
- Serve filling comfort foods like pasta instead of meats.
- Serve only wine and beer instead of mixed cocktails.

- Serve home-baked desserts instead of purchased delicacies.
- Hire local cheerleaders or marching-band members to act as your "catering and clean-up staff" in exchange for a donation to their group's fund-raising effort.
- Move the dinner outdoors, where paper and plastic goods can comfortably replace china and silver.
- Utilize readily available seasonal décor, like pumpkins in the fall or wildflowers in the spring.
- Handcraft your own favors.
- Plan well ahead to take advantage of sales, and shop at bulk warehouse stores for rehearsal-dinner essentials.
- Set budget priorities and forgo those things that cost money but simply don't matter that much.

Even a cost-saving choice for just one or two issues can help keep the budget from overinflating. And your guests won't even give it a thought if you serve a delicious pasta primavera instead of filet mignon.

#439 *A Change of Seasons*

There's no rule stating that the rehearsal dinner has to have the same theme as the wedding, so why not take this opportunity to surprise your dinner guests with something completely different?

If it's the dead of winter and everyone is freezing, choose a beach theme for the rehearsal dinner, complete with coconut drinks and swaying palms. If it's the sweltering, stifling, dog days of August, consider winter-wonderland décor or traditional holiday foods, served buffet style at a rented ice-skating rink.

A change of seasons for the rehearsal dinner is easily achieved, and unexpected merriment is its priceless payoff.

#440 *For Your Favor*

A limited guest list for the rehearsal dinner makes it a more intimate gathering than a wedding reception, and intimate tokens of remembrance are fitting.

Ready-made favors are acceptable, but handmade treasures may mean more. From a custom-crafted bookmark to a homemade delectable treat, the rehearsal-dinner favor is a tangible way for the bride and groom to say thank you.

Favors do not have to match. In fact, customizing gifts for specific recipients shows a great deal of caring on the part of the bride and groom. Spending a certain amount is not important, since the quality of a thank-you is not measured in dollars and cents. It's measured by sincerity.

Give favors to all in attendance, even wedding-party members who will also receive attendant gifts. Personalize them with handmade hangtags, and don't be shy. The rehearsal dinner is the perfect time to wear your gratitude on your sleeve.

#441 *Here's to You!*

The host or hostess of the rehearsal dinner (the one who pays for it) traditionally makes the first toast. If the groom's parents foot the bill for the event, the father of the groom offers the first toast to the wedding couple. Toasts by other parents and wedding-party members can follow, but before all is said and done, the bride and groom should seize the opportunity to stand and deliver.

Individual, from-the-heart toasts to those who helped you reach this monumental moment are well deserved. Choose to toast only your parents and the maid of honor and best man, or take the time to toast everyone for their contribution.

A toast is about caring, and caring should not be directed only toward the bride and groom. It should also emanate from them, and the rehearsal dinner is the ideal platform with which to bring the appreciation and well wishes full circle.

#442 *Roses or Robots?*

Invite guests to the rehearsal dinner with an informal phone call, or send an invitation two to three weeks ahead of the dinner. If a printed invitation is your choice, feel free to make it playful.

Unlike the traditional formality of a wedding invitation, a rehearsal-dinner invite can be carefree and fun. Bride-and-groom cartoon characters with dialogue bubbles imply "good times ahead!" Cowboy boots and lassos indicate a casual, country-style affair, perfect for a barbeque or a dinner at a down-home bar and grill.

The invitation sets whatever tone you desire. If a formal rehearsal dinner is the goal, a border of delicate roses is an option. But if the rehearsal dinner is meant to be more free spirited, a robot wedding couple beaming your invitation details in a futuristic font sets the stage for out-of-this-world laughs.

#443 *Attendant-Gift Presentation*

The rehearsal dinner is the time to thank your attendants with a gift. It's perfectly fine to give identical gifts to all bridesmaids or to all groomsmen, but the maid of honor and best man should receive unique gifts commensurate with their honored roles in the wedding party.

Gifts do not have to be expensive, but they should be thoughtful. Personalized gifts with etched monograms or embroidered names are always welcome. Unfortunately, many wedding couples inscribe their own monogram or their own names, in the mistaken belief that it makes the gift more memorable. Don't do it. Personalized gifts for wedding attendants should include the attendants' names or initials, not those of the bride and groom.

Give the gifts to wedding-party members after dinner dishes have been cleared. If you plan on toasting bridesmaids or groomsmen, the distribution of the gifts is a perfect time to do so.

#444 *Stirring the Pot*

For a great, interactive rehearsal-dinner experience, throw a fondue dinner party.

Fondue has been popular since the 19th century. It's attraction is not only the delightful taste of the melted cheese or the luscious chocolate, it's also the interaction and playfulness of the dipping and eating experience.

Use several pots that feature different flavors of cheeses for dipping breads, vegetables, etc. Some pots can hold creamy, light-to-dark flavors of chocolate for dipping cake squares, fruits, and other dessert morsels. A third style of fondue pot holds hot oil for quick-frying meats or tempura vegetables. Choose any or all of these fondue options to create a fabulous rehearsal dinner.

Plenty of delicious fondue recipes are available online and in cookbooks, and if purchasing the pots is not desirable, rentals are available. To ensure a sanitary and healthful experience, give each guest a dipping fork for each style of pot and a separate eating fork for consuming the food.

Rehearsal dinners are about unwinding and having fun, and fondue has a way of inspiring both.

#445 *A Room with a View*

If your wedding rehearsal happens to coincide with a major or minor league home game, it may be time to think "inside" the box for the rehearsal dinner!

Renting a skybox at a stadium or indoor arena can result in the rehearsal dinner of a lifetime. Skyboxes come with seats for viewing the action, as well as wide-screen TVs and facilities for food and drinks. Inside a private skybox, you'll enjoy toasting to your heart's content, dining on whatever delectables you've selected, and wandering over to view a touchdown, a grand slam, a slam dunk, or an amazing slide of a puck between a goalie's legs. And if sports aren't your passion, those same skyboxes are available during concerts and other entertainments.

Making a spectacular sporting event or a great concert the backdrop for your rehearsal dinner will score plenty of gratitude points. Most skybox rentals include a block of tickets, and most deals are negotiable.

Rehearsal dinners don't have to be all about the wedding all of the time, and there's nothing like a room with a view.

#446 *Celebrity Roast*

Brides and grooms are wedding celebrities, and what's more fun than roasting a celebrity? Rehearsal dinners are perfect venues for a good old-fashioned roast of the bride and groom. Toasts are nice, but roasts are a hoot! Keep the insults light, the tributes heartfelt, and the inspired falsehoods heavy on the humor.

To allow time to hone their roasting skills and prepare their material, rehearsal-dinner invitees should receive plenty of advance notice that a roast is on the agenda. To avoid real embarrassment, you should also let everyone know that you've given the roast a movie-style "rating" — G, PG, or, for the brave of heart, R. Take into account where the rehearsal dinner will be held. Roasts are laugh-out-loud events, so holding one smack-dab in the center of a fine-dining restaurant may not be the best choice.

#447 *Sentimental Journey*

When considering rehearsal-dinner locations, look first to the wedding couple's history. Holding the rehearsal dinner where the couple first met, first kissed, or became engaged allows the bride and groom to relive a special moment, as they share the memory with guests close to their hearts.

Let the location be your guide to the rehearsal dinner's style. Weave the attributes of the location into décor, food, and entertainment choices. First kiss at the beach? Sand-sculpture centerpieces. Met at a bar? Re-create the music and the drinks of the evening. Said "yes" to the proposal at dinner? Serve the same meal.

Taking a sentimental journey as part of the rehearsal-dinner celebration is a unique way to include friends and family in a life-changing event they were unable to attend the first time around.

#448 *Movie Magic*

Take the rehearsal dinner to the movies by bringing your own.

Today's video recorders are small enough to fit inside everything from a ballpoint pen to a cell phone, so there's no reason not to document every moment of the wedding-planning process. And when all of those hours of footage are pared down to a highlight reel, there is no better time to share it than at the rehearsal dinner.

The events that led to the day before the wedding are sure to have as many funny moments as poignant ones, and a visual stroll down memory lane is entertaining for everyone. All you need is the DVD movie you've made, a TV screen or computer, and a DVD player. Most banquet facilities have multimedia equipment, but if your venue doesn't, it's easy enough to bring it along.

For an especially effective movie, use short scenes. No one needs to see the gown being hemmed or the groom's entire haircut. Be brief. Be selective. Be creative!

#449 *Karaoke on the Half Shell*

Like finding a jumbo black pearl in your oyster, karaoke at the rehearsal dinner will bring a giant smile to your face.

Karaoke is a musical smorgasbord that peels away inhibitions and lets every guest's inner diva shine. Whether it's country or heavy metal, everyone has a secret repertoire of songs they're just dying to unleash. And that's the beauty of karaoke. It doesn't matter in the least if you can sing a note. Good and bad voices are equally entertaining!

Some guests might balk at warbling in front of a room full of strangers, but going to a karaoke bar isn't necessary. Karaoke machines are portable and reasonably priced. Pick one up. Add some music, and you're ready to give rehearsal-dinner guests their prime-time moment in the spotlight.

#450 *Let Them Eat Cake . . . Early*

Lots of attention is paid to the wedding cake, and rightly so. But there's no reason to wait to taste something spectacular. Let the rehearsal dinner showcase the wild and wacky cake you would have designed if elegance wasn't so important to the wedding day.

A rehearsal-dinner cake can share dreams and aspirations with dinner guests, such as the wedding couple's desire to someday climb Mt. Everest. Or it can playfully denote conflicting passions, like her favorite and his favorite rival sports teams. The cake is a messenger, and messages both sincere and fanciful will hit the mark.

Rehearsal-dinner cakes are much smaller than wedding cakes, but there's no reason they can't be as awe-inspiring as they are delicious.

#451 *Game On!*

Games at the rehearsal dinner can turn an ordinary meal into an adventure. Whether it's a wedding-themed murder mystery, a culinary scavenger hunt, or a classic round of charades, games provide high spirits.

Guest interaction can sometimes stall when conversation is the only entertainment, but give a guest a role to play or a task involving mental or physical exercise, and the atmosphere in the room suddenly sparks.

Prizes are nice, and clever mementos are created by matching the prize to the game, like a faux detective shield for the murder-mystery winner, or bride- and groom-signed pocket dictionaries for the winning charades team.

Rehearsal-dinner games don't have to be extravagant. Some of the simplest games guarantee tried-and-true fun every single time they're played.

#452 *At-Home Slow-Cook Fever*

There's little that can't be made deliciously in a slow cooker, and with the hustle and bustle of wedding planning, an at-home rehearsal dinner is a breeze when blessed with stuff-it-and-leave-it cooking.

Early in the day, fill the cookers with everything from seasoned sloppy joes and savory stews to a luscious pot roast, then go ahead and decorate the church or put those finishing touches on the bridal veil. The slow cooker's fringe benefit is the gift of time to do other things.

There are thousands of slow-cooker recipes to choose from, and appetizers, entrées, and desserts are equally suited to the slow-cook method. Borrow extra cookers from family and friends if need be to create a variety of great fare for the rehearsal-dinner celebration. Toss a cool salad, add a cold relish tray, and you're done. Food will be hot when it's time to eat, and your at-home rehearsal dinner will inspire a relaxing good time without requiring you to spend all day in the kitchen.

#453 *Guess Who?*

Rehearsal dinners don't have to be fancy, just enjoyable. So while you might not wish to use a paper place mat at the wedding reception, doing so at the rehearsal dinner can be an inspired choice.

Create a list of questions that revolve around the bride, groom, wedding party, family, and anyone else who may attend the rehearsal dinner. Make the questions fun, like "Who only wears blue socks?" or "Who won their elementary school's perfect-attendance award?" Weave a bit of wedding artwork around the questions, then print them onto 11" x 17" paper of any color to create quick, one-of-a-kind placemats.

Guesses will begin to fly as soon as guests are seated. Use the place mats as conversation starters, or make it a more organized event by giving everyone a pen with which to jot down guesses next to the questions. Later reveal the correct answers, and award a prize to the winner. Compose a few extra questions not listed on the place mat to use as verbal tiebreakers. Expect plenty of shared laughs as you ask and answer your way to a sole winner.

#454 *Guess Who's Coming to Dinner?*

Remember how excited you were as a child when Halloween was coming, and all you could think about was who or what you were going to "be"? Costume parties come with extra entertainment value, and the childlike excitement of becoming someone else isn't any less fun when you're all grown up. So why not throw a costume-party rehearsal dinner?

The rehearsal dinner is a time to shake off all the wedding-planning stress and settle your wedding-day nerves before they twist you into a knot. Friends and family in costumes do the trick. Costumes release inhibitions and break the ice, and no one ever has to worry that they aren't dressed "appropriately" for the event.

Give rehearsal-dinner guests plenty of notice, and give them a theme. You don't want a ghost showing up with a Santa Claus. Or do you? It's your rehearsal-dinner party. Invite all the ghosts, scientists, celebrities, literary geniuses, or nursery-rhyme characters you wish. A costume-party rehearsal dinner is your world to design.

#455 *The Rehearsal Dinner That Isn't*

A traditional rehearsal dinner takes place after the rehearsal, but there's no law that prohibits you from hosting a rehearsal "lunch," "brunch," "breakfast," or "picnic" instead. Organize your rehearsal day any way you wish. Holding the gathering earlier in the day gives you more time the night before your wedding to tend to last-minute details or to relax and clear your mind. This is often beneficial to your venue as well. Churches and other ceremony sites must frequently juggle different wedding parties into tight rehearsal slots, because most choose late afternoon to rehearse. A morning rehearsal followed by a picnic in the park, a luncheon, a brunch, or a breakfast may be just the ticket to opening up your wedding eve to other pleasant options. Besides, not having a big meal the evening before your wedding can be a very good thing.

#456 *Name That Wine!*

For a creative icebreaker at the rehearsal dinner, enlist everyone's assistance in naming your wine for the night. Peel the label from a wine bottle before the dinner starts, and set the bottle on the table. Give each guest a large, blank peel-and-stick label along with a supply of colored pens to share, and ask each to create a wine label to honor the bride and groom's wedding, complete with a name, a logo, and their signature in one corner.

When all guests are finished, the bride and groom will read all of the entries aloud as if they are being judged. No doubt, some labels will be affectionate and some will be funny. But instead of actually choosing a lone standout, you will deem it impossible to decide, and you'll declare everyone a winner. With a flourish, affix every last label to the bottle, covering it completely. Pop the cork and share the wine, and at the end of the night, take the bottle home, shellac it, and turn it into a vase or candle holder full of rehearsal-dinner memories. If you want to reward the guests with a prize for their efforts, give everyone a keepsake corkscrew or bottle stopper as a rehearsal-dinner memento.

#457 *Chefs in the House*

With the unstoppable popularity of the Food Network, it would seem that men, women, and children are eager to test their culinary acumen. So let them! Pick a small restaurant for your rehearsal dinner, and rent out the entire facility. Tell the restaurant that you want to give everyone a taste of true chef magic by allowing each guest to contribute to the meal preparation. Just pick one or two exotic dishes that guests would not usually experience, and give each person one small task in making that dish.

It can be pretty funny to see Dad trying to turn a radish into a flower, or to watch the best man shucking corn. You shouldn't choose jobs that involve danger, like cooking over an open flame or filleting a salmon. Leave those tasks to the actual restaurant chef and his staff. But everyone, young and old, will find a certain pleasure and satisfaction in eating a meal they had a hand in creating. And the perfect take-home gift is a bride-and-groom-inspired apron. Making everyone an honorary chef is an activity that produces entertainment and delectable fare, and it also puts the "dinner" in "rehearsal dinner."

#458 *The Easy, Breezy Buffet*

For a few dollars per person, you can cater your rehearsal dinner with beverages and pizza or hoagies and chips, or perhaps something a bit more substantial if you cook it yourself. Or, for about the same amount of money, you can invite everyone to the private banquet room of a buffet restaurant. Your guests will have to serve themselves, but the choices will be vast. And with a private room, you can still enjoy all of the traditional rehearsal-dinner toasts and activities.

Not all buffets are created equal, so before choosing, dine there more than once to gauge the quality of the food, the level of service, and the restaurant's cleanliness and décor. Whether you select a nationally known buffet like Golden Corral or a mom-and-pop buffet with a name that only locals would recognize, privacy is important. If there is no private room or you cannot at least have a corner location separated by plants or screens, the festivities may feel muted. Fortunately, private dining areas for large parties are the norm, not the exception.

A casual buffet allows everyone to let their hair down and fill their bellies with oodles of delicious choices. And it's a one-price-fits-all option that helps keep rehearsal-dinner costs from spiraling out of control.

#459 *Centerpiece Clouds*

To avoid the expense of floral arrangements at the rehearsal dinner, yet still have tables that look pretty and inviting, consider soft-as-a-cloud cotton-candy centerpieces. Wispy cotton candy, displayed in a cut glass bowl and accented with edible butterflies, bumblebees, or greenery, is a creative and adorable centerpiece. It will look great when guests are arriving, and before they leave, it will be gone. All you'll have to take home are the bowls. A cotton-candy centerpiece is the ultimate disposable decoration and fanciful treat.

#460 *Frozen Fortitude*

Rehearsal dinners are the perfect venue for an ice-cream cake. Unlike the reception, the cake won't have to sit around for hours before cutting, and there's no need for a big production when the first slice is extracted. An ice-cream cake can also double as the groom's cake, which is often served at the rehearsal dinner. Order it from your favorite ice-cream shop, and assign someone to pick it up and deliver it to the rehearsal-dinner location. Just keep it on ice until it's time to serve.

Many wedding couples wish they could have an ice-cream cake for the wedding, but it's impractical in most reception situations. There is, however, no good reason to avoid an ice-cream cake altogether. The rehearsal dinner is one wedding event where cold and creamy can easily be the treat of the day.

#461 Dinner Dress Code

A common faux pas of the rehearsal-dinner invitation is not mentioning a dress code for guests. With any invitation to an event, guests benefit from knowing what is expected of them, and no one wants to show up overdressed or underdressed. That little embarrassment can easily be avoided by indicating your preference on the invite, such as "This rehearsal dinner is all about fun! Come as you are!" or "Cocktail attire is a perfect fit for our sunset rehearsal dinner." You simply need to share your guidelines in a congenial tone. Do so, and you'll get the ambiance you hoped for, while your guests will get peace-of-mind knowledge they can rely on.

#462 M&M's Cake Bake

Who doesn't love M&M's? And the Mars company, makers of M&M's, even offers customized candies for your special event. You can have them printed with your own message, likeness, or clever clip-art design. Or you can just go to the local grocery store and grab bags of traditional M&M's, and turn them into a game of "M&M's Top Wedding Baker" at your rehearsal dinner.

After the meal dishes are cleared, pass out bowls or bags of M&M's to each guest, ensuring that each gets the same amount of candies. Now give everyone five minutes to use those candies to build a wedding cake. It takes a steady hand to stack M&M's, so if there's been wine at dinner, the efforts will no doubt get even more hilarious. The cake shapes can be of any design, and the bride and groom will judge the results. Award a related, fitting prize to the winner, like a basket containing a cake mix and other ingredients needed to make a real cake or a gift certificate to a cake shop. Of course, everyone wins in the end, because all guests get to eat their building materials — those addictive little M&M's. An M&M's "cake bake" contest is easy, entertaining, and downright delicious.

#463 *Party Town*

If you're looking for an upbeat rehearsal dinner with lots of fun, check out restaurants where the fun is built in. National chain restaurants like Dave & Buster's offer food, drinks, ambiance, and plenty of games. A private dining room is a must for a rehearsal dinner, but after the dinner and related entertainments, guests who wish to wander off to play games can do so, while guests who just want to sit and visit can continue to chat.

Search your area for restaurants that offer games, dinner theater, or stage acts, then drop in for a meal to check them out. Never book a venue that you haven't personally visited to taste the food, listen to the noise, see the room, and ask questions about your private event. To ensure a great dinner, you need firsthand knowledge.

If you'd like to let someone else pitch in on the entertainment side of your rehearsal dinner, investigate the possibilities. Restaurants with such bonuses are waiting to assist.

Part Three

THE
DETAILS

STATIONERY

CHAPTER EIGHT • *Stationery*

I t's a common fact of life that no job is ever finished until the paperwork is done. But when that job is getting married, the paperwork had better be special!

There's more to wedding "paperwork" than wedding stationery. There are invitations, place cards, menu cards, programs, thank-you cards, announcements, save-the-date cards, escort cards, RSVPs, guest books, wedding certificates, and more. It's a long list.

This chapter addresses traditional printed materials as well as some unconventional alternatives. The way you present yourself on paper will affect how your guests perceive your wedding. You can spend a small fortune on fancy printed materials if you wish, but you don't have to. Elegance is just as easily incorporated through thrifty means. On the flip side, elegance isn't the only choice. You may wish to show your fun-loving personality, your unique area of interest, or your artsy, imaginative side instead. As the bride and the groom, you are the decision makers. You really can have it your way.

The stationery needs of a wedding may be vast, but no wedding couple should feel obligated to embrace every variety of wedding stationery. Aside from the invitations and the thank-yous, everything else, even if it's considered traditional and expected, is optional. Most wedding-related paper goods have valid reasons for existing, and their use adds to the overall wedding ambiance. But as you'll see, inventive alternatives are an easy way to reduce the expense of printed materials.

#464 *Your Own Wedding Stationery*

Wedding stationery can be personalized and purchased from any number of printers, but for stationery no other bride in the world could ever have, make your own.

Making paper from recycled scraps is a fairly simple process, and it's a fun way to involve the whole family, even children, in a prewedding project. Customize your paper by adding wedding-color threads or glitter, bits of dried flowers or grasses that represent your bridal bouquet, a bride-and-groom monogram cut from beautiful wrapping paper, or whatever other inventive accents you may find appealing.

Adding a bit of liquid starch to the paper mix mitigates bleeding in stationery used for writing.

Once the paper is dry, cut it into any shapes and sizes you need. "Uniquely you" handmade paper is ideal for invitation inserts, place or escort cards, or any number of other wedding communications. No two sheets will ever be truly identical, and that's makes the paper even more distinctive and beautiful.

#465 *The Paper Trail*

Wedding stationery includes any and all printed-paper products needed for the wedding. But to keep it straight and on target, use a system.

Set aside an area just for wedding paper products, and as each paper item arrives, mark the top and the end of the box with the "must be in the mail by" or "must be handled by" date. Stack boxes of stationery products according to date priorities. This prominently written clue serves as a deadline reminder for that particular stationery item, helping you stay on track for mailings or for hand-personalization tasks. Mismanaging timelines attached to save-the-dates, invitations, RSVPs, programs, place cards, etc., causes havoc when dealing with venues and vendors, who require specific information to do their jobs effectively.

Unlike other supplies easily kept in suitcases for transport to the event, you'll need ready access to stationery supplies from the moment they are acquired. Keeping all stationery items stacked in their boxes and dated in a timeline-driven, orderly fashion adds efficiency and reliability to the paperwork side of getting married.

#466 *Save the Date!*

Clever save-the-date notifications may have been designed by companies looking for yet another product to sell to wedding couples, but this product is worth its expense. Save-the-dates produce results, and they further the goal of perfect wedding-day attendance.

Do everyone a favor by giving both local and out-of-town guests as much notice as possible. Life is busy. Time off from work, vacation planning, babysitting, animal care, gift or clothes shopping, and rescheduling of appointments are just some of the issues wedding guests may need to address before your wedding. Sending a save-the-date reminder at least six months before the wedding benefits everyone. An e-mailed save-the-date message is easily forgotten, making the Internet a far less effective method of save-the-date delivery. A notification guests can actually hold in their hands does the job best.

#467 *Hang 10 ... or 500!*

Some wedding favors include personalized hangtags at no additional cost, but others charge a hefty fee for the tags. Thanks to today's quality at-home printers, you can avoid this unnecessary expense by making your own hangtags. It's easy!

A visit to your local office-supply store or a tour of online Web sites will produce plenty of templates and tag sheets for ink-jet or laser printers. Create your master in a word-processing program, and you're ready to print.

Some tag sheets come with predrilled holes, but for those that don't, a simple paper punch does the trick.

Another advantage of producing your own tags is that you'll never have to worry that the tags will arrive on your doorstep bearing the wrong information. You will, of course, be responsible if you make your own typos while preparing your tag art and text, so walk on the safe side. Have someone proof your work before you print.

#468 *Menu Cards with a Surprise*

Menu cards are not a wedding-reception requirement, but they are a gracious effort that adds to wedding-table décor. There is something quite sophisticated about an attractive, formal listing of the meal's delights. Utilizing a single, full-size, elegantly printed menu card for each table is acceptable, but to turn that menu card into something fun, consider individualizing it with a fortune-cookie influence.

Feature the menu courses, including preparation style or primary ingredients if you wish, on smaller cards you create yourself. In a bordered area at the bottom, in the style of a wedding-day Confucius, impart a bit of bride-and-groom wisdom, or lift the recipient's spirits with an impending good fortune. When each card is unique, an ordinary menu card becomes a keepsake.

Compose sayings that are funny or heartfelt, then mix or match them as you wish. Make some of them fortunes, some pearls of wisdom, and some funny reflections on the getting-married journey. Position a menu card at each place setting, and icebreaking conversations will no doubt ensue.

#469 *Wedding Programs with Zing*

There's nothing wrong with a traditional trifold wedding program, but there are other inventive program options to consider.

The elements of the program will be the same no matter how you deliver the information. If your wedding is on a hot summer day, a program printed on a paper hand fan is a thoughtful gesture. If you're an avid believer in "a picture is worth a thousand words," consider a miniature photo-album program. If either the bride or groom is blessed with artistic talent, a scrapbook-style program filled with original art could be "the one." And if you're all about the age of technology, consider a CD or DVD program. Make a mix tape of the wedding couple's favorite songs and burn them onto a CD, or create a DVD of wedding-preparation highlights. Enclose either in a CD case, and print the liner with the wedding program information. Guests will know the schedule of wedding events, and have something to look forward to at home.

Wedding programs give guests a sense of participation, and infusing the program with a little original zing never hurts.

#470 *Hog Wild and Regretful*

Before sending save-the-dates, finalize the guest list. A save-the-date means an invitation is imminent, and it's never a happy occasion to "uninvite" someone to your wedding. Determinations about inviting "plus ones" and children need to be made before notifications are sent, because the proper form of address is just as important on a save-the-date as it is on an invitation.

It's perfectly acceptable to invite a person who, for whatever reason, did not receive a save-the-date, but not inviting someone who did is taboo, except in rare circumstances. One example would be a married guest's divorce. Removal of one previously notified guest from the guest list may be warranted if only the husband or the wife, and not the couple together, is a friend of the bride or groom.

Using a lovely, printer-friendly calligraphic font for written communications saves money and guarantees uniformity. Many can't tell the difference between printed calligraphy and its handwritten counterpart, especially if the font is raised. But some can, and if ultimate elegance is of importance to you, hiring a professional calligrapher is the answer.

Calligraphy pros require plenty of time to produce their work, and you should expect to pay anywhere from $1 to $10 per envelope, depending upon the calligrapher's résumé. Place cards, inner envelopes, and other single-line calligraphy can cost 50 cents and up per piece. Calligraphy is a specialized art that requires talent, experience, and expertise, and fees charged by calligraphers are warranted.

But if the cost of handwritten calligraphy is prohibitive, it's comforting to know that choosing a commercially printed calligraphic font rarely costs more than choosing any other font.

#474 *Tangible, Collectible Save-the-Dates*

Postcards and paper notices are fine, but the goal of a save-the-date is not only to notify, it's to act as a continual reminder.

Photo magnets stuck to a fridge, bookmarks in favorite tomes, custom sun catchers on windows, and hand-painted, river-rock paperweights on desks share a common trait. They all have a reason to stay put. And if the save-the-date stays put instead of getting tossed into the trash or the recycling bin, that's a big plus.

A save-the-date is anything you want it to be, but choosing a format and style that entices its recipient to keep the notice in plain view, day after day, makes for a great perpetual reminder.

#475 *The Thank-You Box*

It's never too early to think about expressing your appreciation for wedding gifts and helpful kindnesses, and an easy way to make certain no one is forgotten is to create a thank-you box.

Any box, drawer, or tote will do. Early in the wedding-planning process, fill your chosen container with thank-you cards, stationery, envelopes, pens, stamps, an address book, and small, token gifts like bookmarks, miniature boxes of chocolates, decorative candles, etc.

Except for gifts actually received at the wedding, it's not necessary to wait until after the wedding to say thank you. It's easier to express your gratitude throughout the wedding-planning process. An always-ready, well-stocked thank-you box makes the task efficient and stress free.

The save-the-date and the invitation are equal partners in the invitation process. Don't go hog wild in the giddiness of the moment and send save-the-dates to the "maybes" on your list. Remember that every save-the-date must be followed by an invitation. Be confident in your guest list before mailing any notifications, and you'll never have to say, "I'm sorry."

#471 *A Stamp of Approval*

Wedding-themed postage stamps are available from the United States Postal Service or from certain commercial printers, with designs ranging from commonly recognized wedding icons, like a wedding cake or wedding rings, to a one-of-a-kind photo of the bride and groom. A wedding stamp adds visual expression to any envelope.

All stamps bear appropriate postage, but only stamps from the US Post Office are available without surcharge. Expect to pay more than the face value of the actual postage when ordering stamps from any other source. For more design choices, however, commercial printers have the edge.

Since postage must be purchased for wedding-related mailings anyway, choosing little wedding works of art is a clever way to get the job done.

#472 *Sealed with a "Wow"*

A letter seal may conjure an image of a blood-red pool of wax bearing a monarch's crest, but seals have never been just for royalty. Throughout history, the wax seal has been the symbol of authentic identity for people from every walk of life, and for wedding invitations, the seal is the ultimate finishing touch.

Inexpensive seal kits that feature an initial or a wedding-themed crest are readily available from arts-and-crafts stores or stationery retailers. If it's uniqueness you desire, hand-stamp makers can create custom designs.

If the idea of stamping wax isn't appealing, order ready-made or custom sealing stickers from wedding-supply retailers and certain printers.

Attention to detail always defines the best of the best. For an unexpected and elegant invitation "wow," give it your own "wedding seal" of approval.

#473 *Romance by Hand*

It's thrilling to see your name artfully styled in romantic calligraphy, and calligraphy-addressed envelopes are likely to get opened first.

Calligraphy is personal, elegant, and enticing, but it no longer has to be handwritten. Printers now have many calligraphy-style fonts available for invitations, envelopes, and other wedding-day cards, tags, and notices.

#476 *Fabulous Favor Wrappings*

Some wedding favors come in presentation packaging and need no additional wrapping, but others could definitely use a bit of sprucing up. Wrapping paper, tissue, and organza bags readily come to mind, but it's nontraditional paper goods that really make a fabulous wedding-day statement.

Printable paper allows you to experiment with art, text, or color combinations as you create one-of-a-kind favor wraps. You could "scroll wrap" favors in papyrus paper printed with a special poem, make a paper pouch of monogrammed metallic velum, or cut printed parchment paper into strips and weave them into beautiful miniature baskets that cradle candied almonds.

Favors do "favor" a clever wrapping!

#477 *Not Your Life's Story*

The biggest mistake wedding couples make with save-the-date notices is trying to provide too much information. The most effective save-the-date gets to the point then quits "talking." The bride's and groom's names, the wedding date, and the general location of the wedding (like city and state) form the substance of the message, and the only other required language is "Save the Date" and "Invitation to Follow." Include the URL for your wedding Web site, if you have one.

Resist the urge to include any extra information that would force a reduction of the font size. A save-the-date should be bold and eye catching. The less bold the information, the less effective the message. Of course, since a picture is the best visual reminder of all, the inclusion of a photo of the bride and groom is most welcome.

#478 *Bridal Letterhead Is More Than Lovely*

Many a wedding component has gone awry from simple miscommunication, and letterhead stationery effectively ensures that vendors, suppliers, and others with whom communication is necessary will always have your correct personal information at hand.

Purchase beautiful wedding-themed, printer-friendly paper to create DIY letterhead, or opt for custom, raised-font letterhead from a professional printer.

Wedding letterhead should include the bride's and groom's names as well as primary mailing, e-mailing, telephone, fax, and wedding Web site information. If the wedding date is set, the inclusion of the date is a helpful reminder.

When utilizing a professional wedding planner, it is also acceptable to include, or to substitute, his or her contact information beneath the bride's and groom's names, so that communications go directly to the planner.

#479 *Rip-and-Go RSVPs*

A traditional RSVP consists of a return card and a stamped envelope included in the wedding invitation, but modern trifold invitations offer the option of a perforated RSVP postcard instead.

The postcard portion can include printed postage, or stamps can be used. A postcard RSVP requires little effort on the part of the guest, since separating the card from the invitation and dropping it in a mailbox is easy. The design promotes immediacy and can improve prompt RSVP return rates. As a bonus, postcard postage costs less.

Postcard RSVPs may not be for those who crave the ultimate in formality, but they could be just what the environment and the cost-savvy bride ordered.

#480 *Deliciously Fun DVD Invitations*

Modern technology allows virtually anyone with a camera and a computer to create a movie, and a custom DVD wedding invitation is pretty unforgettable.

From childhood photos of the bride and groom to profiles of the wedding-event venues include anything and everything. Add background music to photo montages, create interspersed frames of wedding-couple trivia, include live messages from the bride and groom, or script a wedding-invite movie. There are no hard-and-fast rules. Make your DVD wedding invitation as simple or as elaborate as you wish.

Create a printed, wedding invitation the size of a DVD liner, and slip it into the transparent lid of the DVD case. Tuck your DVD and your RSVP inside a padded DVD mailer, and send it off. DVD wedding invitations can be elegant or fun, or both. You and your intended are the directors, the producers, and the stars of the show. Do it your way!

#481 *The Memory Lane DVD Thank-You*

Whether or not you send a DVD invitation, a DVD after-wedding thank-you is a warm and welcome way to show gratitude.

A keepsake DVD thank-you will feature photos and video footage from the wedding and reception, including close-ups of the wedding guests. It could also include personal messages from the bride and groom, as well as honeymoon snippets. Universal words of thanks make it easy to copy the DVD for everyone, and a personalized, handwritten thank-you for a specific gift or an act of kindness can be included in the DVD case's lid. Ambitious brides and grooms may wish to record a private thank-you to each guest on the DVD itself. If each DVD is personalized, be sure to employ a foolproof labeling system to ensure that "Sally's" private message isn't inadvertently mailed to "Aunt Betty."

A DVD thank-you will mean a great deal to friends and family. And remember — people love to see themselves on film. Even though you and your new spouse are the stars, be sure to use plenty of "guest" shots.

#482 *Yesteryear Stationery*

Wedding stationery made with modern methods doesn't have to look modern. Vintage papers, designs, and font styles can take your stationery to any era you choose. The distinctive hallmarks of yesteryear's weddings can give today's stationery ensembles more than a unique flair. They inspire reminiscence for some and wonder for others. Whether the era is medieval, Wild West, Victorian, Roaring '20s, or any other moment in time, it's likely to evoke a specific emotional response that typical modern stationery will not generate.

It's fun to look back!

#483 *"We're Hitched, and Here's the Scoop!"*

When it's not possible to invite everyone to the wedding or an elopement has occurred, a mailed wedding announcement shares the news. Lest it be construed as an invitation, the wedding announcement should always be mailed after the nuptials are over.

Most wedding announcements have standard, formal wording, such as:

Mr. and Mrs. Harry Hill
are pleased to announce the wedding of their daughter
Sandy
to
Dave Woods
son of Mr. and Mrs. Burl Woods
on December 14, 2012
at Surfside Beach Resort
Ocean Blue, California

This type of elegant, single-sided announcement is traditional, but there's no reason your wedding announcement can't be much more. From funny anecdotes of the wedding experience to details of wedding-day attire, it's the little things coupled with the big moments that give wedding-announcement recipients a feeling of inclusion. Incorporate both candid and formal photographs to give your announcement plenty of spirit, and add personal thoughts to give it heart.

There's nothing wrong with sticking to tradition, but since those who receive the announcement couldn't attend the wedding, a more elaborate, news-style communication that colorfully shares wedding details is more than an announcement. It's a gift that says, "I wish you could have been there."

But be sensitive. Sending an "it-was-so-wonderful" collection of memories to friends or family who were specifically left off the guest list may add a bit of insult to injury. Carefully consider the circumstances of the wedding, as well as the recipients of the announcement, and let your instincts guide your style choice.

#484 *The Fore and Aft of Military Rank*

When the bride or groom is a member of the armed forces, most information included on the wedding invitation is identical to civilian wedding invites. The only discernible difference is the inclusion of military rank and service affiliation.

Here's a little ditty to help remind you where to put what:

"Below a captain, behind you stay. A captain or above leads the way."

Example: John Manners, Private First Class, United States Army (under a captain, the rank follows the name)

Example: Major Roger Dean, United States Air Force (a captain or above, the rank precedes the name)

High-ranking officers continue to use their military rank even after retirement, and both men and women express designated rank on invitations and announcements even when in combination.

Example: Captain Mark Bell, United States Marine Corps, Retired (retired, but a captain or above), and Angela Bell, Lieutenant Junior Grade, United States Navy (active, but below a captain), request your attendance . . .

Note: The rank of captain in the army, air force, or marines is equivalent to a lieutenant in the navy, and designations should be adjusted accordingly for naval ranks.

Most military branches provide detailed wedding and marriage tutorials for service brides and grooms. Remember the "fore and aft" rule, and you'll already be in the right "military zone."

#485 *Thirst-Quenching Escort Cards*

Escort cards most commonly make their appearance as tented cards, aligned alphabetically by last name, on a table just outside the reception doors. These cards direct guests to their assigned tables, but not to an assigned seat. Seat assignments are the job of a place card.

But to kill two birds with one creative stone, consider delivering the escort cards via wine glasses. By tying an artistically designed escort card to the stem of a glass with a lovely ribbon, you not only alert guests to their assigned tables, you immediately get refreshment into their hands. Fill the glasses with a sparkling punch, lemon water, or other liquid starter drink of your choice, then group the glasses by alphabetical designations (As and Bs here, Ts there, etc.) on tall, linen-covered cocktail tables just outside or just inside the reception-hall doors. Assign a house-party member to monitor each table and help guests locate their drinks.

Early refreshment is always welcome, and it comes with a worry-free bonus. With the escort card affixed to the glass, there's little chance of losing it.

#486 *RSVP Booster Postcard*

In today's busy world, RSVPs often end up in the "meant to do that" box. People have good intentions, but life gets in the way. If the RSVPs for your wedding are not arriving in a timely fashion, consider a follow-up postcard.

Postcards featuring a nice photo of the bride and groom on one side, with space for the address and message on the other, are not expensive. Some online printers produce postcards in quantities as low as 25 pieces, at a cost of only pennies per piece.

On the message side of the postcard, write a brief reminder that the RSVP has not been received. This will also alert guests who may have actually returned their RSVP that it didn't arrive as planned.

Adopt a formal tone or a friendly and conversational one. Adding a reference to a cut-off date spurs action. For example, after a notation that the RSVP hasn't been received, add, "Our caterer requires a final meal count by June 1st. Thanks!"

A telephone call or in-person reminder requires an instant response, while an attractive bride-and-groom postcard reminds without putting guests on the spot. The postcard allows a little more time but imparts a decided nudge.

#487 *Puzzle Fun!*

Wedding guests must endure a wait before the ceremony. To keep things fun and to pass the time, add a puzzle-sheet insert to the wedding program.

There are plenty of free online crossword, word search, and other word-puzzle creators. You simply supply the answer words and the hint, and the puzzle maker turns your words into fun. This easy process allows you to make the puzzles completely customized to the bride and groom, and you can create as few or as many puzzles as you like. More sophisticated puzzle-maker software is available for purchase, but for a wedding-day puzzle or two, you'll likely need no more than what is available for free.

Add a batch of bulk pencils (bride-and-groom personalized or not) for those who don't have a pen in their pocket or purse, and everyone is good to go.

Wedding couple–inspired puzzles are a boon for idle hands and wandering minds.

#488 *Signing Up for Romance*

A traditional guest book does its job well, but there's fun to be had with a little guest-book tweaking. Rather than collecting only typical sign-ins, spark guests' imaginations, and let them write your very own honeymoon romance novel.

Stack individual pages on the guest-book table, and on each page include a teaser line, followed by unfinished sentences. Separate the sentences with plenty of white space for writing. For example:

"John and Angela can't wait for the honeymoon!
They will travel to _____.
John will wear _____.
Angela will pack _____.
John will insist on _____.
But Angela will say, "_____."
And in the end, they will _____.

Include an "Author" signature line for the guest to sign at the bottom of each page. Your guest-book attendant instructs guests to complete their stories at their leisure, then deposit their page(s) into a designated receptacle.

Make the story line anything you wish, and fashion sentence beginnings in any combination. Provide only a few sentence prompts or an entire page full of sentence fragments, but to create a whole "story," you'll need a variety of topic pages.

To provide inspiration fire the imagination, and make your guests smile, display a fun computer-generated mock-up of the bride and groom portraying the hero and heroine on the cover of a romance novel.

After you return from your real honeymoon, save these literary gems for your own enjoyment, or compile all of the heartfelt and hilarious content into a keepsake book to share with guests. Send a copy of the book with each thank-you card, or share the amusement by posting the finished masterpiece on your wedding Web site.

#489 *Marriage-Certificate Art*

The marriage certificate signed at the wedding may not be the gorgeous work of art you imagined, but it's legal. It's fine, however, to have both the legal certificate and a more artistic one that better lends itself to framing and display.

Heirloom marriage certificates are produced by a number of printers. Order them with the details already imbedded, or have someone blessed with a beautiful cursive talent complete the certificate for you.

Aesthetically, the sky's the limit. Choose from plenty of attractive stock designs, or order a custom certificate to feature any colors or theme you wish. The certificate can feature accents like foil, glittering, or cutouts, and when custom ordering, its possible to select a certificate of any dimensions, from poster to postcard size.

If elegance isn't your choice, make the certificate humorous, or personalize it with a photo or a specific piece of art. When it comes to keepsake certificates, you don't have to settle. Get what you want.

#490 *Send an Invite, Save a Tree!*

Could we live without paper? Probably not. But do thousands of trees have to die to quench our paper thirst? Absolutely not!

Wood isn't the only paper source. Paper from hemp, papyrus reed, grain-residue straw, sugar-cane husk, flax, and even old rags is possible. And when paper is crafted from rags or grain residues, it springs to life from an already-recycled source. Nothing has to be specifically grown and harvested to support the making of the paper.

Beautiful wedding invitations, letterhead, and other paper goods can all be found in tree-free versions. Even when not totally following a "green" theme, it's still possible to commit words and art to paper without draining the life from a tree.

Tree-free paper products help reduce a wedding's negative impact on the planet, and elegance needn't be sacrificed to reap the benefits.

#491 *The Sweetly Stuffed Wedding Program*

Wedding programs end up in the trash because they aren't worthy of becoming a keepsake. If they include little more than ceremony and reception schedules, they do their job, but they don't endear themselves to wedding guests. To create an emotionally charged program that entertains, amuses, and makes guests want to take it home, pump up the content.

The biggest "wow" comes from the element of surprise. Printing your guest list at the back of the program is one surprise that really makes guests feel included. Guests are often overlooked as valued participants of the wedding, and even the simplest acknowledgement and thanks go a long way.

Other surprise entries include funny confessions, like "the bride sleeps with a tiny teddy bear under her pillow" or "the groom hates orange marmalade," or perhaps a bride- and groom-written essay on how they envision spending their 50th wedding anniversary.

Details about wedding-party members, a description of the bride's "something old, borrowed, and blue," the reason for certain wedding-song choices, the story of the proposal, a transcript of the personal vows, and candid photos all contribute to an enjoyable wedding program.

By all means, include the schedule and a list of who's who in the wedding party, but for a program that engenders smiles, chuckles, and maybe a tear in the corner of one eye, stuff it with memorable content.

#492 *Fleet of Foot*

Plenty is mentioned about message delivery in the digital age, and while digital invitations are expedient, they're generally void of romance. Hark back to the early 20th century, when sharply dressed delivery boys would put a sealed telegram directly into the recipient's hand. Excitement spiked as he made his way up the walk or into someone's place of employment. Hand delivery is a dead art, but there is never a better time to resurrect it than at wedding time.

For all guests who live in a single town or in a relatively clustered area, hand delivery is a delightful option. Enlist the aid of a friend willing to don whatever costume you choose. It doesn't have to be a telegram-delivery costume. For a formal wedding, it could be a butler carrying the invitation on a silver tray or a "Queen's" messenger who pulls the invite from a velvet pouch emblazoned with the "bride and groom's royal seal." For a more casual, fun wedding, choose Cupid or even Elvis. Any costume will deliver the same pleasing impact on surprised guests.

A friend, a costume, and an economical car, bicycle, motor scooter, or even horse, and you've turned the invitation process into something worthy of watercooler buzz.

#493 *Theme Weaving*

Wedding stationery benefits from a cohesive theme, but not all pieces need identical embellishment. For example, if the invitation features an embossed dove, consider an artistic bird's-nest design for the place cards. A cascade of purple orchids on the letterhead goes perfectly with a lone purple hydrangea blossom on the wedding program or a bouquet of purple petunias on the RSVPs.

Choose similar but not necessarily identical components of any larger theme to give your stationery depth and personality. Begin with the one special bit of artistic expression that matters most to you. Make a sketch of it in the center of a blank piece of paper. Think of it as the "sun" of your theme concept. Let that sun inspire ideas, and jot them down on the paper as they pop into your head. Soon plenty of creative "planet" ideas representing all of your different stationery needs will orbit your central-idea "sun."

Theme weaving keeps ideas from becoming stale and expected. It gives any theme artistic wings.

#494 *Stationery Saving Graces*

When creating your stationery supply, adhere to few important dos and don'ts to shave a bit of stress from the wedding-planning process.

Do seek the expert opinion of a stationer familiar with papers, inks, foils, embossing, and other finishing touches before making a stationery decision. Not all papers and all treatments work well together.

Do order as early as possible for every stationery need. If something goes wrong with the order, plenty of time will be required to correct it. This is especially important when ordering stationery online, where shipping each way adds days.

Do proofread. Once you sign off on a design, it's a done deal.

Don't give up on your stationery dream. If a stationer can't provide what you truly desire, keep looking.

Don't employ any stationer or printer with a less-than-stellar reputation. Your wedding is no time to roll the dice and hope for the best.

Don't change your mind. Changing your mind about design or paper styles after the order has been prepped for print is costly. You'll likely have to pay for the creation of both the old and the new design templates.

To avoid being saddled with paper products that don't meet your expectations, approach stationery creation with a bucketful of high hopes in one hand, and a bucketful of common sense in the other.

#495 *By My Hand*

To add a very personal touch to wedding communications, turn your own handwriting into a computer font. Font-generator software is inexpensive, and it works by converting a scanned handwriting sample into a full alphabetical and numerical font style that is uniquely you.

Substitute your personal handwriting font anywhere you would use a traditional computer font, to infuse wedding letters, postcards, labels, and other documents with individualized style.

All font generators are not the same. Some offer better resolution and more character options, so do your homework. Look them over with a discerning eye and read reviews before choosing.

#496 *Invitation to Grow*

Seed wedding favors are common eco-friendly reception gifts, but waiting until the reception to offer guests a reason to plant is not necessary. Begin with the wedding invitation.

Recycled paper embedded with wildflower seeds makes gorgeous, Earth-conscious invitations with as much formality as you like. Purchase seeded invitations from any number of invite stationers, or give your invitations the ultimate personal touch by crafting and printing the seed paper yourself.

Seeded invitations are more than early gifts to guests. They make the statement that minimizing the waste of natural resources is an important part of your wedding vision.

#497 *Sweetheart Escort Cards*

"Be My Wedding-Day Valentine!"

That's the endearing message you deliver when children's valentines become your clever, yet inexpensive, wedding-reception escort cards. Those adorable little cards, boxed in quantities designed to share with classroom friends, create a delightful welcome panorama for wedding guests.

It doesn't have to be a Valentine's Day wedding. In fact, using them at any other time of the year adds a greater degree of surprise. Just wait until Valentine's Day is over, then swoop into your local stores and buy up your "escort-card stock" at a huge discount. Be sure to buy extra. Discovering you don't have enough when your summer, fall or winter wedding draws near means you'll have a slim-to-none chance of adding to your stock at that time.

Use the valentine envelope for the guest name. Or, to allow the colorful, bigger-than-life designs and messages of the valentines to shine, write the names on small banners cut from any nice white paper, then glue a banner at an angle across the lower right corner of each card. Make the valentine stand upright via its own instant easel by gluing just the top of a stiff paper strip to its back.

Center a large heart wreath on your escort-card table. Surround it with your valentines, and you've created a "just-gotta-talk-about-it" escort-card presentation.

#498 *It's All Business*

Gracing the retail counter or executive's desk at each wedding-vendor site is a card holder filled with business-card reminders of who and what the business is. But as a bride and groom, you are also a business, and depending upon the budget, you may actually be a fairly big business. So treat yourselves with respect, and spring for your own business cards.

> *Bride:* Marcia Doe *Groom:* John Smith
> *Wedding date:* June 30, 2015
> *E-mail special promotions or individual offers to:* marciajohn@mysite.com
> *Fax to:* 999-555-2222, *Mail to:* 645 E. Jupiter Lane, MyCity,
>   MyState 00000

The inclusion of a telephone number is a personal decision. Not including one prevents unwanted solicitation calls, but to permit quick contact, a phone number is necessary.

The use of the "special promotions" language tells vendors that you are ready to shop but are serious about securing the best deals.

Add a photo or icon to the card to make it distinctively yours, then stock your purse or pocket with them for use anywhere and everywhere during the wedding-planning process. Business cards are inexpensive investments with the potential of helping you achieve great savings. Plan your wedding with a happy heart and a business brain.

#499 *RSVPs by the Number*

Identify your RSVP cards. Sometimes guests just don't think about filling in the blanks. They pop the RSVP into its envelope and send it off without including their name, number of people in their party, or other pertinent information. Without a clue of where the RSVP came from, you cannot correct the problem. Fortunately, there are two effective ways to prevent blank-card bother.

Engage in the time-consuming task of filling in the guest's name before sending the card, or simply assign every guest on your list a number, discreetly placed on a lower backside corner of the RSVP. With a numbering system, an RSVP that arrives blank is still identifiable when compared to the numbered list, and other necessary information can be subsequently retrieved via telephone or e-mail. Numbers lightly penciled onto a back corner are unobtrusive yet do their jobs as precisely as if they'd filled in the blanks themselves.

#500 *The Extra Personal Mile*

To surprise and amaze your guests, turn your escort cards into personalized messages. The customary language for an escort card includes the name of the guest plus his or her table number. But there's reason to say more.

With tent-style cards, write a personal message to each guest on the inside of the card. It doesn't have to be a long note — just a few words to convey a sincere welcome. Make it personal by using the guest's name and, if appropriate, include a reference to something unique to your relationship with that individual.

Here's an example for someone you know well, like a dear friend:

Sally, who knew when we were in third grade that we would still be so close today? Thank you for being here . . . always!

Or, for someone you don't know well, like a boss and his wife:

Mr. and Mrs. Haven, we are so honored you have chosen to share our day with us. Thank you!

For an escort card with an envelope, tuck your message inside. For unusual escort-card designs, add a folded message via a ribbon attachment. No matter the style of card used, there's a way to make it personal.

There's often a human disconnect at a wedding, and any number of guests may feel like fish out of water. Spending a few nights in front of the TV writing personal messages makes every person feel as if he or she is the most important guest of all.

#501 *Postcards of Love*

If you know where the honeymoon will be, bring a touch of it to the reception by replacing the traditional guest book with postcards depicting your honeymoon locale. To acquire the postcards, contact the gift shop at the hotel where you will be staying, or use the Internet to search for area gift shops that carry postcards. The Chamber of Commerce can also direct you to an appropriate seller. Once you've located your postcard retailer, order a variety of colorful postcards of the location then set up your guest-book table with the postcards, a basket of pens, and a cleverly crafted "mailbox." An artfully designed sign or a guest-table attendant will instruct guests to write their names and addresses on the address side of the postcard, and any message to the bride and groom on the content side of the card. You get lots of lovely sentiments, along with the names and addresses of guests, and guests get a unique peek at your honeymoon haven.

#502 *Skip It!*

Stuffing envelopes is not the most enjoyable job, and if your guest list is long, you may dread the task of sending out invitations. Speed up the process by skipping the envelope. Clever paper shapes create flaps that easily and neatly fold over to close the invite. Add a personalized sticker to seal the flaps in place, and you've shaved hours of stuffing time from your to-do list. These user-friendly invitations can be as playful and whimsical or as elegant and formal as you wish. Elegance isn't tied to your envelope. It's tied to your overall presentation. If sophistication is your wish, envelope-free invitations nail the fine points of elegance just as effectively as their more traditional counterparts.

#503 *Languages of the World*

America is a true melting pot of cultures. If you invite guests for whom English is a second language, consider bilingual or foreign-language invitations. Some stationers will split the printing run into different languages for a translation fee, resulting in separate English and foreign-language invitations. Others will accommodate a bilingual or trilingual invitation at no additional charge if you provide the foreign-language copy exactly as it should be. In this scenario, all languages appear together on one invitation. To decide whether multilingual invitations are desired, consider what language your guests speak in their own homes, taking into consideration that, while someone may have picked up enough conversational English to speak and understand it, reading it may be another issue altogether. Foreign-language invites are not required, but they are a thoughtful courtesy when your guest list looks a bit like the roll-call roster at the United Nations.

#504 *Screened to a "T"*

Wedding invitations don't have to be made with fancy paper. In fact, they don't have to be made with paper at all. Use silk screening to apply your invitation graphics onto almost any medium — wood, fabric, glass, ceramic, metal, etc. Design your invite and do the screening yourself with a screen-at-home kit, or take the labor and worry out of the equation by giving your project to a professional silk screener.

Think of the possibilities. For a high-tech wedding theme, screen your invitation onto a mouse pad. Garden wedding? Use a flowerpot. Why not delight guests with a miniature saddle blanket or a leather bookmark for that Western-themed wedding? Wine-and-roses theme? Add a rose to your graphics, then silk-screen the design onto wine glasses.

Some silk-screened items will cost more than paper invitations, but depending upon the quality of the paper invitation, some alternative items would be in the same financial ballpark, especially if you order in quantity from a company that sells promotional products and is equipped to silk-screen just about any design onto just about any item. Check it out. You may find that you can be clever and creative for about the same amount of investment as being elegant and formal.

#505 *Leftovers*

Almost all wedding couples wind up with extra invitations. What do you do with them? They can easily be recycled, but that's often an emotionally tough thing to do. Give them new life instead by awarding them a place of honor as the "photo" in the lid of a photo-frame box. Purchase a finished box then slip your invite behind the glass in the hinged lid, or buy an unfinished photo-frame box from a craft store and design it to be whatever you wish it to be. A smaller box makes a clever jewelry box, and a larger one is ideal for storing scarves or mementos. Your extra supply of invites can also be transformed into clever paper ornaments to add to packages for family and friends the first holiday after your wedding, or laminated for use as coasters and underliners. It may prove surprisingly joyful to reach for a coaster and retrieve a memory instead.

#506 *He Said, She Said*

If you have strict formality in mind, being cute and clever won't hold appeal, but if you want your wedding invitations to not only invite but to surprise and tickle, his-and-hers invitations are for you. Each guest gets two invites — one from the bride and one from the groom. One of them is fairly traditional, but the other is unexpectedly hilarious. Send them separately, or to save postage, send them together by making the funny one slightly smaller than the traditional one. (Just seal it in its own envelope, then slip it in with the bigger invite.) If the traditional invite is white with black printing, make the funny one black with white printing, or choose any fabulously funky color combination. Write something fun and inventive on the casual invitation, like: "Hey! Don't even think about missing our wedding. We've got drinks you've never tasted before!" or "Yep, I finally chased hard enough to let myself get caught. Now come to the wedding and witness the miracle!" Will your guests grin and laugh? Will they shudder with disbelief? Who knows? Will they remember your invitations? Absolutely.

#507 *Thank-You Out Loud*

Talking greeting cards are everywhere — those with prerecorded music and those with voice-recording capability. But instead of choosing an existing design, make your own and turn it into a personal thank-you card. Cards with flat mini recorders are a sweet deal for newlyweds who hate writing what they would really rather say. Audio-recording modules can be purchased in bulk then added to any blank card. Choose the traditional type that hides inside the folds of the card, or explore the self-contained versions that come with a sticky back, allowing them to be attached to anything. The price of the module depends primarily upon its recording length, which customarily ranges from 8 to 60 or more seconds. Individual units purchased at traditional retail outlets, like Radio Shack, are pricey. For the best deal, check wholesale sources online and compare prices. Voice cards will still cost more than small, paper cards, but if thanking Aunt Mary with the sound of your own voice is more appealing than a simple written card, the option is there for the taking.

#508 *Softly Personal*

Tissue-paper inserts for wedding invitations originated back in the day when the printing process was prone to smudges. With modern printing methods, that problem no longer exists, yet tissue papers are still included in invites because they simply feel formal. If you like the formality of the insert, but find that an ordinary scrap of tissue doesn't really represent your personality, consider alternatives. If you're having your gown or veil hand sewn, slip squares of the actual tulle or lace used to make them into the invitations. The beautiful designs of Japanese washi paper provide an insert with a splash of color. If your wedding is in the fall, consider a beautiful dried leaf or, for the spring, a sprig of dried herb. Tissue-paper inserts are traditional, albeit unnecessary. You can skip them altogether, or think of them as an opportunity to make your invitation a bit more formal and expressive.

#509 *Dressing the Invite*

Die cutting, embossing, gold leaf, metallics, and other professional embellishments can add significantly to the cost of wedding invitations. But it's easy to create an invite that looks amazing without the huge "ka ching." If you have a top-quality printer, you can print your own invitations. Alternatively, purchase them from a large online printer, like Vistaprint, or an entrepreneurial site, like Zazzle, then dress them up yourself. Use glue-on seed-pearl halves to highlight the face of the invite or a thin satin ribbon to create a tie around the fold. Tiny silk tea-rose heads with adhesive backs give your invite a focal point and depth, while flat-backed gems and peel-off bridal art can turn ordinary paper into a beautiful, custom expression. Begin with an invitation kit, or just gather the materials yourself. In the end, you will likely save money and produce a one-of-a-kind invitation in the process. Everyone loves custom invitations, and guests never have to know that you didn't pay an entire month's food budget to create them.

#510 *Thoroughly Us*

Everyone knows what a traditional wedding invitation looks like. It's elegant, formal, and subtly fashioned. Maybe that's you. Maybe it isn't. If sending an invite that instantly identifies the "real you" holds appeal, consider a modern art or personal-photo invitation. Instead of a words-only invite, print a photo or a piece of art on one side of your parchment or linen paper and the invitation information on the other side. Purchase bulk quantities of "full view" envelopes with plastic-film "windows." Wedding-stationery envelopes are pricey, but full-view envelopes in a variety of sizes are inexpensive in packs of 50 or more. Slip your invite into the envelope with the photo or art facing the window, and place any additional inserts behind it. Address the nonwindow side of the envelope. To dress up the plain white envelope, have custom, artistic labels made. Use the labels to add a splash of color, a wedding-perfect border, gold or silver metallic accents, or whatever design you wish. The labels add the "wedding" to the envelopes, but it's the only-you photo or art that will give your wedding guests something to smile about.

#511 *Raised to Perfection*

If you enjoy a hands-on process, you can make any of your stationery items more beautiful with the use of embossing powders. Embossing powders work in conjunction with rubber stamps and a heat gun. You stamp the paper, dust the powder over the image, shake off the excess, apply the heat gun, and in less than a minute you've created a professionally styled raised design. Not all embossing powders are created equal, so read reviews and chat with craft-store personnel before choosing. You'll want printed materials to be embossed quickly but display great, professional-looking results. It's an easy process to learn, and once you do, your speed will pick up, and you'll produce tons of work in no time. You'll need to purchase a heat gun, whatever stamps you like, and the powders. Some advocate using a hair dryer as the heating element, but hair dryers can blow the powder off instead of merely heating it to the correct temperature. Besides, once you own the gun and the supplies, you'll find a million occasions to use them.

#512 *One More Time*

Invitations are lovely and often expensive, but in the end, they are trash to 99% of their recipients. Very few wedding guests keep the invitation after the wedding is over, but you can give those printed ambassadors a boost by designing them a bit differently. Use a beautiful photograph or piece of art on the cover, at the top, or elsewhere in the invitation where it is un-touched by text. Then enclose a small note inviting guests to forward their invitations on to a charity that will make extraordinary good use of them. Invitations will be sent to:

> St. Jude's Ranch for Children
> 100 St. Jude's Street
> Boulder City, NV 89005

As they have done for decades, the children at St. Jude's Ranch will give your invitations new life as all-occasion greeting cards. Just remember to design your invitations so that photos and art are free of text on the front or back. It's easy, and all it costs your guest to participate in this charitable endeavor is the price of a stamp to get their invite to St. Jude's. Everyone benefits, especially the children who raise money by transforming the cards, and you will know that your invitations are spreading joy far beyond your wedding. St. Jude's Ranch accepts donations of everything from a single card to a box-load, so if you wish to expedite the process, ask your guests to bring their invitations to the reception, where they can be deposited into a decorated box. After the reception, transfer the invites into a single, flat-rate postal box for mailing, and send them all off at once. Whether sent individually or all together, a charitable end for your invitations is a wonderful thing.

#513 *"Forever" and the Postage Kitty*

When planning for stationery needs, the postage to send all those wonderful pieces is often overlooked. Don't let that happen. Postage can really add up, and it literally pays to be ahead of the curve. Create a postage kitty. Beginning at the moment of engagement, you and your intended will routinely donate change to the kitty, and when the time comes to purchase postage, you'll have a nice nest egg to tap. Another way to stay one jump ahead of your postage costs is to purchase "Forever" stamps. Postage prices are always going up, but a "Forever" stamp's value will always be equal to whatever the current first-class rate happens to be. A postage kitty and some savvy stamp shopping helps whittle postage pressures down to size.

#514 *To Label or Not to Label*

It has long been considered "not nice" to use labels for wedding invitations and thank-you cards. It's so impersonal. On the other hand, all that writing can be excruciating, and the cost of hiring a calligrapher is often exorbitant. So what's a great compromise? Beautiful, artistic labels that mean something. There's no law that says a label must have only the mailing address. It can also have its own charisma. For example, design a label with a special message from the bride and groom that forms a continuous border around the edge of the label. Or add a photo, and print the labels on your color printer. Another option is to print ordinary labels then fingerprint them with a beautiful ink, using both the bride's and groom's fingertips. Labels don't have to be taboo. If you elevate them beyond their functional purpose, no one will gasp, "OH! THEY USED A LABEL!" They will simply think, "Oh, how lovely and creative."

#515 *Words for a Lifetime*

A lot of consideration is given to printed materials going out from the bride and groom to others, but there will also be a fair amount of printed materials coming to the wedding couple from guests. Most wedding-day cards end up in boxes, stored deep in closets and forgotten. Their enjoyment doesn't live on, but it could. Revisiting the kind wishes tucked in your wedding cards is a spirit booster when you need it. It's a pleasant remembrance of one of the most beautiful experiences of your life — one that should be readily at hand.

You can plan ahead and purchase a greeting-card album for your cards. These albums have traditional photo-album-style covers and plastic sleeves for the cards. But the truth is that your cards will endure even without protective sleeves or rigid covers.

To make your own keepsake card album, craft a front and a back cover from heavy cardboard and cover them with wedding fabric and adornments. Use a paper punch to punch two aligned holes in the cards and the covers — one in the upper left corner and a second hole about half way down the left side. Using snap-together binding rings, slip the back cover, the cards, and the front cover over the rings and snap them closed. Now you have a beautiful wedding card book that is personally you and is shelf or table worthy, ready and available for a revisit anytime you wish.

#516 *Thinking of Thanks*

If standard thank-you cards just won't cut it for you, devise a more original plan. Before the wedding, have a beautiful large "Thank You" sign made. During the official wedding-day photo session, have a few shots taken of the wedding couple holding the sign. Later, one of those photos will become the face of your thank-you cards.

If a sign is too ordinary, spell out "Thank You" in wooden letters along the top of a fence or on a garden bench, and take a photo that features just the head and shoulders of the bride and groom positioned behind the letters. Or spray paint "Thank You" onto an old, weathered board. Rest the board upright at your feet, and have the photo taken as you share a kiss. The eclectic options are many. Whatever signage method you choose, your efforts will give birth to a one-of-a-kind thank-you card that will be anything but standard.

#517 *Loving Greetings*

The night before the wedding is a wonderful time to express your feelings to your parents, but you don't have to do so face-to-face. Imagine how much it would mean to them to know that even in the hustle and bustle of last-minute wedding details, you remembered them with a special card, hand delivered on your wedding eve. Choose a commercial card if it conveys what's in your heart, or simply do what you did when you were a child and wanted to show your mom and dad how much you loved them. Make the card yourself. Do the same for that special grandparent, or anyone else in attendance who has made a profound difference in your life. Enlist of the assistance of your maid of honor, best man, or another reliable friend to see that the cards are delivered after the rehearsal dinner but before bedtime. It may just be a simple card filled with your thoughts. But to the recipient, it's the act of sending it that is worth the world.

#518 *Secret Security*

To keep track of RSVP cards without marking them with visible codes, numbers, or names written in back corners, send them out with those necessary codes, numbers, or names written in invisible ink. Use a black-light pen to code your cards, and if they come back with missing information, you'll know exactly where they came from. Simply shine your black light on the returned form, and anything written in invisible ink will show right up. RSVPs with missing information are common. A black light and a black-light pen take care of that, and your guests will be none the wiser.

#519 *Sweet, Sweet Thanks*

Want thank-you cards that do more than express your gratitude? Make them edible! Purchase or print small, round stickers sized to fit on the bottom of Hershey's Kisses or Reese's Peanut Butter Cups. A simple thank-you message on the stickers is perfect. Snuggle several pieces into an organza bag tied with a ribbon bow, then add a tag that reads: "This sweet thank-you comes from our hearts. Enjoy!" Be sure to sign each tag by hand (something you can do long before the wedding). If your thank-yous will be mailed in the hot months, switch from chocolate candy to bite-sized cookies. Wrap them individually in a pretty cellophane wrap, affix the stickers to the bottoms, and bag as you would the candies. Mail the thank-you treats in small craft boxes. Edible thank-yous may cost a bit more than traditional thank-you cards, but they're much more surprising and enjoyable to receive!

#520 *The Eyes Have It*

Clever and artistic. That's what you get when you replace your guest book with an eye chart. Use one of the free, online eye-chart makers to create whatever "eye catching" message you wish, such as "Here's to Happily Ever After" or "A Wedding Today Is for All the Tomorrows." The chart maker scales the letters from large to small to make your phrase look like a real eye chart. Take your creation to a copy facility capable of blowing it up to poster size, mat it, and place it on an easel at the reception entrance. Provide permanent markers for guests to use to sign the mat. After the reception, it's ready for framing. Soon it will be a memorable, lifelong conversation piece in your home. It's easy and fun, but if you're not inclined to create eye-chart art yourself, look for crafty entrepreneurs who will create your custom eye chart for a fee. And to really pump up the "clever," set your basket of marker pens next to an arrangement fashioned from flowers and old eyeglasses.

#521 *Miniature Panache*

Give ordinary place cards a bit of "formal" fun with the addition of miniature bow ties. Make them yourself out of anything from felt to beaded ribbon, or look for packages of ready-made bow ties where crafts are sold. They are usually sold in packages of 20 to 24 and cost pennies apiece. Touch a dab of glue onto one corner or the top center of the place card, press the bow tie against it, and that's it. Your plain cards now have wedding personality. To spice things up, don't restrict yourself to formal black ties. Try a gingham print, polka dots, or bow ties made from fluffy angora yarn. It costs very little to add a bit of splash to your place cards, and the payoff is worth much more than the small investment in time and money.

#522 *Hello Hankies*

Sometimes the best stationery isn't stationery at all. It's a hanky. Imagine their delight as prospective guests open an envelope and pull out a lovely, functional save-the-date handkerchief instead of a typical card? With silk screening and embroidery, anything that can be said on paper can be said on a hanky. Want to ask someone to be a bridesmaid and give her a keepsake in the process? Pose the question on a beautifully designed hanky. Want to guarantee that your wedding program doesn't end up in the trash? Print your day's events on a hanky. Handkerchiefs can substitute for paper in any number of circumstances. They come in all sizes, and ordering custom hankies in bulk will result in discounted pricing. You may find that sending an enduring, informative gift doesn't cost any more than sending out a paper notice, but doing so will no doubt elevate your wedding's memorability tenfold.

FLOWERS

CHAPTER NINE • *Flowers*

One of Earth's most precious gifts to mankind is its vast tapestry of beautiful, fragrant flowers. With their crucial role in pollination, the world's flower blossoms literally keep the life cycle moving forward. But it's their special impact on human emotions that makes people love flowers so profoundly. Humble flowers provide a respite from a fast-paced world. In their gentle presence, humans can find their own sense of serenity.

Wedding flowers are meant to be beautiful; they help to unify a theme or highlight a color palette as they transform everything from gowns and tuxedos to tables and walls. Even the most gorgeous photograph of a city skyline cannot compete with the simplest snapshot of a flower garden. That's because flowers don't need compositional skill to make them appealing. Their appeal comes naturally.

Unfortunately, wedding flowers can be quite expensive. In the pages of this chapter, you will find ideas about exquisite flower choices, as well as beautiful alternatives to traditional floral pieces. It is absolutely possible to create a stunning floral atmosphere without emptying the local flower shop.

As you will see, wedding flowers are extremely versatile. They can express a "fun and fabulous" vibe just as easily as they can enhance an elegant one. Whether your chosen motif is country, Victorian, tropical, exotic, or any other formal or informal theme, the way you present the floral creations, as well as the specific blooms themselves, can bring the desired ambiance to life. With amazing floral displays providing the backdrop and setting the mood, you — and your entire wedding — will look even more beautiful.

#523 *How Does My Garden Grow?*

The cost of wedding flowers is frequently astronomical, especially if unique blooms are desired for bouquets, pew arrangements, and centerpieces. But do flowers have to be purchased?

When weddings are planned many months in advance, there's plenty of time to get in touch with your earthy side and create a personal wedding-day floral tapestry. Grow your wedding flowers in a backyard garden or in patio pots, and enlist friends and family to grow for you as well.

There's something amazing about carrying a bouquet of flowers you've nurtured to maturity. A little research about timing and varieties, paired with a few self-watering globes, good soil, and a bit of sunshine (real or artificial), and your wedding-day flowers will be ready when you are.

If you're partial to expensive flowers like lilies or orchids, expect to pay a premium at the florist for each bloom. But growing your own can save a bundle, and as a bonus, you get to enjoy a source of welcome relaxation during the hectic wedding-planning phase.

#524 *Corsages for the Ladies in Your Life*

The answer to the question of who needs a corsage or wristlet is simple. If the word "mother" is in the description, the lady gets one. Mothers, grandmothers, godmothers, and stepmothers are honored guests at the wedding, and each should receive a wedding-day corsage or wristlet. The floral display doesn't have to be elaborate, but it should be suitable. Soft, neutral colors are best, so that she can change her mind about her attire at the last moment if she wishes.

Some wedding couples provide corsages only to mothers and grandmothers, but doing so can understandably result in hurt feelings. It's certainly acceptable to slightly alter the corsages according to the relationship — ivory roses for mothers, white carnations for grandmothers, spider mums for godmothers, etc. — but leaving someone off the list may generate unwelcome wedding-day animosity.

It's far better to choose less expensive corsages for everyone than to choose more expensive flowers for a few and leave others out completely. Corsages should convey love and respect for the influential women in your life.

#525 *Flowers Make the Man!*

Boutonnières for the groom and his groomsmen are often afterthoughts. But a man's floral accent can surely be more than a single selected bud that matches the bride's bouquet.

Ask a man what flowers he prefers, and he's likely to look at you as if you've grown an extra head. He couldn't care less. But you care, and when those wedding-day photos arrive, you'll be glad you gave the issue some dedicated thought. The right boutonnière adds flavor and character.

Men generally like things to be, well, manly, so don't go all delicate on him. Give him something substantial that suits his personality. Whether it's a single sturdy bloom or a boutonnière "arrangement," stay within your broad floral theme, but match the flowers to the man. He may not voice his approval, but he'll be thinking it.

Boutonnières for fathers, grandfathers, stepfathers, and godfathers should follow the same guidelines but be crafted of neutral colors to more easily complement whatever attire each may be wearing.

#526 *The Allure of Silk*

Well-made silk flowers in wedding bouquets can anchor unusually inventive creations and solve many floral issues. Whether the bouquet is fashioned completely of silk or silk blooms and greens are incorporated merely as accents, the result is impressive.

Use silk when allergies prevent the use of real flowers, or when it's the only way to include your favorite out-of-season flower in your arrangements. Silk flowers don't die, and you may find that turning your bouquet into a permanent keepsake after the wedding is less challenging than doing so with real flowers.

Weddings planned during potentially adverse weather seasons can benefit from silk flowers, which won't be affected by precipitation, extreme heat, or bitter cold.

There are plenty of reasons to incorporate silk flowers into bouquets, centerpieces, and pew arrangements, but the most important one is that you find them beautiful.

#527 *Knock on Wood!*

The very idea of wooden flowers may seem strange, but that could be because you haven't had the pleasure of seeing the exquisite wooden roses, orchids, lilies, and other blooms created by talented wood craftspeople. Some wooden flowers take your breath away.

Carry wooden flowers in bouquets, use them in vases, or weave them into centerpieces. Embrace their natural earthy colors, or paint them any color of the rainbow. In spite of their sturdy beginnings, wooden flowers crafted from thin birch and other woods are delicate, and how they are carved is key. Begin your search for wooden flowers online, where craftspeople showcase their work and wholesalers offer bulk options.

Some wooden flowers come with fabric leaves and bendable wire stems, making them easy to manipulate into arrangements. It's possible to create dozens of floral works of art with them at a fraction of the cost of doing the same with the real flowers, and you can do well in advance of the wedding day. And since wooden flowers don't die, the pieces from the reception will make engaging, permanent additions to the homes of friends and family.

#528 *When Less Is More*

Wedding flowers add more than color to the occasion. They magically intertwine a sensation of serenity with the excitement of a fairy tale. But a "the more the better" approach is not always the best way to achieve this enchanting effect.

Some of the most cleverly designed bouquets have no more than three stunning flowers cascading down woven grasses. And centerpieces that feature a single spectacular bloom rising from a bed of variegated greens can add artful sophistication to tables.

Choosing deliberately sparse florals will likely save money, but depending upon the flower choices, savings may be diminished. A single-flower centerpiece featuring a Casablanca lily is going to cost significantly more than one featuring a spider mum. But both have their place, and because sometimes less really is more, both can look amazing.

#529 *Razzle-Dazzle Bouquet Jewels*

Even Mother Nature could use a little bling now and then, and bridal-bouquet jewels add personality to ordinary florals.

Colorful Swarovski® crystals sprinkled in the heart of an open rose, or a tiny crystal bumblebee clutching the rim of a sunflower, add just enough sparkle to wow, but not enough to distract from the beauty of the flowers.

Affix crystal bridal-bouquet jewelry with picks, clips, or wires. From single crystals to gentle waterfalls of gems, options are limited only by the imagination. Even sparkling initials or monograms are easy to create.

Bridal-bouquet jewels are so versatile they can also be incorporated into centerpieces, and even into wedding-cake décor. But their most fabulous asset is their ability to reflect each bride's dazzling individuality.

#530 *Remembrance Accents*

When sentiment takes precedence over artistic design, heirlooms in the bridal bouquet are perfect.

Heirloom jewelry doesn't necessarily sparkle, and sentimental adornments may not be jewels at all. Tiny seashells gathered with a loved one, a special charm received as a child, and even segments of great-grandma's broken pearl necklace can all be woven into bouquets with great success.

When emotional connection is important, heirlooms in the bridal bouquet add that extra little something special that can't be achieved any other way.

#531 *No Bouquets?*

Allergies, expense, and the desire to be unique are all reasons a bride might choose to forgo a traditional bouquet on her wedding day. Fortunately, there are viable alternatives.

Small lanterns with flameless or flickering candles, carried by the bride and her attendants, can turn a nighttime wedding magical. Large, open seashells filled with a waterfall of pearls are beach-wedding perfect. A frosted-pinecone nosegay suits a winter wedding, and a bouquet of herbs and grains is ideal for autumn. A book of poetry or a parasol occupies the hands and adds intimacy. Religious brides may wish to carry a token of their faith.

There are plenty of nonfloral options for brides and bridesmaids. If it's meaningful, accents the wedding theme, and looks good, it can be lovely.

#532 *Submerged and Gorgeous*

Not all flowers need air to breathe. Flower blooms completely submerged in water can create stunning tabletop displays.

Begin with a tall, cylindrical glass vase, or choose a variety of heights if you wish to create a cluster. Precut your flower stems to whatever lengths you wish — maybe a very short stem for the bottom flower with different lengths for the bloom or blooms positioned above it. The stems will keep the blooms from sinking onto each other. For a more ethereal look, remove the stems entirely, and replace them with clear plastic straws that support the blossoms without distracting from them. Or, for a richer presentation, replace the stems with floral wire covered with crystal beads.

Once the flowers are positioned, very gently add water, taking care not to pour it directly on the blooms. Voilà! You've made centerpiece magic. Float a final flower on top of each cylinder if you wish.

A dense flower like a rose works well, while a more fragile flower, like a lilac, may flake in the water. Experiment with your favorite blooms to find the combination that pleases you the most.

#533 *Lilies of the Valley for Me*

One of the most cherished wedding-day flowers is the tiny powerhouse known as the lily of the valley. It's delicate, graceful, and blessed with a beauty that complements virtually every other flower. Unfortunately, it's also pricey, easily wilted, difficult to work with, cursed with an incredibly short growing season, and sometimes downright impossible to find. Furthermore, the blooms are so small that it often takes numerous stems just to accent a floral piece, and with a single stem starting at over $10, it's easy to see how quickly this divine flower can become cost prohibitive. But who says those lilies have to be fresh?

Any bouquet or arrangement can include silk lilies of the valley. Integrating silk and fresh flowers is easy when the silk ones are so small. Unless guests plan on running their hands through the flowers, no one is likely to know that the lilies of the valley are silk while the rest of the flowers are fresh.

The lily of the valley stands for purity and happiness, and a quality silk version can bring as much magic to the wedding day as its living inspiration — without the need to hock a family heirloom to cover the cost.

#534 *Freeze-Dried before the Wedding?*

Freeze-drying bridal bouquets preserves them as keepsakes after the wedding, but that process may also provide a wedding-day benefit.

If you're not married to the idea of fresh flowers, a freeze-dried bouquet, centerpieces, and pew décor may be for you. Freeze-dried flower arrangements are easily purchased in advance, shipped to destination locations, and stored for long periods. Because the moisture is removed from the flowers, the bouquets weigh less than their fresh counterparts, and there is no worry throughout the day that the bridal bouquet is wilting, thereby preventing later preservation.

Freeze-dried flowers are especially fitting for the crispness of fall weddings, and they perform well on blistering days that challenge fresh flowers to stay beautiful for more than an hour or two.

Some freeze-dried arrangements will cost about the same as fresh flowers, while others, like the tossing bouquet, may cost considerably less.

Comparing the look and feel of a freeze-dried bouquet to a comparable fresh one is the best way to decide which works best for your wedding. Freeze-dried flowers are sometimes a very welcome saving grace.

#535 *The Glamorous Tussy Mussy*

Borrowing from history can have its perks, and the tussy-mussy bouquet is one of them.

A tussy mussy (alternatively known as a tussie-mussie) is a handheld cone-shaped vase that holds bridal-bouquet flowers. The tussy mussy has been around for centuries and is customarily made of sterling silver or silver plate, and it may be embellished with Victorian designs. Some modern tussy mussies are fashioned of other materials and adorned with crystals, beads, or original art. They make carrying wedding flowers easy, and most come with stands that permit the tussy-mussy bouquets to be displayed upright at the reception, turning them into centerpieces or cake-table accents.

A tussy-mussy vase also makes a useful after-wedding remembrance piece for the home. Add a few seasonal blooms, and the memories stay as fresh as the day of the "I do."

#536 *Twinkle, Twinkle Little Flower*

A bride walking down the aisle with a pulsating, strobe-lit bouquet is probably not conducive to the romance of a wedding day. On the other hand, discreet and strategically placed accent lighting in a bridal bouquet can easily raise the elegance quotient.

Small LED lights secured deep inside a bouquet can give flowers, especially white ones, a soft, ethereal glow without exposing any actual lights. Tiny bulbs lightly sprinkled throughout a bouquet can add just the right amount of sparkle, and lighted strings woven into greens and ribbons are an inspired finishing touch. The key to effective bouquet lighting is restraint. Less is plenty.

Lighted bouquets are especially effective at nighttime weddings, but even when carried on a sun-drenched beach, the hint of light in a bouquet captures the eye and the imagination.

#537 *Leis with the Aloha Spirit*

Most everyone knows that "Aloha" means both hello and good-bye, but few realize that the true spirit of aloha is so woven into the fabric of Hawaiian life that it's actually referred to in Hawaiian law.

In short, aloha is about welcoming others with kindness and friendliness. It's about love, compassion, and selfless giving. The aloha spirit is a beautiful underscore for any wedding day, and the nonverbal expression of that spirit is the floral lei.

Leis are ideal for men or women, and they can replace bouquets, corsages, boutonnières, and even centerpieces. Purchase professional leis, or handcraft your own using fresh blooms, dental floss, and an appropriate needle. Plumerias, gardenias, and orchids are just a few of the many flowers that make gorgeous leis.

A beach wedding dressed with leis is understandably perfect, but don't disregard leis for landlocked weddings, or even for those during frosty winter months. Because leis are as effectively fashioned from winter flowers as from tropical ones, they bring the aloha spirit to life even when icy trees and snowmen dominate the landscape.

#538 *Ballerina Tulle*

The soft fullness of a ballerina's tutu is an ingenious foundation for a bridal bouquet.

Sometimes the wedding budget doesn't allow for mountains of flowers, or sometimes a bride simply wishes to have something different. A ballerina bouquet features flowers nestled into a gentle cloud of tulle or flowers separated by tulle arcs. In either case, fewer flowers are needed to increase a bouquet's size.

Whether it's economics or artistic expression that leads you to a ballerina bouquet, a soft allure is guaranteed. Adding tulle to the bouquet broadens design and color possibilities, and saves money in the process. There's a lot to be said for something so simple that can do so much.

#539 *The Glory of Giants*

Even though all flowers are beautiful, some manage to reign head and shoulders above the rest, simply because they are head and shoulders above the rest. These are the giant blooms.

When considering first impressions, giant flowers know no equal. It's hard to look away from the six- to eight-inch girth of a giant football mum, or to ignore the in-your-face beauty of a giant lime zinnia. From stunning pew décor to simple but compelling centerpieces, giant blooms accomplish much. With such a large presence, you'll only need one to three flowers for most floral applications. Add a bit of greenery and a bow if desired, and you've created something statuesque.

Whether it's the rich purple globe of a giant allium or the expansive breadth of a mammoth sunflower, big blooms offer a lot of floral bang for the buck.

#540 *Traveling Flowers*

The Internet is a way of modern life, and there's little that can't be ordered online. Wedding flowers are no exception. Ship wholesale and retail wedding flowers to your door from virtually anywhere in the world, but exercise caution. Never is the reputation and stability of a company more important than when ordering something perishable online. If you open a shipment of wilted flowers, there will be no down-the-street florist to fix the problem.

Can wedding flowers be successfully ordered online? Absolutely. The key is to deal only with well-vetted companies whose references you have personally investigated.

The two primary reasons flowers are ordered online are to save money or to acquire out-of-season flowers from a location where they are currently in season. If flowers are ordered in bulk, you will be responsible for whipping them into bouquets, corsages, centerpieces, and other floral needs. Some online floral sellers offer certain styles of ready-made bouquets.

Weather and delivery delays are important considerations. While some online florists and wholesalers offer limited guarantees, it would be rare to find one who would insure against Mother Nature or a labor strike.

Take care in selecting either a local florist or an online provider. Each has something unique to offer, but the most important criterion is your level of comfort with your ultimate choice.

#541 *A Touch of Floral Essence*

It's sad to note, but today's flower shops are filled with flowers that should smell amazing but simply don't. In decades past, walking into a flower shop bursting with roses, lilacs, and other wondrous blooms would wow the senses, but flowers bred to be hearty became longer lasting at the expense of their signature fragrances. In many cases, a rose can no longer be distinguished from a daisy in a blindfold test.

Wedding-flower preparation has become a two-part process: buy the flower, then add a drop of floral scent. It's shameful that fragrance has to be added back to the very thing it came from, but if it's important that your wedding flowers actually smell like flowers, essential floral essences can help. Apply the oil to the stem, just below the bloom, to protect delicate petals.

It may seem silly to try to give a flower back its scent, but that may be the only remedy when growers value quantity over quality. Of course, you can always grow your own fragrant wedding-day blooms, or reap the benefit of Mother Nature's fresh and aromatic bounty by picking wildflowers.

#542 *Frosty, Sweet Floral Art*

It's no surprise that edible sugared flowers show up on wedding cakes, but did you know that, with a few delicate flowers, floral wire, tape, egg whites, and superfine sugar, you can create stunning accent flowers for the bridal bouquet?

Sugared flowers begin with real flowers, and any bloom with thin petals works well. Once the blossom is fully opened and picked, its stem is reinforced with floral wire and floral tape, then the flower is allowed to air dry long enough to eliminate any excess moisture that may linger on the petals. A small artist's paintbrush gently applies an even, thin layer of the egg white (the glue) to each petal, and then superfine sugar is sprinkled evenly over the egg-white wash.

The petals go limp during the process of sugaring, but when the flower dries, it hardens. Accenting the bouquet with just a few sugared flowers turns an ordinary floral array into something magical. The frosty white covering doesn't hide the color of the bloom, but it makes the bloom look as if it has been kissed with pixie dust.

Sugared flowers make beautiful accents for floral bouquets any season of the year, and a few sugared blooms in a bud vase create a simple but stunning focal point for tabletops.

#543 *Bridal-Bouquet Confetti*

Whether freeze-drying, pressing, or dipping in silica gel, professionally preserving the bridal bouquet is costly, and the result is a large decorative piece you may or may not want to look at for years to come. A versatile alternative is confetti.

Turn your bridal bouquet into confetti at home by separating the bouquet and hanging the flowers upside down to dry. Leave them for at least two weeks, until all moisture is gone and the petals are crisp. Take them down and use scissors to cut the blooms into confetti pieces.

Buy potpourri or aroma lockets, and fill them with confetti to create keepsake jewelry for yourself or your mother, sister, grandmother, or any other woman close to your heart. Or fill crystal perfume bottles with confetti for tabletop décor, and use confetti sprays to embellish a framed wedding invitation or photograph.

#544 *The Glorious Gilded Rose*

Sometimes simple is better. If nosegays don't appeal to you, consider carrying a single, long-stemmed, gilded rose.

Gold-dipped roses aren't just golden anymore. Real roses are preserved at the peak of their beauty, then forever encased in gold, silver, or platinum. Alternately, you may choose one that is lacquered and merely trimmed in a precious metal, preserving the rose's actual color.

A bride carrying a single silver or platinum rose, with her bridesmaids carrying gold ones, is a minimalistic but lovely sight. In lieu of boutonnières, the groom and his groomsmen can opt for gilded leaf pins that look as if they were plucked from the ladies' roses. And, of course, there is no need for preservation after the wedding. These flowers are already forever blooms.

Always comparison shop, and ask to see a real sample. Gilding roses is an art, and you only want the best-quality workmanship at your wedding.

#545 *Fall-Fantasy Wedding Flowers*

Autumn brides are treated to bold, seasonal options that make bouquets, centerpieces, and floor vases pop. The stately sunflower leads the pack. With its size, deep color contrast, and perfect symmetry, only a few well-placed blooms are needed to create impressive floral art.

Fall gerbera daisies, cosmos, hydrangeas, chrysanthemums, and dahlias offer a depth of colors as well as unique decorating attributes. For example, cosmos are not all created equal. Some have elongated petals, while others have petals tipped with ruffled, lacy borders. And the scent of a chocolate cosmo even mimics a chocolate bar with a vanilla finish.

Fall flowers also create powerful connotations. Sunflowers represent adoration, while dahlias mean dignity, and chrysanthemums stand for excitement. Mix these richly hued and symbolically potent autumn flowers with white roses and accents of the season, like bronzed fallen leaves and ornamental cabbage, to fill the wedding and reception with floral masterpieces that simply aren't possible any other time of the year.

#546 *Floral Sunlight*

Some churches have little natural light, but with just a few subtle floral changes, it's possible to brighten the surroundings considerably.

Flowers in shades of fuchsia, lime green, yellow, and marine blue, as well as pastel tones like white, pale yellow, and soft pink, can create the illusion of light even when there is none. Just changing pink roses to hot-pink roses can make a discernible difference, especially in darkened locations.

So factor the brightness of the ceremony venue into your floral scheme. There's no point in spending hard-earned cash on beautiful bouquets of flowers that blend into the shadows. If the facility is dim, let your flowers shine their own light on the occasion.

#547 *Sprinkle Flowers*

Think outside the centerpiece. Instead of large, expensive centerpieces for each table, consider using a candle cluster or a piece of table art along with sprinkle flowers.

Sprinkle flowers are individual flower stems paired with a bit of baby's breath, heather, or another floral accent, then placed in a water tube, taped with floral tape, and tied with a ribbon. Think of them as boutonnières with longer stems. Sprinkle flowers are an easy, breezy decorating delight, perfect for "sprinkling" on dining tables, throughout buffet dishes, on the bar, at the guest-book table, and anywhere else that might need sprucing up.

It's easy to create sprinkle flowers at home from blooms purchased in bulk, so labor costs associated with big centerpieces are eliminated. Water tubes (not to be confused with water picks, which have stems on the bottom) are inexpensive, as are floral tape and floral wire (advised for delicate flowers, but not necessary for hearty blooms). Purchase accent ribbon in bulk to further reduce expenses.

Big floral centerpieces are gorgeous, but sprinkle flowers are just as beautiful in their own way.

#548 *Imagination-Inspired Practice Bouquets*

A bride and her attendants need something in their hands at the wedding rehearsal to learn how to carry their bouquets on the wedding day. But springing for extra flowers just for rehearsal bouquets is not very appealing. Invent them instead.

As long as they are the approximate size of the real bouquets, practice bouquets can be fashioned from anything. Surprise your attendants with bright paper blooms tied with a ribbon or a collection of lollipops pierced through a saucer-sized paper plate. A grouping of popcorn balls on bamboo sticks is perfect for autumn rehearsals, and bagged cotton candy on paper cones is summertime fun.

Let your imagination run wild. The wedding rehearsal doesn't have to be all business. Some lighthearted touches, like off-the-wall practice bouquets, are just what the relaxed and happy bride ordered.

#549 *Magnificent Spring*

Spring brides are lucky. Freshly bloomed lilies of the valley, lilacs, tulips, gardenias, and poppies are just a few of the fragrant, delightful flowers available to spring brides, without incurring "out of season" expenses. Accent with blossoms from once-a-year flowering trees like peach, apple, cherry, and magnolia, and it's easy to see why flowers from the season of rebirth are so coveted.

Other spring flowers, like blooming begonias or geraniums, are perfect for decorating on a grand scale. Use them to create living walls and arches.

Just a few dahlias or hyacinth blooms transform darkened corners or stark tables into garden spots, and potted dogwood trees or tall stalks of pussy willows infuse any ceremony or reception space with spring fever.

#550 *Gift-Table Inspiration*

Centerpieces add elegance to the gift table, but the best centerpiece for a gift table is . . . a gift. A beautifully wrapped box, tied with an oversized ribbon and a floral-spray bow on top, is perfect. No gift-toting guest will need to ask, "Where do I put this?" Position the gift-box centerpiece on a decorative pedestal to make the gift table self-evident. As a bonus, you'll likely use fewer flowers than required for a traditional centerpiece, cutting floral costs without sacrificing aesthetic impact.

Place a sheer silk or lace overlay atop the tablecloth, and center the pedestal and gift-box centerpiece toward the back if the table is against a wall or in the center if it's not. Add an attractive card receptacle, either on the table or beside it, and your gift table will be a reception highlight.

#551 *Flowers Too Hot to Handle*

Commercial enterprises share a common bad habit. They raise prices just because they can, and florists are no different. The higher the demand, the higher the price.

Planning a wedding near peak floral-selling events like Mother's Day, Valentine's Day, Christmas, or Easter, or even during prom season, is an invitation to pay more. A surcharge on flowers can really impact the wedding budget, but you're not without options.

The obvious choice is to avoid holding the wedding when flowers are at a premium. But sometimes it's unavoidable. Perhaps Mother's Day weekend is the one and only time everyone can get together, or you've always had your heart set on a Valentine's Day wedding. Whatever the reason, you may find your wedding competing with a floral holiday. If so, the next best choice is to sign your flower contract as early as possible.

Florists want your business, and a floral reservation with a lot of lead time is a valuable bird in the hand. Even though the florist knows how busy the holiday will be, an order with a deposit made during leaner times may help you avoid higher charges. It's a win-win transaction: the florist gets a solid order and a nonrefundable deposit when it's really needed, and you get flowers during a peak holiday, without stretching the flower budget.

Floral supply and demand creates flowers too financially hot to handle during certain times of the year, but with careful planning and shopping, it's possible to find a florist willing to help keep costs in check.

#552 *Uniquely "Her" Corsage Pin*

To make those mother and grandmother corsages something to remember, consider custom-made corsage pins. Create beautiful beaded pins from supplies found at typical craft stores, or if you're craft challenged, search for "beaded corsage pins" online. You'll discover a wealth of talented crafters ready to fashion unique designs just for you. Make the pins as elegantly simple or as richly elaborate as your wedding theme, or individualize them to each recipient in the vintage or modern style befitting that particular person.

Original, keepsake corsage pins look gorgeous on the wedding day, and after the wedding is over, they live on as stylish hat or lapel pins.

#553 *Floral-Budget ABCs*

Florists love flowers and profits, and rightly so, but to avoid single-handedly inflating those profits, stick to your floral budget by sticking to your ABCs:

Arrive prepared. Don't go to the florist with no ideas of your own. The florist will begin by showing you expensive pieces without price tags. You'll fall in love with something exotic, only to discover that it's way beyond your budget. Disappointment follows, and before you know it, you're tempted to cast your budget to the wind. Before a single design book is cracked, instruct the florist to show you only the sections with bouquets and arrangements in the price range you specify.

Be strong. It's hard not to buckle under the pressure of desire, but to stay on budget, you need fortitude and mental incentives. Stick to your guns by reminding yourself that every dollar you save from the flower budget is a dollar more to spend on the honeymoon or on something beautiful for your new home.

Close the deal quickly. The quicker you negotiate for all your floral needs and sign on the dotted line, the less likely you are to thoughtlessly exceed your budget. Exercise careful consideration of all floral pieces long before you ever get to the flower shop, then get in and get out before the florist has the opportunity to say that budget-killing line, "Oh, you just have to see this!" Flowers are addictive. You'll want them all, and the longer you stay on the premises, the more likely the flowers, and the florist, will win the day.

Remember your ABCs, and you won't have to worry about busting the budget. Forget them, and your budget may bloom bigger than the flowers you crave.

#554 *Pretty Paper Expressions*

Certain paper-flower designs are complicated and require diligent, time-consuming work. Other patterns are so simple that even children can turn a scrap of paper into a beautiful blossom. Whatever the design, the key to a paper flower that you would be proud to display at your wedding is cleanliness — clean cuts, clean glue applications, and clean floral taping of the wire stems. Make each step polished, and your paper-flower bouquet may garner more appreciation than its real counterpart.

To create truly personal, distinctive paper-flower centerpieces, begin with photographs. Using a color copier, print digital photos onto vellum paper, which you will transform into flower blooms. Use any simple flower pattern found online or at a craft store to create flowers for a vase or a centerpiece. Tailor each group of flowers to a specific theme. For example, use childhood photos for flowers for the parents' tables or vintage wedding photos for a guest-book bouquet.

No longer are paper flowers the flat, construction-paper creations of your elementary-school days. When created with care and original materials, today's paper flowers are absolutely wedding worthy.

#555 *Flowers in Satin and Lace*

Wire or wicker baskets, boxes, tin cans, buckets, and bowls are all potential centerpiece bases. All work well in their natural state, but to bestow the kiss of elegance upon them, wrap them in rich fabrics like satin and lace.

Use a round, flat-bottomed, pillowcase shape to slip the container into, then tie it with a ribbon. Or carefully braid fabrics, in different but complementary tones, to build row upon row of braids, making a dense and interesting sheath. Another option is to cut the fabrics into 2½-inch circles, and then hot glue only the center of each circle to the container, allowing the outer edge to hang free. Squeeze the circles close together for a soft, fluffy appearance. To add sparkle, glue rhinestones or beads to the center of each fabric circle.

Save money by hitting garage sales and thrift stores to find dresses, coats, ties, lace linens, and other garments or fabrics to cut up. Buying new material with which to decorate centerpiece bases is not necessary when an old prom dress with a splotch still has a skirt full of useable fabric.

#556 *Fresh Floral Escort*

How many reception tables will you have? How many flowers are there in the world? Even if your answer to the first question is a huge number, the answer to the second question will dwarf it. That's good news. It means you can forgo individual escort cards and direct your guests to their tables via beautiful, one-of-a-kind floral presentations.

Create a vase centerpiece featuring a different fresh or silk flower for each table. On the table near the vase, place a small, decorative tent card that includes the flower's name and its symbolic meaning.

Combine one or more of all the different flowers into a generous bouquet, and place it on the escort table at the reception entrance. Surround the bouquet with one upright 5" x 7" escort card for each table, denoting the names of the guests to be seated at that table, along with an image of the flower that adorns it. To make your escort cards, you can find or take a photo of each flower variety, design the cards on your computer, then print the cards with a color printer. Alternately, you could paint the flower on each card, or you could simply add a silk or fresh blossom for identification. Be sure to include the flower's name at the top of each card. Many flowers look similar, and a name guarantees that "daisy" guests won't pull up a chair at the "sunflower" table.

When tables have distinct floral identities, the room not only looks amazing, but the guests are also treated to a quick visual reminder, so that after they've shared a dance or visited the buffet, restroom, or bar, wandering back to the wrong table won't be a problem.

#557 *Meaningful Petals*

Most engagements last for several months or more, and during that time, romance is pretty high on the daily agenda. That can mean plenty of "special occasion" or "no special reason" floral gifts from the groom-to-be to his intended. Instead of watching those flowers wither and die, put them to good use.

After enjoying the blossoms for a time, but well before wilting begins, gently remove the petals from each flower stem. Dry the petals in an ordinary food dehydrator, then store them in airtight plastic containers.

Use your petals to decorate the aisle, sprinkle on tabletops, or scatter anywhere you wish at the wedding. They won't be just any flowers. They'll be petals rich with romantic sentiment.

Keep the petals' special history as a private connection between you and your groom, or share their unique, meaningful origins with all of the guests via a notation in the wedding program.

#558 *Wrapped in Ivy*

The intertwining nature of ivy is widely believed to represent fidelity, making it popular for bouquets and boutonnières. But even if ivy doesn't suit your bouquet design, it's still possible to enjoy its symbolism by using only the leaves.

Tuck a few ivy leaves into two small satin pouches. Slip one into the groom's pocket and hide yours beneath your gown, or affix it to your garter. Because ivy sometimes provokes allergic reactions, and it can mildly discolor clothing, real ivy should be isolated in a pouch before being added to attire. To forgo pouches, choose silk ivy leaves instead.

The ivy doesn't have to be seen. Just knowing that it's there, and what it represents, will add a sweet, personal touch to your wedding.

#559 *The Green Stretch*

When the floral budget is straining, stretch it with greens.

Greenery is far less expensive than flowers, but with just the tuck of a ribbon here or the addition of an ornament there, greens can stand alone to create beautiful arrangements and decorative accents. You can select ferns, ivy, magnolia leaves, eucalyptus, grasses, and any number of other foliage to gather together bouquet-style, intertwine into garlands, group into vases, or simply drape upon tables, shelves, pew caps, and even along floors.

Flowers always look richer when supported by greenery, but greenery doesn't always need flowers to look its best. To stretch the budget and add natural beauty, rely on the Earth's abundant greens.

#560 *The Floral Buddy System*

If you're planning your wedding at a busy venue, consider the buddy-system approach to ceremony flowers.

When more than one ceremony a day is scheduled at a church, garden, or other venue, think about sharing the cost of the venue flowers with the other brides and grooms who will precede or follow you. Ask the venue coordinator to contact the other wedding couples on your behalf to see if they have any interest in a floral collaboration.

If the venue is decked out in all white or ivory, this scenario is easy. Every wedding couple chips in on the cost of the venue flowers but indulges their own color choices for nosegays, boutonnières, and special ceremonial flowers.

Sharing the cost of venue flowers can result in steep savings for all wedding couples involved, but it only works if a universal color and style is chosen. Brides and grooms looking to be completely unique may not wish to share even their venue flowers with others. But most ceremonies are short, and the cost of decorative floral pieces is high. A floral buddy system is one easy way to stretch the floral budget.

#561 *Crystal-Art Bouquets*

Flowers make beautiful bridal bouquets, but they aren't the only stunning option. If you're handy with beads and wire or know someone who is, consider a bouquet made from crystal beads. It will look heavenly on your wedding day, and just as spectacular on your 50th wedding anniversary. From floral patterns to bursts of "fireworks" to bouquets that create the illusion of dancing waters, crystal-bead strands can bend, weave, and form unique shapes that flowers cannot achieve. Take a class at the local craft boutique, then use those quiet nights before the fire or the TV to create a bouquet unlike anyone else's. If making it yourself is not feasible, there are plenty of crafty people to hire. Craft boutiques often have bulletin boards full of crafters looking for commissions, but be sure to see a sample or two of their work first to make sure it meets your standards.

#562 *Imaginative Boutonnières*

Many men aren't wild about flowers, so why not offer them nonfloral, or barely floral, boutonnière alternatives? For example, for a Western-themed wedding, choose a sprig of fern topped with a sheriff's badge for the groom and deputy badges for the groomsmen. For a vintage wedding, let the men sport vest chains, stick pins, or watch fobs instead of flowers. Two-inch pewter, silver, or gold lapel pins backed with a green leaf or two are perfect for formal affairs, while a single, unusual, oversized button nestled over a sheaf of natural grasses complements more casual events. If you want to add a personal touch, custom lapel pins are easily created with the assistance of jewelers, engravers, or pin makers. Flowers may be traditional, but they aren't the only boutonnière game in town.

#563 *Spend Your Bouquet!*

You can easily spend a ton of money on bridal bouquets and boutonnières, or you could spend your money on . . . money. Flowers, butterflies, hearts, stars, and bows are all objects that can be created from ordinary, folded dollar bills. Look for instructions online, in craft shops, or in books and magazines, explaining how to make everything from stunning rose patterns to whimsical birds. Paper folding doesn't destroy the money, so when the big day is over, and your "flowers" have been dutifully photographed for posterity, simply unfold the bouquets and bank the bills. If the color of money isn't your favorite, brighten the arrangements with real baby's breath and ribbons, or settle a jewel-tipped pin into the center of each flower to add sparkle. Money florals don't merely trim the flower budget. They recycle it!

#564 *Solar Blooms*

Not all gorgeous flowers push themselves up from the earth. Some get pushed down into the earth! Consider solar garden flowers. Solar-flower blooms are made of a pliable, rubbery plastic in realistic designs and with a light tucked deep inside each blossom. Long stems (green stakes) insert easily into the ground to hold the flowers upright, and a small, green solar box extends from each stem to harness the sun's power. Unlike those dancing solar flowerpots for windowsills often seen in toy stores and specialty shops, these are majestic faux flowers intended for the outdoors. They are available as violets, roses, lilies, snowdrops, and other floral varieties, so it's easy to create a lighted garden for your outdoor wedding. Place them in direct sunlight during the daytime festivities, and as evening falls, the blooms will light up. Use as many as you like to line walkways, set a perimeter, or form decorative floral groupings. These clever blooms are especially helpful in adding romance to places with no power source, like the beach or a desert park. Be sure to follow the manufacturer's instructions, and give them plenty of sun in the days leading up to your wedding day. When new, solar flowers need a day or two of sunlight to fully charge. After that, there's nothing to do but to give them their daily dose of sun and enjoy their beautiful glow at night.

#565 *Belly-Button Bouquets*

It seems pretty simple to grab your bouquet, hold it with both hands, and walk down the aisle. Unfortunately, nerves can trick you and your brides-maids into holding your bouquets awkwardly and at odd heights. You won't think a thing about it until you see your photos or video and realize that, as you walked to your intended, you held your bouquet so high that you inadvertently gave yourself a strange, triple-mountain bosom, while your maid of honor carried her bouquet so low that it looked like a bowling ball she was ready to roll.

Prevent embarrassment and disappointment — and save wedding photos and footage — by taking nervousness out of the mix. At the rehearsal, use the belly button as the starting point, then zero in on the perfect bouquet location. Experiment. Find the best level by taking digital photos and then looking at yourself the way others will see you. Do you want the blooms right at the belly button, or should they be higher, with only the stems or handle at belly button level? It pays to resolve these types of issues before the wedding — especially since wedding-day photos and video happen once, but last forever.

#566 *Size Matters*

Floral photo books help you pick out centerpieces and bouquets, but photos rarely list the dimensions of those creations. If you order a centerpiece thinking it's going to be a foot tall and a foot wide and it's delivered at half that size, you'll be quite dismayed. To prevent being blindsided, it pays to conduct a little research and experimentation.

Keep in mind that price does not necessarily correspond with size. Depending upon the type of flowers selected, it's possible to pay $100 for a centerpiece the size of a coffee mug or $20 for one the size of a bread box.

What should matter first and foremost is how flower arrangements complement their surroundings. For centerpieces, first choose your tables, then try different faux arrangements on them (using any materials, as long as the shape and size are correct). Study the test arrangements from all angles, and gauge how a centerpiece's size will affect the overall look when combined with dinnerware and glassware. Some towering centerpiece styles so overwhelm a table that they stop being beautiful and become gaudy. And no matter how pretty the flowers, too-small centerpieces underwhelm and unbalance a table.

The same is true of bouquets. Stand before a mirror and hold objects of different sizes before you. You will easily see if something pizza-pan size is too big for your small frame, or if something the size of a saucer makes you look as wide as a house. Flowers should enhance, not detract. To make sure the scale of your bouquet flatters you, do your homework, then carry snapshots and a tape measure with you when flower shopping. Discuss dimensions with your florist, not just flower styles and dollars, and you'll increase your odds of getting exactly what you want — and what you thought you ordered.

#567 *The Brilliant Brooch Bouquet*

Let's see. Shopping for vintage jewelry . . . fun. Carrying a one-of-a-kind bridal bouquet . . . more fun. Having no worries about wilted flowers or after-wedding preservation . . . get-out-of-jail-free kind of fun!

All of this wedding fun is found in a beautiful brooch bouquet. Instead of flowers, the bouquet is crafted from brooches and other brilliant jewelry. You get to scour flea markets, thrift stores, and estate sales, and recruit friends and relatives who would love to be included in the wedding by donating a piece to your wedding bouquet. If you wish, make "vintage brooch and pendant jewelry" your bridal-shower theme, and let everyone contribute.

You can fashion the bouquet in all the colors of the rainbow, or stick to a specific color scheme and search only for jewelry that fits that palette. Do the same for materials — all metal, all rhinestones, all crystals, etc. Keep to a theme, or mix and match. You can even paint the finished bouquet to make it all silver, gold, platinum, blue, or any other perfect shade. The sky is the limit on design accents, too, like a feather here, a pearl-tipped silver waterfall there — whatever you can imagine is possible.

Purchasing a custom brooch bouquet made by an artisan won't save you a lot of dollars in lieu of flowers, but making the bouquet yourself surely will. If you weren't born with a crafty design gene, enlist the aid of friends who were. A brooch bouquet is proof positive that diamonds aren't the only things that sparkle.

#568 *Violets and Dandelions*

Childhood was a time to enjoy the fine art of stringing flowers into jewelry. There was something wonderfully peaceful about sitting on the lawn in the waning sun of a summer day, twisting dandelion tails or violets together to make necklaces. The gift of those youthful, homespun trinkets pleased Mom more than any fancy bouquets or priceless jewels ever could.

Your wedding day may be the perfect occasion to recreate that heartfelt experience. Instead of corsages for Mom and Grandma, consider a bracelet of strung flowers — not the heaviness of a wrist corsage, but the gentle flutter of a single strand of flowers that will circle her wrist and brush softly against her hand. You don't have to hope for a dandelion- or violet-filled yard from which to gather your materials. Any favorite flowers will do. As an added benefit, you'll likely cut costs from your flower budget, but that's not the important part. Taking your mom and your grandma back to a time when life was simpler is a special surprise. Whether you make the bracelet yourself or leave it to your florist, your thoughtfulness will be as lovely as the flowers.

#569 *A Beautiful Spread*

Gorgeous, lace hand fans purchased in bulk are an affordable enhancement to your floral centerpieces. Open the blades and anchor the fan to a base by gluing, taping, or stapling it to whatever flat piece you choose. Cover the base in moss or greenery and add small, corsage-sized nosegays of real or silk flowers to either side. In just moments, a beautiful centerpiece will emerge, with the open fan adding height to your display so expensive flowers won't have to. If you prefer a painted-scene fan with the art only on one side, simply place two open fans back-to-back before adding the floral accents. To make the presentation more dramatic for an evening event, seat votive candles in glass holders behind the florals, next to the fan. Alternatively, use the florals to hide small, battery-operated lights positioned next to the fan. The flicker of the candles or the glow of the lights will add warmth to the table.

#570 *On the Button*

Flowers made of buttons are fashionably eclectic. Buttons come in all sizes, shapes, and colors, and they can be styled into flowers that complement a multitude of wedding themes and décor. Brightly colored and patterned buttons impart "uptown fun," while rhinestone buttons lend an "Art Deco nightlife" vibe to the occasion. Whether a collection of single-button flowers is used to add originality to the buffet table, or full centerpieces of brass buttons and white raffia grace all the tables, button flowers are extremely versatile. Any modern or vintage buttons work, from jumbo and imposing to delicate and dancing on the ends of seed-pearl-encrusted floral wire. Button flowers stand alone or blend wonderfully with real florals, proving that it really is possible to make décor as "cute as a button."

#571 *Under the Bloom*

It can be challenging to maintain the liveliness of a fresh boutonnière. With very little room for a water reservoir, boutonnières tend to wilt faster than bridal bouquets, leaving the groom to wander about his reception with a droopy bloom. You could refrigerate a second, identical boutonnière and have him don it for reception photos. Even better, you could give him a creative, "under the bloom" surprise that's perfect for a ceremonial reveal just before the first dance, the cake cutting, or any moment you choose.

Engrave a flat lapel pin with whatever he wishes to say, such as: "Proud to Be Mary's Husband," "First a Groom, Now a Husband," "It's True, I Love Her," or whatever sincere or funny sentiment works for both of you. Place the lapel pin on the jacket and cover it with the boutonnière. When it's time, simply remove the boutonnière with a flourish and toss it away, revealing the special message underneath.

#572 *Sumptuous Succulents*

By definition, weddings are usually soft, flowing occasions, making an array of gorgeous, gentle flowers an obvious and ideal decorative choice. But sometimes "gorgeous and gentle" can be replaced effectively with "gorgeous and succulent."

Succulents are water-retaining plants that come in so many unique varieties that you could choose a different one for each table at the reception and still have more to choose from. Not all cacti are cursed with a bad case of the prickles, and others possess spines that are actually soft to the touch. But cacti and other succulents do all share several wedding-friendly traits. They are hearty, and you can easily purchase them in advance of the wedding day without worry of wilting. They come in rich, deep natural colors that blend well with virtually any decorative design. They are easily gathered into gardens or aligned to make walkways in environmental conditions where flowers would have a hard time surviving. Mix succulents with votive candles or scattered flower petals if you wish to add softness, but many succulents already boast a plush and gentle appearance all on their own.

There's no denying the beauty of flowers, but Mother Nature has also been kind enough to offer a heartier — and usually cost-saving — alternative in succulents. And the best part is that they are just as happy at your uptown, seaside, or mountaintop event as they would be if you were marrying in the heart of the Sahara desert.

#573 *The Spice of Centerpiece Life*

Variety. That's the spice of life, and when it comes to reception center-pieces, variety can transform a reception's look from uniform and elegant to elegant with personality. Using the same color palette and floral choices, have your florist create centerpieces in a range of sizes and styles: some low; some high; some round; some square; three little ones in a cluster on this table, versus one large one on the next; one with long, sweeping tendrils, and one with neatly trimmed sides. Weaving the same colors and flowers into a variety of presentations adds flair without spending additional money. Uniformity is beautiful, but so is creative abandon. Spice up the reception by choosing centerpieces that show all the facets of your style.

#574 *Buds for All*

A centerpiece, a favor, and a place-card holder equal a beautiful trio. That's what you get when you create bud-vase-cluster centerpieces for your tables. Glass bud vases are easily and inexpensively acquired from a dollar store or from floral-supply wholesalers. Purchase as many bud vases as you have guests. Fill each vase with water, a single flower, and a sprig of greenery. When placing them, match the number of vases to the number of guests at a table. For example, at a table of ten, cluster ten flower-filled vases in the center of the table, and loosely tie them together with a wide ribbon that culminates in an elegant bow.

Add an additional bow to the opposite side of the cluster if you wish. At the base of each vase, add an outward-facing place card that includes the guest's name and these words: "This bud vase and its beautiful flower are yours to keep. Thank you for sharing in our celebration."

Unlike some other wedding favors, bud vases are always welcome and useful to those receiving them. But before they scatter to the homes of your guests, they will make your reception tables look fabulous. Even better, they will significantly reduce table-flower expenses and eliminate favor costs altogether.

#575 *'Tis the Season*

Fields of poppies as far as the eye can see. Cherry-blossom trees bursting into gentle, romantic colors. Wildflowers springing up to blanket hillsides with their vibrant, living tapestries. How beautiful is the "season"?

Flowers that bloom in wide swathes, but only for a short period of time, present an extraordinary opportunity for brides and grooms to turn their weddings into something spectacular. If you're planning an outdoor event, or an indoor one at a facility that boasts a panoramic view of nature, consider timing your wedding to this season of abundance. Marrying during those few weeks a year when Mother Nature works her special magic is almost like being married in the glorious but fictional village of Brigadoon.

No matter where you live — from coast to coast, from the desert to the mountains — there is likely to be a certain time period when something special blooms for just a little while. Plan your wedding to take advantage of this natural beauty, and you and your guests will never forget the sights of the day.

#576 *Keeping It (Almost) Real!*

Real flowers can't be beat. Or can they? Sometimes real blooms are just too risky for an extremely hot day, a bitterly cold day, an exceptionally long day, or when allergies turn nature's floral gift into a floral curse. So solve your floral worries with some convenient technology.

Certain contemporary silk flowers known as "real touch," "soft touch," or "natural touch" could fool Mother Nature herself. These very high-quality silk flowers look real, feel real, and in some cases, even smell real. From a distance, most silk flowers are impossible to distinguish from their real counterparts, but a closer inspection spoils the illusion. Not so with these modern silk marvels. And as an added bonus, there's no need to preserve your bouquet after the wedding — it's already a forever bouquet.

Use these outstanding silk blossoms anywhere you would use traditional florals. They are especially appropriate where floral water picks would be troublesome to conceal, like in pew arrangements or boutonnières. Lovely to look at and lovely to handle, "real touch" flowers are a possibility worth investigating.

#577 *Summon Up a Scarf*

There are many wonderful patterns for making fabric flowers. Some are sewn. Some are not. Some create soft blooms. Some create firm ones. When dutifully followed, all patterns will effectively turn fabric scraps into artful flowers, ready to spice up the ceremony or reception.

But to make those fabric flowers a cut above, consider using scarves. When purchased at thrift stores, scarves are a bargain, but still blessed with gorgeous vintage patterns and colors. Your scarf collection can be eclectic, or it can be devoted to a particular subject, like "travel," "music," or even "flowers." Choose the designs and shades that complement your wedding theme or décor, and fashion the scarves into accent pieces for everything from water-pitcher handles to doorjamb arches to tree adornments. If an area is in need of a brightening, create a beautiful display of scarf flowers created from your inexpensive thrift-store finds. Free flower patterns are easily found on the Internet, and if you enlist the aid of a few friends and family members, crafting the flowers won't even cost you a lot of time.

Why scarves? For a momentous occasion like your wedding, scarf designs are often far more interesting, unique, and delicate than anything you can find in the remnant bin at the fabric store.

#578 *No Rain — Just a Leafy Domain*

If your reception tables are long and rectangular, consider filling their centers with floral gardens. Begin with flat-bottomed, plastic rain gutters. An entire ten-foot section costs only a few dollars. Cut it into two-foot sections, seal off the ends with gutter end caps and reposition the sections end-to-end on the table, as if the rain gutter were still one long piece. Leave the gutters in their original color, or decorate them with sparkling spray paint or with hand-brushed, artistic swirls of paint in any color you like. Fill them with potting soil, inexpensive houseplants, and lots of moss or soft ferns to drape over the sides. If you wish, add ribbons, candles, or flower blooms in water picks. The result is an extensive, beautiful, and affordable tabletop garden that makes rectangular tables look fabulous.

After the reception, your long gardens easily separate into their smaller, self-contained sections and become living gifts for special family members or friends. Once home, they are ready for any patio, windowsill, or shelf. Long, rectangular planters positioned end-to-end will serve the same purpose, but unless you find them at a closeout sale, they'll likely cost much more than easily modified rain gutters.

#579 *I'll Take a Rainbow, Please*

Have you ever seen a rainbow rose? It's quite amazing. A rainbow rose is just what you'd imagine: a rose with multicolored petals, some softly hued and others so vibrant that they look as if they've been dipped in a rainbow. And in a way, they have been. Their creation begins when a grower carefully splits the stem and places each individual stem strand into a different container of specially dyed water. As the rose drinks, its petals absorb the color of each water source. The result is a truly magnificent rainbow effect. The flowers are real. They aren't painted — they are simply fed with "magic" water.

For the bride who just can't seem to decide on her colors, rainbow roses come to the rescue. If you want custom colors, that's possible, too. Rainbow roses are pricier than traditional roses, so you may wish to make them a focal point of bouquets and centerpieces rather than composing the entirety of them. But seeing large groups of them together is a wonderful experience. Mother Nature may not have plucked a rainbow from the sky and wrapped it around these roses, but if you use them at your wedding, that's exactly how you — and your dazzled guests — will imagine it must have happened.

#580 *Martini Posh*

If you want your groom to have a boutonnière like no other, give him an early gift: a set of beautiful, gold-plated, crystal-topped martini picks. Not only are they great for drinks, they are wonderful additions to boutonnières. Designer picks are less than three inches long, but adding one to any boutonnière gives it an instant distinction. Since they are inexpensive and usually come in packs of 10 or 12, you could also include picks in the groomsmen's boutonnières. Or give the groom the sole honor, and keep the rest tucked away for that first-year anniversary party.

#581 *Beautiful Sides*

Pew clips designed to attach floral décor to church pews don't always work well on chairs. Chair backs come in so many different shapes, and with such disparities in thickness, that you can wind up with the flower arrangement hanging on the back of the chair instead of the chair back's side, where it absolutely needs to be to create an aisle effect. If the chair back has any top knob or protrusion on the upper corners, it's easy to hang the flowers from a loop. But if the chair back is solid and smooth, whatever is hung on an edge will likely slip off unless secured.

Do this by giving the chair a tulle "shawl." Wrap soft tulle over the inside "shoulder" of the chair back, and drape it to a point just below the outside (aisle) shoulder. Attach your floral spray to the knot you create by tying the two ends of the shawl together. The "up and over" part that covers the inside shoulder of the chair will keep the tulle from slipping down, and the weight of the floral arrangement will keep the knotted side from wandering. If you feel the need to add a little extra security, apply a strip of invisible, no-residue mounting tape between the tulle and the chair back. With a bit of support assistance, it's possible to affix floral arrangements to even the thinnest of chair backs, and with tulle, you add an additional décor element as well.

#582 *Manipulative Mums*

Those adorable poodle pups and ice-cream sundaes made with chrysanthemums always make people smile. Yet even though dog- and dessert-shaped floral arrangements are clever, you may not find them to be particularly appropriate for your wedding.

Fortunately, mums are very versatile flowers. The sturdy mum is the perfect candidate for manipulating into limitless works of art. Perhaps you would like floral hearts, angels, musical instruments, or even bride-and-groom bears. Whatever the design, the mum and a talented florist can achieve it. Think of unique mum creations as your very own miniature, floral parade floats, beautiful to look at and ready to delight your guests. Chrysanthemums are often overlooked by brides seeking more exotic flowers, but mums are design workhorses with a charm all their own.

#583 *Of Clay and Color*

If there are areas of your venue that would benefit from a floral presence, but the thought of springing for even more fresh flowers makes you want to weep, consider clay flowers. These beautiful blooms are highly realistic, and they cost about the same as a fresh-flower arrangement. The difference is that they will stay beautiful for years, not days or hours. You could choose a stunning clay variety like orchid plants in pots to dress up your décor, then fill your home with them after the wedding.

Because the clay is formed and painted by hand, the flowers look less "artificial" than many of their fake-flower relatives. If you want to venture into floral design, make your own clay flowers at home. Will they look as exceptional as those created by flower artisans? Maybe not, but so what? They will have a unique beauty, since a bloom made by your own hand has a sentimental value no prefabricated flower can possess.

#584 *Friendly Foam*

There are scores of tutorials available online and at craft stores that teach you how easy it is to make foam flowers. But flowers made of foam will not fool anyone into thinking they are real, branding them an unlikely adornment for your wedding — unless, that is, you send them where real flowers wouldn't care to go.

Foam flowers are ideal accents for wall art, high-arch decorating, or inventive tabletop décor. You could never mix real flowers and gemstones in a glass vase or a jar without quickly crushing the delicate petals. But foam flowers can be combined with crystals, stones, beads, or twigs without harm. Even partially burying them in sparkling sand won't hurt them. The petals peek out from any surrounding filler, creating interesting, one-of-a-kind centerpieces or buffet accents. Durable foam flowers make great embellishments for disposable guest slippers or flip-flops, and they can take a carefree ride on your wedding car. Foam flowers may not corner the market on realism, but they don't have to. When the job requires it, they can take a little rough handling.

#585 *Maple Leaves Transformed*

For fall weddings, roses made from maple leaves not only fit the season, they are undeniably beautiful and easily crafted. As the nip in the air grows bolder, the supplies you will need simply float to the earth, and while most folks will be raking and bagging, you'll be gathering your wedding décor.

Plenty of tutorials exist to get you started, and if you live where maple trees shed their leaves in abundance, you can fold and tie your way to a tiny wedding-flower budget. Maple-leaf roses are suitable for everything from boutonnières to centerpieces. Use them exclusively, or mingle them with real favorite flowers. The natural colors of the leaf are what make the roses so appealing. When done with care, they actually look like something Mother Nature herself would have created.

#586 *Tufts of White*

Have you ever seen a cotton field in bloom? Tufts that resemble snow-white marshmallows are called bolls, and they emerge from dark, dusty stems to create a mesmerizing vision, and that's what you bring to your wedding when you incorporate cotton bolls into your décor.

Use long-stemmed bolls in vases, or short ones in boutonnières. Tie them in staggered positions then wrap the stems with raffia, and lovely wall art will emerge. Several stems clustered together make a unique bouquet, and tucking just one to three bolls with clipped stems into a glass bowl or a crystal vase creates a quick, easy centerpiece. Let the cotton shine all on its own, or add colored marbles or river rocks to each container. Bolls can be obtained from some florists, and are always available online. When it comes to your floral needs, cotton is a natural performer.

#587 Quicksand — The Good Kind

The word "quicksand," with its connotation of never-ending suction, doesn't inspire a feeling of comfort. But sometimes "quicksand" is a good thing. Such is the case with the Quicksand rose.

Quicksand roses are the epitome of "vintage." Their dusty beige petals culminate in a pale pink center, and the roses look as if they were born in the Victorian era and never left. With an exceptionally delicate appearance, they are beautiful in a way that other roses aren't, making them a favorite for bridal bouquets. If your wedding is classic or vintage in theme, there are Quicksand roses somewhere with your name on them.

#588 Gorgeous Goblets

For unusual centerpieces that eschew cut flowers but celebrate living greens, consider tree saplings or herbs planted in vintage goblets. Hunting for the goblets at antique shops, thrift stores, and estate sales will be fun, and they absolutely do not have to match or even be the same size. In fact, the more variety, the better. Fill each vessel with the appropriate potting soil, add a sapling or herb, then cluster the goblets together in the center of the table. Loosely tie a ribbon around them if you wish, or set them on a mirrored tray or tile. Later you can distribute them as gifts, which gives the plants new life and the recipients, a lovely goblet to reuse however they wish. To enhance a more robust decorative theme, use tankards and steins instead of goblets. Whether it's a vintage goblet, stein, or tankard, it can have a distinguished place at your table.

#589 A Flurry of Feathers

Feather bridal bouquets have something most floral bouquets don't have, and it's not just feathers. It's softness. They have an ethereal look and feel, and downy soft feathers drawn together in a bouquet can be stunning. Choose feathers only for your bouquet, or delicately blend a selection of flowers and feathers. With a variety of soft and stiff feathers you can turn a bouquet into an instantly identifiable expression of elegance, whimsy, romance, mystery, or daring.

Feathers are perfect for any season, and they won't die before, during, or after the wedding. Many crafters create and sell custom feather bouquets, but it's also one of the easiest bouquets to make on your own, if you are so inclined. A feather bouquet is likely to be far less expensive than a floral one, but only if you make it yourself. There's a fair amount of labor involved, and a crafter who custom makes your bouquet will rightly charge for his or her time and expertise. Check out some of the exquisite designs that can be found online and use them as inspiration. Both feathers and flowers are beautiful, but one will always be softer and more long-lived than the other.

DECORATIONS

CHAPTER TEN • *Decorations*

Inspired decorations please the eye, fire the emotions, and make people feel joyful and worry free. That's the gift of decorative style.

If decorations don't transport you to somewhere better, they fail. The theme or color scheme won't have an impact if the decorations don't simultaneously blend into the background and stand out from it. The theory may sound contradictory, but it isn't. It's that perfect, harmonious mix of subtlety and star power that generates amazing, effective décor.

Ideal wedding decorations create a seamless overall ambiance, yet feature "wow factor" focal points. Envision a smartly tailored winter coat made of fine wool. It's very pleasing to the eye, but when a silver-flecked cashmere scarf is tucked beneath the coat collar and matching gloves are donned, the eye focuses on the stunning accessories while still "seeing" the coat in the background. Take the coat away, and the accessories no longer stand out. The background and focal points bear equal responsibility in creating a lovely vision.

From the nuts and bolts of decorating technique to whimsical, elegant, or outside-the-box decorative components, the pages of this chapter will help you visualize a cornucopia of decorative possibilities and opportunities.

If you want your wedding guests to enter a new world — your world — and experience an event that will be impossible to forget, choose your décor thoughtfully. Going the extra mile doesn't always mean spending an extra dollar. Sometimes it merely means engaging in a bit of do-it-yourself labor or utilizing a clever, unusual presentation.

Beauty is in the eye of the beholder, but inspired wedding-day decorations make people feel beautiful for as long as they are near them.

#590 *Fill Up the Fishbowls*

"Living in a fishbowl" is uncomfortable because people can't stop staring. But when it comes to your wedding, staring is awesome! You'll inspire plenty of admiration simply by utilizing inexpensive, clear glass fishbowls to decorate your reception. What you put in the bowls is up to you, but the possibilities for generating eye-pleasing splashes of beauty are endless.

Floating candles or flowers are always great fillers, but fishbowls offer the opportunity to express yourself and your wedding theme in a myriad of delightful ways. Consider filling the bowls with ribbon-tied, his-and-hers horseshoes resting on a bed of straw to celebrate your Western theme, or try black-and-white candies for an Art Deco touch at your elegant wedding. Fishbowls easily hold small wedding favors on each table or can add an inventive element to a centerpiece.

Make fishbowls as stationary or as alive with animation as you like. Whether it contains colored sand, crystal beads, or miniature dioramas, the fishbowl does more than hold its contents. It makes them stare worthy, and on your wedding day, that's not a bad thing.

#591 *Chalk It Up to Creativity*

When planning a wedding, school may be just a distant memory, but there's one old-school piece of nostalgia that's wedding-reception perfect: a chalkboard. Some of the world's greatest art has been reproduced in chalk, and adding chalkboards to the reception can release everyone's inner artist.

Smartly framed black chalkboards or chalkboard easels can inspire plenty of fun communications. Using colored chalk, you or an artistic friend can draw a beautiful wedding-day work of art across the top quarter of the chalkboard, leaving the rest blank for the messages and doodles of your guests. Nestle the chalkboards between two tall potted plants to blend them into wedding décor, then provide a variety of chalk in a decorated basket.

You will love the photo opportunities that arise as the reception progresses. Chalkboards are wonderfully interactive, and when the reception is over and the messages have been photographed for posterity, donate the cleaned chalkboards to schools, preschools, churches, or clubs.

Chalkboards have been helping people communicate for centuries, but weddings are only just discovering their delightful potential.

#592 *Behold the Treasures of the Nile*

Give your wedding reception the exotic flair of a journey down the Nile by decorating with sprays of tall grasses and reeds. Stencil clay pots and vases with faux fossils and love-inspired hieroglyphics, then fill them with greenery obtained from craft stores, florists, or nurseries. Earthy, natural colors may be the perfect choice, or choose from a rainbow of tinted grasses.

Sprinkle lotus-flower accents among the grasses and reeds to add romantic focal points. Create simple grass "reed boats" to evoke the essence of Cleopatra's reign. Fashion the boats into a number of sizes and use them to present foods or favors, hold gift cards, enliven the band or DJ area, or to form an underliner that extends the reach of centerpieces on tables. And if children will be in attendance, consider providing each child with an activity bag of straws, paper "grasses," string, and simple instructions for making an Egyptian reed boat of their own. An entertained child at a wedding reception is a blessing.

After the celebration is over, share the "Nile's bounty" by bestowing some of the beautiful, enduring decorations upon family and wedding-party members.

#593 *Don't Eat the Decorations! No, Wait! Go Ahead...*

If you're a kill-two-birds-with-one-stone kind of bride, you can't go wrong with edible decorations. Let guests feast with their eyes, then tickle their taste buds. Fruit "flower" arrangements, hard-candy swizzle sticks, favors made from custom chocolate molds, gingerbread dioramas, frosting leaves, popcorn twigs, and M&M's portraits are just a few of the inventive decorations fashioned from food. And what could be better than providing décor and snacks at the same time? Virtually no cleanup, that's what! When the guests eat the decorations, there's less to tidy up, a smaller wedding-day carbon footprint, and less "stuff" to transfer from here to there after the wedding is over.

Get the bridesmaids, relatives, and house-party members together and make those tasty, decorative treats while enjoying a fun prewedding get-together. Or if doing it yourself is not your thing, enlist the aid of food-industry professionals, like candy makers, fruit stylists, chocolatiers, bakers, and caterers. And don't forget culinary students, who love to spread their creative wings.

When it comes to weddings, it really is possible to have your decorations and eat them, too!

#594 *Totally Fabulous Topiaries*

From tiny potted varieties that make ideal place-card holders and wedding favors to majestic creations that inspire awe and wonder, topiaries are wedding-day fabulous. Sculpted living plants shaped like hearts, angels, doves, wedding bells, or virtually any other imaginative design are functional and eco-friendly.

It's easy to foster a theme or pay tribute to a lifestyle with custom topiaries. Use them to create a uniquely vibrant wedding aisle or to add life to reception décor. Leave topiaries in their natural state, or adorn them with decorations like ribbons, crystals, or miniature white lights. If you have plenty of wedding-planning time, grow your own topiaries from vines or sculpt them from potted shrubs. If you weren't blessed with a green thumb, commission custom topiaries from professional gardeners. And if it's the look but not necessarily the living aspect of a topiary that's important to you, choose creations crafted from silk flowers and faux greenery.

Imagine how memorable it would be to gaze upon your yard, garden, or patio on your 25th wedding anniversary and see the spiral topiary pair that proudly guarded your wedding-cake table so many years ago.

#595 *Dancing on Art*

One of the smoothest wedding-décor ideas to come down the pike is the dance-floor decal. Available in numerous sizes, the decal design can be a simple but artistic bride-and-groom monogram or an elaborate and evocative fine-art rendering of the wedding couple. One large, centrally placed decal, along with several smaller decals, can really transform a reception dance floor. The large center decal could feature the bride's and groom's names, the wedding date, a photo, and a personal message, or it could showcase specific, meaningful artwork, such as a tattoo. Imagine the large decal as the "sun" of the dance floor, then choose smaller decals to orbit around it.

Clever phrases that encourage enjoyment, like "Dance as If No One Is Watching!" or "Free Your Dancing Spirit!" are invitations to guests to let their hair down and have a good time. If you wish for a bit more subdued dancing experience, opt for a single, tastefully designed decal that is more of an ambassador of welcome than an invitation to boogie.

Whether sentimental, lively or simply regal, the right floor decal is a dance-floor centerpiece.

#596 *Joyful Ringing — Even When Silent*

The peal of bells has long marked the joyful union of two people, and bells are the most recognized of all wedding symbols. The bell has been produced in mediums ranging from tissue paper to platinum, and has been celebrated in art, music, poetry, and literature.

Shimmering silver, pristine white, glittering gold, or perfect pastel bells add romance to wedding-day décor. Choose from working bells, candle bells, bubble bells, paper bells, or a world of other unique bell incarnations for instant wedding-day ambiance. And don't forget "kissing" bells for guests to ring in lieu of applause, or as a signal that it's time for the bride and groom to pucker up … again!

Wedding bells are full of charm and tradition and can dress everything from walls to tables to ceilings. Don't worry that most decorative wedding bells are silent. The message of the wedding bell always rings loudly in the imagination.

#597 *Begin by Backing It Up*

The beginning of the reception-design process is the right time to choose one or more inspiring backdrops.

Think of a stage play. It is the artistic backdrop that instantly transports the audience to a fictional world in another place and time. Modern wedding couples have the same creative opportunity. Backdrop companies that once provided amazing scenes only to theaters now do the same for weddings. Choose the wonders of the sea, the panorama of a Roman holiday, an angelic glimpse of the heavens, or virtually any scenic creation from your imagination, then use the backdrop to frame your reception and take your guests on a fantastic journey.

Some backdrops can be made of paper or fabric, while others are achieved by the use of a video presentation aired on pale walls. Use backdrops to make a large hall feel more intimate or to draw down the height of a too-tall ceiling. Whether you choose a single backdrop or multiple scenes, you have the ability to bring your own wedding vision to life, while adding magic in the process. Custom creations may cost more than renting stock backdrops, but with so many stock styles to choose from, customizing may not be necessary.

Reserve your backdrops early. The most coveted backdrops are secured months in advance of the big day — for good reason.

#598 *Bridal Arches with Heart*

Bridal arches can be crafted from a wide range of materials, including balloons, metal, and naturally woven living branches, all with beautiful results. But instead of merely employing the bridal arch as a picturesque frame for the wedding couple, think of it as an opportunity for inclusion and remembrance.

An arch is the perfect place to blend two families into one and to remember those who could not attend the wedding. Throughout the arch, artfully weave small charms or ornaments that represent members of the two families as an expression of the joyful merging of two whole families, not just of the bride and groom. This allows everyone you love to symbolically join you at the altar, including beloved relatives who have passed or those who cannot physically attend the ceremony.

The bridal arch is appropriate for both indoor and outdoor ceremonies, and when constructed with heart, it's more than just a lovely accent piece. It's a gift to both families.

#599 *Yes, That Picture Really Is Worth a Thousand Words*

Photographs immortalize life's moments. There is no other inanimate object as full of heart as a photograph, and pictures are not just for after the wedding. Incorporating photographs into reception décor enhances the sense of family and provides guests with an intimate connection to the wedding couple.

Collages of the bride and groom, made with fun and contemplative photos spanning youth to the wedding day, can be blended with centerpieces, framed and displayed on easels, or hung on walls as murals. If you wish, include photos of family, favorite pets, hobbies, or wedding-party members as well.

If your reception is all about fun, highlight the photos with accents and colors that encourage laughter. If you are planning a formal reception, display the photos with black-tie elegance against a champagne background.

Old photos document the life path that brought the bride and groom to the monumental destination of their wedding day. After the wedding, there will be new photos to cherish, but the wedding reception is a perfect time to cherish those you already have.

#600 *Let There Be Light!*

Even dull and drab surroundings are transformed by inspired lighting, and factoring creative lighting into the wedding-décor budget is money well spent.

Bright or dim, soft or harsh, white or tinted, direct or indirect, lighting instantly sets a mood. Professional lighting artists bring fairy-tale themes to life, or you can consider a DIY job if your ceremony or reception venue allows you to erect lighting on your own. Some venues will permit you to do so, provided you carry the proper liability insurance. Others will only permit such lighting if done by a professional service.

If you get the okay to do it yourself, visit facilities that make good use of decorative lighting, and study the strategic setup. Ask questions. Make notes. Even a home-improvement store's lighting department can offer visual guidance. What you produce may not be as effective as what a lighting artist can do, but it will always be better than a room with no creative lighting at all.

Weigh all factors when deciding whether or not to hire a professional service. Remember, to do it yourself you must buy or rent the lights, design the setup, ensure safety, and provide the labor for setup and takedown. At the end of the day, a professional service may prove to be the better bargain.

#601 Water, Water, Everywhere

Is there anything more peaceful than the sound of flowing water? From the famed Trevi Fountain of Italy to the dancing waters of Disneyland, moving water draws the attention and admiration of millions. Today it's easy to add that magical ambiance to your wedding reception.

Water fountains large and small are available to rent or buy. There are battery-powered, tabletop fountains and corded wall and pedestal fountains. Replace traditional floral centerpieces with a cascade of water by choosing tabletop fountains in a variety of styles. From an earthy and natural stone structure to an intricately detailed fairy-tale castle, choices are plentiful. Fountains can also be lit with colored or white light for a dramatic effect. Large fountains that stand on the floor or those that adorn walls may greet guests at the entrance, frame the bride and groom's table, or bestow the essence of an exotic garden upon an ordinary buffet.

Decorative water fountains produce a lot of "splash" for the buck.

#602 Dandy Brandy Snifters

A brandy snifter is a robust piece of glassware with a plump bowl atop a pedestal base. This hearty stemware is a versatile option for couples contemplating their reception décor. Snifters come in many sizes, and creating an interesting grouping is a breeze.

For inventive tabletop décor, fill the snifters with whatever imaginative contents you desire, and decorate snifter bases with ribbons, mica flakes, flowers, or charms. Some companies offer etched brandy snifters at reasonable bulk prices, making it easy to tie your decorative theme together. Offer an after-dinner brandy or a nonalcoholic substitute, like cooled chocolate coffee, in personalized snifters that double as wedding-favor keepsakes.

Since the 16th century, brandy drinkers have appreciated the full, round shape of the brandy snifter because it allows the hand to warm and swirl the liquid inside, but brides will appreciate the decorative style and versatility that those same snifters bring to the reception table.

#603 *The Loveliness of Lace*

Everyone associates lace with wedding gowns or honeymoon lingerie, but rarely does it come to mind when decorations are planned. That's a waste of a very lovely resource. Like a white horse and a pumpkin carriage, lace and a wedding are a perfect union.

Starched and stiffened lace is easily shaped into everything from nut cups to napkin holders. Bits of lace ribbon can add a delicate touch to centerpieces, and lace runners atop ordinary tablecloths add romance. For a larger design statement, fashion a few yards of lace fabric into framed columns or folding screens. Simply attach a large lace panel to a flat, colored surface. Slip the lace-covered panel into a stylish frame, then mount the finished product on a supportive base or hang it on a wall. Lace over cool mint is perfect for a summer-afternoon celebration, while lace over deep purple or formal black is nighttime elegant.

Watch for sales, haunt thrift shops, and rummage through fabric-store remnant bins to score wonderful lace finds, which are easily transformed into richly attractive yet inexpensive wedding décor.

#604 *Move Over, Little Birdie*

Oh, the engineering marvel that is the bird's nest! A brilliant talent for weaving gives birds large and small a welcome and durable place to call home, wherever they may be. For brides, bird's nests bring warmth and coziness to reception décor.

Craft stores and florists offer bird's nests in a variety of sizes and materials. The humble bird's nest offers plenty of decorative inspiration, whether you prefer the earthiness of natural twigs, the richness of burnished or silver wire, or the airiness of raffia.

Use nests to hold pens at the guest-book table, serve candy treats on the buffet, present swizzle sticks at the bar, offer keepsakes on reception tables, or any number of other creative endeavors. Augmenting the nests with lovebirds, doves, hearts, charms, and theme-colored ribbons adds personality.

Their irregular, woven shapes give bird's nests a more interesting dimension than what is achieved through the flatness of trays or the sameness of bowls. Whether your wedding décor is down-home country or uptown posh, bird's nests fit right in. After all, all wedding couples are lovebirds on their wedding day.

#605 *On the Hook*

You don't have to be herding sheep to appreciate the usefulness of a shepherd's hook. Those tall, elegant hooks, once used only by nomad sheepherders, are now helpful friends to gardeners, landscapers, and wedding couples far and wide. Customarily forged of metal, the hooks support your decorative creations with sturdy grace.

For outdoor weddings, drive shepherd's hooks directly into the ground to create an aisle, a pathway, or a backdrop for an altar. Affix them indoors to the ends of pews, or anchor them into pots to present fabulous floral art or wedding-themed mobiles at the ceremony, reception, or both. Clustering several hooks back-to-back in a circle forms an impromptu sculpture or a central focal point, perhaps with a fountain in the center of the cluster. Straight-line groupings can line the wall behind the head table, thereby framing the wedding party.

Topiary balls and floral baskets are traditionally hung from the curve of a shepherd's hook, but you can use anything — bows, strands of beads, crystals, hearts, or even theme-inspired items like decorated cowboy hats at a Western wedding.

Shepherd's hooks are versatile, aesthetically satisfying, and useful long after the wedding day is done.

#606 *If It Sparkles, It Must Be Magic!*

Sparkles have long been associated with magic, but wedding-day shimmer doesn't have to rely on sequins or rhinestones. Wedding décor can produce its own sparkle without the need for bedazzling.

Sparkle sand is full of glistening minerals that catch the light and the eye. It's available in a rainbow of colors, and it's not hard to match your wedding-day palette. Fill glass containers with one or more colors of sand, then top the sand with a single flower for quick, effective centerpieces and table accents. Scatter sand atop the tablecloth on the cake or guest-book table, add sprigs of greenery as desired, and cover everything with a sheet of glass or acrylic. This simple decorative method turns an ordinary table into a sophisticated and stylized work of art.

Sparkle sand is not expensive, and you don't need to be an artistic genius to use it. Anyone can layer sand in a vase or goblet, and making several one-of-a-kind reception accents is a fun project for the whole family. Creating decorative sand pieces also makes an entertaining addition to a bridal shower.

Sparkles are fairy-tale magic at your fingertips.

#607 *Fabulous Fencing*

Whoever said "don't fence me in" wasn't preparing for a wedding day. Fences make great wedding neighbors!

Creative fencing works indoors or out, and it can quickly change the look of any venue. From small border fencing to tall privacy fencing, there are plenty of reasons to include fences in your ceremony and reception designs.

Search for decorative fencing shaped like everything from angels to butterflies. Fencing can be made of wood, plastic, metal, or resin. Most artistic fencing is available in dozens of colors, but any color is possible with paint.

Why use fencing? Well, why not? It's charming and functional. Fencing beautifully partitions play areas for children, dance floors, gift gardens, photo-booth setups, or other specific areas while still leaving them easily accessible. Fencing that encircles tables not only looks fabulous, it can hide supplies and prevent accidental snagging of tablecloths. Pity the bride who watches her wedding cake fly off the table because someone accidentally caught the cloth with a shoe heel or purse.

Fences are both protective and lovely to look at. They can resize a room or keep an outdoor wedding from being overrun by uninvited guests, making them fine wedding-day vanguards.

#608 *The Power of Parasols*

For an outdoor wedding, you can create a dramatic, eye-catching effect by lining both sides of the aisle with a row of brightly colored, open parasols, made of silk or paper. They add a touch of grace at a fraction of the cost of other aisle decorations. Color coordinate your runner with the parasols and you'll provide the perfect flourish for your procession. Buy enough matching parasols so that there's one for every aisle seat, on both sides of the center runner. Open the parasols and make sure the handles are secured directly underneath the seats. (Your best bet are paper parasols from Asia that have straight bamboo handles, which are easier to use for this purpose than curved handles.) To set an extra magical mood, add accent or twinkle lights to the parasols.

After the recessional, guests seated on the aisle will be able to take the parasols with them, resulting in a unique parade behind the bride and groom. The parasols will come in handy, particularly if your guests are looking for a little shade on a sunny day.

After the ceremony, you can also use the parasols to create inventive photo backdrops, then transport them to the reception to form an aisle for the bride and groom's grand entrance.

Parasols come in hundreds of colors and designs, and they can even be personalized to honor the bride and groom. They are perfectly suited to wedding themes like Victorian, Asian, Celtic, and country. Parasols are available in bulk, reducing costs even further.

And to take full advantage of the motif, don't forget miniature drink parasols for the bar!

#609 *Say It with Ribbon!*

For an easy way to customize wedding-day items, use personalized ribbon. It can accentuate favors, welcome bags, nosegays, and centerpieces, and it can perpetuate a color or design theme throughout multiple events. Employ personalized ribbon at the shower, rehearsal dinner, bachelorette party, bride's luncheon, ceremony, and reception to create instant continuity and recognition. Fashion it into bows, wrap it around vases, trim tables, lace it through arches, or use it to create tails for decorative kites. Wherever ribbon is welcome, personalized ribbon excels.

Adding the wedding couple's name and wedding date is customary, but not absolute. Say whatever you wish. Use the ribbon to convey a special message to your guests or to highlight something dear to the bride and groom's heart.

A wedding without ribbon would be a rare occasion indeed. There's a reason for that. Ribbon is a hard-working decorative asset. Personalized ribbon is even more special.

#610 *The Wonderful Wedding Wreath*

Wedding wreaths add just the right dash of welcome color in a too-white wedding world, and they can convey everything from sheer elegance to humor.

Wedding suppliers, craft stores, and florists sell ready-made wedding wreaths, but making your own can guarantee a wreath specific to you. Make your wreaths from simple patterns that involve ribbons and silk flowers over wire, fresh flowers in a wet-foam base, intertwined vines, or any number of other design options.

Small, delicate wreaths make unique bouquets for bridesmaids or triumph as beautiful candle rings on tables. Medium-sized wreaths lend themselves to pew decorating or accenting the buffet or wedding cake. Large wreaths add life to doorways, walls, and bridal arches.

Embrace a color scheme, but style each wreath differently to add interest and spice. Overlap a cluster of wreaths to create 3-D wall art. Replace some flowers on each wreath with small photos that tell the story of the bride and groom's courtship. Insert a shaped wreath, like a heart or a dove, into a round wreath to produce a creative work of wedding art.

Wreaths are cost-effective decorating aids, and as a bonus, they are easily shared with family and friends following the big event.

#611 *Fluff and Fold*

If you're willing to trade some effort for budget dollars, origami can save you plenty of cash. Those incredibly intriguing swans, doves, flowers, butterflies, hearts, and other designs crafted from hundreds or thousands of tiny scraps of paper are viable substitutes for floral centerpieces, buffet-table accents, wedding favors, and room décor. And when recycled paper is used, origami also befriends the Earth.

A white origami swan resting on a small mirror representing water makes an effective and original centerpiece. Other origami centerpiece options might include flowerpots filled with a wildflower bouquet, a single tulip in a glass vase, butterflies on flexible wires springing from greenery, peacocks resting on real twigs, or angels nestled among wispy clouds of angora.

Origami is a process, but it's not one that must be undertaken in a marathon crafting session. Work on it when the mood strikes, then walk away and return to it later. Folding the little papers is something that anyone of any age can accomplish in front of the TV, riding in a car, or while relaxing in a lawn chair amidst the sights and sounds of nature.

Instructions for different designs are available in books or online, and video tutorials created by origami enthusiasts are available on social video sites. If saving is not the objective, hire a professional origami artist. Origami is labor-intensive, and the fee for having custom creations made may be substantial.

The centuries-old art of origami adds beauty and grace to the wedding. Use origami as a minimal accent or as the focal point of wedding décor, and consider simple origami kits for children to keep them busy at the reception.

#612 *Flickering Ambiance*

Few decorative accents carry the impact of a flickering candle. Candlelight conveys warmth, romance, and elegance, and incorporating candlelight into wedding décor transforms ordinary stillness into beautiful, gentle movement.

Candles secured in hurricane glass gently light the aisle to the altar, and floating candles sprinkled in fountains or atop water-themed centerpieces are mesmerizing. Candle gels are fashioned so that flowers, shells, or other items encased inside are easily seen, making them ideal accent pieces for restrooms and the guest-book table. Specialty candles shaped to resemble everything from flowers to wedding cakes serve well as wedding favors, and jar candles in a rainbow of colors stack nicely into artistic pyramid shapes.

From the impressive stature of pillars and tapers to the versatility of small votives and tea lights, candles turn any space into a wonderland.

If real flames concern you, consider the realistic glow of battery-operated, "flameless" candles, purchased individually or in bulk. They come in nearly as many styles and varieties as real candles, but since LED "wicks" don't produce real fire, there's no worry that knocking one over will ignite a wedding-day catastrophe.

#613 *Customizing the Captivating Candle*

All candles are captivating, but custom candles, with their own style and character, elevate décor by leaps and bounds. Uniquely crafted candles can tell a story or capture the bride and groom's wedding journey. Whether it's the love of a mutually enjoyed hobby or the depiction of moments from your courtship, you have freedom of expression with custom-molded candles.

If custom candles are not in the budget, consider presenting ordinary candles in unique candleholders, like cowboy boots, Cinderella castles, angel wings, lotus cups, motorcycles, or whatever candleholder style best reflects the essence of your wedding.

Adding adornments like charms, a seashell cluster, or a monogram fashioned from crystals will turn plain candles into personalized décor.

#614 *Sophisticated Silhouettes*

Use a readily available photo software program to generate elegant and charismatic silhouettes, then print and mount them to create works of art. Select a variety of profile headshots of the bride and groom. Print out the black silhouettes in large sizes, overlay them against a white paper or white damask background, then frame them in inexpensive black, white, or silver frames. Creatively cluster the finished frames around the room or affix them to folding screens to build tall, artistic focal points. Use them individually as table décor.

To integrate and celebrate the concept, also include a bride-and-groom silhouette on the wedding program and on escort or place cards.

Silhouettes mesh beautifully with any wedding décor, but they look especially striking with a black-and-white, Art Nouveau, or crystal theme.

#615 *Beyond the Nut Cups*

Whether your wedding favors are simple sugared almonds or engraved crystal, packaging provides a decorative opportunity.

Unpackaged favors can look lonely at a place setting, but creative favor boxes and bags can spruce up your presentation. Today's favor holders offer more style choice and convenience than the gathered-and-tied tulle circles that once dominated wedding receptions. The circles are still available, and they still make a delicate wrap for a spoonful of nuts, but filling them is more work than merely dropping the nuts/candy/gift into a ready-made organza bag and closing the drawstring top. The bags come in a multitude of sizes and colors, and some are embellished with lace, contrast stitching, monogramming, faux jewels, embroidery, or even charms. Adorn any bag with a sprig of dried herbs, a silk flower, ribbons, or other accents.

If bags aren't "your bag," consider favor boxes that come in a variety of shapes, like snowflakes, castles, palm trees, and a world of other designs. For the best selection, search several wedding-favor companies to find clever styles that are not carried by every merchant.

Place nuts, candies, or gifts into virtually any object capable of holding something inside: quirky jelly jars, ring boxes, tiny beach bags, mini popcorn boxes, little water pails, beer koozies, shaped tins, and shot glasses are just a few of the unique options.

Use an embellished bag, an elaborate box, or an unusual vessel to personalize the wedding and enliven reception décor.

#616 *Incredible Ice*

Stunning ice sculptures have highlighted buffets since ice was first chopped from a frozen lake. Just one of these skillfully carved showpieces adds instant refinement to a room.

A professional ice sculptor carves from a single block of ice to breathe life into creative designs. Sculptures can cost upwards of $200, but a monumental, commissioned piece isn't the only way to enjoy ice art.

Making your own ice-sculptures is as easy as purchasing inexpensive molds, filling them with crystal-clear spring water, and freezing them for a couple of days. You can find ice sculpture molds online and in craft stores.

Do-it-yourself sculptures are usually about a foot tall. They're small when compared to the sculptures a hotel restaurant might display, but placing several of them on clustered, tiered pedestals creates an effective presentation as wonderful as one giant piece of ice art. Angels, brides and grooms, doves, hearts, and other relevant designs easily join forces to beautify any setting.

Small sculptures melt much more quickly than large ones, so using the more petite sculptures outdoors may risky. Indoors or out, ice sculptures must rest in decorative bases capable of absorbing surface melts.

Whether it's ice on a winter tree or ice shaped like a rising phoenix, frozen water is the embodiment of artistic "cool."

#617 *The Tiny Garden Within*

Your wedding and reception may not be held in the heart of a rain forest, but that's no reason to deny your wedding day the spiritually uplifting pleasure of living plants. Just use a smaller scale.

Terrariums are the Earth in microcosm, and no two are ever truly alike. Glass enclosures house artistic, living displays that bring a garden-like essence to your wedding, with no worry that leaking water, scattered dirt, or falling leaves will affect your day. Use terrariums as centerpieces, or place several on potted-plant towers that rise from the floor to frame the cake table or create a walkway.

Plant your terrariums early in the wedding-planning process, and be creative. Use succulents to represent the desert or exotic plants to add tropical flair. For uniformity, use terrariums of the same size and shape. For eclectic variety, use terrariums of many different sizes and shapes. Keep them authentically natural, or add clever embellishments that promote the wedding theme or tickle the funny bone, like tiny bride and groom characters walking down a terrarium path or miniature doves flying in a heart formation above the greenery.

With terrariums, it's possible to have a garden experience even if the reception is held in the dead of winter.

#618 *Electric Starlight*

One of the fastest ways to create intimacy in a room is to use chandeliers. Branches of lights not only give the illusion of a lower ceiling, they cast pools of illumination that highlight the areas beneath them.

You don't have to use big, crystal chandeliers with scores of bulbs. They look amazing, but they may not be in the budget or be appropriate for a semiformal wedding. Instead, create your own inventive chandeliers.

Wrap white LED light strings around a workable base, and hang the finished product from the ceiling with fishing line. Fashion the base from something as simple as an inexpensive, upside-down wire basket. Weave the lights throughout, using a little or a lot, depending upon your preference. And voilà! You've created a chandelier.

If there's no power source for your chandeliers, replace lights requiring a plug-in outlet with battery-operated strands.

Seasonal indoor/outdoor lighted designs, like white stars or angels, can also be adapted as chandeliers. Turn the piece face down and affix fishing line at each corner, then draw the corner lines together into one center hanging line. Many ready-made, lighted, decorative pieces cost little, especially at the close of holiday periods.

Give chandeliers a try. You may find that adding a bit of sparkling, electric starlight to the occasion will turn an ordinary room into a fabulous one.

#619 *A Touch of the Sheik*

Imagine it's the 19th century and you've been slogging through hot, white sands for miles, when on the horizon you spot a sheik's encampment. Rising from the parched earth is a beautiful tent of colorful, flowing fabrics that swirl in a cooling breeze seemingly of their own making. Hopeless doldrums give way to excitement as you hurry toward the comforts and hospitality you know lie just ahead. This is the welcoming spirit you can create for your wedding reception with the use of ceiling canopies.

Long, sheer panels of fabric gathered at a center point, with their tails floating in the air, turn any uninteresting space into an enchanting environment. Refreshment reigns as beautiful, sweeping arcs of fabric stimulate the eye.

Ceiling canopies are a vision unto themselves, and they may be adapted to any wedding theme by changing the fabric and the configuration of panels. Take a cue from a sheik's passion for lush surroundings, and create a wedding oasis of your own.

#620 *Regal Runners*

Table runners are not tablecloths. Tablecloths cover an entire table. Runners are strips of cloth that "run" from one end of a table to the other, often overlaid on top of tablecloths as accent pieces. There are multitudes of available fabrics, patterns, and color choices, especially for custom-made runners. But for something different, consider runners made from materials other than fabric.

Imagine the length and width of a typical runner, then fill that space with something else. Sprinkle flower petals from one side of the table to the other for a fairy-tale effect, or let raffia tendrils stretch out from the centerpiece for an organic, earthy feel. Glitter, sparkling sand, or mica flakes dusted across the tabletop add magical flair, and gently braided ribbons adorned with small flower buds that match the bride's bouquet add personalization.

Runners add to table décor. But traditional cloth runners aren't the only paths to an intriguing table.

#621 *Living Dolls*

Dolls have come a long way. It's now possible to purchase custom dolls that look just like you. That's pretty fun, even if you're all grown up.

Picture a pair of straight or spiral miniature staircases populated by bride, groom, and wedding-party dolls in the center of the buffet table. The bride and groom dolls stand on the top bridge that connects the staircases, and each bridesmaid and groomsman doll claims a staircase step of its own. Dress the dolls in wedding-party attire reminiscent of the real garments of the day, and finish with miniature bouquets and boutonnières.

The dolls don't have to be spitting images to generate smiles, they will be enjoyed even without customized faces. At the end of the day, give each doll to its respective human counterpart to keep, and reserve those uniquely-you bride and groom dolls for the children you may have someday.

#622 *Totally Awesome Table Art*

A unique table setting focuses on the centerpiece, but you're not required to fill the center of a table with flowers. Sculptures, busts, photo cubes, and artistic renderings on miniature easels can all command attention, inspire conversation, and add eclectic beauty.

Table art represents the bride's and groom's personal styles. Choose from any medium, like metal art, charcoal florals in pyramid frames, framed photos hanging from spiral bases, and sand or clay sculptures. Any artistic object works if it is the right size for the table. Add a flower bloom here and there as desired.

Unlike floral centerpieces, table art is forever. Give the pieces as reception prizes or as gifts to friends and family, or keep them all for your new home.

#623 *Drawn, Stenciled, or Stamped*

It's common to personalize cake and favor bags that are ordered in bulk from commercial vendors or printers. But if creating your own bag holds appeal, it's simply a matter of embellishing a stock bag with the stencil or stamp of your choice.

Decorate your bags with a freehand design, or for easy uniformity, purchase a customized stencil or stamp. Combine the best of both worlds by using a ready-made stamp or stencil in an appealing design, then embellish it with the bride's and groom's names and the wedding date in calligraphy or other artistic application.

Give your bags a soft, ribbon handle or a stiff, paper-cord one and you've created a fleet of practical, inventive wedding-day bags.

#624 *Rocking It!*

Rocks may not be the first decorative accent that comes to mind when thinking about weddings, but don't ignore those earthy specimens. Simple stones really can rock your décor.

Imagine the beauty of a rock-and-mineral garden, then visualize the opportunities for re-creating that beauty at your wedding and reception. Fashion amethyst- and quartz-cluster centerpieces or river-rock fountains with candle pools. Accent the buffet with sprinkles of fool's gold, or use ordinary rocks to spell out the bride's and groom's names on the lawn outside the wedding venue or reception hall.

Use rocks in their natural state, or paint them with wedding trivia or wedding colors, and use them as weights to secure aisle runners, programs, and tablecloths at outdoor weddings. Inside, turn them into connected borders or individual accent pieces.

Rocks have decorative moxie. They're natural and beautiful, and unless you seek out only the most precious minerals, they are either inexpensive or blissfully free.

#625 *The Kiss of Faux Ice Crystals*

Is there anything more seasonally universal than ice? Whether it's the breathtaking vista of icy trees on a winter morning or the sight of an ice-filled glass on a blistering summer's day, ice triggers an emotional response.

It can do the same for any wedding, at any time of the year, but it doesn't have to be made from water.

The very realistic illusion of water-formed ice is achieved with acrylics or silicone rubbers, which look the part without any dripping or melting worries. Acrylic cubes that come in crystal-clear or brilliant colors are perfect for filling vases, adding sparkle to tabletops, or decorating darkened corners. Pair silicone-rubber ice with a hot-glue gun to create sculptures, backdrops, or garlands.

Whether to contribute to perfect winter-wedding décor or to gift guests with the essence of cool in the heat of summer, faux ice is a decorative treat.

#626 *"Our Life" Billboards*

"The Billows Wedding"
"John and Mary's Wedding"
"The Andrews-Billows Wedding"

These are examples of ordinary wedding signs that pop up every day. You'll find them on streets leading to venue sites or at the entrance to a reception hall. In their current state, they effectively relate the required information, but why not go the extra mile and turn your signage into personalized works of art?

Take the opportunity to celebrate your theme. For example, for a medieval motif, try "Hear Ye! Hear Ye! This Way to the Royal Billows Nuptials!" Shape the sign like a castle flag, and add turret art or other medieval designs to give your sign that "wow" factor. Use decorative signs throughout the reception, such as "Partake in the King's Wedding Feast!" at the buffet tables or "The Giddy Grog" at the bar.

For a wedding with no theme, express your personalities or passions through your signs. If you're avid bicyclists, use bicycle-themed signage. If you met at a coffee shop, consider two cups of coffee with their handles intertwined and the message "This Way to Steve and Nan's Freshly Brewed Wedding Celebration."

When wedding signs become clever little billboards, they do more than inform. They create a sensation.

#627 *Inspired Tabletops*

White linen tablecloths are a wedding-day staple, but they often come with a hefty linen-rental rate.

Instead of renting, consider using white or pastel sheets. Make sure they're clean and crisp, then top them with white, silver, or gold wrapping-paper runners you've purchased at a deep discount after the holiday season.

If a paper runner is not your cup of tea, search thrift stores for thin or lacy shawls that look beautiful when spread flat, or choose to top the tables with a spray of palm fronds.

Old drapes are another option. Drapes have a nice hem and are easily joined together to make circular or rectangular tablecloths. Dye them to create a matched blend, or portray an eclectic spirit by connecting drapes with different patterns via a common color scheme. Damask drapes work especially well.

When tables are covered with white butcher paper or natural cream paper and creative place mats, simply wrap the legs in coordinated paper ribbon. Or use a piece of fabric as a short tablecloth and cover the legs by making long fabric tubes to slip over each leg. Secure the tubes with a bow at the table's edge. Make the sheaths about twice as long as the table leg to create a gentle, rippled finish.

If the bare tabletops are already nice, you may need nothing more than a spray of glitter or sparkling sand down the center.

Floor-length linen tablecloths are indeed elegant, but they aren't the only way to graciously top a table.

#628 *99 Bottles of...*

The bottle is a wedding decorator's cost-saving friend. From beer bottles to perfume-bottles, the sizes, shapes, and colors of bottles created throughout the years are endless.

Replace floral centerpieces with clusters of diversely shaped bottles filled with colored water, sparkling sand, crystal beads, faux-ice twigs, or even colored popcorn. Tie them together with a wide satin ribbon and bow. For singular accents on tables, in the restrooms, or at the bar, paint the outside of bottles with designs that rise up from the bases, then top each one with a single flower.

Use individual clear bottles to tell the story of the bride and groom's courtship by nestling clues inside the bottles, like a tiny model car, a miniature picnic basket, or even a handwritten message. Just about everything is produced in miniature. Look for charms or accessories made for dollhouses or model-train dioramas. Little tokens inside the bottles keep guests talking as they try to figure out just what the tiny symbols represent.

Many fine liquor bottles are already beautifully designed, yet they just end up in the recycling bin. Fish them out and put them to good use. Bottles with a bit of ribbon or lace and something interesting tucked inside will cost little but deliver much.

#629 *Mellow Movement*

Even the most breathtaking indoor reception décor doesn't have something outdoor weddings naturally enjoy: movement. A gentle breeze adds a beating heart to all surroundings. Fortunately, visual movement within four walls is possible with the use of battery-operated wind spinners.

Choose beautiful white, silver, or gold spinners or those with themed centers, like a dragonfly, sun, angel, butterfly, or flower. Attach each one to an inexpensive battery-powered spinner motor, available online. Cover the battery packs with satin ribbon, and hang them from the ceiling or from shepherd's hooks imbedded into large, weighted pots. The silent motors spin at a gentle speed, creating just enough movement to give the room a breath of life.

Use a few to accent here and there, or use several at varying heights to create dynamic clusters — for example, on either side of the band. Hang one or more above the guest-book table to add vibrancy to your welcome, or place a different one over each station of the buffet table to differentiate food groups.

Wind spinners draw the eye upward, making the room feel expansive and alive, and after the wedding, they bless your home patio with the same full-of-life flair.

#630 *Red-Carpet Treatment*

Create a dais effect for the head table by framing it with carpet. Even if the table is not elevated, the use of a bordering carpet creates the illusion that it is.

Because the tablecloth likely drapes to the floor, you'll need carpeting that is only about 18 inches wide. Apply it to the floor in the front and on both sides of the table (or in a circular pattern for a round table), with just a couple of inches tucked under the hem of the tablecloth. Use double-sided carpet tape to secure it safely to the floor. Purchase ready-made runners for each side, or buy an inexpensive carpet remnant, cut it into the shape you need to surround the table, and have the edges finished by a rug binder or a custom-car shop that makes floor mats. Or you could finish the edges of the remnant yourself with cleverly designed carpet-binding tape, available at home-improvement stores.

Choose a rich color that fits your theme but contrasts with the tablecloth, like deep-purple carpet for a "royal" wedding or spring green for a "garden" theme. Even if the room is already carpeted, adding a head-table carpet is aesthetically striking and gives the wedding couple the special "elevated" treatment they deserve.

#631 *Studded*

Boutonnière pins do more than just secure a flower to the groom's lapel. These little treasures can turn just about any decorative object into something fabulous.

Use wire cutters to trim the pins to whatever size works best for the project, then adorn anything that needs a little extra flair. Stud candles with faux-pearl or diamond-topped pins, or stick pins into the hearts of individual flowers in centerpieces. Add elegance to the buffet table's decorative carved fruits and vegetables by outlining the designs with pinheads, or use the pins to highlight monograms, names, or the wedding date on banners and signs.

#632 *Bountiful Balloons*

Balloons have not only stood the test of time as decorative workhorses, they've evolved into majestic works of art. Balloon artists turn simple balloons into sculptures shaped like everything from columns and arches to actual brides and grooms. Balloons paired with lights are elegant, while clusters of helium hearts promote a whimsical atmosphere.

Create intimacy by adding free-hanging ribbon tails to balloons amassed on the ceiling or under canopies, or inspire a centerpiece to reach for the stars via a balloon bouquet rising from its center.

Balloons are versatile, and when assembled by your own hand, they're inexpensive. If a balloon artist is hired to do the work, expect to pay for that person's talent and expertise, just as you should. Anyone can fill a balloon with helium and tie a ribbon to it, but it takes a great deal of skill and experience to sculpt balloons into masterpieces. Not all balloon artists possess the same skill, so choose an artist only after seeing his or her actual work. Someone else may have made those gorgeous balloon sculptures you see in a portfolio.

When decorating your wedding or reception with balloon décor, consider going above and beyond. Hire a balloon artist to sculpt on-site to entertain your guests.

#633 *Memory Lane Table Runners*

It's easy to create photo and art iron-on transfers on a home computer, so why not turn digital photos of the bride and groom, family, pets, scenery, nature, classic art, or whatever other concept appeals to you into table runners? Use the transfers to make a collage on the fabric strip of your choice, and trim the runner with a fabric border befitting your color scheme.

Make the runners short or long, wide or narrow. Use color photos to add vibrancy to the tables, or choose to print in black-and-white for an Art Deco feel or for a formal, black-and-white wedding theme. Print in sepia tones for a vintage "daguerreotype" look.

Be creative, and you'll transform your reception tables into more than just a place to eat, drink, and talk.

#634 *Beautiful Projection*

Perhaps you want to put giant photos of you and your groom on the walls of your reception, but the venue says, "No way! No wall attachments!" Well, no problem! With a projector, any design, photograph, artwork, or other image is placed on the unit and projected on the wall as small or as large as you like. Tuck the projector behind a potted plant or a tall fern, and let it be your muralist. You can even assign someone to periodically change the images if you wish, providing ever-fresh wall décor. Check out art-projector rentals from companies that offer supplies for business meetings and seminars.

"No" doesn't have to mean "No!" Just impress the venue, and your guests, with clever, projected wall art.

#635 *Magic and Mystique*

Floor arrangements can be costly, but they fill up a room and add pizzazz to décor. Fortunately, a floor arrangement doesn't have to mean hundreds of dollars worth of plants or flowers. Simply create magical displays with ordinary twigs adorned with Mardi Gras masks.

You can purchase the masks in bulk; go for those masks with cat-eye or oval-shaped eye slits in silver and gold or the rich purples, greens, and other bold colors of Mardi Gras. Masks may be metallic, glittered, feathered, or plain. Opt for a variety, or stick to the look you like best.

Head to the backyard and trim some long, thin branches from assorted trees, then strip them of their leaves. You can paint the twigs black, white, silver, or gold, or leave them in their natural state. Using glue or a glue gun, affix the masks to the twigs here and there, as if they were blooms sprouting from the bark. Cluster groups of the finished twigs in large floor pots, or position them horizontally on walls to create intriguing wall art. If the pots will not be positioned against a wall, cover the backs of the masks with other masks facing the opposite direction.

When all is done, you will have spent only a few dollars on your "mask arrangements," but they will enliven a room like the work of a $100-an-hour decorator.

#636 *Oh, the Classics*

Dickens, Shakespeare, Hemmingway, Austen, Twain, and Mitchell are all names blessed with respect and recognition. Inviting them and many of their ancient and modern literary peers to your wedding reception provides you with a unique decorating opportunity.

Vintage books found at estate sales, thrift stores, flea markets, and antique shops make impressive wedding decorations. Sew sheer organza bags at home, or purchase a ready-made bag for each book. Slip the book into the bag, gather the top together, and tie the fabric with a white ribbon. Group the well-dressed books into flat or upright clusters to support florals, candles, or dishes on the buffet. Arrange creative stacks to serve as cupcake stands.

Use any vintage-book collection, or match the books to the passions of the bride and groom. If you are avid hikers, choose outdoorsy books with titles that suit your lifestyle. If you are closet chefs, use cookbooks. The diaphanous sheaths permit the titles to be read but give the books that certain wedding essence. At the close of the reception, keep those books you especially like, and donate the rest to a nursing home, a hospital, or your neighborhood library.

#637 *Darling Dollhouse Furnishings*

Dollhouse chairs make clever place-card holders. Place cards attach easily to the chair backs, and a wrapped mint or an organza bag of nuts rests comfortably on the chair seat. Most craft stores carry a line of unfinished balsa-wood chairs, to be personalized or finished in any art style you wish. Chairs can also be handcrafted with little more than stiff paper, scissors, and glue. Simple, easy patterns are available online or in craft shops. When creating them yourself, make the chairs into tiny reflections of your real wedding-reception chairs. Whether they are made from scratch or acquired from stores that sell miniatures, tiny chairs fit nicely into reception-table place settings.

#638 *All Tied Up*

Interesting, eye-catching knots and braids can transform ordinary décor. And it won't cost you a single penny to add them to your decorations. From table skirts and ribbons to greenery and drapes, anything that can be manipulated can be enhanced through knotting and braiding. Practice with different knotting styles, then sprinkle those learned techniques throughout your décor. Knots and braids also lend themselves to adornment, providing the opportunity to add sparkling or sentimental objects where otherwise there would be nothing to hold them.

Not every decorative accent costs hard-earned dollars. Some simply rely on effort and creativity.

#639 *Kindergarten Cones*

Remember kindergarten, when crafts were the joy of your life, and bringing that paper cone filled with paper flowers home to Mom was the best feeling ever? Those rolled-and-glued paper cones are still a hit, and they're still easy and inexpensive to make.

For perfect pew arrangements, use paper cones with bows on the bottom and a tuft of florals at the top. They're lightweight and form easily from any color or texture of paper. Paper loves decoration, and adding adornments is as simple as wielding a hot-glue gun. For an exotic paper cone, use rice paper or floral pressed paper you've made yourself. For a formal look, try glossy black or silver wrapping paper, rolled with a heavier construction-paper insert. Add a personalized sticker if you wish, or for a more intimate touch, handwrite a message on each cone. Pew cones can also be used as gentle remembrances of friends and family who could not attend your wedding.

At the reception, slip paper cones into crystal glasses for instant centerpieces. Fill your cones with flowers, herbs, grasses, or whatever arrangements fit your theme.

Who said kindergarten was all about child's play? Versatile paper cones prove otherwise.

#640 *Pennies from Heaven*

Everyone's heard it: "Find a penny, pick it up, and all the day you'll have good luck!" And who needs more good luck than a newly married couple?

Use shiny new pennies to create eclectic, glistening table runners and centerpiece bases that are all about good fortune. Place a single penny on small white leaves fanned out from the center of the table, or use the pennies alone to create intricate patterns against the tablecloth. Long clusters of pennies wending this way and that create a 3-D table runner reminiscent of a meandering, coppery creek. You could also toss them in bowls of water topped by a floating lily or a candle cluster.

Banks need time to get new coins from the Federal Reserve, so order rolls of pennies from your bank well in advance. Not all banks are "coin cooperative," but if your bank won't help you acquire the coins for your wedding, maybe you need a different, friendlier bank for your new married life — one that knows the value of a penny.

With penny décor, you're not buying adornments, you're simply borrowing them from yourself. After the wedding, recycle your pennies back into dollars, or stuff the pennies into piggy banks or jars to donate to children's charities. Either way, you'll be perpetuating the good fortune.

#641 *Embroidered Medallions*

Inexpensive embroidery hoops, most commonly made of wood or plastic, come in a variety of sizes and are a wedding decorator's friend. If a family member is gifted with needle skills, custom-embroidered designs will make your wedding décor personal. But even if embroidery is not an option, the hoops still provide beautiful decorating possibilities.

Stretch white lace or other fabric over the hoops, then trim the edges close to the hoop frame. Circle the hoop with ribbon and add a bow to cover the tension-control knob. Hang each hoop individually with white ribbon, or to create a floating, ethereal look, use fishing line. Vary the sizes you hang, and the large and small white medallions will fill empty spaces with something simple but beautiful. A cluster of hanging hoops also adds visual interest when used to frame the cake table.

#642 *The Plush Menagerie*

Instead of big floral centerpieces, consider lions and tigers and bears, oh my!

Long before the big day, start collecting good-looking stuffed animals you find at yard sales, thrift shops, or discount stores. It's best to choose animals that can be fixed into a sitting position and those that are comparable in size. You'll need two for every table and a few extra to position in other locations.

Pair the furry creatures into "brides" and "grooms," and dress them accordingly, with something as simple and easily made as veils and top hats. If you or someone in your family possesses sewing savvy, go the extra mile and dress each pair in a wedding outfit that represents weddings from around the world.

Position the sitting pair back-to-back, and tie the stuffed animals together with silk or satin ribbons with loose bows on each side, allowing the tails of the ribbons to stream out across your tablecloth. The tiny bouquets held by the animal "brides" are all the flowers you need for your tables. And when the wedding is over, keep the pairs you can't "bear" to part with, and donate the rest to a children's organization.

Animal brides and grooms have a huge "awe" factor, and with a bit of savvy hunting, you can save a bundle on the centerpiece budget and still have divine tables.

#643 *A Beautiful Shake*

To create an inventive centerpiece arrangement, tap into snow globes. Snow-globe scenes are beautiful, whimsical, or both, and if you make your own, they're personal. Craft a snow globe from virtually any jar with a screw-on lid, or purchase snow-globe kits ranging from inexpensive plastic globes to glass globes with gorgeous wooden bases.

Inside the globes, you will use miniatures to create wedding scenes or tell stories from your life as a couple. Feature favorite pets or honeymoon-location scenes, or simply insert jeweled monograms in each. Nestle the globes in a bed of greenery, but make them accessible. Guests will want to pick them up and give them a shake. And why shouldn't they? Snow globes are interactive art. Beyond looking fabulous, they provide pleasant little bursts of entertainment.

#644 *The Lantern Connection*

Vintage or modern, full-sized or miniature, lanterns add romance to any wedding theme. No matter how eclectic and diverse other decorations may be, the addition of lanterns seems to pull everything together. Tuck candles inside them, or create unusual centerpieces by filling them with interesting florals. Wedding guests always have a use for miniature candle-lantern favors, and large lanterns hanging from shepherd's hooks add height to a room or style to an outdoor setting. Lanterns with real or electric candles inside light up the ceremony aisle when used as pew décor, and adorned lanterns easily replace bouquets for bridesmaids. Think of lanterns as universal decorative tools — like a bit of unifying magic.

#645 *Beautiful All in One*

Reception tables customarily boast a centerpiece, place cards, and favors — three entities, three expenses. Sometimes it makes sense to streamline your efforts and combine all three into one spectacular table display.

Take a beautiful tabletop tree branch in white, silver, gold, or its natural color, and depending upon the available space on your table, position it upright in a weighted pot or rest it on its side with the branches reaching outward and upward. Choose glass ornaments shaped like balls, birds, butterflies, hearts, or other shapes. Enlist the help of someone with a talent for script or calligraphy to personalize each ornament with the guest's name. Add the custom ornaments to the tree with whatever additional accents you wish, and you're done! The table looks stunning.

If escort cards are not used, guests locate their table via their names on the ornaments. If escort cards are used, the individualized ornaments on the table are simply a beautiful surprise. At each place setting guests discover a small, decorative box with tissue paper inside and a thank-you note from the wedding couple that also instructs guests to take their ornaments home in the box when they depart. If you wish to assign seats at the tables, guests' names can be added to the boxes as well as the ornaments.

Wedding guests are used to seeing décor bearing the names of the bride and groom. Finding their own names on décor is pleasingly unexpected.

#646 *The Table Template*

You may not set up your own reception tables, but you are the one with the vision of what you want them to be. To make them all that you imagined, leave nothing to chance. Make a photo template.

After you've decided on the centerpiece, table linens, dinnerware, glassware, flatware, place cards, favors, and chair décor, create a mock-up. Purchase your exact centerpiece from the florist, and rent, borrow, or purchase everything else you need to create a single perfect table.

Ask your reception venue if you may come during an off time to set up and photograph your table. If that's not an option, use the kitchen table at home. Take photographs from multiple angles, including overhead shots. Measure distances. Exactly how far from the plate do you want the place card? Place settings should be how far from the centerpiece? Answer every question by making a notation to accompany the photos. Compile the finished work into a notebook for those setting up your reception, and you won't have to worry that your vision will get lost in the construction process.

A table template may cost you an afternoon and a few extra dollars, but for those brides who wish to realize the reception scene of their dreams, it's a worthy investment. For those who couldn't care less where a fork falls or if the centerpiece is decidedly off center, skip the notebook. Never devote precious wedding-planning time or money to something that doesn't matter to you.

#647 *Anywhere Walls*

Whether the walls of your venue are just ugly or there are no walls at all, erecting portable "walls" can change the look dramatically. Begin with typical, diamond-patterned, eight-foot-tall sections of wooden or white plastic lattice, in either two-foot- or four-foot-wide sections. For use indoors, make the sections freestanding by adding crosspieces to the bottom, or if they are meant to add intimacy to an outdoor wedding, attach long stakes to the back side to anchor them into the ground. Use vines, flowers, bows, butterflies, or whatever you wish to decorate the panels. To make your walls look opaque, poke the centers of white or multicolored tissue or cellophane squares into the diamond holes, leaving the fluffy edges on the forward-facing side.

Just a few of these decorated panels transform any venue into something quite different, and easily added battery-operated or electric twinkling lights are a bonus. It doesn't take a lot of money to remodel walls or to create interesting wall sections, but the results will look as if it did.

#648 *Pictures in Motion*

This is the digital age, and digital photo frames that used to cost an arm and a bit of a leg are now far less expensive but just as impressive. It probably won't break the budget to add one or more to the wedding reception. Load them with photos of the bride and groom, from childhood through the present, then set them where people gather and mingle, like at the bar, the buffet table, or the cocktail tables in the dance-floor area. Watching the succession of small personal pictures is entertaining and emotionally satisfying. If you choose candid photos, they will surely spark conversation, and that's just what you're hoping for.

#649 *Uncommon Treasures*

For DIY brides, wedding décor and supply ideas spring from anywhere, especially the home. Most homes are bursting at the seams with stored items that have seemingly outlived their usefulness. Give new life to those old treasures by transforming them into fabulous wedding accents.

Got a creaky old occasional table buried in the corner of the garage? Get it out, découpage the tabletop with bride-and-groom photographs and dried flower petals, give it a few coats of clear varnish, and presto — you have created a customized "talk about it" guest-book table.

White spray paint and silver ribbons transform old holiday wreaths into wedding wall art or candle rings for tables. Sketch a pattern, then glue bits and pieces of broken dishes onto a rustic board to create a monogrammed yard sign for outside the ceremony or the reception venue. Turn old ice-cube trays into chocolate or caramel molds, and add zest to that never-ending stash of straws by turning them into sweet, retro pixie-dust sticks. When it comes to creative, DIY wedding style, there really is "no place like home."

#650 *Fluff and Fold*

Wouldn't you love to give every guest a beautiful rose or an exotic bird of paradise? With a little time and effort, you can. Just put an extraordinary napkin at each place setting.

Napkin folding has come a long way from the standard accordion fold. Ingenious people have figured out how to turn napkins into flowers, animals, stars, boats, and just about everything else under — and including — the sun. How about an adorable white bunny napkin for your wildlife theme, or a pinwheel napkin that represents everlasting love? Want to give your guests a private thank-you message? Tuck your note inside a cleverly folded envelope napkin. Napkin folding is a cost-free way to add decorative panache to the reception. All it takes is a bit of learning and a lot of folding.

#651 *Pop Up Some Beauty*

With the pop-up card, greeting cards have evolved. They are no longer merely great vehicles of communication — they also lend dimension to your décor. Pop-up cards without writing on them come in stunning designs like floating butterflies, hearts, fairies, angels, and even wedding couples.

Simply open two cards and place them back-to-back. Glue the backs together, or hold them in place with jeweled clips. The two cards together will create one piece of art that is 10 to 12 inches long and about 5 to 7 inches tall. Use your finished work as the basis of quick and effortless centerpieces or as buffet-table accents. Die-cut, origami, and adorned paper designs that spring into suspension when a pop-up card is opened add all the loveliness of custom decorations with virtually none of the work.

#652 *A Hint of Irish Hills*

Stretching your decorative dollar is often easiest when you think big. For example, if the head-table area is plain and open, nestle that table in a valley surrounded by lush, green, rolling hills reminiscent of an Irish countryside.

Place the table on a carpet of artificial grass that stretches out a few feet in front of and on the sides of the table. Mold chicken wire into round hills and dales, making the peaks reach table height or a bit taller. Two chicken-wire structures will flank the table on either side, taking up where the artificial turf ends but leaving room to walk around the table. Cover the inexpensive chicken wire with rolls of equally inexpensive moss, then accent it with lighter shades of lichen and a smattering of tiny white flowers. In no time you'll have a gorgeous meadow setting for your head table.

To inexpensively finish the décor, hang ceiling-to-floor spirals of moss sprinkled with lichen and flower buds behind the table. Or spend a bit more and rent a scenic backdrop instead. Something along the lines of a stunning Thomas Kincaid cottage scene, paired with the rolling hills you've created, would take your breath away and give guests something magical to gaze upon every time they glance your direction.

#653 *Charge On!*

A charger is a big, decorative plate used as an underliner for dinner courses. Some chargers are boldly colored to add pop to table décor, while others are stately, with intricately carved or decorated edges. Nearly every bride would love to have charger plates to brighten her tables, but chargers are expensive to buy and even to rent. So be creative and make your own.

Visit a dollar store,(the same store online may have more options than its physical store), and buy picture frames in bulk packages ranging from 4 to 36 pieces. When buying in bulk, each 8½" x 11" "document" frame will cost only about a dollar. Paint the wooden frame whatever color works for your theme, and add whatever you wish behind the glass, such as beautiful scrapbook or wrapping paper, dried herbs or flower petals, photo collages, or colored sand. Virtually anything that will fit in the frame works. To complete the look, choose rectangular dishes for the dinner courses.

Let the frames double as favors, and let each guest take their custom frame/charger home to use as a tray or a picture frame. Other charger alternatives include stiffened felt that has been fashioned into exotic shapes with cutout silhouette interiors, and doilies placed beneath a glass overlay. Chargers don't have to be made of gold or porcelain to be stunning. They just have to add charm to the table.

#654 *Antiquing on the Road*

If you love those antique-appraisal shows on TV, consider your very own antique-hunting road trip. Antique and vintage items look beautiful when woven into wedding décor, and later, they'll look beautiful in your home.

The hunt can be a series of day trips, or you can plan an extended jaunt to several antique hot spots and stay at quaint bed-and-breakfast inns along the way. To keep everything from becoming all about work, brides and grooms need adventure during the wedding-planning process. Antiquing on the road is a wonderful way to have that adventure while still addressing wedding-planning concerns.

After the wedding day, keep your favorite antiques and give the rest to friends and family as mementos of your beautiful occasion. Wall, ceiling, floor, and table décor are all opportunities for antique and vintage influences, as are favors, guest registers, and just about any other wedding-day accent. Somewhere, most modern items have antique cousins.

#655 *Living Chandeliers*

There's no denying the impact of a crystal chandelier, but it isn't the only gorgeous suspended option. A living chandelier is blessed with just as much impact, but with far less cash outlay.

Traditional outdoor hanging baskets of greens and flowers festooned with candles or mini white lights make a beautiful décor statement, indoors or out. If the reach of the greens or florals is not low enough, add hanging vines or silk ribbons that flutter downward, and finish each with a floral bud at its tip.

The definition of a chandelier is "a decorative light that holds multiple bulbs or candles and hangs from the ceiling." Nowhere does it say that a chandelier must be composed of expensive crystal or leaded glass. Living chandeliers are useful and beautiful long after the wedding, and you won't break the bank to create them.

#656 *Mismatched and Fabulous!*

There are no wedding police. And there are no laws that say everything at the reception must match. In fact, there's plenty of decorative impact at a wildly eclectic wedding. Feel free to use different linens and place settings at each table, candles of every shape, color, and size, or wildflowers here and perfectly sculpted nosegays there. All that matters is that you can step back and admire what you see.

Mismatching may also help the budget. It opens the doors to shopping possibilities that wouldn't otherwise exist. You cannot walk into a discount store and find 200 identical items, forcing you to go to pricey wedding-supply vendors. But it's easy to find 10 or 20 of one thing and 10 or 20 of another thing at most retailers. By shopping at multiple stores and outlets, you can piece together some fabulous tables, often with a nicely reduced price tag.

#657 *Flying the Flags*

Bunting created from pennant-shaped flags has replaced crepe-paper streamers as the hanging of choice at weddings. You can purchase flag bunting in a cornucopia of colors and designs, in lengths ranging from four to more than a hundred feet.

Wedding-flag bunting is the same style of bunting you see flapping above used-car dealerships, but with a pretty, bridal twist. Some versions have letters to spell out wedding sentiments, while others are silk-screened with a photo of the bride and groom. Fortunately, ordinary plastic or paper flags are not the only choice. If you create the flags yourself, you can make them from anything — bridesmaid-dress material, lace, old clothes or handkerchiefs, or even grocery sacks that have been crinkled multiple times then flattened to resemble weathered parchment. White lettering or a design on sack paper creates an appealing aesthetic. You can even make the flags out of photographs. Making the flags yourself also allows you to add fringe, sequins, or glitter as you wish.

Flag bunting can be tasteful or tacky. It's all in the flags you choose and how you display them. But with its color presence, its potential for movement, its easy personalization, and its ability to cover large, barren areas, flag bunting is something to think about.

#658 *Bobble, Bobble*

To put the fun in your wedding-cake topper or the chuckle in your bar décor, re-create yourselves as bobblehead dolls. From your photo, your likeness is affixed to the faces of a bobblehead wedding couple. Some providers even offer custom gown and tuxedo accents, and many offer bodies that reflect work or pastime passions, like firefighting or motorcycling.

Custom bobbleheads come in a variety of price ranges, but if spending a fair amount to be forever immortalized as bouncy-headed dolls is not an option, look for wedding bobbleheads that have small picture frames where the faces should be. It's easy enough to simply slip your head shots into the frames.

Bobblehead dolls are great conversation starters at the wedding and at home.

#659 *Welcome!*

Your reception is a huge "Thank you" to your guests, so why not put out the welcome mat right away? A customized mat placed at the reception entrance or just in front of the guest-book table shows guests how welcome they truly are.

Indoor/outdoor personalized mats come in a multitude of colors and price ranges. They can be thick or thin, fluffy or flat, and they can bear just the wedding date and the names of the bride and groom or something far more imaginative to match your theme. Having a *Wizard of Oz* theme? Choose a mat that says, "Welcome to Oz!" Want to address your guests directly? Try one that reads, "Welcome, Dear Friends … From Your Hosts, Mary and Dave." Or maybe you want to create a mat that both reflects the magic of the day and is suitable for your future front door, like "Mr. and Mrs. Smith Welcome You."

A welcome mat is not a wedding-day necessity, but it is a wedding-day nicety.

#660 *Endearing Twisted Trees*

For the DYI bride, a great way to recycle old crafting beads or broken jewelry is to create wire trees adorned with pearl or gemstone "leaves." The result is a dazzling, eclectic forest right inside your reception venue.

Wound-wire shapes formed to resemble mighty oaks or weeping willows create the tree trunk and its branches, and faux pearls or other gems glued sparingly to the branches become the lovely, whimsical leaves. In lieu of gluing, beads may replace gems and be threaded onto the wire tips, then held in place by a twist of the wire itself. You don't need to blanket the branches with gems or beads. Sometimes "sparse" is more beautiful than "loaded."

Use the trees as focal points in centerpieces or as stand-alone décor on the buffet or guest-book table. To make them sparkle, set them in the path of a light beam. The cost of making each tree is minimal, even if you have no gems, beads, or wire at home and must purchase all supplies from a craft or discount store. If gems aren't your preference, consider adding tiny origami birds or charms to the branches.

Real trees are a gift to the Earth, and wire trees are a gift to wedding décor.

#661 *Bonsai Poetry Trees*

Real or faux bonsai trees make exotic centerpieces, and they can become even more relevant when paired with a meaningful sentiment.

Use your computer to print a poem onto an elegant paper stock of your choice. Print each stanza so that it can stand alone, then cut the stanzas apart and frame them in miniature round, oval, and square hanging frames (purchased in bulk). Hang the framed stanzas from the bonsai tree, and place the tree on a decorated lazy Susan in the center of the table. The tree will charm from all angles, and guests will be able to spin the turntable to view all of the frames.

If poetry is not your choice, use religious passages, song lyrics, or love quotes. Poet Alfred Joyce Kilmer penned, "I think that I shall never see / A poem as lovely as a tree." Does that make a tree combined with poetry even lovelier? Quite possibly.

#662 *Tatted Chair Art*

A lovely alternative to a chair cover is a stiffened doily. Starch modern or vintage doilies to create immobile works of art, then hang them from the backs of chairs via a tulle bow with tails.

Tatted or crocheted doilies are full of intricate, decorative style, but any starched doily will work. Make them all the same design, or allow every chair to have its own personality. Cut the doilies into hearts, angel wings, or other shapes if you wish, or use them as is.

Both old and new doilies are easy to find, and starching them is a simple process. A little hunting, a little stiffening, a little tying, and you will transform your chairs without spending several dollars apiece for chair covers.

#663 *Ostriches and Friends*

To create beautiful hanging art, use ostrich feathers, plus feathers from a few of their bird friends, to fashion faux ceiling fans. Stick the ostrich feathers around the circumference of a moss-covered Styrofoam ball, positioning the feathers in a flat formation to resemble ceiling-fan blades. Use the smaller, fluffier plumage of a partridge or a guinea fowl to cover the moss and create a vibrant center. Hang the feather fans with fishing line, and they will appear to be floating on air. Make several fans to create a false ceiling for your reception, or hang just a few above your dance floor to add intimacy. Feathers have their place in wedding décor, and "in the air" is one of those places.

#664 *Butterflies Are Free . . . Almost*

If a flower or bow will work in a specific decorative application, so will a butterfly. Silk, nylon, paper, and other materials are crafted into beautiful butterflies of all sizes, and many can be found for only pennies apiece when purchased in bulk. If the floral budget is getting out of hand, substitute butterflies for flowers in centerpieces and bouquets. If bulk ribbons are costlier than you had imagined, use a smaller bow with a butterfly accent to achieve the impact of a larger bow standing on its own. Group butterflies together into wall décor, and sprinkle them among the dishes on the buffet table. Handcrafted butterflies are lovely, and they come as close to being free as just about any decorative treasure you can find.

#665 *Bountiful Beads*

When you need to fill a big, empty space or to create a "wall" where none is, bead art works beautifully. Use long lengths of jute, wire, ribbon, or fishing line, and place beads at appropriate intervals on each line, so that a pattern is revealed when the beaded strings are hung in a row. Create a hummingbird, a cross, a monogram, or virtually any design from hanging beads.

One easy way create a design is to hang your lines from a long length of decoratively sheathed PVC pipe that can later be suspended from ceiling hooks or supported by upright stands. Place your hanging strings against a light-colored wall, and project an image over it using an art projector. Trace the outline of the art you've chosen by marking dots on the strings where you will add beads. If an art projector is not available, draw your pattern on butcher-paper pieces, lay the hanging strings against it, and mark the beading "start and stop" locations on each line.

If the labor involved in creating a beaded portrait is not appealing, consider random beading instead. You won't have a "picture," but you will still have a beautiful decorative piece that can add ambiance to the ceremony site, and can be transported to the reception for double duty as a backdrop or room divider. The beauty of beaded art is that it is both functional and easily customized.

#666 *Worthy Napkin Rings*

Ordinary napkins easily transform into extraordinary table art with the help of clever napkin rings. Fortunately, there's no need to spring for a hundred wedding-bell napkin rings you'll never use again. If an item can be made to contain a napkin, it's a contender.

Stretchable, beaded bracelets or friendship bracelets purchased in bulk can add a splash of color without incurring great expense. A custom-crafted fabric bookmark encircling the napkin and tied with a tassel gives the table a personal touch and doubles as a favor. A napkin encompassed by a simple strand of raffia finished in a bow is all a woodsy wedding needs, and a strip of stiffened lace is ideal for a Victorian theme. For the fun-loving wedding couple, consider a laminated cartoon strip that becomes a ring by using a dab of glue to bind its ends. Replicate the same cartoon strip for all guests, or save strips over time and give everybody a different one, encouraging icebreaking smiles at the tables.

Napkin rings add plenty to table ambiance, but with imagination, they needn't be more than a tiny blip in the wedding budget.

#667 *Crackle It!*

Since the 16th century, glass artisans have submerged piping-hot glass into frigid water to create crackle glass. This technique results in a beautiful overall pattern in the outer layer of the glass. Adding crackle-glass pieces to your reception décor is easier than you think. Instead of searching for expensive ones at boutiques, antique shops, and department stores, check out purveyors of garden supplies!

Crackle-glass bird feeders, garden globes, and even pear-shaped fruit-fly catchers all have the makings of stunning wedding décor. They are available in a wide variety of colors, and as a bonus, they often cost far less than traditional "home décor" crackle-glass pieces. From accents for buffet tables to guest-table centerpieces and hanging décor, crackle glass easily transforms "ordinary" into "extraordinary."

#668 *Sublimely Submersible*

For a quick, eye-catching centerpiece, consider submersible illumination. Submersible lights that resemble votive candles feature steady white lights or pastel lights that continually change colors. Drop one or more of these inexpensive little LED units into any glass container, add water, and float rose petals or a single lily blossom on top.

Or for a one-of-a-kind presentation, begin with photos of the bride and groom. Place them back-to-back with other photos, pieces of wedding-related artwork, or a special message to guests. Cut the combination photo/backing pieces into interesting shapes and individually laminate them, leaving a little extra lamination at the bottom of the photo after trimming. Poke a tiny hole in the extra plastic and thread a length of fishing line through the hole. Anchor the tail to the bottom of your glass container, or weigh it down by tying it to marbles, river stones, or the lights. Stagger the lengths of your fishing line so that each submerged photo "floats" upright at a different height, and you've created incredibly personal table art without an incredibly hefty expense.

If you worry about using a water element in your décor, just fill small punch bowls with any ornaments of your choice and mingle the lights throughout the bowl's contents. Submersible lights are just as pretty and work just as well out of the water.

#669 *Full of Life and Love*

Consider forgoing traditional centerpieces in favor of bride-and-groom treasure boxes filled with mementos of the wedding couple's lives and shared love. Begin with clear, acrylic lidded boxes. If the cost of ready-made acrylic boxes is cost prohibitive, use boxes designed to hold tissues or napkins. Fill each box with bits and pieces that tell a story or inspire curiosity, like concert-ticket stubs and pressed flowers. Think of each box as a three-dimensional scrapbook.

Make each box different so that guests wandering the reception hall get to enjoy the variety. One box may focus on your favorite hobbies, while another depicts where you first kissed or where you plan to honeymoon. Finish the boxes by inserting small floral or greenery sprays in the top slots where the tissues or napkins would ordinarily emerge. Tissue or napkin boxes frequently have no bottoms, so you may need to fashion a box bottom from a thin, sturdy board then cover it with fabric, lace, or any other material that complements your décor.

Life and love are treasures worth celebrating, and on this occasion, thinking "inside" the box is the perfect way to do so.

#670 *Towering Splendor*

Think big and cover a lot of decorative area quickly with the use of tower vases. Also known as Eiffel Tower vases because of their similar shape, these glass vessels come in various colors and sizes. Purchase them wholesale or retail in bulk to keep the price reasonable.

Cluster them in "forests" of glass by using all heights, from small 8-inch vases to tall, refined 30-inch styles. Set clusters of tower vases in staggered heights on your reception tables, and fill them with whatever strikes your fancy, or simply leave them empty. Just the glass collection catching rays of accent lighting will add beauty. For an eclectic look, hit the thrift stores and collect vintage bridal hats and veils to perch atop the tower vases.

#671 *Bottle Bright*

Give battery-operated, small-bulb Christmas lights or fiber-optic strands a simple but elegant home at your wedding reception. Stuff them into colored bottles, jars, or lidded bowls. The lights shine through just enough to create ambiance but not enough to cause a glare, making them per-fect tabletop accents. Combine them with centerpieces, or group them around the room to enhance the mood. Use the same-color glass containers throughout, or create eclectic blends of subdued colors that evoke intimacy or bright colors that feel like a party.

Vessels filled with battery-operated lights are ideal alternatives at venues where candles are prohibited. A little light goes a long way in décor, and these inexpensive light creations will last for hours on a new battery.

#672 *Smiles from the Newlyweds*

While some limousine services provide stock wedding-car decorations that won't harm the vehicle, feel free to add your own personal enhancements. Large, customized window-cling decals can be applied in an instant, and they peel off at the end of the event without leaving so much as a streak.

Choose any art or sentiment you wish. Stick to the bride's and groom's names and wedding date, or express your unique spirit to the world with something like: "The World's Newest, Hottest Newlyweds!"

Window clings work on any limousine, vintage car, sports car, or monster truck. If it's got wheels and glass and it gets you there, it's suitable for the addition of personalized window art. And the decals are sure to make your spectators smile.

#673 *Oh, to Sparkle*

When in doubt, add Swarovski crystals. Any decorations look better when accented with cut glass that glistens in rainbow hues, and Swarovski is the master at creating such glass. There will always be areas at the ceremony or the reception that will benefit from the lovely flash of crystals. To be ready, purchase a bag or two of crystals and have them on hand as the decorations are installed. Some online retailers sell Swarovski crystals in bulk to the public at wholesale prices, or you can visit any jewelry findings retailer. And when you discover that the potted fern you placed at the guest-book table looks duller than you had imagined it would, you'll just pull out your crystals and a tube of clear glue and add a beautiful, instant accent. You may be surprised at the difference something so small can make.

#674 *Soulfully Shaded*

If your reception area has large stretches of plain walls, break them up by hanging colorful window shades at uniform intervals. Consider pleated shades for a modern effect, woven waterfall shades for a warm, homespun look, or tulip Roman shades for formal elegance. To add an interesting depth to the room, mount or hang the shades so that they stand out about six inches from the wall. Add a few floor plants here and there, and a big expanse of empty space is suddenly transformed into something pleasant and inviting.

Plenty of styles and colors make finding the right shades easy. And if you choose carefully, shades that are today's wedding-reception décor can be tomorrow's window accents in your new home.

#675 *Be Still My Quilling Heart*

Religious devotees who decorated book covers and other faith-inspired items were once the only practitioners of a rolled-paper art known as quilling. Later, 18th-century genteel ladies gathered at afternoon teas to roll paper around quills then turn the strips into exquisite art. Today, there are fabulous quillers who market their skills to create art for others. But quilling isn't just for artisans. With practice, anyone can do it, and quilling patterns, tools, and precut papers are now readily available online and in craft stores.

When quilling is done well, the result will knock the socks off your wedding guests. From monogrammed hearts to birds, angels, and even brides and grooms, if it can be designed on paper, it can be made from paper. To see masterful examples of quilling, check out the art of Yulia Brodskaya on any number of Web sites featuring her breathtaking designs.

Adding quilled art to your wedding and reception brings a whole new meaning to decorative, artistic endeavor.

#676 *For More Than the Birds*

When looking for beautiful and quick accents for the reception, consider birds. Birds love to bathe and eat, and humans love to watch them. Fortunately, many birdbaths and bird feeders are gorgeous, especially fused-glass birdbaths and feeders that come in wonderful colors, patterns, and designs. Fused glass resembles stained glass, but without the lead dividers. Some fused-glass birdbaths or feeders cost an arm and a leg, but others are delightfully inexpensive yet just as beautiful.

Collect a few, but instead of inviting birds to bathe in or dine from these fine structures, use them at the ceremony to hold programs or escort cards. Or turn them into elegant snack servers at the reception by filling them with quick treats for guests. For a lovely decorative effect, cluster a few here and there and fill them with water and floating candles. The glass art will shine through the water, and the candle flames will add to the impact. If the baths or feeders come with ground stakes at the bottom, simply sink them into pots of soil and add some greenery.

Birdbaths and bird feeders really aren't just for the birds — not when they are so wonderfully decorative and functional as wedding-day accents.

#677 *Buckle Up!*

If you want your chairs to be chic but different, forget the bow and slip the sash into a rhinestone-studded buckle. Chair buckles are simply a round, oval, or square shape with a solid center bar. You push the fabric through one side of the bar, over its top, and out the other side. It's clean and beautiful. But chair buckles can be pricey. Fortunately, old-fashioned shirt buckles can serve the exact same purpose.

In the 1980s, every woman wearing a T-shirt had one corner of it drawn into a clever, stylish T-shirt buckle. These buckles may not be as easy to find as they were in the '80s, but they're still around. Plastic buckles with rhinestones, or even buckles shaped like flowers, animals, or letters, will instantly transform your chairs. And check online and at retro and thrift shops to find new or vintage specimens, or if you're crafty, you can easily make your own creative buckles.

Buckles or bows, the choice is yours. But before you automatically award the job to those ever-present bows, give buckles a chance to shine.

#678 *Voluptuous Vellum*

Vellum paper is the modern version of ancient vellum. *Vellum* refers to animal skins that have been specially prepared to accept writing inks, but today's vellum paper is made from cotton. Fortunately, the modern paper version retains the stiff, translucent look of the real thing, making it ideal for color craft projects.

If you have a color laser printer, applying art to vellum is a breeze. A color ink-jet printer will also do the job but requires extra drying time, and the opportunity for smudging may be greater. Art can also be applied to vellum freehand.

It is possible to create virtually any design, including butterflies, bumblebees, hearts, clovers, initials, and wedding bells. Just find colorful, free-to-use art online and print it onto the vellum via your color printer, or draw the designs directly onto the paper. Cut out each image, then add glitter or pearlized paint or leave it unadorned. Vellum lends itself to holding a bend, so if you want butterflies with their wings up, it's easy to make that happen.

Use the flat creations as inserts in invitations, to scatter on tables, or to glue onto printed materials like programs or menu cards. Affix folded, three-dimensional versions to the corners of escort or place cards, or fill glass jars with them for table décor. The artful possibilities are endless, and vellum is the go-to paper for bringing your ideas to life.

#679 *Hearts of Love*

When decorating the ends of pews or chairs along the aisle, consider soft, plush, and simple-to-make heart-shaped pillows. If you place a ribbon loop near the top of the backside, they will hang or tie on most pews or chairs with ease. Create them in any color you wish, and adorn them in any way you wish. One option is a white heart with a fabric flower atop a lace overlay in one corner, but any design is possible. Many ready-made heart pillows are available at retailers and from crafters, and if you don't wish to start from scratch, you could buy the pillows and then embellish them.

After the ceremony, move the hearts to the reception and hang them from tree twigs, shepherd's hooks, or doorways, or attach them to the ends of long, wide ribbons you've already positioned behind your cake table. When the reception is over, share the pillows with mothers, grandmothers, and anyone else you wish to have one. Unlike typical pew décor, a pillow will always have a place in the home.

#680 *Dark Glasses*

During the early 20th century, black glass was incredibly popular. It's beautiful and artistically stark, making it a perfect mate to virtually any other décor color or theme. Today, vintage black-glass pieces are found at antique shops or online auction sites, but they may be cost prohibitive. Fortunately, you'll find black-glass reproductions that may not have the age or the pedigree, but still have the look.

To add sophistication to your reception, cluster black-glass vases, bowls, dinnerware, baskets, and even jewelry around the room, and use interesting pieces to support or accent centerpieces or underscore candles. Pair the black glass with gold or silver for a formal effect, or surround it with pastels, like lilac or blush rose, for a semiformal ambiance. Black glass is also breathtaking all on its own. You don't have to fill it, stuff it, or otherwise alter it. Just give it accent lighting to bring out its luster, and it will do its decorative job beautifully.

#681 *Welcome Spring!*

If you're planning a spring wedding, why not add a colorful Maypole to the décor? Mount it behind the cake table, and stretch its ribbons in all directions by suspending their tails from the ceiling with fishing lines. Or you could position it on the dance floor to create a beribboned false ceiling. Set one up outside with its ribbons loose for children to play with, or create miniature, tabletop Maypoles to use as centerpiece focal points.

You can't think of a Maypole without thinking of spring. They're colorful, festive, and easy to make, and if you're a spring bride, a Maypole is a natural addition.

#682 *Fragrant Greetings*

When using potpourri at the reception, do so only at the entrance near the guest-book table. Because some guests will be sensitive to such smells, using potpourri, incense, or air fresheners inside the reception is never a good idea. But a nicely scented basket at the entrance provides a welcome yet fleeting aroma. Guests aren't in the vicinity long enough to trigger a scent sensitivity, and the subtle fragrance foreshadows the celebratory atmosphere inside.

Potpourri does have its place at the wedding. It simply needs to know its place and stay there.

#683 *A Sense of Warmth*

For fall or winter weddings or those with a woodsy theme, bring on the fireplace logs. Faux fireplace logs are real logs that come with the electrically produced color and crackle of a real fire without a real flame. They won't warm a body, but they will warm a room's décor, making it seem cozier. Other faux fireplace logs are made of realistic resin and are notched to hold tea-light candles, providing the flicker of actual flames without any heat. Battery-operated tea lights will also fit the logs, to accommodate venues where candle flames are prohibited.

If you want to add that intimate, comforting feeling that only a fireplace can provide but a real fireplace is simply not an option, faux fireplace logs sitting on a fire grate are a great substitute.

#684 *Fairies, Angels, and Brides*

Centerpieces need to be interesting and attractive to be successful, and some with no flowers at all meet that criteria and soar beyond it. Imagine a beautifully unique fairy, angel, or bride doll nestled in a bed of greenery on every table. After the wedding, you can donate the dolls to a charity that gives gifts to children, providing young ones with a new friend to cherish.

Dolls come in all manner of designs, materials, and expressions. Go for realism, or push the limits of artistry. Use soft dolls, functional dolls, or rigid dolls meant for shelves. If it's color you want, use fairy dolls with iridescent, rainbow-hued wings. If you want dolls that children can later enjoy dressing and redressing, choose articulated bride dolls, and for dolls with a special connection, consider angel dolls that will bring a touch of magic to a child's living space.

When you choose doll centerpieces, they will add a special atmosphere to the wedding day, and they will reach beyond the event in a meaningful way.

#685 *3-D Magic*

Walls at commercial venues sometimes present difficult decorating challenges, but if you think "3-D," then visualizing a whole new look for that wall is not hard at all. Imagine the wall dotted with beautiful 3-D dragonflies, ladybugs, or butterflies in various sizes, their delicate wings spread as if the swarm were flying to the ends of the Earth. If the wedding is in winter, use glittering 3-D snowflakes or warm, woodsy pinecones.

Ask your venue for permission to attach your artistic treasures to the wall. Most won't mind, as long as you use good-quality, no-harm, removable mounting tape to affix the pieces. When removed, the tape leaves no residue on the wall.

With their gorgeous shapes and gentle ambience, arrays of snowflakes or die-cut flying insects — whether iridescent, pastel, or pure white — can turn any dull wall into an artful vision.

#686 *Sophisticated Ribbons*

Ribbons already pack a lot of decorative punch, but to elevate them into the sophistication stratosphere, give them the ribbon-buckle treatment. Ribbon buckles are customarily the exact width of the ribbon, and they can be made in simple, refined colors or bejeweled with shimmering rhinestones or crystals. They slip on easily, and once in place, only the outer edge of the buckle is visible. Match the buckle to the ribbon size to keep the ribbon flat, or select a slightly smaller buckle to create a "pinch" in the ribbon.

Use buckled ribbons to dress up favors, or weave them throughout the buffet table to add charm. If you try to brighten the room by hanging lengths of ribbon in clusters down a wall, they'll still look like ribbons hanging on a wall. But place beautiful buckles here and there, and those hanging ribbon strips become colorful wall art. Thread buckled ribbons into floral arrangements, or fashion them into ribbon wreaths to surround flameless candles.

Buckles transform ribbons that are already lovely into ribbons with distinction.

#687 *Mirror, Mirror*

Mirrors enlarge and enlighten a space, and tabletop mirrors do wonders for wedding décor. Mirrored cubes used by stores to display perfume or jewelry are beautiful but pricey. Simply make your own instead, using ordinary hand mirrors.

Align four hand mirrors facedown on a table so that they touch edges in a line, with the handles pointing away from you. Apply two long strips of clear packing tape across the mirror backs, positioning one just beneath the handle area and the other toward the bottom of the mirror. Stand them up and fashion them into a square, with the mirrors facing outward and the handles reaching upward. Reach inside the unit and affix another piece of tape to secure the mirrors into a square position. Your new mirror box is now ready for decorating as you see fit.

The use of vintage-style mirrors with beautiful frames and handles makes a lovely display, but even ordinary mirrors can be enhanced through the embellishment of their handles.

Once finished, set whatever you wish inside the square. The size of mirrors used will dictate what will fit inside, and additional hand mirrors can be added to change the shape or enlarge the scale of your structure. Large mirrors will make a stunning outer covering for a flowerpot, a bowl of delectable treats, or a floral spray. Greenery that trickles through the handles looks especially nice. Depending upon the handle lengths, you may need to settle a covered support inside the mirrors as a riser to elevate whatever you wish to set inside.

Frameless, purse-sized mirrors can also be hot glued to any acrylic box, like a photo holder or tissue box, and inexpensive mirror tiles from a home-improvement store can be used flat as trays or glued together to create a more traditional square cube.

Mirror décor makes everything look better, but it doesn't have to be expensive.

#688 *Not Just for Walls*

Beautiful wallpaper is not just for walls. Damask wallpapers make quick and lovely table runners, especially when combined with a rustic décor. A flocked damask wallpaper design against a real wood table is striking. Wallpaper can also be mounted into picture frames of all shapes and sizes to create instant wall or easel décor, and you can easily cut it into strips to spiral around tree twigs to give ordinary branches an eclectic, artistic finish. You can even cut out the individual flocked designs from the wallpaper to affix to anything from wedding-card boxes to menu cards, or press them beneath a sheet of glass atop the guest-book table.

Gorgeous wallpaper and wallpaper borders are quick and easy design tools for brides. Search the closeout bins, and stock up.

#689 *Skyline Mystique*

There's something breathtaking about a skyline at night. All those lights glowing across a panorama of interesting building shapes makes you want to embrace someone you love and just gaze at the view.

Having that mesmerizing skyline at your wedding is easier than you think. Simply purchase some large, six-foot-foam core or cardboard sheets, and cut the upper third of each sheet in the shape of a different "building top." (There's no need to cut the bottom two-thirds of the foam core or cardboard, since you're only interested in the tops of the buildings.) The rooflines don't have to be pristine — your "city" can be as fanciful and artistically interpretive as you wish.

Spray paint the finished pieces midnight blue, align the individual buildings facedown, then place supporting strips along the backs to secure them together. String strands of small white lights (twinkling or constant) across the cutout tops, and place your cityscape against a wall. Hang a moon and stars above the buildings to add even more skyline mystique.

Even if you marry in a field of cows, you can still bring the magic of city nightlife to your celebration.

#690 *Alphabet Art*

Never underestimate the decorative power of your ABCs. Freestanding wooden letters spell out whatever you'd like them to say — the wedding couple's names, a message to guests, a favorite phrase, or simply "We Did!" Some custom sign makers allow you to choose any font, and then they cut the letters accordingly. Arrange the words on tabletops or on the floor to create an inventive border for a miniature garden or even the dance floor. If you want "floating" words, hang the letters from the ceiling with fishing line.

There's a lot to be said for "spelling it out." After all, there's no better occasion for communicating your sentiments than a wedding.

#691 *Just for Two*

Instead of individual chairs for the bride and groom at the head table or sweetheart table, try a bench for two. A bride-and-groom love seat, a dual throne, or a beautiful park bench unite the wedding couple and enhance the décor.

A white-wicker, porch-style love seat is ideal for a spring or summer wedding, while a rough-hewn, natural wood bench adorned with seasonal floral touches is perfect for an autumn celebration. There are even throne-style love seats with oversized backs that make you feel like you're tucked into a cozy booth.

With so many essentials to buy, a wedding-couple love seat might not be a top priority in the decorating budget. But if you plan ahead, you may find the perfect, affordable seat at a yard sale or estate sale. And if you let it be known that you're looking, you may receive one as a gift, or a friend may offer to loan you one. You could also check into renting one from theater prop houses or trade-show furniture suppliers. If you decide to purchase a wedding-day love seat, think beyond the wedding, and choose one that you will enjoy cuddling on at home for the rest of your lives.

#692 *Star Treatment*

Who doesn't crave their 15 minutes of fame? And who says you have to wait for it to come along in its own good time? You can make it happen! There are oodles of online sites ready, willing, and able to put you and your groom on the cover of hot-topic "magazines."

Create just one faux magazine cover to use for invitations or announcements, or go all out and design multiple covers in a variety of fun magazine genres, then frame them and place them around the reception. You not only get to choose the photo, you also get to add headlines and text, and your covers can be humorous, serious, or a little of both. They will be a hoot for guests, and if you want, you can even surprise your parents or best friends with a cover or two of their own. Imagine their delight at finding them at your reception.

Fame is fleeting. Your wedding is a perfect reason to indulge in a few hours of the star treatment.

#693 *Gorgeous Glow*

Every bride needs a little bit of decorative magic in her pocket, and FloraLytes provide it. FloraLytes are little one-use lights that activate with a pull of a tab. They stay lit for a minimum of a day, and can be used anywhere and with anything. Want lighted boutonnières? Nestle a single FloraLyte into each of them. Have tower vases that would look so much better with a glow? Set two or three activated FloraLytes into each vase's bottom. Looking for something safer than a candle for your paper lanterns? FloraLytes do the trick. Weddings are very much about tradition, but it's nice to know that modern, nontraditional tools like FloraLytes can make even the most classic wedding look brighter.

#694 *A Fine Figure*

Some wedding couples simply don't want their head table or sweetheart table laden with floral arrangements. If you prefer a clean, sleek look for your table, forego the flowers and add a single, beautiful figurine instead.

Set the figure on a soft spray of greenery, a mirror round, or a silver tray, or keep the look elegantly stark and simple by using only a white or crystal figurine with no further embellishment. Choose an artsy bride-and-groom statuette, intertwined hearts, or even a lone, beautiful tree. Whatever art you care to present is the perfect choice. An elegant porcelain cake topper can also be effective on the table.

Inspired, wedding-perfect figurines can complement or replace flowers, giving you the sophisticated and minimalistic look you crave.

#695 *Bubble Up*

How do you turn ordinary water into a clever, colorful cluster of beads? Let the water meet its match in water beads.

Water beads come in several colors, and when added to liquid, they absorb it, holding the water inside and then slowly leaching it back out to whatever flowers or plants reside in the container. Use water beads to accent floral presentations or to create a colorful, polymer river that "flows" through your buffet table. Add FloraLytes or candles if you wish.

It takes several hours for the beads to fully absorb the water they have been placed in, so plump them a day ahead. Don't worry that they won't last throughout the reception, because they have a very long life, shortened only by long-term exposure to bright light. After the wedding, take them home and place them in your indoor bamboo garden.

Lots of plants love water beads, and you'll love how they transform the look of your table décor.

#696 *Something Fishy*

To find lovely glass orbs to hang from tree limbs, shepherd's hooks, or the ceiling, consider a nautical option. Once the fisherman's tool of choice for keeping fishing nets afloat, glass fishing floats are beautiful glass balls secured in knotted nets. Today, real glass floats, as well as inexpensive reproductions, are available for decorative use. They come in several sizes and a rainbow of colors.

Individually hung from the ceiling on staggered lengths of fishing line, these orbs make great drop-down décor to frame the bandstand or guest-book table, or to simply add splashes of color that catch and reflect the light. You can also cluster the glass floats in bowls or baskets wherever table décor is needed.

The fish probably didn't like glass floats circling above them, but humans enjoy them thoroughly.

#697 *Perfect Pops*

How amazing are pop-up place mats? Made of paper, the place mat lies flat against your table linen as any ordinary place mat would, but its secret weapon is an intricately carved design that graces the top. Pop up that design, and you have an instant, built-in place card. The hole left by the pop-up allows the table-linen color to show through, beautifully integrating the mat with the table. It's a wonderfully clever concept that results in the kind of décor accent that people buzz about, transforming reception tables into something different and special.

Use the same design for everyone, or mix it up and choose several artistic designs to create a fascinating tablescape. What may seem so simple is really a little touch of genius.

#698 *Fascinating Frames*

For quick, easy, and impressive wall décor, try empty picture frames. Go on the hunt for interesting frames in all sizes, shapes, and vintages — the glass and backing are unnecessary. Old frames can be found at consignment shops, thrift stores, antique shops, and at just about every garage sale on the street.

Vintage frames are lovely for a classic wedding style, and modern frames work beautifully for a contemporary theme. Paint them if you wish, but frames in their natural state are already blessed with visual appeal.

Mount a grouping of the empty frames on the wall using harmless, removable frame hooks. Hang them completely unadorned, or add a corsage-sized floral spray to one corner of each frame. Oval, round, square, rectangular, and oddly shaped frames come together to add interest and beauty to otherwise barren walls, and it won't cost a lot of money to make it happen. Frames are fabulous even when nothing is inside them.

#699 *A Sucker for Love*

When looking for sparkly splashes of color to add to centerpieces and other décor, don't overlook the simple, inexpensive lollipop. With their crinkly cellophane wrappers and white sticks, hard-candy suckers do more than keep the kids happy. Clustered together, jewel-toned pops make gorgeous centers for oversized silk or paper flowers. Add a silver-ribbon stripe to each stick (modeled after the circular, descending stripe of a barber's pole), then fill Mason jars with them to sit on the bar, buffet, or guest-book table, or hang the jars from shepherd's hooks, tree limbs, or the rafters. Add a custom tag with a clever quote, then serve suckers with hot tea or hot chocolate for use as sweet swizzle sticks. To envision their decorative possibilities, look at suckers with an eye toward art, instead of with a hungry craving.

FOOD & DRINK

CHAPTER ELEVEN • *Food & Drink*

I f you want happy wedding guests, you must feed and water them. There are few things more essential to a good time than refreshments. Taste-bud pleasers boost the spirit, jump-start energy, and bring satisfaction.

From cold, bottled water for a preceremony wait in the hot sun to a Viennese dessert table in the wee hours of the reception, generosity in the food-and-drink department is the foundation of a comfortable and memorable event. Refreshments are a priority for the wedding, so budget accordingly. Whether you will be serving a full meal or merely an array of scrumptious munchies, and whether champagne or fruit punch is the beverage of the day, fulfilling your guests' culinary desires is a major, tangible aspect of thanking them for attending your wedding.

This chapter presents ideas about both traditional and unusual food and drink selections. From the wedding cake to buffet boosters to foods that lead double lives as entertainment, décor, or favors, the following pages are filled with ways to please the palate, ensure dining safety, and create unique presentations of delectable delights.

Who doesn't love to eat or lift a glass when partaking in social interaction? You and your intended are the guests of honor at your wedding, but you are also the hosts of the celebration, and all good hosts know that flavorful, satisfying fare is the cornerstone of celebratory success.

#700 *That Warm, Embracing Cup of Joe*

Coffee is dear to the hearts and palates of millions, and a coffee cart at your wedding reception is a guest-pleaser. Set up a self-service coffee bar with button-activated hot pots, or opt for a full-service bar by bringing in your very own knowledgeable and entertaining barista.

From standard black brew to espressos, cappuccinos, and exotic blends, your coffee cart promises to be a refreshment comfort zone. Even with free-flowing bubbly and cocktails, there will come a time when the party hearties will embrace a warm cup of joe.

Operate your coffee cart from the start of the reception, or open it later to enjoy with dessert and that all-important slice of wedding cake. Following a few coffee dos and don'ts will ensure success:

- Don't serve hot coffee in paper cups, unless utilizing paper cups with sipping lids made specifically for hot drinks.
- Do provide at least three coffee choices to give your coffee cart appeal.
- Don't forget the coffee accessories, like stir sticks, sweeteners, creamers, napkins, and wet wipes.
- Do consider tying your coffee cart to your wedding favors by giving your guests personalized cups or mugs as wedding keepsakes.

The universal love of coffee makes a coffee cart a most appreciated gift!

#701 *Sit Down, but Choose First!*

For your sit-down dinner, give guests a choice by asking for an entrée preference on the RSVP.

Courtesy calls for specifics. It's not enough to ask guests to choose from "fish," "beef," "chicken," or "vegetarian." Entrée preparation is an important decision-making consideration. Listing ingredients is not necessary, but describing an entrée choice as "Baked Halibut," "Beef Bourguignon," "Chicken Kiev," or "Vegetarian Lasagna" provides enough information about expected tastes.

To absolve you of any angst should a guest not designate a preference, identify a default entrée on the RSVP.

Entrée choices should be based on universal appeal and cost. While lobster may be your favorite food, it's not only costly, it's also a love/hate meal that may excite half of your guests and repulse the rest. Choosing entrées that don't break the budget, and those that a majority is likely to enjoy, will make the sit-down experience sweetly satisfying.

#702 *It's a Small-Bite World*

One of the joys of wedding reception refreshments is the thrill of circling the globe of good tastes. Whether you're planning a sit-down dinner, a buffet meal, or no formal meal at all, an international spread of delectable appetizers will deliver on the culinary front.

In Spain, small servings of food are known as tapas, and eating only bites of a variety of foods can easily add up to a filling and scrumptious meal. Sampling foods from many cultures adds fascination.

Imagine following the zing of an Egyptian curried-eggplant dip with the understated mildness of a Chinese spring roll. Or how about a spicy Mexican taquito snuggled up to a melt-in-your-mouth square of Greek baklava? It's fireworks for the taste buds!

Identify your dishes and decorate your international spread by adding framed or mounted postcards depicting scenes from around the world.

Dining doesn't have to be about large, weigh-you-down meals. Wedding-reception dining can mean snacking "the world" to your heart's content!

#703 *Wedding-Cake Surprise!*

Wedding-cake filling is traditionally butter cream or Bavarian cream, fruity mousse, chocolate ganache, or perhaps lemon curd. But who says you have to be traditional? Seize the day and fill your cake with whatever flavor you fancy.

Tap into flavors like nuts, fruits, spices, liqueurs, candies, jellies, and syrups to invent a filling that blows the lid off tradition and makes your wedding cake a memory all its own.

Coconut and key lime, pistachio and blackberry, maple and cream cheese, gingerbread and caramel, pumpkin and hazelnut, and toffee and marshmallow are just a few of the flavor profiles you can create by listening to your taste buds.

Not every filling will be appropriate for every cake. Some fillings are reliant upon a certain temperature. Others are heavy and are only appropriate for sheet cakes or the lower layers of tiered cakes. Your baker knows which dream flavors will work and which ones won't. But if a baker says no to your idea, get a second opinion just to be sure. You don't want to give up that peanut-butter-and-banana filling at your Elvis wedding just because you've stumbled upon a lazy baker!

#704 *Welcome to Candy Kingdom!*

When the Aztecs first plucked the fruit pod from the cacao tree, little did they know they were about to start an eternal, worldwide addiction that would last for all eternity. Chocolate is loved throughout the world, and wedding-reception candy spreads are a sweet idea indeed.

Make a candy-filled mini buffet for guests to visit, or provide an assortment of candies in wedding-theme-appropriate containers on each table. Age plays no role. Adults and children alike clamor for jellybeans, mints, lollipops, caramels, and most of all, chocolates. Whether light, dark, white, milk, filled or solid, chocolates are the headliners.

Saying "Thank you for being here!" with a bounty of sinfully rich and sweet goodies can't ever be wrong.

#705 *Why Have a Football at the Wedding?*

The groom's cake is a gift from the bride to her groom, and unless it's consumed at the rehearsal dinner, it's customarily displayed near the bridal cake at the wedding reception.

The groom's cake used to be no more than a small cake with minimal décor, but times have changed. Now, more often than not, it rocks a clever theme. Brides make an effort to create a cake that matches their groom's passion for this or that, or one that pays tribute to his personality. Bakers no longer blink when asked to incorporate even the wildest concepts into their confection. Nothing is off limits.

The groom's cake is customarily cut up at the reception, and small portions are tucked into cake-slice boxes and sent home with guests. For single female guests, an additional tiny sliver of cake is slipped into a plastic bag and added to the take-home box. This individually wrapped sliver is meant for tucking under her pillow that night so that Miss Single Female will dream of her future husband.

Groom's cakes are not mandatory, but they are an honor for the grooms who receive them.

#706 *Stuffed and Guiltless!*

Wedding receptions aren't for worrying about calories, but there's no reason you have to send your guests home with an extra pound of flesh either. Low-calorie versions of hors d'oeuvres and entrées can be every bit as delicious as their heftier counterparts.

Instead of cream-cheese-stuffed, bacon-wrapped dates, try an herbed-goat-cheese, whole-grain crostini. Consider replacing a fried-shrimp entrée with grilled shrimp atop seared portobello mushrooms and brown rice. Even a simple exchange, like whole-grain, high-fiber rolls instead of yeast rolls, makes a healthful and filling difference.

While it probably wouldn't endear you to your guests to break out the rice cakes and watercress, it's certainly possible to present culinary delights that won't attach themselves to the hips of the guests before they've even departed the reception.

#707 *The Fresh Palate*

With an abundance of food and drink, the palate can become inundated with flavors that refuse to leave. Lingering tastes overwhelm and alter the next flavor choice. That's why a clean palate is dining's best friend.

Fine-dining restaurants frequently provide a light sorbet, usually lemon, to cleanse the palate between courses. Do the same for wedding guests by providing a unique sorbet bar beneath an ice sculpture.

Create a circular moat of sorbet by placing suitable containers in an ice bed at the base of the ice sculpture, making certain it's far enough away from the sculpture to avoid melting drips. Provide small tasting spoons (like those in ice-cream shops) in decorative containers dotted here and there in the ice, and position a decorative receptacle nearby for used and discarded spoons. If you wish, add a small sign that alerts guests to the palate-cleansing pleasures of the sorbet bar. It might read:

This Sorbet Bar Is the Perfect Source
For a Palate-Cleansing Refresher between Each Course

Any sorbet flavor will do, but the lighter the taste, the better the cleanse.

#708 *Pizza — That's Amore!*

If you're a beer-and-pizza kind of couple, there's no reason to change your stripes for your wedding. Go ahead and choose caviar on toast points if your heart's set on fancy food, but if it's just a good time with friends and family that matters, there's nothing wrong with a beer-and-pizza reception.

A buffet filled with a variety of pizzas, a tossed-salad bar with tasty fixings, and a few inventive dipping sauces for breadsticks is the epitome of a comfort-food spread. Pizza is a universal love fest, and it's one of the easiest wedding feasts to accomplish. You don't need a caterer. You just need the phone number of your favorite pizza joint.

Add courtesy and personality to the mix by providing custom bibs to protect attire from pizza-sauce drips. Even the swankiest eateries include disposable bibs with potentially messy foods, but no five-star restaurant could ever have bibs as fun and as clever as your wedding-day pizza bibs!

#709 *With This Cup, I Do Express*

Most receptions kick off with a cocktail hour, and personalized glassware at the bar is a memorable, above-the-call-of-duty touch.

Bulk glassware customized with names, images, or any desired message is not expensive. From shot glasses to tumblers to wine flutes, unique glasses can rule the cocktail hour as bonus keepsakes or as stand-alone wedding favors.

Add personalized or wedding-themed swizzle sticks, and your reception bar will soar above ordinary. Custom glassware is not necessary. It is, however, an impressive plus.

#710 *Have You Tried the Sam-and-Mary Sunrise?*

There's no need for a degree in mixology to create a custom drink, so why not add zip and zing to your reception by offering your own custom cocktail?

A custom drink may tickle the taste buds, but it's an even better conversation starter. Wedding guests eager to try your stylized drink will no doubt have plenty of lively discussions about your one-of-a-kind libation.

Consider turning custom drinks into a friendly, prewedding competition by asking the wedding party and family members to come up with their own unique drinks. They can be told in advance about this fun, informal competition in any way you choose — in person, by phone, or via e-mail. The wedding couple will judge the concoctions, and the winner's drink will be offered at the reception, alongside the bride and groom's special brew. If the wedding couple's drink is alcoholic, make the contest entries nonalcoholic, or vice versa, so that no matter what other drink is created, it won't compete with the bride and groom's masterpiece.

Inventing custom drinks doesn't require bartending experience, but a little imagination goes a long way.

#711 *Savory Stations*

If you're planning a buffet-style dinner at your reception, consider taking a tip from popular buffet restaurants. Divide your buffet into savory stations.

One long buffet inevitably means congestion and slow lines. Instead of end-to-end rectangular tables, use freestanding round tables for your buffet, and give each station its own beautiful centerpiece. Divide tables by food ethnicity — Mexican dishes on this table, Italian fare on that one. Or designate tables by style of food — salads and side dishes here and entrées there, or vegetarian to the left and meat-lover's to the right.

Round tables provide easier access to buffet dishes and more centralized room for decorative, themed accents, condiments, relishes, breads, and spreads.

Thinking "in the round" is a great beginning to a pleasant buffet experience.

#712 *Minty Refreshment*

After-dinner mints are an easy way to give more for less. Whether you choose inexpensive, pastel "pillow" mints in your wedding colors or opt for more costly chocolate-covered mint wafers, mints go with every dinner. Smaller mints can be purchased in personalized tins, or you could add a unique message to custom candy wrappers for larger mints.

Mints are a delectable, mouth-refreshing gift. A few mints nestled in an organza bag or wrapped in tulle serves the purpose quite nicely. If you want to go that extra mile, fill hand baskets with individually wrapped mint gifts and have the flower girl, ring bearer, or junior bridesmaids deliver mints to each guest at the conclusion of the meal.

#713 *Grown-Up Nut Cups*

Little paper nut cups are a wedding-reception staple, but opting for much larger cups can turn nuts into functional, flavorful centerpieces.

Fill white, silver, or pastel cupcake cups with a variety of tasty nuts, then settle the cups into the metal rings of cupcake trees. Place one cupcake tree in the center of each individual table, or use several trees at even intervals down longer tables. Add a decorative container of mini tasting spoons or mini scoops for extracting the nuts, and a stack of artfully flared cocktail napkins for holding them. Decorate the base of the tree stand with greenery, flowers, or ribbons, and a beautiful centerpiece is born.

Unusually styled votive candleholders, or martini glasses with their stems tied together with ribbon, make viable substitutes for cupcake trees. Building your own unique tree using easily accessible materials like cardboard or decorative wire is not difficult. If you need help with this, you are sure to find information online or at a craft store.

Nuts are always wedding perfect. It's nice to know their versatility permits them to do double duty as delightful decorations.

#714 *Kid-Friendly Drinks*

If children are invited to the reception, they will no doubt arrive all clean and tidy in their Sunday-best clothes. Help those clothes make it home in the same condition by offering only nonstaining drinks for kids.

Flavored waters or punches made from clear liquids and fruit essences can tickle kids' taste buds and protect moms and dads from cherry or grape-stained clothing. Some garments are never the same after the intense cleaning it takes to remove deeply colored stains, and with the high cost of children's clothing, it's nice to avoid destruction where possible.

Kid's drinks don't have to be brightly colored. They just have to taste great.

#715 *Vegetarian Vittles*

There are degrees of vegetarianism. Some vegetarians don't eat meat but do eat fish, eggs, and dairy. Others use no products derived from living creatures whatsoever, not even honey for sweetening or lard for cooking. While only a small percentage of the overall population is vegetarian, chances are that someone in your circle is. It's always a good plan to include at least one vegetarian main dish in the wedding-reception menu.

The rule of thumb is to make the dish completely vegetarian without any trace of animal ingredients so that even the strictest vegetarian can enjoy it. There are plenty of delicious veggie-based recipes to choose from, and it's easy to incorporate a vegetarian dish into any theme or flavors. Vegetarian hors d'oeuvres are even easier.

A rule to remember: Nonvegetarians can certainly enjoy a vegetarian dish, but the reverse is not likely to be true.

#716 *Food Safety First!*

A wedding-day buffet is anything you want it to be, but to keep guests safe, the first criterion for any buffet dish is that it is able to stand the test of time. Buffet foods are exposed to more potential danger than plated foods. The room temperature, sitting time, exposure to lights, and even glitter falling from decorations can affect the safety of buffet dishes.

The rules are simple. Hot foods must be served with a continuous heat source like electrical hot servers and trays or chafing dishes over odorless, clean-burning, and disposable chafing fuels. Cold-food dishes should be nestled in ice beds.

If your event is catered, these concerns will fall on the caterer. But if you are whipping up a fabulous spread in your own kitchen, you will be responsible for maintaining the food's temperature and for shielding dishes from the fallout generated by embellished decorations, wild hairdos, and other floating menaces.

It's not as hard as it sounds. Professional serving equipment can be rented, or if your reception is held where a kitchen is available, as in some church basements, chances are that you can borrow whatever equipment you may need from the facility.

To feed your guests well, feed them safely.

#717 *Precious Gems for the Taste Buds*

If you want your reception to look like a million bucks, give it the Midas touch. Metallic, edible dusting sugars are a decorative, delicious plus for wedding culinary art, adding ooh-la-la to wedding-day foods.

From hors d'oeuvres to desserts, pump up the sparkle and the magic by accenting delectable treats with the shimmer of gold, silver, or pearl dusting sugar. Dusting sugar has a finer consistency than edible glitter, and each works best for certain circumstances. For example, dip punch glasses into silver glitter as you would dip a Margarita glass into salt, or brush glitter onto the wedding-ring designs atop cupcakes. The finer consistency of an edible dusting sugar works well on overall applications, like turning a white-finished cookie into a shimmering, pearlized gem good enough to eat!

#718 *Get Your Wedding-Cake Groove On*

Cake bakers moved into the 21st century with an animated bang, and cakes can now shake their frosting as if they were alive.

Animated cakes add excitement to the cake-cutting ceremony. Whether it's a waltzing wedding couple atop the cake or uniquely decorated layers that spin in opposite directions, wedding cakes don't have to merely sit and look pretty anymore.

Utilize animation to create a surprising spectacle for all guests. Birds that chirp, flowers that open at the moment of cutting, and angels rising high above the top tier are just a few animation possibilities.

Not every baker has the skills or experience to animate your wedding cake, so if animation tickles your fancy, search well for that creative baker with "extreme" cake-baking talent.

#719 *Setting an Able Table*

For brides planning to serve a reception dinner without the help of a caterer, amassing enough china, crystal, and flatware for the event is a challenge. Rental immediately comes to mind, but at a price of anywhere from a quarter to more than a dollar per dish, it's easy to see how the costs quickly add up.

Convenient and inexpensive disposable paper goods can work if the reception is not formal and the food is not overly messy. But there is a middle ground between paper and china. These versatile serving items are Resposables by EMI Yoshi.

Resposables are made of high-quality plastic, but they are patterned and cut to look like china and crystal. They are aesthetically more appealing than traditional disposable goods, but are still completely recyclable. Some resposable flatware has such a silver sheen that it's hard to distinguish it from real silverware, until you pick it up and feel its lighter weight. The rental of a knife, fork, and spoon for 50 guests can cost $40 and up (as long as none goes missing, requiring an inflated, lost-item purchase price to be added to the rental fees), while the same service in high-grade resposables would cost less than $20, with no penalty for missing pieces, no washing, and no pickup or return.

Resposables are not for every bride, but there are certainly wedding receptions where a nice-looking, recyclable-plastic version of china, crystal, and flatware is just perfect.

#720 *A Rose by Any Other Name ...*

In Shakespeare's *Romeo and Juliet*, it was Juliet who said, "What's in a name? That which we call a rose by any other name would smell as sweet." So what is in a name? Does it matter? Yes.

The word *wedding* seems to automatically escalate cake costs. Cake price lists reveal different pricing structures from bakery to bakery, but there's a common thread among all of them. Wedding cakes are more expensive.

A sheet cake decorated with roses at one bakery provides 24 servings and costs about $1.00 per serving. But a wedding cake that also serves 24 people from that same bakery costs $4.50 per person. Granted, wedding cakes are shaped and decorated differently. They no doubt require more labor. But do they warrant four-and-a-half times the cost of a typical decorated cake?

For brides and grooms looking to trim the budget, the cake's name may indeed make a difference. To save money, order what would essentially be the top tier of a traditional wedding cake, then order ordinary satellite cakes to place on lower, staggered pedestals. These cakes "orbit" around your intimate wedding cake, creating a dramatic presentation. And when the time comes, they'll taste just as delicious.

You could also order your cake by theme name. For example, call the bakery and ask for a "cherry blossom–themed" cake or a "nautical-themed" cake. The cake will be beautiful and tasty, but without "wedding" in its name, it'll likely come with a more agreeable price tag.

The wedding cake, for some brides and grooms, is no place to scrimp and save. But for others, changing the name to prevent paying a premium for something destined to disappear down the gullet makes perfect sense.

#721 *The Heritage Viennese Table*

A Viennese table is a dessert buffet on wheels, stocked with pastries, mousses, pies, cakes, cookies, tortes, and whatever other lip-smacking desserts the imagination can conceive. It is often accompanied by a coffee and espresso spread, and the table customarily makes a grand entrance at the end of the reception. The fanfare of rolling out the Viennese table to dramatic music and resounding applause is as much fun as eating its offerings. Sparklers make it even more exciting.

Any combination of desserts is acceptable, but to wrap up your reception with more than just sugar, let your Viennese table convey the personal heritage of the bride's and groom's families.

Choose desserts that represent the cultures of the combined families down through the ages. This is a great place to share great-grandma's special recipes, even if the caterer is doing the baking.

Turning an ordinary Viennese table into a heritage Viennese table puts a nice cherry on top of your dessert fest and concludes your reception with a meaningful surprise.

#722 *Eclectic Chocolate Expression*

There's very little on the planet that moves people the way chocolate does, so go ahead and personalize your wedding with your own custom chocolate mold.

Standard candy molds like wedding bells, doves, etc., are absolutely fine for wedding-day chocolates, but a one-of-a-kind mold made just for the bride and groom takes personalization to a whole new level. Use your white or dark chocolate creations as favors, after-dinner treats, decorations, and centerpiece accents. Choose any design, from the family crest to the wedding getaway car to a representation of the wedding theme. It's possible to forge virtually any shape with chocolate.

Make your own mold from food-grade silicone, or hire a professional candy-mold maker. A professional can create a mold sheet that includes several of your designs, permitting many chocolates to be made at once. Melt the chocolate and fill the mold yourself, or give that job to a candy maker and just wait for the chocolate delights to arrive.

When you say it with chocolate, you speak a language everyone understands!

#723 *Blown-Glass Individuality*

Cake toppers complement the wedding cake, with effects ranging from extreme elegance to side-tickling humor, but none do for a cake what a blown glass cake topper can do.

Glass blowing requires artistic talent, and no two custom blown-glass cake toppers could ever be truly identical. The sky is the limit for designs. Are you motorcycle lovers? Try a sculpture of a bride and groom catching the wind from the seat of a hog. Do you have pet names for each other? Animate those names by creating glass wedding "pets."

Blown-glass cake toppers reflect your passion for each other or for hobbies, occupations, faith, nature, traditions, animals, military life, or anything else dear to your hearts. Choose clear glass that resembles ice or frosted glass with a creamy finish. Oil-based paints and metallics accent a piece and pay homage to wedding color schemes.

Check with your baker on permissible weight and dimensions before ordering any custom glass creation. Machine-manufactured glass toppers are less expensive than custom blown glass, but even toppers created just for you by a glass artisan are usually reasonably priced.

Traditional toppers are rarely seen after the wedding, but a blown-glass cake topper is a work of art perfect for home decorating.

#724 *Favorite Finger Foods*

Grazing is fun. A bite of this and a taste of that go a long way toward satisfying that common side effect of alcohol consumption known as the "munchies." And since finger foods keep guests filled to the brim, meals may not need to be quite as elaborate or quite as expensive.

Potato chips, chopped veggies, sushi, sliders, tiny egg rolls, and taquitos all qualify. If it's small, portable, and consumed without utensils, it's a finger food.

Give finger foods their own designated areas at the reception. Instead of keeping them all together, cluster bowls and trays of grab-and-go foods on cocktail tables here and there to make them easily accessible without waiting in lines. Add stacks of napkins on each table, and provide a decorative receptacle for waste nearby.

Finger foods are wedding reception ideal. Whether you're planning a buffet or a table-service meal, adding a never-ending supply of finger foods to the agenda guarantees full bellies and tantalized taste buds.

#725 *The Temptations of Autumn*

When the weather turns crisp and leaves tug from their branches, weddings reap the rewards. Harvest time enables reception buffets or sit-down dinners to offer fresh, seasonal fare befitting a king and queen.

From cheese-stuffed figs and pumpkin bisque to gingerbread, turkey, and a bounty of colorful vegetables, autumn offers a unique opportunity to eat heartily but at a savings that comes from choosing from the just-filled horn of plenty.

Seasonal fruits like apples, pears, elderberries, raspberries, blueberries, cherries, and grapes inspire everything from salads to desserts, and the rich colors and tastes of autumn vegetables mean that the vegetarian dish you include at your reception is destined to be amazing.

Don't forget the spiced cider and buttered rum drinks, or the nut cups filled with freshly hulled black walnuts. To enjoy autumn fare to the fullest, instruct your caterer to embrace the season at every turn.

#726 *Flowers Good Enough to Eat*

Parsley and sculpted radishes are common garnishes, but for weddings, think floral. Serve a different edible flower with each dish or course, and take your guests on a most unusual culinary journey.

Scores of edible flowers are beautiful to look at and an experience to eat, and they set your wedding apart.

Not all flowers are edible. Some are mildly toxic, while others are extremely poisonous, so enlisting the aid of a culinary expert with a background in floral foods is important. Inform your caterer that you wish to have flowers on the menu. Consider the caterer's recommendations, then do your own research to verify that every flower garnish considered is truly safe to eat. University botany departments have professors and experts well versed in the subject of edible flowers, and botanical garden specialists are another viable resource.

Garnishes aren't a big wedding concern. But little details make an event spectacular. Replacing traditional garnishes with edible flowers is a little detail that packs a lot of punch.

#727 *A Cube of Pure Delight*

Sugar was once a priceless delicacy, and sugar cubes were among the earliest of wedding favors. Modern wedding couples no longer consider a cube of sugar to be an elaborate gift, but that doesn't mean those wondrous little bites shouldn't make a wedding-day appearance.

Flavored, colored, and uniquely shaped cubes are available to purchase, or you could try your hand at flavoring your own. Adding lemon juice gives the sugar a tart little kick, and the result is a delightful pop any sweet tooth would enjoy. A hint of vanilla bean or orange wraps a cube in surprise. Experiment with colors and flavors, or simply order what you like from sugar experts.

Colored cubes in crystal bowls look fabulous on reception tables. Providing tongs or a spoon with each bowl will allow guests to grab a sweet treat at will, or to plunk one or two into a cup of coffee or tea.

The common sugar cube isn't so common at weddings anymore, but that only makes its dressed-up appearance at your wedding reception even more unique and delicious.

#728 *Feed Them!*

There's nothing worse than a grumpy band, but if musicians are forced to watch wedding guests stuff delectables into their mouths while their own bellies growl, grumpiness creeps in.

It's easy to overlook the band, the wedding planner, and other hired help when budgeting for food. While you aren't required to provide meals for anyone who is not a guest, it really makes sense to do so. Hired or not, it's miserable to be on the outside looking in when hunger strikes. It benefits your day to have happy, satisfied help, and it's especially considerate to provide food for photographers, videographers, musicians, and others who spend hours on-site. Serve them a meal from your guest menu, or choose simpler fare to be served behind the scenes.

Ensure happiness. When the savage, hungry beast growls, feed it.

#729 *A Taste of This, a Taste of That*

Hire a caterer only after tasting the company's fare. Taste matters, and reputable caterers routinely offer a tasting session, or invite you to a catered event to taste the food and see the team in action.

Some caterers charge for a tasting session, while others do not, and any fee should be discussed up front. You won't be provided every dish the caterer offers, but you should be able to sample at least something from every course — appetizers, salad, soup, entrée, etc. If everything you sample is well prepared, it's probably a fair assumption that other foods the company prepares will also meet those standards.

The greater your catering needs, the harder the caterer will work to secure your business. Don't be afraid to ask for tastes of specific dishes you are particularly interested in.

Tipping your tasting session server is at your discretion, but unless specifically prohibited by the caterer, doing so is the sincerest way to say thank you.

#730 Ye Olde Wedding Cake

Per wedding tradition, the top tier of the wedding cake is frozen intact to be enjoyed by the wedding couple on their first anniversary.

When this practice first began in the late 19th century, cakes were of a much denser consistency than modern cakes. Today's cakes do not freeze as well for long periods, especially in refrigerator freezers. The moisture and flavors of the cake are sacrificed, and if the cake is covered in fondant, preservation is more difficult. Fondant freezes fine, but thawing causes moisture loss to the cake beneath it.

To help your wedding cake taste amazing on your first anniversary, make that top tier juicy, and cover it in butter-cream frosting. A nice fruit or rum cake freezes well and sustains its flavor longer than traditional cake.

As soon as possible, freeze the cake uncovered for a couple of hours to set the frosting, then wrap the cake in plastic wrap and foil. Secure it in a cake box, and tape all sides completely closed before putting the box in a freezer bag. Squeeze out any air, then tightly seal and tape the outer bag. In the alternative, secure the quick-frozen cake in plastic wrap inside an airtight plastic container.

Air is the enemy. Keep your cake deep frozen and free from air seepage, and chances are good that you'll enjoy a tasty, memorable dessert when that first anniversary arrives.

#731 Spitting-Image Cake Topping

An easy and lovely way to top your wedding cake is with a miniature likeness of your wedding-altar scene. Are you using a decorative arch? Make a tiny replica of that arch with a bride and groom "exchanging vows" beneath it. Use individual bride and groom figures, and place them exactly as you plan to stand during the real ceremony.

To recreate a kneeling bench, a unity candle, or a unity sand ceremony, use dollhouse furnishings or other miniatures to capture that single ceremonial moment on the cake top.

You'll know exactly how your ceremony is expected to look long before the wedding day arrives, allowing plenty of time to create the scene in miniature. Be meticulous, and use the same flowers, candle arrangements, etc. The more accurate you are, the more impressive the cake top.

A cake-top re-creation of the ceremony will surprise guests and deliver your own sweet déjà vu moment during the cake cutting.

#732 *Little Mouths to Feed*

It pays to feed children from a special child's menu. Most kids aren't interested in fancy food and just want something tasty and fun to eat. After all, it's a party. Give them special-occasion, but not necessarily expensive, foods they might not regularly get at home.

Ask your caterer about a child's plate for your guests under the age of 12. Children's portions, even if from the adult menu, can result in cost savings. But choosing less expensive foods to begin with makes the savings even more substantial.

Take a cue from fast-food joints and add a toy, game, or other entertainment to kids' meals. Even the littlest puzzle inspires busy hands and a contented mind. Such foresight permits each child to eat foods he or she enjoys and have a bit of fun in the process. Meanwhile, those busy little hands help guarantee peaceful dining for the child's adult companions.

#733 *Bridal-Couple Platter*

Eating at the wedding reception works well for guests, but not always so well for the wedding couple. Much is going on, and with so many interruptions, you may not even realize you haven't eaten until your belly loudly protests its emptiness at the most inopportune time.

To ensure that a lack of food doesn't waylay the wedding night, ask your caterer to prepare a "to go" platter just for the two of you. Enjoy your snacks just before you leave the reception, in the car while en route to your wedding-night destination, or in the privacy of your room after you've arrived.

There's always the option of a fast-food fill-up as you travel from Point A to Point B, but is cruising through a drive-thru really a wedding-night desire?

Order a platter. You won't regret it.

#734 *Sunday Dinner*

Wedding-reception meals are customarily table-service or buffet, but there is another viable alternative: family style. In lieu of individual plates of food, the courses are served in bowls and on platters set in the center of the table then passed from guest to guest as if they were sitting down to a Sunday dinner with loved ones.

Sharing food in this intimate, inclusive manner stimulates conversation and fosters a bonding that doesn't always occur with other meal-service styles.

To create the best of both worlds, utilize family-style service for salads and sides, even when plating your most expensive course, the entrée.

#735 *Yummy but Sugar Free*

Calories aside, some of your guests may need to avoid sugar for important health reasons. With the alarming increase in diabetes across all ethnicities, it's a safe bet that at least some of your wedding guests will deny themselves the enjoyment of your wedding cake. Don't leave them out of the festivities. Give them a sugar-free dessert option.

Make one layer of your tiered cake sugarless, or create a collection of sugarless cupcakes, cookies, and other dessert choices for wedding guests who cannot consume natural sweeteners or corn syrups.

Offering sugar-free dessert options, especially during the cake-sharing portion of the reception, conveys a sincere regard for your guests.

#736 *Bars and More Bars*

What do diners love in a restaurant? They love an establishment that sports a salad bar, a baked-potato bar, a sundae bar, or any other kind of bar. There's something universally appealing about having the freedom to doctor a food to your own personal tastes. Bars at receptions are just as enticing.

To inspire guests to acclaim your reception's culinary delights, feature a comfort food and give it a cornucopia of possible toppings. Be creative. Try a potato-chip bar, a yogurt bar, or a waffle bar. Offer exotic toppings that one might not expect, like chocolate on the potato-chip bar or potato-chip crumbles on the yogurt bar. Encourage experimentation via an array of unusual choices.

If a food can be topped, it can star in its own fabulous bar.

#737 *Yum on a Stick!*

Need a unique wedding favor, a decorative touch for the dinner plate, or an edible bouquet? Create any of these with versatile candy kabobs.

Run a bamboo skewer through candies or chocolates, add a ribbon bow to the top and bottom of the kabob, and you're done! If the candies aren't too messy, skewer them without individual wrappers then wrap the whole thing in clear or colored plastic wrap. Alternatively, forgo any wrapping and lay the "au naturel" candy skewer upon a white paper doily or rest it in a decorative-paper banana boat.

Miniature cookies also make tempting kabobs. Bake the cookies yourself, and skewer them while they're hot to prevent breakage that might occur from piercing a cold, brittle cookie. To double the treat, alternate candy with cookies on your kabobs.

Vary the kabob components for colors and tastes, and use the ribbon accents to complement any wedding theme or to brighten any color palette.

#738 *The Champagne-Challenge Party*

There's nothing like a champagne toast at your wedding, but does the brand of champagne really matter? It might. Top-shelf, vintage champagnes generally cost a pretty penny, and champagne connoisseurs will tell you that the taste is worth the extra expense. But how many of your guests will actually be champagne connoisseurs?

To choose a bubbly for your wedding, first throw a champagne-challenge party. Invite friends for an evening of music, conversation, hors d'oeuvres and champagne. Serve the champagne in flutes only — no bottles in sight — and be sure to stock a variety in all price ranges. Tie a colored satin ribbon to each flute stem, but keep the mystery alive. Only you will know which color matches which bottle.

Serve all choices, then after a few drinks and some lively repartee, present your guests with a ballot, and ask them to vote for the colored ribbon that adorned the best champagne. You may find that a $12 bottle is just as popular as a $50 bottle and save yourself a tidy sum on champagne for the wedding. You get a prewedding party and firsthand champagne opinions — a win-win!

#739 *Farmers to the Rescue*

If you're planning a wedding when the tomatoes are ripe on the vine and the corn is sweet and tender, bring that glorious freshness to your reception by planning your menu around the finds at your local farmer's market. There's nothing more satisfying than fresh, wholesome food. After you've set your wedding date, check with local vendors at the farmer's market to learn which fruits and vegetables will be peaking just as your wedding day draws near. Make advance arrangements to garner the cream of the crop and perhaps score a nice quantity discount in the process. Whether you plan to do the cooking at home or employ a caterer to handle the culinary duties, fresh delights from the farmer's market will lay the foundation for an unforgettable meal your guests won't see coming.

#740 *Posh Presentation*

Even when serving simple foods, your table can scream "Fabulous!" The key is presentation. An ordinary scoop of seafood salad is not necessarily much of a visual stimulant. But serve that scoop in a safely bleached clamshell, and it suddenly has a "wow" factor.

Change it up. Instead of ordinary china, think butterfly-shaped bowls or colorful, glass candy dishes for sides, and leaf- or flower-petal-shaped plates for entrées. Serve mashed potatoes in martini glasses or chilled soup in brandy snifters. If your wedding is earthy in nature, consider an array of wooden or bamboo dinnerware. Unusual dinnerware choices bring instant character to the food, even if it's only a serving of macaroni and cheese. It's true. Macaroni and cheese hugged by a bumblebee dish simply isn't ordinary at all.

#741 Say Cheese, Please

Fancy hors d'oeuvres are fine, but cheese is fun! Everyone loves to pick and choose from an eclectic cheese spread. Lots of flavorful cheese cubes pricked with colored toothpicks make tasty, filling hors d'oeuvres. Cheese looks nice whether it's served in fancy crystal or scattered across a wooden cutting board. But the best part of cheese is its versatility. You can carve it to make cheese hearts or angel wings that reign majestically over your cheese spread, or easily transform cheese cubes into the building blocks of unusual sculptures.

And cheese is pretty clean. Even when cheese tumbles from a toothpick and falls into a lap or down a shirt front, the resulting "damage" will be far less serious than that left by a meatball or a bacon-wrapped fig.

Cheese, grapes, and berries make beautiful hors d'oeuvre bedfellows.

#742 Fun and Fruity Rock Pops

Crystal rock-candy pops come in assorted fruit flavors and tantalizing colors. They look like sparkly, cave-inspired stalactites on wooden sticks. You kill two birds with one "rocky" stone when you use these crystal candy pops as both décor and sweet treats. Cluster them in crystal or cut-glass bowls to add splashes of color to any reception location. Put them on the bar, the buffet, or on dining or cocktail tables, and when a sweet tooth calls out for satisfaction, the guest with the craving won't have to suffer in silence. Relief will be just a crystal rock-candy pop away.

#743 Soup's On!

If you want your guests to feel full and satisfied, don't forget the soup. Soup before an entrée means the expensive proteins that follow can be a touch smaller, yet few will notice. When a hearty soup is served before the main course, especially when paired with bread, the body begins to feel well nourished long before the main course arrives. Soup is a classic stretch of culinary resources that does its job well, and there's no need to fear that soup will be messier than any other food. Those who dribble soup from their spoons are just as likely to fling beef Wellington from their forks. If soup can grace the tables of five-star restaurants, there's no reason to shun this universally loved and dollar-stretching dish at your wedding.

#744 *Simply Refreshed*

Not every guest consumes cocktails, beer, or wine, and even guests who do often enjoy liquid reprieve between drinks. To add true refreshment to traditional bar and dining beverages, consider pitchers of citrus-infused water for guests to enjoy at will.

Ordinary water gently infused with oranges, lemons, limes, grapefruits, and the more exotic citrus hybrids, like tangelos, has a pleasing, cleansing tickle. Use spring water or filtered water to achieve the best flavors.

Citrus-infused waters are an easy-to-make, inexpensive extra. They're also perfect as a quick refreshment for hot guests at overly warm ceremony venues. Fruit slices floated in each pitcher identify the water's flavor and look great in the bargain.

#745 *Your Own Private Chef*

How many people in your circle of friends would jump at the chance to hone their cooking skills under the tutelage of a professional chef? Glorious meals aren't just for dining out. At-home cooks are eagerly learning how wonderful it can be to produce amazing culinary delights in their own kitchens.

If you plan to hold your reception in a venue equipped with a kitchen, why not "cater" your own event by hiring a private chef willing to work with family and friend volunteers? The volunteers get spectacular insights and hands-on experience they would otherwise have to pay handsomely for, and you get a beautifully prepared meal for the cost of the chef and the food supplies. Serve the food buffet style, and you won't even need servers, just a volunteer or two to watch over the buffet. It's liberating to work with your own private chef, and after the meal, you can publicly thank your volunteers with a round of applause from your grateful guests.

#746 *Cake-Go-Round!*

Single-layer wedding cakes are beautiful when artfully displayed, and most often those displays consist of a staircase presentation or individual cake stands arranged at staggered heights. Such displays are exquisite, but if you want your cakes to soar beyond exquisite, give them movement. Who doesn't love a merry-go-round?

Building a revolving carousel for your cakes is not as difficult as you may imagine. Carousel revolutions are powered by a simple, turntable-style mechanism. Use traditional horse designs as "seats" for your cakes, or replace the horses with hearts, angels, or whatever motifs you prefer. "How to make a carousel" instructions are available online and in craft shops. Or, if wielding tools is not your cup of tea, enlist the aid of a craftsperson in your area. When the wedding is over, sell your carousel to a party-supply house, donate it to a charity, or tuck it away for your children to someday enjoy. A slow-moving wedding-cake carousel catapults the cake table into a whole new dimension.

#747 Keep On Truckin'

Food trucks once offered quick, greasy, fast-food fare and were barely regulated for sanitation. Not anymore. Modern food trucks are rigorously monitored and offer everything from piled-high gourmet sandwiches to fine French cuisine entrées. Many executive chefs have even taken their culinary show on the road via their own food truck. So what do food trucks have to do with weddings? Plenty — especially if you are thinking of an out-of-the-way wedding location.

Food trucks are self-contained food-service marvels, and just because the food comes from a truck doesn't make it any less delicious than if it came from a fine-dining kitchen. If the food's good, it's good — period. With a self-powered food truck, it's possible to serve great food in the heart of the woods, out by a lake, or at virtually any facility that sits somewhere near a road. Just add a small waitstaff to serve the food to your guests.

You can provide real dinnerware if you wish, or negotiate a fee for the food-truck operator to replace typical, disposable table-service settings with china-like, recyclable dishes and flatware. Food-truck entrepreneurs love guaranteed work, so negotiate on the price. A good deal is one that makes you, your guests, and the food-truck operator happy.

A food truck is also a great surprise for the wee hours of a lively, we-don't-want-it-to-end reception!

#748 Ornamental Story

Most wedding cakes are topped with a single cake topper, often a wedding-couple figurine. One way to cut the cost of the wedding cake, yet make it so clever that guests won't stop talking about it, is to order a tiered cake with little finish work. Elaborate scrolling, flowering, and piping generate nearly all of the labor costs. Decorating a wedding cake requires talent and expertise, and you rightly must pay for your baker's skills. But if, for example, you order a three-tiered cake with only minimal décor to add texture, you can considerably reduce the price of the cake.

To compensate for the lack of all that piping and decoration, use multiple cake toppers. Cake-top figurines come in so many bride-and-groom styles that it's easy to create a story by placing one beside the other. Ring each tier with bride-and-groom toppers in various poses and configurations, and you'll create a unique, one-of-a-kind cake that wraps humor, romance, love, and laughter into one clever and appealing cake star. If you wish to add a floral component, add a small nosegay to the top tier only. Cake ornaments are centuries old, but never in history have there been so many wonderful figurine choices.

#749 Candy-Cane Sweethearts

When just the right touch of red will make the décor pop, candy-cane hearts are perfect. They're lovely and edible, and they're the accent of choice for black-and-white or holiday themes.

Place regular, unpackaged candy canes on a nonstick baking sheet (or use a bit of baking spray on a regular cookie sheet), and heat them at about 225 degrees for ten minutes or so. They will melt just enough to permit remolding of their shapes. Make them into twists, hearts, letters, or apple shapes, or whatever your creative mind imagines, then use them at place settings, or add ribbons to them to create hanging décor. To use them in centerpieces, insert a bamboo skewer into the base of the design while the candy is still hot. As it cools, it will harden around the stick. Only do a few at a time to prevent cooling before you have the chance to mold them. Crushed candy canes also make delectable sprinkles on and around cupcake trees or when mixed with nuts in nut cups. Those familiar red-and-white stripes aren't just for holiday overindulgence anymore.

#750 A Catering Two-for-One

Reception halls can be pricey. Catering can be pricey. One way to potentially shave costs is by utilizing a catering company that also has its own banquet facility. Some caterers throw in the use of the hall if you book your catering job with the company. Others offer a significant discount. As a bonus, you'll know the food will be prepared on-site in a kitchen the staff knows well. There's no fear that something will be left behind during transportation, because the only traveling the food will do is from the kitchen to your tables. Make judicious use of the Internet and your telephone, and schedule early tastings with those caterers who promote a "hall plus food" two-for-one deal. You may not find the perfect, all-inclusive catering hall, but if you set your sights on trying, you might be surprised at what you unearth.

#751 *Mr. and Mrs. Signature BBQ*

If your reception is a down-home celebration, and a good old-fashioned barbeque tickles your fancy, make that barbeque an experience to remember. Invent your own sauce! For barbeque lovers, nothing is more satisfying than a tender piece of meat or poultry married to a mouthwatering sauce. It's your wedding, so why shouldn't you have a Mr. and Mrs. signature sauce? Serve your fabulous barbeque, then keep the fun rolling by sharing the sauce as wedding favors. Safely bottle extra sauce into small glass jars, then seal and tie them with red gingham ribbon and raffia. If you're not comfortable giving out the sauce, give out the recipe! Making a barbeque sauce that's uniquely yours isn't difficult. It's simply a matter of experimenting with spices and flavors until you sample a mixture that makes your taste buds dance and your tongue dart out to capture any errant drips that dare to cling to your lips.

#752 *A Passion for Potluck*

While many wedding-etiquette experts harbor the opinion that a potluck reception is a big fat no-no, there are times when a potluck is just perfect. For any number of reasons a wedding may need to happen more quickly than anticipated, or there may be very little money for a reception. Enter the "in lieu of gifts" potluck wedding celebration party.

Invite guests to bring a dish of food, and its recipe, instead of a wedding gift. The homemade dishes will be a culinary adventure, and the recipes, complete with the guests' names and addresses, will be your guest book and, ultimately, a very personal wedding-day keepsake. Snap a photo of each guest with his or her dish, and later place the recipe and the photo into a commemorative recipe album. Potluck isn't a dirty word, and if your guest list is small enough, a potluck wedding-celebration party can be a beautiful, bonding occasion. Finding just the right wedding gift is often a trial for guests. If they can bring food instead, you may have a lot of very happy revelers on your hands.

#753 *Cake Double*

Movie stars have stunt doubles, and platinum-selling musical artists lip-sync at their own concerts. So why, against your better judgment, must you spend big bucks on a wedding cake? Many of today's wedding cakes are as fake as a Mona Lisa with a toothy grin. So what are those phony tiers made of? Usually they're Styrofoam, covered in the same frosting or fondant as a real cake.

It's easy to rent a fake cake for display and serve slices of substantially less expensive, but equally delicious, sheet cakes or cupcakes to your guests. You may indeed save money by forgoing an elaborate real cake, but money isn't the only driving force behind fake wedding cakes. Sometimes the reception location, the weather, or the design choice makes the use of a real, delicately structured cake difficult. But even with fake cakes, you have options. Choose a totally fake cake with a back-side cutout that houses a couple of real cake slices for use in the cake-cutting ceremony, or opt for a primarily fake cake with one real cake tier that can be cut and tasted as usual. Fake cakes are just as aesthetically appealing as their real counterparts, and as a bonus, they ship far more securely than a real cake ever could. No one can even tell that the stunning exterior of your awe-inspiring cake hides a heart of hard, cold foam blocks.

#754 *The Wedding-Cake Safe*

Once you've made the decision to have a fake cake at your wedding, go ahead and give it your own twist. Have a real top-tier cake supported by hollowed-out fake tiers beneath it, and use those empty tiers to hide a surprise. Think of it as a combination fake cake and piñata! If you are giving small wedding favors, like key chains, thimbles, tape measures, etc., that don't really make a significant statement at table settings, stuff them into your cake structure. After you've cut your real tier, cut into a predetermined opening in your "cake safe," and let the surprises spill forth. It's an unexpected way to finish off a cake ceremony and a clever way to distribute wedding favors. There's no reason to keep your customized fake cake under wraps. Let it earn its keep!

#755 *Delicious Place-Card Favors*

Take the intent of a place card and mix it with the treat of an edible favor, and you have a functional, delectable, table-friendly cookie place-card favor. The cookies direct guests to their seats and tempt their taste buds. Personalize each cookie with the guest's name, slip it into a cellophane bag (bought in bulk online or at craft stores), gather it closed with a ribbon, and place it atop the correct place setting. To add elegance, tuck a sprig of greenery, a silk flower, or a dried herb into the ribbon or on the plate beneath the bagged cookie.

The cookies can be any shape and size as long as they are big enough to hold the guest's name. Consider gingerbread brides and grooms, sugar-cookie hearts, snickerdoodle wedding bells, or sweet almond butterflies. Choose whatever design and flavor works best with your theme. An edible place-card favor consolidates two wedding budget expenses into one, with a dose of good taste thrown in.

#756 *Photogenic Punch*

If you want to inexpensively add color to your tables, think of liquid refreshment. Carafes of punch, in whatever flavors and colors complement your theme, add as much vibrancy as flowers and as much convenience as having an ever-present waitress hovering over the table. With punch carafes, no one ever has to wander off to refill a glass. Group the carafes around centerpieces, or forgo the centerpieces and simply settle the carafes onto a lush greenery base or arrange them around a tall candle. Carafes filled with colorful punch are very photogenic, especially if you float flower-blossom ice cubes inside.

#757 *Fresh Pop!*

Popcorn is inexpensive to make, easy to serve, and enjoyed by almost everyone, wedding guests included. Provide continuous fresh popcorn via a popcorn cart or tabletop machine rental, or buy already popped popcorn in bulk packaging to serve in large baskets or oversized bowls. Place stacks of cocktail napkins or small popcorn bags and a scoop next to the baskets, and guests will serve themselves when the munchies strike. If the sound of popping corn is not exactly what you had in mind for your wedding, stow the machine behind the scenes.

Look for a nearby popcorn vendor. If the vendor isn't otherwise engaged at a carnival or festival on the day of your wedding, you might find that bringing in a vendor for your cocktail hour is the easiest way of all to treat your guests to bites of delicious popcorn.

#758 *Buttering Up the Guests*

Whenever food can serve a dual purpose at your wedding, it's a big win. Butter is one of those versatile foods. Almost all meals come with bread of some sort, along with butter pats. To exhibit an incredible attention to detail and to enhance table décor, let your butter generate smiles before it generates taste. Use butter molds to turn butter into art.

From seashells to horseshoes, butter can be molded into endless shapes. It can even be scored with the wedding couple's monogram. Use small, decorative butters at each place setting, or opt for a larger butter sculpture shared by two or more people at a table. For obvious reasons, beautiful butter designs work best in climate-controlled areas. Serving butter daisies at your summer outdoor wedding would require storing them in an iced-down cooler and serving them at the last minute rather than displaying them on the tables. Real butter is delicious, but there is no reason it can't first be a delight to behold.

#759 *Glamorous Comfort Food*

What's your favorite food? The answer to this question is rarely Peking duck or beef Wellington, yet those fancy bites often find themselves at the forefront of caterers' meal suggestions. If your favorite Italian food is pizza and not fusilli with roasted eggplant and goat cheese, or you prefer deviled eggs to eggs Florentine, there's no reason to contract for fancy foods just because they have fancy names. If you like comfort foods, simply tweak them to make them wedding friendly. Pizza doesn't have to be round or square. Pizza dough can be crafted into a spiral, a heart, a star, or a ring that sits on the outer edge of a plate, so that you can fill the inside of the plate with a salad or a trio of dipping sauces. To add flair to your deviled eggs, serve them in nests of seasoned quick-fried noodles, with a tiny edible bird perched on the edge.

Technique and imagination can turn any comfort food into an amazing dish. When shopping for caterers, ask what unusual food presentations they have done in the past. Tell them that you want to give your favorite comfort food an upscale makeover, since your wedding guests would probably never say Peking duck or beef Wellington is their favorite food, either. Comfort foods don't have to look like paper-wrapped fast foods. They, too, can sport gourmet outerwear. It's all in the style.

#760 *Lofty Cakes*

An easy way to save money on your wedding cake is to deconstruct it. Three individual cakes of varying sizes are customarily less expensive than a three-tiered wedding cake. Tiered pedestal cake plates are sold individually or in sets of three at no great expense. Purchase a set and use one for each of your three cakes (or six for your six cakes, etc.). Create sturdy base supports for the pedestal plates using wooden boxes, columns, or upside down, flat-bottomed bowls or pans. As long as the base sits firmly on the table and has a smooth, flat top to hold the cake pedestal, any viable support will help you create an interesting, staggered-height cluster. Once the bases are in place, drape a lovely cloth over each one, tucking it in here and there until your display looks like the moguls of a snow-covered mountain — soft, flowing, and inviting. Place your cakes on their pedestals and position them on the bases, placing the biggest cake on the lowest tier and the smallest cake on the highest. Add a sprinkling of flowers or greenery as you wish, and the result will be a lush and lovely cake table that didn't break the bank.

#761 *Seventh-Inning Stretch Snack Box*

It isn't only baseball games that need a seventh-inning stretch. Just about every party comes to that moment in time when people need a pick-me-up. Spur the excitement with a snack box. Long after the dinner and well before the last dessert table, bring in the boxes. You can fill them with something unusual, like pizza rolls, or something simple, like a giant blueberry muffin. If you want to lighten things up, stuff your box with a fruit cup and a gingersnap cookie. Got your eye on a midnight breakfast surprise? Try pigs in a blanket or a bacon-and-egg burrito. Surprise your guests with a late-reception treat, and watch the rejuvenation kick in!

#762 *Gluten Be Gone*

The percentage of the population with gluten sensitivity is growing. It's unlikely that gluten in wheat, rye, and barley is becoming more harmful. It's that people are finally learning the source of the miserable symptoms they've been suffering. Add gluten-free foods to your menu and your desserts, and you won't cause gluten-sensitive guests to suffer or abstain. Gluten-free dishes are not less appetizing. It's even possible to have a gloriously delicious gluten-free wedding cake.

Find out for yourself. Visit a designer cupcake shop that offers gluten-free goodies. You may discover, without being told, that you can't tell the difference. But like all foods, not all gluten-free items are created equal. Find a catering chef who knows how to work gluten-free dishes into the menu, or do it yourself by seeking out gluten-free recipes everyone raves about. You don't have to have a totally gluten-free reception, but adding a few to your menu is a thoughtful gesture.

#763 *Have Your Cocktail and Eat It Too*

Is the wedding going to be a hot summer affair? Then bring on the "cool." Surprise your guests by stocking the bar with a selection of frozen-cocktail ice pops and slushies. Imagine enjoying a "champagne mimosa" on a stick, or the sweet-and-sour bite of a hard-lemonade slushie. Of course, not all frozen pops and slushies need be alcoholic. Make alcoholic and nonalcoholic versions of similar flavors, like a frozen mint julep for cocktail lovers and a frozen mint lemonade for teetotalers. Experiment at home with delicious frozen-drink recipes until you find just the right ones for your reception. Make them in advance, and keep them under wraps in the freezer until the big day when your bartender will serve them from decorated vintage coolers packed with ice. Cocktails that require nibbling are a summer surprise. Just be sure to clearly mark the alcoholic ones so that no one is too surprised.

#764 Donut Totems

Who doesn't love to splurge on a to-die-for donut? Coconut, chocolate, sprinkled, sugared — whatever your pleasure, donuts are a sweet and special-occasion indulgence with broad appeal. Consider placing a few clever "donut totems" on your dessert table, or as stand-alone treats late in the reception. Acquire a few upright paper-towel dispensers to use as your totem bases, then simply slip the donuts over the pole. Keep each totem to a single flavor, and guests won't have to remove two or three from the top to get to the one they want. Be sure to provide some bakery tissue squares or large tongs for retrieving the donuts, along with saucer-sized paper plates to hold them. Donut totems are a perfect pairing with a self-serve coffee bar or a late-night coffee service. Negotiate a discount with your favorite donut shop, make the donuts yourself, or pick them up in the bakery sections of grocery and big-box stores, then let those donuts raise the "happy" level.

#765 Tower of Chocolate Delight

Even without a dessert buffet, you can still satisfy your guests' sweet-tooth cravings by creating boxed-chocolate centerpieces. Use different sizes of boxed chocolates with the lids removed — a large box for the base tier, a medium box for the middle tier, and a small box for the top tier. Cake-tier separators work nicely to elevate the second and third boxes. Add picks of decorative ribbons here and there, along with a few sprigs of greenery tucked around the bottom box, and you've created a beautiful, no-hassle, scrumptious centerpiece. An added bonus is less disposable waste.

#766 Soda-Fountain Fun

To spice up the party, turn ordinary drinks like coffee, tea, and soda into soda-fountain delights. Offer a few flavored syrups, and your guests will think they've stepped back in time to the corner soda fountain! Vanilla, cherry, chocolate, and almond are popular options, but some syrup companies offer dozens of flavors to choose from. Place bottles affixed with one-ounce dispensing plungers near the beverage bar, and guests can flavor their refreshments at will. Or, to add an extra dose of fun to the mix, fill disposable eyedroppers or test tubes (inexpensively available in bulk) with different flavors, and arrange them in candy dishes to create inventive table-top décor. Use your home printer to create tiny labels that identify each dropper or test tube's contents to prevent the cherry lover from accidentally choosing licorice, and you're done. You've gone above and beyond for your guests' taste buds, and they know it.

#767 Bread Bonanza!

Bread sticks, onion rolls, raisin twists, French baguettes, sourdough bagels — these are just a few of the many delightful and delicious breads you can serve your guests. But breads do more than fill bellies. Use oversized bread-baskets or white wicker cornucopia baskets overflowing with bread treats instead of floral centerpieces for round tables, and long, wooden planks topped with a "bread spread" for rectangular tables. Accent with splashes of greenery and a sprinkling of candles, and your tables will not only look amazing, they'll keep guests plenty satisfied. To add color, consider tucking individual-sized jars of jam or bear or bumblebee-shaped honey dispensers into the bread feast. With all-bread centerpieces, you create a warm, welcoming environment, pare plenty of dollars from the floral budget, and keep guests from feeling hungry, even if the entrée portions are modest.

#768 Two Scoops of Wedding Cake, Please!

How fun would it be to serve your wedding cake in a cone? If paying for a giant wedding cake isn't appealing, forget the cake and pack the freezer!

"I Do! I Do! Wedding Cake" ice cream by Blue Bunny boasts buttercream-flavored ice cream with morsels of white cake and swirls of raspberry ribbons. If a cone won't work, have your catering staff scoop the ice cream into martini glasses. Or, if you simply must have cake, place a red velvet, chocolate, or other darkly colored and richly flavored cupcake in an elegant banana-split dish, and snuggle a scoop of the luscious wedding-cake ice cream up to the cupcake's side. Like the bride and groom, that's a perfect pairing! Add a mint leaf for a pop of bright color, and you've presented a unique reception dessert bound to garner rave reviews. Inexpensive martini glasses and disposable banana-split dishes that look like real crystal are available at a variety of special-event suppliers, wholesalers, and retailers.

Ice cream thrills young and old alike, and what could be more fitting for your celebration than one that actually has that special wedding-cake flavor all wrapped up in its creamy goodness? And if you can't find wedding-cake ice cream, you can always create your own home-churned version.

#769 *Pop Goes the Cake!*

What's better than cake? Candy-coated cake on a stick! Cake pops are sized just right and taste just great. Simple cake-pop recipes call for mixing dry, baked cake and frosting, forming the mixture into balls or squares, piercing the shapes with a lollipop stick, dipping them in the candy coating of your choice, and sprinkling, piping, bejeweling, or sugaring to your delight.

These delectable big bites make ideal wedding favors, dessert-bar treats, or edible centerpieces. Once finished and cooled, they take to being cellophane wrapped and tied with a bow as if they were proud to show themselves off. Of course, you can skip the "stick" part if you wish and nestle your pops into paper cupcake cups or arrange them in candy dishes, but doing so means you'll likely have guests looking for forks or wet wipes. Besides, anything on a stick is just downright entertaining. Cake pops add a special zing to cake consumption, and they know how to multitask to boot.

#770 *A Comfortable Margin*

If you're serving a buffet meal or a Viennese dessert table, be mindful of the table spacing. With food dishes, utensils and underliners, and decorative accents, serve-yourself tables can become quite loaded, and sometimes, in order to reach food or to keep a dish from moving while trying to scoop from it, people need to set their plate down. If you haven't allowed even a scrap of an edge to do that, plates can easily tip and slide to the floor or, worse, pitch food onto someone's clothes. Even if your caterer sets up the buffet, designate someone to check the buffet table for "rest areas." Use an actual reception plate and set it down in various locations. If it sits well, you're good to go. If it's precarious, you'll know that adjustments need to be made. That two-minute check will save you and your guests from an avoidable, messy disaster.

#771 *Marvelous Meringues*

Simple, delicious, and fabulously versatile, meringues are decorative and dining all-stars. All meringues are made with egg whites and fine sugar, but the flavor possibilities are endless — coffee, chocolate, raspberry, almond, peppermint, and so many more. The beauty of meringues for weddings is not only how delightful they are to pop into the mouth, but also how adaptable they are for decorating. Beautifully swirled meringues in whatever color/flavor combination you desire easily replace flowers at table settings. Just place a single meringue on a small, white, lace paper doily and rest it atop the dinner napkin or plate. It's as colorful and appealing as a flower bloom, but far more desirable to the guests who get to eat it. Meringues in oversized martini glasses, with the glass stems adorned with ribbon and greenery, make inspired centerpieces, and meringues at the coffee bar are a welcome treat. Meringues are simply a sweet touch all the way around.

#772 That's Just Nuts!

Nuts are healthy and tasty, and bowls of nuts with scoops, alongside cocktail napkins or paper nut cups, are a quick and easy addition to the cocktail party. They also fill guests up a bit before dinner or the buffet. Nuts are super satisfying, but if they are salty, guests will likely drink more. To keep the nut noshing from driving the bar tab into the stratosphere, serve nuts in their shells.

Pistachios and peanuts are easily hand shelled, but if you want to add more exotic nuts, you can include any nut in the shell by setting up a "cracking bar." Include a variety of clever nutcrackers, and you've provided snacks and entertainment at the same time. Be sure to dot the cocktail tables and cracking bar with "shell spittoons" to hold the discarded shells. And if you really want to increase the entertainment value, add a few empty coconut-shell halves so that guests can challenge each other to a friendly "shell game" while they are enjoying their nuts.

#773 All-American on a Bun!

Cocktail snacks are nice. Dinner is better. Cake is awesome. But later, with all that dancing-induced hunger, nothing hits the spot like a good old-fashioned hot dog. There's no need to bother the caterer. Just hire a local hot-dog-cart vendor. The cart's wheeled in, and the hot dogs fly out. What could be easier? If you want the vendor to dress a certain way, provide him or her with a jacket, hat, scarf, or whatever attire befits the occasion or theme, and the hard part is done. All that's left is enjoying the ultimate good-time food.

#774 Bottles of Sweet Satisfaction

Not every guest wants to hit the bar. Soda people love their sodas, and when looking for a delicious treat, there's little that beats an old-fashioned, throwback soda in a bottle. Throwback sodas are made with real sugar, the way they were before many of your guests were probably even born. Fortunately, plenty of those vintage-style sodas are still being made in Mexico and shipped to U.S. stores nationwide. From real Coke and real Pepsi to the best orange, grape, root beer, and lemon-lime sodas you'll find, there's plenty to choose from to evoke a sense of nostalgia in your older guests and expose younger ones to a whole new soda experience. Just bring in decorated washtubs, and fill them with ice and soda bottles. Provide wedding-themed bottle openers and recycling receptacles for the empties, and you'll be a hit with the soda lovers. As with love and life, when it's the real deal, it's just plain better.

#775 *Wafer Wonders*

Unexpected details always contribute to the "wow" factor, and edible rice papers pack a big "wow" factor punch into tiny expressions. Rice paper, or wafer paper, beautifully transforms into any design you imagine — butterfly, flower, snowflake, bird, etc. Rice paper can be sugared and colored with edible-ink pens, or even run through a printer with the use of edible printer ink. Choose solid or lacy designs. When laid onto frosting, rice paper art is absorbed, leaving behind the image on the cake or the cupcake.

But you don't need cake. Free-formed paper designs stand alone. Just a dab of light corn syrup "glues" a rice-paper butterfly or heart to the edge of a cup or a dinner plate. Wedding guests would arrive to find a gentle dragonfly resting on the edge of their plate, or a heart on their wineglass, and it's all perfectly safe to eat. If you don't want to tackle the wafer-making task yourself, craft artisans who do lovely wafer work are available for hire. Sugar wafer attachments aren't required décor, but they are "wow" -factor décor that literally melt in the mouth.

#776 *Nests of Love*

Cleverly designed sweet treats that greet guests as they arrive at their seats are always welcome, and none more so than little birds' nests filled with a pair of edible lovebirds. Choose bird-shaped sugar candies to place in edible nests you make from chow mein noodles and chocolate. The nests are fun and easy for kids to make, too, so if you have young ones eager to help with the wedding, making bird-nests is a wonderful way to let them pitch in. Plenty of bird nest recipes are easily found online. Vary the chocolate according to your décor and the season — milk-chocolate nests in the spring, white-chocolate nests in winter, dark-chocolate nests in summer, and a dark-chocolate/milk-chocolate mix for nests in the fall. If you prefer color, add food coloring that's specifically designed to be combined with white chocolate. These little nests with their loving occupants are also perfect as special escort cards. Just add a little flag to the nest with the guest's name and table assignment, then settle all of the nests among stretched-out decorative branches for guests to pick up. Whether at the entrance as an escort card or at the table setting as a sweet treat, edible birds' nests give guests a visual delight, followed by a sweet-tasting one.

#777 *A Slice of Cheese?*

Some people think "savory" beats "sweet" any day of the week, and if you're not excited about a wedding cake, dare to be different. Make your wedding cake from cheese!

Each "cake" layer is a variety of different cheese balls or wedges, from sweet to sharp flavors. Instead of a slice of wedding cake, guests would get scoops or slices of cheese to go on exotic breads and crackers. Include sweet options like raisin or cranberry breads alongside more traditional breads and crackers. A sweet bread combined with a wonderful bite of cheese creates a nontraditional but excitingly fresh celebratory dessert. One thing's for sure. Your cake of cheese will generate plenty of conversation. And don't worry that it won't be beautiful enough. A cake of cheese can be decorated as gorgeously as any cake made from flour. Bon appétit!

#778 *Candy Wonderland*

To turn your reception decorations into teasing, tempting delights, replace all florals with candy — candy topiaries, candy centerpieces, candy bouquets and wreaths. Wrapped candies are available in bulk, and the Styrofoam needed to hold the pieces is easily carved into a variety of shapes and sizes. If you choose lollipops on sticks, you won't even have to use a glue gun to attach the candy pieces to the forms. To make your designs fluffier, insert tufts of tissue paper between the candies.

They're fun. They're tasty. And they're simple to make. Patterns and instructions are available at craft stores and on the Internet, or you can simply hire them made as you would floral pieces. Let your guests eat them at will, or use them as prizes and gifts.

Candy art can be all about fun by using a variety of colors and styles, or it can be simply elegant by using only a single candy color and blending it with gold or silver tissue tufts.

#779 *Grandma's House*

Why did the food always seem to taste better at Grandma's house? It was due to her many years of culinary experience, but at least a part of it was because it was served on dishes with beautiful patterns and even the occasional chip or two. Those were dishes infused with love.

Setting your tables with vintage dinnerware is a wonderful way to make the reception more intimate and add a warm, welcoming feel to the occasion. Settings don't even have to match. Hunt for each place setting individually, and if each has a matching plate, cup and saucer, and perhaps a bread-and-butter plate, it's perfect. A setting covered with roses can go next to a setting of dogs in the field or apple trees full of fruit. The eclectic differences make the tables spectacular. Suddenly your dinnerware is more than just plates and cups. It's entertainment — lovely, individualized entertainment. Wait until you see how the camera phones pop out for such tables.

Mix it up. Go vintage. Make each guest feel as if he or she were dining at Grandma's house, many decades ago.

#780 *The Soothing Sounds of a Cake Fountain*

If there's one thing that looks and sounds sweeter than a fountain, it's a fountain surrounded by a wedding cake. Cake fountains are made to sit beneath, in the middle of, or surrounded by beautifully appointed cakes. Consider the fountain to be one tier of the cake. It sits on its own pedestal or tabletop area of the cake table, with the cake arranged around it in any artistic configuration you wish. A lighted, running fountain turns even a plain cake into an amazing cake, and it's even possible to tint the color of the water to accent your cake and your décor. Use a cake fountain to instantly and easily upgrade your cake display, then take it home and use it to instantly and easily soothe the stress of a momentous day.

#781 *Tasty Fun*

You may think that biting your groom's head off should be a right reserved just for you, but with edible photos, your guests can nibble away at his smiling face and yours, too, whenever the mood strikes. Edible photos are available from any number of cake makers or online suppliers, or you can purchase edible inks and photo sheets for your inkjet printer and print your own edible photos. Frosting photos adhere to the frosting you place on cakes, cookies, or cupcakes. Affix them to iced cookies on sticks, wrap them in cellophane, and add a bow, and you'll have clever wedding favors.

Top wedding cupcakes with them, and your actual wedding cake can be smaller and just for the two of you. If you have photos of guests, you can make them edible, too.

If you don't want to invest in the inks and photo sheets, shop around for the best prices and the most experienced, reputable bakers. Professionals who routinely make edible-photo desserts are accustomed to the process and may do it better and quicker. On the other hand, most charge by the photo, even if multiple photos are on one sheet, so even with the purchase of the supplies, if you plan to make quite a few photos, you may find it more equitable to give it a whirl yourself. Whatever happens, you can always eat the rejects!

#782 *Stand Up for Our Cake!*

If the Food Network has taught the world anything, it's that cakes can be fashioned into absolutely any shape. Unfortunately, cake stands didn't follow a similar creative path, restricting our choices to the same pedestal designs of yesteryear. Pedestal stands are lovely, but if you want your cake to really "stand" out, consider having your cake stand custom made.

Perhaps you want your wedding cake to be crafted in the shape of your new married monogram. Currently, the only option would be to present that clever cake flat on the table or elevated on one big square, round, or rectangular platform. But if you went to a wood or metal artisan, you could commission a cake stand that would follow the exact same pattern as your cake, lifting it off the table with only the pedestals showing underneath. No unsightly platform in sight. Check with local craft-show companies who may have wood or metal craftspeople on their rosters, or search online for woodworkers who specialize in custom wood art, or metalworkers who advertise custom metal-art creations. The talent to create your unique cake stand is out there. You just have to connect to it.

#783 *Cheese Dip — BIG Cheese Dip!*

Cheese fountains are a gooey, hot flow of delicious! Many home chocolate fountains have cheese capability with appropriate temperature control to keep it moving, and they are super inexpensive to boot. They're smaller than commercial fountains, but even renting a commercial unit can set you back a lot more than simply using your own, smaller one. If you think a small, home-sized machine won't be sufficient for your large guest list, buy two or more units. You'll still save a ton over renting. If you have more than one fountain, you can even offer a variety of cheese flavors — nacho flavor in one, Swiss in another, and maybe a nice Port wine cheese to wrap it up. Just add breads and veggies, and your guests will keep themselves full and happy at all hours.

#784 *Gourmet Comfort*

Want to simplify the menu and avoid picked-at plates? Throw out the fancy-pants foods, and set up the biggest, baddest burger bar in town! No need to ask if there are vegetarian guests — you'll provide delicious vegetarian burgers alongside the gourmet versions, and everyone will be happy.

The trick to a successful burger bar is the toppings. Roll out the usual and the unusual, and guests can turn any burger into a bleus burger, a fiesta burger, a Hawaiian burger, or a monster burger with toppings three times higher than the burger itself. Add a variety of gourmet buns, and finish it off with fries with dipping sauces. Veggie lovers and the burger averse can make a salad from the toppings bar, which will already include lettuce and dressings.

To make the burgers sing with flavor, bring on the grill. Many steak restaurants have mobile grills they take to festivals and catering events. Give them a call. Tell them you want to create a burger bar extraordinaire. Of course, for smaller weddings, you can always call on your family burger master and create the spread yourself. Burgers and fries are an American institution for good reason. People love them!

#785 *Dapper Keg*

Etiquette gurus will tell you that, unless the reception is taking place on some outside turf, having a beer keg at a wedding reception is tacky. It's not so much the idea of having beer on tap that so offends the senses, because honestly, the finest bars on the planet have beer on tap. It's the sight of the keg that rankles. A keg just screams "frat party!" So cover it up. Even if the keg is behind a bar, give it a dapper "suit of clothes." Give it a koozie. Just like the koozies that keep your soda can cold, an insulated Keg Koozy fits over the keg to keep it chilled and make it dapper. Think of it as the keg's own wetsuit. Without the need for ice, the koozie will keep the keg cold for about six hours. You can even order custom koozies printed with the bride's and groom's names, or with whatever you wish to say. If you're going to have a keg at your wedding, help it fit in. A well-dressed keg should keep the naysayers at bay.

#786 *A Passion for Pasta*

It's easy to think of beef or chicken as reception entrées, but to save money and add homey comfort to your reception, consider making pasta the main course. Steer clear of a big plate of spaghetti with marina sauce, and opt instead for a delicate dish like angel hair Alfredo or a stuffed pasta shell topped with the wedding couple's monogram. Pasta isn't just a poor man's dinner. It can be fabulously posh and exceptionally delicious when prepared with a delicate sensibility.

#787 *Cake in a Cone*

What's the easiest cupcake to eat? The one baked in an ice-cream cone, of course! Ice-cream-cone cupcakes are made by filling the cones with cake batter and baking the goodness right inside. Finished with beautiful frosting and embellishments on top, this wedding treat won't crumble down your guests' formal finery. Leave the cones themselves unadorned, or gussy them up by attaching sugar wafers, edible pearls, or tasty gems to the outside. If you want them to be as fabulously dressed as you will be, brush the cones with a bit of clear syrup and dust them with edible glitter, or add an edible bow tie to half of your cupcakes and an edible "diamond" necklace to the other half. If you have something to say, personalize your clever cupcakes with a toothpick sign sticking out of the top. Cake in a cone — how utterly fun!

MUSIC

CHAPTER TWELVE • *Music*

The world just wouldn't be the same without music. From lullabies that soothe tiny hearts to songs with driving beats that make feet want to tap and hips to shake, music is as much a part of human life as breathing. On the wedding day, the judicious use of music can underscore all of your ceremonial and celebratory events. It's a poignant backdrop, a melodic punctuation mark. It's entertainment. The music you choose will matter to all who attend.

The ideas on the pages that follow will help you consider your musical choices from both traditional and nontraditional angles, enabling you to construct a memorable musical wedding score. The possibilities are many, and you don't have to conform to what is expected. On the other hand, dominating the wedding day with your own musical guilty pleasures isn't the best choice either. If you're a heavy-metal-loving couple, you had better make sure that every single guest shares your heavy-metal affinity, or you'll risk driving some guests right off the premises. The same approach applies to any musical genre. Whether it's country or hip-hop, gospel or show tunes, be kind and sprinkle your personal favorites among a widely varied musical mix. "A little something for everyone" is a key component to wedding-day happiness.

As a truly universal language, music builds bridges between cultures. It calms nerves, aids healing, and protects memories from fading. There is little else on Earth with the soul-deep impact of music. That's why musical choices for the wedding day shouldn't be made in haste. Begin early. Take your time. Listen well. From the ceremony prelude to the last dance at the reception, every note counts.

#788 *Underscoring the "I Dos"*

Primary musical needs for the ceremony include the prelude, the processional, and the recessional. Prelude music underscores guest seating and provides preceremony entertainment. Processional music delivers the wedding party to the altar, and recessional music accompanies the wedding party's exit.

In addition to the big three, soloists or musicians are often called upon to provide musical interludes during ceremonial events like candle lighting, wine sharing, glass breaking, and other symbolic moments.

Feel free to enjoy whatever style of music you like throughout the ceremony, as long as your musical choice doesn't violate any mandates imposed by your religious venue. Most wedding couples choose gentle music for the occasion, but if you would rather boogie in or boogie out to something with a stronger beat, that's absolutely your prerogative.

#789 *Musical Milestones at the Reception*

Music moves the reception, and you will choose favorite songs for the following traditional reception events:

- your grand entrance
- your first dance
- the father-daughter dance
- the mother-son dance
- the cake-cutting ceremony
- the bouquet toss
- the garter toss
- your last dance
- any unique dance, like a money dance, a feature dance with the winners of the bouquet and garter tosses, a bride-and-gents dance, or a groom-and-ladies dance

Add a personal influence by providing your own prepared playlist to the band or DJ well in advance of the big day. Ask the bandleader or DJ to notify you right away if your song selections cannot be played for any reason.

Music is personal. Not everyone likes the same genre of music or the same songs within a genre. But if you're country at heart, don't worry that some guests may not like country music. Choose the country songs you like best. If it's rock 'n' roll, big band, or jazz that you prefer, then go for it.

It's miserable to ride in someone else's car when the driver relentlessly plays tunes you don't enjoy. That's why it's important that at your reception you are the driver. For important, milestone moments, choose music that fills you with pleasure. If some guests don't like your musical selections, they will soon forget about it. But if you don't like the music on your wedding day, you will never forget it. Supplement your chosen songs with an eclectic collection of music that others might enjoy, and you'll have the best of both worlds — music you love when it matters most, and music for the masses when your special songs aren't playing.

#790 *Wonderful Whispering Winds*

Musicians, soloists, and prerecorded music are all wedding-ceremony staples, but wind chimes can add a uniquely peaceful harmony to the occasion.

The pleasant tinkle of chimes at outdoor weddings easily creates a sweet accompaniment for guests arriving at the ceremony, but with a bit of planning, wind chimes work just as well indoors. Choose battery-operated chimes, or create movement for standard chimes by directing a small fan toward them. Tuck the fan discreetly behind a floral decoration, and instruct ushers to silence the melodic tinkling just before the ceremony begins.

Chimes are crafted from a variety of materials to create different tones. From the lightness of intertwining crystals to the earthiness of bamboo, choosing the perfect wind chimes for your wedding is simply a matter of deciding which sound you like best. Attach angels, wedding bells, monograms, and other decorative accents to the chimes if desired.

Wind chimes can last forever, and when hung in your home or on your patio after the wedding, the soothing melodies of the chimes may bless every day with fond memories.

#791 *Musical Physical Fitness*

Before choosing musicians for the ceremony or reception, consider how much space will be needed to accommodate them, any restrictions that may be imposed by the venue, and how appropriate an instrument will be.

You don't want to learn on your wedding day that the church forbids the bagpipe recessional you've always dreamed of, or that the harp music you selected for your outdoor wedding is so easily swept away by the breeze that only the two people closest to the harpist can hear it.

After asking the venues about any restrictions, speak with prospective musicians to learn of their specific needs. Trying to squeeze an eight-piece band onto a six- by six-foot stage doesn't work, and expecting a band to play in the blazing sun without a cover is just wrong.

There's more to choosing music than simply selecting songs. Music at the wedding is important, but the music must fit the venue both aesthetically and physically. For smooth musical sailing, it pays to work out the kinks before the contracts are signed.

#792 *DJ or Live Band?*

DJs and live bands both bring something unique to the table. Consider the following:

- A DJ plays songs performed by the song's original artists. A band performs songs using its own interpretation.
- Both a DJ and a band have an extensive playlist, but requested songs that are not on the playlist will have to be learned in advance by a band, while a DJ can likely obtain existing recordings with little notice.
- For small venues, a DJ can adjust the volume lower, while a band's volume can only go so low.
- A band can add visual impact to a reception theme through sheer size and costuming. A DJ is just one person, so any thematic impact is minimal.
- A DJ takes up less room than a multipiece band.
- Most bands cost more than a DJ.
- A live band can add exceptional entertainment value by allowing guests to sit in. Guest interaction with a DJ is not likely, unless he or she is also a karaoke host.
- Live bands have that "wow" factor that a DJ may or may not have.

Personalities matter. It's important that a band or DJ lead ceremonial events like cutting the cake or the first dance without being intrusive. Over-the-top performers intent on stealing the bride and groom's wedding-day thunder should be weeded out in the auditioning process.

Before your wedding, whether you're considering a band or a DJ, try to watch a live performance and thoroughly check references: these are the keys to making beautiful music.

#793 *It's in the Can*

Technology has opened the door to a whole new generation of canned music, and for some wedding couples, songs from an iPod, laptop, or CD player may make an effective substitute for a band or a DJ.

It's a surefire way to get the songs you want, and it can definitely trim some entertainment dollars from the budget. But it isn't exactly free. Even if your reception is small, you will need to buy or rent an amplification and speaker system to prevent a weak, faraway sound that only a few close guests can hear. Practicing with the system is essential to avoiding buzzing, feedback, or other problems.

When utilizing only recorded music, overcome the loss of a master of ceremonies by assigning someone to monitor the music player and make appropriate announcements for ceremonial or special events.

One considerable downside to a canned-music reception is the loss of visual impact. Human performances are far more entertaining than any machine — unless, of course, you plan to conceal the iPod, laptop, or CD player inside a roving robot.

#794 *I Hear a Flute*

One of the most inspirational and lyrical instruments for a wedding ceremony is a flute. Flute music is ethereal, gentle, and stylized. Whether it's the hauntingly beautiful melody of a Native American flute, the spirited call of an Irish flute, or the peaceful, poignant tonal breaths of a traditional flute, the sounds produced by a talented flautist are perfect for a wedding ceremony.

Flute music during the quietest moments of the ceremony is extraordinarily moving, and with the airiness of a flute, you never have to worry that the sound will be overpowering.

Find a flautist by contacting a local symphony or orchestra, or by contacting agents or management companies that provide wedding musicians. Search online for flute players who specialize in unique themes, and audition them via a live performance or a recorded CD. As with any musician, give your flautist plenty of time to learn special requests.

#795 *Soloists and Musicians, Oh My!*

There's something important to understand about singers and musicians. They're artists, and artists with creative minds routinely think outside the box — about everything. If you don't want your soloist or musicians to show up with cotton-candy-pink hair or shoeless with a bright Hawaiian shirt, you need to be clear about your desires before you do the hiring.

If you audition a pink-haired, shoeless soloist, it's possible that successfully altering his or her appearance just won't happen. Don't expect to change someone's fundamental personality. On the other hand, it's your wedding. If pink hair and hairy toes are not to your liking, and you have little confidence that the soloist or musician will agree to your wishes, move on. Hire someone else. Just remember that you don't have the right to tell a hired musician to buy something specific to wear for the occasion, but you do have the right to specify the style of attire and the presentation you desire.

The more famous the soloist or musician, the less influence you are likely to have. But then, scoring a chart-topping artist for your wedding would no doubt blind everyone to appearances anyway. With an A-list entertainer as your soloist, it would be hard to go wrong.

#796 *Music in Your Soul*

Are you a singer or musician at heart? If so, join the fun. Ask the band you are thinking of hiring if it's okay for you or your new spouse to sit in for a few songs. A bride singing at her own reception or a groom hitting the skins for a wild drum solo is always a crowd pleaser.

Some band members are understandably reluctant to allow someone else to play a cherished instrument. But unless it's the drums, it's pretty easy to have your own instrument standing by. A band may charge extra if you want to rehearse your songs with them, but most are so professional that following your lead without a rehearsal is no problem. Just give plenty of notice about which songs you want to perform.

If a band won't allow you to sit in, look elsewhere. Hire an amenable band, and spread your musical wedding-day wings!

#797 *Lyrics of Love*

Wedding couples routinely write their own vows, but how great would it be to hear your own song lyrics at the ceremony or reception? Writing lyrics is just a hop, skip, and a jump from writing vows, and it requires only the addition of a little rhythm to the words.

The easiest way to write lyrics is to alter the words of an existing song. Simply change the details in the song, like the names of people or places, or adjust a line to reflect something personal in your life. Songs are copyrighted and protected, but as long as you have no intention of recording or distributing the song, it's unlikely that changing "Sandy" to "Sarah" or substituting "my big, bad Harley" for "my big, bad Chevy" on your wedding day is going to incur the wrath of the original songwriter.

Of course, if your inner muse is dying to get out, write enough lyrics for a full song, including the verses and chorus, and hire a songwriter or a musician to set those words to music. A custom song for your wedding, especially one you had a hand in creating, will be sweetly satisfying.

#798 *Bagpiper Fanfare*

The lilt of a bagpipe feels instantly ceremonial, and a bagpiper at a wedding is truly special.

Most bagpipers play traditional mouth-blown pipes that produce a rich, full tone, as well as smaller bellows-blown pipes that generate a mellower, softer sound. The big pipes work well for the prelude, processional, and recessional, while the bellows-blown pipes, known as Scottish smallpipes, beautifully underscore ceremonial rituals without blowing the doors off.

To create a dramatic entrance or exit, let the bagpiper lead the processional or the recessional instead of playing from a stationary position. A talented bagpiper in full tartan regalia is a moving, memorable sight.

As with all musicians, not all bagpipers are created equal. Bagpiping is a complex art that takes years to master, and auditioning your bagpiper, either in person or by video, is a must. Hear the music and see the attire for yourself.

Scottish roots are not a prerequisite to embracing the melodic wail of a bagpipe. If you love the majesty a bagpiper brings to the wedding day, indulge and enjoy.

#799 Strings and More Strings

There's a reason string ensembles are staples at art galas and state dinners. Classical chamber music is beautiful but completely unobtrusive. The only time you think about the music is when the musicians stop playing, and you suddenly realize that the gentle melodies are no longer filling your soul and soothing your psyche. It is this intimate, understated quality that makes string ensembles wedding-day ideal, especially for formal weddings.

Strings at your wedding can mean anything from a solo cellist to a full string ensemble that may include the cello, violin, viola, bass, harp, and even piano. The most common ensemble is the string quartet, consisting of two violins, a cello, and a viola.

String music is more than just classical, and many string quartets infuse modern music into their repertoires.

When auditioning your string ensemble, inquire about music stands. Music stands get messy, and they may not be the wedding-day image you desire. A well-rehearsed ensemble no longer needs to read music while playing, but if music stands are necessary, protect the aesthetic appeal of your wedding by requiring that they be solid, opaque, and clutter free.

Take the time to look, listen, and inquire when hiring, and your string ensemble will make you proud.

#800 The Soul of the Soundtrack

In their quest for a few songs guaranteed to make their wedding different, brides and grooms have been known to agonize over a never-ending parade of "maybe" tunes. But choosing a musical theme can hasten the selection process and produce the exceptional final result you're craving.

Movie and musical soundtracks already accomplish the most important task by only including songs that fit a single expressive theme. Embrace your love of Disney movies, Broadway shows, *Harry Potter*, *Twilight*, *Grease*, *Hairspray*, or any other movie, play, or TV series that delights you. Select favorite soundtrack songs for all aspects of the ceremony. The music will already be cohesive, yet adaptive to your wedding.

Soundtracks boast full, rich melodies that can be replicated by live musicians or played from a CD via a sound system. When it comes to creatively weaving songs into a musical tapestry, it's hard to top the amazing composers and musicians found at the core of musical soundtracks.

#801 *Do the Mash*

A music mash-up is the blending of two or more songs into one musical performance. It's usually the "best of" portions of each song. Mash-ups may feel like a recent technological phenomenon, but they've been around for generations.

When Elvis Presley combined "Dixie" with the "Battle Hymn of the Republic" decades ago, the result was a musical miracle that left no dry eye in the house and no heart untouched. More recently, the TV show *Glee* assumed the mantle of mash-up master.

To create musical magic for your wedding, work with your musicians to combine certain passages of favorite songs and turn them into one unforgettable rendition. It's a direct path to an expression that sets your wedding apart.

A mash-up allows you to choose more songs by utilizing only parts of them, but most important, it provides the artistic freedom to be yourselves.

#802 *A Horse of a Different Color*

The hauntingly beautiful Carpenters' song "We've Only Just Begun" is one of the most performed wedding songs of all time, but some couples don't include it in their wedding for that very reason.

If you love a certain song but fear that its tried-and-true nature is a detriment, give the song a new lease on life by taking it out of its comfort zone. Change up the instruments.

"We've Only Just Begun" performed on the piano sounds very different than it does when plucked from the strings of a harp, teased from the reeds of a harmonica, or soulfully emerging from the bell of a saxophone. Instruments color a song and alter its sound. You still get the essence of the song, but it's wrapped in a more inventive and unexpected package.

There's no reason to give up on a well-loved wedding song simply because it's made countless wedding-day appearances. Just season it with a new instrumental flavor to make it fresh.

#803 *Here Comes the Bride . . . Maybe*

Millions of brides have walked down the aisle to Richard Wagner's 1850 "Bridal Chorus," more commonly known as "Here Comes the Bride." It's become so prevalent at modern weddings that most brides think it's a ceremonial requirement.

Choosing another song for the bride's entrance can be dramatic and beautiful, but it can also be confusing to guests who already know to stand and face the bride when they hear those first five, instantly recognizable, pounding notes of "Here Comes the Bride." If you choose to walk down the aisle to a nontraditional bride's-entrance song, simply give your family the heads-up in advance so that they can stand and turn at the appropriate time. When they do, all other guests will follow suit, even if they've never before heard the song.

A great number of equally amazing songs have been written since 1850, and choosing one of those to underscore that momentous walk may be just what the bride ordered.

#804 *Synthesizer Surprise!*

Brides and grooms rarely want to don oversized shoes and red ball noses to get married, but a light comedic touch can turn an ordinary ceremony into something guests can't wait to chat about at the office watercooler.

The earliest synthesizer equipment required a dolly and some heavy lifting to transport. But today, synthesized sounds are easily created by using small, handheld electronics. Adding a synthesizer to the wedding ceremony may lighten the mood and tickle the funny bone when least expected.

Think how wide eyed and smiling the guests would be if the pops and whistles of exploding fireworks filled the air as your lips met for the first kiss, or if you turned to your guests and raised clasped hands to a synthesized rendition of "We Are the Champions."

A dash of humor doesn't suit every wedding couple, but for others, lighthearted moments dazzle and delight. And for those couples, a synthesizer is the perfect instrument.

#805 *Melodic Prose and Poetry*

Readings before or during a wedding ceremony are often underscored by gentle music, but a more dramatic choice is melodic prose and poetry. The difference is in the execution. The music underlying a reading provides only a soft background of sound. But in melodic prose and poetry, the music is as much of a star as the words being read.

To successfully combine a reading of a poem or a passage of prose with a musical score, the reader and the musician must work together as a team. As with typical readings, the music softly supports the reader as he or she delivers poetic lines or words from a story. But unlike typical readings, the reader pauses at predetermined moments to let the music build. During these intervals, solo melodies can transport the listener and evoke a wide range of emotional responses. Music is a language all its own, and blending that musical language with a meaningful spoken piece is spellbinding.

When thoroughly rehearsed and performed well, melodic prose and poetry create unforgettable wedding memories.

#806 *"Oops" Songs*

A wedding day is about hope, love, and inspiration, and music plays a huge role in conveying those positive emotional attributes. But the mood goes awry if the song catalog includes tunes better left to the music player back home.

To ensure an uplifting day, ban songs that wail on about the opposite end of the emotional spectrum. Songs about breaking up, hurting, loss, hopelessness, or "you done me wrong" aren't great choices for weddings, even when the melodies are beautiful. If you must, go ahead and treat guests to Roy Orbison's haunting "It's Over" or *NSYNC's lively, danceable "Bye Bye Bye," but consider using instrumental versions only. You get the music you prefer, but you don't get lyrics that make a great marriage seem like a pipe dream. No one needs to hear negative sentiments undermining the wedding vows.

Choose your music carefully, and you won't subliminally send the wrong wedding-day message.

#807 *Creative Keyword Song Selection*

Finding online song lists categorized by wedding events is easy, and many Web sites have extensive resources that cover songs for the first dance, cutting the cake, etc. But to find popular songs to fit your own unique needs or wishes, engage multiple search engines using a direct keyword phrase.

These days, all search engines are not created equal. Enter a specific keyword phrase and you'll likely receive different first-page results from Google.com, Bing.com, Yahoo.com, and any number of other search engines. Don't be shy about using them all to increase your chances of finding just the right songs.

For example, for a song about togetherness, enter the keyword phrase "songs with the word together" or "songs that include together." The more specific your phrase, the more viable the results will be.

No one knows the answer to "How many songs have ever been written?" The number is staggering. But that's good news for brides and grooms looking for popular songs that speak to them musically and lyrically. Finding them is a matter of searching well and searching wisely.

#808 *Song Searching at the Source*

Finding the perfect music is not always easy, especially if the song is obscure or received little to no airplay. It's hard to remember the thousands of songs you've heard over the years, and it's even harder when you remember only part of a title or just the artist who sang the song. That's where ASCAP, BMI, and SESAC can help.

These are the agencies that collect royalties for songwriters, and each of them has a searchable database. Not every song is listed with all agencies, so if the song you're looking for is not on the ASCAP Web site, search BMI or SESAC. Each has its own "repertory search" function with defining criteria like the name of the artist, songwriter, title, and publisher. Remembering only one of these, or a portion of one of these, doesn't prohibit a search, but the closer you get to the complete title or artist, the less "results" scrolling you'll need to do. For example, perhaps you want the song "I Believe in Miracles," but you only remember that it's a song about miracles. Enter the word "miracles," and search all available results until the full song title appears and you have that "aha!" moment of recognition.

Once you've nailed down the correct title and recording artist, give the information to your musicians or your DJ for inclusion in your wedding playlist. Little-known songs make toes tap just as enthusiastically as those played hundreds of times a day on the radio, and little or big, if the songs are published, you'll likely find them listed on ASCAP, BMI, or SESAC.

#809 *Bum-Note Symphony*

Many churches and ceremony venues make an on-site piano or organ available for your wedding. That's a welcome offer, but before jumping in to provide a piece of sheet music to the pianist or organist, you should graciously ask this question: "When was the instrument last tuned?"

Not surprisingly, pianos and organs at ceremony venues may not receive routine tuning, and there's little worse than a middle C that plunks out like a B flat. You may not be able to identify how far off the notes are, but guests with good pitch will squirm in their seats with each foul note.

Be proactive. Inquire about the last tuning and listen to the instrument. If it's not up to par, hire a musician who comes with his or her own "in tune" portable piano, organ, guitar, cello, or other instrument.

Bum notes at a wedding are just awful. Don't give them the chance to sour the sweet sounds of your nuptials.

#810 *Something for Everyone*

When selecting dance music for the reception, take your guests' musical inclinations to heart. Pick a hot dance song from every decade, and play the songs in progression, beginning with the oldest.

For Grandma and Grandpa, just hearing "Happy Days Are Here Again" may bring a flood of memories, along with the inspiration to get up and cut a rug one more time. Mom and Dad might melt at the first strains of the "Tennessee Waltz" or feel like cutting loose to "Stayin' Alive."

It's safe to say that many age groups will attend your wedding, and not everyone shares your love of a particular musical genre. Including at least one or two songs from different eras is fun for all. It's a walk down memory lane for those who enjoyed the songs when they were at their peak of popularity, and it's a musical adventure for those who wonder what it was like to have lived and loved during those bygone days.

#811 *Piano Virtuoso*

What if you could have Bach or Beethoven entertaining your guests? How about Ray Charles, Duke Ellington, Jerry Lee Lewis, or Billy Joel? Hiring a world-class pianist for the cocktail portion of your reception may not be in the budget, but that doesn't mean you can't have world-class piano music. Simply rent a player piano.

Player pianos have character, the dancing keys are fun to watch, and the piano itself encourages guests to gather round and tap their feet or sing along. Song choices cover the gamut of musical styles. Begin your search by contacting piano stores in your area. When utilizing the right equipment, moving a piano isn't as hard as it sounds. Renting a player piano is a viable choice for brides and grooms who want to give their guests an inventive and entertaining musical experience.

#812 *With a Light Heart*

Everyone remembers to choose music for the ceremony and the reception, but prep time benefits from a little mood music, too. Fill those audio players with lighthearted wedding songs — one for the bride's room and one for the groom's. Nerves are at their worst during preceremony dressing, pacing, and clock watching, and music soothes those frazzled nerves. Choose upbeat tunes, like "You're the One That I Want" from the movie musical *Grease,* or the Beach Boys' version of "Chapel of Love." The music doesn't need to be loud to work its magic. It just needs to be present.

#813 *A Cappella Blends*

Is there anything more uplifting than a choir? Even if the ensemble is only a quartet or a sextet, the blending of voices without instrumental accompaniment is a musical gift. One way to make ceremony music unforgettable is to forgo instruments and hire a choir instead. The musical selections can be as modern or as classical as you wish. Believe it or not, there are words to the traditional wedding march (commonly known as "Here Comes the Bride"), but if you don't want lyrics during your grand entrance, the a cappella group can hum its harmonies. Or you can choose any other beautiful love song with words that matter to you.

An a cappella group adds volume and impact to a wedding ceremony. Utilize these talented singers before the ceremony to entertain guests and throughout the ceremony for interludes and ceremonial events like candle lighting. Musical instruments are wonderful inventions, but a beautiful human voice is the greatest musical instrument of all.

#814 *Shower Me with Songs*

The bridal shower is a great time to get help with your wedding-day playlist. Via bridal-shower invitations, ask guests to bring along CDs or MP3s of their favorite love and dance songs, no matter what genre of music those songs come from. Provide players, and play the songs your guests suggest, making a note of the titles and artists you enjoy most. The shower hostess can play the guests' favorites as background music when serving refreshments or between games. You will no doubt hear great songs that you would not have even thought to consider.

It's difficult to find just the right songs for all of the different music-driven ceremonial events, but with a little help from your friends, that chore can be cut down to size and generate a good time in the process.

#815 *Music-Box Lilt*

The voice-amplification system at your ceremony works for other sounds as well, like those that drift from a music box. If you don't have a musician to underscore your unity candle, sand, flower, or tree ceremony, bring your favorite music box along. Place it near a microphone, and when the time is right, have your maid of honor trigger its start. Some music boxes play longer than others. Experiment with the timing so that whichever one you use won't have to be restarted in the middle of the activity. The lilt of a music box is lovely to the ears and a sweet accompaniment to loving, ceremonial acts.

#816 *Under the Umbrella*

What happens if you book a band for your wedding then a band member can't make it? If the band is large, you may not even notice. But if it's a three- or four-piece band, that missing musician could spell disaster. In short, you wouldn't be getting what you paid for. Even if a replacement musician joined at the last moment, you may not get the sound or the continuity of the original band.

Some bands, however, will ensure the success of your event by having backup musicians already in the mix. Much like an umbrella that saves you from misery on a rainy day, a substitute musician can save the wedding day. These "umbrella" bands have multiple people playing the same part in the group, rotating in and out as schedules permit, but always performing under a single "umbrella" name that remains constant. Bands formed on college campuses are good examples. The beauty of hiring an umbrella band is that there are always backups available, and even though band members may change, it's highly likely they've participated often enough to know the band's special nuances for every song. So when auditioning bands for your big day, ask them what happens if a band member can't make it. Just who is under their umbrella?

#817 *Sweet or Sour Solo?*

A soloist plays an important role in creating the right ambiance at the wedding, but not all soloists are wedding perfect. When auditioning ceremony soloists, consider the venue. Does the altar feel miles away from the back pews or chairs? If so, your soloist needs to possess the art of projection. Is it an intimate venue? Then your soloist must be able to personally connect with the audience. Is the ceremony outdoors? If it is, choose a soloist with a full voice and a commanding presence that won't get lost in wide-open spaces.

If you have specific songs you want your soloist to sing, have soloists audition with those actual songs. Gauge the soloist's vocal range. Do the highest notes get weak or the lowest notes fade away? Do the soloist's upper and lower registers sound like two different people? Listen to part of the audition with your eyes closed to hear vocal nuances the eyes sometimes misapprehend.

A wedding is special, and you want a special soloist. Some people are fabulous singers or entertainers, but their vocal gymnastics or their annoying stage presence makes them poor candidates for a wedding performance. Think of your soloist as the beating heart of your ceremony, and choose one that beats strong and sure but doesn't threaten to vocally flatline or race uncontrollably. For your wedding, you want a soloist who simply hits the sweet spot and stays there.

#818 *What You See Is What You Get*

Consider the type of music you want at your wedding before signing a contract with a band. If you hire a group that consists of a couple of guitar players and a drummer, that's the music you will get — music that comes from guitars and drums. If your favorite songs are filled with the lush notes of strings or the exciting runs of harmonizing brass instruments, you may miss those sounds if you choose a band that simply can't provide them. What you see is what you get. Sure, some sounds in a song can be synthesized, but that doesn't mean a band will have the ability or the talent to make those synthetic sounds work. Reflect on what is musically important to you, then save yourself some time by eliminating from the audition process bands that can't make the music you want to hear.

#819 *An Orchestral Wedding*

Imagine a 19th-century castle ballroom filled to its gilded rafters with music and formally clad dancers gliding to and fro across a polished floor. If you were to look behind the dancers, you would find a full and well-balanced orchestra. Nothing but the biggest and best would do.

If you want to create a formal event like no other, a full orchestra can make that happen. Any fewer than 18 to 20 musicians would likely fall short of the incredible impact of an orchestral wedding experience. But that's a lot of musicians, and the cost will be substantial. You'll have to weigh the expense against the desire and see if you can cut the budget somewhere else in order to free up more funds for the orchestra.

Smaller orchestras can be hired directly or through booking agents. For larger orchestras, it may be possible to reduce the expense by booking a reception venue where an orchestra already resides. Sometimes a theater, an outdoor amphitheater, or a concert hall with an orchestra in residence is available for receptions. Ask if it is possible to time your wedding reception to an orchestra's dress rehearsal. Or, inquire about a reduced rate. Since there would be no need to set up and tear down at another facility, orchestra members would save time and effort. Not every venue will be receptive to a reduced-fee proposal, but it never hurts to ask. Finally, consider a nonprofit, public orchestra that survives on donations.

There's no better way to achieve ultimate formality than with a full, multidimensional orchestra that's all yours for an entire evening. If an orchestral wedding experience appeals to you, it's worth the effort to investigate the possibilities.

#820 *Never-Ending Music*

No band or DJ works without breaks, and a typical musical set is 40 minutes on and 20 minutes off. What happens in those 20 minutes out of every hour when the music is silent? The loss of music can make any party's spirit dip. Most bands and DJs flip a switch and play canned music during their breaks, and that's better than nothing. But an even better solution would be to pass the time with performances by alternate entertainers. Hire a flamenco guitarist, a pianist, or even a musical comedian to fill the gaps. These performers maintain the flow of entertainment and add variety to the reception experience.

Music is the "electricity" that keeps the celebration lit up. There's no reason to let it dim, even for a moment.

#821 *Booking Agent — Should I or Shouldn't I?*

Finding the right musicians for your wedding can be challenging. But booking agents earn their keep helping you do just that. You shouldn't be concerned that you will pay more when using an agency to book your band or soloists, because the agent's fee comes from the musician's income. For peace of mind, be sure to verify this important detail up front with whatever agency you approach.

Big companies like GigMasters are nationwide and have a huge online presence, complete with customer reviews of entertainment acts and local searches, while other agencies may serve only your own locality. Both can be beneficial in helping to locate the perfect entertainment. Will it be cheaper to book your musicians directly? It may be. But unless you check out a multitude of available acts in your area, you might settle for "Band A," not knowing that the superior "Band B" was just around the corner.

A reputable agency may prevent disappointment from the unknown, as it connects you to entertainers with reliable reputations.

#822 *Take It with You!*

Most bands and solo artists these days have a CD. Unlike years ago, when a band had to spend massive dollars to record, press, and package their music, today's musicians can produce a great-sounding product in their home studios or with the aid of their computers. Because it's cheaper for them to create it, it's cheaper for you to buy it.

When signing your musicians for the wedding, ask if they have a CD. If they do, and you like it, ask if you can purchase CDs in bulk as wedding favors for your guests. Giving CDs of your actual wedding band is an all-around win. It helps to promote the band, gives guests a favor they can identify with and enjoy after the wedding, and easily checks off one more task from your wedding to-do list. Just add a ribbon, or slip the CD into a gift envelope. You're done quickly, and the music plays on.

#823 *Daddy's Little Girl*

If you are close to your father, the father-daughter dance is especially meaningful. It's a bonding moment that creates a lifetime memory. To make it even more special for Dad, surprise him by playing a song from his heyday — a time when you were still his little girl.

Choosing one of his favorite songs from decades ago is a gift he won't be expecting. The song will take him back in time, while forever connecting the two of you in the present. Just pick a year from your childhood, then go online to research the songs of that era. If necessary, secretly ask other relatives what his favorite songs were. Somewhere in your research, you'll find the song destined to belong to just the two of you. Sometimes the best gifts don't cost a thing.

#824 *Music by the Numbers*

If you don't want to spring for a live band or a DJ, but you want your song selections to be more impulsive than what comes from an MP3 playlist, rent a jukebox! How fun it is to let guests have a hand in choosing the music! Just load the box with songs from all eras and all types of artists, then let the music roar to life.

Allow guests to choose songs, or give each guest a "jukebox card" to fill out. The guest checks out the song options on the jukebox, then lists three choices on his or her card, like D3, J10, and A4. The cards are handed over to your designated "Jukebox Master," who will enter the selections at random. Guests will never know when their songs will pop up, and hearing what others chose can be a hoot when everyone starts asking, "Okay, who picked that song?" A jukebox can take a pretty long list of numbers at once, so the Jukebox Master won't have to hover over it.

At one time, jukeboxes were the hottest musical ticket in town, and their appeal has never really waned. They're just too fun.

#825 *Ballads for Brunch*

If you're planning an after-wedding breakfast or brunch, don't forget the music! Unless you're holding the get-together in the main dining area of a restaurant, you'll provide your own background tunes. It's a perfect time to create a mix CD of your favorite songs, perhaps including the "runners-up" songs that didn't get chosen for the first dance, mother-son dance, father-daughter dance, etc.

The rule of thumb is "keep it gentle." Digestion and head-banging music don't get along, especially for older guests. Love songs, instrumentals, New Age selections, or even the sounds of nature are all contenders, depending upon where the meal will take place. Of course, you can always hire a live guitarist, harpist, or pianist if you wish, but a mix CD is easy, inexpensive, and personal.

#826 *When the Heart Melts*

To make the dinner hour stand out at the reception, forgo the background music and hire a crooner. There are millions of singers in the world, but crooners are an elite bunch. When a true crooner sings, your heart melts just a little from the moving, mellow inflection that underscores each note. Bing Crosby, Nat King Cole, Dean Martin, Tony Bennett, and Frank Sinatra are just a few of the crooning legends. Modern-day crooners, like Michael Bublé, keep that musical romance alive.

Hiring a crooner just to perform during the dinner hour of the reception is a special treat. Audition singers and judge their abilities for yourself. Someone may call himself a crooner, then turn out to be anything but. Have each candidate sing "Strangers in the Night." If you don't want to close your eyes and just drift away on the melody, your crooner probably isn't one at all. A real crooner can move mountains with his voice.

#827 *Soup and a Song*

Never dismiss the memory-generating power of a musical surprise. Secretly plant a few great singing servers within your catering staff, and let them serenade guests when it's least expected. Entire restaurants have been built around a staff that sings, and they are usually one of the top choices for treating out-of-town guests to a good time.

If you can't find real singing servers, hire a small, a cappella choral group, dress the members as waiters and waitresses, and no one will be the wiser. It's a delight to have your server burst into song — as long as the server can actually sing. Servers who have only gathered around a table to clap and join in on a happy-birthday song don't count. Look for real singers who can carry a tune as well as they can carry a tray.

#828 *Unplugged*

Sometimes favorite songs by favorite artists are just too loud or overproduced for wedding-ceremony needs. If you really want a certain song to be played before or during your ceremony, find out if that artist has an "unplugged" version. Stripped-down versions of popular songs are often recorded when the artist performs on a TV special, during a radio-station appearance, or in conjunction with another artist. Don't give up on the song without checking the artist's Web site, record label, or with the song's publisher. The perfect acoustic rendition of a beloved song, sung by the original artist, may be out there somewhere, and you'll be happy that you took the time to find it.

#829 *My Favorite Song*

Here's another kind way to add guests' favorite songs to your reception playlist: ask them in advance. Include a request on your RSVP for the guests' favorite song and artist, then build your playlist to include those selections. Guests will appreciate your generous consideration, and they'll enjoy dancing to a favorite tune, or simply listening to it as it's played during dinner or the cocktail hour. Play the songs without announcement, or create a list for your DJ or bandleader, enabling him or her to announce, "This song is courtesy of Mr. and Mrs. John Weeks."

Involve your guests in the celebration, and the celebration will be more memorable. Your thoughtful request will give them a sense of belonging.

#830 *The Cutting Edge*

If you are looking for prelude music like no other, consider hiring a sawyer. A sawyer is someone who plays the saw. These saws are sometimes referred to as musical saws or singing saws. If you've never heard an accomplished sawyer play, do yourself a favor and visit the International Musical Saw Association Web site, and listen to some of the sweet, ethereal music that master sawyers can create. It's a lovely, melodious sound on its own, but it's especially haunting and captivating with piano or guitar accompaniment. Saw music at your wedding will make your guests talk about the experience for a very long time.

It takes years of practice to coax a saw into making such beautiful melodies, so don't hire Uncle Joe and his toolbox. Use the Association to help you find a master sawyer in your area, then surprise and enchant your guests with something very different and very impressive.

#831 *So Long, Farewell*

The last song of the night is more than a swan song. It's the period that seals in the memories of the day. And like the epilogue to a great book, you want it to be amazing. Sure, you can choose old standby favorites like "Last Dance" or "(I've Had) the Time of My Life," but maybe that's not enough.

If you're the kind of person who remembers what it feels like to carry a kiss on your lips long after the kiss is over, take the time to select a last song that will leave you with that same lingering joy. Pick a song that's soft, slow, and gentle, or choose a blow-the-doors-off, rocket-fast, dizzying good-bye tune that knocks your socks off. Just choose a song that means something to you — the one you'll want playing on an endless loop in your head as you embark on your wedding night. If, on your 50th wedding anniversary, your last song still takes you back to that one perfect moment in time, you'll know you chose the perfect musical send-off.

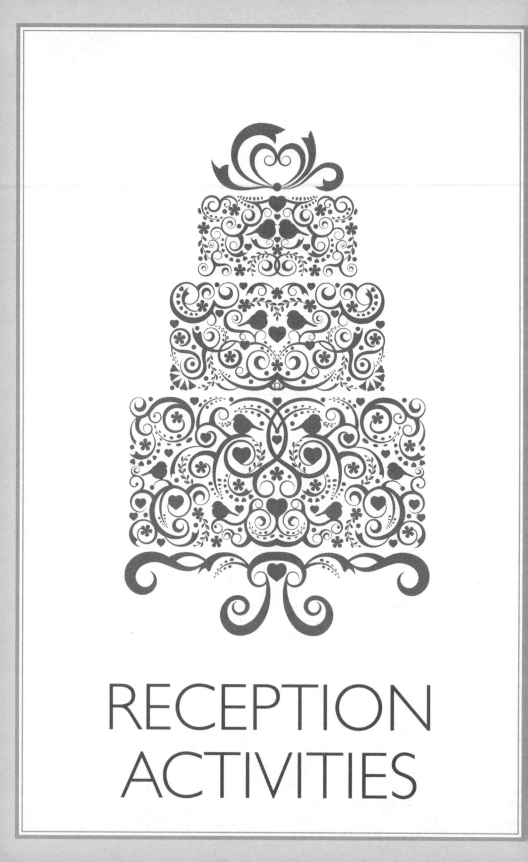

RECEPTION ACTIVITIES

I t's a fundamental truth: the wedding is all about the bride and the groom. Or is it?

It goes without saying that the bride and the groom are the most important people at the wedding. No one will argue that point, and every wedding couple deserves a dream-come-true celebration. But a wedding that includes guests is simply not all about the wedding couple.

Some brides and grooms openly express their belief that guests should consider it an honor to be invited to the wedding. But there's a great deal of presumption in that mind-set. After all, the only way for a wedding to be 100% about the bride and the groom is for the wedding couple to say "I do" with just an officiant and a witness in attendance.

A wedding invitation comes with strings. You are asking people to dress up for you, give their time to you, incur travel expenses because of you, buy a gift for you, toast you, salute you, and wrap you in well wishes. That's a lot to ask, so why not reciprocate with the one thing you can give back: a good time.

This chapter is full of "good time" components for your reception. Some ideas work alone, while others are easily incorporated into bigger, broader concepts. Most wedding couples want their guests to enjoy themselves, and why not? Bored, unhappy guests are no picnic for the bride and groom either. So check out the possibilities. Maybe you'll find a special wedding activity that will make your guests remember your wedding event as one of the best times they've ever had. That's the goal, for if your guests have great memories, yours are sure to be even greater.

#832 *What Do I Do?*

All too often, reception guests are left to wonder if they should eat, drink, and be merry before the bride and groom arrive. Put their minds at ease.

Assign a reception host or hostess to ensure the comfort of the guests. The host oversees the serving of hors d'oeuvres and a light nonalcoholic drink, like punch or sparkling water, and signals the band or DJ to play suitable background music. The bar may be open or not, as desired. Dancing, eating (beyond hors d'oeuvres), and other partying should wait until the bride and groom appear, but leaving guests to mingle without refreshment or music is cruel and unusual punishment for those who have come to help you celebrate.

As they await your arrival, guests can also enjoy an amusing diversion. For example, when setting up the reception, scatter easels around the perimeter of the room. On each easel, place a framed white poster board with a large photo (either funny or sentimental) of the bride and/or groom attached in the center. Use an attractive frame and a sturdy backing, with no glass covering. Place a brandy snifter full of pen-style markers next to each easel, and have your host invite all guests to write photo captions on the poster board surrounding the picture. Guests are entertained as they move from photo to photo, and you get a wealth of touching and hilarious memories in the bargain.

#833 *Good Times at the OK Kiddie Corral*

Children are adventurous. Impromptu games of hide-and-seek underneath the cake table or the inside of the bass drum can result in sudden disaster. To keep both younger and older guests happy, consider a wedding-reception activity corner just for kids.

Border the designated area with decorative fencing, and make it pop with kid-friendly décor and plenty of games and toys. Offer puzzles, Lego, stuffed animals, and other intriguing but quiet entertainments.

It's not fair to ask super-energized little ones to sit quietly at a wedding reception, but an even worse faux pas is leaving them to their own devices. Addressing the unique needs of children by providing a little world all their own is more than worth the time it takes to arrange it.

#834 *Meet and Greet!*

The receiving line may be held immediately following the ceremony, but it is usually conducted just after the wedding couple arrives at the reception. This is the wedding couple's opportunity to receive good wishes from the guests and, in turn, thank those guests for coming. If the guest is unknown to either the bride or the groom, an introduction by the one who knows the guest is in order.

Custom dictates that the bride's parents head the receiving line, followed by the bride and groom, the groom's parents, and, if desired, the rest of the wedding party. But formal receiving lines aren't the only way to have an effective meet and greet at the wedding reception, and plenty of modern couples opt for alternatives.

Greeting each individual guest is important, but doing so can be accomplished by an extended cocktail-hour mingle before the meal, or by a casual tour of the tables by the bride and groom and their parents. Depending upon the number of guests, a mingling interaction may prove easier on tired backs and sore toes. Many men and women dress up only occasionally, and fancy shoes and tight clothing contribute to the discomfort of a prolonged receiving line, for both the guests and the wedding party.

A receiving line adds a noble air to the proceedings, and it's an efficient way to greet each guest, but choosing a less formal method of greeting shouldn't make you or your guests feel any less royal. It may, in fact, make everyone happier.

#835 *Calling Fred and Ginger*

Organized activities at a wedding reception can provide laughs and memories you can't buy at any price. One such great event is the old fashioned dance-off.

Prepare for it by compiling a long, varied medley of up-tempo and slow songs for the band or DJ to play. Create contestant numbers by using two sheets of 8½" x 11" paper for each person, with the same number boldly marked on each sheet. Use long strips of yarn to connect the two sheets via punched holes in the upper corners. The sandwich-board-style numbers will slip over a guest's head, with a length of yarn resting on each shoulder, making the number visible from the front and back. The yarn protects clothing and is not as potentially damaging as staples or tape.

While the medley plays, the bride and groom judge the friendly competition, deciding on each couple to be eliminated. The maid of honor and best man assist by tapping the shoulders of the booted couples and escorting them back to their seats. When only two couples are left, the winner is decided by applause.

A great prize is a funny, handmade trophy from the bride and groom, proclaiming the winners to be the "[insert the wedding couple's last name here] Wedding Dance Champions!" Award additional token prizes to the couple eliminated first, or to those deemed worthy for any other reason.

A dance-off is a crowd pleaser, and it's especially fun later in the reception, when merriment peaks.

#836 *Champagne Surprise*

Beautiful toasting flutes customarily await the wedding couple at the reception. Sometimes these wine glasses are adorned with flowers and ribbons. Sometimes they are etched with the words "Bride" and "Groom" or with the names of the wedding couple. But it's nice to turn these special glasses into more than mere champagne vessels.

After the toasting flutes are purchased, the bride and groom each take possession of one and choose a message to add to the very bottom of the stemware base. Whether it's a single word, like "Forever," or a small phrase, like "You Are My Heart." This is a private message from one half of the couple to the other. Write the words on the underside of the base with permanent silver or white paint or a metallic wine-glass marker. If you prefer a more delicate finish, take the flutes to an engraver to have the message etched into the glass.

The personalized glasses are entrusted to the sworn-to-secrecy maid of honor, who delivers them to the reception without the bride or groom having ever seen the other's finished glass. The private message from one to the other will be revealed when the wedding couple lift their glasses in a toast for the first time.

These toasting flutes are keepsakes for a lifetime. It's nice to know that they can "speak" to you again and again throughout the years.

#837 *It's a Toss-Up*

The traditional bouquet toss doesn't always work well in the 21st century. Couples are getting married later in life, and frequently most or all of the female wedding guests are married, making them ineligible to catch the bouquet. But life is nothing if not flexible. If single women are scarce, alter the ceremonial bouquet toss to include all female guests.

Invite all ladies to the floor for a special floral toss. Instead of using a typical bouquet, gather a bunch of individual flowers in your hands, with a unique message tied to each stem. When you toss the flowers into the air, they will separate and scatter so that many female guests can claim a single flower, along with a message of hope, inspiration, or love.

This ceremonial event doesn't have to be about a young maid catching the bouquet and being next on the marriage list. It can simply be about engaging in a fabulously fun moment with the women in your life.

#838 *Slippers Please!*

As much fun as it is to get dressed up, it's even more fun to dress down, kick off your shoes, and ease into a world of comfort. It's hard to enjoy yourself when your feet hurt.

If you want your reception to never end and your guests to dance the night away, you may wish to ward off the agony of aching feet by providing your guests with flip-flops or slippers.

Spa-goods providers, medical suppliers, import wholesalers, and others sell disposable flip-flops and slippers in bulk. They are inexpensive, and most are one-size-fits-all. Baskets of slippers by the dance floor are a special gift from the bride and groom. Guests will understand that they are not only allowed to kick off their uncomfortable shoes, they are encouraged to do so.

To accommodate pantyhose and socks, slider-style slippers and flip-flops work better than those with a toe divider.

Flip-flops and slippers help to protect feet without inflicting high-heel backaches, sore toes, blistered heels, or injuries from less-than-twinkle-toed dance partners. They are quite the wedding reception treat.

#839 *Toasters — Not the Pop-up Kind!*

Every wedding couple runs the risk of receiving enough toasters to open a breakfast diner, but there are some toasters all wedding couples cherish — the human kind.

Toasting the newly married couple during the reception festivities is traditional, but modern wedding couples can stretch that tradition any way they please. While the best man's toast will always hold a position of honor, encouraging spontaneous toasts by any and all friends and family members opens the door to plenty of entertainment and unexpected sentiment.

How fun would it be to watch the seven-year-old flower girl raise her glass of apple juice and share her best and brightest marriage tips for the bride and groom? And heart-touching moments, like Great-Grandma's toast backed by 80 years of life and wisdom, or the words of an old college friend who traveled 2,000 miles to attend the wedding, may reside in your heart forever.

Notify your guests that all toasts are welcome by including a business-card-sized note to that effect in the invitation. Only some will take advantage of the offer, and that's perfectly all right.

#840 *Celebrating Your Married Guests*

If your guest list includes a number of married couples, invite them to remember their own weddings at yours. Include a separate notice in the invitation that encourages married couples to mail you a color-photocopied wedding photo, or to send a digital photo via e-mail that you can print on your own.

At the reception, arrange the guests' wedding photos in a large wall display or on an easel, with the couple's name and wedding date listed beneath each photo. Add distinction by decorating the display with wedding-themed accents, and position it against a backdrop of tall potted plants. A runner carpet in front of the display turns it into a bona fide walk of wedding memories. Add interest to the display by placing hearts next to the photos of the longest-married couple, the pair that traveled the farthest to your wedding, or any other recognition you wish to bestow.

The wedding day is all about the bride and groom, but sharing your moment with those who have walked the wedding path before you will only make your occasion more memorable. Viewing and talking about the array of wedding photos will be an unexpected pleasure for all guests, married or not.

#841 *Sparks of Love*

Who doesn't love the magical dance of fireworks? Fireworks for a wedding reception come in all sizes and forms. Full outdoor aerial displays are expensive, but they quite literally send the newlyweds off with a spectacular bang. If, however, an aerial display costing thousands of dollars is not in the cards, inexpensive handheld sparklers will light up the cake or become a shimmering backdrop for the first dance. Moderately priced floor pyrotechnics can add sizzle to a shared kiss or spell out words of love during champagne toasts.

Most fireworks, even small ones, require city permits, additional liability insurance, firefighter notification, and permission from the venue. But if your heart is set on finishing off the reception with breathtaking bursts of sparkles, tackle the logistics and let the fireworks fly!

#842 *Wedding Sleight of Hand*

Magicians who've mastered sleight of hand are fun table-side entertainers at the wedding reception.

To find the perfect performer, interview magicians and watch them work. If you are wowed, your guests will be wowed, too. Once you've decided on a magician, ask him or her about personalizing the act. Plenty of tricks convert well to a wedding theme, like substituting standard coins or cards with ones that bear pictures of the bride and groom. Some illusions require specialized props that can't be altered, but even sprinkling a few "wedding" elements among the regular ones will add pizzazz to reception performances.

There's definitely magic in the air at weddings, but only a real magician can share up-close-and-personal magic with guests.

#843 *Ballroom Glory*

For an unforgettable reception surprise, hire a professional ballroom-dance couple to perform for your guests — and to dance with them.

Since ballroom dancers can rumba, waltz, or paso doble to any genre of music, don't worry that a full orchestra will have to be squeezed onto the bandstand. But with a professional male dancer for the female guests and a professional female dancer for the male guests, everyone can have a shot at "dancing like a star."

Anytime you go above and beyond the traditional call of "reception" duty and provide unique activities for your guests, you show your giving spirit. A professional ballroom couple is a gift of great magnitude.

#844 *Wedding-Day Sweethearts*

The head table at a reception is always reserved for the bride and groom and the wedding party. But the use of a continuous long table is not written in stone. As an alternative, consider a sweetheart table for the bride and groom and satellite tables for the wedding party.

A smaller sweetheart table, sometimes placed on a slightly raised platform, allows the newlyweds to feel a bit more regal and permits private moments that can rarely be enjoyed at a typical head table.

The bride and groom sit at the center sweetheart table, and wedding-party tables are positioned to their left and right. Unlike a traditional head-table configuration, the sweetheart/satellite layout permits the significant others of wedding-party members to join them at their table. This is a welcome consideration for wives or husbands or partners of wedding-party members who would otherwise be relegated elsewhere.

The bride and groom are definitely wedding-day sweethearts. It's more than okay to act like it.

#845 *Pucker Up!*

Wedding guests who hunger for a little public display of affection often use kissing bells to get the bride and groom to share a smooch. Signaling that it's time for a kiss gives guests an entertaining power that's all in good fun.

But if you don't want a lingering ringing in your ears, try replacing the little bells with tiny flags bearing the wedding couple's picture, monogram, or family crest. Whoops and hollers will no doubt accompany whatever signaling method is chosen, but since flag waving is blessedly silent, you'll hear only the robust calls, not shouts on top of ringing.

If you want to limit the number of times your lips are called to duty, use party poppers. One pull of the string produces a single bang and an explosion of colorful streamers, but once it's been popped, it's over. Every guest who pops his or her popper has no way to call for a kiss down the road.

Calls for kisses are reception staples, but with a little creative thinking, you won't have to kiss your lips raw before the honeymoon even begins.

#846 *The Who and What of the First Dance*

The first dance of the reception is reserved for the bride and groom and usually takes place immediately after the completion of the receiving line. The master of ceremonies, reception host/hostess, or bandleader introduces the bride's parents, groom's parents, the wedding party, and finally the bride and groom. Each person, couple, or group makes their way into the room when their name is announced. Entering last, the bride and groom proceed to the dance floor to await the start of their first dance.

Alternatively, the wedding couple proceeds directly to their seats, and the first dance is postponed until after the meal. If this scenario is chosen, the bride or groom signals the announcer when the wedding couple is ready to dance.

As the first dance progresses, an announcement invites the wedding party to join in. It is also perfectly fine to wait until the last bars of the song before inviting everyone to join you.

The first dance happens once in a lifetime, and although it begins with only two, ending it with many feels pretty warm and wonderful.

#847 *First-Dance Song Fever*

Brides and grooms always choose a meaningful song for their first dance. It's a memory that doesn't fade, and choosing the right song is important. Unfortunately, there is often too much pressure to choose a slow song for the dance when the couple is far more fun loving than traditional.

The first dance doesn't have to be performed to a gentle love song. The perfect song comes from any genre, suits the wedding couple's personalities, and highlights their dance skills. No wedding couple wants to feel embarrassed while lurching through a dizzying waltz if their feet are better suited to a different beat.

A surprise first dance is always a big hit. If you both have rhythm to spare, consider a professionally choreographed dance routine that will make guests' eyes pop with amazement.

The important thing is to memorialize that first dance by dancing to the beat of your own drum, whatever musical stylings that drum may produce.

#848 *Photo-Booth Paparazzi*

The glare of the flash, funny faces, and impromptu poses are the makings of a great photo spread. But you don't need the paparazzi on hand to capture those priceless moments. You just need a photo booth.

Photo-booth rentals for the wedding reception are not only great entertainment for guests, but they quickly produce tangible keepsakes. Most booths provide instant photos for guests and a master copy of all photos for the bride and groom. Some booths have external video screens that allow live feeds of the shenanigans inside to tickle the funny bones of guests on the outside, and some photo-booth companies offer a limited-time, after-wedding Web site address where the photos are posted for all guests to enjoy. To ensure receiving all the features and services you want, exert due diligence in selecting a photo-booth rental company.

Photo booths break the ice, create excitement, and allow the bride and groom to see reception images they would likely otherwise miss. And don't forget to provide a few props if you really want to encourage the photo-booth antics!

#849 *The Great Centerpiece Capture*

Reception centerpieces are almost always a point of contention. Lots of friends and family members want to take one home, but there are never enough to go around. A fun way to resolve after-wedding centerpiece ownership is to turn the "who gets it" into a game.

Any audience-pleasing game will do. Choose a contest as potentially hilarious as a hoola-hooping marathon on the dance floor (with the centerpiece going to the contestant with the longest spinning hoop), or one as demure as guessing the number of wedding-themed items in a giant jar.

Create a new game for each centerpiece, or simply repeat a chosen game until all centerpieces are won. It's fair. It's fun. And no one experiences hurt feelings when you don't choose him or her as a centerpiece recipient.

#850 *Quilting for Memories*

Wedding events are routinely captured in photographs and on video, but as the excitement of the wedding day settles into the deep recesses of the memory, photo albums and videos are viewed less and less often. For a wedding keepsake that provides comfort and everyday sweet memories, consider the wedding quilt.

Insert a handwritten request into the wedding invitation, asking each guest to arrive at the reception with a small, eight-inch-square piece of fabric in any color, pattern, or material style. Place a "Quilt Square" basket near the guest-book table to collect the swatches.

Purchase a bed-sized piece of sturdy, colorfast cotton fabric in white or a pastel, and cut it into eight-inch squares. Fill vases or glass bowls with plenty of permanent fabric pens, and place them next to a basket containing the blank squares. Add a framed tabletop sign that invites guests to use a pen and a blank square to write whatever funny or heartfelt message they wish. The sign should also instruct guests to put the finished pieces in the "Quilt Square" basket.

After the wedding, fashion the written squares into a quilt, and use the colored, patterned swatches donated by the guests to create borders, wedding-ring patterns, and accents. The result is a tangible, beautiful, and perpetually useful display of priceless words and emotions that need never fade into storage. If you aren't a quilter or don't have a quilter in the family, consider a "quilter for hire," found online or via craft and sewing centers. Whether or not you fashion it with your own two hands, the quilt will be just as memorable.

#851 *The Circle of Love*

The cake-cutting ceremony is often the first official act that newlyweds jointly share, and it symbolically represents unity. The bride and groom share the task of cutting the first slice by each placing a hand on the knife, or by one person controlling the knife while the other rests his or her hand atop the hand doing the work. It's a beautiful moment. But brides and grooms who wish to give the cake-cutting ceremony even greater emotional depth can invite family and friends to help.

The bride and groom stand side by side behind the cake, making sure that the bride stands to the groom's right. They jointly hold the knife, with the groom using his right hand and the bride using her left. That position leaves the outer hands of both free to clasp the hand of someone dear to his or her heart. The circle of hand-holding continues with family, wedding attendants, and special friends, until the line extends from behind the table and around the sides, where all wedding guests join in. In this way, every last person in the circle is part of the cutting of that first slice of cake. It's an incredible moment of bonding for everyone involved, especially when underscored by the perfect music.

After the first slice is cut, family and guests return to their seats, and when ready, the bride and groom feed each other those first precious bites.

Note: Make sure your videographer is inside the circle, and allow him enough time to pan across everyone in the room holding hands before the cake is cut. It is a scene definitely worth watching again.

#852 *The Milestone-Anniversary Dance*

It's always wonderful to embrace the commitment and longevity of marriage, and a "Milestone-Anniversary Dance" at the reception is a clever way to involve the guests in the celebration.

Invite only married couples to the dance floor for a gentle, slow dance. At about the 30-second mark, announce that the floor is now open only to those couples married more than one year. Continue making announcements every half minute or so by adding years, months, and days as necessary, until only one couple remains. Eventually, the longest-married couple will be dancing alone. At the dance's conclusion, award the couple a special prize for being the ones to set the bar for your new married life, and have the photographer capture a photo of you and your new spouse with the longest-married couple. Later, frame a copy of the photograph for the couple and send it along with your thank-you note.

Watching the eliminations of the Milestone-Anniversary Dance is fun, even for those who don't get to dance too long, or for singles not qualified to join in.

#853 *Begone, Little Black Book!*

Plenty of modern wedding couples aren't wild about the traditional garter toss. For some, having the groom root around under the bride's skirt, then fling a frilly garter to a fairly uninterested group of guys, has lost its zing. But add a little humorous surprise to that garter, and everyone will take notice.

One of the best garter tosses involves the groom's "little black book." Symbolically launching a groom's romantic past into the air can do wonders for a new bride, and the guys on the receiving end battle far more ferociously to claim the prize. It's spirited entertainment.

But it doesn't have to be an authentic little black book. In fact, in this day and age, handing out real names and telephone numbers is considered taboo. Instead, use a little black book that's really a notepad, and fill it with "Tips for Getting the Girl!" as authored by the groom. Make the tips heartfelt and genuine, or funny and outrageous. The guests won't know it's not a real little black book attached to the garter, and that's what makes it so deliciously fun.

The garter toss doesn't have to get "tossed" for lack of interest. Just spice it up and give it new purpose.

#854 *The Watering-Hole Effect*

Even though your reception is stocked with tables and chairs for all guests, consider also including tall cocktail tables without seats. Decorate these elevated tables to coordinate with dining tables, but situate them in designated areas near the bar, on the edges of the dance floor, and in interesting clusters around the perimeter of the room.

People enjoy mingling, and a cocktail table gives those not seated a place to lean and chat. They're also great for holding drinks during dances. And if beautifully decorated, they add plenty of aesthetic appeal to the décor. Their height alone adds artistic flavor.

Like an oasis in the desert, cocktail tables provide relief and rejuvenation to those who happen upon them. And they look great in the bargain.

#855 *Favor Fanfare*

Whether the wedding favors are simple or spectacular, make them even more guest pleasing with a great presentation. Most favors are simply added to each guest's table setting, but a unique display of favors really adds to the reception's atmosphere.

Pile keychain favors into a wedding-decorated pedal car, and use the car as the focal point of the buffet table. Giving sun-catcher favors? Hang them from ornamental table trees, and kill two birds with one stone by turning the favors into centerpieces. This works for any hanging favor, like bells, lanterns, miniature birdhouses, cookie cutters, or even organza bags of treats.

Or consider distributing the favors by "special delivery." At a theme wedding, arrange for someone to appear in an appropriate costume to personally deliver the favors to guests at their tables. Having a Western theme indoors? Use a cowboy. For an outdoor Western reception, use a pony and rider. Pirate theme? Blackbeard toting a treasure chest of favors is a sight no one is likely to forget.

Presentation adds value and the element of surprise, making even the least expensive favors more appealing.

#856 *First-Dance Magic*

When choosing the style of your first dance as husband and wife, choose a dance so intense that you lose sight of anyone but each other.

Swaying in each other's arms qualifies as a first dance, but a truly unforgettable first dance should leave you and your guests breathless. A waltz is elegant and full of romantic spirit. A tango is fiery, bold, and intimate. A country reel is playful but mesmerizing. Whatever the dance style, practice makes magic.

Consider your attire. A full-skirted gown is ideal for a waltz, but it could derail a tango.

Consider your personalities. If you're not comfortable doing the dance, no one will be comfortable watching it.

And finally, consider the guests. A hot and sensual rumba may make you feel like the sexiest people on the planet, but it may make little Johnny and Great-Grandma flee the room.

When it comes to the first dance, total immersion is golden — just don't forget that you have an audience.

#857 *Silly Silhouettes*

For a fun and whimsical reception game, take photos of the bride and groom engaged in various "action" poses, then use a photo software program to turn those photos into silhouettes. Make a game of the silhouettes by printing two copies of every pose. Frame one copy from each silhouette pair, and place those framed copies in various locations around the reception hall. Add the words "What Are We Doing?" to the bottom of each frame. Mount the other copy onto white poster board. On the back of each board, place a large copy (or photocopy) of the original picture from which that particular silhouette was made. As guests mingle and enjoy the reception, they'll amuse themselves by forming lively opinions of what the bride and groom are up to.

Later, have the maid of honor and best man — or any quick-witted, silver-tongued pair — play game-show hosts by displaying the first poster-board-mounted silhouette and asking guests to reveal their theories about what is going on in the image. The first person to guess correctly wins a token prize, and the silhouette is flipped over to reveal the actual photograph. Repeat until all silhouettes have been displayed and all prizes awarded. Be prepared for some pretty out-there commentary! But then, the more off base the guesses, the more they're bound to tickle the masses.

#858 *The Blessing Tree*

Begin by drawing a tall, leafless tree on a life-sized poster board or on a folding screen. Make the tree wide, with plenty of branches, large and small, stretching in all directions, and "carve" the words "Blessing Tree" into the trunk. Place your tree in a prominent location at the reception, and on a small bench near its base, provide pens and pads of "leaf" sticky notes. Die-cut sticky pads are available in many shapes, including oak, maple, and other tree leaves.

A small, elegant sign invites guests to write whatever blessing they wish on a leaf, then attach it to the tree. By their participation, guests actually have a hand in creating your décor as they make the tree bloom.

For a three-dimensional experience, use a real or artificial potted tree that stands alone, and instead of sticky notes, use paper leaves fitted with hanging string.

All blessings are wonderful, but those immortalized by hand will endure far beyond the wedding day.

#859 *Get Ready to Rumba!*

In the world of sports, before boxers in the ring throw the first punch, the round is announced by beautiful, scantily clad women holding "round identifying" signs for all to see. Why? The round could just as easily be announced via the public address system. The reason is excitement. The around-the-ring parade gets the crowd going. So why not do the same for your wedding guests? Just tweak things a bit to add wedding flair.

Understandably, enlisting women in bikinis is not the answer, but how about the ever-adorable flower girl and ring bearer? Or you could give the job of parading the signs across the floor to other children who wish to participate in the wedding. This works especially well if the wedding theme allows children to dress in fun costumes.

Signs could indicate any imminent event, from the bride and groom's entrance to the cake cutting to specific dances, such as the first dance, the father-daughter dance, and guest-participation dances, like a line dance or a limbo. Use the signs to announce that the buffet is now open or that it's time for the garter and bouquet tosses. Any reception activity is fair game.

For a funnier take on the activity-announcing process, use a robot or a wedding-decorated remote-controlled car. Affix a tall, waving pennant, which can be changed as needed, and steer the device in a circle around the dance floor before each event.

Clever announcements serve a valid purpose by directing guests' attention to events they won't want to miss.

#860 *Late-Night Karaoke Kicks!*

Almost everyone has a secret singer inside just waiting to take the stage by storm. Singing lifts the spirits and soothes the soul. Wait until it's getting late — that's the ideal time for everyone at your reception to let loose.

Karaoke is just as much fun for those who listen as it is for those who sing, and you'll never have to worry about entertainment value. Wedding-party participants and guests *are* the entertainment.

Think of karaoke as your reception after-party. Just because the band or DJ has come and gone doesn't mean the revelry must end. A personal karaoke machine can substitute for its bigger, more state-of-the-art professional cousin, for no matter the size or quality of the machine, the performances will be just as melodically delicious.

#861 *Fortune-Cookie Fandango!*

Custom fortune cookies are playful and yummy, and funny fortunes, bride-and-groom trivia, or heartfelt wishes can pop from those sweet cookies. But to create a fortune cookie with a thrill, use your custom cookies to set the stage for a "Fortune-Cookie Fandango."

Choose humorous or serious messages for all cookies except two. In those two special cookies, have your cookie supplier print the word "Fandango!" on the strip of paper. Following the traditional dances, pass out the cookies. When the cookies are cracked, two people will discover the "Fandango!" message and become the first guests honored with a dance with the bride and groom.

A fandango is a lively Spanish courtship dance, made even more exciting by the use of castanets. Have some on hand to highlight the talents of your new partners, for whether they prove to be rhythmically gifted or decidedly uncoordinated, they'll be a treat to watch.

Of course, any style of dance will do. But choosing something spirited ratchets up the fun for guests. Not many people actually know how to fandango, but that makes it all the merrier. Of course, you'll have the inside track, so go ahead and practice before the big day. Your fandango expertise will dazzle the crowd.

#862 *The Funny-Face Forum*

Whether ornate, whimsical, or simply modern, picture frames at your reception stir up good old-fashioned fun.

Tour garage sales or visit thrift stores to find large frames in a variety of shapes. Remove the backs, the glass, and whatever artwork or photographs the frames held. The goal: an eclectic collection of frames, each large enough to encompass two heads but light enough for one person to hold.

Set up a small area against a wall, defined by a U-shaped border of tall potted plants or folding screens, and stack your frames along the wall. Using blank business cards, write a funny scenario on each one, like "you just saw a leprechaun," "you lost your keys," or "Elvis just kissed you." Write as many different scenarios as you wish (the more the better, but duplicating ideas is also fine), and put all of the cards in a fishbowl.

Invite guests to visit the funny-face forum to be photographed. Once there, guests pull a card from the fishbowl, choose a frame, and hold it before their faces as they enact the emotion inspired by the scenario on their card. To make it more outrageously fun, add a basket of suitable props.

Use a professional photographer, or ask a friend blessed with a nice digital camera and a good eye to do the honors. After the photo is taken, the guests write their names on the reverse of the card. The photographer takes the card and marks it with a number that corresponds with the photo number on the camera so that names and scenarios can later be matched to the proper photograph.

A funny-face forum keeps guests busy and entertained as a hilarious photo collection is created. Put the photos on your wedding Web site, or make a CD of them to include with thank-you cards. Everyone will want a copy.

#863 *Ring Around the Tree*

Whether it's July, September, or March, you can bring a Christmas tree to the party.

Begin by covering a round table (42-inch diameter or larger) with a smooth, white cotton tablecloth. Add a white, silver, or gold tabletop tree in the center, and hang bride-and-groom photos in small, ornament-sized frames as decorations. Tie them to the tree with delicate ribbons. Place glass bowls filled with permanent fabric markers in whatever colors you prefer under the tree, and erect a small, artistic sign that reads:

"This tablecloth is destined to be our Christmas-tree skirt. Please celebrate the holidays with us for the rest our lives by adding your message to our cloth."

After the reception, cut the tablecloth to tree-skirt size, create a slit for tree-trunk access, and hem raw edges with a wide, colorful, holiday-themed trim fabric. It's a perfect marriage of wedding memories and holiday spirit.

#864 *Conga!*

Conga lines aren't just fun, they're irresistible dances that banish shyness. Guests with a touch of "shrinking violet syndrome" come out of their shells when the bride and groom conga past, reach out a hand, and personally draw them into the merriment.

Begin with two lines. The bride and several wedding-party attendants lead one, and the groom and the rest of the attendants lead the other. Snake both lines around the room until all able guests have been invited to join in, then merge the two dancing snakes into one super conga line that rocks the reception hall.

A conga is designed to include everyone, and as an all-encompassing entertainment, it works every time.

#865 *Conversations Galore*

Conversation cards have grown in popularity because they work. Packs of interesting, thought-provoking questions get people talking.

Purchase wedding-specific, ready-made card sets, or choose those that address a variety of topics, like music, sports, history, or imagination. Sets range in size from a few dozen to hundreds of cards. You can break up the sets and tuck a single card into the napkin of each place setting; use a clear, double-sided frame to mount questions back-to-back for tabletop display; or simply scatter several cards amidst confetti on each tabletop.

To make the discussions specific to you and your wedding, write your own questions on small squares of decorative card stock.

Conversation cards cover a wide range of subjects, but it will be best to stick to those areas that inspire fun or tease curiosity. Save talk about religion and politics for another time.

#866 *Follow the Script*

Every event, especially a wedding reception, benefits from a behind-the-scenes script. A mental vision of reception entertainments is not enough. You need a concrete plan.

Begin with a list of all potential activities. Include everything from the reception's opening moments to the final cleanup, then arrange each activity on the list into a time frame. Doing so helps you to understand what will and won't work. Once you see the schedule, you may realize that there just isn't time for 12 differently themed dances. What seemed like a good idea in theory may not be viable in reality.

To keep things lively and moving along, your wedding coordinator, host or hostess, and DJ or emcee should all have copies of the reception script.

A schedule is never written in stone, and you don't have to abandon an entertaining activity just because "its time is up." Think of your script as a willow, not an oak, and let it bend and sway, as long as it always returns to its original position at certain points in time.

Instead of the curse of chaos, give your reception the gift of a wildly enjoyable, completely doable script.

#867 *Tabletop Scavenger Hunt*

Remember that giddy, victorious feeling when you scored at Go Fish? How about when you watched *Let's Make a Deal* on TV and realized that everyone in the audience just couldn't stop grinning? That's the power of gaming fun, and for all ages, the thrill of discovery games is as alive as ever. Bring that contagious energy to your reception.

Provide your emcee or DJ with a list of at least a couple of dozen items. Make some of them easy, like pink shoes, a mustache, a silver belt buckle, four quarters, etc., and some outrageous, like belly-button lint or "a woman wearing a man's watch."

Each table of guests is a team, and as the emcee calls out each item, it's up to the table to produce it. A "game-show assistant" verifies that a table has the called item, and if so, places a marker, like a poker chip, a marble, or other token, on the table. After all items are called, the table with the most markers wins a special, exclusive hors d'oeuvres platter or a big box of sinful chocolates to share. Use a backup list of items to break any ties.

Keep it lively. Only allow 10 or 15 seconds to produce an item. Added pressure produces added laughs.

#868 *Crystal Ball*

You're getting married, so while you're at it, why not plan some entertainment for, say, your tenth anniversary? Let your wedding guests look into their mind's eye and predict what your life will be like in 10 (or 20, or 50) years.

Set up a small table with a beautiful crystal-ball centerpiece. Add several notepads and pens and a sealed box with a slot in the top. Via a tabletop sign, invite guests to gaze into the crystal ball and "see" your future, then jot down their vision on a sheet of paper, sign it, and slip it into the box slot.

When the reception is over, seal the slot closed and tuck the box into the far reaches of a closet. Don't be tempted to peek! You don't want to find out early that you will be rich beyond your wildest dreams, or that your baby will grow up to be the commander of an intergalactic space station. Knowing too much too soon would simply spoil all the fun for that special anniversary down the road.

#869 *Jigsaw Puzzler*

Before the wedding, take an awesome photo of the bride and groom, and turn it into a jigsaw puzzle with more pieces than there are guests. Plenty of online sources turn photos into puzzles.

Use a marker pen to print a different number on the back of each piece, then create a small tag that reads:

You are Number [write whatever the number is here]!
Find the puzzle board and place your piece where it belongs.
Hold on to your tag. You'll need it later!

Place each puzzle piece and its corresponding tag into a small, ziplock plastic bag. Or inexpensive little bags used for jewelry findings can be bought in bulk at most craft stores.

Don't give guests border puzzle pieces, only internal ones. Use the border pieces to create the puzzle's framework, and place it on a designated table at the reception. At the back of the table, prop a framed photo showing the actual puzzle picture.

Attach the individually bagged pieces to your escort cards so that every guest receives one, or place a basket at the reception entrance with instructions to "Take One."

The puzzle is a great way for guests to pass the time as they await the bride and groom's grand entrance. It's also a terrific icebreaker, because guests must rely on each other to complete the puzzle.

Later, when the puzzle is finished and the meal, cake cutting, and primary dances are over, the bride and groom randomly select puzzle pieces to remove from the puzzle. The guest holding a tag with the same number as the removed puzzle piece wins a prize. Anything quirky, like a giant candy bar wrapped in a paper version of the bride-and-groom puzzle photo, or the photo printed onto a calendar or mouse pad, is a fitting prize.

Jigsaw some fun into your reception, but remember to record it. Since your professional photographer will be occupied with you while the puzzle is being assembled, don't forget to assign someone else to snap pictures or take video clips of the masterpiece being brought to life. All of that combined brainpower deserves to be preserved for posterity, and you definitely don't want to miss it.

#870 *Artful Memories*

Wedding photos are beautiful. Video is timeless. But there is nothing like an artist's rendering to capture one extraordinary moment in time. For a wedding-reception treat, hire a painter or a sketch artist. Think of the artist in a courtroom who immortalizes the expressions on participants' faces, or the painter who captures the hustle and bustle of a town square with just the stroke of a brush.

Decide on the medium you prefer, such as charcoal, watercolor, etc., then enlist the services of a professional, freelance "artist for hire," or check with local art schools and university art programs to find someone whose work you appreciate. Designate a prime, perhaps elevated, location for the artist to erect his or her easel and palette, and give no instructions other than to create as many works of art during the reception as is feasible.

Watching the artist turn a canvas or drawing paper into reception vignettes entertains guests and provides you with unparalleled, one-of-a-kind keepsake art. Reduce, then reproduce, one of the art pieces to create your thank-you cards, and frame a favorite selection as a special gift for parents.

Pictures are indeed worth a thousand words, but unique art with a human touch is priceless.

#871 *Extra! Extra!*

Your wedding is big news. So share it! Create several feature stories about your lives, engagement, wedding sentiments, and honeymoon plans. Add headlines, photos, and even a few clever advertisements and cartoons, then print your very own wedding-day newspaper. Have fun with it. Advertisements or classifieds could be all about selling used "singles'" supplies, like the groom's well-worn little black book, the bride's leftover portion of a dating-service contract, or a dog-eared copy of a pickup-line book. Use traditional newsprint paper, and make your hot-off-the-presses edition as many pages as you wish.

For table impact, choose a black-and-white color scheme for linens and dinnerware. Fold or roll your newspaper, finish it off with a red ribbon, and place one on each table setting. For your centerpiece, use a single red-and-white striped popcorn box (easily purchased in bulk, with or without the word "popcorn"). Slip a plastic cup into the box to support a black-and-white floral arrangement. Your tables will pop with the splash of red provided by the popcorn boxes and the ribbon on the newspaper, but that will be nothing compared to the pop of delight your guests will experience as they read your special-edition *Wedding-Day Times*.

#872 *Wedding-Guest Balloon Float*

Balloons with shimmering ribbon tails make impressive décor when snuggled up to the ceiling, a bit like bringing dozens of puffy, gentle "cloud nines" inside. Begin by floating a few balloons, then let your guests do the rest. Loosely tie the ribbon tail of a helium-filled balloon to each place setting, attaching it to either the wedding favor, napkin ring, or dinner knife, whichever is heavy enough to anchor the balloon. Use each balloon as a place card by attaching a tag with the guest's name at the juncture where the ribbon meets the balloon. Once guests have found their seats, they will release the balloon to the open space above their tables. Soon your reception will be filled with floating balloons and dangling ribbons, and your ceiling will look fabulous. For an even sweeter touch, choose balloons with sparkling designs that will catch the light and give your "clouds" a fairy-tale shimmer.

#873 *Pop Goes the Cork!*

If the champagne will flow freely at your wedding reception, turn it into a game for your guests. Every time there's a need to open a new bottle, decide who will do the honors by drawing a guest's name from a hat. The goal of the game is to pop the cork in such a way that it lands on a designated bull's-eye. Use butcher paper or a large poster board to create a target, featuring a funny bride-and-groom photo as the bull's-eye, for the floor. Place the target in one corner, away from tables and the dance floor. Several feet away, arrange potted plants in a horseshoe formation, where the contestant will stand to vie for cork-popping bragging rights. Those who hit the bride-and-groom bull's-eye win a prize.

For safety's sake, always be sure the bottle is pointing toward the target, where no people are allowed. For the contestants' sake, provide a pair of decorated goggles and a full plastic apron to protect their clothes in the event of a bubbly splash. The goofy gear will only add to the humor of the contest. It doesn't matter if a guest has never before opened a champagne bottle. In the spirit of good fun, all participants are allowed to have a coach, or an army of coaches, to egg them on.

#874 *Too-Cute Doggie Bags*

What do animal lovers do when they dine out? They think of the furry, four-legged "babies" they left at home and wonder what delectable morsel they should bring back in a doggie bag. If you're an animal lover, why not remember the critters who gave up time with their humans so that those humans could help you celebrate your important event?

Behind the wedding favor at each place setting, add a fancy little doggie bag for those left behind. In a small, ziplock plastic bag, place a smattering of natural kibble or a dry dog treat for the canines, and in another plastic bag, place some catnip or a dry cat treat for the kitties. Insert the sealed bags into an opaque, decorative bag. Add a tag that reads:

"Love is for sharing. This wedding doggie bag is for the precious animals you left behind so that you could be with us on our important day."

There's no great cost involved, but this extra little effort will spawn plenty of surprised smiles. Brides and grooms who think of their pets as members of their family understand others who feel the same way.

#875 *Hot Shots*

When the JumboTron at a sporting event flashes audience shots, all eyes are upon it. Everyone loves watching the crowd, and wedding guests are no exception. For easy entertainment, set up your own live feeds with strategically placed video cameras that stream images in real time. Use one large screen or several smaller ones to display reception activity. You will, of course, want cameras poised to capture any ceremonial events, but you will also want shots of the tables, the bar, and especially the dance floor.

Rent the live-feed equipment, or simply use large monitors and the miniature cameras of a security system. The purchase of a security-camera package is a valid reception investment. Later, you can install the system at home and enjoy the comfort and safety of a securely monitored environment for your new married life.

A live-feed system does not replace a videographer who concentrates on capturing specific, key moments that you will want to cherish forever. While some live feeds can indeed be recorded as they are airing, their real purpose at the reception is simply to provide real-time, fun-to-watch entertainment.

#876 *The Great Wedding-Guest Band*

Music is a universal language, and even tone-deaf people harbor dreams of creating melodious tunes. So why not turn every guest into a member of the band? Dig up some old instrument cases — a guitar case here, a trombone case there — and fill them with kazoos, maracas, finger cymbals, jaw harps, mini tambourines, tiny tom-tom drums, bells, claves, triangles, and even bottles for blowing. Any small instruments will do.

Add a sign that reads: "Come on. You know you want to! Join the band!" If you simply want the guests to bust loose and have fun, no further explanation will be necessary, but if you wish to keep clinker notes and questionable rhythm from interrupting your first dance or other special moments, designate only certain songs to be performed by "The Great Wedding-Guest Band." Involve your emcee or real bandleader so that he or she can make an announcement when it's time for guests to join in.

#877 *Celebrities in the House!*

Did you know that some celebrities would attend your wedding for an appearance fee? That's always an option, if you can afford it. But if your budget doesn't quite cover that hefty expense, do the next best thing — hire a celebrity impersonator. Don't hire one to walk in and entertain right off the bat. Just hire him or her to be a guest, and like every other guest, let your "celebrity" bring a date. Don't make any grand announcement. Just greet that Whoopi Goldberg, Johnny Depp, or Paris Hilton look-alike with a hug and a kiss, and let the speculation begin. Save any "celebrity performance" until later in the reception.

Guests will have a blast trying to figure out how you know that person. Expect plenty of rubbernecking and sideways glances! To give the scheme maximum impact, use only current celebrities from film, TV, music, politics, or sports, and make sure you've seen the impersonator in his or her full look-alike regalia before signing a contract. You don't want an impersonator that only marginally looks like a celebrity. You want a dead ringer! The more spot-on the look and the mannerisms, the more fun your guests will have. And to really seal the deal, make sure that your celebrity arrives fashionably late, to catch guests completely by surprise.

#878 *Voilà! The Cake!*

The wedding cake is always settled onto a beautifully appointed table for all the guests to see before the cake-cutting ceremony. So be different. Keep your cake under wraps. Have it placed on the table as usual, then position an exquisite, opaque, silk-paneled folding screen around it. The screen panels can be hand painted with your wedding-theme colors and motif or display silk-screened photos of the bride and groom.

At an appointed time before the cake-cutting ceremony, create a big "Voilà!" moment by having the cake reveal announced by the reception host or bandleader. Then, with a drumroll or a crescendo of music, the maid of honor and the best man ceremoniously remove the screen to reveal the cake, giving guests plenty of time to make their way over for a close-up look before it's time for the cutting.

A similar grand entrance is made when the cake is wheeled into the reception on a rolling cart or is carried in by the baker, but everyone has seen enough funny home videos to know that a stub of the toe or a bump under a wheel can be more than enough to send that beautiful cake into never-never land. The screen reveal provides the same "wow" factor, without any of the "will it or won't it make it" worry.

#879 *Glowing with Love*

If you're having a nighttime reception and you want to depart with a "glowing" send-off from friends and family, custom glow sticks do the trick. Just before it's time to go, have wedding-party members steer guests into two lines facing each other. Once in position, the attendants will pass out personalized glow sticks bearing the bride and groom's names, a message of love, or whatever symbol or icon you choose to emblaze on them. A simple snap activates the neon lights, and soon all guests will be holding their glow sticks high in the air as you make your way out of the facility and off to your wedding night.

It's bright. It's colorful. It's the perfect tribute. And as a bonus, there's no cleanup of rice, confetti, birdseed, or other traditionally tossed "goodbye and good luck" paraphernalia.

#880 *Cheering the Newlyweds*

Many venues no longer allow tossing anything at the bride and groom when they leave the ceremony or the reception, so turn your guests into cheerleaders instead. Pom-poms create visual impact and encourage a playful spirit. Order inexpensive, promotional pom-poms in bulk, or make them yourself, using paper strips and colored fabric tape for the grip. Any soft paper will do. Try wrapping paper, tissue paper, newsprint, or even lightweight printer paper. Just fold the long strips in the center, gather a bunch together, and bind with the tape. Presto! You've created a pom-pom. Make them as thin or as fat as you wish. As long as they shake freely in the hand of an excited guest, they're perfect!

#881 *Comfort Permission*

Etiquette dictates that a gentleman does not remove his jacket in the presence of ladies. At a wedding, it's especially rude to do so if the groom and the groomsmen have not first removed theirs. But if it's stiflingly hot and the dance floor is jumping, or the reception is outdoors in the heat and humidity, it's a given that the men are suffering.

Take pity, and give them permission to remove their jackets. Just have the DJ, bandleader, or reception host make a simple announcement on your behalf, such as: "Gentlemen, the bride and groom want you to enjoy their wedding to its fullest. If you wish, please feel free to make yourselves more comfortable by removing your jackets." The choice to do so will then be up to each individual guy (and perhaps his wife). It's a little gift to your male guests, but it's a generous and appreciated one.

#882 *Shared Surprises*

There's no denying that the wedding day is all about the bride and the groom. But it's this very fact that makes surprises for guests all the more precious. At the reception, set aside some moments to thoughtfully recognize others. For example, did your soldier brother miss his and his wife's anniversary because he was away on a tour of duty? Surprise both with a dance in their honor at your wedding. Take a moment to publicly thank and pay tribute to both sets of parents with a special keepsake of the day, or ask your cousin with the beautiful voice to join the band for a song. It is your day, so why not enrich the experience and fill it to the brim with the joy of giving, as well as the joy of receiving?

#883 *Subtle Instigation*

Instead of an organized wedding-trivia game at the reception, consider a more spontaneous and informal approach. Print your cocktail napkins with trivia questions about the bride and groom, and let your guests start their own conversations and develop their own theories. Make the questions fairly obscure, without readily apparent answers. If you make the questions too easy, the interactions will wane quickly, but tougher questions will prompt your guests to dig in and try to figure out the answer by asking questions of other guests. If you are directly approached for an answer, just smile coyly and say, "All in good time." Let the guests stew and wonder for as long as you like, then later have them share their guesses with the crowd, or simply put everyone out of their misery and spill the beans. This entertainment won't be organized, like a typical trivia game, but guests will still get to enjoy plenty of shared speculation.

#884 *Rejuvenate!*

Everyone is dressed up. Ladies are in heels. Men are wearing stiff, formal shoes. There's an abundance of dancing and standing. That's the nature of a wedding reception. So it's understandable that guests get tired and start to think about going home and getting off their feet. If you want to tempt your guests into staying longer and encourage a happier, more comfortable frame of mind, treat their feet!

Pick a corner of your reception venue, and make it semiprivate by using decorative fencing, tall potted plants, or folding screens. Inside the area, provide a few comfy chairs and an equal number of electric foot massagers to go with them. Most home massagers, whether vibrating or shiatsu, are reasonably priced, and they provide just enough of a tootsie workout that in only a few moments stress is relieved, energy is increased, and the guest gets a second wind. Purchase the massagers, or poll your friends and family to see if units can be borrowed. Foot massagers are a thoughtful amenity that keeps on giving as the celebration carries on, and on, and on.

#885 *And the Weddy Goes to . . .*

Awards for everything from traveling the farthest to the wedding to being married the longest to being born the same year and month as the bride or groom, etc., provide interactive reception fun. To make the activity even more entertaining, create your own personalized "Weddy" awards. As with any major award show, there will be presenters, music, an enraptured audience, appropriate trophies, and acceptance speeches.

If you dig through your guest list, you will be able to conjure up awards for just about anything. Someone has the same pet as the bride and groom? Award worthy! Someone introduced them? Definitely award worthy! The award categories are endless. Spike the level of enjoyment by sprinkling off-the-wall categories among the real ones. For example, bestow the Lifetime Achievement Award for Flirting upon your grandma or grandpa.

The trophies can be beautiful or funny. Simply begin with any common item, then personalize it to make it pertain to your wedding. Include your band or DJ in the ceremony so that music can be played as the winner approaches to accept the award, and also, of course, to cut off the acceptance speech, just like all those televised award shows routinely do. Pick a host who's quick on his or her feet, and every guest will hope to be a "Weddy" winner.

#886 *Improvise!*

Have you ever wandered into a comedy club, fair, or theater and stumbled upon an improv group that kept you so thoroughly entertained that you hated to see their performance end? Those talented groups are everywhere, just waiting to be hired for your reception. If you haven't personally seen such a group, check out the agencies that represent wedding-related talent. Many of them list improv groups on their roster, and an improv group with a history of performing at weddings already knows how to make it all about the bride, the groom, and the guests. Most have videos available as audition pieces, or you may be invited to see them in person.

Hiring an improv group means that the entertainment will be spontaneous, but you set the tone. The group will keep their material as G-rated as you wish, as long as you convey your guidelines in advance. If it's in the budget to enlist entertainment beyond your dance band or your DJ, consider making it a funny-bone hire. Guests will be delightfully surprised.

#887 *Walk the Walk*

Wedding walks used to be a common and charming practice. It isn't done much anymore. But why not? If your ceremony and reception venues are just a short distance from each other, you could easily choose a central parking area between the two facilities and direct guests to park there before walking the short distance to the ceremony. After the ceremony, lead your guests en masse to the reception in a wedding walk. This procession was once a wedding-day highlight, as the wedding couple and their entourage made their way to their reception amidst a chorus of honking horns and shouts of congratulations from passersby.

After the reception, guests will have an equally short walk back to their vehicles. You'll save the cost of limo service between the ceremony and the reception, and create a happy memory in the process. If guests don't wish to participate in the wedding walk, they don't have to. There will be plenty of others who will follow you to the ends of the Earth — or to the reception, whichever comes first.

#888 *Wedding's Got Talent*

As an entertaining surprise for wedding guests, hold your very own reality-show-style talent competition. You can have a spur-of-the-moment, casual event, with contestants from within your circle of family and friends. Or you can raise the stakes and hold a bona fide talent contest.

Advertise in the local paper, and audition contestants in the weeks and months before the wedding. Choose ten acts to compete at the "[bride's and groom's names here] Wedding Finals" at your wedding reception, with your guests acting as judges and crowning the winner. Make it known that you will be awarding a prize, and invite the local press to cover the event if you wish.

It will be entertaining for everyone, especially you, since the competition will give you time to breathe. Wedding couples list "no time to relax and enjoy" as one of their biggest reception regrets. Taking the focus off of you for the half hour or so of the competition will be a gift, and everyone will enjoy it. Unless you have no eye for talent and you pick ten truly horrible finalists, the talk-about-it-forever factor is all but guaranteed.

#889 *Well Wishes and Smiles*

If you plan to have a receiving line at the reception, give the line its own photographer, one who will stand behind you. The biggest mistake with photos of the receiving line is that guests' faces are routinely obscured as the photographer angles for a better shot of the bride or groom. But the priceless images you want to remember — the expressions on those guests' faces — can only be captured if the camera is facing them, not you.

You will have many wedding-day photos of yourselves. Photos of your guests as they greet you in the receiving line will increase in sentimental value as the years go by. Treat yourself by making your guests the stars of the show for that one ritual. Memorializing that solitary moment when they express their congratulations is a choice you'll not regret.

#890 *Pint-Sized Greetings*

Children rarely get to sign a wedding guest book, so why not let them "sign in" with a "greetings" book all their own? Use a plain paper scrapbook, and write "NAME:" followed by a straight line at the top of each page. Place the book on its own kid-sized table next to the guest-book table, but make it every bit as elegant as its full-sized counterpart. Add a bucket of crayons and colored pencils, and a special welcome sign that invites your young guests to write or draw whatever they wish on their very own page in their very own greetings book. You've invited children to the wedding, and this little effort shows them that they matter. When all is said and done, you'll no doubt have some pretty memorable pages from some pretty memorable kids.

#891 *Dance by Numbers*

Mix it up on the dance floor by generating random dance-couple pairings. Write a tiny, discreet number on each guest's place card, and use pieces of paper or small, blank price tags from an office-supply store to create a complete set of corresponding numbers. Place that set into a decorated fishbowl, and every so often, draw two numbers from the bowl. The guests with those numbers on their place cards will become a dance couple. Of course, you will get man/man and woman/woman couples, as well as man/woman and young/old couples, making the dance even more fun. Draw just two names at a time, or draw five or six sets of numbers to populate the dance floor with random pairings. And, of course, you will want the songs for these dances to be as eclectic as the couples who swing and sway to them!

#892 *Everybody's Cake Ceremony*

If your reception tables are round, a round floral centerpiece is a natural addition. But so is anything else that is round, like a cake. Instead of one enormous wedding cake, imagine a reception with as many cakes as there are tables. Small wedding cakes would replace traditional flower center-pieces in the center of each table, with the wedding couple's cake being the largest of the group.

Conduct the cake-cutting ceremony as usual, but instead of serving cake to guests at the ceremony's conclusion, invite everyone to simultaneously have their own cake cutting right at their tables. Choose small two-tier cakes or single cakes perched on short cake pedestals, and you eliminate cake-cutting fees, separate centerpieces, and the need for servers to distribute the wedding cake.

All small cakes can have décor similar to the newlyweds' cake, or each cake can sport its own unique design. Your centerpiece cakes don't have to be ultra fancy, just ultra enticing. And they'll achieve that effect just by sitting there and teasing guests with the promise of what's to come.

#893 *Plugging the Gap*

Sometimes, due to unusual circumstances or venue availability, there is a considerable delay between the ceremony and the reception. It may be a great opportunity for the wedding couple to pose for a vast array of photos, but that same lag time can be unpleasant for wedding guests with nowhere to go for an hour or more. Plug that gap with an adventure. Send your guests on a local treasure hunt.

As with any treasure hunt, prepare a long list of common and not-so-common items for guests to gather from the community. The items can be as simple as a smooth rock or as challenging as a 1954 penny. The list has to be long so that no one will have a chance of finding every object before the reception begins.

Whoever finds the most items is awarded a nice prize, like a restaurant gift card. Be sure to have guests sign in on a "Treasure Hunt" sheet at the reception entrance. In the event of a tie, this will enable you to grant the prize to the one who signed in first with the winning number of items in tow.

If you will have to inconvenience your guests with an overly long wait, you can either humbly ask their forgiveness or give them something to do that makes the time fly.

#894 *A Word or Two*

One of the biggest complaints of wedding guests is that the wedding couple didn't say, "Thank you for coming." If you don't have a receiving line, it's a courtesy for the bride and groom to chat with guests one-on-one. But even with the best intentions, someone may get overlooked.

To keep the inadvertent snubs to a minimum, have a plan. Make the rounds of your senior guests first. Older people may tire more quickly and leave early, completely missing the opportunity to speak with you. For everyone else, keep a guest list at the head table, and each time you return to your seat, give it a glance. Names will begin to pop out at you, reminding you that you haven't engaged with them. In your next foray away from the table, you will want to find those guests to share a word or two. There's no better touch than the personal one, and a private conversation, even a ten-second exchange, breathes a lot of good will into the festivities.

#895 *Class of "Our Wedding Day"*

Years after the last guest has left the reception, that guest and many others will begin to fade from memory, especially if the guest list was large. You will have your guest book and other mementos, and even images of guests in photographs and videos, but it's unlikely that every single attendee will have been photographed.

If you don't want to find yourself trying to recall your wedding guests down the road, ask your photographer to take a "yearbook" photo of the whole reception "class." It will be fun, and it will be worth it. The photographer will need to bring along a ladder and a wide-angle lens to fit you, the wedding party, and every last guest in a single shot. When you receive the photo, you will see that it was well worth the effort to capture that one moment in time, when all those people gathered to help you celebrate.

Give a ten-minute warning before the photo so that no one wanders off to the restroom or elsewhere. You won't want to miss anyone. It's history — your history. Preserve it forever.

#896 *Links of Love*

Long before tinsel, people adorned their Christmas trees with Victorian garlands, linking together paper loops to create a decorative chain. If you love the holidays, invite your wedding guests to help you make the best "forever" garland for your home, but with a bridal twist.

Instead of paper, cut ten- by two-inch lengths from white vinyl tablecloths (without flannel backing) picked up at discount stores or from fabric stores' sale racks. Be sure to have a strip for each guest, plus some to spare. Buy inexpensive, silver no-sew snaps in bulk bags, and affix the snaps to the tails of the strips so that the ends will create a circle when snapped together. For a fancier finish, use pearl-button snaps. Once the snaps are attached to each end, place the flat strips in an oversized basket with a handle, along with permanent markers in the holiday colors of your choice.

Attach a bow to the basket's handle, along with written instructions, such as:

We want to always remember this moment, and with your help, our holidays will be forever blessed with the joy of our wedding day. Please decorate or add any message you wish to one strip. Sign it, then using the snap, add your strip to the garland to create a link in our special chain of memories. When you are finished, pass the basket along to others. Thank you so very much! Each holiday, when this garland graces our home, we will think of you.

Be sure to start the chain with a few connected links as an example. Give the basket to one table of guests, and let it make its way throughout the reception at its own leisurely pace. In the end, your basket will hold a wonderful keepsake garland that is easily stored by unsnapping the links and tucking the flat strips into a box until the next holiday arrives.

#897 *Down, Down, and Away!*

Balloons and "up, up, and away" go together like peanut butter and jelly, but balloons can also come down with as much festive fanfare as those that drift ever skyward. A balloon drop at the wedding reception serves multiple decorative purposes. A large net (part of a balloon-drop kit) is loaded with air-filled balloons and hoisted upward, forming a whimsical ceiling of colorful "clouds." Then, at any big moment you choose (first dance, cake cutting, bouquet toss, etc.), the music soars and the balloons are released to float downward over you and your guests, like confetti on a parade. Once on the floor, the balloons transform the look of the reception and give it an exciting, vibrant feel. You may want to release them over the dance floor only, or in several locations around the hall. Balloons going down instead of up are a beautiful — and affordable — wedding-reception spectacle.

#898 *Wedding World Tour*

You're having a small wedding. Money is no object. You simply must have the most memorable reception ever. Any of these statements is a good reason to have a "satellite reception," which includes multiple venues.

After the ceremony, all guests are provided transportation (buses, vans, or cars, depending upon the size of the guest list). The destination? Only you know! You whisk your guests to a prearranged stop at a winery for your cocktail hour, then on to dinner at the restaurant or banquet hall of your choice. Next it's a twilight cake cutting at a scenic overlook, then finally you're off to a pavilion to dance the night away.

Utilizing different locations for each major reception component elevates the entertainment value of the wedding experience. Wedding receptions are usually quite predictable. The "keep them guessing" element engages your wedding guests in a way they won't forget.

Underscore the satellite theme by creating personalized paper "passports" for each guest, making the passport "photo" a funny-face icon and giving each guest a unique passport number. Upon arrival at each location, stamp the passports with a custom stamp that expresses something funny or loving about the wedding couple. At the end of the night, draw from a top hat filled with copies of all the passport numbers, and award a "Timeless Traveler" prize to the guest whose number is drawn.

If you're looking for "unforgettable," a satellite reception provides it in spades. It's not for everyone, since it does require extensive planning. But the rewards are fabulous. Just be sure to assign someone to monitor the shuttling of your guests back to their own vehicles, once they are ready to retire from their "wedding world tour."

#899 *Wicked Wine Tasting*

A wine tasting at the reception is a great treat for guests. But to make it even more entertaining, turn that tasting into a challenging game by using blindfolds.

The first part of wine tasting is looking at the wine to check its clarity and brilliance. Eliminating that option by blindfolding the tasters makes the tasting more formidable. When blindfolded, even experienced chefs can have their palates confused by foods they've worked with a million times. The same holds true for wine tasters who can't see what's being poured. Without the benefit of sight, even telling red from white can be difficult for some. So instead of assigning the traditional ratings for clarity, color, aroma, taste, and aftertaste, have blindfolded guests attempt to identify the wines by type, region, maker, and added flavors instead. And the wines don't all have to be fabulous. To increase the humorous aspect of the contest, go ahead and add some dreadful brews to the mix.

You can have everyone taste at once by passing out inexpensive blindfolds at the tables and then having servers administer the tastes, or you can set up a designated area with a wine host or hostess, and guests can wander over at will during the reception to make their taste attempts. Be sure to keep all bottles covered by bottle bags or paper sacks. No peeking for contestants awaiting their turn! Award a nice bottle of wine or a clever corkscrew to those who most accurately describe their wines, or draw contestants' names from a hat to select random winners.

#900 Love Is . . .

Give your wedding guests something to ponder and something to share by asking them to contribute to a perpetual poem for the bride and groom. Choose an art-paper roll in whatever color you wish, and securely attach one end of the rolled paper to a wall or to a hard-backed easel. Stock a nearby vase or basket with permanent markers with fine or medium tips. At the top of the paper, write something like:

On this 4th day of April in the year 2016, Michael and Sarah have pledged their love to each other. Help them always to remember the many incarnations of love by sharing your 'love is' thoughts in this perpetual poem. Your lines don't have to rhyme. They only have to remind.

Then begin the poem with an example, such as:

Love is the beauty of a sunset and the gentle rise of the moon. Love is …

Soon the continuous paper will begin to fill with your guests' own philosophies of what love is, and you'll get more than an extraordinarily personal wedding keepsake. You'll learn about ways to love life — and each other — that you may have never considered before.

#901 2,468!

Whatever your wedding theme, it's easy to create a quick challenge for guests. Fill a large water jug, a fishbowl, an aquarium, or any other see-through container with a whole lot of "somethings." Golf theme? Use golf tees. Vegas theme? Use dice. You get the picture. Stuff the container to the brim, then have guests estimate how many items are inside. The one closest to the correct amount without going over wins a themed prize.

Count the items as you fill the container, then write the correct answer on a slip of paper. Fold it and tape it to the bottom of the container. Instruct everyone to write their guess on the back of their place card, and when the time is right, everyone will look at their card as the slip of paper is removed from the bottom of the container and the correct amount is announced, determining a winner (or winners). The more items you place inside, the less likely it will be that you will have multiple winners. If you can't think of a small, commercially produced object that matches your theme, craft your own themed items by making and decorating little cookies or candies to stuff inside. Or go old-school and simply use a blend of uncooked black and white beans to represent the bride and groom. "Theme jugs" are quick and easy, yet they offer plenty of passive entertainment as guests speculate, evaluate, and calculate.

#902 *Perpetual Light*

Birthday cakes have candles to commemorate a joyful milestone and send wishes off to be granted. Candles are lit in memory of lost loved ones, or to wish healing or good fortune for someone in need. When someone lights a candle for you, it's a gesture of kindness and caring. What could be a better wedding-day tribute than to have every wedding guest light a candle of hope and promise for the bride and groom?

If your reception venue permits candles, set aside a secure area that is inaccessible to children and far from curtains or drapery. Cocktail-height tables are a good choice. Settle a candle lantern, inscribed with the bride's and groom's names, atop a greenery or floral base in the center of the table. Surround the lantern with votive candles in candle cups, and provide a vase of wooden lighting sticks. The sticks, candles, and cups are all relatively inexpensive and available in bulk. Add a small tabletop sign, perhaps printed on a beautiful china plate mounted on a plate stand, which invites guests to capture the flame from the lantern and use it to light a candle to the bride and groom's happiness. Be sure to have enough candles so that every guest will have one to light.

When all of the candles are lit, you will not only experience the love and well wishes of your guests, you will have a spectacular addition to the reception's décor. The flicker of the flames will seem never ending, just as you intend your marriage to be. Enjoy the vision, but be safe. Keep a fire extinguisher nearby, or use flameless candles that each guest merely has to switch on. Whether the flames are real or faux, the effect will be just as beautiful.

#903 *Get in Line!*

Line dancing is blessedly simple and always fun. Some find it hokey and think it should be stomped out of existence. Others couldn't care less that it may be hokey. If it's fun, it's fun, period.

Line dancing is the easiest way to get reluctant guests up and dancing. There's no pressure because everyone faces the same direction — no one is looking you in the eye — and everyone is in it together. You can choose old favorites like Boot Scootin' Boogie or the Electric Slide, and actually include that information as a wedding-invitation insert, allowing guests to learn the steps in advance if they wish.

There are scores of line-dancing songs and corresponding dance steps, covering every musical genre. But for an original twist, make up your own simple line dance. Choose a song with a good beat. Teach the dance to your wedding attendants before the wedding, and then you and your wedding party will teach it to your guests at the reception.

Don't let perceptions sway you. Line dancing is fun to do and fun to watch. If you want a dance that everyone of any age can do, just line 'em up.

#904 *That's Me!*

They're all the rage at beaches, amusement parks, fairs, and shopping villages from coast to coast. They can also be all the rage at your reception. They are caricature artists.

Caricatures are a blast, and guests don't even need to pose. Just hire an artist to work his or her magic from table to table, guest to guest. Provide a "gallery" area where finished pictures can be displayed during the reception. Everyone will get to enjoy them before guests take their personal sketches home as favors.

Before hiring an artist, check out his or her work. Have the artist sketch you and your groom and if the final result meets your approval, use that large picture as the focal point in the reception "gallery." Guests' pictures can be smaller if you wish. Also ask about the length of time needed to create a portrait. You need a quick, talented artist capable of producing enough volume per hour to cover all guests. If you have a large guest list, a pair of artists may be necessary.

Caricatures are so charming because they take a vision from real life and exaggerate it until the humor rises to the top. Pushing humor to the top is a great way to enjoy life.

#905 *Black-Light Boogie*

Black lights used to be all the rage. When the regular lights went off and the black light went on, the glowing neon colors and shimmering whites that were revealed instantly transported the crowd to fantasyland.

Surprise your wedding guests with a black-light moment they won't expect. During the reception, announce an "everybody dance" boogie. When the music begins, hit the lights and let the surprises shine. Use black-light-reactive fabrics for the linens, which will look normal under regular light then pop to life under black light. There are ordinary-looking figurines that are black-light receptive, or you can use invisible ink on everything from twigs to candles, setting the stage for a black-light surprise destined to give everyone an unforgettable wedding experience.

Have a custom black-light hand stamp made, and ask your guest-book-table attendant to stamp everyone's hand as they enter. The ink is invisible, so they won't know what's there until the black lights come on. And when they do, everyone will literally have a "hand" in making the black-light moments even merrier. Getting your boogie on is fun, but not nearly as fun as doing it in black light.

#906 *Lucky Horseshoe*

A typical reception-table configuration looks like what you'd find in a restaurant or a lounge: tables everywhere, with a designated dance floor off to one side. This setup almost always means that someone is relegated to the back of the room, with little or no view of the bride and groom or their activities. Try the "horseshoe" approach instead.

Set tables in the shape of an imaginary horseshoe, bordering the outer edges of the room. Create walk-through space every couple of tables. Place the head table at the opening of the horseshoe, and leave the floor space in the middle empty for games, dancing, the garter and bouquet tosses, etc. Position the cake table to one side of the head table, or raise the head table onto a dais and place the cake table just before it. All of that wide-open floor space means that everyone gets to enjoy an unobstructed view of the wedding couple. The buffet, band, gift table, etc., would go behind the horseshoe on the round end.

A horseshoe-shaped table layout works best in a large, rectangular hall. Some reception venues won't be large enough to accommodate it. But if your site is ample, you may want to think about giving your guests the gift of wonderful visual access. The "good luck" of the "horseshoe" shape doesn't hurt a bit either.

#907 *With a Song in Your Heart*

Even those who don't know the difference between a high "C" note and a Hi-C juice box still love to warble, and there's always comfort in company. Sing-alongs are lively entertainment. Without being singled out, guests get to lift their voices in song, which is just plain good for the soul.

You don't have to raise the roof all night, but a sing-along sprinkled here and there will add to the celebratory feel of the occasion. Perhaps a chorus or two is what is needed to get a kiss from the bride and groom. Or think of it as a vocal version of musical chairs: if the band stops playing, everyone has to sing an a cappella version of a predesignated song to get the band going again. Assign a family member or a wedding attendant to be the vocal leader. That person will start each sing-along segment, and guests will chime right in.

To avoid hearing a lot of vocal mumbling, choose familiar songs with easy lyrics. Consider each song's original artist. Just about everyone can sing along to Neil Diamond songs because of their great repetitive hooks. Or select classic songs from artists like Elvis, who cross over musical genres and are as popular today as they ever were. You could also adhere to a theme, like picking songs for the season or only singing love songs. Whatever songs you choose, provide lyric cheat sheets for the tables. Someone is bound to need one.

#908 *Piano Dance*

Are you a bride and groom with mad dance skills? If both of you have great rhythm and musicality, think what a fabulous surprise it would be for guests to watch you begin your first dance . . . on a keyboard!

Who says the first dance has to be only about romance? Instead, begin it with the emphasis on fun, then end it in a more traditional, romantic style. The dance will be just as touching, but it will also be wildly entertaining for guests. Purchase one or two piano mats that lay on the floor and play musical notes as you step on the keys. These musical mats are easily found at toy stores or online. When the first dance is announced, have the best man and maid of honor precede you to the dance floor with the mats in tow. In a flourish, they will unfurl the mats across the floor, and the two of you will dance the music right out of them. With practice, you can create a magical song that will have guests clapping and hooting. At the completion of your keyboard boogie, the band or DJ will begin to play your real first-dance song, and you will segue into your romantic dance, as helpers retrieve your mats. That romantic song could be the same tune you just played with your dancing feet or a completely different one. Later, when wedding guests are partying hard, you may want to pop out the mats once more, and let your guests forge a few musical "foot" stylings of their own.

#909 *Kisses All Around*

Your wedding is all about falling in love and sharing a future. Why not spread the love with a subtle, silent invitation to your guests to share a kiss beneath a mistletoe arch or a kissing ball? Mistletoe isn't just for Christmas. In fact, it was woven into primitive wedding ceremonies centuries ago and is believed to foster life and fertility, and possess aphrodisiac qualities to boot.

Grow your own mistletoe, or purchase it from growers. Then attach sprigs to the inside of any decorative arch, or fashion the sprigs into a lush, round ball and dangle it from a beautiful ribbon in a doorway or directly from the ceiling. Add a scripted sign to your arch or hanging ball that reads: "Our love is in the air, and we wanted to share!" Or choose any message you wish. A "mistletoe spot" is a sweet, unobtrusive reception activity that just keeps on giving.

#910 *Starry, Starry Night*

If you love the universe (and who doesn't?), why not let your guests enjoy it up close and personal? Stargazing is a magical experience, but tying it to your wedding makes it even more special.

Set up one or more telescopes outdoors, or inside before a window, and add a sign that reads:

"When love is as vast as the universe, even the stars
are invited to the celebration."

Guests can wander over at their leisure to embrace the wonders of space. It's a passive entertainment enjoyed by young and old alike. Tie a constellation chart to the telescope stand with a beautiful bow to help guests zero in on special stars. Borrow, rent, or purchase the telescope equipment, and let the stars entertain in their own beautiful and unique way.

#911 *THANK YOU!*

What's a great prelude to after-the-fact, down-the-road thank-you cards? It's a larger-than-life thank-you that guests will see the moment they arrive at the reception. To thank your guests for sharing in your celebration, give them a greeting card that expresses your gratitude — not a card for each guest, but one enormous, handmade greeting card that is so big and so amazing that guests will want to be photographed with it.

Begin with two 48" x 96" cardboard sheets, which cost about $5 per sheet. (Staples, the office-supply store, will ship a bundle of five sheets to a store location near you, with no shipping charge. Other retail outlets have similar options.) Connect two upright cardboard sheets with duct tape, thereby making the card's "fold," then spray paint the whole piece a solid color that complements your wedding décor. Once it's dry, add whatever lettering and art you desire. Just be sure that the front has a huge "Thank You!" as its focal point.

Inside the card, write: "To our friends …" then write every guest's name on the two inside panels. After all of the names are listed, add: "We love you for being here with us today," or whatever sentiment you prefer, then in big, sweeping letters, sign it with both the bride's and groom's signatures. Place your giant greeting card in a location where the lighting is good for pictures, and let it surprise, please, and continually thank your guests on your behalf.

This giant sentiment of appreciation does not replace those traditional, after-wedding thank-you cards that are specific to individuals and their gifts. It's simply a welcome, and surprising, addition to them.

#912 *Fire in the Hole!*

Cutting the cake, the first dance, entering the reception, the last song — any and all of these singularly important wedding functions can be ratcheted up a notch by using a confetti or streamer cannon that blows sparkling confetti or color streamers into the air. Check with your venue to make sure that the use of the cannon is permitted. If it is, you can buy or rent one for the big day. They're quite expensive to purchase, so unless you and your intended are major party animals, you probably don't need to own one. Renting is a better option, and rentals can include an experienced operator as part of the rental package. It really feels like a celebration when things are sailing through the air. And if it's a winter white ambiance you seek — one without the shivering cold — consider the cannon's cousin, the snow machine.

Confetti cannons and faux-snow machines work well indoors or outdoors. Where and when that exciting explosion occurs is up to you.

#913 *Technically Advanced*

The disposable cameras that used to dot reception tables have all but disappeared. Why? Because it's a digital era, and developing pictures from film is going the way of the dinosaur. Today, photos are captured with tiny digital cameras, cell phones, and watch-sized video recorders.

But even though the technology has changed, candid photos are still very desirable. Guests often capture some of the best photos of the day. So instead of dotting your tables with disposable cameras, dot them with CDs. For each guest, provide a blank CD in a beautifully designed CD mailing sleeve. The reverse side of the mailer bears the guest's name and table assignment, making it suitable for use as an escort card or place card. Beneath the guest information is a request for the guest to transfer any wedding photos he or she takes onto the CD and return it to you by mail. The other side of the mailer is where you will fill in your mailing address. You can also affix the correct postage if you wish. Blank CDs and mailing sleeves designed specifically for weddings are available from some retailers, but you can easily create your own sets as well.

#914 *Mail Call*

Stuck for a place to put your wedding cards at the reception? Get real — a real mailbox, that is. Of course, you can always use a birdcage, a decorated box, or any other traditional card repository. But everyone needs a mailbox anyway, and there are so many beautiful ones these days, why not simply get yourself a new mailbox that will stay with you for a lifetime? The pedestal types are especially lovely, and you can anchor one in a large flowerpot for the reception, then take it home and introduce it to your mailman. Cleverly designed post-top or wall-hang mailboxes are also available from artisans, and you can custom order one shaped like a dog, a house, a bug, a car, or any other design that works with your lifestyle or your wedding theme. Once in a while, the most obvious answer is actually the most beneficial one. A real mailbox for the wedding cards may be money very well spent.

#915 *Man's Favorite Garter*

Go ahead. Spice up the garter toss in a way that will make every man in the place run to participate. Use a flask garter! You don't have to wear it all day. Just quietly slip it on behind the head table before you come to the dance floor to do the garter toss. When your new husband pulls that garter from beneath your gown, guests will roar. Fill the flask with a swallow of whatever liquid you wish, then watch the men's eyes light up when that flask garter goes airborne. It's still a garter toss. It's just way more fun!

#916 *Pseudo Super 8*

Super 8 movies featured graininess, jerky action, and washed-out colors, but they were home movies and everyone clamored to make them. Long before today's smart video cameras, there were Super 8s. And in spite of their obvious quality issues, they have an inexplicable appeal. That's why photographers searched for ways to make modern videos look like vintage

Super 8 films. They succeeded. For wedding couples, this means an opportunity to create something truly unique and delightful for wedding guests.

Use footage you already have, or create a whole new video. Later, you'll be able to try your hand at video-effects software to give it the Super 8 treatment. You may wish to go all out by selecting a 1960s-style wardrobe for the bride and groom, family members, attendants, and anyone else you wish to include in your cast of characters, then make your own unforgettable movie. Use a traditional video recorder, and later add effects with the software, or use a cell phone or notebook video recorder along with a Super 8 app, which applies the effects as you record. Play your silent film during the cocktail hour, or create a longer, endless-loop version to play during the reception. Why is a Super 8 film more fun to watch? No one knows. It just is.

#917 *Fabulous Finish*

When your venue won't allow fireworks to send you off on your honeymoon in style, don't give up. Let lasers fill the void. A professional laser-light show can be just as exciting as fireworks but without the associated risks. Indoors or out, lasers create bursts of exciting colors and images to rival the explosions of pyrotechnics. A laser show is not inexpensive, so budgeting for one may take a lot of long-term planning. But if you have your heart set on a spectacular finish to your reception, go ahead and investigate. If there are laser artists in your area, you may have found your wedding reception's fabulous pièce de résistance!

#918 *Go BIG!*

Don't dismiss real games at your reception — supersize them instead. If you have the space, consider setting up a huge floor chessboard or a giant game of checkers. Other choices include a larger-than-life tic-tac-toe or pickup sticks. Certain companies specialize in oversized versions of traditional games. These are games that adults can dive right into, and have loads of fun playing. Not everyone will be a dancer, and having a game or two waiting on the outskirts of the tables, on the lawn or patio, or in an adjoining room will keep both rowdy party hounds and gentle bookworms happy. Besides, what's not to love about giant games? If you're going to go gaming, go big!

#919 *Walking on Air*

Yes, you will no doubt be walking on air on your wedding day, but if you want to add a dash of whimsy to the reception, you can invite a few "characters" to walk on air with you. AirWalkers balloons are large, human-height, helium-filled balloons. They are weighted to make them stay upright yet move about the room at will, as if they are walking among your guests. They come in a multitude of shapes, including brides and grooms, flowers, popular movie and cartoon characters, and even pink flamingos. AirWalkers are a hoot. They sneak up on you when you least expect it, and don't be surprised if a guest or two tries to invite one to dance.

#920 *Who, Me?*

Trivia cards at reception tables are great icebreakers, but they're even more effective when the questions apply specifically to those sitting at the table. To create engaging, personalized trivia cards for each table, first ask your guests to participate via their RSVP.

Include a section on the back of the RSVP, or on an additional insert, where you ask guests to share five fun, quirky, or mysterious things about themselves that others might not readily know. Add lines to the card for their answers. After the answers are in, create your trivia cards by printing the questions on blank, perforated business-card sheets you buy at the office-supply store. If someone wrote, "My first dog's name was Dimwit" and "I got to ride a horse in a rodeo when I was ten years old," the trivia questions might look like: "Whose first dog was named Dimwit?" and "Who was a rodeo rider at the age of ten?"

If you want to give your guests helpful hints when asking them to participate via the RSVP, send along a list of general questions as examples. Even if every guest doesn't comply, most will, and you will have custom, table-ready material that everyone will get a kick out of.

#921 *Girl Power!*

Sometimes girls just have to kick up their heels, and there's no better time to do it than at your wedding celebration. Pick a great song, like "Girls Just Wanna Have Fun" or "Redneck Woman," and sashay out to the dance floor, joined only by your maid of honor and bridesmaids. As the music plays, dance with joyful abandon. Whether you choose to free dance or actually learn some group choreography before the big day, it will be a great bonding moment.

Though your girls'-only song will begin with just you and your attendants, you will, in short order, invite your heel-kicking moms to join in. Soon after, you'll open the invitation to all of the female guests. And once the place is jumping with "girl power," you'll prove that girls really do know how to have fun.

#922 *Of Fine Stature*

How fun would it be for guests arriving at the reception to encounter gorgeous, life-size statues of the bride and groom, or perhaps Eros and Aphrodite, the Greek god and goddess of love? Only the statues wouldn't be made of stone or marble. They would be human performers in full-body makeup, transformed into realistic statues. The patient souls remain perfectly still, and some people don't have a clue that the statue isn't real until it turns toward them or gives them a wink. Especially entertaining for the cocktail hour, your human statues not only add a big, beautiful, decorative element, they add the element of surprise, again and again.

Hire your human statues as you would any performer. Look for an agency that represents them. Or you could always go up to a statue on the street and ask it if it's available for private events. If it doesn't answer you within ten minutes, move along. You're talking to stone.

#923 *Missing and Loved*

What do you do when everyone expects a father-daughter or a mother-son dance, but the mother or father has passed away? Skipping the dance is one option, but is that what your late parent would want? Only you can decide. But if you would like the dance to go on in memory of your father or your mother, simply dance with the remaining parent in honor of the other one.

Or, when it's time for the parent-child dance, invite honorary partners to share the dance. For example, if your father is not with you, have your master of ceremonies announce, "To honor her father with a father-daughter dance, the bride would like to invite any fathers in the room to join her." The fathers won't be able to abandon their seats fast enough to line up, and you will have many substitute fathers to share your moment with. Similarly, a groom who is missing his mother could share his dance with the mothers in the room.

The honorary partners are parents. They understand. It won't be the same as dancing with your real father or mother, but it will be special, not only for you but for everyone in attendance.

#924 *Our Five Minutes*

It's been a long, exciting day, and you've just had the last dance of the night. It's time to invite guests to gather in the hall or outside to prepare for your grand departure. Let them go. Let everyone go. Empty the room, and take five minutes for just the two of you.

In spite of the wedding being all about you, you will discover that you likely haven't had a moment alone like you hoped you would. These precious five minutes are your time. If the DJ or bandleader leaves soft music playing as he or she exits, go ahead and enjoy one last dance alone, or simply hold each other and reflect on the day. You can do whatever you wish in that swan-song moment. It feels good to give the heart a wrap-up that you share only with each other.

Guests can wait five minutes to see you off. The band can wait to tear down, and the caterer can wait to clean up. Five minutes may not seem like a lot of time, but at the end of your spectacular day, it will feel like the best wedding gift ever.

FIX IT!

CHAPTER FOURTEEN • *Fix It!*
Wise Preventions & Quick Solutions

In spite of their joyous nature, weddings have their fair share of persnickety problems, and uncomfortable issues can crop up when you least expect them. Under everyday circumstances, such situations might seem like little bumps in the road. But on your wedding day, even the smallest bumps can feel like giant mountains of stress and woe. The best way to deal with these predicaments is to prevent them from happening in the first place. The second-best solution is to soundly and swiftly nip them in the bud.

This "Fix It!" chapter shares ideas on how to address unpleasant circumstances from the perspectives of both prevention and resolution. Sometimes there's no time for prevention, and the problem just blindsides you. But don't despair. There's always a solution, and thinking about resolutions before problems occur is a great first step toward not feeling defeated by them.

The best way to problem solve is to give an issue your focused attention, understand it, and apply the "fix" to the best of your ability. On your wedding day, there is an additional step that matters — the "fuhgeddaboudit" step. A wedding-day problem shouldn't be allowed to steal your bliss. Fix it if it can be fixed, and then walk away. Walking away is hard to do when you've dreamed of wedding perfection your whole life, but the truth is simple. Unless a UFO swoops down and snatches someone from the wedding party, there's not much else that should hamper your spirit for more than a heartbeat or two.

This chapter will give you the knowledge you'll need to prevent many predictable problems from popping up. But no amount of brainstorming can foresee all potential pitfalls. So if some mishap does occur on your big day, just remember to handle it quickly, "fuhgeddaboudit," and have a glorious wedding anyway.

#925 *Spare Wheels*

While every princess needs a beautiful carriage, the smart princess has a backup plan.

Even the finest of limousines can have a flat tire or an engine that sputters and fails, and when it happens there may not be enough time for the limousine company, the horse-and-carriage service, or the purveyor of whatever means of transportation you have engaged to get a replacement to you in time. Plan ahead.

When booking your transportation service, book a backup within your closest circle of friends and family. That designated person will have a clean car ready and available to you, should wedding-day transportation gremlins rear their ugly heads. Mr. or Ms. Transportation Ace in the Hole should be in close proximity. Choose someone who is already scheduled to be on hand during preparations and the ceremony.

Designating a backup car and driver avoids stressful delays or the unfortunate experience of climbing into the closest, not-so-spic-and-span vehicle on your wedding day.

#926 *Take an Aspirin and Crush It in the Morning*

The big day has arrived. You wake up with a bright smile and an eager heart only to discover an ugly new blemish right between your eyes. Don't despair. As long as you have no allergies to ordinary aspirin, a helpful quick fix is at hand.

Crush a single aspirin into a small bowl and add just enough water to make a paste. Apply the paste to the blemish and leave it on for about 20 minutes, while you attend to other wedding-day preparations. The aspirin dries the blemish and helps remove redness. Soon the unwelcome spot should be manageable enough to be camouflaged by your favorite concealer. Just remember to remove the paste residue with clean water and allow your skin to thoroughly dry before applying makeup.

If aspirin is not for you, an application of ice followed by a few dabs of witch hazel may also improve the condition.

Don't try to squeeze a blemish into submission. All you are likely to accomplish is the enlargement of the bull's-eye on your face. No bride needs that.

#927 *The Wedding Crashers*

The appearance of uninvited guests at the wedding is a more common occurrence than you would imagine. It's not usually strangers who wander in, although that can happen. Wedding crashers are more likely to be former husbands, wives, girlfriends, boyfriends, or partners. Sometimes they are distant relatives or coworkers who simply invite themselves without notice. Embarrassment and conflict are unwelcome at your wedding, and uninvited guests should be addressed quickly.

Choose your most diplomatic friend or family member to act as your wedding-day ambassador, and if possible, arm your lookout with an advance list of potential crashers. If you have no idea that someone is going to crash until you see him or her walk through the door, an on-the-spot decision is necessary. Should that person get to stay, or will his or her presence cause disruption? The answer to that question dictates the response.

If the uninvited person came to the wedding with nefarious intentions, asking him or her to leave is important. No one wants hurt feelings, but it's your wedding. Anguish shouldn't be a part of it.

Don't handle the issue personally. Rely on your designated ambassador to run interference on your behalf. Addressing the issue as soon as possible may prevent the eruption of a bigger problem later.

#928 *A Hundred Left Feet*

What do you do when the dance floor at your reception is an empty wasteland?

When the music is playing but no one is dancing, something has gone wrong, and your wedding reception has entered the dreaded land of boredom. Fix it!

People decline to dance for any number of reasons, but the most common one is that they don't want to be embarrassed by their two, big left feet. Instead of hoping that the open bar will release wedding guests' fears and inhibitions, try a little friendly persuasion.

Call all male wedding guests to the dance floor for a group dance with the bride and her bridesmaids. Teach the men a dance move, even if it's only a rhythmic sway or a simple bounce. The bride and the bridesmaids switch from partner to partner in a brief, lively dance with each guy. Once the dance is in full swing, have the groom and his groomsmen hand deliver the women guests to the floor to find their partners.

When left on their own, a few will no doubt wander back to their chairs, but you'll be surprised at how many will remain to get their groove on. Once the ice is sufficiently broken, the dancing, and the feel-good thrill that comes with it, will follow. All it takes is showing your guests that dancing with two left feet is just as fun as dancing on air.

#929 *Zip It!*

Zippers have a mind of their own. If the zipper in the bride's gown or the groom's tuxedo pants suddenly won't budge, it pays to have a trick up your sleeve.

Everyone knows that bar soap is a great zipper motivator, but what if only messy liquid soap is available in the bride's or groom's dressing room? An easy substitute is lip balm. Someone is sure to have lip balm in a purse or pocket, and sliding it across a stuck zipper can work as well as soap or petroleum jelly. Just remember to protect surrounding fabric with a cloth or tissue when using any lubricant, and use only clear versions. Flavored lip balms may contain dyes that can stain fabrics.

If the zipper has snarled itself on a sliver of fabric, and gently jockeying the zipper pull won't dislodge it, use a toothpick, an opened paper clip, or a straight pin to squeeze a touch of lubricant under the fabric sliver, then gently pull the fabric away from the zipper as it moves.

If the zipper has broken, the best solution is a needle and thread. Closing the zipper opening with a quick whipstitch can solve the problem without anyone being the wiser. Of course, stitching the groom into his trousers may produce obvious adverse side effects. Getting him another pair of pants as soon as possible after the "I dos" and the subsequent photos is, to say the least, a priority.

#930 *Hot Flash!*

A broken air conditioner at your summer reception can be a mood killer. The venue management should provide assistance, including fans to circulate air and cool the room, while the AC is being worked on. But relying solely on venue personnel to solve the problem may mean that the problem doesn't get solved.

An emergency run for electric fans, hand fans, and block ice can save the day.

Situate ice in disposable turkey-roasting pans, with a towel placed in each pan bottom to collect the melting ice. Air blowing across ice or water will cool the area more effectively than air generated by a fan alone.

For individual cooling, folded paper is a quick substitute for hand fans. The wedding program will do, but if you haven't provided one, construction paper works nicely.

A quick trip to the closest discount store for construction paper, electric fans, roasting pans, towels, and block ice (or bagged ice, if block ice isn't available) is a job easily accomplished by only a couple of people, and the cost and effort will be worth it.

Rescheduling a reception when a cooling catastrophe strikes is impossible, but with a little imaginative substitution, it's possible to make yourself and your guests more comfortable as you celebrate.

#931 *Sole-ful Calamity*

Snapped heels, broken straps, and split soles can happen to the best of shoes, making a barefoot stroll down the aisle feel like a frightening possibility.

With no shoe-repair facility nearby, no spare pair of heels, and no one willing to go shoeless on your behalf, you will need to make a quick repair. This means never leaving home without your favorite super glue.

From reattaching heels and soles to mending broken straps, super glue can usually provide enough of a fix to see you through the day. Carefully and neatly apply the glue to the heel or sole that requires reconnection, then align and hold it in position for as long as possible.

Broken straps should be reinforced by gluing the two ends together and gluing a piece of fabric long enough to span a good length of the strap underneath the break. Cull the fabric from a hem, a handkerchief, a thin hand towel, or whatever flat fabric scrap is available.

Quick shoe repair is all about diligence and patience. Carefully applying the glue, properly aligning the repair, and holding it in position as it sets make all the difference between a sloppy shoe repair that everyone notices and a tidy one that easily conceals just how close to barefoot you actually came.

#932 *Employ Due Diligence*

Horror stories abound about wedding vendors who fail to live up to their obligations, ruining some or all of the wedding day. While this problem isn't 100% preventable, its occurrence can be substantially reduced with proper due diligence.

The Internet gives you access to a wealth of supplies and options that might be otherwise unavailable, but with that access comes greater opportunities for failure and fraud. However, local vendors with fabulous storefronts aren't necessarily the solution to the problem, because they can turn out to be just as unreliable as services found online. The best way to protect your day is to investigate every vendor to the fullest.

In addition to always checking the references provided by the vendor, and considering recommendations provided by the venue or the wedding planner, wise wedding couples should check out each vendor by utilizing information from:

- the Better Business Bureau
- the state Department of Corporations
- the city or state licensing authority for that type of business
- public legal records
- online reviews

It takes time to be thorough, but peace of mind is worth the effort. A good offense really is the best defense against wedding-day glitches and disappointments.

#933 *Cool and Comfortable Blooms*

Bridal bouquets, corsages, and boutonnières all share a common risk: wilting. Even flowers delivered close to the wedding time may have been made as much as a day in advance. Flowers are dead the moment they are cut, and keeping them looking beautiful requires dedicated attention. The florist keeps them cool and comfortable in a floral refrigerator, but what happens to delicate blooms if the bride takes an extra-long time to dress, the minister is unavoidably delayed, the day is unseasonably warm, or any other scenario occurs in which time may not be on your side?

A simple fix is a cooler. Have a family member stick a cooler or two in his or her trunk, along with a few half-filled, frozen water bottles. Flowers should never come into contact with actual ice, but a frozen water bottle tucked inside a paper bag cools the flowers without freezing them. Don't leave the cooler in the trunk of the car, unless it's a very cool day with no sun. Bring it inside.

That cooler is your mobile refrigeration. You may not need it, but if you do, you and your flowers will be glad it's there.

#934 *The Sound of Music*

Whether it's a freeway traffic jam or an alleged alien abduction that prevents the ceremony soloist, the band, or the DJ from arriving to perform at your wedding, don't despair. Music is always at hand.

Before the wedding, create a CD, MP3, cell phone, or laptop music file for each wedding-day musical need. Put the songs in the order they will be heard in, but to prevent accidentally hearing your father-daughter dance song in the middle of the "I dos," make individual, easily accessible recordings that are specific to the ceremony and the reception.

If you don't already own compact external speakers, treat yourself. If your musicians thankfully perform as scheduled, you'll find plenty of uses for those handy speakers in everyday life.

Prerecorded music can fill a void created by missing musicians, but you have to prepare it in advance. You don't want to have to resort to a radio station rife with car-insurance ads, or to the mood-killing silence of a search for just the right song on a commercial CD.

If you pack your selected music, speakers, and all of the necessary cords and jacks in your emergency music kit, there will be nothing left to do but plug them in and celebrate.

#935 *Drunk as a Skunk*

A drunk at the wedding reception can quickly turn the occasion ugly, and drunken disruptions should be nipped in the bud.

If the offending person arrived with another guest, that guest can run interference. But if the person is alone, or his or her significant other is not inclined to intervene, your assigned reception host or hostess should step up. Ignoring disagreeable behaviors can only lead to hurt feelings, humiliation, and increased liability.

The first course of action is compassionate engagement. Instigate a conversation with the person while providing him or her with a nonalcoholic beverage. Encourage food consumption. High-fructose foods and juices may be especially helpful. Exercise speeds up metabolism, so try accompanying the inebriated person on a walk outside.

Drunks corner the market on belligerence, so don't ever try to be accusatory or dominant with the offender. If the situation is irreparable, escort the person from the premises and have him or her driven home in a cab or by a sober friend. Do not let an obviously inebriated person drive away from your reception.

Brides and grooms shouldn't have to deal with a drunken guest on their own, but sometimes just a worried word conveyed from the wedding couple to the offender will do the trick. Drunks rarely wish to intentionally harm or disappoint anyone.

#936 *Rushed and Rattled*

Popular wedding venues often book events back-to-back, with little down time in between. This scenario may result in one wedding party or the other being hustled through postceremony photos or being shown the door while the reception is still in full swing.

To eliminate the possibility that you will be rushed and rattled, choose a ceremony and reception venue that guarantees only one wedding per day. Emotions always run high at weddings, but you can prevent the stress that comes from prematurely getting the boot because bride and groom number two have arrived, or because your officiant is unexpectedly stuck in traffic.

It's almost always a failing proposition to expect to precisely schedule your event down to the minute. Things go wrong that only time can fix. By choosing venues where you are the sole queen and king for the day, you can prevent major disasters.

#937 *Party of Plus One ... and One*

It's bound to happen. An invited guest shows up with an additional, unexpected person in tow. It's sometimes understandable. It may be a surprise out-of-town guest or a child of a divorced parent whose circumstances suddenly changed.

A last-minute, uninvited guest of a guest is not the same as a wedding crasher. This is not someone you will wish to show the door, but it is someone who will require a seat. If simply adding an extra chair to the guest's assigned reception table is not an option, it's time to shuffle.

If your party of two is now a party of three, scan the seating chart for a table that includes at least one couple plus a single guest who might be relocated with little fuss. If that proves impossible, ask that another table be erected.

Don't hurt other guests' feelings by asking them to move to a less desirable seat. The guest who brought the extra person can't complain if they find themselves sitting at a new table in the back of the room.

To avoid being blindsided by the unexpected, plan for it. Leave an empty seat or two when making the seating chart, and order a few extra servings of food. Thinking ahead creates a comfort zone for everyone.

#938 *Shoo, Spot!*

When that solitary, nerve-settling sip of wine manages to dribble down your dress, or your ring bearer races in with mud splotches on his britches, it's time to unleash your stain-removal arsenal.

Club soda, talcum powder, hair spray, baking soda, stain-removal pens, clean cloths, cotton balls, water, and tape are essential aids for quick stain removal. Pack a kit, and don't leave home without it. Use powdery cures for oily stains, club soda for colored stains, and hair spray for inky stains. Stain-removal pens may work best on darker-colored fabrics, and tape lifts residue like crumbs or mud.

No quick fix will be perfect, and fabrics should always be tested on an underneath site first, but when there's no time for dry cleaning or laundry, impromptu stain removal is certainly better than nothing.

Just remember the stain-removal mantra: "Dab and blot, never rub!"

#939 *Don't Cry, Be Happy*

Even if the rehearsal went off without a hitch, a wedding-day walk down an aisle bordered by staring strangers can terrify young flower girls and ring bearers. Instead of a flutter of petals or an adorably presented ring pillow, you get tears, wails, and balking.

Comfort is key for young ones. Plan ahead, and send your littlest attendants down the aisle with something to hold on to besides their ceremonial objects. A stuffed, white teddy bear incorporated into the flower girl's basket, or a tuxedo-clad bear that's holding the ring pillow between its paws, can help stave off discomfort. Soft bears with gentle expressions make children feel less alone and inspire bravery ("If the bear can do it, so can I!").

Teddy bears have been turning frowns into smiles for generations. And they just might be a magic fix for a wee problem on your wedding day.

#940 *Unfloat the Bloat*

What were you thinking when you served salty ham at the rehearsal dinner? And you know you only made matters worse by washing it down with three flutes of carbonated champagne. Now, here you are, cursed on your wedding day with puffy feet and a bloated belly. Your beautiful gown and your stylish shoes are going to punish you for your culinary indiscretions, and you must resign yourself to suffering and regret — or you can choose to be proactive instead.

If you've partied yourself into a gassy, water-retentive version of your former self, get up and get going. Rise early on your wedding day and work out. Exercise fires all systems, and internal functions operating at their optimum levels help the body process and eliminate. Follow your workout with a stint in a sauna, bath, or hot tub. If the water doesn't make you sweat, it's not hot enough. After the heat, take your normal bath or shower.

Indulge in dandelion tea, a natural diuretic, and snack on a whole-grain muffin or toast, along with some fresh pineapple and papaya. Cutting back on water is not helpful. Drink plenty of water to stay hydrated.

You may not be able to undo all of the effects of overindulging, but a little concentrated effort definitely makes a difference in the way you feel as you walk down that aisle.

#941 *You're Fired!*

Stuff happens, and sometimes it becomes necessary to eliminate a member of the wedding party. Emotions can be intense during the wedding-planning process. If a bridesmaid or a groomsman causes conflict or ill feelings, replacing that person may be the wisest course of action to prevent further disruption down the road, however unpleasant this seems.

If you have to "fire" someone from your wedding party, speak with him or her privately about your concerns. An honest, levelheaded conversation might change the offending attendant's attitude, or it might prove be the straw that breaks the "friendship" camel's back. Be prepared for either outcome. The important thing to remember is that it is your wedding, and the path to that wedding should be as worry free as possible. Saying "you're fired" doesn't come easily, but it's far better than a sour, disruptive wedding attendant who spoils the joy of the occasion.

#942 Weddding Woes!

No, the word "wedding" should not have a third "d," but if you're not careful, yours might. One of the most frustrating of all wedding mistakes is the inclusion of preventable typos in stationery, programs, invitations, and other printed wedding materials.

Once a typo settles itself into the printed product, it's pretty permanent. The cost of reprinting and the time needed to do so is usually too significant for it to be feasible, leaving you bright red with unnecessary embarrassment. The solution is to double down and enlist not one, but two, independent proofreaders.

Choose professional proofreaders or best friends, family members, or coworkers with a discerning eye and a command of grammar. Never rely on a printing company for proofing. All commercial printers have disclaimers that put the burden on you. But it's even worse to rely solely on your own proofreading. When you write — even when you are writing your own name and address — it is possible to miss the same mistake over and over, because your brain often causes you to see what you meant to write, not necessarily what was actually written.

Two proofreaders are always better than one, and humans are better than computers. Computer programs catch only certain errors. "Buy," "bye," and "by" all look fine to a computer, but they are definitely not interchangeable. Observant humans catch those mistakes, and a good catch can save your printed wedding materials from a bad case of "say what?"

#943 Nest That Handbag

Brides could take a cue from those clever little containers known as Russian nesting dolls.

Bridal handbags are tiny and hold next to nothing, but throughout an event as long and as demanding as a wedding day, women simply need more than next to nothing. Lugging around a big purse is not very bridal chic, but that doesn't mean you can't have one nearby.

Choose an oversized purse with big pockets as your anchor purse. Fill it with absolutely everything you'll need for the entire day, but in one pocket place only a soft cloth. For your bridal purse, choose a traditional, small clutch that complements your gown.

Take the anchor purse to the bride's room at the ceremony, retrieve items from it as needed, then depart with your bridal purse containing only the immediate necessities. Assign a bridesmaid to transport your anchor purse to the reception and to discreetly place it beside your seat and beneath the table before you arrive.

Once seated, slip your bridal purse into the soft, protective cloth that you had it stowed in earlier, and tuck it into the anchor purse until it is needed. Now all of your supplies are accessible for your next "personal" break. Just reach in and transfer the desired items to your bridal purse, and be on your merry way. You'll look fabulous toting your small, elegant clutch, and no one will suspect that you are working from a purse the size of Mount Everest.

#944 *Speed Dial*

Where's that vendor? Who's picking up Grandma? Shouldn't the minister be here by now?

Organization is the key to a smooth and satisfying wedding day. But many things can go wrong. The best way to avoid those little annoyances is to create a master list of contact information that covers everyone connected to the wedding.

Compiling phone numbers, e-mail addresses, street addresses, and contact names — with the information listed both alphabetically and by category — prevents frustration. Make several copies of the list. Prior to the wedding day, distribute them to key people, including the wedding coordinator, the wedding host or hostess, the maid of honor, and the best man. All recipients should be familiar with who's on the list and why each person is on it.

A master list is a wedding-day tool that is essential for your peace of mind. With luck, you won't need it — and if you're well prepared, you'll be less likely to need luck at all.

#945 *Out-of-Towner Blues*

Out-of-town wedding guests need more than just a room to rent and a map to the wedding. They need attention. Unfortunately, as the bride and groom, you may be too busy to give it to them. To solve the dilemma, assign each out-of-town family its own wedding concierge.

As soon as the guests arrive in town, have the concierge (a bridesmaid, groomsman, family member, etc.) pay a visit to the guests' hotel to welcome them and provide them with the concierge's contact information (both phone and e-mail). Bringing along a welcoming gift basket is a plus.

The concierge helps out-of-towners navigate their surroundings, find necessities, and discover local entertainments. He or she keeps the guests apprised of wedding events and helps to arrange transportation if necessary.

Your wedding concierge is not responsible for any expenses incurred by the visiting guests. The role is simply one of courteous assistance.

Being a concierge to a visiting family is not a full-time job. After that initial, icebreaking meeting, the concierge may just become a friendly voice on the other end of a telephone call. But knowing that a smile and a helping hand are available is comforting to guests who are out of their element.

#946 *Ship It!*

A honeymoon is the wedding afterglow, but it's a whole lot less fun if that trousseau you so carefully assembled winds up in the icy Arctic, while you're sifting the white sands of the tropics between your toes.

Luggage that travels on airplanes sometimes goes on a journey all its own. Most luggage that is lost during airline transfers is found within a day or two, but not always. Other losses occur when bags are left in taxis, on shuttle buses, or next to an airport bench. To minimize the potential for disappearing belongings, give your luggage a leg up. Ship it.

Luggage-delivery services used to be only for the well heeled. But with airlines now routinely charging for bags, the cost of shipping is no longer seen as an extravagance. Whether your luggage travels on your airplane or through a delivery service, you'll pay by the pound, so packing light is wise. And since not all luggage-delivery companies offer the same services, be sure to do your homework.

For a comfortable experience at the airport, pack a single small, carry-on bag filled with one change of clothes and essential toiletries for both the bride and groom, and ship everything else. How great would it be to not have to handle luggage? With door-to-door luggage delivery, you'll find your bags waiting for you at your hotel or in your cruise-ship cabin, and you won't even have to break a sweat to get them there.

#947 *Blowin' in the Wind*

Walking down the aisle at your outdoor wedding should be every bit as serene and graceful as if you were indoors. But if a sudden gust of wind picks up the tail of your aisle runner and wraps it around you like a whirlwind, you'll probably wish you could fly away to Oz.

The best solution is to have no aisle runner outdoors and to lay a pathway of petals instead. Petals whipping up in a breeze are actually pretty. But if walking to the altar without a runner is not an option, choose wisely. Don't be tempted to use ordinary paper or fabric runners over dirt, grass, or sand. They are easily punctured by heels and can cause a fall.

Instead, purchase a tear-resistant runner or a white tarp (the thicker the better), and cut it to the size and length you need. Line the edges with decorative rocks and attach the leading edges to a heavy metal bar suitable for securing to the ground with tent stakes or strong, U-shaped hooks. Keeping the runner taut is essential. The looser it rests upon the earth, the more dangerous it may prove to be.

You're getting married outdoors for a reason, and since aisle runners don't exist in nature, maybe one shouldn't be invited to your wedding.

#948 *Who Ignored the Business?*

There's a business side to marriage preparation, and brides and grooms who wed without addressing the hard stuff may set themselves up for unpleasant realities later on.

The time to begin discussions about real-world issues is soon after the question has been popped and the affirmative answer has been given. You will both benefit from sharing your individual views regarding family financial planning, existing debt, community-property laws, health care, elderly support, children, tax liability, government benefits, continuing education, business ownerships, insurance, and more. Finding out after the marriage that the bride intends to pursue her master's degree, but the groom saying "What for?" could throw the couple's budget and plans for the future into turmoil, easily leading to relationship woes.

Too many couples believe that love conquers all. In truth, without the willingness to face the not-so-exciting business end of uniting two people, love can get weak in the knees and refuse to hold up the relationship.

Prevent financial and emotional minefields from appearing after the wedding by having some real conversations now.

#949 *Photos That Only a Mother Could Love*

If you've seen wedding photos that, well, could have been great but just weren't, you know how easy it is to ruin an incredible shot. Don't let it happen to you.

Rule #1: Fancy equipment doesn't guarantee superior photos. Only the skill of the photographer can do that. Take control by thoroughly examining any potential photographer's work.

Rule #2: Don't allow flash distractions. While the professional photographer is working, ask guests not to snap photos of their own. That once-in-a-lifetime moment of gazing into each other's eyes won't have any emotional impact if there's a ghostly white streak across your faces.

Rule #3: Embrace space. Leaving just a bit of distance between the two of you when performing a ceremonial function helps to ensure a clean view of each participant. The result is a photo that doesn't make the two of you look like a fused body with extra odd limbs.

Rule #4: During milestone dances, avoid smoke, mist, or pulsating lights that can wreak havoc for the camera lens.

Rule #5: Be yourselves. Letting your personalities shine through will lead to memorable photos. Emulating dolls on a cake top is not the goal.

Wedding photos matter. They are the defining link to one of the most momentous occasions of your life. Avert potential disasters by understanding how your own actions can help make those photos amazing.

#950 *Bless the Prewedding Honeymoon*

Everyone recognizes how stressful it is to plan a wedding, and unfortunately that stress can build up in the bride and groom until they're ready to blow a gasket. If it feels like this might happen to you, get up and get away.

A prewedding honeymoon doesn't have to be lavish or expensive. It must, however, involve the completely carefree joy found on a real honeymoon. One- or two-day outings that involve relaxation, sightseeing, exploration, decadent food, and physical pursuits like bicycling, dancing, swimming, or other sports are enough to release the pressure and keep the bride's and groom's lids from blowing off.

Try a couples' massage or a picnic in unknown territory. Check into a hotel just to watch movies and order room service. Do whatever you want, but don't do it at home. Making your getaway feel like a honeymoon, with the same relaxing benefits, is only possible if you truly escape the wedding-planning pressures.

Whatever your pleasure, indulge. Set aside at least one day a month to leave behind the rigors of wedding planning, and do something good for the soul.

#951 *Too Hard to Handle*

A roomful of squirming, uncomfortable guests is not what you hope to observe at your reception.

Remember this rule: It's always better to put a smaller person on a larger chair than to put a larger person on a smaller chair. Your choice of reception chairs makes a big difference. For example, those pizza-ice-cream-parlor chairs with small, round seats and hard, bony backs aren't meant for long-term sitting. They look great, but they quickly cease to feel great.

Ensure the contentment of the masses by selecting chairs with ample seats, supportive backs, and no unnecessary trim or ridges that cut into shoulder blades or the backs of thighs. Make the chairs welcoming. More cushioning means longer-lasting comfort.

Chairs with arms provide extra comfort for some people, while completely destroying the comfort of others. If having both styles in not an option, choose only armless chairs.

When decorating reception chairs, make sure that chair covers won't interfere with repeated scoots of the chair as guests come and go from tables, and only affix decorations to the center back, to prevent décor from irritating the seated guest.

No wedding couple sets out to torture their guests, but it can happen if chair comfort isn't considered. Strive to put your most difficult guest at ease, and no one with bummed buns will be forced to invent a lame excuse for leaving early.

#952 *Where Is Everyone?*

Elopement is an extraordinary experience, but the exclusion of those close to you may put a damper of guilt on your nuptials. Fortunately, you can make your loved ones a part of the action by setting up a wedding Web site.

Create a personal Web site with a blog, and you can make friends and family feel like a part of the adventure. Upload messages, diary entries, videos, and photos, and even stream live video to your site. In a virtual world, anything is possible, even vicariously experiencing a wedding via the Internet. Sharing daily details creates real-time involvement and takes the sting out of being left behind. It also goes a long way toward lifting the mantle of guilt from your shoulders.

Once you return to your humble abode, a postwedding party is the perfect celebratory finish to your elopement. Guests will have the opportunity to congratulate you face-to-face, and you'll have the chance to thank everyone for understanding your choice to say "I do" in a land far, far away.

#953 *The Spotlight Syndrome*

Stress should not be invited to the wedding, but traditions like the first dance and reciting personal vows can cause fearful palpitations. Those unaccustomed to being center stage may feel an anxiety bordering on dread. But wedding-day fears can be conquered with knowledge. Knowledge is power, and power bolsters confidence.

If the worry is that your "twinkle toes" are more like buffalo hooves, seek the guidance of a professional dance instructor. Even the most rhythm-challenged person can improve dramatically with a true understanding of how and when to move a body part. Furthermore, a professional can assess your skills and help you choose a dance that suits hidden talents you didn't even know you had.

If you are fearful of speaking your vows in a hushed venue with all eyes upon you, the answer is to narrow your focus. Forget the guests are there. Speak only to your betrothed, as if the two of you were the only persons in the room, and let the unwelcome fears evaporate. Meditation teaches you how to direct your focus away from the peripheral "noise" and connect only with the one you love. If speaking to your soul mate in private is easy, saying your vows without succumbing to your nerves is achievable.

Embrace the power of knowledge. The more you know, the less there is to fear.

#954 *How to Get Blood from a Budget Turnip*

Exceed a wedding budget, and you're in debt for years. Underestimate how much you'll need to save up, and you won't get everything you want. But if you engage in some clever shopping strategies, all of your wedding wishes can come true.

One of the secrets to buying more for less is to shop in the off-season. When planning a wedding for next fall, shop for décor items just as this year's winter season is beginning. In many stores, fall items will be slashed by as much as 75% to 90%. Apply this "just after" formula to whatever season your wedding falls in.

Style changes aren't drastic within a single year, so take advantage of the retailer's off-season and buy bridesmaid dresses early. For custom-made dresses, snag wonderful fabrics for a deep discount during end-of-season fabric-store sales. You'll also save a bundle by buying off-season embellishments and décor, so don't forget materials needed for decorating and for table or chair coverings.

Watch for out-of-season sales of gift items that make great wedding-party gifts, and check wedding-favor sites for clearance items. There's nothing wrong with closeout favors. They've merely been replaced with something different, not necessarily something better.

Smart shopping means getting more for less by being prepared. Sign up for retailers' e-mail lists to get early notices of sales. Enlist family and friends to help you identify sales for items you really want. And don't be afraid to ask a retailer how long they expect something to stay on the shelf, or if there's already a plan for an upcoming sale.

#955 *Outdoor-Wedding Survival*

Outdoor weddings are beautiful, but they come with unique issues that, if left unaddressed, have the potential to spoil an otherwise magnificent day. To avoid Mother Nature–inspired catastrophes, practice preparedness. Items that you should have on hand to alleviate outdoor-wedding problems include:

> clips to hold tablecloths in place
> umbrellas for shade
> hand fans for individual cooling (if it is warm outside)
> insect deterrents
> flags, balloons, or lanterns to dissuade birds from joining the celebration
> designated access for disabled guests
> space heaters (if it is cool outside)
> a beverage station with cold or hot drinks (as the weather dictates)
> shelter for the cake table
> pins, ties, tape, and clips to secure altar and reception decorations
> moist towelettes for guests
> clean, portable restroom facilities
> a portable dance floor
> a backup tent

To eliminate the worry that a sudden gust of wind will send your wedding cake flying into Aunt Mary's lap, or that a flock of curious birds will add a little "flavor" to the guacamole, give every component of your outdoor wedding due consideration.

Ask yourself, "What could go wrong?" Visualizing detrimental possibilities makes it easier to prevent them.

#956 *That's Not What I Remember!*

Wedding vendors are human. They make mistakes and forget things just like brides, grooms, and every other person on the planet. But misunderstandings are stopped in their tracks with an inexpensive digital recorder.

When visiting a bridal show or a wedding vendor, turn on your recorder before discussing products, policies, prices, or plans. Small digital recorders fit in the palm of your hand, but when conflict arises, their value is anything but small. They are keepers of truth. Consulting your recorder prevents the embarrassment of making false accusations against a vendor, but on the other hand, if you're remembering a situation correctly, you can quickly share that fact with a vendor who thinks otherwise.

Don't try to be a spy. Put your recorder out in the open, and tell the vendor that remembering every wedding-planning conversation is impossible without it. An objection is unlikely, but if there is one, take a closer look at the source. It's possible that you wouldn't care for his or her service anyway, and it's best to move on.

#957 *What Am I, Chopped Liver?*

You've done the unthinkable. You've left someone off the place-card list, and no seat has been assigned. You have a wanderer.

A wanderer will feel pretty slighted when everyone else is honored with a specific seat but he or she is left out in the cold. It's especially egregious if the offended person is part of a group and everyone else has been duly remembered. Turn those proverbial lemons into lemonade by transforming your wanderer into a star.

Make the wanderer the wedding couple's special guest of honor, and give that person his or her pick of seats, adjusting table configurations accordingly. And to really alleviate any tension, award your wanderer a prize. A little extra something to take home is always welcome, so be sure to have a few unisex gifts on hand to use as prizes and gifts for situations you hadn't envisioned. Gifts not used at the reception can always be given out at birthdays down the road.

A quick and clever remedy can transform any perceived slight into a special remembrance, and planning ahead means not having to think on your feet to resolve the situation. No, you won't really fool anyone into thinking the faux pas was planned, but lighthearted, quick actions will mitigate hurt feelings.

#958 *Cooling Your Heels in Customs*

Extreme efficiency isn't always the wisest choice. Just ask any bride who spent her first honeymoon night cooling her heels in an airport customs office. Her crime? She changed her maiden name to her married name too early.

International travel requirements are stricter than ever, and all documentation must match without question. Even a letter out of place can cause unnecessary nightmares. When planning to cross borders on your honeymoon, wait until you return home to begin the name-change process.

If, for some reason, there is a significant delay between your wedding and your honeymoon, there may be enough time to change your name and receive all your new documents, but you should allow at least eight weeks to receive all new forms of ID.

Anything can hinder the arrival of documents, and if even one piece is missing, expect difficulty.

Avoid spending your honeymoon with customs officers and embassy representatives, or being denied entry into the country where you dreams await. Don't rush the name change.

#959 *Something's Come Up*

Sometimes the best-laid plans just don't work. Life is unpredictable, and anything from a natural disaster to a personal one can cause a wedding to be postponed or cancelled. How guests are notified depends upon how quickly the wedding date is approaching.

A written communication using a nicely printed card and envelope is best, but keep the message brief and to the point. The sender of the wedding invitation can do the honors, or the message can come directly from the bride and groom.

If the decision to postpone or cancel occurs too close to the wedding date for the mail to be effective, use e-mail and telephone calls. Of course, if you are trying to avoid the "why" conversations that are sure to ensue, the use of a telephone is the less desirable method.

If a postponement is unavoidable or a cancellation is imminent, notify your guests as early as possible. Be polite. Be direct. And be quick.

#960 *Red Alert*

Anything may cause the dreaded bloodshot eye — partying too hard at the rehearsal dinner or Uncle Frank's passion for cigars.

Makeup can work wonders in other areas, but it's powerless against the red web threatening to mar your wedding day. But all is not lost. Begin by taking a time-out. Shoo everyone from the room, dim the lights, put on the gentlest music you own, and recline. Apply a small ice pack or a cold gel pack across the eyes to help constrict the blood vessels. This also helps to diminish around-the-eye puffiness. Use this time in repose to clear your mind before the day's events.

After the ice treatment, allow your eyes to return to normal temperature, then use homeopathic or conventional over-the-counter allergy eyedrops.

Prevention really is key, and vitamin C is beneficial in preventing bloodshot eyes. Plan ahead and eat plenty of vitamin C–rich foods in the weeks leading up to the wedding. You'll help ward off the dreaded red eye and feel healthier in the process.

Tears of joy are a wedding staple. Keep your gel pack and your eyedrops handy for a quick time-out when needed. And, of course, all of your eye makeup must be waterproof, lest you end up with black tears and even redder eyes.

#961 *First-Aid Fixes*

Every activity comes with the potential for boo-boos — a pinprick here, a skin scrape there. Even the most glamorous weddings aren't immune to the unexpected and annoying little drops of blood that threaten everything from attire to décor. Prepare for this possibility and resolve the situation quickly by having a first-aid kit on hand at the ceremony and reception.

Create your own kit by acquiring supplies individually, or take the easy route and purchase a ready-made kit that includes first-aid supplies for ten people. A kit intended for workplaces is stocked with dozens of quick-fix items and generally costs under $25, an amount far less than buying those same supplies individually. Add some wedding-specific aids to your kit, like eyedrops for tearful eyes and heel and toe pads for sore, blistered feet.

Kits with supplies for more than ten people are usually not necessary. If your wedding is somehow nicking and pricking more than ten people, forget first aid. It's time to hunt down the source and eliminate it.

#962 *Tears Need Tissues*

Weddings are sentimental events that tend to open the emotional flood-gates. Crying at weddings is as natural as eating a hot dog while watching the baseball play-offs. It's the customary thing to do.

Unfortunately, many guests are caught unprepared when they well up. In the heat of the moment, they wipe their tears and stuffy noses on undeserving shirtsleeves or on whatever scrap of paper they can find (including your beautiful wedding program). Have a heart, and provide tissues for all guests.

Choose purse-sized tissue packs, then make them wedding lovely. Insert them into decorated envelopes that promote your wedding theme, or slip them into organza pouches that complement the colors of your décor. Place a basketful of tissue packs at the entrance to the ceremony. Guests can grab their own pack, or for an even sweeter service, ushers can distribute them from the basket as guests are seated.

Tissues are an easy, inexpensive way to provide comfort, but they are often overlooked during the wedding-planning process. Like brides and grooms, tears and tissues belong together.

#963 *But I Didn't Order That!*

Your wedding day is no time to discover that a vendor or two has slipped you an unexpected and unwelcome surprise. Can you take anyone to task for it? Maybe. Maybe not.

Some vendors ask you to sign contracts with language like "subject to availability" and "reserves the right to substitute." Agreeing to these terms means that you won't have a leg to stand on when pink pansies arrive instead of pink poppies, or when metal-backed chairs replace those beautiful, wooden spindle-backed seats you so wanted.

Read the fine print on the contract, and if a situation may legitimately warrant a substitution (such as a drought killing the poppies), insert one viable substitution of your choice before signing. Leaving the substitutions up to the vendor by signing a contract with nonspecific language increases the risk of wedding-day disappointment.

A substitution may be unavoidable. If it must happen, at least ensure that the substituted item is of your choosing, not the vendor's.

#964 *Elemental Shoe Survival*

Unless you plan to marry in your living room, there's a real possibility that your beautiful wedding shoes will suffer a nature-induced splotch or two as you move from here to there. It doesn't have to be pouring rain or blizzard conditions outside. Even green grass, oil residue on concrete, or the Earth's ready supply of surface dirt can do the unthinkable to your delicate heels.

Sometimes wearing another pair of shoes until it's time to slip into your fine footwear is the answer. Sometimes it isn't. If, for example, you wish to take photos down by the lake before the service, you might arrive at your ceremony in shoes riddled with stains. Prevent this type of disaster by using high-heel overshoes.

Transparent rain boots created especially for high heels come in a variety of styles, from discreet sole covers to slipover knee boots. Some even have lacy accents, so that if the toe peeks out during a candid photo, the foot will look amazing.

Satin-finished shoes don't get along well with Mother Nature's unruly mud and muck, but with a little thoughtful protection, they can stand up to the elements and still look fabulous on the dance floor.

#965 *Shine Patrol*

Important elements of a wedding photo shoot include the bride and groom, the wedding party, the photographer, and a "shine" cop.

Sunshine and hot lights have a way of turning a shining cheek or a glistening forehead into a photo disaster. Brides, grooms, and wedding-party members often break a sweat while posing for pictures, but doing so won't spell disaster if there's an "eagle eye" on the job.

Designate an astute house-party member to attend the photo shoot with tissues, pressed powder, lip balm, and a mirror in hand. As soon as those rascally beads of perspiration appear, your shine cop comes to the rescue, handing off the tools that quickly combat unwelcome shine. Those being photographed can't see themselves, and an objective eye that is not glued to the camera viewfinder helps to ensure picture-perfect shots.

#966 *Fit for a Wedding*

Most wedding vendors are professional and experienced, but not all of them extend those attributes to their attire. Avoid having a photographer in blue jeans or bartenders in wrinkled shirts by providing a dress code for all vendors attending the ceremony or reception.

Workers need to wear comfortable clothing to do their jobs, but it's possible to be comfortable without looking out of place. Don't try to put them into formalwear, but inform each vendor of your wedding's degree of formality (no ratty sneakers at your white-tie event) and your color scheme (perish the thought of the videographer arriving in a bright red shirt when your colors are peach and green). Your dress code should tell vendors that you expect them to dress in a manner befitting your occasion, without mentioning specific attire.

It's perfectly within your right to inquire about vendor appearance, and as long as you're not approaching the issue from a misguided sense of superiority, vendors usually honor your request with a smile.

#967 *Wizard Time*

One of the worst-case scenarios for brides and grooms is the failure to be ready for the big day. Once you fall behind on wedding-planning projects, it's hard to catch up, and the accompanying stress can percolate until you simply wish it would all go away. That's no way to begin a marriage, so give yourselves the gift of time — wizard time.

Like magic, set your life ahead by two weeks. Take every task in your timeline and bump it forward. If the final menu is required four weeks ahead of the wedding, give it to the caterer six weeks ahead. If the gown alterations are to be finalized one week before the ceremony, reschedule them to be accomplished no later than three weeks ahead. The extra two weeks will work for you again and again, allowing you to change your mind or address adverse issues that crop up unexpectedly.

Planning a wedding on wizard time lets you breathe much more deeply.

#968 *Senior Shuttle*

Some seniors don't drive much, or they may not wish to drive in bad weather or after dark. To avoid senior guests' staying home when they would really like to come to your wedding, consider organizing a senior-shuttle system.

Don't worry if springing for a limo isn't in the cards. Enlist the aid of friends or family members with comfortable cars or vans to collect seniors from their homes and transport them to the ceremony and the reception, then take them back home when the festivities end. If there are many seniors invited, organize pickups by territory, so that one driver isn't heading in opposite directions to collect passengers. Of course, the drivers should be teetotalers. Drinking and driving is never allowed, especially not with such precious cargo on board.

A courtesy car service benefits senior guests by providing them with competent, free transportation, and it benefits the bride and groom by permitting them to share their biggest day with some really incredible people.

#969 *Speak Up!*

When marrying in a large church, outdoors, or in any cavernous room, guests may have trouble hearing what's going on at the altar. And if they can't hear, what's the point of being there?

When you know that the acoustics are going to be less than satisfactory, fix the problem by doing what news anchors do. Wear discreet, cordless lapel microphones.

Some churches with large congregations have microphone systems, but if your ceremony venue doesn't offer public-address assistance, speak up with the help of a rental system. Many audio/visual vendors rent systems at reasonable rates. The important part is negotiating a package deal that includes both the rehearsal and the wedding day. Rehearsing with microphones before using them at the wedding is important.

And remember, once the microphones go live, they broadcast whatever you say from wherever you are, so even when you're waiting to make your entrance, be conscious of quips that may tumble from your lips.

#970 *Apple to the Rescue*

In filmmaking, it's important to keep people and props centered in a shot, but not everyone or everything is of comparable height. Enter the apple box. An apple box is a wooden box frequently used to give a boost to a shorter person doing a scene with a much taller one. An apple box at the altar could work wonders for some brides and grooms.

If one half of the wedding couple is much shorter, the first kiss may cause an awkward shot for the photographer and videographer. The taller person almost always overshadows the shorter one. So why not correct the height difference for that once-in-a-lifetime moment? Level the "kissing field" with a beautifully decorated apple box.

Cover the box in whatever design you wish, and place it at the altar before the ceremony begins. When it's time for the kiss, the best man positions the box. Don't try to do it discreetly. Give it fanfare! It will tickle your guests, and when you see your photos, you'll love that you gave yourself a boost.

#971 *Flower Wrangler*

Imagine glancing out from the altar only to discover that Grandma is not wearing the beautiful corsage you had ordered for her.

With all the hustle and bustle in the bride's room, it's hard to know what is, or isn't, going on beyond your doors. Seeing to it that flowers are appropriately disseminated is a job for one responsible person chosen from your house-party members.

A comprehensive list that denotes the flowers by the recipient's name, arrangement style, and colors prevents floral mix-ups. And unless the wrangler knows everyone on sight, add a small photo of the recipient next to the listing for each floral bouquet, corsage, or boutonnière. This way, Grandma B. won't get the corsage meant for Grandma C., and if the florist has inadvertently left someone off the list, the mistake will be discovered immediately, allowing time to correct the oversight.

A flower wrangler should be privy to all floral plans. If floral decorations need to be placed, the flower wrangler should have a sketch of locations.

Flowers, especially small units like corsages, have a way of getting mislaid and forgotten. With a flower wrangler, the worry of misplaced or misdirected flowers is eliminated.

#972 *Defeating Droops and Loops*

It's time. All you have to do is make your way from the bride's room to the aisle for your grand ceremonial entrance, but as you turn to head for the door, you realize that one sleeve is sitting cockeyed on your shoulder. You can't imagine why you never noticed it before, but there's no time for tailoring. Don't worry. Armed with double-sided fashion tape, you're home free.

Every model in the world has her outfit taped somewhere to her body as she sashays down the runway. It's the easiest way to tame flapping, drooping, and looping fabric. Fashion tape isn't only a model or a designer's best friend. It's a bride's quick savior. From minor repairs to minor adjustments, double-sided fashion tape is a mighty weapon in the war against unexpected droops and loops.

#973 *Get Me to the Church on Time!*

Excitement, nerves, and party-hearty rehearsal dinners can keep brides and grooms up way too late the night before the big day, and when you fall behind the next morning, misery multiplies as the clock ticks away. Even worse is a clock that quits ticking, or one that malfunctions, randomly adding or subtracting minutes. Remove the worry over inaccurate timepieces by going atomic.

Invest in an atomic clock for anyone whose relationship to the alarm clock is testy at best. An atomic clock never gets the time wrong. Think of it as your wedding-event heartbeat, and let it keep you steady. Brides and grooms who arrive late to their own wedding with the old excuses of "my alarm didn't go off" or "but my clock said it was only …" start their day with one foot already in wedding-day quicksand. It's a terrible feeling.

An atomic clock and a fresh battery are a small price to pay for a wedding day free of time-induced stress.

#974 *I Love You, Mom, But . . .*

It's your wedding, so why do you feel like a bridesmaid instead of a bride? If it's because Mom has taken over, and the only thing you recognize about the wedding choices is that you didn't make them, it's time to step up.

Mom loves you and you love her, but allowing her to steamroll through the wedding planning may cause resentment and regret for the rest of your life.

Mothers of the bride and groom should definitely have important roles in wedding planning, but only those you delegate to them. It doesn't even matter if Mom is single-handedly footing the bill. It's your wedding.

Talk to her. Explain that a bride's choices are among the biggest joys of the wedding experience, second only to actually taking your vows. You don't want to relinquish those choices, and without them, you may as well jump into the jalopy and head for the justice of the peace. After all, a wedding without you at the helm is no better than a wedding with no bells and whistles at all.

Be lovingly sympathetic, but be strong. If Mom's overzealous assistance disturbs you, address it and fix the situation. You won't get a second chance.

#975 *Combing the Beach*

Most of the time, beach weddings are gorgeous. Unfortunately, a wedding at the beach can come with plenty of unwanted "guests" like cigarette butts, plastic bags, ketchup-smeared fast-food wrappers, slimy piles of seaweed, broken beverage containers, and even the occasional stinky, dead marine creature. So be prepared to clean as you go.

Bring a long-handled strainer or a sand rake, as well as a trash container with a snap-on lid, and assign someone to keep an eye out for unwelcome intruders that could impact guests. Decorate the trash bin to fit the theme, and guests won't give it a second thought. If something ugly dares to intrude on your wedding, simply have your helper scoop it up, drop it into the container, and snap the lid back into place.

No one wants to leave a wedding with more than simple sand on their shoes or clothes, and no one wants to sniff a dead fish during the "I dos." Combing distasteful debris from a beautiful beach shows that you care about your guests and the land they walk on.

#976 *No Sagging Stems*

You've elected to save money on reception centerpieces by arranging bulk cut flowers in vases instead. But when those bulk flowers come out of their wrappers the day of the wedding looking more like wet noodles than beautiful blooms, you're shocked. Flower stems can weaken for any number of reasons, leaving your lilies loopy and your daisies droopy. But you can resolve the issue quickly with a box of inexpensive milkshake straws.

Straws made for milkshakes and smoothies have a larger circumference than regular drinking straws, and they come in lengths of 18 inches or more. Most flower stems will slip right in and stand tall and proud with the assist. If the stem is still too wide, simply take a razor blade or a sharp knife and score down one side of the straw, then slip the stem through the slit. Pastel or neon straws can actually add style to the bouquet, or you can hide the straws from view with greenery or baby's breath.

No sagging stems means no straggling blooms trying to make a break from the pack, and if the straws are never needed for the flowers, you'll have a ready supply for picnics and barbeques in the future.

#977 *Wise Disguise*

Inexpensive, inflatable buffets resemble swimming-pool rafts, but with wide, rounded sides. Filled with ice, they hold drinks, cold foods, or even ice-cream cups. The problem is that they usually come in bright colors and wild, party-inspired patterns that aren't exactly wedding perfect.

But you don't have to have frolicking monkeys or neon polka dots at your wedding. Simply line the cooler buffet with a white vinyl tablecloth that spills out over the sides, creating a "damask" or "lacy" border. If white is not your preference, use tablecloths that incorporate your wedding color scheme. Some inflatable buffets come in solid white, but they still have that "beachy" look, which you can alter with the tablecloth of your choice.

A tablecloth disguises the buffet's true colors and gives it a decidedly wedding-appropriate appearance. Later, you can forgo the tablecloth and use the buffet au naturel for many parties to come.

#978 *Uh . . . What's Your Name Again?*

Chances are that not everyone at your wedding reception will know each other, and the odds of strangers' ending up at the same table are fairly good. Of course guests will surely introduce themselves, but for some, remembering new names is an exercise in futility.

Help them out. Make two identical place cards for every guest, and position the cards back-to-back in the place-card holder. All of the guests around a table will be able to see the names of their tablemates, and no one will have to be embarrassed by calling Sue by Rosie's name or by referring to Harold as Joe. It takes a teensy bit more effort on your part, but your guests will be put at ease by your helpful and considerate preparations.

#979 *Ridiculously Cheap Organization*

Organization saves the day when it comes to wedding preparation, and an unexpected resource can help you put your supplies in order. It is the common, very cheap, no-frills paper plate.

Take makeup, for example. If you want to see at a glance whether all of your makeup is ready to transfer to the bride's room, first dole it out on white paper plates: eye makeup on one plate, lipsticks and glosses on another plate, and foundations, powders, and blushes on a plate of their own. You will notice right away if something has been forgotten, allowing you to include any missing items before you're at the venue and realize you left without them.

When your inventory is complete, scoop each paper plate with its treasures into a zippered plastic bag (one plate of supplies per bag), and place all bags in a tote. Upon arrival at the bride's room, spread out your paper plates of necessities, and never worry about having to hunt or dig for something as precious preparation moments fritter away. Everything will be visible, organized, and ready to go.

The paper-plate system works for all components of wedding preparation. It's clean, inexpensive, and effective!

#980 *Shopping with Eyes Wide Open*

There will be oodles of purchases made during wedding preparations, and odds are that you will end up with something, or many things, that aren't quite what you hoped they would be. It's not you. It's them! Stores, especially certain boutiques, go all out for décor and ambiance, when what the customers really need is good lighting to shop by.

If you don't want to get your goodies home only to discover straggling threads, smudges, holes, cracks, and suspicious labels on everything from clothing to glassware, don't shop alone. Take two "friends": a pocket flashlight and a strong magnifying glass. Scan everything with the magnifying glass. It's no fun to think that you've purchased a name brand only to discover under scrutiny that "Pearl" is spelled "Peurl," and it isn't a designer item at all. There's a reason detectives use flashlights when investigating a crime scene, even during daylight hours. Focused light gives your eyes a boost.

Don't be caught unawares. Take your shopping "friends" along for important purchases, and let them do their jobs.

#981 *The Wedding Buzz*

It took a year to plan, and then it passed in the blink of an eye. What happened?

Weddings and receptions run the risk of being remembered as one big blur, if you don't literally stop to smell the roses. Brides and grooms often forget the most important part of their wedding day — each other. Don't let the buzz of activity swallow your day. Make a promise that, for at least five minutes out of every hour, you will devote yourselves only to each other. Make time to enjoy the decorations from every angle, savor your food, dawdle over a shared toast, or play a sexy game of footsie under the table. The big things about the wedding day come and go, but it's the little things, those moments of deep connection with each other, that are the memories you will never forget. If you're too busy to share those moments, there won't be anything to remember but the "buzz."

#982 *The Five-Finger Rule*

When shopping for wedding vendors, it's inevitable that you will fall in love at first sight with one or more of them. Don't. Discipline yourself to sign no contract until you've filled a five-fingered-hand with quotes and offers from similar vendors.

Negotiating with at least five vendors offering the same product is valuable. The information gleaned from each will help you negotiate the absolute best deal, even if you eventually choose the very first vendor that wowed you. This rule also helps you to remember and understand details that might slip through the cracks if you allowed yourself to commit before learning all you can about the subject. Furthermore, it protects you from the pain of regret.

Nothing's worse than locking in with a vendor only to find a better one down the road. Stick to the rule. Use all five fingers. Once you have a vendor for each digit, let your head lead your heart as you choose.

#983 *Soothing Scents*

Avoid panic and soothe those bridal nerves with the calming effect of an aromatherapy locket. Brides go through a lot, but a scented locket may be just the ticket to unfrazzling the frazzle.

Consider using the essential oils bergamot or ylang-ylang to help ease the stress that's lodged between your shoulder blades. Or you may wish to choose scents befitting the task. For example, shoe shopping might be a lavender occasion, while standing for a long fitting might call for chamomile. Vanilla may smooth the rough edges of a really bad soloist audition, and lemongrass could be the perfect antidote for grumpy vendors.

Unless scented oils disagree with your nose, take advantage of the soothing little miracles locked inside them. An aromatherapy locket is a gift full of bridal benefits, since a peaceful bride-to-be leaves happiness in her wake. Just ask the groom-to-be.

#984 *Clodhoppers and Flood Pants*

Brides try on every bridal garment multiple times leading up to the wedding day. It's simply part of the process, and part of showing off her fairytale treasures to others.

Grooms, on the other hand, may not be so diligent, and pity the poor fool who shows up to the wedding with his formal attire in its garment bag only to discover that something he tried on at the tux shop was delivered in a different size altogether. No groom with size 10 feet can clomp around on his wedding day in size 12 shoes, or tug down britches with pant legs that are four inches too short.

So unless it's Pee-Wee Herman attire you hope to see waiting at the altar, don't leave this issue to fate. Preventable wedding-day faux pas do not make good memories. This scenario happens all too often, but it's easily avoided by the implementation of a best-man review.

The best man should set up a time to inspect the groom decked out in his full wedding-day attire, as soon as the formalwear has been picked up or delivered. From the tip of his toes to the top of his head, the groom should look and feel great in his duds. To ensure that this once-over happens, explain this responsibility in writing for the best man. Things do go wrong, but if you catch serious wardrobe errors early, guests will never have to know that the groom almost got married in his flip-flops.

#985 *Close but Not Quite*

It should be a bridal mantra that blue is not blue and pink is not pink. Every color comes in multiple shades and even more "color-merged" derivatives. The worst possible time to figure that out is when the wedding cake arrives all decked out in green buttercream florals that look like day-old pea soup against the green accents of the table decoration.

Order nothing without providing swatches to the vendor, baker, or candlestick maker. Anyone involved in any creative aspect of your wedding should be provided with a full palette of swatches. It's a simple, preventative fix for a problem you absolutely won't want to have on your wedding day.

#986 *Scrunch It!*

When the tablecloth is dangerously long, scrunchie it. When the drapes won't stay put, give them the scrunchie treatment. Couldn't find the napkin rings you wanted? Use scrunchies!

Hair scrunchies go beyond the ponytail. They are versatile little problem solvers, and it pays to have a stash of them at the ready. Need a bit of extra décor for that flowerpot or vase? A scrunchie slips on in a heartbeat and adds a pop of color. You can even use them as blindfolds if needed for reception games.

They're super easy to make using scrap fabric, and in no time you have a whole supply of wedding-perfect scrunchies on hand. If there's a problem that a rubber band would fix, a scrunchie will do it too, but with a greater sense of style.

#987 *Hairpalooza!*

Not all bride's rooms are created equal. Some are comfortably temperature controlled, while others are hothouses of distress. What good does it do to spend big bucks on a gorgeous hairdo, if the stuffy heat and uncontrolled humidity in the room are going to wilt that 'do before you even make it to the altar?

If you are marrying in a venue without air-conditioning, as with many older churches and other facilities, arm yourself with some simple dehumidifying tools. Stagnant air is the enemy. To dehumidify a room, you must first move the air. Bring along a few small, inexpensive fans (electric or battery operated) to stir the air and help dry it out.

If you don't happen to have real desiccants like silica gel on hand, grab some rock salt or uncooked white rice from home. Place it into bowls, and set the bowls about the room. Moisture loves rice and will navigate toward it. Salt is also a natural for drying. Rice or salt is not the quickest fix of all — that would be a portable, mini dehumidifier. But if springing for the real deal isn't an option, the fans and the kitchen supplies will at least give your beautiful hairdo a fighting chance.

Quick fixes work best in small areas. If you are dressing in a large room with no temperature control, you should escape as soon as possible. Get dressed, then go wait in an air-conditioned car. You can't expect your hair to stay fresh and vibrant when humidity is running amok.

#988 *Your Personal Cake Prompter*

"Oh, that wedding cake was to die for!" If a chorus of similar statements is the only way you have of knowing how good your cake really was, then you've missed a great wedding-day joy — eating that beautiful creation.

One scrawny, cake-cutting bite isn't the best way to enjoy your cake. Actually eating it is. But so many brides and grooms never take the time at the reception to savor a real piece of their cake. The reception is busy. You forget. Well, don't let this happen.

Buy yourself a little, inexpensive, silver cake charm and add it to your place setting. If you wander off to dance or to mingle, the charm will remain to vigilantly remind you upon your return that YOU FORGOT TO EAT CAKE! Eventually, the charm will do its job, and you will never have to regret that you let the whole reception pass you by without doing what brides and grooms absolutely should do at their reception — enjoy themselves to the fullest. That definitely includes eating your own once-in-a-lifetime cake.

#989 *Ignored Amenities*

If you pay good money for a photo booth or to make a beautiful "sweet treats" buffet at the back of the reception hall, you surely want people to enjoy them. However, guests may not know you've provided any entertainments unless they've actually stumbled upon them on their own.

Before the wedding, make a list of everything available to reception guests, from self-serve foods to amusements and photo ops. Then instruct your DJ, bandleader, or reception host/hostess to announce the items on the list, one at a time. You don't want a laundry-list-style recitation that makes guests feel like they should take notes, but individual mentions of different items between songs is a perfect way to ensure that guests get to enjoy themselves in every way you imagined they would.

#990 *Forever Lips*

The ceremony: beautiful lips.

Midway through the reception: what beautiful lips?

Brides rarely realize that their lipstick faded away at some point during the festivities — not until their wedding pictures tell them so, that is. If you love the way your lipstick enhances your smile, remember to reapply it. With all the kissing, drinking, eating, and lip biting, even the heartiest and most long-wearing lipsticks can fade into nothingness. Unfortunately, even disappearing color and gloss won't faze your photographer, who will just keep shooting.

Remind yourself to refresh your lip color by attaching a small mirror to the back of the floral arrangement at the head table. Only you and those sitting on either side of you will even know it's there, but each time you take your seat, your own pale lips will remind you to take a moment to renew that beautiful wedding-day smile.

#991 *Dork Dancing*

Not everyone was born with the dancing gene, and some cannot even snap their fingers in rhythm to the music, let alone get their toes to match a beat. If this description applies to the bride or the groom, how do they not embarrass themselves during that highly anticipated first dance? Easy. Pick an undanceable song!

Some artists put out songs that are virtually impossible to dance to. Many jazz tunes fall into this category, and so do songs from the rock 'n' roll, folk, and country genres.

If you don't want to feel like a dancing dork, choose a song that is not rhythmic. Then simply hold each other, sway, and dip. Throw in a kiss or two, and the guests will cheer. It will be the best dance of your life, because everyone will realize how difficult it would be to dance to the song. Even the guests won't be able to tap their feet in rhythm.

An impossibly off-the-wall tune is a welcome wedding gift to the dance challenged.

#992 *Return to Vendor*

You had a wonderful wedding and a fabulous honeymoon. How horrible would it be to come home to a staggering debt for rented linens and charger plates that were never returned as agreed, because everyone thought someone else was handling it? Who's in charge?

If you do not have a wedding planner to handle returns, you must guarantee that the task is handled in your absence. To prevent garbage bags stuffed with tablecloths from being tossed out with the trash, or boxes of stemware from rattling around in someone's trunk for two weeks, you need to appoint a "check and balance" team.

Assign one person to gather the items from the reception and another to mark the items off a printed checklist after those items are loaded into a vehicle. Instruct the two people to communicate every day until the items are returned as scheduled. To add insurance to the plan, give the contact information of your team members to the vendor who supplied the rented items so that, if all else fails, the vendor can follow up.

A checks-and-balances system spreads out the burden and helps eliminate human error that could end up costing you more than you spent on your honeymoon. There's no valid defense for failure to abide by a rental contract. Dole out the responsibility to the two people you would trust with your bank account, because as long as the rental items are in their possession, they are quite literally controlling your money.

#993 *Two by Two*

Is the world just one big fuzz ball without your glasses? Does the groom hobble without the knee brace that combats his old football injury? When it comes to the wedding day, a "two by two" approach to personal essentials is mandatory.

If you can't properly experience life without a certain item, always have a backup. Otherwise, breaking your eyeglasses in the bride's room could mean either seeing a blurry groom waiting at the altar or whipping out the duct tape and walking down the aisle in serious geek mode. A spare pair in your essentials bag will ward off disaster. The same goes for absolutely any item you can't live without. An extra "whatever" is a quick fix you'll be grateful to have if pesky gremlins try to wreak havoc on your day.

#994 *The Sticky Fingers of Uncle Sam*

An all-too-common mistake nearly every wedding couple makes when planning their wedding budget is to forget about Uncle Sam. If the wedding will cost some $25,000, as the average wedding does, the sales-tax burden on that amount could easily be close to $2,500, depending upon your state and locality. That's a serious budget buster.

To avoid the pain and shock of Uncle Sam's sticky fingers, determine your maximum budget, subtract 10% from it, and then use the lower figure as your "buying" budget. You'll be glad that you gave the old uncle his due before you got down to the wire, and only then realized you were out of money with several necessary purchases still to be made.

Sales tax is an unavoidable wedding expense, but putting it on the list at the onset of wedding planning takes the sting out of it.

#995 *Upended Registry*

You picked a beautiful china pattern and registered with just the right retailer, with many months to spare. All is well, until the china manufacturer decides to discontinue your pattern, rendering your carefully considered choice obsolete. The sad part is that some retailers will fail to notify you, and will simply sell the stock they have on hand to your unsuspecting guests.

Before you register with any retailer, ask for a copy of their written policy on back orders and discontinued items. Set your own parameters when you sign up, such as "cancel any back orders not received within 35 days" or "in the event of discontinuation of my pattern, I must be notified within ten days of the manufacturer's notice to you." Make sure that you will have the ability to switch patterns, and that any items sold from the discontinued pattern may be exchanged for the new one without restocking fees or surcharges. If the store won't abide by your wishes, register elsewhere.

Manufacturers cannot be expected to maintain a low-selling pattern just because your wedding is on deck a year down the road, and the retailer has no control over manufacturer discontinuations. Retailers do sometimes discontinue items in the store that are not discontinued by the manufacturer, in which case notification would ensure that you could simply register elsewhere, with a retailer still offering the line. In either scenario, you need the ability to control what happens if such an unfortunate event occurs. Don't end up with three pieces of this and eight of that because you didn't know what was happening. Communicate with the retailer at the time you register.

#996 Flaming Feet

Unless she's wearing flip-flops or sneakers beneath her gown, it's pretty hard to find a bride who isn't suffering with burning, aching feet by the time she reaches the reception. Ice those flames!

Just before it's time for the reception to begin, have the caterer or other assigned helper place a full, sealed bag of ice atop a thick layer of absorbent towels, and place everything in a sheet-cake pan or similar container. Toss a thin terry or cloth towel over the whole concoction, and slip it beneath the tablecloth of the head table, just before the bride's seat.

That ice-cold footrest will feel like a slice of heaven when you kick off your shoes for a quick refresh. And even if the ice melts, it is sealed inside its plastic bag, with the cushion of towels to catch any drips.

No matter how many times you get up to dance or partake in other activities, your cool-as-a-cucumber footrest will be awaiting your return. The ice should last a long time, but if it doesn't, the water left inside will still feel like a foot-sized waterbed you won't want to leave. Even if you have changed into more comfortable reception shoes, your feet will thank you for treating them so well.

#997 Nature's Signature

Of course you want to pose on the hill or the riverbank because the setting is just so picturesque, and you know the photo will be amazing. On the other hand, leaving the spot with an autograph from Mother Nature, in the form of a grass stain or a mud smear, isn't quite so picturesque for your wedding gown.

No problem! Take along a circular piece of fabric that matches your gown, and settle it onto the place where you will stand. Make it the same diameter as your gown, and once you are standing on it, it won't even be noticeable. What it will do is take the swipe from Mother Nature, so you don't have to. Simply lift your gown as you walk to the scenic spot, and then step onto your matching round of fabric before releasing the skirt from your grip. Life, and the health of your gown, will be infinitely good.

#998 *Those Ain't Wedding Bells!*

It should go without saying, but say it you should. Chatting and texting have become epidemic, and there's a cell phone in every pocket. Add a notation to your wedding program to remind guests to turn off their cell phones during the ceremony. No wedding couple wants to hear some off-the-wall ringtone in the middle of their vows. Just to be on the safe side, also have your ushers mention turning off cell phones as they seat guests and hand out programs.

It may seem a bother to bring it up, but a single call can ruin the moment in a big way. The offending guest or attendant will be as sorry as can be, but it will be too late. Eliminate any cell-phone danger with a preemptive reminder.

#999 *Redress the Excess!*

There's a fine line between gorgeous and ghastly. Some wedding-reception décor is so overblown that you can't squeeze a toothpick onto a tabletop or take a step without bumping into something that glitters, jiggles, or flashes.

Contrary to popular belief, not every scrap of available space has to be overly adorned. If you're going to have a mirror-topped table, do you really need stripes flowing out from underneath it, boldly patterned napkins, towering candles, fat florals, charger plates, waterfalls, and a ring of roses encircling the edge? Have you planned for centerpieces so big that the glassware will have to be tucked between encroaching leaves like cars in a garage?

Before you buy, rent, or hoard it, give it the gorgeous/ghastly test. Imagine where that decorative accent will go and what it's meant to accomplish. If you're acquiring it just because you love it, thinking you'll decide where to use it later, don't do it. That's how receptions become so overly decorated that guests need therapy just to process all the "stuff" in their line of vision.

"Beautiful" and "bountiful" are not interchangeable words, and even weddings that cost hundreds of thousands of dollars can wind up looking completely hideous if the brakes aren't judiciously applied at some point. Photos exist to prove it.

#1000 *Belt It or Zip It!*

Being prepared is a cardinal rule of honeymoon travel. Unforseen events do happen, and never being separated from your money and essential documents should be the first rule of preparation.

To ensure safety and security, especially when traveling in a foreign country, carry your vital necessities on your person. The use of a money belt or fanny pack, or both together, prevents accidental abandonment of your items in a restaurant, store, entertainment venue, or public-transportation vehicle. It also lessens the opportunity for theft or for loss resulting from luggage mishandling.

Wear it to save it, and spare yourself the headaches and heartache of a ruined vacation.

#1001 *Happy Heels*

You bought the most beautiful pair of heels for your wedding, but your photographer has decided he wants you to pose under the apple tree — after you walk down a brick path and tromp through grass to get there. Stilettos on bricks? In grass? Seriously? This is why you don't want to be without heel protectors — those clear slip-ons for the heel that increase the heel-tip surface and make it easy to walk on grass, sand, woven carpets, or other soft surfaces without sinking, tripping, or staining your heels.

Some venues ban stilettos because they damage floors. No problem. Heel protectors help protect floors, so if you've asked guests not to wear stilettos, and the message didn't sink in, having a few extra pairs of heel protectors on hand will no doubt rescue you from an uncomfortable situation. It's no fun to ask guests to lose their shoes after arriving at your wedding, even if you had already told them about your venue's restrictions. Heel protectors can save the day, but they are not created equal. Read the reviews online and shop smart.

INDEX

stepparents, 150, 154, 292, 293
storyboarding wedding events, 51–52
streamer cannons, 473
stress reduction, 20, 35, 41, 44, 45, 58, 235, 425, 487–488, 494–495, 496, 505, 509–510
stress test for bridal gowns, 202
string ensembles, 419
stuffed animals, 133, 145–146, 348, 489
succulents, 313–314
sugar cubes, flavored, 387–388
sugar wafer attachments, 406
sugared flowers, 300
sugar-free desserts, 391
suitcase-delivery services, 492
summer weddings, 23, 38, 59, 77–78, 113–114, 115, 131, 155, 188, 266, 303, 330, 340–341, 368, 401–402 See also outdoor weddings; weather, preparing for
Sunset Hills Memorial Park, 78
sunshine theme, 112–113
Super 8 movies, 474–475
supper club theme, 111
suppliers See decorations and supplies; vendors and service providers
surprise weddings, 135

Swarovski crystals, 294, 361
sweat See heat, solutions for
sweaters, 218
Sweet Apple Farm, 88
sweetheart/satellite head table layout, 441
swizzle sticks, 380
synthesizers, 421

T
table assignments See escort cards; seating charts
table runners, 338–339, 341–342, 344–345, 367
table styles and placements, 49, 59, 350, 368–369, 380–381, 386, 404, 441, 446, 470, 488, 507
tablecloths, 341–342, 507
tabletop scavenger hunts, 452
taffeta, 195
talent competitions, 461–462
talking thank-you cards, 283
task-a-day calendars, 35
tattoo concealer, 220
tax refunds, 44
tea theme, 142–143
technology theme, 129
telescopes, 74–75, 85, 472
temperature See weather, preparing for
tennis shoes, 103, 206
terrariums, 337
Thanksgiving weddings, 107, 117

thank-yous See gifts and thank yous
theater theme, 111–112
themes, 101–146, 316, 318, 325, 326, 333, 338 See also destination weddings; seasons and holidays; specific theme
backdrop rentals, 167–168
bouquets, 104, 106, 107–108, 113, 115, 117, 118, 121, 125, 128, 129, 135, 136, 146
for bridal showers, 34, 52, 55–56, 311
music, 95, 105, 106, 115–116, 135–136, 416, 419–420
reception activities, 341, 446–447, 448, 466–467
rehearsal dinners, 248, 251, 254
stationary, 38, 271, 277, 282, 283
transportation, 22–23, 31, 102
Thornewood Castle, 76–77
3-D wall art, 366
tiaras, 181, 185, 221
timeless beauty, 195–196
"timeless" theme, 144
timeline for reception activities, 451–452
tinsel, in hair, 208
tipping, 12–13, 388–389
tissue-paper inserts for invitations, 283

toast- and speech-giving
reception activities, 58, 227, 232–233, 438, 439, 440, 459
rehearsal dinners, 247, 249, 250
topiaries, 326
toppers for wedding cake, 50, 383, 386, 389, 395–396
tower vases, 360, 369
train theme, 82, 90–91, 97, 104–105
trains, on bridal gowns, 196–197, 230–231
transportation, 12, 14–15, 22–23, 31, 51, 57, 102, 228, 232, 361, 461, 466, 482, 503
Trapp Family Lodge, 68–69
travel See destination weddings
travel theme, 82, 90–91, 97, 104–106
traveling overseas, planning for, 161, 499, 517
treasure hunts, 463–464
Treasure Island theme, 113
tree decorations, 129–130, 140, 141–142, 153–154, 303, 320, 345, 349–350, 356–357, 448, 450–451
tree unity ritual, 153–154
tree-free stationary, 275, 281–282, 289
trends, avoiding, 10–11, 195–196
trivia games, 459, 476

ACKNOWLEDGMENTS

It was a joy to bring this book to life, and I couldn't have done it without those who matter most. I am ever grateful to my family (Mom, Dan, Steve, Kim, LuAnn) for their endless love and support. I owe an additional heartfelt thanks to my mom, LaWanda, who frequently provided me with her "wedding thoughts" lists as I navigated my way through this book, and I deeply appreciate my *more-like-a-sister-than-a-cousin*, LuAnn, for her generous research assistance. I'm especially thankful to my husband, Mark, who didn't bat an eye when I asked him to water twenty-five baby trees at our wedding altar so many years ago. Thirty years later he still supports my dreams, old and new, even as he alone fulfills the most important one.

I owe this book in large part to friend and author, Karen Berger, who patiently guided me forward. From the inspiration of her writing savvy to her selfless sharing, she has been, and is, a blessing in my life. I thank my friend, Chris, who has on many occasions been my "first look" editor, and I cherish my agent, Marilyn Allen, from the bottom of my heart for simply being the amazing, patient, encouraging and talented person she is. I am grateful to Megan Hiller for enabling me to progress with ease as she listened to my thoughts and shared her perspective, and I wholeheartedly thank publishing director and editor Robin Haywood, for spearheading this massive undertaking with such foresight and focused enthusiasm.

No one ever really accomplishes a great feat alone, and whether the endeavor is large or small, having someone in your corner as you pursue it means everything. I'm very fortunate to have had my corner filled to capacity as I worked hard to make this book worthy of those preparing for their most momentous occasion, and I owe my final and grandest thanks to the brides and grooms whose love and optimism inspire me every day.